Lazuli Finch
JOHN J. AUDUBON

Management Science

Management Science

Sang M. Lee
University of Nebraska

Laurence J. Moore
Virginia Polytechnic Institute
and State University

Bernard W. Taylor
Virginia Polytechnic Institute
and State University

wcb

Wm. C. Brown Company
Publishers
Dubuque, Iowa

wcb group **Wm. C. Brown,** Chairman of the Board
Mark C. Falb, Corporate Vice President/Operations

Book Team
G. W. Cox, Editor
Lynne M. Meyers, Production Editor
Marla A. Schafer, Designer
Faye M. Schilling, Visual Research Editor

wcb
Wm. C. Brown Company Publishers College Division
Lawrence E. Cremer, President
Raymond C. Deveaux, Vice President/Product Development
David Wm. Smith, Assistant Vice President/National Sales Manager
David A. Corona, Director of Production Development and Design
Matthew T. Coghlan, National Marketing Manager
Janice Machala, Director of Marketing Research
William A. Moss, Production Editorial Manager
Marilyn A. Phelps, Manager of Design
Mary M. Heller, Visual Research Manager

Library of Congress Catalog Card Number: 80–65222

ISBN 0–697–08046–3

Second Printing, 1981

Printed in the United States of America

To Laura

To my wife, Nancy and my children Becky, Andy, and Stefani

To my wife, Diane

Contents

Part 2 Deterministic Models: Mathematical Programming 23

Preface

The field of management science encompasses a number of quantitative techniques and a logical methodology for applying these techniques to decision-making problems. The purpose of this text is to provide the reader with a fundamental coverage of the techniques that comprise management science and to demonstrate their applications. This textbook is intended primarily for graduate and upper-level undergraduate students in business and administration.

Management science is a relatively new but increasingly accepted area of required curriculum in academic programs of business and administration. In the past, many of the quantitative techniques currently included in management science were taught almost exclusively in engineering, science, or doctoral-level business programs. The application of these techniques to management decision-making problems was conducted almost exclusively by specialists in the field with advanced technical degrees. However, the increased emphasis on the quantitative skills of undergraduate business students has facilitated the inclusion of management science as an integral component of the business degree programs at most colleges and universities. This has resulted in more and more graduates entering the professional business environment with management science skills. The successful application of management science techniques by these graduates has, in turn, increased the popular acceptance of the field.

As a result of this increasing popularity, most business schools now offer advanced courses (or sequences of courses) in management science at the undergraduate level, required courses in management science at the master's (including the master of business administration) level, and doctoral programs in management science. It is to these courses and students that this text is aimed.

Although this text has been written for advanced undergraduate- and graduate-level courses in management science (or quantitative methods), we have attempted to maintain a basic, straightforward presentation of the topics. The process of applying management science to decision-making problems consists of identifying and analyzing the problem, building a mathematical model of the problem, and then solving or testing the model using various quantitative techniques. To demonstrate this process and the various techniques, examples are employed wherever possible in lieu of a proliferation of complex mathematical formulas. We have attempted to provide the student with conceptual knowledge concerning the properties, assumptions, and limitations of management science models and the realities of the decision environment. The advanced nature of the text is derived from its detailed and in-depth coverage of each individual topic and the inclusion of all the topics most frequently associated with management science.

The degree of mathematical sophistication required of the business student using this text varies with the particular topic being covered. For example, chapters 1 through 5 require only college algebra as a prerequisite. Chapters 7 (Inventory Models), 11 (Simulation), 15 (Advanced Topics in Linear Programming), and 16 (Nonlinear Programming) require some calculus. Chapters 6 (Network Models), 8 (Decision Theory and Games), 9 (Markov Analysis), 10 (Queueing Theory), and 11 (Simulation) also require some preliminary foundation in probability and statistics. However, we have provided comprehensive appendixes for linear algebra and matrices, calculus, and probability, which can be used as either teaching or review aids for these fundamental prerequisites.

Because of the extensive and detailed coverage of topics in this text, it can be used in conjunction with a variety of course outlines. In general, it is not possible to cover all of the topics in this text in a one-quarter or one-semester course. Typically, an introductory M.B.A.-level course in management science will include the basic topics of linear programming contained in chapters 2 through 5 plus one or more advanced topics in linear programming, such as goal programming (chapter 13), integer programming (chapter 14), or several optimization topics, such as network models (chapter 6), inventory (chapter 7), or simulation (chapter 11). A typical two-quarter sequence might cover Part 2 (Deterministic Models: Mathematical Programming) and Part 3 (Network and Inventory Models) in the first quarter and Part 4 (Probabilistic Models) and a portion (such as dynamic programming) of Part 5 (Advanced Topics in Mathematical Programming) in the second quarter. An academic year sequence could cover all topics in the text.

Alternatively, selected portions of the text can be used for advanced undergraduate and graduate courses that are more specialized. For example, Part 5 could be used exclusively for a course in advanced topics in mathematical programming. Portions of the text can also be used for courses in such areas as linear programming and probabilistic models. The figure on page xix shows the text chapters grouped by major subject areas and their approximate relationships in the overall subject matter of management science.

Each chapter is accompanied by questions or problems that serve to give the student practice in the solution techniques and to demonstrate the applicability of management science to decision-making problems. The solution of these problems in conjunction with the textual material should provide the student with a thorough understanding of the individual quantitative techniques and an overall comprehension of the management science process.

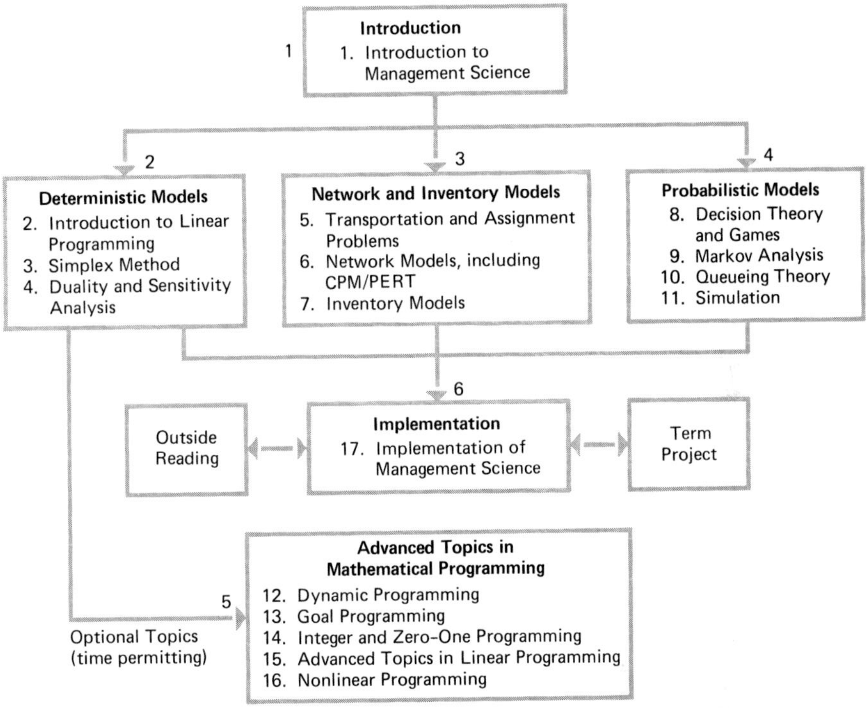
1
Introduction
1. Introduction to Management Science
2
Deterministic Models
2. Introduction to Linear Programming
3. Simplex Method
4. Duality and Sensitivity Analysis
3
Network and Inventory Models
5. Transportation and Assignment Problems
6. Network Models, including CPM/PERT
7. Inventory Models
4
Probabilistic Models
8. Decision Theory and Games
9. Markov Analysis
10. Queueing Theory
11. Simulation
6
Outside Reading
Implementation
17. Implementation of Management Science
Term Project
5
Optional Topics (time permitting)
Advanced Topics in Mathematical Programming
12. Dynamic Programming
13. Goal Programming
14. Integer and Zero-One Programming
15. Advanced Topics in Linear Programming
16. Nonlinear Programming

Acknowledgements

In writing and developing this text we owe our gratitude to a number of individuals. Our special thanks are reserved for Professor Eugene Kaczka of Memphis State University who reviewed the entire manuscript and made many valuable comments. We are also indebted to Edward Clayton, Belva Cooley, and Dick Deckro, our faculty colleagues at Virginia Tech, for their many helpful suggestions; and to David Olson, C. S. Kim, J. P. Shim, Joyce Anderson, Jane Chrastil, and Cindy Gnirk at the University of Nebraska-Lincoln; Lori Franz at the University of South Carolina; and Robert Barrett, Leslie Gwynn, and Alan Turner at Virginia Tech. We are also grateful to Gerry Chenault, Vicki Owen, and Judy Vassar at Virginia Tech for their typing and editorial assistance through several drafts of the book.

Sang M. Lee
Laurence J. Moore
Bernard W. Taylor, III

Part 1

Introduction

1

Introduction to Management Science

Management science is the application of the methods and techniques of science to the problems of management decision making. The primary objective of management science is to help managers make better decisions by solving problems more effectively. In pursuing the goal of helping managers to become more effective problem solvers, a number of mathematical techniques and systematic procedures have been developed and adapted from other disciplines, such as the natural sciences, mathematics, and engineering. Management science has applied these various techniques and methods to the problems of management.

At first glance, it may seem incongruous to combine the terms *management* and *science* since management is often thought of as more of an art than a science. However, there has been an increasing effort during this century to systematize much of the management process. Early industrial engineers began at the turn of the century to apply scientific techniques to industrial management. F. W. Taylor and Frank and Lillian Gilbreath were instrumental in the development and application of such scientific approaches to management as work standards, job design, and motion study. H. L. Gantt pioneered in scheduling with the Gantt Chart, which serves as a foundation for some of the most widely used scheduling techniques today. While these developments may seem simplistic to the sophisticated student and management scientist of today, at the time they represented significant "scientific" breakthroughs.

The interest in applying the methods of science to management problems has increased with the passage of time. It received a strong impetus during World War II with the development of **operational research** in England. The British brought together groups of scientists from various disciplines to apply scientific methods to military problems, i.e., to do "research" on military "operations." This approach was credited with the successful deployment of radar installations that were instrumental in the victory of the Battle of Britain. This same approach—bringing together scientists from different disciplines to apply various scientific techniques to logistical and operational problems—was later adopted successfully by the American military forces.

It was only natural that a return to peacetime saw the development of an environment conducive to operations research in business and industry. The accelerated growth of the war economy, both in the United States and abroad, created a favorable environment for innovations in industry, new products and inventions, expanded industrial capacity, and increased consumer demand. This expansion, in turn, resulted in an increase in the number and complexity of management problems. It was in this environment that some managers and management analysts began to experiment with new problem-solving methods and techniques derived from the fundamentals of operations research. These managers were interested in solving problems and were receptive to new ways to do it.

One new problem-solving approach that encompassed the principles of operations research involved analyzing problems with the assistance of mathematical representations of problems, known as models. With the aid of various quantitative techniques, models were experimented on and manipulated to obtain solutions, which, in turn, assisted the manager in reaching better decisions. This general approach to problem solving also came to be known as *management science*. However, the applications of these techniques and models to problem solving in general were limited by the capacity of people to solve them. The development of the electronic computer in the 1950s and 1960s provided the necessary capacity to solve large and complex problems very rapidly, eliminating a roadblock to the development and application of management science.

Today management science is a recognized and popular discipline in the field of business management. Applications of the quantitative techniques comprising management science are widespread, and they have been credited in numerous instances with increasing the efficiency and productivity of management. This increased popularity is mirrored in the number of colleges and universities offering undergraduate and graduate management science courses and degree programs in management science (also called operations research, quantitative analysis, and decision science). It is now part of the fundamental curriculum of most programs in business administration.

It is our purpose in this text to provide an introduction to the more frequently used management science models and techniques. In conjunction with this objective, the methodology and logic behind mathematical model building will be discussed in each chapter. In addition to developing mathematical models, several other elements must be considered for a thorough understanding of management science.

First, management science can be applied to a number of different types of organizations. In other words, management science can be used to solve problems in such fields as government, military, business and industry, academia, and health care. The field of management science has evolved to the point where its application of scientific tools has become an invaluable aid in solving problems in a multitude of decision-making environments.

Second, the mathematical techniques presented in this text require manual solution. However, in every case, programs or capabilities exist for computerized solutions. Such computer programs are not presented in this text, but one should always be aware of their existence since many realistic problems can only be solved in a reasonable period of time if a computer is employed. For this text, this absence does not constitute a difficulty since our purpose is to teach techniques and their application, a necessary prerequisite for subsequent computer application.

Finally, although the numerous quantitative techniques and examples of model building and their applications are stressed in the text, it should be remembered that management science consists of more than just a collection of techniques. Management science also involves a philosophy of approaching a problem in a logical manner as does any science. In other words, the logical, consistent, and systematic manner of problem solving employed by management science is even more basic to effective management than the knowledge of the mechanics of the quantitative techniques themselves.

The Scientific Method

As noted in the previous section, management science encompasses the application of a scientific approach to problem solving. The objective of scientific decision making is to make good choices from the existing alternatives by utilizing systematic approaches to providing information concerning the decision environment and evaluating the range of decision alternatives in a logical, precise manner. Thus, management science includes a carefully constructed methodology for analysis. This methodology has been adapted from the natural sciences and is termed the *scientific method*.

The scientific method follows a generally recognized set of steps. Whether these steps are followed in precisely the order described often depends on the nature of the problem being studied and the individuals performing the analysis. However, a basic premise of scientific analysis is a rigorous and careful approach to all phases of the analysis.

Observation

This first step of the scientific method involves the continuing study of the system (organization) in an attempt to identify problems. It is essential that the management scientist be always alert for operational problems. Once a problem is indicated, the management scientist must analyze it carefully as a basis for subsequent steps in the scientific method.

Definition of the Problem

Before solutions to a problem can be considered, an accurate definition of the problem must first be formulated. It has often been reported by organizations that failure in problem-solving has resulted from an incorrect definition of the problem.

In addition to defining the problem, this step includes identifying the possible *alternatives* available to management. Also, the *objectives*, or *goals*, of the system under analysis must be clearly defined. The stated objective helps to focus the attention of the analyst on the problem and its effects on the total organization. Finally, in order to evaluate the performance of a proposed solution, *measurement criteria*, such as cost or profit, must be specified.

Model Construction

The classical description of this third step in the natural sciences is *formulation of the hypothesis*. For our purposes this step involves formulation of a *model* by which the system can be manipulated and experimented on. Models are abstractions of reality in which only those *components* relevant to the problem being analyzed are included. Thus, a major portion of model construction involves identification of relevant components and description of the *relationships* between these components.

A model can take any of several alternative forms. It can be a graph, a flow chart, a network, or a set of mathematical equations. This latter form is often referred to as a symbolic model, and it is the type we will be most frequently concerned with in this text.

Model Validation

This step requires that all assumptions employed in the construction of the model be identified and validated. In other words, the model must be checked to see if it correctly reflects the operation of the system it represents. The manager must operate and experiment with the model to make sure it reacts in the same way as the real system.

Problem Solution

Although the classical statement of this step is *experimentation with the model,* in reality, this step may involve solution or operation of the model in order to observe its performance under different conditions. Whether or not the problem reflected by the model is solved depends on the nature of the study and the objective of the analysis.

At this stage the various quantitative solution techniques and methods that are a major part of management science enter the process. Problem solving generally implies the application of one or more of these techniques to the model.

Implementation

This last step is the logical result of model development and problem solution. A scientific study is of little value unless it is ultimately put to use in some form. The true value of the process is the impact that implementation has on the performance of the system studied. A critical aspect of this step is the interface between the management scientist (the model builder) and the management environment, not only at the end of the model development and solution but throughout the analysis procedure. To begin the scientific process the model builder abstracts from reality; however, to complete the process the opposite must be achieved in that the model must be reestablished in reality.

The management science process includes all of the steps discussed. However, the primary focus of this text is on two steps: model construction and solution. Therefore, a more careful delineation of model types and solution techniques is presented.

Model Classification

Models may be categorized into two groups: (1) **deterministic models** and (2) **probabilistic models.** Deterministic models are models developed under conditions of assumed certainty. They are necessarily simplifications of reality since certainty would indeed be rare. However, the advantage of such models is that they can generally be manipulated and solved with greater ease. Thus, complicated systems can often be modeled and analyzed if it can be assumed that all the numerical components of the system are known with certainty.

The second model category, probabilistic models, includes cases in which uncertainty is assumed. However, although incorporating uncertainty into the model may yield a more realistic representation of the situation, such a model is generally more difficult to analyze.

In this text, the first seven chapters deal predominantly with deterministic models. Chapters 2 through 4 deal exclusively with linear programming, one of the most familiar and frequently used management science techniques. Chapters 5, 6, and 7 present the additional deterministic techniques of network and inventory models, although some aspects of these models are probabilistic. Chapters 8 through 11 present the probabilistic models and techniques of decision theory, game theory, Markov analysis, queueing, and simulation. Chapters 12 through 16 cover some of the more advanced topics in mathematical programming including dynamic programming, goal programming, integer programming, and nonlinear programming.

A Modeling Example

Consider a manager of a plant who is concerned about the costs of the material kept on hand to produce products. The manager desires to have this inventory cost be as low as possible. The manager has determined that there are two primary costs associated with how much material is ordered and kept in inventory. First, there is the cost of ordering the material, that is, the costs involved with having the order processed, loaded on trucks, and delivered by the supplier. Second, there is the cost of carrying the material as inventory prior to its use. This cost includes the value of the storage space taken up by the material and lost interest on money invested in inventory. The manager has determined that the sum of these two costs rises or falls depending on the amount of material ordered. Figure 1.1 is a graphic representation (a model) of these inventory costs for various order sizes developed by the manager.

Figure 1.1 Graphic model of the inventory problem.

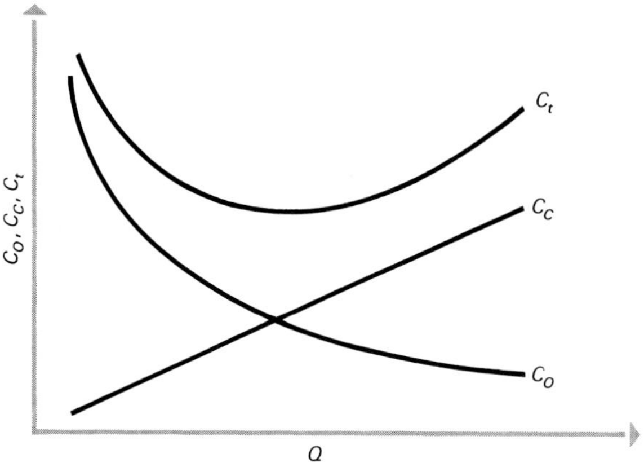

The graph of figure 1.1 illustrates the relationship of three variables, C_o, C_c, and C_t, to a fourth variable, Q. The model is a simplified representation of inventory costs in which inventory carrying cost, C_c; ordering cost, C_o; and total inventory cost, C_t, are related to the quantity of material ordered, Q. For larger orders, the inventory carrying cost (C_c) is greater, whereas the ordering cost (C_o) is lower since fewer orders are required. For smaller orders, the carrying cost is lower, but the ordering cost is greater due to an increase in the number of orders. Total inventory cost (C_t) first decreases and then increases, as a function of order size. The objective is to determine the order size (Q) that minimizes the total of the two types of inventory cost ($C_o + C_c = C_t$). The purpose of such a model is to represent the system and provide the framework for obtaining a solution to the problem.

In the process of presenting the graphic model of an inventory problem, the symbolic model has been introduced. The mathematical symbols for inventory costs, C_o, C_c, and C_t, and for order size, Q, represent the important components of the model. Mathematics is a very important language for the management scientist. It includes a set of rules to guide the manipulation of symbols, which insures consistent results.

At this point, however, the relationships of the symbols C_o, C_c, and C_t to Q have only been specified graphically. Now we shall express the relationship of C_c to Q in the following linear equation form:

$$C_c = a + bQ$$

where

C_c = carrying cost

Q = order size

a = vertical axis intercept of the straight line, C_c

b = slope (rate of change in C_c relative to Q)

The preceding is an example of a mathematical model. Note that this mathematical model of the relationship of C_c to Q is only a component of the total inventory model. (We will not attempt, at this stage, to further develop the mathematical relationships describing this inventory problem. This will be done in the later chapter on inventory models.) Wherever possible, models will be illustrated graphically. Graphical presentation greatly enhances the communication value of management science models. In fact, an intuitive understanding of the solution process can be facilitated in many cases by a graphical illustration. In studying figure 1.1, it is obvious that the optimum value for Q in the inventory modeling case is at the point where the lowest level of total inventory cost (C_t) is achieved.

Elements of Model Construction

The inventory cost model in the previous section contains several elements that were combined in the construction of the model. These elements include **variables** and **parameters,** and their relationships. In this section these elements will be defined in greater detail. As an aid in presenting these elements and their relationships in model construction, a break-even model will be used as an example.

Break-even analysis is often referred to as cost-volume-profit analysis. This is because the purpose of the analysis is to study the relationship of cost, volume, and profit to determine the volume that equates revenue and cost. Break-even is defined as the volume (level of operation in terms of unit quantity, dollar volume, or percentage of capacity) required to arrive at the point where total revenue equals total costs.

For example, a book publisher is concerned with determining the quantity of book sales required to cover the fixed costs of publishing a new book. If the new book includes costly design and typesetting features, then fixed costs will be high and the resulting break-even volume will be higher than normal. If the book must compete with several similar books, forcing the publisher to offer the book at a competitive price, then the publisher can undertake the project only if projected sales volume at the competitive price exceeds the computed break-even point in revenue versus cost.

A manufacturing firm considering investment in automated equipment for production operations can make use of break-even analysis to determine the feasibility of it. Although investment in automated equipment may reduce the variable costs of production, the benefits of reduced variable costs may not offset the increase in the fixed cost required. Break-even analysis can assist in determining the level of operation required to make such an investment beneficial.

Identification of Model Components

The first step of model construction is to abstract from the system of interest the elements that are essential to the problem analysis. The usual approach is to translate the essential elements and components into various symbols, to facilitate model construction and manipulation.

The major components of the break-even analysis model are total revenue, fixed costs, variable costs, and volume (or quantity).

Total Revenue

Total revenue reflects the sales forecast for the planning period and consists of the selling price multiplied by the quantity sold.

Fixed Costs

Fixed costs are costs not directly related to volume of production or sales. Fixed costs remain constant in dollar amount regardless of the level of output. Some examples of fixed cost are

Depreciation on plant and equipment
Executive and office staff salaries
Property insurance and taxes
Property rent
Interest on investment
Lump-sum advertising expenses

Variable Costs

Variable costs are often referred to as direct costs and are directly related to the volume of production or sales. Total variable costs are computed as the variable cost per unit multiplied by the level of operation (quantity). Some examples of variable costs are

Direct materials
Direct labor
Sales commissions
Packaging
Freight out

Volume

The **volume** (quantity) of the operation is the level of operation, as specified by (1) unit quantity, (2) dollar volume, or (3) percentage of capacity. Both total revenue and total variable costs are related to the level of operation (volume of production or sales).

Variables of the Model

The **variables** of a model are subdivided into at least three categories: (1) the solution or decision variable, (2) the criterion variable, and (3) exogenous variables.

Solution Variables

The first and most important type of variable that must be identified in any modeling process is the **solution (decision) variable.** A solution variable, which typically represents what the manager is making a decision about, is expressed as a mathematical symbol (as are all variables). It is called a *variable* because the value it takes on can vary over a range of values as defined in the mathematical model. In the case of break-even analysis, the solution variable is the break-even volume, or quantity, that is to be solved for. In this model Q will be designated as the symbol for quantity. Since the solution value of this variable is often the basis for a decision, the solution variable is sometimes referred to as the decision variable. Alternatively, because the solution value of this variable results in a decision on the part of the manager, it is also said to be a controllable variable (i.e., the manager has control over decisions).

Criterion Variable

The **criterion variable** is the variable to be measured in order to evaluate various solutions. The criterion for evaluation of the example model is **profit,** where profit equals total revenue minus total cost. For example, at one level of output the profit might be negative, whereas at a higher level of output the profit might be positive. In the break-even model, the objective is to solve for the quantity of output at which total revenue equals total cost, i.e., profit equals zero. Thus, profit is designated as the criterion variable for our model and is denoted by the symbol Z.

Exogenous Variables

Exogenous variables are variables that derive their value from outside the system being modeled and, generally, cannot be controlled by the decision maker. The basic break-even model assumes a perfectly competitive market such that price is a value determined by market forces and cannot be manipulated by the decision maker. Additionally, under such conditions the firm can produce and sell any quantity desired without affecting price. Thus, price, P, is an exogenous variable to the break-even model.

Parameters of the Model

The **parameters** of a model are the remaining elements of the model that complete the formulation of the relationships among the variables. Parameters are generally constant (numerical) values, which change only for different cases of the same problem.

In a model represented by a mathematical equation, the parameters of the model are the coefficients of the equation. The purpose of representing the parameters of the model as symbols is to obtain a solution to the model in a general form. A generalized mathematical model allows different cases of the same type of problem to be solved by substituting new values for the parameters into the general form. In this way, solutions can be obtained for specific problems without resolving the entire model.

The parameters of the break-even model are fixed cost and variable cost. Fixed cost will be denoted symbolically by *FC* and variable cost by *VC*.

It should be pointed out here that it sometimes becomes difficult to distinguish between exogenous variables and parameters. The given exogenous variable, price, might also be thought of as a model parameter, since it is assumed to be a given constant for the model. Likewise, although a model component may be a parameter or exogenous variable in the model for one problem, it may become the decision variable for another problem. In the case of break-even analysis, both price and fixed cost can take on the roles of decision variables under certain conditions.

Since the break-even model is concerned with the point at which total revenue equals total cost, we will also assign each of these two model components a symbolic representation. Total revenue will be denoted by *TR*, and total cost will be denoted by *TC*.

Most management science models are composites of submodels. It is generally simpler to construct each of the submodels separately and then aggregate the submodels into the overall model as a last step. Construction of the break-even model demonstrates this approach by constructing the submodels for total revenue and total cost and then linking the two together into an overall model.

The model symbols are summarized as follows:

Q = quantity (solution variable)

Z = profit (criterion variable)

P = price (exogenous variable)

FC = fixed cost (parameter)

VC = variable cost (parameter)

TR = total revenue (submodel variable)

TC = total cost (submodel variable).

Model Relationships and Construction

The construction of the model consists of identifying the relationships between the system components. Where possible, the functional relationship among the variables and parameters is specified explicitly. This can be done in the case of the break-even analysis model. The model is in fact a profit model (profit equals total revenue minus total cost).

In order to analyze any model and arrive at a decision, the relationship of the criterion variable to the solution variable must be specified. In break-even analysis, profit (Z) is the criterion variable, and quantity (Q) is the solution variable. Thus, the following relationship must be developed:

$$Z = f(Q)$$

(Read as: Profit, Z, is functionally related to order size, Q.)

We also know that the relationship of the criterion variable to the two submodels, TR and TC, is

$$Z = TR - TC.$$

We will, therefore, develop each submodel separately, and join the two as our last step.

Total Revenue

Total revenue is simply price multiplied by the quantity produced or sold. Therefore, our first submodel is

$$TR = P \cdot Q.$$

Total Cost

Total variable cost is the unit variable cost multiplied by quantity. Fixed cost is a constant dollar value, independent of volume. Thus, the second submodel is

$$TC = FC + VC \cdot Q.$$

Profit Model

The profit model is given in terms of the criterion variable, solution variable, exogenous variable, and parameters as

$$Z = P \cdot Q - FC - VC \cdot Q$$

or

$$\text{Profit} = \text{price} \cdot \text{quantity} - \text{fixed cost} - \text{variable cost} \cdot \text{quantity}.$$

Solution of the Model

We must now solve for the value of the solution variable (Q) in terms of the other variables and parameters of the model. An objective in break-even analysis is to determine the value of Q for which profit (Z) equals zero. Therefore, the solution procedure to be employed here is to set the model for profit equal to zero and solve for Q. The solution procedure is illustrated as follows:

$P \cdot Q - FC - VC \cdot Q = 0$	Setting profit model equal to 0
$P \cdot Q - VC \cdot Q = FC$	Transposing FC
$Q(P - VC) = FC$	Collecting Q separately
$Q_{BE} = \dfrac{FC}{P - VC}$	Dividing through by $P - VC$.

We identify Q_{BE} as the break-even point quantity. At the point where the volume of operation equals Q_{BE}, profit will equal zero (and total revenue will equal total cost). Note that $P - VC$ is the commonly known term, **unit contribution.** Thus, break-even is determined by dividing fixed cost by unit contribution.

The model solution illustrates the previously discussed general form of a solution; that is, the break-even quantity can be determined by inserting the values for fixed cost, price, and variable cost for the symbols FC, P, and VC in the Q_{BE} equation and obtaining a solution directly. Not all models can be solved in a general form, but whenever possible it is preferable.

The Graphic Model and Solution

The preceeding break-even model is displayed graphically in figure 1.2. The graph illustrates that the break-even quantity Q_{BE} occurs at the point where profit Z equals zero (and where total revenue equals total cost). If we refer back to the model solution process, we see that the break-even point occurs where quantity multiplied by unit contribution is equal to fixed cost, or

$$Q(P - VC) = FC.$$

Thus, as quantity is increased from zero to Q_{BE}, the total contribution toward fixed cost (quantity times unit contribution) is progressively covering a larger portion of fixed cost, and the loss is being reduced. As quantity is increased beyond Q_{BE}, the expression $Q(P - VC)$ exceeds fixed cost in the form of increasing profit.

Figure 1.2 Graphic model of the break-even analysis.

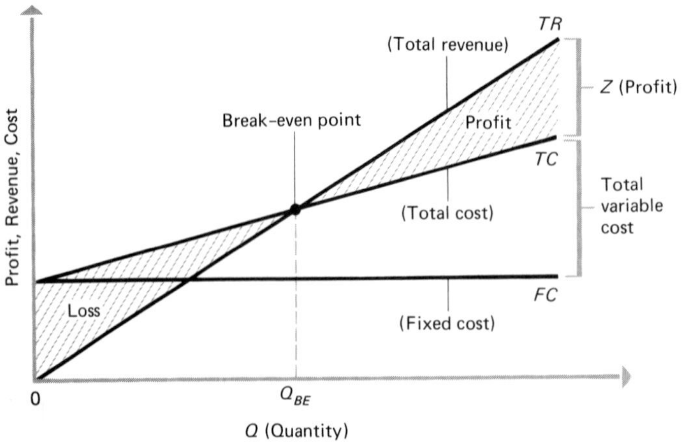

Examples of Management Science Models

In this section a brief cross section of some of the model types presented in this text will be reviewed. These models will, by necessity, be somewhat simplified for definitive purposes.

Example 1.1 Product Mix Decision

A wood products firm produces two kinds of paneling, colonial and western. The paneling is processed through two operations, pressing and finishing. The decision problem facing management is how many sheets of each type of paneling should be produced in a month in order to gain the most profit.

The problem confronting management is that unlimited production of paneling is not possible—the firm is limited by the amount of resources available to produce the products. The problem then is to allocate the resources in the optimal manner in order to maximize profit.

The firm has resources in terms of plant hours available for pressing, hours available for finishing, pounds of wood product, and a dollar budget. The resource requirements and availabilities for each type of paneling, which constitute the parameters of the model, are as follows:

	Resource Requirement per 100-Sheet Lot		Total Resources Available
Resource	Colonial	Western	per Month
Wood product	20 lb.	40 lb.	5,000 lb.
Pressing	4 hr.	6 hr.	400 hr.
Finishing	3 hr.	4 hr.	500 hr.
Cost (budget)	$40	$60	$7,000

The firm receives $80 profit for every 100-sheet lot of colonial paneling and $100 profit for every 100-sheet lot of western paneling.

Following the management science process, now that the problem has been defined, the next step is to develop a model of the system. In other words, a mathematical formulation is to be developed.

First, solution, or decision, variables must be defined. Since the decision in this problem concerns solving for the amount of each type of paneling to produce, the two solution variables are defined as follows:

x_1 = the number of 100-sheet lots of colonial paneling to produce in one month

x_2 = the number of 100-sheet lots of western paneling to produce in one month.

Next the objective of the firm, to obtain the maximum possible profit, is transformed into a mathematical equation expressing this objective.

$$\text{Maximize profit} = \$80x_1 + \$100x_2$$

In management science terminology, this equation is referred to as the **objective function.** It is the amount of profit received for any values of x_1 and x_2. For example, if $x_1 = 10$ and $x_2 = 20$ (10 lots of colonial paneling and 20 lots of western paneling), the profit is \$2,800—an amount achieved by substituting the given values of x_1 and x_2 into the objective function. The objective is to maximize the value of the function by determining the best values for x_1 and x_2.

The firm's problem, however, is to maximize profit within the limitations of their available resources. The next step is to transform the resource requirements and availabilities into mathematical relationships. For example, there are 5,000 pounds of wood product available to make paneling—each lot of colonial requires 20 pounds and each lot of western requires 40 pounds. Thus, the amount of wood product used for colonial paneling is $20x_1$ (20 pounds per lot times the number of lots) and the amount of wood product used for western paneling is $40x_2$. The total amount of wood product used must be 5,000 pounds or less. The other three constraints for pressing, finishing, and budget are developed in a similar manner.

$$\begin{aligned}
&\text{Wood product:} && 20x_1 + 40x_2 \leq 5{,}000 \text{ pounds}\\
&\text{Pressing:} && 4x_1 + 6x_2 \leq 400 \text{ hours}\\
&\text{Finishing:} && 3x_1 + 4x_2 \leq 500 \text{ hours}\\
&\text{Cost (budget):} && 40x_1 + 60x_2 \leq \$7{,}000
\end{aligned}$$

These relationships are referred to as **constraints** because they specify that the utilization of each resource cannot exceed the total amount of resources available. The $\leq$ inequality signs indicate the limitations of these relationships (i.e., the firm could use less but not more than these resource amounts).

The mathematical model formulation can now be summarized as:

$$\text{Maximize } Z = \$80x_1 + \$100x_2$$

subject to

$$\begin{aligned}
20x_1 + 40x_2 &\leq 5{,}000\\
4x_1 + 6x_2 &\leq 400\\
3x_1 + 4x_2 &\leq 500\\
40x_1 + 60x_2 &\leq 7{,}000.
\end{aligned}$$

The next step would be to solve this set of mathematical relationships to determine values for x_1 and x_2, which both satisfy the constraints and achieve the objective. However, this step will be explained later in the text. This is, in fact, a **linear programming** model, a topic that will be covered in chapters 2 through 4. It is an example of a deterministic model that *optimizes* the specified criterion, subject to limited resources. That is, uncertainty is not considered in the model, which is formulated to determine the one "best" or "optimal" solution.

Example 1.2 Transportation Problem

An asphalt company produces asphalt at three plants within a geographic region. The asphalt is then transported in trucks from the plants to construction sites where roads are being paved. Presently the company is under contract to supply asphalt to three road-paving locations. The decision problem for the management of this company is to minimize the cost of transporting asphalt from plants to construction sites. More specifically, management desires to know the number of truckloads to ship from each plant to each road-paving site at the lowest cost, given the availability of asphalt at each plant and the requirement at each construction site. The transportation costs from each plant to each site are given in tabular form as follows:

Plant	Transportation Costs to Each Paving Site 1	2	3	Supply (in truckloads)
A	$40	25	30	120
B	75	50	60	80
C	15	45	50	80
Demand (in truckloads)	150	70	60	280

The constraints of this problem are the maximum amounts of asphalt that the company is able to supply from each of its three plants and the amounts demanded at each site for the planning period. This information is given in the column labeled *supply* and the row labeled *demand*.

This problem can be formulated mathematically as a linear programming model within the following general framework.

Minimize total transportation cost

subject to

Supply constraints

Demand constraints

Within this model, the decision variables are the amounts transported from each site to each destination.

The supply constraints represent the fact that only a limited amount can be supplied from each plant (120, 80, and 80 truckloads respectively). Thus, for plant A, regardless of which of the three sites the asphalt is shipped to, the total shipments cannot exceed 120. Similarly, a limited amount is demanded at each site (150, 70, and 60 truckloads respectively). So regardless of which plant(s) the asphalt comes from, the total delivered to site 1 should not exceed 150 truckloads. The objective function signifies that the truckloads should be allocated in a manner that will meet the demand at the sites, not exceed the supply at each plant, and do so at the lowest transportation cost. Since the actual model formulation is somewhat more complex than the linear programming discussed previously, we will refrain from presenting it here. This model type is a special case of linear programming that will be presented in detail in chapter 5.

Example 1.3 Construction Scheduling Problem

A construction company has contracted to build a new office building. The company's management wants to develop a construction schedule that will allow them to finish within the allotted time. They have identified five major steps in the building's construction: finalizing the design, digging footings, building the foundation, transporting steel and other materials, and building construction. The objective of the company is to complete the project on time.

As an aid in planning and scheduling, a precedence diagram for the different construction activities has been developed. (See figure 1.3.) By allocating time to each building activity, this precedence diagram becomes a CPM/PERT **network,** which can be used to determine overall project duration. This type of project network can also be used to determine the time at which each event should occur in order to maintain the project schedule. (The circles in the network in figure 1.3 indicate the completion of an activity and the start of another.) CPM/PERT is just one of the network model types that will be presented in chapter 6.

Figure 1.3 A CPM/PERT network.

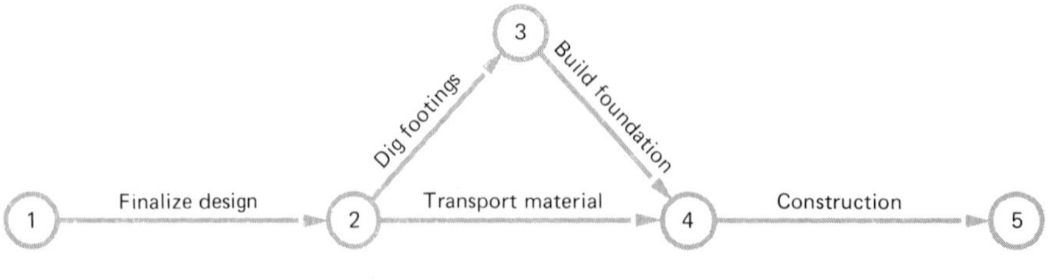

Example 1.4 Feasibility Study for Facility Expansion

A bank's management is considering the installation of another drive-in window or windows to supplement the single drive-in window already in use. The bank operations officer has observed that on occasion the waiting line for the present drive-in window is so long that customers leave or become irate with the teller. The bank's management has requested the operations officer to analyze the teller system and determine how many additional windows would be required to achieve a reasonable waiting time for customers. The officer has also been instructed to compare the construction and operating costs for the window(s) with the estimated losses resulting from customer ill will when they must wait for service.

This is a classic problem in **queueing,** or waiting line, analysis. In chapter 10, various queueing models will be presented that would enable the operations officer to perform the analysis requested by management. Information that can be obtained from these models includes such factors as the average time a customer must wait prior to service, the average number of customers waiting in line to be served, the average time a customer is at the bank (both in line and being served), the probability that a certain number of customers will be in line, and the percentage of time the teller is idle. This information can then be used to determine the cost trade-offs associated with building and operating new drive-in windows. Such information would allow the operations officer to determine the expected waiting time of customers at two windows instead of one and then to compare the construction and added operating costs with the decrease in losses resulting from dissatisfied customers. Note that the type of output generated from a queueing model is probabilistic and descriptive. In other words, queueing models are examples of models that do not optimize (do not seek a "best" solution) but provide operating statistics that describe the system being analyzed (e.g., average waiting time is a statistical descriptor).

In many cases queueing problems are so complex that they cannot be analyzed by the traditional queueing models. In such cases **simulation** is a possible alternative modeling form. In a simulation a computerized description of the problem situation is constructed and used to generate the sort of operating statistics described previously. Simulation, which can be used as an alternative to many analytic models (i.e., models with a mathematical formulation and solution), is the topic of chapter 11.

Example 1.5 Machine Acquisition Problem

A manufacturing firm is attempting to decide how many of three different types of new machines it must purchase to keep pace with normal plant growth and increasing product demand. The three machine types are small-, medium- and heavy-duty, and their costs are \$1,500, \$3,500, and \$5,000 respectively. The purchase of machines is constrained by space limitations, budget limitations, and maintenance capabilities. The firm's management staff has developed the following linear programming model for this decision problem:

$$\text{Maximize Sales} = \$2{,}000x_1 + \$5{,}000x_2 + \$8{,}000x_3$$

subject to

$$40x_1 + 70x_2 + 100x_3 \leq 750 \text{ ft}^2$$
$$\$1{,}500x_1 + \$3{,}500x_2 + \$5{,}000x_3 \leq \$20{,}000$$
$$x_1 + x_2 + x_3 \leq 7$$

In this model, the values for x are nonnegative integers, which are the decision variables representing the number of machine purchases of each type. The objective function is the increase in dollar sales resulting from the new machines. The constraints reflect (1) the space limitations in the plant, (2) the budget limitation for the purchase of machinery, and (3) the total number of machines that can be purchased and maintained.

This model structure is similar to the model structure for the linear programming model in our first example. However, the crucial difference in this model is that the values of the decision variables that optimize the solution must be integers—it is not possible to purchase fractions of machines. This difference requires a substantial adjustment in the solution technique used in a normal linear programming model. Therefore, the topic of **integer programming** is presented as an advanced topic of mathematical programming in chapter 14.

Summary

The examples presented in this chapter are only a sample of the many problems that may be attacked by management science modeling and solution techniques. Although the examples have been necessarily brief and simplified with actual solutions not discussed, the construction of these model types and others will be presented in detail, illustrated with examples, and their solutions demonstrated in later chapters. This method offers the reader a broad spectrum of knowledge in the mechanics of model building and problem solution. However, the ultimate test of the management scientist, or any person who applies the management science process and techniques, is the ability to transfer textbook knowledge to the real world. In such instances there is an ''art'' to the application of management science, but it is an art predicated both on practical experience and a sound basic knowledge of the tools of management science. The first of these necessities is beyond the realm of textbooks; however, the second is the purpose of this text.

References

Ackoff, Russell L., and Sasieni, Maurice W. *Fundamentals of Operations Research*. New York: John Wiley & Sons, 1968.

Beer, Stafford. *Management Sciences: The Business Use of Operations Research*. Garden City, New York: Doubleday & Co., 1967.

Churchman, C. W.; Ackoff, R. L.; and Arnoff, E. L. *Introduction to Operations Research*. New York: John Wiley & Sons, 1957.

Fabrycky, W. J., and Torgersen, P. E. *Operations Economy: Industrial Applications of Operations Research*. Englewood Cliffs, New Jersey: Prentice-Hall, 1966.

Hillier, F. S., and Lieberman, G. J. *Operations Research*. 2d ed. San Francisco: Holden-Day, 1974.

Taha, Hamdy A. *Operations Research*. 2d ed. New York: Macmillan, 1976.

Teichroew, P. *An Introduction to Management Science*. New York: John Wiley & Sons, 1964.

Wagner, Harvey M. *Principles of Operations Research*. Englewood Cliffs, New Jersey: Prentice-Hall, 1975.

Wagner, Harvey M. *Principles of Management Science*. Englewood Cliffs, New Jersey: Prentice-Hall, 1975.

Study Questions

1. Discuss the history and development of management science.
2. List and discuss the steps of the scientific method.
3. In figure 1.1 indicate how the value of Q that would result in the lowest cost would be determined. Based on this graphical analysis explain how the lowest cost value of Q could be determined mathematically.
4. In relation to management science define the term *model*.
5. Define the following model components and discuss their relationships: *decision variables, criterion variable, exogenous variables,* and *parameters*.
6. Construct the break-even model from the model components Q (quantity), Z (profit), P (price), FC (fixed cost), VC (variable cost), TR (total revenue), and TC (total cost).
7. Derive the formula for determining the break-even quantity from the break-even model.
8. An electrical manufacturer produces radios. On a daily basis the fixed cost for producing radios each day is $10,000 while the variable cost is $5 per radio. Each radio is sold for $25. Given this information, determine (a) the daily break-even quantity, (b) total break-even revenue, (c) total break-even cost, and (d) total break-even profit.
9. Develop a graphic model of the break-even analysis in problem 8.
10. Define *management science* and the field of study it encompasses.
11. Why has management science as an academic discipline increased in popularity during the past several decades?
12. Distinguish between *probabilistic* and *deterministic* models. Classify the various topics in this text according to these two categories.
13. Consider a product mix decision problem where an electrical manufacturer is attempting to determine how many clocks and radios should be produced. Verbally describe the types of resource constraints that could exist, the possible objective(s) of the firm, the decision variables, and the possible model parameters.
14. Develop a mathematical model for the transportation problem in this chapter (ex. 1.2), using the general model framework given in the problem explanation as a guideline.
15. Identify types of problems other than the construction scheduling problem (ex. 1.3) for which a precedence diagram could be used.
16. Describe several different examples of problems to which waiting line analysis could be applied like the bank facility expansion problem (ex. 1.4).
17. Identify several examples of decision-making problems that require integer solutions like the machine acquisition problem (ex. 1.5).

Part **2**

Deterministic Models: Mathematical Programming

2

Introduction to Linear Programming

Linear programming is perhaps the best known and one of the most widely used techniques of management science. It is a mathematical method of allocating scarce resources to achieve an objective, such as maximizing profit. Linear programming has found wide application in business, as most managerial problems involve resource allocation. For example, management decision problems such as production planning, capital budgeting, personnel allocation, advertising, and promotion planning are concerned with the achievement of a given objective (profit maximization or cost minimization) subject to limited resources (money, material, labor, time, etc.). Linear programming involves the description of a real world decision situation as a mathematical model that consists of a linear objective function and linear resource constraints. In this chapter a brief history of linear programming will be presented followed by several example problems demonstrating the mathematical model formulation process, a general linear programming model and its properties, and a graphical interpretation of linear programming.

History of Linear Programming

Although the origin of mathematical programming techniques dates back to the theories of linear and nonlinear equations, George B. Dantzig is generally recognized as the pioneer of linear programming. Dantzig's work was primarily in the search for mathematical techniques to solve military logistics problems when he was employed by the U.S. Air Force during World War II. His research was encouraged by other scholars, such as J. Von Neumann, L. Hurwicz and T. C. Koopmans, who were working on the same general subject. The original name given to the technique was *programming of interdependent activities in a linear structure,* later shortened to *linear programming*.

After the war, many scholars joined Dantzig in the further development of the concept of linear programming. The first paper on a workable solution method (now known as the simplex method) was published by Dantzig in 1947. Dantzig collaborated with Marshall Wood, Alex Orden, and their associates in developing the simplex method while working on research projects for the U.S. Air Force.

Early applications of linear programming were predominantly to military problems such as logistics, transportation problems, and procurement problems. In addition, Wassily Leontief's input-output analysis provided a base for the application of linear programming to interindustry economic analysis.

Since 1947, researchers such as A. Charnes, W. W. Cooper, A. Henderson, and W. Orchard-Hays have joined Dantzig in developing and exploring new applications for linear programming. Linear programming was soon being applied to a large number of public and private sector problems. Linear programming was found to be a powerful problem-solving approach for managerial decision analysis in business. The number of linear programming applications has increased in recent years with the rapid development and sophistication of electronic computers.

Model Formulation and Examples

Linear programming has been successfully applied to a wide spectrum of problems across many different fields. However, business and industry, agriculture, and the military have made the most extensive use of linear programming. The typical decision problem confronted by management groups in various settings is the optimum allocation of scarce resources. Resources can be money, labor, material, machine capacity, time, space, or technology. Management's task is to achieve the best possible outcome with these limited resources. The desired outcome is either expressed as the maximization of some measure, such as profit, effectiveness, welfare, or return, or the minimization of such elements as cost, time, and distance.

Once the problem has been identified, the goals of management established, and the applicability of linear programming determined, the next step in solving an unstructured, real-world problem is the formulation of a mathematical model. This entails three major steps: (1) the identification of solution variables (the quantity of the activity in question), (2) the development of an objective function that is a linear relationship of the solution variables, and (3) the determination of system constraints, which are also linear relationships of the decision variables, that reflect the limited resources of the problem.

In this section, six different examples are presented that demonstrate the steps of linear programming model formulation. The following examples are typical of linear programming applications and have been widely used to demonstrate model formulation. By careful analysis of each of these examples the reader should be able to grasp the major characteristics of model formulation and the fundamentals of linear programming.

Example 2.1 Product Mix Problem

A manufacturing company wishes to determine how many of each of three different products they should produce given limited resources in order to maximize total profit. The labor and material requirements and the contribution to profit for each of the three products are as follows:

	Resource Requirements Labor (hr./unit)	 Materials (lb./unit)	Profit ($/unit)
Product 1	5	4	$3
Product 2	2	6	5
Product 3	4	3	2

There are 240 hours of labor available daily for production. The supply of materials is limited to 400 pounds per day. The decision problem is to determine the quantity of each product to produce in order to maximize total profit. This problem meets all the requirements of a linear programming problem (requirements that will become apparent as additional examples are studied). Now we shall formulate the problem as a linear programming model.

Decision Variables

The three decision variables in the problem are the quantities of products 1, 2, and 3 to be produced on a daily basis. These quantities can be represented symbolically as

x_1 = quantity of product 1
x_2 = quantity of product 2
x_3 = quantity of product 3.

Objective Function

The objective of the product mix problem is to maximize total profit. It should be obvious that total profit is the sum of profits gained from each individual product. Profit from product 1 is determined by multiplying the unit profit, \$3, by the number of units produced, x_1. Profit for products 2 and 3 are determined similarly. Thus, total profit, Z, can be expressed as

$$\text{Maximize } Z = 3x_1 + 5x_2 + 2x_3$$

where

$3x_1$ = profit from product 1
$5x_2$ = profit from product 2
$2x_3$ = profit from product 3.

System Constraints

In this problem the constraints are the limited amounts of labor and material available for production. Production of each of the three products requires both labor and material inputs. For product 1, the labor required to produce each unit is 5 hours. As such, the labor requirement for product 1 is $5x_1$ hours. Similarly, product 2 requires $2x_2$ hours of labor and product 3 requires $4x_3$ hours. The total number of labor hours available for production is 240. Thus, the *labor* constraint is

$$5x_1 + 2x_2 + 4x_3 \leq 240.$$

The constraint for material requirements is formulated in the same manner. Product 1 (x_1) requires 4 pounds for every unit produced, product 2 (x_2) requires 6 pounds per unit, and product 3 (x_3) requires 3 pounds per unit. Since there are 400 pounds of *raw material* available this constraint is expressed as

$$4x_1 + 6x_2 + 3x_3 \leq 400.$$

We also restrict each decision variable to a positive value since it would be illogical to produce negative quantities of a product. These restrictions are called **nonnegativity constraints** and are expressed mathematically as

$$x_1 \geq 0,\ x_2 \geq 0,\ x_3 \geq 0.$$

Most linear programming applications have nonnegativity constraints. However, the linear programming solution procedure is capable of handling negative decision variable values if for some reason the problem requires it and the model is appropriately formulated. Negative values frequently occur when the decision variable defines a rate such as a growth or inflation rate, which can increase or decrease. Its decrease would be denoted by a negative value. Instances where this condition occurs and the procedure for handling it are discussed in chapter 3.

One might also question the exclusive expression of the constraints as inequalities ($\leq$) rather than as equalities ($=$). A strict equality would imply the total use of production capacity; whereas a $\leq$ inequality allows the use of full capacity only *if* that is what the optimal solution requires. It also allows for some unused capacity if that is what the optimal solution requires. In many cases a solution with some unused production capacity will result in a better solution, meaning greater profit, than a solution requiring the use of all resources. The $\leq$ inequality simply allows the flexibility for either occurrence.

Now the complete linear programming problem can be summarized as a mathematical model:

$$\text{Maximize } Z = 3x_1 + 5x_2 + 2x_3$$

subject to

$$\begin{aligned} 5x_1 + 2x_2 + 4x_3 &\leq 240 \\ 4x_1 + 6x_2 + 3x_3 &\leq 400 \\ x_1, x_2, x_3 &\geq 0 \end{aligned}$$

By solving this model for the optimum values of the decision variables, x_1, x_2, and x_3, the total profit, Z, will be maximized.

Example 2.2 Diet Problem

The preceding product mix problem was an example of a maximization problem. The following diet problem is a minimization problem.

A hospital dietician must prepare breakfast menus every morning for the hospital patients. Part of the dietician's responsibility is to make certain that minimum daily requirements for vitamins A and B are met. At the same time, the menus must be kept at the lowest possible cost to avoid waste. The main breakfast staples providing vitamins A and B are eggs, bacon, and cereal. The vitamin requirements and vitamin contributions for each staple are:

	Vitamin Contributions			
Vitamin	mg/Egg	mg/Bacon Strip	mg/Cereal Cup	Minimum Daily Requirement (mg)
A	2	4	1	16
B	3	2	1	12

The cost of an egg is four cents, the cost of a bacon strip is three cents, and a cup of cereal costs two cents. The dietician wants to know how much of each staple to serve in order to meet the minimum daily requirements while minimizing total cost.

Decision Variables

The diet problem contains three decision variables that reflect the number of units of each type of food placed on the menu.

x_1 = number of eggs served

x_2 = number of bacon strips served

x_3 = number of cups of cereal served

Objective Function

The objective of this problem is to minimize the total cost of each breakfast. The total cost in this case is simply the sum of the per unit cost from each serving of eggs, bacon, and cereal. Thus, total cost, Z, is expressed as

$$\text{Minimize } Z = 4x_1 + 3x_2 + 2x_3$$

where

$4x_1$ = cost (cents) of eggs per serving

$3x_2$ = cost (cents) of bacon per serving

$2x_3$ = cost (cents) of cereal per serving.

System Constraints

In the diet problem, the constraints reflect the minimum daily vitamin requirements established by the dietician. Each type of breakfast food yields the previously specified quantity of vitamins (in mg) per unit. The constraint for vitamin A is

$$2x_1 + 4x_2 + 1x_3 \geq 16$$

where

$2x_1$ = vitamin contribution of eggs (in milligrams) per serving

$4x_2$ = vitamin contribution of bacon (in milligrams) per serving

$1x_3$ = vitamin contribution of cereal (in milligrams) per serving.

Unlike example 2.1, this example uses $\geq$ inequalities specifying the minimum amount of vitamins needed. In other words, *at least* 16 milligrams of vitamin A must be achieved. In the simplest and most general form of linear programming, maximization problems employ $\leq$ inequalities, while in minimization problems, $\geq$ inequalities are used. However, this is not an absolute rule as more complex problems frequently have both $\leq$ and $\geq$ constraints as well as equalities.

The constraint for vitamin B is constructed similarly,

$$3x_1 + 2x_2 + 1x_3 \geq 12.$$

The complete linear programming problem can now be summarized.

$$\text{Minimize } Z = 4x_1 + 3x_2 + 2x_3$$

subject to

$$\begin{aligned} 2x_1 + 4x_2 + 1x_3 &\geq 16 \\ 3x_1 + 2x_2 + 1x_3 &\geq 12 \\ x_1, x_2, x_3 &\geq 0 \end{aligned}$$

By solving this model for the values of the decision variables, x_1, x_2, and x_3, the dietician will obtain the minimum total cost (minimum value of Z) possible, while at the same time meeting the minimum requirements for vitamins A and B.

Example 2.3 Blend Problem

A refinery blends four petroleum components into three grades of gasoline—regular, premium, and low lead. Management wishes to determine the optimal mix of the four components that will maximize profit. The maximum quantities available of each component and the cost per barrel are as follows:

Component	Maximum Barrels Available/Day	Cost/Barrel
1	5,000	$ 9.00
2	2,400	7.00
3	4,000	12.00
4	1,500	6.00

In order to insure the proper blend for each gasoline grade, maximum or minimum percentages of the components in each blend have been determined. The blends as well as the selling price of each grade are given:

Grade	Component Specifications	Selling Price/ Barrel
Regular	Not less than 40% of 1	$12.00
	Not more than 20% of 2	
	Not less than 30% of 3	
Premium	Not less than 40% of 3	18.00
Low Lead	Not more than 50% of 2	10.00
	Not less than 10% of 1	

Decision Variables

The blend problem is somewhat more complex than the previous two examples and, as a result, requires some additional thought in defining the decision variables. At first glance it is tempting to define three decision variables, x_1, x_2, and x_3 that would represent the quantities of regular, premium, and low-lead gasoline produced respectively. However, these decision variables do not reflect the decision problem proposed by management. They not only want to know the amount of each grade to produce, but also the amount of each component blended to produce each grade.

In addition, management desires to maximize profit. However, if three decision variables for gasoline grades are used, only information on selling price would be included in the mathematical model. Since profit is determined by subtracting cost from selling price and cost information is available only on the four petroleum components, it is necessary to include the quantity of components produced as well as the quality of grades produced in the decision process.

As such, in this problem the decision variables must reflect the quantity of each component used in each grade. These quantities can be represented algebraically as

x_{ij} = barrels of component i used in gasoline grade j per day, where $i = 1, 2, 3, 4$ and $j = R$ (regular), P (premium), and L (low lead).

This results in twelve decision variables. As an example, consider one decision variable x_{2P}. This variable represents the amount of component 2 used in the production of premium grade gasoline per day. Thus, the amount of each grade of gasoline produced is actually made up of the sum of the four components used in each grade, as follows:

Regular: $x_{1R} + x_{2R} + x_{3R} + x_{4R}$
Premium: $x_{1P} + x_{2P} + x_{3P} + x_{4P}$
Low Lead: $x_{1L} + x_{2L} + x_{3L} + x_{4L}$.

Objective Function

The objective of the blend problem is to maximize total profit. This requires that the cost of each barrel be subtracted from the revenue obtained from each barrel. Revenue is determined by multiplying selling price by the total amount of each grade of gasoline produced. For example, the selling price of regular grade is \$12 per barrel, which must be multiplied by the total quantity of regular grade gasoline produced from each of the four components, $x_{1R} + x_{2R} + x_{3R} + x_{4R}$. On the other hand, the cost of component 1 is found by multiplying the cost per barrel, \$9, by the total quantity of component 1 used for each grade of gasoline, $x_{1R} + x_{1P} + x_{1L}$. Computing the revenues and costs for the other grades and components in a similar manner results in an objective function that combines all costs and revenues.

$$\begin{aligned}\text{Maximize } Z = \;& \$12(x_{1R} + x_{2R} + x_{3R} + x_{4R}) + 18(x_{1P} + x_{2P} + x_{3P} + x_{4P}) \\ & + 10(x_{1L} + x_{2L} + x_{3L} + x_{4L}) - 9(x_{1R} + x_{1P} + x_{1L}) \\ & - 7(x_{2R} + x_{2P} + x_{2L}) - 12(x_{3R} + x_{3P} + x_{3L}) \\ & - 6(x_{4R} + x_{4P} + x_{4L})\end{aligned}$$

Combining terms results in the following simplified objective function:

$$\begin{aligned}\text{Maximize } Z = \;& 3x_{1R} + 5x_{2R} + 6x_{4R} + 9x_{1P} + 11x_{2P} + 6x_{3P} \\ & + 12x_{4P} + 1x_{1L} + 3x_{2L} + 4x_{4L} - 2x_{3L}\end{aligned}$$

The negative term, $-2x_{3L}$, in the objective function results from the fact that the cost of component 3 is greater than the selling price of low lead.

System Constraints

In this problem, the model constraints reflect the limited amounts of each component available and the blend requirements for each grade. The availability constraints show that the total quantity of each component used in all three grades of gasoline is limited to the barrels of component available per day.

$$x_{1R} + x_{1P} + x_{1L} \leq 5{,}000$$

$$x_{2R} + x_{2P} + x_{2L} \leq 2{,}400$$

$$x_{3R} + x_{3P} + x_{3L} \leq 4{,}000$$

$$x_{4R} + x_{4P} + x_{4L} \leq 1{,}500$$

The blend requirements are slightly more complicated. Looking at just the first requirement for regular grade gasoline, it is specified that component 1 must constitute at least 40% of the total amount of regular. This constraint is reflected as

$$\frac{x_{1R}}{x_{1R} + x_{2R} + x_{3R} + x_{4R}} \geq .40$$

where $x_{1R} + x_{2R} + x_{3R} + x_{4R}$ equals the total amount of regular gasoline.

This constraint can be rewritten in a form more consistent with linear programming constraint inequalities:

$$x_{1R} \geq .40(x_{1R} + x_{2R} + x_{3R} + x_{4R})$$

and finally

$$.6x_{1R} - .4x_{2R} - .4x_{3R} - .4x_{4R} \geq 0.$$

This latter constraint reflects the linear form into which all linear programming constraints must be converted before eventual solution. This format requires all decision variables to be on the left-hand side of the inequality and all constants on the right-hand side. Also, all quantities on the right-hand side must be nonnegative values.

The other two blend requirements for regular grade gasoline can be transformed into constraints in a similar fashion as

$$-.2x_{1R} + .8x_{2R} - .2x_{3R} - .2x_{4R} \leq 0$$

$$-.3x_{1R} - .3x_{2R} + .7x_{3R} - .3x_{4R} \geq 0.$$

The single blend requirement for premium grade gasoline is

$$\frac{x_{3P}}{x_{1P} + x_{2P} + x_{3P} + x_{4P}} \geq .40$$

which converted becomes

$$-.4x_{1P} - .4x_{2P} + .6x_{3P} - .4x_{4P} \geq 0.$$

The two blend requirements for low-lead gasoline are

$$-.50x_{1L} + .50x_{2L} - .50x_{3L} - .50x_{4L} \leq 0$$
$$.90x_{1L} - .10x_{2L} - .10x_{3L} - .10x_{4L} \geq 0.$$

The complete linear programming formulation for the blend problem can be summarized as

$$\text{Maximize } Z = 3x_{1R} + 5x_{2R} + 6x_{4R} + 9x_{1P} + 11x_{2P} + 6x_{3P}$$
$$+ 12x_{4P} + 1x_{1L} + 3x_{2L} + 4x_{4L} - 2x_{3L}$$

subject to

$$x_{1R} + x_{1P} + x_{1L} \leq 5{,}000$$
$$x_{2R} + x_{2P} + x_{2L} \leq 2{,}400$$
$$x_{3R} + x_{3P} + x_{3L} \leq 4{,}000$$
$$x_{4R} + x_{4P} + x_{4L} \leq 1{,}500$$
$$.6x_{1R} - .4x_{2R} - .4x_{3R} - .4x_{4R} \geq 0$$
$$-.2x_{1R} + .8x_{2R} - .2x_{3R} - .2x_{4R} \leq 0$$
$$-.3x_{1R} - .3x_{2R} + .7x_{3R} - .3x_{4R} \geq 0$$
$$-.4x_{1P} - .4x_{2P} + .6x_{3P} - .4x_{4P} \geq 0$$
$$-.5x_{1L} + .5x_{2L} - .5x_{3L} - .5x_{4L} \leq 0$$
$$.9x_{1L} - .1x_{2L} - .1x_{3L} - .1x_{4L} \geq 0$$
$$\text{all } x_{ij} \geq 0.$$

By solving for all values of x_{ij} in the previous model, the optimum quantities of each grade of gasoline will be obtained as

Regular:

$$x_{1R} + x_{2R} + x_{3R} + x_{4R}$$

Premium:

$$x_{1P} + x_{2P} + x_{3P} + x_{4P}$$

Low Lead:

$$x_{1L} + x_{2L} + x_{3L} + x_{4L}.$$

In addition, the optimum quantities of each component will be determined as

Component 1:

$$x_{1R} + x_{1P} + x_{1L}$$

Component 2:

$$x_{2R} + x_{2P} + x_{2L}$$

Component 3:

$$x_{3R} + x_{3P} + x_{3L}$$

Component 4:

$$x_{4R} + x_{4P} + x_{4L}.$$

In this model, profit (Z) is maximized by simultaneously considering revenues for gasoline grades and costs of components.

Example 2.4 Crop Mix Problem

A farm owner wants to know how many acres of three different crops to plant on three different plots in order to maximize profit.

The farmer's tract of land consists of 2,000 acres. He has subdivided the tract into three plots and has contracted with three local farm families to operate the plots. The farm owner has instructed each sharecropper to plant three crops: corn, peas, and soybeans. The size of each plot has been determined by the capabilities of each local farmer. Plot sizes, crop restrictions, and profit per acre are given in the following tables:

Plot	Acreage
1	500
2	800
3	700

Crop	Maximum Acreage	Profit/Acre
Corn	900	\$600
Peas	700	450
Soybeans	1,000	300

Any of the three crops may be planted on any of the plots, however, the farm owner has placed the following restrictions on the farming operation. At least 60% of each plot must be under cultivation. To insure that each contractor works according to his potential and resources (which determined the acreage allocation), the owner wants the same proportion of each plot to be under cultivation. The owner's objective is to determine how much of each crop to plant on each farm in order to maximize profit.

Decision Variables

The decision variables for this problem define the amount of each crop planted on each farm. These amounts are expressed symbolically as

x_{ij} = acres of crop i planted on plot j where i = c(corn), p(peas), s(soybeans) and $j = 1, 2, 3$.

This results in nine decision variables.

Objective Function

The objective of the farm owner is to maximize profit. Profit is determined by computing the product of the profit per acre for each crop and the total number of acres of the crop planted on all three plots. Thus, the objective function reflects the profit gained from each crop.

$$\text{Maximize } Z = 600\ (x_{c1} + x_{c2} + x_{c3}) + 450\ (x_{p1} + x_{p2} + x_{p3}) + 300\ (x_{s1} + x_{s2} + x_{s3})$$

System Constraints

The system constraints are constructed to reflect the limited resources of the farm and the operating restrictions established by the owner. The first set of constraints defines the upper and lower limits of cultivated acreage on each plot. The upper limit, naturally, is the acreage allocation established by the owner while the lower limit is the 60% of the available acreage that must be planted. This results in the following constraints:

$$300 \leq x_{c1} + x_{p1} + x_{s1} \leq 500$$

$$480 \leq x_{c2} + x_{p2} + x_{s2} \leq 800$$

$$420 \leq x_{c3} + x_{p3} + x_{s3} \leq 700$$

However, since these constraints do not fit the normal linear programming format—all decision variables on the left side of the inequalities and quantities on the right side—they must be transformed. This can be achieved by transforming each constraint into two constraints for maximum and minimum acreages. This results in six constraints:

$$x_{c1} + x_{p1} + x_{s1} \geq 300$$

$$x_{c1} + x_{p1} + x_{s1} \leq 500$$

$$x_{c2} + x_{p2} + x_{s2} \geq 480$$

$$x_{c2} + x_{p2} + x_{s2} \leq 800$$

$$x_{c3} + x_{p3} + x_{s3} \geq 420$$

$$x_{c3} + x_{p3} + x_{s3} \leq 700$$

Also, the previously stated restrictions on the total number of acres of each crop that can be planted are shown by

$$x_{c1} + x_{c2} + x_{c3} \leq 900$$
$$x_{p1} + x_{p2} + x_{p3} \leq 700$$
$$x_{s1} + x_{s2} + x_{s3} \leq 1{,}000.$$

The final set of constraints reflects the owner's desire that all three plots cultivate an equal proportion of their total acreage. This has the effect of imposing equal work and output standards on all three contract farmers. These constraints are computed as ratios.

$$\frac{x_{c1} + x_{p1} + x_{s1}}{500} = \frac{x_{c2} + x_{p2} + x_{s2}}{800}$$
$$\frac{x_{c2} + x_{p2} + x_{s2}}{800} = \frac{x_{c3} + x_{p3} + x_{s3}}{700}$$
$$\frac{x_{c1} + x_{p1} + x_{s1}}{500} = \frac{x_{c3} + x_{p3} + x_{s3}}{700}$$

These three constraint ratios equate the proportion of cultivated land for all three crops to total acreage for each plot. However, these equations are not in the proper form for a linear programming problem so they must be transformed by cross multiplying, resulting in the following three constraints:

$$800(x_{c1} + x_{p1} + x_{s1}) - 500(x_{c2} + x_{p2} + x_{s2}) = 0$$
$$700(x_{c2} + x_{p2} + x_{s2}) - 800(x_{c3} + x_{p3} + x_{s3}) = 0$$
$$700(x_{c1} + x_{p1} + x_{s1}) - 500(x_{c3} + x_{p3} + x_{s3}) = 0$$

By carefully observing these three constraints, it is apparent that the third constraint is redundant. That is, if plot 1 is in proportion to plot 2 and plot 2 is proportional to plot 3, then plot 1 is automatically proportional to plot 3 and the equation reflecting this ratio can be eliminated.

The complete linear programming model is:

$$\text{Maximize } Z = 600(x_{c1} + x_{c2} + x_{c3}) + 450(x_{p1} + x_{p2} + x_{p3}) + 300\,(x_{s1} + x_{s2} + x_{s3})$$

subject to

$$\begin{aligned}
x_{c1} + x_{p1} + x_{s1} &\geq 300 \\
x_{c1} + x_{p1} + x_{s1} &\leq 500 \\
x_{c2} + x_{p2} + x_{s2} &\geq 480 \\
x_{c2} + x_{p2} + x_{s2} &\leq 800 \\
x_{c3} + x_{p3} + x_{s3} &\geq 420 \\
x_{c3} + x_{p3} + x_{s3} &\leq 700 \\
x_{c1} + x_{c2} + x_{c3} &\leq 900 \\
x_{p1} + x_{p2} + x_{p3} &\leq 700 \\
x_{s1} + x_{s2} + x_{s3} &\leq 1{,}000 \\
800(x_{c1} + x_{p1} + x_{s1}) - 500(x_{c2} + x_{p2} + x_{s2}) &= 0 \\
700(x_{c2} + x_{p2} + x_{s2}) - 800(x_{c3} + x_{p3} + x_{s3}) &= 0 \\
x_{ij} \text{ for all } i, j &\geq 0.
\end{aligned}$$

Example 2.5 Multiperiod Investment Problem

An investment firm has \$1,000,000 to invest in four alternatives: stocks, bonds, savings certificates, and real estate.

The firm wishes to determine the mix of investments that will maximize the cash value at the end of six years. Investment opportunities in stocks and bonds are available at the beginning of each of the next six years. Each dollar invested in stocks at the beginning of each year will return \$1.20 (a profit of \$0.20) two years later and can be immediately reinvested in any alternative. Each dollar invested in bonds at the beginning of each year will return \$1.40 three years later and can be reinvested immediately.

Investment opportunities in savings certificates are available only once, at the beginning of the second year. Each dollar invested in certificates at the beginning of the second year will return \$1.80 four years later. Investment opportunities in real estate are available at the beginning of the fifth and sixth years. Each dollar invested in real estate will return \$1.10 one year later.

In order to minimize risk, the firm has decided to diversify its investments. The total amount invested in stocks cannot exceed 30% of total investments and at least 25% of total investments must be in savings certificates.

Firm management wishes to determine the optimal mix of investments in the various alternatives that will maximize the amount of cash at the end of the sixth year.

Decision Variables

In order to fully comprehend the types of multiperiod investment decisions that must be made in this problem, it is helpful to employ a diagram of the investment process as shown in figure 2.1.

Figure 2.1 Investment scheme.

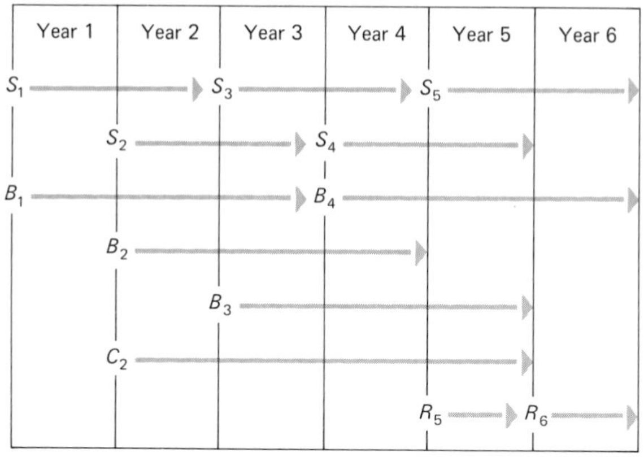

Figure 2.1 depicts each type of investment, the years in which it can be made, and time to maturity. For example, S_1 represents an investment in stocks at the beginning of year one. The arrow leading from S_1 goes to the end of year two when the return is realized. Using the same notation as in figure 2.1, the decision variables are defined as follows:

S_i = amount of money invested in stocks at the beginning of year i, i = 1, 2, 3, 4, 5.

B_i = amount of money invested in bonds at the beginning of year i, i = 1, 2, 3, 4.

C_2 = amount of money invested in savings certificates in year two.

R_i = amount of money invested in real estate at the beginning of year i, i = 5, 6.

I_i = amount of money held idle and not invested at beginning of year i.

Objective Function

The objective of the investment firm is to maximize cash value at the end of the sixth year. From figure 2.1 it can be seen that the amount of money at the end of the sixth year will be based on the values of S_5, B_4, and R_6. These amounts must be multiplied by their respective returns to yield their cash values at the end of the sixth year. In addition, the amount of money not invested at the beginning of the sixth year is included. This results in the following objective function:

$$\text{Maximize } Z = \$1.20\, S_5 + 1.40\, B_4 + 1.10\, R_6 + I_6$$

System Constraints

In this problem there are two types of constraints: equations that define the investment opportunities in a given year and inequalities that prescribe the investment policies established by management.

At the beginning of the first year the only investments available are in stocks and bonds. There is a maximum amount of \$1 million available for these two investment alternatives. However, since the minimum length of maturity for the two alternatives is two years, if all the \$1 million is invested in S_1 and B_1, there will be no funds available for investment at the beginning of the second year. If we signify the amount of money not invested at the beginning of year one as I_1, the investment opportunity constraint in the first year is

Year 1:

$$S_1 + B_1 + I_1 = \$1,000,000.$$

In the second year, the investment opportunities will be S_2, B_2, and C_2. These opportunities plus the amount not invested (I_2) must equal the amount not invested in year 1 (I_1).

Year 2:

$$S_2 + B_2 + C_2 + I_2 = I_1$$

For the remaining years the constraints are formulated in a manner similar to that in years one and two. The only difference is that the return and principal on the earlier investments will be available for reinvestment starting with year three. For example, in year three the amount available for investment is I_2, the amount not invested the previous year, plus \$1.20 S_1, the matured value of the stock investment at the beginning of period 1.

Investment Opportunities — *Amounts Available*

Year 3:

$$S_3 + B_3 + I_3 = I_2 + 1.20\,S_1$$

Year 4:

$$S_4 + B_4 + I_4 = I_3 + 1.20\,S_2 + 1.40\,B_1$$

Year 5:

$$S_5 + R_5 + I_5 = I_4 + 1.20\,S_3 + 1.40\,B_2$$

Year 6:

$$R_6 + I_6 = I_5 + 1.20\,S_4 + 1.40\,B_3 + 1.80\,C_2 + 1.10\,R_5$$

These six constraints must also be converted to the proper equation form. Two constraints must also be formulated for the firm's investment policies.

First, it was determined that the total amount of investment in stocks, $\sum_{i=1}^{5} S_i$, should not exceed 30% of total investment in various alternatives, $\sum_{i=1}^{5} S_i + \sum_{i=1}^{4} B_i + C_2 + \sum_{i=5}^{6} R_i$, which yields the following constraint:

$$\sum_{i=1}^{5} S_i \leqslant 0.30 \left(\sum_{i=1}^{5} S_i + \sum_{i=1}^{4} B_i + C_2 + \sum_{i=5}^{6} R_i \right)$$

Second, at least 25% of total investment must be invested in savings certificates, C_2.

$$C_2 \geqslant 0.25 \left(\sum_{i=1}^{5} S_i + \sum_{i=1}^{4} B_i + C_2 + \sum_{i=5}^{6} R_i \right)$$

Rearranging these last two constraints into the standard linear programming form results in the following two constraints:

$$0.7 \sum_{i=1}^{5} S_i - 0.3 \sum_{i=1}^{4} B_i - 0.3C_2 - 0.3 \sum_{i=5}^{6} R_i \leqslant 0$$

$$-0.25 \sum_{i=1}^{5} S_i - 0.25 \sum_{i=1}^{4} B_i + 0.75\, C_2 - 0.25 \sum_{i=5}^{6} R_i \geqslant 0$$

The complete linear programming formulation for the multiperiod investment problem can now be summarized.

Maximize $Z = 1.20\,S_5 + 1.40\,B_4 + 1.10\,R_6 + I_6$

subject to

$$S_1 + B_1 + I_1 = \$1{,}000{,}000$$

$$S_2 + B_2 + C_2 - I_1 + I_2 = 0$$

$$-1.20\,S_1 + S_3 + B_3 - I_2 + I_3 = 0$$

$$-1.20\,S_2 + S_4 - 1.40\,B_1 + B_4 - I_3 + I_4 = 0$$

$$-1.20\,S_3 + S_5 - 1.40\,B_2 + R_5 - I_4 + I_5 = 0$$

$$-1.20\,S_4 - 1.40\,B_3 - 1.80\,C_2 - 1.10\,R_5 + R_6 - I_5 + I_6 = 0$$

$$0.7\sum_{i=1}^{5} S_i - 0.3\sum_{i=1}^{4} B_i - 0.3\,C_2 - 0.3\sum_{i=5}^{6} R_i \leq 0$$

$$-0.25\sum_{i=1}^{5} S_i - 0.25\sum_{i=1}^{4} B_i + 0.75\,C_2 - 0.25\sum_{i=5}^{6} R_i \geq 0$$

$$S_i, B_i, C_i, R_i, I_i \geq 0$$

Example 2.6 Transportation Problem

An appliance manufacturer ships refrigerators from three warehouses to three retail stores on a monthly basis. Each warehouse has the following number of refrigerators available for shipment each month:

Warehouse	Capacity
1. St. Louis	200
2. Philadelphia	150
3. Atlanta	300
	650

Each retail store has the following monthly demand for refrigerators:

Store	Demand
A. New York	100
B. Chicago	300
C. Houston	250
	650

The cost for shipping refrigerators from each warehouse to each store differs according to the mode of transportation and distance. The shipping cost per refrigerator for each route is given as follows:

From Warehouse	To Store A	B	C
1	$10	5	12
2	4	9	15
3	15	8	6

The appliance firm desires to know the number of refrigerators to ship from each warehouse to each store in order to meet the demand at each store at the total minimum shipping cost.

Decision Variables

This problem contains nine decision variables that reflect the number of refrigerators shipped from each of the three warehouses to each of the three stores. The variables are expressed algebraically as

x_{ij} = the number of refrigerators shipped from warehouse i to store j, where $i = 1, 2, 3$ and $j = A, B, C$.

For example, variable x_{2B} represents the number of refrigerators shipped from warehouse 2 in Philadelphia to store B in Chicago.

Objective Function

The objective of the appliance manufacturer is to minimize total shipping cost. Since each shipping route has an associated cost per refrigerator, the objective function reflects the total cost for shipping all units demanded.

$$\text{Minimize } Z = \$10x_{1A} + 5x_{1B} + 12x_{1C} + 4x_{2A} + 9x_{2B} + 15x_{2C} + 15x_{3A} + 8x_{3B} + 6x_{3C}$$

System Constraints

The system constraints in this problem represent the supply available at each warehouse and the demand at each store. Consider warehouse 1 in St. Louis. It is able to supply a total of 200 refrigerators to any of the three stores A, B, and C. This constraint is written as

$$x_{1A} + x_{1B} + x_{1C} = 200.$$

In other words, the sum of all refrigerators shipped from warehouse 1 to stores A, B, and C must equal 200, the available supply at warehouse 1. This constraint is an equality for two reasons. First, the refrigerators shipped from warehouse 1 cannot exceed the amount available, 200. Second, the number shipped cannot be less than 200 since the total number available, 650, equals the total number demanded, 650. There is a demand at the stores for all refrigerators shipped; thus, all refrigerators at each warehouse will be shipped. The supply constraints for warehouses 2 and 3 are constructed similarly:

$$x_{2A} + x_{2B} + x_{2C} = 150$$
$$x_{3A} + x_{3B} + x_{3C} = 300$$

There are also three demand constraints constructed in the same way as the supply constraints. For example, at store 1, there are 100 refrigerators demanded from any of the three warehouses.

$$x_{1A} + x_{2A} + x_{3A} = 100$$

The demand constraints are also equalities for the same reasons as the supply constraints. The remaining demand constraints for stores 2 and 3 are

$$x_{1B} + x_{2B} + x_{3B} = 300$$
$$x_{1C} + x_{2C} + x_{3C} = 250.$$

The complete linear programming model for this problem is summarized as

$$\text{Minimize } Z = 10x_{1A} + 5x_{1B} + 12x_{1C} + 4x_{2A} + 9x_{2B} + 15x_{2C} + 15x_{3A} + 8x_{3B} + 6x_{3C}$$

subject to

$$x_{1A} + x_{1B} + x_{1C} = 200$$
$$x_{2A} + x_{2B} + x_{2C} = 150$$
$$x_{3A} + x_{3B} + x_{3C} = 300$$
$$x_{1A} + x_{2A} + x_{3A} = 100$$
$$x_{1B} + x_{2B} + x_{3B} = 300$$
$$x_{1C} + x_{2C} + x_{3C} = 250$$
$$x_{ij} \geqslant 0.$$

The Generalized Linear Programming Model

From the detailed example problems just presented we are able to observe a distinct pattern for the general formulation of a linear programming problem. In each problem, decision variables, an objective function, and system constraints were defined, which together formed a mathematical model of a real-world-type situation. It would be wise for the reader to commit the general model presented in this section to memory since the general symbolic notation will be referred to often in the discussion to follow.

Decision Variables

In each problem, decision variables, which denoted a level of activity or quantity produced, were defined. For our general model, n decision variables are defined as

$$
\begin{aligned}
x_1 &= \text{quantity of activity one} \\
x_2 &= \text{quantity of activity two} \\
&\ \vdots \\
x_j &= \text{quantity of activity } j \\
&\ \vdots \\
x_n &= \text{quantity of activity } n
\end{aligned}
$$

or

$$x_j = \text{quantity of activity } j, \text{ where } j = 1, 2, \ldots, n.$$

Objective Function

The objective function represents the sum total of the contribution of each decision variable in the model toward an objective. It is represented as

$$\text{Maximize } Z = c_1x_1 + c_2x_2 + \ldots + c_jx_j + \ldots + c_nx_n$$

where

Z = the total value of the objective function

c_j = the contribution per unit of activity j $(1, 2, \ldots, n)$.

The alternative form for the objective function is to *minimize* rather than maximize.

System Constraints

The constraints of a linear programming model represent the limited availability of resources in the problem. We will let the amount of each of m resources available be defined as b_i (for $i = 1, 2, \ldots, m$). We also define a_{ij} as the amount of resource i consumed per unit of activity j ($j = 1, 2, \ldots, n$). Thus, constraint equations can be defined as

$$
\begin{array}{ccccccccc}
a_{11}x_1 & + & a_{12}x_2 & + \ldots + & a_{1j}x_j & + \ldots + & a_{1n}x_n & \leqslant & b_1 \\
a_{21}x_1 & + & a_{22}x_2 & + \ldots + & a_{2j}x_j & + \ldots + & a_{2n}x_n & \leqslant & b_2 \\
\cdot & & \cdot & & \cdot & & \cdot & & \cdot \\
\cdot & & \cdot & & \cdot & & \cdot & & \cdot \\
a_{i1}x_1 & + & a_{i2}x_2 & + \ldots + & a_{ij}x_j & + \ldots + & a_{in}x_n & \leqslant & b_i \\
\cdot & & \cdot & & \cdot & & \cdot & & \cdot \\
\cdot & & \cdot & & \cdot & & \cdot & & \cdot \\
a_{m1}x_1 & + & a_{m2}x_2 & + \ldots + & a_{mj}x_j & + \ldots + & a_{mj}x_n & \leqslant & b_m \\
 & & & & x_1, x_2, \ldots, x_j, \ldots, x_n & & & \geqslant & 0.
\end{array}
$$

This general relationship shows all constraints as $\leqslant$ inequalities. Functional constraints can also be of the form:

$$a_{i1}x_1 + a_{i2}x_2 + \ldots + a_{ij}x_j + \ldots + a_{in}x_n \geqslant b_i$$

and

$$a_{i1}x_1 + a_{i2}x_2 + \ldots + a_{ij}x_j + \ldots + a_{in}x_n = b_i.$$

The general form of the linear programming model can be summarized as

Maximize (or minimize) $Z = c_1x_1 + c_2x_2 + \ldots + c_jx_j + \ldots + c_nx_n$

subject to

$$
\begin{array}{ccccccccc}
a_{11}x_1 & + & a_{12}x_2 & + \ldots + & a_{1j}x_j & + \ldots + & a_{1n}x_n & (\leqslant, =, \geqslant) & b_1 \\
a_{21}x_1 & + & a_{22}x_2 & + \ldots + & a_{2j}x_j & + \ldots + & a_{2n}x_n & (\leqslant, =, \geqslant) & b_2 \\
\cdot & & \cdot & & \cdot & & \cdot & & \cdot \\
\cdot & & \cdot & & \cdot & & \cdot & & \cdot \\
a_{i1}x_1 & + & a_{i2}x_2 & + \ldots + & a_{ij}x_j & + \ldots + & a_{in}x_n & (\leqslant, =, \geqslant) & b_i \\
\cdot & & \cdot & & \cdot & & \cdot & & \cdot \\
\cdot & & \cdot & & \cdot & & \cdot & & \cdot \\
a_{m1}x_1 & + & a_{m2}x_2 & + \ldots + & a_{mj}x_j & + \ldots + & a_{mn}x_n & (\leqslant, =, \geqslant) & b_m \\
 & & & & x_1, x_2, \ldots, x_j, \ldots, x_n & & & \geqslant & 0.
\end{array}
$$

To demonstrate this general notation refer back to example 2.1. The model formulation in that problem is

$$\text{Maximize } Z = 3x_1 + 5x_2 + 2x_3$$

subject to

$$5x_1 + 2x_2 + 4x_3 \leqslant 240$$
$$4x_1 + 6x_2 + 3x_3 \leqslant 400$$
$$x_1, x_2, x_3 \geqslant 0.$$

Thus, in the general model notation, the problem is given as

$$\text{Maximize } Z = c_1x_1 + c_2x_2 + c_3x_3$$

subject to

$$a_{11}x_1 + a_{12}x_2 + a_{13}x_3 \leqslant b_1$$
$$a_{21}x_1 + a_{22}x_2 + a_{23}x_3 \leqslant b_2$$
$$x_1, x_2, x_3 \geqslant 0$$

where

$$c_1 = 3, c_2 = 5, c_3 = 2$$
$$a_{11} = 5, a_{12} = 2, a_{13} = 4, \quad b_1 = 240$$
$$a_{21} = 4, a_{22} = 6, a_{23} = 3, \quad b_2 = 400$$

Finally, making use of the concise algebraic form of the summation sign, the generalized linear programming model is given by

$$\text{Maximize (or minimize) } Z = \sum_{j=1}^{n} c_jx_j$$

subject to

$$\sum_{j=1}^{n} a_{ij}x_j \ (\leqslant, =, \geqslant)\ b_i, \text{ for all } i\ (i = 1, 2, \ldots, m)$$

$$\text{all } x_j \geqslant 0.$$

Using this notation, the example 2.1 problem is given as

$$\text{Maximize } Z = \sum_{j=1}^{3} c_jx_j$$

subject to

$$\sum_{j=1}^{3} a_{ij}x_j \leq b_i, \text{ for } i = 1, 2, 3$$

$$x_j \geq 0, \text{ for } j = 1, 2, 3.$$

The c_j, a_{ij}, and b_i values are the *parameters* of a linear programming problem that are assumed to be known constants.

Properties of the General Linear Programming Model

The general linear programming model contains certain implicit properties that must exist for its definition as a linear programming problem to be valid. These properties require that the functional relationships in the problem be linear and additive, divisible, and deterministic. The reader may have already discovered these properties through the analysis of the example problems. However, in this section these properties will be explained in greater detail.

Linearity and Additivity

The primary requirement of linear programming is that the objective function and all related constraints must be **linear.** In other words, if a constraint involving two decision variables were graphed in two-dimensional space it would form a straight line. Likewise, a constraint involving three decision variables would yield a plane (a flat surface), and, in general, a relationship of n decision variables would result in a hyperplane (a flat geometrical shape) in n-dimensional space. If an equation of n solution variables were graphed in n-dimensional space it would form a straight line for $n \leq 2$, a single point for $n = 1$, and a hyperplane for $n > 2$.

The term *linear* also implies that relationships are directly proportional. **Proportionality** means that the rate of change, or slope, of the functional relationship is *constant,* and, therefore, changes of equal size in the value of a variable will result in exactly the same *relative* change in the functional value. For example, if $a_{11} = 5$ and $x_1 = 2$ then $a_{11}x_1 = 10$. If x_1 is increased by 5 percent it becomes 2.1, then $a_{11}x_1$ now equals 10.5, which is also a 5 percent increase.

Linear programming also requires that the total measure of outcome (the objective function) and the total sum of resource usage must be additive. For example, the total profit (Z) will equal the sum of profits earned from individual activities, c_jx_j. Also, the sum total amount of resources utilized for activities, x_j, must be exactly equal to the sum of resources used for each individual activity, $a_{ij}x_j$.

Divisibility

This property requires that the solution values obtained for the decision variables, x_j, not be restricted to integer values. This means that the x_j variables can take on any fractional solution value. Therefore, these variables are referred to as **continuous** variables, as opposed to **integer** or **discrete** variables.

This condition is acceptable when the decision variables are naturally continuous. For example, if x_j = pounds produced, a fractional value such as 3.4 pounds would be a logical solution. Examples 2.2 (diet problem), 2.3 (blend problem), 2.4 (crop mix problem), and 2.5 (investment problem) all have continuous decision variables. However, examples 2.1 (product mix problem) and 2.6 (transportation problem) have decision variables (products and parts) that are discrete (noncontinuous). For example, if the product was a chair, it would be illogical to produce 5.6 chairs.

In many cases, nonfractional activities can simply and legitimately be rounded to the nearest integer values. This is most often the case when a large number of items, such as a thousand bolts, are being produced. Often this will result in an acceptable solution. However, rounding can also affect optimality, especially when only a few large items are produced, such as transformers or airplanes. As a result, when integer values are strictly required, an alternative linear programming model, integer programming, can be used. This alternative method will be discussed in greater detail in chapter 15. In the interim, the reader is asked to accept the assumption of divisibility and the sometimes inappropriate results it creates.

Determinism

In linear programming, all model parameters (c_j, a_{ij}, and b_i) are assumed to be known constants. Linear programming implicitly assumes a decision problem in a static time frame in which all parameters are known with certainty. In real situations, however, model parameters are rarely deterministic since they reflect future as well as present conditions, and future conditions are seldom known with certainty.

There are several ways to cope with parameter uncertainty in linear programming models. Sensitivity analysis is a technique developed to test solution values to see how sensitive they are to parameter changes. Sensitivity analysis will be discussed in greater detail in chapter 4. Chance-constrained programming, a method that incorporates probabilistic occurrences in model parameters, will be discussed further in chapter 15.

Graphical Interpretation of Linear Programming

Because of the property of linearity, linear programming problems can be illustrated and solved graphically if the problem is two-dimensional (i.e., two decision variables). Although problems in two dimensions are not commonplace in real-world situations, geometric interpretation of linear programming is quite useful. It provides a great deal of insight into the modeling and solution of linear programming problems, which will be valuable in our solution of more complex problems in chapter 3 via the simplex algorithm. However, the reader should keep in mind the limitations of graphical analysis as a solution technique. Considering the difficulty in drawing a multidimensional graph, the limitations of graphical analysis are obvious for problems involving more than two decision variables.

Consider the following simple product mix problem. A company produces two products, 1 and 2. Each product has resource requirements as follows:

Resource	Product 1	Product 2	Total Resources Available
Material (lb./unit)	1	2	10 lb.
Labor (hr./unit)	6	6	36 hr.
Profit ($/unit)	4	5	

In addition, because of demand forecasts, a maximum of 4 units of product 1 will be produced.

This problem is formulated as:

$$\text{Maximize } Z = 4x_1 + 5x_2$$

subject to

$$\begin{aligned} x_1 + 2x_2 &\leqslant 10 \\ 6x_1 + 6x_2 &\leqslant 36 \\ x_1 &\leqslant 4 \\ x_1, x_2 &\geqslant 0 \end{aligned}$$

The model formulation is represented graphically in figure 2.2. In order to graph the three constraint inequalities, it is necessary to treat each as an equality. Then by finding two points common to each linear equation they can be plotted on the graph. A simple way to plot each line is to let one variable in an equation equal zero and then solve for the remaining variable. For example, in the first constraint if $x_1 = 0$, then $2x_2 = 10$ and $x_2 = 5$. Similarly, by letting $x_2 = 0$, $x_1 = 10$. These points ($x_1 = 0$, $x_2 = 5$ and $x_1 = 10$, $x_2 = 0$) are then plotted on each axis and connected with a line as in figure 2.2.

By reinserting the $\leqslant$ inequalities in each constraint, a region is formed that simultaneously satisfies all three constraint relationships. This region, the shaded area *ABCDE* in figure 2.3, is defined as the feasible solution area, since it satisfies all system constraints. (The feasible solution area is restricted to the first quadrant because the variables x_1 and x_2 must be positive—x_1, $x_2 \geqslant 0$). Likewise, any set of x_1, x_2 values outside this region is not a feasible solution since it violates one or more of the constraints. For example, in figure 2.3 points *R* and *S* are feasible solutions, while *P* and *Q* are infeasible.

Figure 2.2 Graphic representation of the product mix problem.

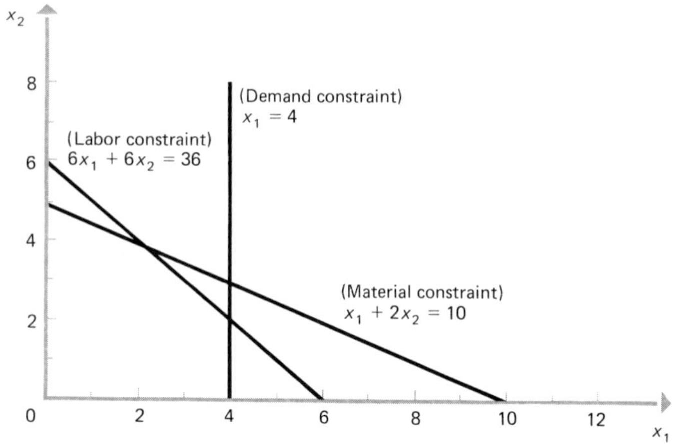

Figure 2.3 Feasible and infeasible solutions.

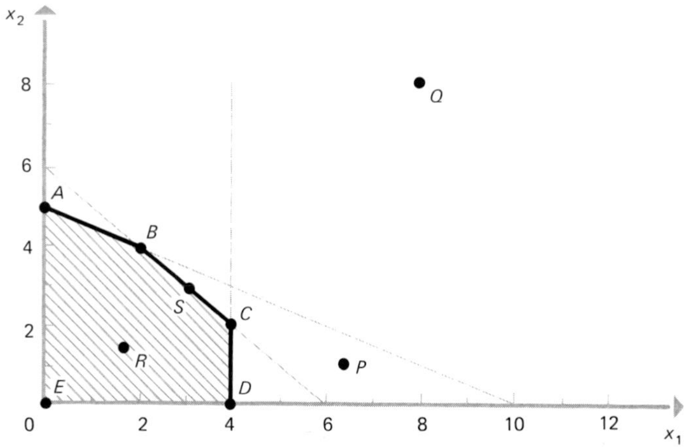

Given the feasible solution space, *ABCDE*, which contains all feasible solutions to the problem, we must now ascertain the point (x_1, x_2) that best fulfills the objective function. In this problem the objective is to maximize profit. In order to find the optimal solution, which maximizes Z (profit), the objective function must also be plotted. However, Z is not the equation of a single line but rather the equation of a multitude of lines depending on the value Z takes on.

Figure 2.4 shows the objective function plotted for several alternative values of Z. For example, $Z = 10 = 4x_1 + 5x_2$ results in the objective function line, Z_1. By increasing the value of Z to 20 we see that another objective function line, Z_2, results. Z_3, Z_4, and Z_5 are also plots of alternative values for the objective function. By observing figure 2.4, several properties should now be apparent relating to the objective function.

Figure 2.4 Slope of the objective function.

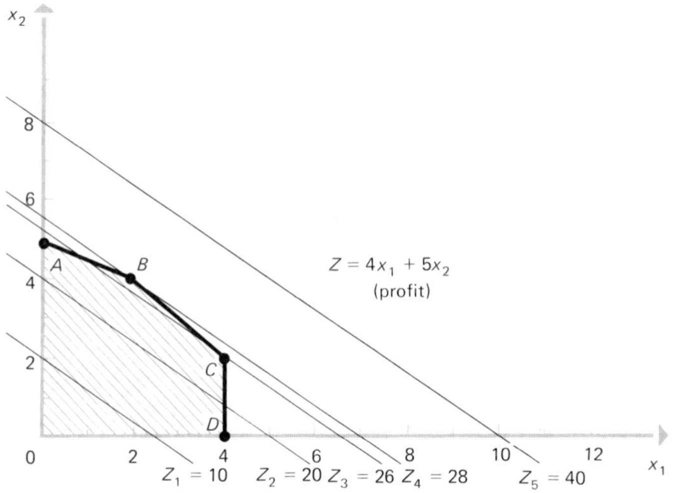

First, all Z_j values are parallel. This is because all levels of the objective function ($j = 1, 2, \ldots$), regardless of the value of Z, have the same slope. By solving the objective function for x_2 in terms of Z and x_1, we arrive at the equation

$$x_2 = \frac{Z}{5} - \frac{4}{5}x_1,$$

which shows the slope of the objective function to be $-4/5$ for any value of Z. For example, if $Z = 10$, we have $x_2 = 2 - 4/5x_1$ and for $Z = 20$, we have $x_2 = 4 - 4/5x_1$. In general, the slope for all Z_j equations in this problem is $-4/5$.

Second, it is also apparent that an infinite number of possible objective function lines exist. These lines begin at the origin and as Z increases move out into the solution space. As a result, the objective function in graphical analysis is often referred to as an iso-function line, reflecting the fact that Z is an infinite number of parallel lines.

Now given that $Z_5 > Z_4 > Z_3 > Z_2 > Z_1$, it is clear that Z_1 is not the best value of Z, because the objective function can take on larger values. However, it is equally apparent that Z_5 is not optimal because it contains no points (x_1, x_2) that satisfy the problem constraints (no point lies within the feasible solution space, *ABCDE*). Z_4 does have a point, *B* (where $x_1 = 2$ and $x_2 = 4$), in common with the feasible solution space and is larger than all other Z_j values within the region. Even the slightest increase in *Z* beyond the value of Z_4 would cause the objective function line to fall completely out of the solution space. On the other hand, if Z_4 were decreased by even a small amount, it would no longer include the best or optimal point. Thus, we have located the maximum value of *Z* at point *B*.

Since the optimal solution is found at a **corner point** formed by the intersection of two constraints, the values of x_1 and x_2 can be found by solving these two constraint equations simultaneously.

$$x_1 = 10 - 2x_2$$
$$x_1 = 6 - x_2$$

thus,

$$6 - x_2 = 10 - 2x_2$$
$$x_2 = 4$$

and

$$x_1 = 10 - 2(4)$$
$$x_1 = 2$$

Substituting $x_1 = 2$ and $x_2 = 4$ into the objective function results in the optimal value of *Z*.

$$Z = 4x_1 + 5x_2$$
$$Z = 4(2) + 5(4)$$
$$Z = 28$$

From this example, several important observations can be made. First, the optimal solution will always lie on the boundary of the feasible solution space. The feasible solution space forms a convex set of points. This means that the boundary of this region is made up of sets of straight lines (or flat planes) that converge at corners (often referred to as extreme points). As a result, there are no indentions in the boundary. (This definition of **convexity** can be verified by observing that a line connecting any two points in the solution space is also in the solution space as in figure 2.5). As a result of the property of convexity, the boundary formed by the constraint equations must contain the set of points that includes a unique maximum value for *Z*. Therefore, the boundary must contain the optimal point.

Second, the optimal solution is not only on the boundary of the solution space but more specifically is at a corner point formed by the intersection of two constraints. This is because the corner points are protrusions, or extremes, in the convex set and, thus, the outermost points on the boundary. For any linear programming problem each extreme point feasible solution is at the intersection of *n*

Figure 2.5 A convex set.

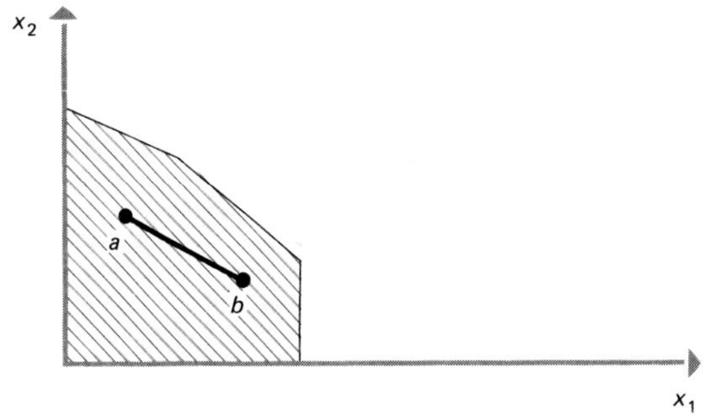

constraint equations where n is the number of decision variables. Thus, the solution at any corner point can be found by solving n simultaneous equations. The exception to this property is a multiple optimal solution that occurs when the objective function is parallel to a constraint line, i.e., the two functions have the same slope. This special case is discussed in greater detail later in this chapter.

Graphical Solution of a Minimization Problem

The graphical solution for a minimization problem is found in much the same way as a maximization problem except for a few fundamental differences.

Consider the following problem:

$$\text{Minimize } Z = 3x_1 + 3x_2$$

subject to

$$\begin{aligned} 2x_1 + 4x_2 &\geq 16 \\ 4x_1 + 3x_2 &\leq 24 \\ x_1 &\geq 2 \\ x_1, x_2 &\geq 0 \end{aligned}$$

The graphical representation of this problem, determined in a manner similar to that employed in the previous example, is shown in figure 2.6. The feasible solution space in this problem is the shaded region, *ABC*. We have already determined that the optimal solution will be found on the boundary of the feasible solution space at a corner point. However, although the optimal value in a maximization problem is at the corner point that maximizes the value of the objective function, the best solution in a minimization problem is at the point yielding the minimum value of Z. A series of iso-function lines are shown in figure 2.7. Note that the values of Z decrease as they approach the origin. The iso-function line that has the lowest value and still remains in the feasible solution space is Z_3. This corresponds to point B, the optimal corner point.

Figure 2.6 Graphic representation of the minimization problem.

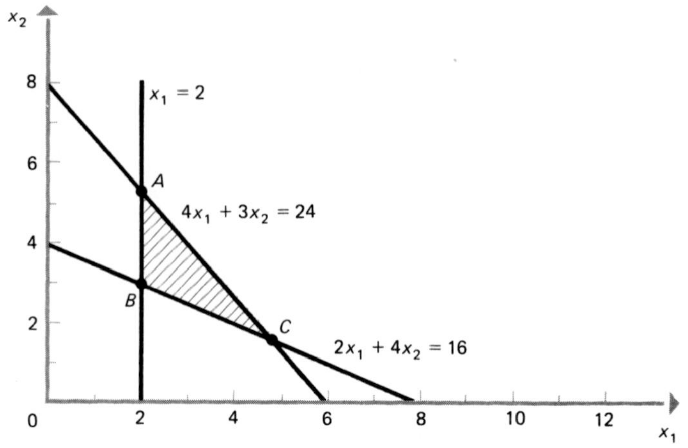

Figure 2.7 Optimal solution point.

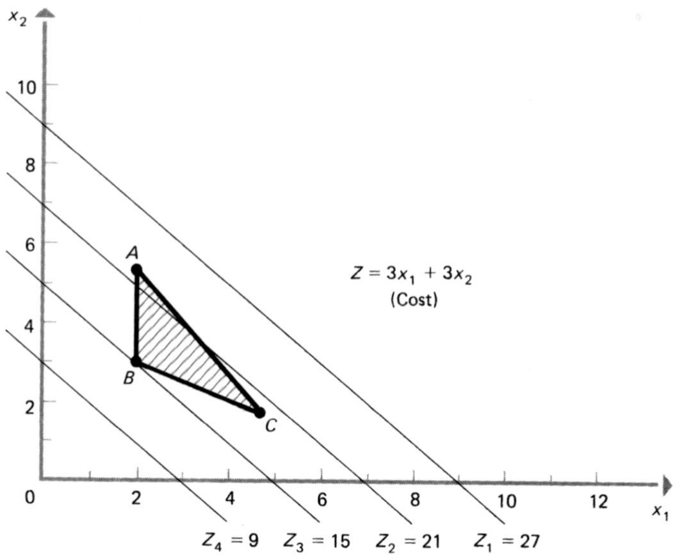

Solving simultaneous equations at point B results in the optimal solution.

$$x_1 = 2$$
$$x_1 = 8 - 2x_2$$

thus,

$$x_2 = 3$$

and

$$Z = 3(2) + 3(3)$$
$$Z = 15$$

In general, the solution in a minimization problem is at the point of the feasible solution space boundary that is closest to the origin. Thus, if we consider the objective function to be a line moving toward the origin through the solution space, the optimal solution is at the last point it touches. This process is the reverse of that in a maximization problem where the objective function moves away from the origin and the last point it touches is the optimal solution.

Special Cases of the General Linear Programming Model

Several exceptions to the general linear programming model exist that have not been referred to previously. These complexities include the presence of multiple optimal solutions, infeasible problems with no solution, and unbounded problems. These exceptions, like the general linear programming problem, can be illustrated via graphical analysis.

Multiple Optimal Solutions

Multiple optimal solutions exist in a linear programming problem when the objective function falls on more than one optimal point. Since the boundary of the solution space is a series of connected straight-line segments, the only way this situation can exist is when the slope of the objective function and one of the constraint equations (straight-line segments) are the same. This results in the objective function passing through two adjacent corner points (constraint intersections). The following problem results in multiple optimal solutions. The problem is shown graphically in figure 2.8.

$$\text{Maximize } Z = 4x_1 + 4x_2$$

subject to

$$x_1 + 2x_2 \leq 10$$
$$6x_1 + 6x_2 \leq 36$$
$$x_1 \leq 4$$
$$x_1, x_2 \geq 0$$

Figure 2.8 Multiple optimal solutions.

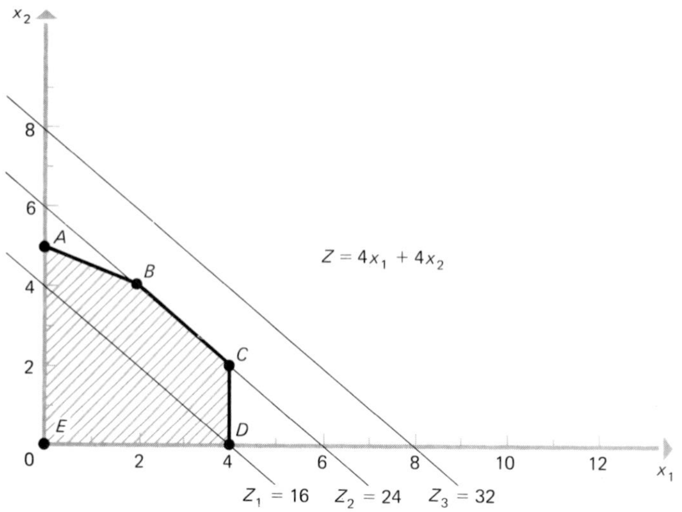

The objective function, Z, in figure 2.8 touches points B and C simultaneously as it reaches its maximum value on the boundary of the solution space (for Z_2). Thus, all points on the constraint line, between and including points B and C, represent optimal values. Typically, however, only points B and C are referred to as the alternate optimal solutions with the realization that an infinite number of points in between are also optimal.

In certain instances, the existence of multiple optimal solutions can benefit the decision maker since the number of decision alternatives or the range of decision options is enlarged. Choosing among multiple optimal solutions allows the decision maker greater flexibility. For example, a manager would have greater choice as to product mix.

An Infeasible Problem

In some cases a linear programming problem has no feasible solution. In other words, there are no points that simultaneously satisfy all constraints in the problem. An example of an infeasible problem is formulated in the following model and depicted graphically in figure 2.9.

$$\text{Maximize } Z = 5x_1 + 3x_2$$

subject to

$$4x_1 + 2x_2 \leq 8$$
$$x_1 \geq 3$$
$$x_2 \geq 7$$
$$x_1, x_2 \geq 0$$

Figure 2.9 No feasible solutions.

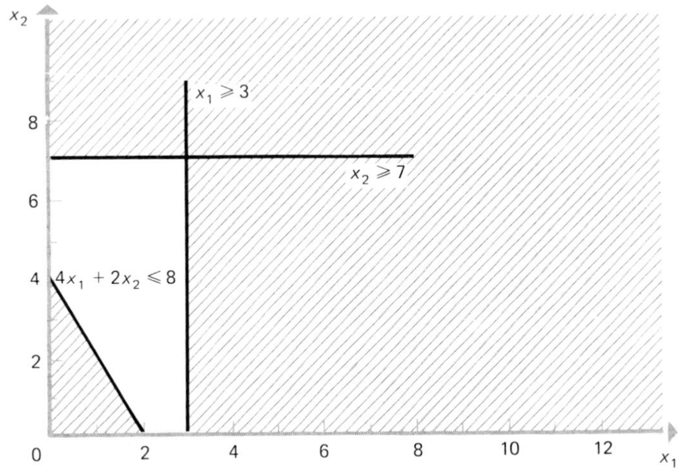

Since the three constraints do not overlap there is no feasible solution space. Thus, the objective function does not pass through any point that meets all three constraints at once. As such, there are no values of the decision variables that satisfy all the requirements posed by the constraints.

An Unbounded Problem

In some problems the feasible solution space formed by the constraints is not confined within a closed boundary. In these cases, the objective function can sometimes increase indefinitely without ever reaching its maximum limit since it never reaches a constraint boundary. The following is an example of this type of problem. (See figure 2.10 for a graphical representation.)

$$\text{Maximize } Z = 4x_1 + 2x_2$$

subject to

$$-x_1 + 2x_2 \leq 6$$
$$-x_1 + x_2 \leq 2$$
$$x_1, x_2 \geq 0$$

Because this is a maximization problem the optimal solution would normally be found on an outer boundary of the solution space. However, as can be seen in figure 2.10, a boundary is never reached as the objective function increases. This results in Z, profit, increasing infinitely without bound. Clearly this is not a realistic problem. Realistic maximization problems have limited resources that make infinitely large profits impossible. Thus, unbounded maximization problems exist only

Figure 2.10 Unbounded solution.

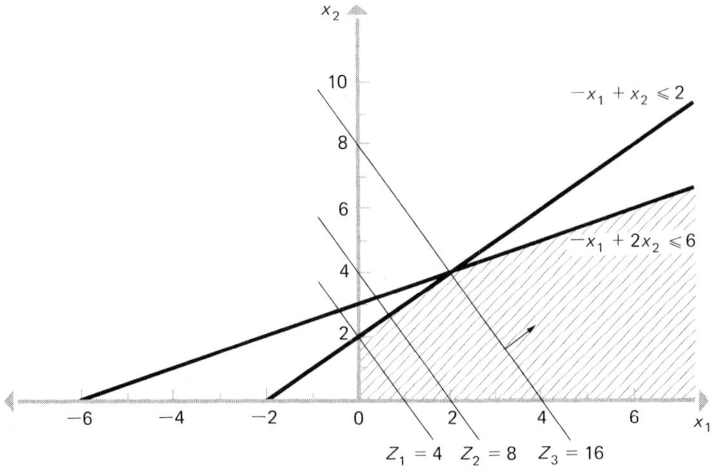

when a mistake in the linear programming formulation has occurred or when a constraint has been inadvertently omitted. Note, however, that in the case of a minimization problem, if all variables are restricted to nonnegative values, the solution would occur at the origin.

Summary

In this chapter, we have studied the formulation of linear programming through several examples, examined its general properties, and presented a graphical interpretation of the model and its solution characteristics. In doing so, the three main components of linear programming were identified: (1) decision variables, (2) objective function, and (3) system constraints. Properties of linear programming that were defined include (1) linearity and additivity, (2) divisibility, and (3) determinism. The graphical interpretation of linear programming pointed out the concept of convex solution spaces and the existence of optimal solutions at the intersection of constraint equations, forming the boundary.

This chapter has provided the necessary insight into linear programming and the background to confront the next important step in our presentation of linear programming, the solution. As we have already noted, graphical solution is quite limited. In the next chapter we will present the simplex method for solving linear programming problems. This straightforward solution technique is one reason why linear programming has become such a popular, widely applied technique in management science.

References

Charnes, A., and Cooper, W. W. *Management Models and Industrial Applications of Linear Programming.* New York: John Wiley & Sons, 1961.

Hadley, G. *Linear Programming.* Reading, Massachusetts: Addison-Wesley Publishing Co., 1962.

Hiller, F. S., and Lieberman, G. J. *Introduction to Operations Research.* 2d ed. San Francisco: Holden-Day, 1974.

Kwak, N. K. *Mathematical Programming with Business Applications.* New York: McGraw-Hill, 1973.

Lee, S. M. *Introduction to Linear Optimization.* New York: Petrocelli/Charter, 1976.

Llewellyn, R. W. *Linear Programming.* New York: Holt, Rinehart and Winston, 1964.

Pfaffenberger, R. C., and Walker, D. A. *Mathematical Programming for Economics and Business.* Ames, Iowa: Iowa State University Press, 1976.

Phillips, D. T.; Ravindran, A.; and Solberg, J. J. *Operations Research.* New York: John Wiley & Sons, 1976.

Taha, H. A. *Operations Research.* 2d ed. New York: Macmillan, 1976.

Problems

1. A company produces two products, *A* and *B*, which have profits of $9 and $7 respectively. Each unit of product must be processed on two assembly lines for a required production time as follows:

	Hr./Unit	
Product	Line 1	Line 2
A	12	4
B	4	8
Total Hours	60	40

Formulate a linear programming model to determine the optimal product mix that will maximize profit.

2. An electrical manufacturer produces three products: clocks, radios, and toasters. These products have the following resource requirements:

	Cost ($)/Unit	Labor (hr.)/Unit
Clock	$ 7	2
Radio	10	3
Toaster	5	1

Demand SP
200 $15
300 $20
150 $12
$2,000 600 hrs.

Maximum daily demand for clocks, radios, and toasters is 200, 300, and 150 respectively. The manufacturer has a daily production budget of \$2,000 and at most 600 hours of labor. In-process inventory space is available for a combined total of 500 units. Selling prices are \$15 for a clock, \$20 for a radio, and \$12 for a toaster. The manufacturer desires to know the optimal product mix that will maximize profit.

Formulate a linear programming model for this problem.

3. A manufacturer makes motorized and manual hand trucks in a factory that is divided into two shops. Shop 1, which performs the basic assembly operation, must work 5 hours on each motorized hand truck but only 2 hours on each manual hand truck. Shop 2, which performs finishing operations, must work 3 hours on each motorized and manual hand truck it produces. Due to a limited number of workers and machines, shop 1 has 180 hours available per week and shop 2 has 135 hours available per week. If the manufacturer makes a profit of \$300 on each motorized hand truck and \$200 on each manual hand truck, how many of each should be produced to maximize profit?

Formulate a linear programming model for this problem.

4. A concrete company produces bags of concrete mix from two ingredients, *A* and *B*. Each pound of ingredient *A* costs \$.06 and contains 4 units of fine sand, 3 units of coarse sand, and 5 units of gravel. Each pound of *B* costs \$.10 and contains 3 units of fine sand, 6 units of coarse sand, and 2 units of gravel. Each bag of concrete must contain at least 12 units of fine sand, 12 units of coarse sand, and 10 units of gravel. The company desires to know the best combination of ingredients *A* and *B* that will minimize total cost.

Formulate a linear programming model for this problem.

5. A manufacturing company produces two products, *A* and *B*, at two different plants, 1 and 2. Plant 1 has resources available to produce 500 units of either product (or a combination of products) daily, while plant 2 has enough resources to produce 800 units. The cost for each product at each plant is:

Product \ Plant	1	2
A	\$50	\$60
B	45	30

Plant 1 has a daily budget of \$20,000, and plant 2 has a budget of \$30,000. Based on past sales, the company knows it cannot sell more than 600 units of product *A* and 800 units of product *B*. Profit for product *A* is \$80 and profit for product *B* is \$70. The company wishes to know the number of units of *A* and *B* to produce at plants 1 and 2 to maximize profits.

Formulate a linear programming model for this problem.

6. A chemical corporation needs to produce 1,000 pounds of a chemical mixture for a customer. The mixture consists of three ingredients that have the following cost per pound:

Ingredient	Cost/lb.
x_1	\$2
x_2	3
x_3	5

The formula for the mixture requires that the following specifications be met:

a. The mix must contain at least 200 lb. of x_2.
b. The mix cannot contain more than 400 lb. of x_1.
c. The mix must contain at least 100 lb. of x_3.

The company wants to know the mixture that will minimize total cost.
Formulate a linear programming model for this problem.

7. A furniture manufacturer produces tables and chairs at two plants. The tables and chairs have the following resource requirements:

Product \ Resource	Wood (lb.)	Upholstery (yd.)
Table	3	—
Chair	5	8

The two products require different production times (in hours) depending on the plant at which they are produced:

Product \ Plant	1	2
Table	3.0	1.5
Chair	2.0	2.5

The standard costs of production for each product at each plant are as follows:

Product \ Plant	Cost 1	Cost 2
Table	$200	230
Chair	150	135

The firm has 1,000 yards of upholstery available weekly. The firm has 200 pounds of wood available weekly at plant 1 and 240 pounds weekly at plant 2. The firm has 100 hours available per week at plant 1 and 120 hours per week at plant 2. The company has a weekly budget of $2,500 for tables and $1,700 for chairs. The firm sells tables for $350 and chairs for $250. The manufacturer wants to know the number of tables and chairs to produce to maximize profit per week.

Formulate a linear programming model for this problem.

8. A mining company owns two mines that produce ore seven days a week. The mines have different locations and, thus, have different production capacities. After crushing, the ore is graded and divided into three classes: high, medium, and low. A contract with a smelting company calls for 12 tons of high grade ore, 8 tons of medium grade, and 24 tons of low grade ore per week. It costs the company $200 per day to run the first mine and $160 per day to run the second. The two mines have the following daily production:

Grade \ Mine	Production/Day (tons) 1	2
High	6	2
Medium	2	2
Low	4	12

The mine owner wants to know the number of days to operate each mine in order to fill the smelting company's order most economically.

Formulate a linear programming model for this problem.

9. A plumbing manufacturer produces plumbing equipment. One of the most profitable pieces of equipment is produced on three assembly lines. The output on each line and the time available for this piece of equipment are:

	Output (units/hr.)	Time Available (hr./week)
Line 1	15	25
Line 2	10	40
Line 3	12	30

The primary raw materials used in producing these pieces of plumbing equipment are steel and copper tubing. The amount of raw material needed to produce the piece of equipment on each line is:

	Steel (lb.)	Copper Tubing (ft.)
Line 1	50	15
Line 2	35	25
Line 3	40	20

At the present time, the company has 40,000 pounds of steel and 20,000 feet of copper tubing each week. The company receives a profit margin of $20 on each piece of equipment. The manufacturer wants to know the number of hours that should be allocated on each line for the production of the pieces of equipment in order to maximize profit.

Formulate a linear programming model for this problem.

10. Grain cooperatives in Kansas, Nebraska, and Iowa ship grain to three warehouses in Louisiana, Texas, and Georgia. The supply of grain per month at each source is

Source	Supply (tons)
Kansas	200
Nebraska	300
Iowa	600
	1,100

The demand at each warehouse per month is

Destination	Demand (tons)
Louisiana	400
Texas	700
Georgia	500
	1,600

The costs per ton for transporting grain from sources to destinations are

From \ To	Louisiana	Texas	Georgia
Kansas	$20	30	50
Nebraska	25	15	30
Iowa	45	17	22

The firm wants to know the optimal amount to ship from each source to each destination in order to minimize cost.

Formulate a linear programming model for this problem.

11. A feed company produces a livestock feed mix from four ingredients: corn, peanuts, oats, and a vitamin supplement. The company produces the feed mix in 2,000-pound batches. The cost per pound of each ingredient is

Ingredient	Cost/lb.
Corn	$0.10
Peanuts	0.05
Oats	0.15
Vitamins	0.20

Each batch must be mixed according to the following specifications:

a. The mix must contain at least 30% peanuts.
b. The mix cannot contain more than 20% oats.
c. Each batch must contain at least 10% vitamin supplement.
d. The ratio of corn and oats to peanuts must be at least 3 to 2.

The feed company wants to know the optimal batch mix that minimizes total cost.

Formulate a linear programming model for this problem.

12. A pollster has been contracted to do a survey the day following a politician's speech. The firm must assign interviewers to perform the survey. The interviews can be conducted during the day shift or night shift or both, either by telephone or in person. The firm has 10 available phones and transportation and equipment for 15 personal interviewers. The number of interviews one person can conduct are

	Telephone	Personal
Day	100	120
Night	150	75

The following criterion has been established by the pollsters to insure a representative survey:

a. There must be at least 3,000 total interviews.
b. At least 1,000 interviews must be at night.
c. At least 1,500 interviews must be personal.

An interviewer will work only one shift (day or night) and will conduct either telephone or personal interviews the entire shift. The pollster wants to know the minimum number of interviewers of each type to be assigned to the survey.

Formulate a linear programming model for this problem.

13. A container company produces two sizes of cans for food products: a 2.5-quart can and a 4-quart can. The contribution to profit is \$.04 for a 2.5-quart can and \$.03 for a 4-quart can. The 2.5-quart cans are processed in 20,000 can lots, and 4-quart cans are processed in 30,000 can lots. Each lot, regardless of the type of can, must pass through two production stations for stamping and coating. Both the stamping and coating stations operate a maximum of 30 days per month. A 2.5-quart-can lot requires 2 days of processing at the stamping station while a 4-quart-can lot requires 4 days. The 2.5-quart-can lot requires 4 days in the coating operation, while the 4-quart-can lot requires only 2 days. The container company uses an outside trucking firm to transport their products. Their contract with the trucking company requires at least enough shipments to keep two trucks busy 18 days per month. A production lot of either 2.5-quart cans or 4-quart cans will keep two trucks busy for 2 days. The company wants to know the optimal number of lots to produce per month to maximize profit.

Formulate a linear programming model for this problem.

14. An auto parts manufacturer makes crankshafts that are sold to auto, truck, and tractor manufacturers. Each of the different vehicles requires a different crankshaft. The auto parts company is in the process of determining their production of each of the three types of crankshafts for the upcoming planning period. Their marketing department has forecasted the following maximum demand for each of the crankshafts during the planning period:

Crankshafts	Maximum Demand
Autos	175
Trucks	65
Tractors	160

The parts company sells auto crankshafts for \$27.75, truck crankshafts for \$34.50, and tractor crankshafts for \$30.00. As a matter of policy, they want to produce no less than 50% of the forecasted demand for each product. They also want to keep production of tractor crankshafts to a maximum of 40% of total crankshaft production.

The production department has estimated that the material costs for auto, truck, and tractor crankshafts will be \$4.00, \$6.00, and \$5.50 per unit respectively. The crankshafts are processed through forge, lathe, and grinding stations. In the upcoming planning period, there will be 360 hours available for the forge where the direct labor cost is \$2.25 per hour. The lathe station has 240 hours available and the direct labor cost is \$2.50 per hour. The grinding station has 480 hours available and the direct labor cost is \$2.75 per hour. The standard processing rate for auto crankshafts is 3 hours in forge, 2 hours in lathe, and 1 hour in grinding. Truck crankshafts require 4 hours in forge, 1 hour in lathe, and 3 hours in grinding, while tractor crankshafts require 2 hours at each station. The auto parts company wants to know the optimal plan for crankshaft production.

Formulate a linear programming model for this problem.

15. A distillery produces custom-blended whiskey. A particular blend consists of rye and bourbon whiskies. The company has received an order for a minimum of 400 gallons of this custom-blended whiskey.

The customer has specified that the order must contain at least 40 percent rye and not more than 250 gallons of bourbon. The customer also specified that the blend should be mixed in the ratio of two parts rye to one part bourbon. The company can produce 500 gallons per week regardless of the blend, and they desire to complete this order in one week. The blend is sold for \$5.00 per gallon. The brewing company's cost per gallon for rye is \$2.00 and for bourbon, \$1.00. The company wants to determine the blend mix that will meet customer requirements and maximize profits.

Formulate a linear programming model for this problem.

16. A manufacturer must meet the following contracted delivery schedule for a particular product over the next four months:

Quantities Contracted to Deliver	
Month	Quantity
1	5
2	6
3	8
4	9

The manufacturer has the option of producing more than is contracted for during any given month and storing the surplus product until needed. Storage cost is given as $1 per item per month.

Items can be produced in regular time or in overtime. The costs associated with each type of production are:

Month	Regular Time	Overtime
1	$1	$2
2	4	6
3	2	4
4	4	6

The fluctuation in unit production costs is due to seasonal resource factors.

There is also a capacity restriction as to regular and overtime production. The maximum number of units that may be produced during regular time in any month is 9 units. The maximum for overtime production is 3 units. The manufacturer wants to know the optimum production schedule to minimize costs.

Formulate a linear programming model for this problem.

17. A meat-processing firm produces wieners from four ingredients: chicken, beef, pork, and a cereal additive. The firm produces three types of wieners: regular, beef, and all meat. The company has the following amounts of each ingredient available on a daily basis:

	lb./Day	Cost/lb.
Chicken	200	$0.20
Beef	300	0.30
Pork	150	0.50
Cereal Additive	400	0.05

Each type of wiener has certain minimum and maximum ingredient specifications:

Wiener	Specifications	Selling Price/lb.
Regular	Not more than 10% beef and pork combined; not less than 20% chicken	$0.90
Beef	Not less than 75% beef	1.25
All Meat	No cereal additive; not more than 50% beef and pork	1.75

The firm wants to know the amount of wieners of each type to produce in order to maximize profits.

Formulate a linear programming model for this problem.

18. A machine shop is planning next week's production. The shop makes cylinders, plates, and bushings. The selling prices are $25 per cylinder, $20 per plate, and $30 per bushing. There are three alternative production routes for each product. The following table gives the hours available, operation times (in tenths of an hour), and the number of products required:

	Cylinders			Plates			Bushings			Machine Hours Available
Routes	1	2	3	1	2	3	1	2	3	
Lathes	.5	.7	1.1	.4	.2	0	.5	.2	0	800
Grinders	.5	0	.3	.5	.3	.3	.3	1.2	1.4	500
Welders	.5	.6	.3	.8	1.5	1.8	1.4	.7	.4	700
Minimum Product Requirements	100			200			300			

The machine shop wants to know the production schedule that will maximize total sales.

Formulate a linear programming model for this problem.

19. A commodities trading firm knows the prices at which it can buy and sell items of a certain commodity during the next four months. It is restricted from following the market trend due to the limited capacity of its warehouse, which is 10,000 bushels. The buying price (c_i) and selling price (p_i) during each of the given months (i) are given as follows:

	Month i			
	1	2	3	4
c_i	$ 5	6	7	8
p_i	4	8	6	7

No storage cost is assumed. Assume that sales are made at the beginning of the month, followed by purchases. At the beginning of the first month, there are 2,000 bushels in the warehouse. The trading firm wants to know the amounts that should be bought and sold each month in order to maximize profit.

Formulate a linear programming model for this problem.

20. A young investor has accumulated $250,000 and has sought advice from an investment counselor on how to invest some or all of the money. With the aid of the counselor, the investor has decided to invest among the following alternatives: common stock, treasury bills, AAA bonds, BBB bonds, income bonds, and negotiable certificates of deposit. The counselor after careful analysis has determined the yield for each investment alternative and a probability that the yield will not be realized.

Investment Alternative	Expected Annual Yield (%)	Probability of Less Yield
Common stock	10.00	.30
Treasury bills	6.50	.01
AAA bonds	8.50	.05
BBB bonds	9.25	.08
Income bonds	13.00	.15
Negotiable Certificates of Deposit	8.00	.02

The investor had decided the sum of the probability of realizing less than the expected yield should not be more than 0.25. In order to diversify the total investment not more than 25% of total should be invested in any one alternative. The investor wants to know the amount to be invested in each alternative in order to maximize the expected return.

Formulate a linear programming model for this problem.

21. A shipping firm desires to know the maximum tonnage of goods it can transport from city A to city F. The firm has contracted railroad cars on different rail routes linking these cities via several intermediate stations as follows:

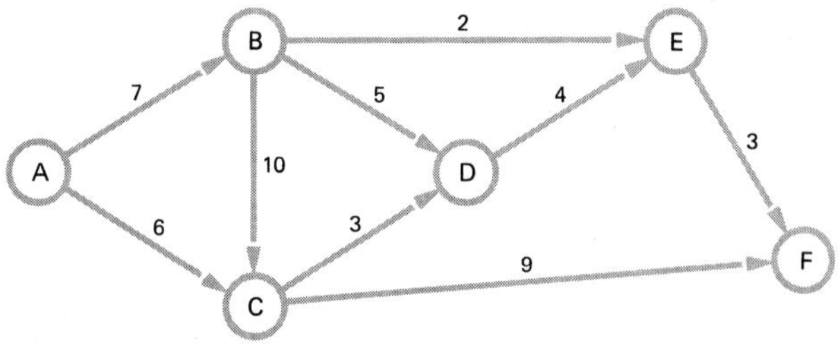

The firm can transport a maximum amount of goods from point to point as shown in the diagram. The firm desires to determine the optimal route over which the maximum tonnage can be shipped from city *A* to city *F*.

Formulate a linear programming model for this problem.

22. A production manager is trying to determine a production schedule for the next five months for a product. From past production records, the manager knows that 2,000 units can be produced per month. An additional 600 units can be produced monthly on an overtime basis. The unit cost of items produced on a regular-time basis is \$10 and \$15 on an overtime basis. Contracted sales are as follows:

Month	Contracted Sales
1	\$1,200
2	2,100
3	2,400
4	3,000
5	4,000

Inventory carrying costs are \$2 per unit per month. The manager does not want any inventory carried over past the fifth month. The manager wants to know the optimal production each month that will minimize total cost.

Formulate a linear programming model for this problem.

23. A retail chain is deciding on the types and amounts of advertising it should use to market its products. The available types of advertising are radio, newspaper, and television. They invited a representative of each media type to make a presentation, the results of which are as follows:
a. The television station representative stated that a TV commercial would reach 25,000 potential customers. The cost per commercial is \$15,000. The demographic breakdown of the television audience is

% of Total	Male	Female
Old	20	20
Young	20	40

b. The newspaper representative claimed that their subscriptions and sales show they reach 10,000 potential customers per ad. The cost of a newspaper ad is $4,000. The demographic breakdown of newspaper readers is

% of Total	Male	Female
Old	40	30
Young	20	10

c. The radio marketing representative said that their audience for a commercial was 15,000 potential customers. The cost of a radio ad is $6,000. The demographic breakdown of radio listeners is

% of Total	Male	Female
Old	10	10
Young	30	50

The retail chain has the following advertising policy requirements:

a. They want at least twice as many radio ads as newspaper ads and as many or more television ads as the other two media types.
b. They want to reach at least 100,000 customers.
c. The company wants to reach twice as many young people as old people.
d. At least 30% of the audience should be women.

Available advertising space limits the retail chain to at most 10 newspaper ads and 12 radio spots. The retail chain wants to know the optimal number of each type of advertising that will minimize total cost.

Formulate a linear programming model for this problem.

24. The owners of a new firm are interested in expanding their operation. After careful examination, they have determined three areas they might invest in: product research and development, sales program, and advertising. The owners have $200,000 available for investment. They can invest in their sales program every year and each dollar invested yields a return of 20% yearly. They can invest in advertising every two years and the return is 30% (at the end of two years). An investment in research and development is for 3 years, at which time a return of 50% is realized. In order to diversify the total investment at least $10,000 must be spent on the sales program, at least $20,000 on advertising, and at least $30,000 on research and development in the first year. The firm wants to know how much to invest in each area over a four-year period in order to maximize the total return to the firm.

Formulate a linear programming model for this problem.

25. A manufacturing firm produces four pieces of equipment, p_1, p_2, p_3, p_4, which can be produced on five machines, m_1, m_2, m_3, m_4, m_5, or purchased from an outside vendor. The machine time required (in hundredths of an hour) on each machine for each piece of equipment is

Equipment	Machine m_1	m_2	m_3	m_4	m_5
p_1	.03	.00	.02	.04	.03
p_2	.00	.07	.06	.10	.07
p_3	.10	.15	.12	.12	.00
p_4	.04	.10	.06	.05	.06

Each machine is limited to 40 production hours per week. Demand for each piece of equipment is 700 units per week. The cost of each part produced on a machine and their respective prices if purchased are

	Manufactured Cost/Unit	Purchase Price/Unit
p_1	\$4.00	\$5.25
p_2	6.00	9.00
p_3	3.75	5.20
p_4	2.80	3.00

The firm wants to know the combination of manufactured and purchased pieces of equipment that will minimize total cost.

Formulate a linear programming model for this problem.

26. Given the following linear programming problem:

Maximize $Z = 9x_1 + 12x_2$

subject to

$$4x_1 + 8x_2 \leq 64$$
$$5x_1 + 5x_2 \leq 50$$
$$15x_1 + 8x_2 \leq 120$$
$$x_1 \leq 7$$
$$x_2 \leq 7$$
$$x_1, x_2 \geq 0$$

Solve graphically.

27. Given the following linear programming problem:

Maximize $Z = x_1 + 5x_2$

subject to

$$5x_1 + 5x_2 \leq 25$$
$$2x_1 + 4x_2 \leq 16$$
$$x_1 \leq 5$$
$$x_1, x_2 \geq 0$$

Solve graphically.

28. Given the following linear programming problem:

Minimize $Z = 3x_1 + 6x_2$

subject to

$$3x_1 + 2x_2 \leq 18$$
$$x_1 + x_2 \geq 5$$
$$x_1 \leq 4$$
$$x_2 \leq 7$$
$$x_2/x_1 \leq 7/8$$
$$x_1, x_2 \geq 0$$

Solve graphically.

29. Given the following linear programming problem:

Minimize $Z = 8x_1 + 6x_2$

subject to

$$4x_1 + 2x_2 \geq 20$$
$$-6x_1 + 4x_2 \leq 12$$
$$x_1 + x_2 \geq 6$$
$$x_1, x_2 \geq 0$$

Solve graphically.

30. Given the following linear programming problem:

Maximize $Z = 8x_1 + 7x_2$

subject to

$$10x_1 + 8x_2 \geq 40$$
$$6x_1 + 16x_2 \leq 48$$
$$x_2 \geq 1$$
$$x_1, x_2 \geq 0$$

Solve graphically.

31. Given the following linear programming problem:

Minimize $Z = 4x_1 + 5x_2$

subject to

$$2x_1 + 2x_2 \geq 8$$
$$x_2 \leq 3$$
$$9x_1 + 3x_2 \leq 27$$
$$x_1, x_2 \geq 0$$

Solve graphically.

32. Given the following linear programming problem:

Minimize $Z = 20x_1 + 16x_2$

subject to

$$3x_1 + x_2 \geq 6$$
$$x_1 + x_2 \geq 4$$
$$2x_1 + 6x_2 \geq 12$$
$$x_1, x_2 \geq 0$$

Solve graphically.

33. Given the following linear programming problem:

Maximize $Z = 3x_1 + 4x_2$

subject to

$$3x_1 + 2x_2 \leq 18$$
$$2x_1 + 4x_2 \leq 20$$
$$x_2 \leq 4$$
$$x_1 + x_2 \geq 2$$
$$x_1, x_2 \geq 0$$

Solve graphically.

34. Given the following linear programming problem:

Maximize $Z = 3x_1 + 2x_2$

subject to

$$2x_1 + 4x_2 \leqslant 22$$
$$-x_1 + 4x_2 \leqslant 10$$
$$4x_1 - 2x_2 \leqslant 14$$
$$x_1 - 3x_2 \leqslant 1$$
$$x_1, x_2 \geqslant 0$$

Solve graphically.

35. Given the following linear programming problem:

Maximize $Z = 5x_1 + 2x_2$

subject to

$$3x_1 + 5x_2 \leqslant 15$$
$$10x_1 + 4x_2 \leqslant 20$$
$$x_1, x_2 \geqslant 0$$

Solve graphically.

36. Given the following linear programming problem:

Maximize $Z = 1.5x_1 + x_2$

subject to

$$x_1 \leqslant 4$$
$$x_1 - x_2 \leqslant 0$$
$$x_1, x_2 \geqslant 0$$

Solve graphically.

37. Given the following linear programming problem:

Maximize $Z = 3x_1 + 2x_2$

subject to

$$x_1 + x_2 \leqslant 1$$
$$x_1 + x_2 \geqslant 2$$
$$x_1, x_2 \geqslant 0$$

Solve graphically.

38. Given the following linear programming problem:

Maximize $Z = x_1 + x_2$

subject to

$$x_1 - x_2 \geqslant -1$$
$$-x_1 + 2x_2 \leqslant 4$$
$$x_1, x_2 \geqslant 0$$

Solve graphically.

39. Given the following linear programming problem:

Maximize $Z = 2x_1 + 3x_2$

subject to

$$x_1 + x_2 \leqslant 4$$
$$3x_1 + x_2 \geqslant 4$$
$$x_1 + 5x_2 \geqslant 4$$
$$x_1 \leqslant 3$$
$$x_2 \leqslant 3$$
$$x_1, x_2 \geqslant 0$$

Solve graphically.

40. Given the following linear programming problem:

Maximize $Z = -x_1 + 2x_2$

subject to

$$-x_1 + x_2 \leq 1$$
$$x_1 - 2x_2 \geq -4$$
$$x_1, x_2 \geq 0$$

Solve graphically.

41. Given the following linear programming problem:

Maximize $Z = 2x_1 + 2x_2$

subject to

$$x_1 - x_2 \geq 0$$
$$-3x_1 + x_2 \geq 3$$
$$x_1, x_2 \geq 0$$

Solve graphically.

42. Given the following linear programming problem:

Maximize $Z = 5x_1 + x_2$

subject to

$$3x_1 + 4x_2 = 24$$
$$x_1 \leq 6$$
$$x_1 + 3x_2 \leq 12$$
$$x_1, x_2 \geq 0$$

Solve graphically.

43. Given the following linear programming problem:

Maximize $Z = 4x_1 + 6x_2$

subject to

$$2x_1 - 3x_2 \leq 12$$
$$-x_1 + 2x_2 \leq 6$$
$$x_1 \leq 6$$
$$2x_1 + 5x_2 \leq 20$$
$$x_1, x_2 \geq 0$$

Solve graphically.

44. Given the following linear programming problem:

Maximize $Z = 2x_1 + 5x_2$

subject to

$$7x_1 + 5x_2 \leq 70$$
$$2x_1 + 3x_2 \leq 24$$
$$x_2 \leq 5$$
$$3x_1 + 8x_2 \leq 48$$
$$x_1, x_2 \geq 0$$

Solve graphically.

45. Given the following linear programming problem:

Minimize $Z = 8x_1 + 2x_2$

subject to

$$2x_1 - 6x_2 \leq 12$$
$$5x_1 + 4x_2 \geq 40$$
$$x_1 + 2x_2 \geq 12$$
$$x_2 \leq 6$$
$$x_1, x_2 \geq 0$$

Solve graphically.

46. Solve problem 1 graphically.
47. Solve problem 3 graphically.
48. Solve problem 4 graphically.
49. Solve problem 8 graphically.
50. Solve problem 13 graphically.
51. Solve problem 15 graphically.

3

The Simplex Method

The **simplex method** of solving linear programming problems was first developed by George B. Dantzig in 1947 and has since been refined by numerous others. The simplex method is based on matrix algebra in that a set of simultaneous constraint equations is solved through the matrix inverse procedure. Although the simplex method may sound formidable, its basic steps are relatively simple. The mathematical procedure employs an iterative process of repeating a set of mathematical operations, until the optimal solution is reached. In other words, in a profit maximization problem each successive operation yields a total profit greater than the profit resulting from the previous operation.

Quite simply, the simplex method is nothing more than a series of mathematical steps or, as some authors have noted, a mathematical "machine." Values from the formulated linear programming model are fed into the simplex machine, and a set of predefined mathematical operations are performed successively until the solution is generated. As such, it would be possible for the reader to solve a linear programming problem by simply following the predefined simplex steps. However, in this chapter we will not only describe the simplex process but also offer the reader insight into the simplex mathematics that will further understanding of linear programming.

Transformation of the General Linear Programming Model to the Standard Simplex Form

In order to employ the simplex method for solving linear programming problems, it is first necessary to transform all inequality constraints in the model to equalities. The simplex method is based on the principles of matrix algebra. As such, it entails the solution of sets of simultaneous equations. However, the constraints of linear programming models are often in the form of inequalities, as shown in many of the examples in chapter 2. Since inequalities are difficult to solve simultaneously, one of the primary requirements of the simplex method is that all constraint inequalities be transformed into equalities. (See Appendix A for the solution of linear programming problems via matrix algebra.) In order to demonstrate this transformation, an example linear programming model of a product mix problem will be used.

Example 3.1 *Product Mix Problem*

A manufacturing firm produces two products, 1 and 2. The requirements for labor and materials for production of each product as well as the resource availabilities are given, as follows:

Resource	Resource Requirements Product 1	Product 2	Total Available Resources
Labor	2 hr./unit	4 hr./unit	80 hr.
Material	3 lb./unit	1 lb./unit	60 lb.

The unit profit for product 1 is \$100 and for product 2, \$80. Management's problem is to determine the optimal product mix that will maximize profit subject to availability of the limited resources. The linear programming model for this problem is formulated as

$$\text{Maximize } Z = \$100x_1 + \$80x_2$$

subject to

$$2x_1 + 4x_2 \leqslant 80$$
$$3x_1 + x_2 \leqslant 60$$
$$x_1, x_2 \geqslant 0$$

where

x_1 = number of units of product 1

x_2 = number of units of product 2

Z = total profit (\$).

In this problem, the $\leqslant$ inequality constraints are converted to equations by adding to each constraint a new variable called a **slack variable.** For this problem two slack variables are needed; one for each of the two constraints. The addition of these slack variables (s_i) results in the following converted constraint equations:

$$2x_1 + 4x_2 + s_1 = 80$$

$$3x_1 + x_2 + s_2 = 60$$

where

$$s_1 = \text{slack variable for labor constraint}$$

$$s_2 = \text{slack variable for material constraint}$$

The addition of these slack variables has a specific function in the linear programming problem that can best be demonstrated via graphical analysis. The product mix problem is shown graphically in figure 3.1.

Figure 3.1 Graphic representation of the product mix problem.

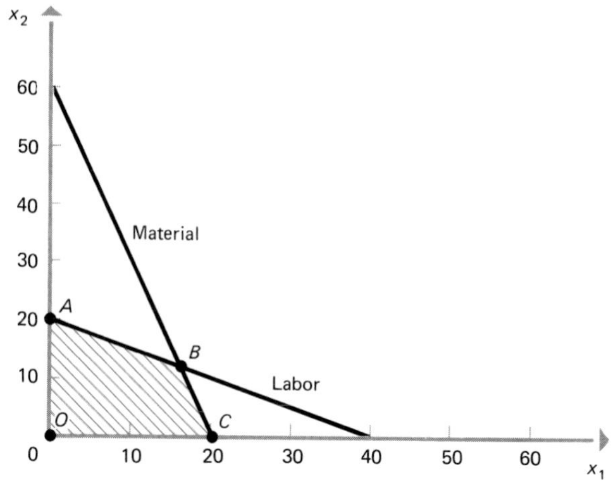

The feasible solution space is defined by the shaded area *OABC*. Every point in the solution space can be defined in terms of the two decision variables, x_1 and x_2, and the two slack variables, s_1 and s_2.

For example, at point C, $x_1 = 20$ and $x_2 = 0$. Substituting these values in both constraints results in the following values for s_1 and s_2:

Labor:

$$2x_1 + 4x_2 + s_1 = 80$$

$$2(20) + 4(0) + s_1 = 80$$

$$s_1 = 40$$

Material:

$$3x_1 + x_2 + s_2 = 60$$

$$3(20) + 1(0) + s_2 = 60$$

$$s_2 = 0$$

Slack, then, in reality is the amount of *unused* labor if twenty units of product 1 and zero units of product 2 are produced. Similar analyses can be performed at points A and B and for all points within the feasible solution space. For any point within the solution space but not on one of the constraint boundaries, slack will be present in both constraints since all possible resources are not being employed. The most dramatic instance of unused resources is at the origin, 0, where both x_1 and $x_2 = 0$. At the origin (which *is* a feasible solution point) $s_1 = 80$ and $s_2 = 60$. In other words, if there is no production, then all of the available resources are unused or *slack*.

From this analysis, it can be ascertained that slack variables, which are defined as the amounts of unused resources, are introduced in order to convert inequality constraints into equalities.

We must now concern ourselves with the effect of the two additional variables on the objective function of the product mix problem. Recall that the original objective function represented the sum of the profit obtained from each product. However, it is obvious that since slack variables are unused resources, they contribute nothing to the profit-maximizing objective of the problem. Thus, the objective function can be expressed as

$$\text{Maximize } Z = 100x_1 + 80x_2 + 0s_1 + 0s_2.$$

The Simplex Method

The simplex method is a process that follows these general steps:

1. The process starts at the origin (i.e., the initial solution is defined as $x_1 = 0$ and $x_2 = 0$.)
2. After the initial solution is selected, the simplex process searches for a better solution (if one exists), i.e., one with a higher Z value. When a better solution is found, the simplex procedure automatically eliminates all other solutions that are not as good.
3. This process is repeated until a better solution cannot be found. The simplex process then terminates and the optimal solution is indicated.

The General Simplex Tableau

One of the characteristics of the simplex method that contributes to its computational simplicity and ease of understanding is the conversion of the standard linear programming model into tableau form. Although several different formats of the simplex tableau have been described in different texts, the functions of the simplex tableau are basically identical. We will employ the format shown in table 3.1.

Table 3.1 Simplex tableau format

c_j \ c_b	basis	b_i^*	c_1 x_1	c_2 x_2	c_3 s_1	c_4 s_2
	z_j					
	$c_j - z_j$					

The symbol definitions used in table 3.1 are as follows:

c_j = The profit or cost coefficients of the objective function; these are shown for each variable as c_1, c_2, c_3, c_4.

c_b = The profit or cost coefficients of the objective function for solution variables in the "basis."

basis = The variables currently in the solution set, i.e., the variables that have values at the present solution point being analyzed. This is referred to as a *basic feasible solution*.

b_i^* = Initially, these are the values on the right-hand side of the problem constraints; as the simplex method iterates toward a solution, these values are the "solution" values for corresponding variables in the solution basis.

The row designations z_j and $c_j - z_j$ are computed values, and, as such, will be defined as we proceed through the solution procedure.

All of these terms, c_j, c_b, *basis*, b_i^*, z_j, and $c_j - z_j$, are labels that appear in all subsequent tableaus. The blank areas (cells) and the variables c_1, c_2, c_3, c_4, etc. will be replaced with values either provided directly from the model or computed.

The Initial Simplex Tableau

The tableau in table 3.1 is set up for the four-variable, two-constraint product mix problem (example 3.1) we have been using in this chapter. The formulation for this problem is given in the following equations and shown in tableau form in table 3.2 with the appropriate cells filled in with the parameters of the problem.

$$\text{Maximize } Z = 100x_1 + 80x_2 + 0s_1 + 0s_2$$

subject to

$$2x_1 + 4x_2 + s_1 = 80$$

$$3x_1 + x_2 + s_2 = 60$$

$$x_1, x_2, s_1, s_2 \geqslant 0$$

Table 3.2 Initial simplex tableau

c_b \ c_j	basis	b_i^*	100 x_1	80 x_2	0 s_1	0 s_2
0 0	s_1 s_2	80 60	2 3	4 1	1 0	0 1
	z_j					
	$c_j - z_j$					

By observing table 3.2 and the formulation of the product mix problem, the sources of the values in table 3.2 become evident. However, in order to promote a better understanding of the simplex process we will explain the origin of the tableau cell values in greater detail.

The column with the heading *basis* in the tableau contains the variables that are in the initial solution set. As we noted previously, the first step in the simplex method is to start with an initial basic solution at the origin and then proceed to better solutions. Given a linear programming problem with m constraint equations and n variables, there will always be $n - m$ nonbasic variables and m basic variables. In other words, nonbasic variables are those variables not in the solution basis and, as such, equal zero, while basic variables have solution values. Note that at each solution point only two of the four variables have values in the basis and the other two are zero by definition. Thus, in each case there are two basic variables corresponding to the two constraints (i.e., $m = 2$) in the problem, and there are two nonbasic variables ($n-m=2$).

We now know that a basic solution for our example problem consists of two basic variables while the other two variables equal zero. The most obvious basic solution and the easiest to identify is at the origin where $x_1 = 0$ and $x_2 = 0$. Therefore, the basic solution is

$$2(0) + 4(0) + s_1 = 80$$
$$s_1 = 80$$
$$3(0) + 1(0) + s_2 = 60$$
$$s_2 = 60.$$

This general property exists for all simplex problems of this type. The initial solution that begins the simplex process is always the solution at the origin. As such, in table 3.2, the two variables forming the solution base are s_1 and s_2. Also note that the number of blank cells (and empty rows) under the column entitled *basis* in table 3.1 corresponds to the number of constraint equations in the problem and, thus, the number of basic variables in the solution. Thus, the total number of rows in the initial simplex tableau (two for this problem) will remain constant for subsequent iterations. (Note that the nonnegativity constraints, x_1, x_2, s_1, $s_2 \geq 0$, are not included in the tableau as constraint rows. This is because the simplex process in its present form automatically excludes negative values. However, conditions where negative values may exist will be discussed later in this chapter.)

The b_i^* column in table 3.2 indicates the *right-hand-side* value of each constraint equation. Thus, in the initial tableau the b_i^* values are 80 for s_1 and 60 for s_2.

The x_j and s_i headings refer to the variables in the model. The tableau format calls for the decision variables (x_j) to be listed first in order of magnitude of their subscript (j) followed by the slack variables also listed from left to right in order of magnitude of their subscript (i). Thus, in table 3.2 the variables read from left to right x_1, x_2, s_1, and s_2.

The values within the tableau in the columns under each variable name (x_1, x_2, s_1, s_2) are the a_{ij} values (coefficients) in each constraint equation. Since the first row represents the first constraint, the a_{ij} values are

$$a_{11} = 2,\ a_{12} = 4,\ a_{13} = 1,\ a_{14} = 0.$$

These values are shown in the row corresponding to s_1 in table 3.2. The a_{ij} values for the second constraint are

$$a_{21} = 3,\ a_{22} = 1,\ a_{23} = 0,\ a_{24} = 1.$$

The c_j values along the top row are the contributions per unit to the objective function of each variable. In the c_j row in table 3.2, $c_1 = 100$, $c_2 = 80$, $c_3 = 0$, $c_4 = 0$. The c_j values are also indicated along the left column of the initial simplex tableau for those variables in the solution basis (denoted by c_b). Since s_1 and s_2 are in the initial solution base, $c_3 = 0$ and $c_4 = 0$ are listed in this column.

This completes the process of filling in the cells in the initial simplex tableau. From this point on, the remaining cell values (z_j and $c_j - z_j$), as well as cell values in subsequent tableaus (i.e., iterations), are computed via the simplex algorithmic procedure.

The Simplex Computational Process

Reviewing briefly the steps of the simplex method, the first step is to identify the initial basic feasible solution at the origin and then proceed to better basic feasible solutions until the optimal solution is found. To complete the initial tableau we need to evaluate the objective function value of the basic feasible solution. This is accomplished by computing the z_j row in the simplex tableau as shown in table 3.3. The values in the z_j row are determined by multiplying each a_{ij} value in the same column by its corresponding c_b value and then summing these products. For example, in the b_i^* column the following computation is made:

$$\begin{array}{rl} c_b & b_i^* \\ 0 \times 80 & = 0 \\ +0 \times 60 & = 0 \\ \hline z_{b^*} & = 0 \end{array}$$

Table 3.3 The z_j values of the simplex tableau

c_b \ c_j	basis	b_i^*	100 x_1	80 x_2	0 s_1	0 s_2
0	s_1	80	2	4	1	0
0	s_2	60	3	1	0	1
	z_j	0	0	0	0	0
	$c_j - z_j$					

The z_j value in the b_i^* column is zero. This represents the total profit contribution of the basic solution. Since the solution base consists of only slack variables (s_1 and s_2), which contribute nothing to profit, the total value of the objective function is zero.

The z_j values are computed in a similar manner for the remaining columns. Thus, under the x_1 column

$$\begin{array}{rl} c_b & x_1 \\ 0 \times 2 & = 0 \\ +\ 0 \times 3 & = 0 \\ \hline z_1 & = 0. \end{array}$$

Similarly, all remaining z_j values (z_2, z_3, and z_4) are also zero.

Now we must compute the bottom row of the simplex tableau, $c_j - z_j$. This is achieved by subtracting the z_j row values from the corresponding c_j values (shown at the top of the tableau), as shown in table 3.4. The $c_j - z_j$ row represents the net increase in profit associated with one additional unit of each variable. This property becomes more apparent if we look at a brief example.

The present simplex tableau is obviously not optimal since the value of the objective function is zero. Thus, one of the nonbasic variables (x_1 or x_2) will become a basic variable. In other words, we will produce units of either product 1 or 2 in order to realize some profit. Now let us suppose that x_1 will become a basic variable. Since the contribution to profit (c_1) for x_1 is \$100, we will increase the objective function by that amount for every unit of x_1 produced. However, if we produce one unit of x_1, then the slack variables must decrease by the a_{i1} coefficients of x_1.

Table 3.4 The $c_j - z_j$ values in the simplex tableau

c_b \ c_j	basis	b_i^*	100 x_1	80 x_2	0 s_1	0 s_2
0	s_1	80	2	4	1	0
0	s_2	60	3	1	0	1
	z_j	0	0	0	0	0
	$c_j - z_j$		100	80	0	0

For example, let

$$x_1 = 1$$

therefore, the resource utilizations by x_1 result in reduced slack values as follows:

$$2(1) + 4(0) + s_1 = 80$$
$$s_1 = 78$$

also

$$3(1) + 1(0) + s_2 = 60$$
$$s_2 = 57.$$

In each constraint we see that the amount of slack (s_1 and s_2) has decreased by the amount of a_{11} and a_{21}, or $\Delta s_1 = -2$ and $\Delta s_2 = -3$ (where Δ denotes the amount of change). Now if we substitute these increases and decreases into the objective function we have

$$Z = \overbrace{100(1) + 80(0)}^{c_j} + \overbrace{0(-2) + 0(-3)}^{z_j}$$
$$Z = 100 - 0$$
$$Z = 100.$$

In the variable columns, z_j represents the decrease in profit associated with the production of one unit of each variable. In this case since the decreases are in slack, there is no actual decrease in profit. Therefore, the total row value ($c_j - z_j$) is the per unit net increase in profit of entering a nonbasic variable in the solution base. Note that $c_j - z_j$ for the basic variables are zero. Since these variables are already in the solution, they will neither increase or decrease the solution profit.

The Entering Nonbasic Variable

Now that the initial simplex tableau has been completed, the solution process can begin. The first step is to determine the nonbasic variable that should enter the solution base and become a basic variable. Observing figure 3.2, we can see the choice existing between the two variables x_1 and x_2. In other words, feasible solution points exist on both the x_1 and x_2 axis.

The **entering nonbasic variable** is the one that results in the largest increase in profit per unit. As noted earlier, the net increase (or decrease) in profit per unit is represented by $c_j - z_j$. The entering variable is x_1, since the $c_j - z_j$ value of 100 is the largest net increase of the two nonbasic variables. The x_1 column, in table 3.5, is referred to as the **pivot column** (the term *pivot* coming from the classical pivot operations in the solution of equivalent simultaneous equations). Referring again to figure 3.2, the identification of x_1 as the entering nonbasic variable means that the solution point will be on the x_1 axis.

Figure 3.2 Selection of the entering nonbasic variable.

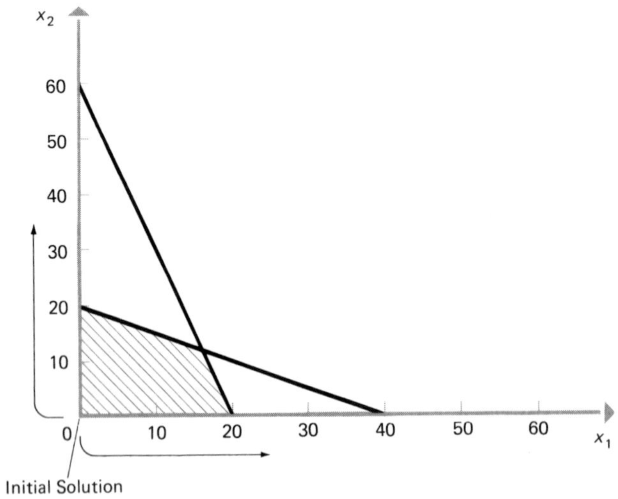

Table 3.5 Determining the pivot column

c_b \ c_j	basis	b_i^*	100 x_1	80 x_2	0 s_1	0 s_2
0	s_1	80	2	4	1	0
0	s_2	60	3	1	0	1
	z_j	0	0	0	0	0
	$c_j - z_j$		100	80	0	0

Pivot Column

The Leaving Basic Variable

Since it has been previously demonstrated that each basic solution contains only two (or m) variables, one of the existing basic variables must leave the basic solution and become zero if x_1 is to enter. Since x_1 provides the greatest per unit increase in profit, it is desirable to produce as much x_1 as possible. Looking at the labor constraint, if all the labor resource is used to make x_1, s_1 is automatically zero and x_1 becomes:

Labor:

$$2x_1 + 4(0) + 1(0) = 80$$
$$2x_1 = 80$$
$$x_1 = 40.$$

In other words, enough labor is available to produce 40 units of product 1. Now observing the material constraint, and using all of the material slack (s_2) to produce x_1 we have

Material:

$$3x_1 + 1(0) + 1(0) = 60$$
$$3x_1 = 60$$
$$x_1 = 20.$$

The analysis of these two constraints indicates that there is enough labor to produce 40 units of x_1 and enough material to produce 20 units of x_1. This restricts the total production of x_1 to 20 units. If 20 units of x_1 are produced, the total material resource will be consumed; thus, $s_2 = 0$. Alternatively, if $x_1 = 20$, there is still some available labor left unused.

Because all clacks s_2 used when making optimal amount of x_1

Labor:

$$2(20) + 4(0) + s_1 = 80$$
$$s_1 = 40$$

As a result, if x_1 enters the solution, s_2 is the leaving basic variable ($s_2 = 0$). This process is demonstrated graphically in figure 3.3. As we move out on the x_1 axis, there are two alternative solution points to choose from, C or E. Point C corresponds to the material constraint and point E corresponds to the labor constraint. Since point C ($x_1 = 20$) is the most constraining, point E ($x_1 = 40$) is infeasible (i.e., it is outside the feasible solution space). In fact, a unique and useful characteristic of the simplex method is that only feasible solution points are considered in the tableau basis. As can be deduced, this eliminates some of the solution points in the problem and contributes to the computational efficiency of the simplex method.

Figure 3.3 Selection of the leaving basic variable.

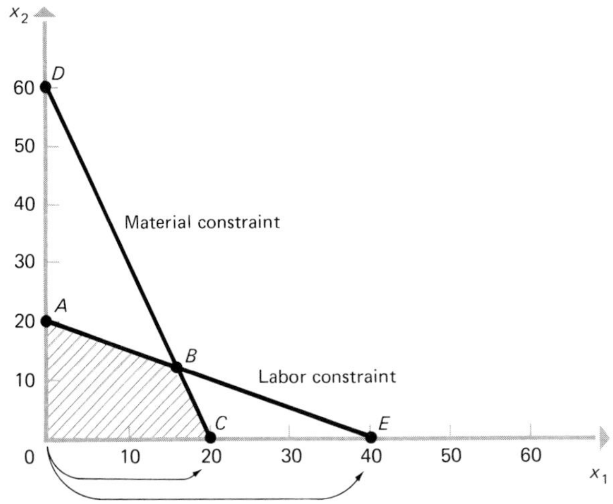

As a general definition, to determine the leaving basic variable each b_i^* column value is divided by its corresponding pivot column value. Select as the leaving basic variable the one that has the minimum positive value or zero.

basis	b_i^*		x_1		
s_1	80	÷	2	=	40
s_2	60	÷	3	=	20 ← pivot row

The leaving basic variable row is referred to as the **pivot row** in table 3.6. The value at the intersection of the pivot column and pivot row is called the **pivot number,** or pivot point, and it is identified by a circle in table 3.6.

Table 3.6 Identification of pivot column, pivot row, and pivot number in the initial simplex tableau

c_b \ c_j	basis	b_i^*	100 x_1	80 x_2	0 s_1	0 s_2	
0	s_1	80	2	4	1	0	
0	s_2	60	(3)	1	0	1	Pivot Row
	z_j	0	0	0	0	0	
	$c_j - z_j$		100	80	0	0	
			Pivot Column				

The Second Simplex Tableau

In the second simplex tableau, the variable x_1 has been substituted for s_2, which has left the basic solution. This new solution base is shown in the basis column of table 3.7. The corresponding c_j value of 100 for x_1 is shown in the c_b column.

Table 3.7 Computation of the new pivot row values in the second tableau

c_b \ c_j	basis	b_i^*	100 x_1	80 x_2	0 s_1	0 s_2
0	s_1					
100	x_1	20	1	1/3	0	1/3
	z_j					
	$c_j - z_j$					
		$60 \div 3 = 20$	$3 \div 3 = 1$	$1 \div 3 = 1/3$	$0 \div 3 = 0$	$1 \div 3 = 1/3$

The second simplex tableau (following one iteration) is the new solution with the basic variables x_1 and s_1. In order to produce the cell values in the second simplex tableau several mathematical operations, called pivot operations, must be performed.

The row values in the second tableau corresponding to the *pivot row in the initial tableau* are computed first by dividing every cell value in the pivot row of the first tableau by the pivot number, 3. The new values, which are referred to as the new pivot row, are shown in table 3.7.

The general formula for this operation is

$$\text{New pivot row values} = \frac{\text{Old pivot row values}}{\text{Pivot number.}}$$

The meaning of these values is given as follows. They represent the rate of substitution of x_1 for every other variable shown at the top of each column. For example, the value 1/3 at the intersection of the x_1 row and s_2 column shows that every unit of x_1 produced requires 3 units of material slack (s_2). Thus, a 1 to 3 substitution ratio exists between x_1 and s_2. All other new pivot row values can be analyzed similarly.

The next operation is to compute all remaining cell values in the tableau. Since there are only two constraint rows in this problem, there is only one other row of values to determine. However, if there were more than one remaining row, all these row values would be determined in the same way. These row values are computed using the following formula:

$$\text{New row value} = \text{Old row value} - \left(\begin{array}{l}\text{Corresponding}\\ \text{coefficient in}\\ \text{pivot column}\end{array} \times \begin{array}{l}\text{New pivot}\\ \text{row value}\end{array}\right)$$

Let us look at the cell value at the intersection of the s_1 row and the b_i^* column. Using the formula,

$$\text{New row value} = 80 - (2 \times 20) = 40.$$

The computation of all cell values in the s_1 row is demonstrated in table 3.8. These values are shown in tableau form in table 3.9.[1]

Table 3.8 Computation of s_1 row values

Columns	Old Row Values	−	Coefficient in Pivot Column	×	New Pivot Row Value	=	New Row Value
b_i^*	80	−	(2	×	20)	=	40
x_1	2	−	(2	×	1)	=	0
x_2	4	−	(2	×	1/3)	=	10/3
s_1	1	−	(2	×	0)	=	1
s_2	0	−	(2	×	1/3)	=	−2/3

Table 3.9 New row values in the second simplex tableau

c_b \ c_j	basis	b_i^*	100 x_1	80 x_2	0 s_1	0 s_2
0	s_1	40	0	10/3	1	−2/3
100	x_1	20	1	1/3	0	1/3
	z_j					
	$c_j - z_j$					

1. The reader may recognize this process as being analogous to the classical Gauss-Jordan process for solving linear equations. For a more detailed account of this process, see Appendix A.

The value of s_1, which is 40, in the new row represents the remaining slack given the production of 20 units of x_1.

$$2x_1 + 4x_2 + s_1 = 80$$
$$2(20) + 4(0) + s_1 = 80$$
$$s_1 = 80 - 40$$
$$s_1 = 40 \text{ hours of unused labor}$$

Completing the Second Tableau

In order to complete the second simplex tableau, the z_j and $c_j - z_j$ row values must be determined in the same manner as in the initial tableau. To review briefly, the z_j row values are computed by multiplying the values in each column by the corresponding c_b values and summing the products. The $c_j - z_j$ values are found by subtracting each of the z_j values from the c_j values in the top row of the tableau. The cell values for the z_j row are found as follows:

$$z_{b^*_i} = (0)(40) + (100)(20) = 2{,}000$$
$$z_1 = (0)(0) + (100)(1) = 100$$
$$z_2 = (0)(10/3) + (100)(1/3) = 33\ 1/3$$
$$z_3 = (0)(1) + (100)(0) = 0$$
$$z_4 = (0)(-2/3) + (100)(1/3) = 33\ 1/3$$

The z_j values and the $c_j - z_j$ row values are shown in tableau form in table 3.10.

Table 3.10 Completed second simplex tableau

c_b \ c_j	basis	b^*_i	100 x_1	80 x_2	0 s_1	0 s_2
0	s_1	40	0	10/3	1	−2/3
100	x_1	20	1	1/3	0	1/3
	z_j	2,000	100	33 1/3	0	33 1/3
	$c_j - z_j$		0	46 2/3	0	−33 1/3

This completes the computation of the second simplex tableau. Note that the solution corresponds to point C in the graphical analysis in figure 3.3. The value of the objective function for this basic feasible solution is \$2,000, which can be verified by substituting the basic solution values in the original objective function.

The Third Simplex Tableau

Once the second tableau has been completed, the simplex process is repeated. Observing the second tableau, we can see that the $c_j - z_j$ value in column x_2, 46 2/3, is the largest positive value indicating the greatest per unit net increase in profit. Thus, x_2 is the entering nonbasic variable and the x_2 column is the pivot column. Dividing the two a_{ij} values in the x_2 column into their corresponding b_i^* column values results in the following values:

$$s_1 : 40 \div 10/3 = 12$$
$$x_1 : 20 \div 1/3 = 60$$

Since 12 is the minimum positive value, s_1 is the leaving basic variable and the s_1 row is the pivot row. The pivot row, pivot column, and pivot number are indicated in table 3.11.

Performing the row operation on the pivot row by dividing each cell value by 10/3 results in the new pivot row in the third tableau (see table 3.13). The remaining row values are computed in table 3.12 and shown in tableau form in table 3.13.

Table 3.11 Pivot column, row, and number for the third tableau

c_b \ c_j	basis	b_i^*	100 x_1	80 x_2	0 s_1	0 s_2	
0	s_1	40	0	(10/3)	1	−2/3	Pivot Row
100	x_1	20	1	1/3	0	1/3	
	z_j	2,000	100	33 1/3	0	33 1/3	
	$c_j - z_j$		0	46 2/3	0	−33 1/3	
				Pivot Column			

Table 3.12 x_1 row values for third simplex tableau

Column	Old Row Value	−	Coefficient in Pivot Column	×	New Pivot Row Value	=	New Row Value
b_i^*	20	−	(1/3	×	12)	=	16
x_1	1	−	(1/3	×	0)	=	1
x_2	1/3	−	(1/3	×	1)	=	0
s_1	0		(1/3	×	3/10)	=	−1/10
s_2	1/3	−	(1/3	×	−1/5)	=	2/5

Table 3.13 Completed third simplex tableau

c_b \ c_j	basis	b_i^*	100 x_1	80 x_2	0 s_1	0 s_2
80	x_2	12	0	1	3/10	−1/5
100	x_1	16	1	0	−1/10	2/5
	z_j	2,560	100	80	14	24
	$c_j - z_j$		0	0	−14	−24

The z_j and $c_j - z_j$ row values in the third tableau are determined in the same way as in the previous two tableaus. The simplex process now requires us to determine the new entering nonbasic variable and leaving basic variable (i.e., the pivot column and pivot row). However, observing the $c_j - z_j$ row, we see that there are no positive values. In the x_1 and x_2 columns, zero $c_j - z_j$ values exist since these are basic variables. In the s_1 and s_2 columns, negative $c_j - z_j$ values are present. This means that if s_1 was chosen as the entering nonbasic variable, the objective function would *decrease* by \$14 per unit and if s_2 were selected, the objective function would *decrease* by \$24 per unit. The fact that there are no positive $c_j - z_j$ values indicates that there are no nonbasic variables that could be selected to enter the solution that would further *increase* profit. Therefore, the simplex process has ended and an optimal solution has been reached. The optimal solution corresponds to point *B* in figure 3.3.

$$x_1 = 16$$

$$x_2 = 12$$

$$Z = \$2{,}560$$

In general, an optimal solution is identified in the simplex process when none of the values in the $c_j - z_j$ row are positive.

Summary of the Simplex Steps

The standard format for performing the simplex process for a maximization problem consists of the following steps:

1. Transform the problem into standard simplex form. This requires the conversion of all constraint inequalities into equations by adding slack variables.
2. Set up the initial tableau. The initial basic feasible solution is at the origin. Thus, the solution base consists only of slack variables. z_j and $c_j - z_j$ row values must be computed.

3. Determine the entering nonbasic variable (i.e., the pivot column). The entering variable will be nonbasic. It is found by observing the $c_j - z_j$ row and selecting the largest positive value.
4. Determine the leaving basic variable (i.e., the pivot row). Divide the values in the b_i^* column by each corresponding pivot column value. Select as the leaving variable the one with the minimum nonnegative value (i.e., the most constraining).
5. Compute the new tableau row values. The new row values corresponding to the old pivot row are computed using the following formula:

$$\text{New pivot row value} = \frac{\text{Old pivot row value}}{\text{Pivot number}}$$

   All other row values are computed using the following formula:

$$\text{New row value} = \text{Old row value} - \left(\begin{matrix}\text{Coefficient in} \\ \text{the pivot column}\end{matrix} \times \begin{matrix}\text{New pivot} \\ \text{row value}\end{matrix}\right)$$

   After computing all new tableau cell values, the z_j and $c_j - z_j$ rows are determined.
6. Ascertain if the new solution is optimal. The new basic solution is optimal if all values in the $c_j - z_j$ row are zero or negative. If a positive value exists, go to step 3 and repeat the simplex steps.

It was pointed out at the beginning of this chapter that the simplex method is based on matrix algebra. In fact, the simplex iterations yield the same results in tableau form as the Gauss-Jordan method for solving simultaneous equations yields in algebraic form. The algebraic approach is demonstrated in Appendix 1 for the same example problem as presented in this section. The interested reader is encouraged to review this supplementary material as it adds further insight into the mathematics of the simplex process. Upon examination of the algebraic method, one characteristic that will become obvious is the existence of an **identity matrix** (i.e., a matrix with ones on the diagonal and zeroes elsewhere) at each iteration. The identity matrix can also be observed in the simplex tableaus in tables 3.2 to 3.13 for the basic variables in each solution. Knowledge of this relationship will prove useful for certain aspects of sensitivity analysis to be presented in chapter 4.

The Minimization Problem

In the previous description of the simplex method only one type of linear programming problem, the maximization problem containing only $\leq$ constraints, has been considered. In this section we will describe the simplex process for a minimization problem with $\geq$ constraints. A minimization problem follows the same basic steps as a maximization problem; however, there are several adjustments that must be made.

Since minimization problems typically involve ≥ constraints, also presented is the problem of converting ≥ constraints to equation form. Recall that for ≤ constraints a slack variable was added to consume the resources not employed in a constraint. However, this technique cannot be duplicated for ≥ constraints. In order to demonstrate the conversion technique for ≥ constraints, let us consider the following example.

Example 3.2 *Diet Problem*

The example described here is a diet problem similar to example 2.2 formulated in chapter 2. The objective of this problem is to minimize the total cost per serving of breakfast while meeting minimal requirements for vitamins A and B. The vitamin contribution of each type of breakfast food, the unit costs, and minimum vitamin requirements are summarized in the following table:

	Vitamin Contribution		
Vitamin	Egg (mg)	Bacon Strip (mg)	Minimum Daily Requirements (mg)
A	2	4	16
B	3	2	12
Unit Cost	4¢	3¢	

The diet problem is formulated as

Minimize $Z = 4x_1 + 3x_2$

subject to

$$2x_1 + 4x_2 \geq 16$$
$$3x_1 + 2x_2 \geq 12$$
$$x_1, x_2 \geq 0$$

where

x_1 = number of eggs

x_2 = number of strips of bacon

Z = total cost (cents).

The first step of the simplex process is to convert the ≥ constraints to equation form. However, instead of adding a slack variable as for ≤ constraints, a **surplus variable** is subtracted. The terms *slack* and *surplus* differ in that slack is added and reflects unused resources while surplus is subtracted and reflects an excess above a stated requirement. Both have identical notations, s_i.

Subtracting a surplus variable from the vitamin A constraint yields

$$2x_1 + 4x_2 - s_1 = 16.$$

To test this equation, set $x_1 = 20$, $x_2 = 0$, and substitute these values into the equation.

$$\begin{aligned} 2x_1 + 4x_2 - s_1 &= 16 \\ 2(20) + 4(0) - s_1 &= 16 \\ 40 - s_1 &= 16 \\ s_1 &= 24 \end{aligned}$$

Therefore, by subtracting the surplus variable (s_1) the equality holds. However, consider the initial solution of the simplex tableau at the origin. At that point, $x_1 = 0$ and $x_2 = 0$, which, if substituted in the vitamin A equation, results in the following:

$$\begin{aligned} 2(0) + 4(0) - s_1 &= 16 \\ s_1 &= -16 \end{aligned}$$

A negative value for s_1 obviously violates the nonnegativity restriction of linear programming and, thus, is inappropriate. This conflict can be observed graphically in figure 3.4. The solution at the origin is outside the feasible solution space and, as such, is infeasible. To facilitate a solution outside the solution space, an **artificial variable** is introduced. The artificial variable has no real meaning except that it allows the simplex process to begin. This results in the needed initial solution at the origin. In subsequent tableaus the simplex process will move toward a basic solution in the feasible solution space.

Figure 3.4 Graphic representation of the diet problem.

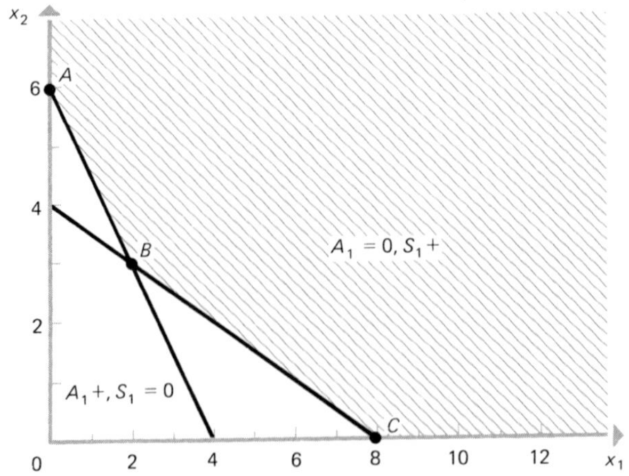

Adding an artificial variable (A_i), our equation now becomes

$$2x_1 + 4x_2 - s_1 + A_1 = 16.$$

Testing the equality condition, let $x_1 = 20$, $x_2 = 0$, and $A_1 = 0$;

$$2(20) + 4(0) - s_1 + 1(0) = 16$$
$$s_1 = 24$$

Now letting $x_1 = 0$, $x_2 = 0$, and $s_1 = 0$ (i.e., at the origin);

$$2(0) + 4(0) - 1(0) + A_1 = 16$$
$$A_1 = 16.$$

The constraint equation holds for either case. It can also be seen in figure 3.4 that A_1 and s_1 are complementary. In other words, if A_1 is positive, s_1 is zero and vice versa.

Converting each constraint to an equation by first subtracting a surplus variable and then adding an artificial variable results in the following equations in standard simplex form:

$$2x_1 + 4x_2 - s_1 + A_1 = 16$$
$$3x_1 + 2x_2 - s_2 + A_2 = 12$$

While adjusting the constraint equations to the proper form, we have also created two new variables, A_1 and A_2, which must be reflected in the objective function. Previously it was noted that the c_j value for a slack variable is zero since it does not contribute to profit. Similarly, the c_j value for a *surplus* variable is also zero since it contributes nothing to cost. However, if a c_j value of zero is assigned to an *artificial* variable, it can end up in the final solution base as part of the optimal solution, just as a slack or surplus variable can end up in the solution. The artificial variable is simply added to the problem to aid in putting the constraint equations into proper form and setting up an initial solution at the origin. Therefore, a means must be devised for insuring that the artificial variables are not included in the optimal solution.

This can be accomplished by assigning a very large positive c_j (unit cost) value to the artificial variable in the objective function. This results in the artificial variable being so costly that it never ends up in the final solution. This method is known as the **large M method** since the c_j value assigned to the artificial variable is M, representing an extremely large positive value (for example, \$1,000,000). This notation results in the following objective function for example 3.2.

$$\text{Minimize } Z = 4x_1 + 3x_2 + 0s_1 + 0s_2 + MA_1 + MA_2$$

The simplex method will now drive the artificial variables out of the basic solution since they cannot possibly lead to the objective of cost minimization.

Final Adjustments in the Minimization Problem

The final adjustment in the simplex method for a minimization problem is to reverse the final row designation from $c_j - z_j$ to $z_j - c_j$. In a minimization problem the final row values represent the net per unit decrease in cost for each variable. Thus, if we left the last row in the tableau as $c_j - z_j$, we would choose the largest negative value for the entering basic variable. However, to be consistent with the previously defined decision rule, $z_j - c_j$ is used, and we continue to use the largest positive value for the entering nonbasic variable.

The adjustments for a simplex minimization problem are summarized as follows:

1. Change all $\geqslant$ constraints to equation form by subtracting a surplus variable and adding an artificial variable.
2. Assign a c_j value of M to each artificial variable in the objective function.
3. Change the $c_j - z_j$ row to $z_j - c_j$.

Given these adjustments, example 3.2 is converted to standard simplex form and solved (tables 3.14–3.16) as follows:

$$\text{Minimize } Z = 4x_1 + 3x_2 + 0s_1 + 0s_2 + MA_1 + MA_2$$

subject to

$$2x_1 + 4x_2 - s_1 + A_1 = 16$$

$$3x_1 + 2x_2 - s_2 + A_2 = 12$$

$$x_1, x_2, s_1, s_2, A_1, A_2 \geqslant 0$$

Table 3.14 Initial simplex tableau

c_b \ c_j	basis	b_i^*	4 x_1	3 x_2	0 s_1	0 s_2	M A_1	M A_2	
M	A_1	16	2	(4)	-1	0	1	0	Pivot Row
M	A_2	12	3	2	0	-1	0	1	
	z_j	$28M$	$5M$	$6M$	$-M$	$-M$	M	M	
	$z_j - c_j$		$5M$-4	$6M$-3	$-M$	$-M$	0	0	
				Pivot Column					

Table 3.15 Second simplex tableau

c_b \ c_j	basis	b_i^*	4 x_1	3 x_2	0 s_1	0 s_2	M A_2	
3 M	x_2 A_2	4 4	1/2 (2)	1 0	$-1/4$ 1/2	0 -1	0 1	Pivot Row
	z_j	$4M+12$	$2M+3/2$	3	$M/2-3/4$	$-M$	M	
	z_j-c_j		$2M-5/2$	0	$M/2-3/4$	$-M$	0	
			Pivot Column					

Table 3.16 Third simplex tableau (optimal)

c_b \ c_j	basis	b_i^*	4 x_1	3 x_2	0 s_1	0 s_2
3 4	x_2 x_1	3 2	0 1	1 0	$-3/8$ 1/4	1/4 $-1/2$
	z_j	17	4	3	$-1/8$	$-5/4$
	z_j-c_j		0	0	$-1/8$	$-5/4$

Notice that A_1 and A_2 are in the initial solution base (table 3.14). The pivot column, pivot row, and pivot number are all determined in the same manner as outlined for the maximization problem. Likewise, the second tableau is computed exactly the same as in a maximization problem (table 3.15).

In the second tableau the A_1 column has been eliminated. This is a simple shortcut. Once an artificial variable leaves the solution base, it will never return because of its extremely high c_j value, M. As a result, this column can be eliminated and the tableau reduced.

The third simplex tableau results in the optimal solution (table 3.16). All $z_j - c_j$ values are negative or zero, and the optimality test holds. Interpreting the simplex solution in terms of the original problem, two eggs and three strips of bacon should be included in each serving. This will not only meet the daily vitamin requirements but minimize the cost per serving at 17 cents.

A Mixed Constraint Problem

The examples examined in this chapter have been of two types: a maximization problem with $\leqslant$ constraints and a minimization problem with $\geqslant$ constraints. However, consider the following problem:

$$\text{Maximize } Z = 20x_1 + 10x_2$$

subject to

$$x_1 + x_2 = 150$$
$$x_1 \leqslant 40$$
$$x_2 \geqslant 20$$
$$x_1, x_2 \geqslant 0$$

This problem differs from our previous examples in several ways. First, it is a maximization problem with a $\geqslant$ constraint. Second, it contains a constraint that is already in equation form. Therefore, before solving this problem by the simplex method, adjustments must be made for these differences.

Converting An Equality Constraint

The equality constraint, $x_1 + x_2 = 150$, seems to be in the appropriate standard simplex form already. However, checking the solution at the origin ($x_1 = 0$, $x_2 = 0$) we find

$$x_1 + x_2 = 150$$
$$0 + 0 = 150$$
$$0 = 150.$$

This is obviously an impossible outcome since zero does not equal 150. The addition of a slack variable or the subtraction of a surplus would be inappropriate, however, because the equality itself indicates a strict condition where there are neither unused resources nor the possibility for overachieving a specified requirement. In order to make this constraint realistic at the origin and still meet the strict equality condition, an artificial variable is added. The constraint becomes

$$x_1 + x_2 + A_1 = 150.$$

At the origin the solution is now $A_1 = 150$.

Converting a $\geqslant$ Constraint in a Maximization Problem

In the case of the $\geqslant$ constraint, $x_2 \geqslant 20$ is converted to equation form in the same way as previously described for a minimization problem. A surplus variable is subtracted and an artificial variable is added.

$$x_2 - s_2 + A_2 = 20$$

However, the c_j value assigned to the artificial variable (A_2) in the objective function is no longer a positive M. Since a positive M would represent a large profit in a maximization problem the artificial variable would be assured of always being in the optimal solution base. Therefore, a negative M value, $(-M)$ must be employed for all artificial variable c_j values in the objective function. The same rule holds true for the artificial variable introduced in the equality constraint.

In standard simplex form this problem becomes

$$\text{Maximize } Z = 20x_1 + 10x_2 + 0s_1 + 0s_2 - MA_1 - MA_2$$

subject to

$$\begin{aligned} x_1 + x_2 + \qquad\qquad A_1 \quad &= 150 \\ x_1 + \quad s_1 \qquad\qquad &= 40 \\ x_2 - \quad s_2 + \quad A_2 &= 20 \\ x_1, x_2, s_1, s_2, A_1, A_2 &\geq 0 \end{aligned}$$

The simplex solution for this problem is presented in tables 3.17–3.20.

Table 3.17 Initial simplex tableau

c_b \ c_j	basis	b_i^*	20 x_1	10 x_2	0 s_1	0 s_2	$-M$ A_1	$-M$ A_2	
$-M$	A_1	150	1	1	0	0	1	0	
0	s_1	40	1	0	1	0	0	0	
$-M$	A_2	20	0	(1)	0	-1	0	1	Pivot Row
	z_j	$-170M$	$-M$	$-2M$	0	M	$-M$	$-M$	
	$c_j - z_j$		$20+M$	$10+2M$	0	$-M$	0	0	
				Pivot Column					

Table 3.18 Second simplex tableau

c_b \ c_j	basis	b_i^*	20 x_1	10 x_2	0 s_1	0 s_2	$-M$ A_1	
$-M$	A_1	130	1	0	0	1	1	
0	s_1	40	(1)	0	1	0	0	Pivot Row
10	x_2	20	0	1	0	-1	0	
	z_j	$200 - 130M$	$-M$	10	0	$-10-M$	$-M$	
	$c_j - z_j$		$20+M$	0	0	$10+M$	0	
			Pivot Column					

Table 3.19 Third simplex tableau

c_b \ c_j	basis	b_i^*	20 x_1	10 x_2	0 s_1	0 s_2	$-M$ A_1	
$-M$	A_1	90	0	0	-1	(1)	1	Pivot Row
20	x_1	40	1	0	1	0	0	
10	x_2	20	0	1	0	-1	0	
	z_j	$1000 - 90M$	20	10	$20+M$	$-10-M$	$-M$	
	$c_j - z_j$		0	0	$-20-M$	$10+M$	0	
						Pivot Column		

Table 3.20 Fourth simplex tableau (optimal solution)

c_b \ c_j	basis	b_i^*	20 x_1	10 x_2	0 s_1	0 s_2
0	s_2	90	0	0	-1	1
20	x_1	40	1	0	1	0
10	x_2	110	0	1	-1	0
	z_j	1,900	20	10	10	0
	$c_j - z_j$		0	0	-10	0

Table 3.21 is a brief review of the different simplex adjustments required for the alternative constraint forms.

Table 3.21 Simplex constraint types and their resolutions

Constraint	Adjustment in Constraint	Objective Function Coefficient: Maximization Problem	Objective Function Coefficient: Minimization Problem
$\leqslant$	Add a slack variable	0	0
$=$	Add an artificial variable	$-M$	M
$\geqslant$	Subtract a surplus variable	0	0
	and add an artificial variable	$-M$	M

Negative Variables

In the linear programming problems we have analyzed to this point, a nonnegativity restriction has been imposed on all model variables. Indeed, in most practical situations decision variables are naturally nonnegative. However, decision variables can, on occasion, define such concepts as production rates. In such a model a negative value for a decision variable would reflect a *decrease* in the rate of production while a positive value would indicate an *increase* in the production rate.

In the simplex method, negative values are not allowed; thus, any problem with possible negative values must be converted to an equivalent problem with positive variables. There are two cases of negativity that will demonstrate the equivalency process: (1) variables that are totally unrestricted (unbounded) and (2) variables that are negative within a given bound.

Unrestricted Variables

In this type of problem, any or all of the decision variables are said to be unrestricted if they can take on negative as well as positive values. In order to solve the simplex problem, the variables that are unrestricted as to sign are converted to positive variables by using the following formula:[2]

$$x_j = \hat{x}_j - \hat{\hat{x}}$$

where

$$x_j = \text{the unrestricted variable}$$

and

$$\hat{x}_j,\ \hat{\hat{x}} \geqslant 0$$

Consider the following example:

$$\text{Maximize } Z = 9x_1 + 18x_2$$

subject to

$$6x_1 + 3x_2 \geqslant 18$$
$$2x_1 + 2x_2 \leqslant 16$$
$$x_1 \sim \text{unrestricted}$$
$$x_2 \geqslant 0$$

where

$$x_1 \text{ and } x_2 = \text{production rates for products 1 and 2}$$

To convert this problem to the standard simplex form with all positive variables, $\hat{x}_1 - \hat{\hat{x}}$ must be substituted for x_1 in the previous problem.

2. $\hat{\hat{x}}$ is not subscripted since it may be used for any number of unrestricted variables in a problem (e.g., $x_1 = \hat{x}_1 - \hat{\hat{x}}$, $x_2 = \hat{x}_2 - \hat{\hat{x}}$).

Maximize $Z = 9(\hat{x}_1 - \hat{\hat{x}}) + 18x_2$

subject to

$$6(\hat{x}_1 - \hat{\hat{x}}) + 3x_2 \geqslant 18$$
$$2(\hat{x}_1 - \hat{\hat{x}}) + 2x_2 \leqslant 16$$
$$\hat{x}_1, \hat{\hat{x}}, x_2 \geqslant 0$$

Expanding terms and converting all inequalities to equation form results in the following standard simplex form:

Maximize $Z = 9\hat{x}_1 - 9\hat{\hat{x}} + 18x_2 + 0s_1 + 0s_2 - MA_1$

subject to

$$6\hat{x}_1 - 6\hat{\hat{x}} + 3x_2 - s_1 + A_1 = 18$$
$$2\hat{x}_1 - 2\hat{\hat{x}} + 2x_2 + s_2 = 16$$
$$\hat{x}_1, \hat{\hat{x}}, x_2 \geqslant 0$$

The solution to this problem is shown in tables 3.22–3.25. The last tableau yields the following optimal solution:

$\hat{\hat{x}} = 2$

$x_2 = 10$

$Z = 162$

Table 3.22 Initial simplex tableau

c_b \ c_j	basis	b_i^*	9 $\hat{x}_1$	−9 $\hat{\hat{x}}$	18 x_2	0 s_1	0 s_2	−M A_1	
−M	A_1	18	⑥	−6	3	−1	0	1	Pivot Row
0	s_2	16	2	−2	2	0	1	0	
	z_j	−18M	−6M	6M	−3M	M	0	−M	
	$c_j - z_j$		9+6M	−9−6M	18+3M	−M	0	0	

Pivot Column

Table 3.23 Second simplex tableau

c_b \ c_j	basis	b_i^*	9 $\hat{x}_1$	−9 $\hat{\hat{x}}$	18 x_2	0 s_1	0 s_2	
9	x_1	3	1	−1	(1/2)	−1/6	0	Pivot Row
0	s_2	10	0	0	1	1/3	1	
	z_j	27	9	−9	9/2	−3/2	0	
	$c_j - z_j$		0	0	27/2	3/2	0	

Pivot Column

Table 3.24 Third simplex tableau

c_b \ c_j	basis	b_i^*	9 $\hat{x}_1$	−9 $\hat{\hat{x}}$	18 x_2	0 s_1	0 s_2	
18	x_2	6	2	−2	1	−1/3	0	
0	s_2	4	−2	(2)	0	2/3	1	Pivot Row
	z_j	108	36	−36	18	−6	0	
	$c_j - z_j$		−27	27	0	6	0	

Pivot Column

Table 3.25 Fourth and optimal tableau

c_b \ c_j	basis	b_i^*	9 $\hat{x}_1$	−9 $\hat{\hat{x}}$	18 x_2	0 s_1	0 s_2
18	x_2	10	0	0	1	1/3	1
−9	$\hat{\hat{x}}$	2	−1	1	0	1/3	1/2
	z_j	162	9	−9	18	3	27/2
	$c_j - z_j$		0	0	0	−3	−27/2

However, in order to determine the solution for the original problem variables, the variables must be reconverted to their original form.

$$x_1 = \hat{x}_1 - \hat{\hat{x}}$$
$$x_1 = 0 - 2$$
$$x_1 = -2$$

and

$$x_2 = 10$$
$$Z = 162$$

The solution to this problem does indeed have a negative value, $x_1 = -2$. The solution can be observed graphically in figure 3.5.

Figure 3.5 Graphic analysis of an unrestricted variable problem.

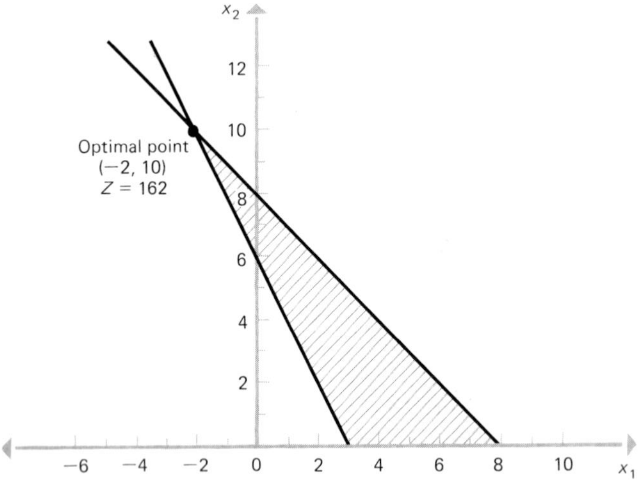

Variables with a Negative Bound

The other form that variables can take is to be negative but bounded. For example,

$$x_1 \geqslant -20.$$

This is actually the same as the previous unrestricted case except that the negative bound, 20, replaces the $\hat{\hat{x}}$ variable in the conversion of x, (i.e., $x_1 = \hat{x}_1 - 20$).

Negative Right-Hand-Side Values

To explain the resolution of a negative right-hand-side value, consider the following constraint:

$$-5x_1 + x_2 \leq -25$$

This constraint in its present form prohibits the solution of its accompanying problem by the simplex method. In the initial solution of the simplex model, $x_1 = 0$ and $x_2 = 0$. Therefore,

$$-5x_1 + x_2 + s_1 = -25$$
$$-5(0) + 0 + s_1 = -25$$
$$s_1 = -25.$$

Clearly the nonnegativity restriction on s_1 has been violated. To resolve this discrepancy, the constraint should be adjusted by multiplying both sides of the original constraint by -1. This reverses the direction of the inequality, which now becomes

$$5x_1 - x_2 \geq 25.$$

Additional Complications and Their Resolutions

Several additional complications that can occur in the solutions to linear programming problems include a tie for the pivot column, tie for the pivot row, an infeasible problem, an unbounded problem, and multiple optimal solutions. Each of these complications and their resolutions are discussed in the following sections.

Tie for the Pivot Column

The nonbasic variable that is selected to enter the solution (i.e., selection of the pivot column) is determined by the largest positive $c_j - z_j$ (or $z_j - c_j$) value. However, in any linear programming problem a tie could result from identical $c_j - z_j$ values. When this occurs the tie can be broken by arbitrarily selecting between the tied values. There is no wrong choice, although the selection of one variable may result in more iterations (i.e., more tableaus) than the other tied variable(s) would have. Regardless of which variable column is chosen, the optimal solution will eventually be found.

Tie for the Pivot Row and Degeneracy

Just as a tie can result when determining the pivot column, ties can also occur when selecting the pivot row. Table 3.26 represents the initial tableau for a maximization problem.

Table 3.26 Simplex tableau with a tie for the pivot row

c_b \ c_j	basis	b_i^*	4 x_1	6 x_2	0 s_1	0 s_2	0 s_3	
0	s_1	40	6	4	1	0	0	$40 \div 4 = 10$ } Tie
0	s_2	16	1	0	0	1	0	
0	s_3	10	1/2	1	0	0	1	$10 \div 1 = 10$ } Tie
	z_j	0	0	0	0	0	0	
	$c_j - z_j$		4	6	0	0	0	
				Pivot Column				

After selecting x_2 as the entering variable in the initial tableau, it is determined that two rows, s_1 and s_3, are tied for the pivot row. If row s_3 is selected arbitrarily the second tableau results as shown in table 3.27.

Table 3.27 Second simplex tableau

c_b \ c_j	basis	b_i^*	4 x_1	6 x_2	0 s_1	0 s_2	0 s_3	
0	s_1	0	4	0	1	0	−4	Pivot Row
0	s_2	16	1	0	0	1	0	
6	x_2	10	1/2	1	0	0	1	
	z_j	60	3	6	0	0	6	
	$c_j - z_j$		1	0	0	0	−6	
			Pivot Column					

In the second tableau we can see that a basic variable (s_1) has assumed a value of zero. This occurrence, which results from tied rows, is referred to as **degeneracy.** The zero b_i^* value can lead to a series of solutions that have the same z_j value, in this case 60. This is referred to as **cycling,** or **looping,** and can theoretically continue infinitely with the simplex method never yielding an optimal solution. However, in practice, after a number of such loops, the simplex procedure will *usually* proceed normally and eventually reach an optimal solution. The main drawback to degeneracy is the increase in the number of tableaus that must be computed, which, in turn, reduces the efficiency of the simplex method considerably.

As a general rule, the best way to break the tie between pivot rows is to simply select one arbitrarily. Tie breaking methods have been developed to prevent infinite looping, but the extra simplex computations these methods require do not warrant their discussion here.

An Infeasible Problem

In chapter 2, a problem with no feasible solution was illustrated graphically (fig. 2.9). This condition occurs when the problem has incompatible constraints, and, as a result, there is no common feasible solution space. However, an infeasible solution may not always be apparent as the problem is formulated or during the simplex process. This is especially true for large linear programming problems that cannot be graphed.

The final simplex tableau shown in table 3.28 demonstrates the identifying characteristics of an infeasible solution. All $c_j - z_j$ row values are negative or zero, indicating an optimal solution. However, observing the solution base, we see that there is an artificial variable in the final solution base and the z_j value is $90 - 2M$. Both of these values are totally meaningless since the artificial variable has no meaning. Therefore, the existence of an artificial variable in the solution base of the final simplex tableau indicates that the problem is infeasible.

Table 3.28 An infeasible problem

c_b \ c_j	basis	b_i^*	10 x_1	15 x_2	0 s_1	0 s_2	$-M$ A_1
10 $-M$	x_1 A_1	9 2	1 0	3/2 -2	1/2 -1	0 -1	0 1
	z_j	$90-2M$	10	$15+2M$	$5+M$	M	$-M$
	c_j-z_j		0	$-2M$	$-5-M$	$-M$	0

An Unbounded Problem

Another difficulty that can occur in a linear programming problem is an unbounded solution, illustrated graphically in figure 2.10. In this type of problem, the objective function can increase indefinitely without ever reaching a constraint boundary. Table 3.29 shows a tableau for a problem with an unbounded solution.

Table 3.29 An unbounded problem

c_b \ c_j	basis	b_i^*	7 x_1	4 x_2	0 s_1	0 s_2	
0 7	s_1 x_1	6 2	0 1	-2 -1	1 0	-1 1	$6 \div -2 = -3$ $2 \div -1 = -2$
	z_j	14	7	-7	0	7	
	c_j-z_j		0	11	0	-7	

Pivot Column

The entering variable in this tableau is indicated as x_2 because it has the maximum positive $c_j - z_j$ value. However, it is impossible to select a pivot row and a leaving variable since both pivot column values are negative. Thus, there are no positive row ratios available to allow a pivot row selection. This tableau does not indicate an optimal solution, yet the simplex process is prohibited from continuing. In other words, as x_2 enters the solution, neither basic variable acts as a bound on the problem (i.e., they increase as x_2 increases). As a result Z also increases indefinitely.

As a general rule, it can be stated that if a pivot row cannot be selected for lack of a positive ratio or if all a_{ij} values in the pivot column are negative or zero, the solution is unbounded.

Multiple Optimal Solutions

The final special case we will discuss in the simplex process is the existence of multiple optimal solutions. This type of problem is illustrated graphically in chapter 2 (fig. 2.8). Consider the final simplex tableau for a maximization problem in table 3.30.

Table 3.30 Simplex tableau with multiple optimal solutions

c_b \ c_j	basis	b_i^*	4 x_1	2 x_2	0 s_1	0 s_2
4	x_1	10	1	1/2	1/2	0
0	s_2	4	0	2	−1	1
	z_j	40	4	2	2	0
	$c_j - z_j$		0	0	−2	0

After examining the $c_j - z_j$ row it can be seen that all values are negative or zero; hence, the solution is optimal. However, x_2 is a *nonbasic* variable that has a $c_j - z_j$ value that is neither positive or negative but zero. Recalling that the $c_j - z_j$ value indicates the per unit net increase in profit that would be realized from entering a nonbasic variable, we can see that entering x_2 would neither decrease or increase profit. It would result in a different solution mix. Selecting x_2 as an entering variable results in the tableau shown in table 3.31.

Table 3.31 Simplex tableau with the alternative optimal solution

c_b \ c_j	basis	b_i^*	4 x_1	2 x_2	0 s_1	0 s_2
4	x_1	9	1	0	3/4	−1/4
2	x_2	2	0	1	−1/2	1/2
	z_j	40	4	2	2	0
	c_j-z_j		0	0	−2	0

A different solution mix exists in table 3.31 but with the same objective function value ($z_j = 40$). Thus, there are multiple optimal solutions. However, it should not be construed that these are the only two optimal solution points. Reviewing figure 2.8 it can be seen that in multiple optimal solutions all points on the constraint boundary between two adjacent corner-point optimal solutions are also optimal. Therefore, the tableaus in tables 3.30 and 3.31 identify the adjacent corner-point solutions between which an infinite number of optimal solutions exist. However, in practice, the identifiable corner-point solutions are said to be *the* multiple optimal solutions.

As a general rule, when the $c_j - z_j$ row indicates an optimal solution, if the $c_j - z_j$ values of any *nonbasic* variables are zero, multiple optimal solutions exist. To find the alternate optimal solution(s), the nonbasic variable with the $c_j - z_j$ value of zero, should be selected as an entering variable and the simplex steps continued.

Computerized Solution of Linear Programming

The simplex method for solving linear programming problems described and demonstrated in this chapter is useful for solving only problems of a relatively small size if done manually. Linear programming problems of only four equations and three variables can result in as many as fourteen iterations (and occasionally even more). A linear programming problem with N constraints has been estimated to have an average of $2N$ iterations. Problems with only five constraints and an average of ten iterations can be so time-consuming that the manual computation of the simplex method becomes impractical.

As a result, computer programs have been developed that replicate the simplex process in the solution of linear programming problems. These "packages" are usually very easy to apply and, depending on the computer system employed, very economical.

The question that is often posed is, "Why learn the simplex method when computer programs to solve linear programming problems are so readily available—especially in the business community?" There are several answers to this question. The most prominent is that learning the simplex process dramatically increases one's understanding of linear programming. In this same vein, learning the simplex process aids in interpreting and implementing the solutions. Just because an unstructured problem has been modeled and solved does not automatically validate solutions as correct. Unless the user knows the fundamentals of linear programming solutions it is difficult to adjust even a computer program. Thus, while the computer is an obvious aid in solving linear programming problems, in-depth knowledge of the simplex method is a necessity for real expertise in the formulation and subsequent solution of linear programming problems.

An additional reason for studying the manual simplex procedure is that it is very useful in understanding the principles and applications of sensitivity analysis and duality, the topics to be presented in chapter 4.

Summary

In this chapter, the simplex method for solving linear programming problems has been presented. This has included a presentation of both maximization and minimization problems and a discussion of the various complications that can occur and their resolutions. In future chapters, variations of the linear programming problem that require special solution techniques will be discussed. However, all of these variations in linear programming are primarily alterations of the basic model presented in chapters 2 and 3, and the alternative solution techniques are predominantly variations of the simplex method. Chapters 2 and 3 have presented the foundation of mathematical programming on which all special variations are based.

References

Charnes, A., and Cooper, W. W. *Management Models and Industrial Applications of Linear Programming*. New York: John Wiley & Sons, 1968.

Dantzig, G. B. *Linear Programming and Extension*. Princeton, N.J.: Princeton University Press, 1963.

Gass, S. *Linear Programming*. 4th ed. New York: McGraw-Hill, 1975.

Hadley, G. *Linear Programming*. Reading, Massachusetts: Addison-Wesley Publishing Co., 1962.

Hillier, F. S., and Lieberman, G. J. *Operations Research*. 2d ed. San Francisco: Holden-Day, 1974.

Kim, C. *Introduction to Linear Programming*. New York: Holt, Rinehart and Winston, 1971.

Wagner, H. M. *Principles of Operations Research*. Englewood Cliffs, N.J.: Prentice-Hall, 1969.

Problems

1. Given the following linear programming problem:

$$\text{Maximize } Z = 3x_1 + 2x_2$$

subject to

$$\begin{aligned} 3x_1 + 2x_2 &\leq 18 \\ 2x_1 + 4x_2 &\leq 20 \\ x_1 &\leq 4 \\ x_1, x_2 &\geq 0 \end{aligned}$$

Solve using the simplex method.

2. Given the following linear programming problem:

$$\text{Minimize } Z = 4x_1 + 6x_2$$

subject to

$$\begin{aligned} x_1 + x_2 &\geq 8 \\ 2x_1 + x_2 &\geq 12 \\ x_1, x_2 &\geq 0 \end{aligned}$$

Solve using the simplex method.

3. Given the following linear programming problem:

$$\text{Maximize } Z = 6x_1 + 2x_2 + 12x_3$$

subject to

$$\begin{aligned} 4x_1 + x_2 + 3x_3 &\leq 24 \\ 2x_1 + 6x_2 + 3x_3 &\leq 30 \\ x_1, x_2, x_3 &\geq 0 \end{aligned}$$

Solve using the simplex method.

4. Given the following linear programming problem:

$$\text{Maximize } Z = x_1 + 5x_2$$

subject to

$$\begin{aligned} 5x_1 + 5x_2 &\geq 25 \\ 2x_1 + 4x_2 &\leq 16 \\ x_1 &\leq 5 \\ x_1, x_2 &\geq 0 \end{aligned}$$

Solve using the simplex method.

5. Given the following linear programming problem:

$$\text{Maximize } Z = 10x_1 + 5x_2$$

subject to

$$\begin{aligned} 2x_1 + x_2 &\geq 10 \\ x_1 &= 4 \\ x_1 + 4x_2 &\leq 20 \\ x_1, x_2 &\geq 0 \end{aligned}$$

Solve using the simplex method.

6. Given the following linear programming problem:

$$\text{Minimize } Z = 4x_1 + 3x_2$$

subject to

$$\begin{aligned} 2x_1 + x_2 &\geq 10 \\ -3x_1 + 2x_2 &\leq 6 \\ x_1 + x_2 &\geq 6 \\ x_1, x_2 &\geq 0 \end{aligned}$$

Solve using the simplex method.

7. Given the following linear programming problem.

$$\text{Minimize } Z = 2x_1 + x_2 + 2x_3 + 1.2x_4$$

subject to

$$\begin{aligned} x_1 + x_3 &\geq 300 \\ x_3 + x_4 &\geq 500 \\ .6x_1 - .4x_2 &\leq 0 \\ x_1 + x_2 + x_3 + x_4 &\geq 1{,}000 \\ x_1, x_2, x_3, x_4 &\geq 0 \end{aligned}$$

Solve using the simplex method.

8. Given the following linear programming problem:

$$\text{Maximize } Z = 10x_1 + 5x_2$$

subject to

$$\begin{aligned} 3x_1 + 9x_2 &\geq 27 \\ 8x_1 + 6x_2 &\geq 48 \\ -4x_1 + 6x_2 &\leq -12 \\ 8x_1 + 12x_2 &= 24 \\ x_1, x_2 &\geq 0 \end{aligned}$$

Solve using the simplex method.

9. Given the following linear programming problem:

$$\text{Minimize } Z = 3x_1 + 6x_2$$

subject to

$$\begin{aligned} 3x_1 + 2x_2 &\leq 18 \\ x_1 + x_2 &\geq 5 \\ x_1 &\leq 4 \\ x_2 &\leq 7 \\ x_1, x_2 &\geq 0 \end{aligned}$$

Solve using the simplex method.

10. Given the following linear programming problem:

$$\text{Maximize } Z = 40x_1 + 60x_2$$

subject to

$$\begin{aligned} x_1 + 2x_2 &\leq 30 \\ 4x_1 + 4x_2 &\leq 72 \\ x_1 &\geq 5 \\ x_2 &\geq 12 \\ x_1, x_2 &\geq 0 \end{aligned}$$

Solve using the simplex method.

11. Given the following linear programming problem:

$$\text{Minimize } Z = 6x_1 + 4x_2$$

subject to

$$\begin{aligned} 3x_1 + 2x_2 &\geq 18 \\ 2x_1 + 4x_2 &= 20 \\ 2x_2 &\leq 8 \\ x_1, x_2 &\geq 0 \end{aligned}$$

Solve using the simplex method.

12. Given the following linear programming problem:

$$\text{Maximize } Z = .7x_1 + 1.2x_2 + .9x_3$$

subject to

$$\begin{aligned} x_1 + x_2 + x_3 &= 2{,}000 \\ x_1 &\leq 1{,}500 \\ x_2 &\leq 400 \\ x_3 &\leq 700 \\ .5x_1 + .8x_2 + .6x_3 &\geq 750 \\ x_1, x_2, x_3 &\geq 0 \end{aligned}$$

Solve using the simplex method.

13. Given the following linear programming problem:

Minimize $Z = 20x_1 + 16x_2$

subject to

$$\begin{aligned} 3x_1 + x_2 &\geq 6 \\ x_1 + x_2 &\geq 4 \\ 2x_1 + 6x_2 &\geq 12 \\ x_1, x_2 &\geq 0 \end{aligned}$$

Solve using the simplex method.

14. Given the following linear programming problem:

Maximize $Z = 30x_1 + 40x_2 + 20x_3$

subject to

$$\begin{aligned} 100x_1 + 120x_2 + 70x_3 &\leq 100{,}000 \\ 7x_1 + 10x_2 + 8x_3 &\leq 8{,}000 \\ x_1 + x_2 + x_3 &= 1{,}000 \\ x_1, x_2, x_3 &\geq 0 \end{aligned}$$

Solve using the simplex method.

15. Given the following linear programming problem:

Maximize $Z = 9x_1 + 12x_2$

subject to

$$\begin{aligned} 4x_1 + 8x_2 &\leq 64 \\ 5x_1 + 5x_2 &\leq 50 \\ 15x_1 + 8x_2 &\leq 120 \\ x_1 &\leq 7 \\ x_2 &\leq 7 \\ x_1, x_2 &\geq 0 \end{aligned}$$

Solve using the simplex method.

16. Given the following linear programming problem:

Maximize $Z = 4x_1 + 5x_2$

subject to

$$\begin{aligned} 2x_1 + 2x_2 &\geq 8 \\ x_2 &= 3 \\ 9x_1 + 3x_2 &\leq 27 \\ x_1, x_2 &\geq 0 \end{aligned}$$

Solve using the simplex method.

17. Given the following linear programming problem:

Maximize $Z = 100x_1 + 75x_2 + 90x_3 + 95x_4$

subject to

$$\begin{aligned} 3x_1 + 2x_2 &\leq 40 \\ 4x_3 + x_4 &\leq 25 \\ 200x_1 + 250x_3 &\leq 2{,}000 \\ 100x_2 + 200x_4 &\leq 2{,}200 \\ x_1, x_2, x_3, x_4 &\geq 0 \end{aligned}$$

Solve using the simplex method.

18. Given the following linear programming problem:

Maximize $Z = 60x_1 + 50x_2 + 45x_3 + 50x_4$

subject to

$$\begin{aligned} x_2 &\leq 20 \\ x_4 &\leq 15 \\ 10x_1 + 5x_2 &\leq 120 \\ 8x_3 + 6x_4 &\leq 135 \\ x_1, x_2, x_3, x_4 &\geq 0 \end{aligned}$$

Solve using the simplex method.

19. Given the following linear programming problem:

$$\text{Maximize } Z = 600x_1 + 540x_2 + 375x_3$$

subject to

$$x_1 + x_2 + x_3 \leq 12$$
$$x_1 \leq 5$$
$$80x_1 + 70x_2 + 50x_3 \leq 750$$
$$x_1, x_2, x_3 \geq 0$$

Solve using the simplex method.

20. Given the following linear programming problem:

$$\text{Maximize } Z = 40x_1 + 35x_2 + 45x_3$$

subject to

$$2x_1 + 3x_2 + 2x_3 \leq 120$$
$$4x_1 + 3x_2 + x_3 \leq 160$$
$$3x_1 + 2x_2 + 4x_3 \leq 100$$
$$x_1 + x_2 + x_3 \leq 40$$
$$x_1, x_2, x_3 \geq 0$$

Solve using the simplex method.

21. Given the following linear programming problem:

$$\text{Maximize } Z = 5x_1 + 7x_2 + 8x_3$$

subject to

$$x_1 + x_2 + x_3 \leq 32$$
$$x_1 \leq 20$$
$$x_2 \leq 15$$
$$x_3 \leq 18$$
$$x_1, x_2, x_3 \geq 0$$

Solve using the simplex method.

22. Given the following linear programming problem:

$$\text{Maximize } Z = 7x_1 + 5x_2 + 5x_3$$

subject to

$$x_1 + x_2 + x_3 \leq 25$$
$$2x_1 + x_2 + x_3 \leq 40$$
$$x_1 + x_2 \leq 25$$
$$x_3 \leq 60$$
$$x_1, x_2, x_3 \geq 0$$

Solve using the simplex method.

23. Given the following linear programming problem:

$$\text{Maximize } Z = 15x_1 + 25x_2$$

subject to

$$3x_1 + 4x_2 \geq 12$$
$$2x_1 + x_2 \geq 6$$
$$3x_1 + 2x_2 \leq 9$$
$$x_1, x_2 \geq 0$$

Solve using the simplex method.

24. Given the following linear programming problem:

$$\text{Maximize } Z = x_1 + 2x_2 - x_3$$

subject to

$$4x_2 + x_3 \leq 40$$
$$x_1 - x_2 \leq 20$$
$$2x_1 + 4x_2 + 3x_3 \leq 60$$
$$x_1, x_2, x_3 \geq 0$$

Solve using the simplex method.

25. Given the following linear programming problem:

$$\text{Maximize } Z = 5x_1 + 2x_2 + 10x_3 + 8x_4$$

subject to

$$2x_1 - 3x_2 + x_3 + 7x_4 \leq 32$$
$$4x_1 + 6x_2 - 2x_3 - 2x_4 \leq 24$$
$$2x_1 - 4x_2 + x_3 + 2x_4 \leq 12$$
$$x_1, x_2, x_3, x_4 \geq 0$$

Solve using the simplex method.

26. Given the following linear programming problem:

$$\text{Maximize } Z = -2x_1 + 8x_2$$

subject to

$$-2x_1 + x_2 \leq 4$$
$$x_1 + 2x_2 \leq 4$$
$$x_1 \sim \text{unrestricted}$$
$$x_2 \geq -2$$

Solve using the simplex method.

27. Given the following linear programming problem:

$$\text{Maximize } Z = 2x_1 + 4x_2 - 2x_3$$

subjct to

$$2x_1 + x_2 - 4x_3 \leq 6$$
$$-4x_1 - 2x_2 + x_3 \leq 5$$
$$2x_1 + 6x_2 = 10$$
$$x_1, x_2, x_3 \geq 0$$

Solve using the simplex method.

28. Given the following linear programming problem:

$$\text{Minimize } Z = 2x_1 - x_2 + 3x_3$$

subject to

$$x_1 + 2x_2 + x_3 \geq 12$$
$$x_2 - 2x_3 \geq -6$$
$$6 \leq x_1 + 2x_2 + 4x_3 \leq 24$$
$$x_1, x_2 \geq 0$$
$$x_3 \sim \text{unrestricted}$$

Solve using the simplex method.

29. Given the following linear programming problem:

$$\text{Maximize } Z = 5x_1 + 7x_2 + 6x_3$$

subject to

$$4x_1 + 2x_2 + x_3 \leq 8$$
$$-2x_1 + 4x_2 + 12x_3 \leq 24$$
$$x_1 + 2x_2 + x_3 \geq 6$$
$$x_1, x_2, x_3 \geq 0$$

Solve using the simplex method.

30. Given the following linear programming problem:

$$\text{Minimize } Z = 3x_1 + 5x_2 + 2x_3$$

subject to

$$x_1 + x_2 - 3x_3 \geq 35$$
$$x_1 + 2x_2 \geq 50$$
$$-x_1 + x_2 + x_3 \geq 25$$
$$x_1, x_2, x_3 \geq 0$$

Solve using the simplex method.

31. Given the following linear programming problem:

$$\begin{aligned} &\text{Maximize } Z = 4x_1 + 2x_2 \\ &\text{subject to} \\ &-2x_1 - x_2 \geq 30 \\ &x_1 - 2x_2 \geq 8 \\ &3x_1 - 2x_2 \leq 12 \\ &x_1, x_2 \sim \text{unrestricted} \end{aligned}$$

Solve using the simplex method.

32. Given the following linear programming problem:

$$\begin{aligned} &\text{Maximize } Z = 10x_1 + 8x_2 \\ &\text{subject to} \\ &-6x_1 + 2x_2 \geq 12 \\ &x_1 - x_2 \geq -2 \\ &x_1, x_2 \sim \text{unrestricted} \end{aligned}$$

Solve using the simplex method.

33. Given the following linear programming problem:

$$\begin{aligned} &\text{Minimize } Z = 2x_1 + 4x_2 + x_3 \\ &\text{subject to} \\ &2x_1 - 3x_2 + x_3 = 4 \\ &3x_1 - 4x_2 - x_3 \geq 1 \\ &x_1, x_2 \geq 0 \\ &x_3 \sim \text{unrestricted} \end{aligned}$$

Solve using the simplex method.

34. Given the following linear programming problem:

$$\begin{aligned} &\text{Maximize } Z = 3x_1 - x_2 + 2x_3 \\ &\text{subject to} \\ &3x_1 + 2x_2 + 2x_3 = 0 \\ &2x_2 + x_3 \leq 400 \\ &6x_1 + x_2 \geq 600 \\ &x_1, x_2 \geq 0 \\ &x_3 \sim \text{unrestricted} \end{aligned}$$

Solve using the simplex method.

35. Given the following linear programming problem:

$$\begin{aligned} &\text{Maximize } Z = 2x_1 + x_2 - x_3 \\ &\text{subject to} \\ &15 \leq x_1 \leq 25 \\ &x_1 + 2x_2 - x_3 = 12 \\ &x_1, x_2 \geq 0 \\ &x_3 \sim \text{unrestricted} \end{aligned}$$

Solve using the simplex method.

36. Given the following linear programming problem:

$$\begin{aligned} &\text{Minimize } Z = x_1 - 2x_2 + 4x_3 \\ &\text{subject to} \\ &-2x_1 + x_2 + 3x_3 = 3 \\ &2x_1 + x_2 + x_3 \geq 1 \\ &x_1, x_3 \geq 0 \\ &x_2 \sim \text{unrestricted} \end{aligned}$$

Solve using the simplex method.

37. Given the following linear programming problem:

$$\text{Maximize } Z = x_1 + 2x_2 + 2x_3$$

subject to

$$x_1 + x_2 + 2x_3 \leqslant 12$$
$$2x_1 + x_2 + 5x_3 = 20$$
$$x_1 + x_2 - x_3 \geqslant 8$$
$$x_1, x_2, x_3 \geqslant 0$$

Solve using the simplex method.

38. Given the following linear programming problem:

$$\text{Maximize } Z = 2x_1 - x_2$$

subject to

$$-x_1 + x_2 \leqslant 1$$
$$-x_1 + 2x_2 \leqslant 4$$
$$x_1, x_2 \geqslant 0$$

Solve using the simplex method.

39. Given the following linear programming problem:

$$\text{Maximize } Z = 4x_1 + 2x_2$$

subject to

$$x_1 + x_2 \geqslant 1$$
$$-4x_1 + x_2 \leqslant 0$$
$$-x_1 + 4x_2 \geqslant 0$$
$$-x_1 + x_2 \leqslant 1$$
$$x_1 + x_2 \leqslant 6$$
$$x_1 \leqslant 3$$
$$x_1, x_2 \geqslant 0$$

Solve using the simplex method.

40. Given the following linear programming problem:

$$\text{Maximize } Z = 9x_1 + 18x_2$$

subject to

$$6x_1 + 3x_2 \geqslant 1{,}800$$
$$2x_1 + 2x_2 \leqslant 1{,}600$$
$$x_2 \geqslant 0$$
$$x_1 \sim \text{unrestricted}$$

Solve using the simplex method.

41. Given the following linear programming problem.

$$\text{Maximize } Z = 4x_1 + 8x_2$$

subject to

$$x_2 \leqslant 6$$
$$x_1 \leqslant 4$$
$$2x_1 + 3x_2 \leqslant 12$$
$$x_2 \geqslant 0$$
$$x_1 \geqslant -4$$

Solve using the simplex method.

The following problems refer to problems in chapter 2.

42. Solve problem 1 using the simplex method.
43. Solve problem 3 using the simplex method.
44. Solve problem 4 using the simplex method.
45. Solve problem 8 using the simplex method.
46. Solve problem 13 using the simplex method.
47. Solve problem 15 using the simplex method.
48. Solve problem 34 using the simplex method.

4

Duality and Sensitivity Analysis

Identifying the optimal basic solution of a problem as outlined in the previous two chapters is not always the ultimate objective of linear programming. Quite often the final simplex tableau provides additional economic information that is even more important than the basic solution to the problem. The importance and depth of the additional information obtained from analyzing optimal simplex tableaus has generated a great deal of interest in this area of analysis. The two major areas of interest related to the study of optimal solutions are **duality** and **sensitivity analysis.** Duality is a unique property of linear programming that allows the economic valuation of constraint resources. Sensitivity analysis is the study of changes in the model parameters and the effects these changes have on the problem solution.

Duality

The term *duality* refers to the fact that every linear programming problem consists of *two* forms. The first, or original, form of the problem is called the **primal,** while the second form of the problem is called the **dual.** Similarly, for every **primal solution** there exists a corresponding **dual solution.** As might be expected, the properties of one problem form are closely related to the properties of the other. As a result, the optimal solution to the primal form correspondingly yields complete information about the solution of the dual form.

There are several important reasons for analyzing a problem in terms of its dual form. The first and most important reason is that the dual solution provides significant information concerning the economic interpretation of the resource parameters of a linear programming problem. As such, the dual can provide information to the manager regarding the value of resources, thereby aiding the manager in making decisions regarding the acquisition of additional resources. A secondary attribute of the dual form is that it may occasionally be easier to solve than the primal form because of fewer simplex computations.

Economic Interpretation of the Primal

Consider the following profit maximization problem for a manufacturing firm. The firm produces two products, 1 and 2. The production of products 1 and 2 is subject to the following resource requirements and availabilities for labor, material, and storage space:

Resource	Resource Requirements Product 1	Product 2	Total Resources
Labor (hr./unit)	1	2	10 hr.
Material (lb./unit)	6	6	36 lb.
Storage (ft.²/unit)	8	4	40 ft.²

Given that profit per unit of product 1 is \$4 and for product 2 it is \$5, this problem is formulated as:

Maximize $Z = 4x_1 + 5x_2$

subject to

$$\begin{aligned} x_1 + 2x_2 &\leqslant 10 \quad \text{(labor)} \\ 6x_1 + 6x_2 &\leqslant 36 \quad \text{(material)} \\ 8x_1 + 4x_2 &\leqslant 40 \quad \text{(storage)} \\ x_1, x_2 &\geqslant 0 \end{aligned}$$

Solving this problem via the simplex method results in the optimal simplex solution in table 4.1.

Table 4.1 Optimal simplex solution

c_b \ c_j	basis	b_i^*	4 x_1	5 x_2	0 s_1	0 s_2	0 s_3
5	x_2	4	0	1	1	−1/6	0
4	x_1	2	1	0	−1	1/3	0
0	s_3	8	0	0	4	−2	1
	z_j	28	4	5	1	1/2	0
	$c_j - z_j$		0	0	−1	−1/2	0

The model results that are most obvious, based on our present knowledge of linear programming, are the optimal basic solution ($x_1 = 2$, $x_2 = 4$, $s_3 = 8$) and the maximum profit ($z_j = \$28$). However, there is additional information in the final tableau related to the constraint resources (labor, material, and space), which has yet to be analyzed. This information is contained in the $c_j - z_j$ row of the final tableau. As previously noted, the $c_j - z_j$ row cell values indicate the per unit increase (or decrease) in profit if the corresponding variable entered the solution base.

Observing the $c_j - z_j$ values under the s_1 and s_2 columns, it can be seen that if either of these variables entered the solution, profit would decline by $1.00 and $0.50 per unit respectively. Recall that s_1 represents unused labor resources and s_2 represents unused material resources. Both s_1 and s_2 (in table 4.1) are by definition equal to zero since they are not in the basic solution, which means that all labor and materials are being used. Therefore, entry of one unit of s_1 into the basic solution is analogous to reduction in the *use of labor* by one unit (i.e., if s_1 moves into the basis and equals one, that represents 1 hour of labor not being used). Likewise, entry of one unit of s_2 results in reduction in the *use of material* by one unit.

Now, if entry of one unit of s_1 (reducing labor usage by one unit) would reduce profit by $1.00, then the reverse process would increase profit by $1.00. The same holds true for s_2 except that the marginal rate at which profit changes as s_2 (the quantity of material resource) changes is $0.50. It can therefore be logically deduced that $1.00 and $0.50 represent the marginal values of these resources. In other words, we could expect profits to increase by $1.00 or $0.50 if another unit of labor or material, respectively, could be obtained. The $c_j - z_j$ values under the slack variables are often referred to as **shadow prices,** since they are, in effect, the maximum price the manager would be willing to pay to obtain more of the resources in order to maximize profit subject to the resource constraints.

Consider for a moment that the manager of the manufacturing firm wishes to place a value on the worth of the resources. Looking at the original model formulation, the manager sees only how much of each resource is required to produce each unit of product, how much of each resource is available, and the profit to be garnered from units produced. There is no indication of the worth (or cost) of those resources. Observing the maximum profit of $28, the manager ascertains that the value of the resources must be defined in terms of their contributions to profit. Thus, the manager must distribute the profit among all employed resources in order to determine the implicit value of those resources in gaining that profit. This resource value is what is shown by the $c_j - z_j$ values under the slack variables in the final simplex tableau. Going one step further, it can be seen that the value of each resource corresponds to the slack variable for each resource constraint. Thus, the $c_j - z_j$ value for s_1 is the marginal value of labor, $c_j - z_j$ for s_2 is the marginal value of material, and $c_j - z_j$ for s_3 is the marginal value of storage space.

Continuing in the economic interpretation of the primal, it can be deduced that if the manager is assigning a value to each resource based on its contribution to profit, the total value of each resource is limited by the profit that exists.

Economically speaking, after assigning the total value of the resources, the return is zero. As a result, the total value of the resources cannot be greater than z_j^* (or \$28 for this example). Conversely, if the manager is accurately assigning a value to each resource by determining the portion of profit accruing from each resource, then the total value of those resources *cannot be less* than the profit, z_j^*. Thus, the value of all resources is always *exactly equal* to optimal profit.

These economic properties can also be examined within the framework of the example problem. First consider the resource constraint for labor,

$$x_1 + 2x_2 \leq 10.$$

Since our optimal solution mix is $x_1 = 2$ and $x_2 = 4$, the total value of the labor resources can be computed. From our prior analysis of the $c_j - z_j$ row values, we know that the value of one hour of labor is \$1.00. Since each unit of product 1 requires 1 hour of labor, and 2 units of product 1 are produced, then the value of labor used in production of product 1 is

(\$1.00/hr.) (2 units of product 1) (1 hr./unit) = \$2.00,

which is

(value/hr. of labor) (quantity of product 1) (labor use/unit of product 1).

Performing the same operation for product 2, where $x_2 = 4$, and the labor utilization is 2 hours per unit of product 2 produced, results in

(\$1.00/hr.) (4 units of product 2) (2hr./unit) = \$8.00,

and summing the results of the previous two calculations yields

2.00 + 8.00 = \$10.00, the value of labor.

The same computations can also be performed for the material resources:

(\$0.50/lb.) (2 units of product 1) (6 lb./unit) = \$6.00

(\$0.50/lb.) (4 units of product 2) (6 lb./unit) = \$12.00

and

6.00 + 12.00 = \$18.00, the value of material

Summing the two resource values yields the total value of resources:

value of labor + value of material = Z

\$10.00 + \$18.00 = \$28.00 = Z

The question might now be asked, "What is the value of s_3, storage space?" The answer is that on a *marginal* basis storage space has no value, since storage is not a binding constraint (i.e., since $s_3 = 8$, this means that 8 square feet are left unused). An extra square foot of storage space has no value to the manager since extra unused storage space already exists.

Thus, the resources of the linear programming problem have value, in the sense in which it is discussed here, only if they represent binding constraints to the problem. That is, the value is in terms of what it would be worth to have available additional units of the resources that are limiting possible production (and profit). The key to understanding the implicit value of resources, as given in the $c_j - z_j$ row in the optimal solution tableau, is to recognize that these are *marginal* values for the optimal solution, which is located on the solution space boundary created by those constraints that reflect resources that have value to the manager.

A unique condition of linear programming models is that the economic properties previously mentioned can be expressed within the dual form. In fact, the term *duality* refers to the fact that a completely symmetrical model form can be developed from the original problem (primal form) in which the decision variables represent the values of the constraint resources.

The Dual Form of the Problem

For a linear programming maximization problem, which we will define as the primal, the corresponding dual is a minimization problem. Conversely, a primal minimization problem has a corresponding dual maximization form. The dual form of our previously discussed example problem is a minimization problem, which is formulated as follows:

$$\text{Minimize } Z = 10y_1 + 36y_2 + 40y_3$$

subject to

$$y_1 + 6y_2 + 8y_3 \geq 4$$
$$2y_1 + 6y_2 + 4y_3 \geq 5$$
$$y_1, y_2, y_3 \geq 0$$

where

y_1 = the marginal value of one hour of labor

y_2 = the marginal value of one pound of material

y_3 = the marginal value of one square foot of storage space

The relationship between the primal and dual formulations can be summarized as follows:

1. The maximization of a primal becomes a dual minimization.
2. The dual variables, y_1, y_2, and y_3, correspond to the resource constraints in the primal problem. Since there are $m = 3$ constraints in the primal, there are $m = 3$ variables in the dual.

3. The right-hand-side elements (b_i) in the primal correspond to the coefficients of the objective function in the dual. The values $b_1 = 10$, $b_2 = 36$, and $b_3 = 40$ form the objective function of the dual, $z_d = 10y_1 + 36y_2 + 40y_3$.
4. The a_{ij} constraint coefficients in the primal are the a_{ji} values in the dual:

Primal (a_{ij})				Dual (a_{ji})
a_{11}	=	1	=	a_{11}
a_{12}	=	2	=	a_{21}
a_{21}	=	6	=	a_{12}
a_{22}	=	6	=	a_{22}
a_{31}	=	8	=	a_{13}
a_{32}	=	4	=	a_{23}

5. The c_j values in the primal are the right-hand-side values in the dual (i.e., $c_1 = 4$ and $c_2 = 5$).
6. All constraints in the maximization primal are $\leqslant$, and all constraints in the corresponding minimization dual are $\geqslant$.

As a review of the example production problem, the primal-dual relationship can be observed in figure 4.1.

Figure 4.1 The primal-dual relationship.

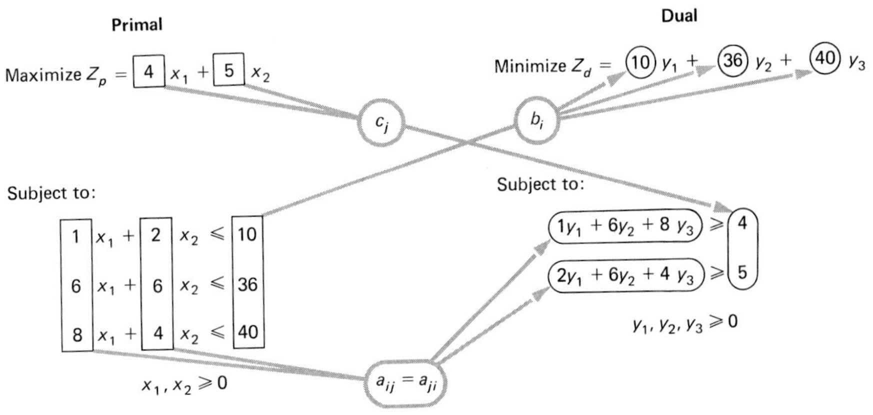

Primal
Dual
Maximize Z_p = 4 x_1 + 5 x_2
Minimize Z_d = 10 y_1 + 36 y_2 + 40 y_3
c_j
b_i
Subject to:
Subject to:
1 x_1 + 2 x_2 ≤ 10
6 x_1 + 6 x_2 ≤ 36
8 x_1 + 4 x_2 ≤ 40
1y_1 + 6y_2 + 8 y_3 ≥ 4
2y_1 + 6y_2 + 4 y_3 ≥ 5
y_1, y_2, y_3 ≥ 0
x_1, x_2 ≥ 0
a_ij = a_ji

The Primal-Dual Relationship in General Form

An important format for expressing a linear programming problem that will be of benefit in the following discussion of the dual is the general form of a linear programming problem. Recall the general linear programming model for a maximization problem originally shown in chapter 2.

$$\text{Maximize } Z_p = \sum_{j=1}^{n} c_j x_j$$

subject to

$$\sum_{j=1}^{n} a_{ij} x_j \leqslant b_i,\ i = 1, 2, \ldots, m$$

$$x_j \geqslant 0,\ j = 1, 2, \ldots, n.$$

Applying the basic primal-dual conversions previously noted to the primal in general form results in the following general form for the dual:

$$\text{Minimize } Z_d = \sum_{i=1}^{m} b_i y_i$$

subject to

$$\sum_{i=1}^{m} a_{ji} y_i \geqslant c_j,\ j = 1, 2, \ldots, n$$

$$y_i \geqslant 0,\ i = 1, 2, \ldots, m.$$

Economic Interpretation of the Dual Form

Now let us analyze the primal-dual economic relationships that were alluded to in our prior discussion of the primal. Tables 4.2 and 4.3 show the final optimal simplex solutions for the primal and dual forms of our example.

Primal

$$\text{Maximize } Z_p = 4x_1 + 5x_2$$

subject to

$$x_1 + 2x_2 \leqslant 10$$
$$6x_1 + 6x_2 \leqslant 36$$
$$8x_1 + 4x_2 \leqslant 40$$
$$x_1, x_2 \geqslant 0$$

Dual

$$\text{Minimize } Z_d = 10y_1 + 36y_2 + 40y_3$$

subject to

$$y_1 + 6y_2 + 8y_3 \geqslant 4$$
$$2y_1 + 6y_2 + 4y_3 \geqslant 5$$
$$y_1, y_2, y_3 \geqslant 0$$

Table 4.2 Optimal simplex tableau for the primal form

c_b \ c_j	basis	b_i^*	4 x_1	5 x_2	0 s_1	0 s_2	0 s_3
5	x_2	4	0	1	1	−1/6	0
4	x_1	2	1	0	−1	1/3	0
0	s_3	8	0	0	4	−2	1
	z_j	28	4	5	1	1/2	0
	$c_j - z_j$		0	0	−1	−1/2	0

Table 4.3 Optimal simplex tableau for the dual form

c_b \ c_j	basis	b_i^*	10 y_1	36 y_2	40 y_3	0 s_1'	0 s_2'
36	y_2	1/2	0	1	2	−1/3	1/6
10	y_1	1	1	0	−4	1	−1
	z_j	28	10	36	32	−2	−4
	$z_j - c_j$		0	0	−8	−2	−4

Observing the two simplex tableaus in tables 4.2 and 4.3, the relationship between the primal and dual solutions can be ascertained. Note that the negative $c_j - z_j$ row values under s_1 and s_2 of the primal tableau correspond to the solution values of y_1 and y_2 of the dual. Considering all $c_j - z_j$ values in the primal solution tableau, we have:

Primal Tableau Column Headings	$c_j - z_j$ Values in Primal	Dual Tableau Basic (b_i^*) Solution
x_1	0	s_1' (not in basis, therefore zero by definition)
x_2	0	s_2' (not in basis, therefore zero by definition)
s_1	1	y_1
s_2	1/2	y_2
s_3	0	y_3 (not in basis, therefore zero by definition)

As noted previously, the dual variables, y_i, represent the marginal value of a unit of each resource, i. As a result, the constraints of the dual reflect the value of resources that are involved in the contribution to profit of each product. Because $c_1 = 4$ in the primal, the use of these resources must result in at least \$4.00 in profit for each unit of product 1. If the resources invested in producing one unit of product 1 do not return at least \$4.00, then it would be better to invest the resources elsewhere.

It can be seen that if the implicit value of labor is \$1.00 per hour ($y_1 = 1$), then the use of 1 hour of labor will be worth \$1.00 to the firm in achieving the profit of \$4.00. Similarly, since one pound of material is valued at \$0.50 ($y_2 = 1/2$), the 6 pounds necessary to produce one unit of product 1 is worth \$3.00 to the firm in achieving the profit of \$4.00. Using these values in the product 1 constraint yields

$$1y_1 + 6y_2 + 8y_3 \geq 4$$
$$1(1) + 6(0.50) + 8(0) \geq 4$$
$$4 \geq 4.$$

Now consider the objective function of the dual.

$$\text{Minimize } Z_d = 10y_1 + 36y_2 + 40y_3$$

The coefficients 10, 36, and 40 in the dual objective function are the b_i parameters from the primal (i.e., the available resources). Since we already know that $y_1 = \$1.00$, $y_2 = \$0.50$, and $y_3 = 0$ (the values of labor, material, and space), it can be seen that the dual objective function represents the product of the total resources and the resource values.

$$Z_d = (10 \text{ hr.})(\$1.00/\text{hr.}) + (36 \text{ lb.})(\$0.50/\text{lb.}) + (40 \text{ ft.}^2)(\$0/\text{ft.}^2)$$
$$Z_d = \$28, \text{ the total marginal value of all resources}$$

Finally, consider the seemingly confusing property of

$$\text{Maximize } Z_p = \$28 = \text{Minimize } Z_d.$$

As already analyzed in our prior economic interpretation of the primal, the values of the model resources are determined such that they are just high enough to give to those inputs a value equal to total profit. That is, the profit is distributed among each resource so that the total resource value equals total profit (and their difference is zero).

This property can also be analyzed analytically employing the general form of the model. Recall the constraints of the general model for the primal.

$$\sum_{j=1}^{n} a_{ij}x_j \leq b_i,\ i = 1, 2, \ldots, m$$

Multiply both sides of this inequality by the sum of all y_i, $\sum_{i=1}^{m} y_i$.

$$\sum_{i=1}^{m} y_i \left(\sum_{j=1}^{n} a_{ij}x_j \right) \leq \sum_{i=1}^{m} b_i y_i$$

However, notice that the term $\sum_{i=1}^{m} b_i y_i$ is also the general form of the dual objective function, Z_d.

Next, recall that the general form of the dual constraints is

$$\sum_{i=1}^{m} a_{ji}y_i \geq c_j,\ j = 1, 2, \ldots, n.$$

If both sides of this inequality are multiplied by the sum of all x_j, $\sum_{j=1}^{n} x_j$, then

$$\sum_{j=1}^{n} x_j \left(\sum_{i=1}^{m} a_{ji}y_i \right) \geq \sum_{j=1}^{n} c_j x_j.$$

From this formulation notice that the term $\sum_{j=1}^{n} c_j x_j$ is also the general form of the primal objective function, Z_p. Observing these several manipulations it is further observed that the terms $\sum_{j=1}^{n} x_j \left(\sum_{i=1}^{m} a_{ji}y_i \right)$ and $\sum_{i=1}^{m} y_i \left(\sum_{j=1}^{n} a_{ij}x_j \right)$ are equal.

Thus, by combining these terms the following relationship is determined:

$$Z_p = \sum_{j=1}^{n} c_j x_j \leq \left[\sum_{j=1}^{n} x_j \left(\sum_{i=1}^{m} a_{ji}y_i \right) = \sum_{i=1}^{m} y_i \left(\sum_{j=1}^{n} a_{ij}x_j \right) \right] \leq \sum_{i=1}^{m} b_i y_i = Z_d$$

and

$$Z_p \leq Z_d$$

This analytical result is known as the **fundamental primal-dual relationship.** Interpreting the relationship literally, the value of the primal objective function is bounded by the corresponding value of the dual objective function. Carrying this relationship a step further, if the optimal solution values (x_j) are feasible and the optimal dual solution values (y_i) are feasible, then

$$Z_p = Z_d,$$

which corresponds to the primal-dual relationship previously noted.

Implicit in the fundamental primal-dual relationship is the property of **complementary slackness.** This property holds that for a positive basic variable in the primal, its corresponding dual variable will equal zero. Alternatively, for a nonbasic variable in the primal (which is thus zero), its corresponding dual variable will be basic and positive.

As an example, consider the primal and dual solutions of the production problem illustrated in tables 4.2 and 4.3. Observe that the basic variables in the primal (x_2, x_1, and s_3) have corresponding dual variables (s_2', s_1', and y_3) that are nonbasic and, thus, equal to zero. Similarly, the nonbasic primal variables s_1 and s_2 equal zero while in the dual the corresponding variables y_1 and y_2 are basic and positive.

Exceptions to the Primal-Dual Relationship

The primal-dual transformation illustrated in this chapter is based on a maximization problem with all $\leqslant$ constraints. From prior illustrations in chapters 2 and 3, it has been shown that this linear programming form does not always exist. The rules for transforming the primal form of a problem into the dual form are altered when the linear programming problem contains mixed constraints (i.e., a combination of $\leqslant$, $=$, $\geqslant$ constraints) and/or unrestricted variables. Each of the possible alternative cases will be considered separately.

An Equality Constraint

The following problem in primal form contains an equality constraint.

$$\text{Maximize } Z_p = c_1x_1 + c_2x_2$$

subject to

$$a_{11}x_1 + a_{12}x_2 = b_1$$
$$a_{21}x_1 + a_{22}x_2 \leqslant b_2$$
$$x_1, x_2 \geqslant 0$$

The equality constraint can also be expressed by the following two inequality constraints:

$$a_{11}x_1 + a_{12}x_2 \leqslant b_1$$
$$a_{11}x_1 + a_{12}x_2 \geqslant b_1$$

Of these two inequalities, the second one ($\geq$) can be transformed to a $\leq$ constraint by multiplying through by -1:

$$-a_{11}x_1 - a_{12}x_2 \leq -b_1$$

Summarizing, the original problem can now be formulated with all $\leq$ constraints.

$$\text{Maximize } Z_p = c_1x_1 + c_2x_2$$

subject to

$$\begin{aligned} a_{11}x_1 + a_{12}x_2 &\leq b_1 \\ -a_{11}x_1 - a_{12}x_2 &\leq -b_1 \\ a_{21}x_1 + a_{22}x_2 &\leq b_2 \\ x_1, x_2 &\geq 0 \end{aligned}$$

The problem is now in the proper form with all $\leq$ constraints to construct the dual. (Note that, in this and the following dual formulations, the constraint coefficients in the dual maintain the subscript notation of a_{ij} of the primal, in order to show where in the primal the dual constraint coefficient come from.)

$$\text{Minimize } Z_d = b_1y_1 - b_1y_2 + b_2y_3$$

subject to

$$\begin{aligned} a_{11}y_1 - a_{11}y_2 + a_{21}y_3 &\geq c_1 \\ a_{12}y_1 - a_{12}y_2 + a_{22}y_3 &\geq c_2 \\ y_1, y_2, y_3 &\geq 0 \end{aligned}$$

This form of the dual of a primal problem is quite acceptable; however, with a few simple manipulations an additional property of the dual of a problem with an equality constraint can be identified. First, all similar terms in the objective function and constraints are combined.

$$\text{Minimize } Z_d = b_1(y_1 - y_2) + b_2y_3$$

subject to

$$\begin{aligned} a_{11}(y_1 - y_2) + a_{21}y_3 &\geq c_1 \\ a_{12}(y_1 - y_2) + a_{22}y_3 &\geq c_2 \\ y_1, y_2, y_3 &\geq 0 \end{aligned}$$

It can now be seen that the term $y_1 - y_2$ in the preceding model is in the same form as if y_1 were an unrestricted variable. Recall from chapter 3 that if a variable, x_j, is unrestricted in sign, then the problem was transformed into proper simplex form by letting

$$x_j = \hat{x}_j - \hat{\hat{x}},$$

which corresponds with the form of the term $y_1 - y_2$. Returning to the original primal problem, this property enables us to develop the dual without transforming the original equality constraint. Thus, the dual of the original primal problem is formulated by treating the primal equality constraint as a $\leq$ constraint and letting y_1 be an unrestricted variable.

$$\text{Minimize } Z_d = b_1y_1 + b_2y_2$$

subject to

$$a_{11}y_1 + a_{21}y_2 \geq c_1$$
$$a_{12}y_1 + a_{22}y_2 \geq c_2$$
$$y_1 \sim \text{unrestricted}$$
$$y_2 \geq 0$$

and

$$y_1 = \hat{y}_1 - \hat{\hat{y}}$$

In general, any equality constraint i in the primal results in an unrestricted variable, y_i, in the dual. The following example demonstrates the primal-dual transformation when there is an equality constraint.

Primal

$$\text{Maximize } Z_p = 3x_1 + 7x_2$$

subject to

$$4x_1 + 2x_2 \leq 24$$
$$x_1 + 7x_2 = 28$$
$$2x_1 + 3x_2 \leq 18$$
$$x_1, x_2 \geq 0$$

Dual

$$\text{Minimize } Z_d = 24y_1 + 28y_2 + 18y_3$$

subject to

$$4y_1 + y_2 + 2y_3 \geq 3$$
$$2y_1 + 7y_2 + 3y_3 \geq 7$$
$$y_1, y_3 \geq 0$$
$$y_2 \sim \text{unrestricted}$$

The opposite condition holds when the primal contains an unrestricted variable (x_j). In this case, the dual constraint (j) is an equality.

A ≥ Constraint

The other constraint possibility that alters the standard primal-dual transformation is the existence of a ≥ constraint. In this case the direction of the inequality is reversed by multiplying the constraint by −1. For example,

$$a_{11}x_1 + a_{12}x_2 \geq b_1$$

becomes

$$-a_{11}x_1 - a_{12}x_2 \leq -b_1.$$

The following example problem demonstrates the primal-dual transformation with all three constraint possibilities (≤, =, ≥) plus an unrestricted variable:

Primal

$$\text{Maximize } Z_p = 10x_1 + 3x_2 + 8x_3$$

subject to

$$\begin{aligned} x_1 + 4x_2 + 2x_3 &\leq 16 \\ 3x_2 + x_3 &= 10 \\ 6x_1 + 2x_2 &\geq 20 \\ x_1, x_2 &\geq 0 \\ x_3 &\sim \text{unrestricted} \end{aligned}$$

Dual

$$\text{Minimize } Z_d = 16y_1 + 10y_2 - 20y_3$$

subject to

$$\begin{aligned} y_1 - 6y_3 &\geq 10 \\ 4y_1 + 3y_2 - 2y_3 &\geq 3 \\ 2y_1 + y_2 &= 8 \\ y_1, y_3 &\geq 0 \\ y_2 &\sim \text{unrestricted} \end{aligned}$$

The Dual Form of a Minimization Problem

A minimization problem can also be transformed into its dual form (a maximization problem). However, in the case of a minimization problem, the proper constraint form would consist of all ≥ constraints. Thus, any mixed constraints must be converted to ≥ form. The following example demonstrates the primal minimization problem and its dual form:

Primal

$$\text{Minimize } Z_p = 3x_1 + 6x_2$$

subject to

$$\begin{aligned} 2x_1 + 7x_2 &\geq 16 \\ x_1 &\leq 10 \\ 4x_1 + 2x_2 &= 20 \\ x_1, x_2 &\geq 0 \end{aligned}$$

Dual

$$\text{Maximize } Z_d = 16y_1 - 10y_2 + 20y_3$$

subject to

$$\begin{aligned} 2y_1 - y_2 + 4y_3 &\leq 3 \\ 7y_1 + 2y_3 &\leq 6 \\ y_1, y_2 &\geq 0 \\ y_3 &\sim \text{unrestricted} \end{aligned}$$

The dual variables (y_1, y_2, and y_3) represent the marginal value of relaxing the constraints of the primal problem in which the objective is to minimize total cost.

Summary of the Primal-Dual Relationships

The various primal-dual relationships are summarized in table 4.4.

Table 4.4 Primal-dual relationships

Primal	Dual
Max $Z_p = \sum_{j=1}^{n} c_j x_j$	Min $Z_d = \sum_{i=1}^{m} b_i y_i$
Constraint i	Variable y_i
Variable x_j	Constraint j
$\leq$ constraints	$\geq$ constraints
constraint i, $=$	$y_i \sim$ unrestricted
$x_j \sim$ unrestricted	constraint j, $=$

The Dual Simplex Method

The **dual simplex method** is an alternate form of the simplex method presented in chapter 3 that is based on the primal-dual relationship, which holds that the solution to a given linear programming problem is *optimal when both primal and dual solutions are feasible*. The term *dual simplex* is derived from this relationship, but the actual simplex method is conducted entirely on the primal form of the problem. The reason for studying the dual simplex is not because it may be more efficient than the regular simplex method, but, because it is very useful in performing sensitivity analysis, the topic to which the remainder of this chapter is devoted.

The dual simplex method applies directly to ''better than optimal'', but infeasible, solutions and works toward feasibility. The corresponding approach in the dual form is to work with nonoptimal but feasible solutions and move toward optimality. In most linear programming problems the initial basic solution is usually at the origin ($x_j = 0$) with all slack variables as basic. However, in minimization problems with a number of mixed constraints, it is necessary to add a number of artificial variables in order to get an initial solution at the origin. For such problems it is often more convenient to begin with an infeasible but better than optimal solution and apply the dual simplex method. This is achieved by converting $\geq$ constraints to $\leq$ constraints by multiplying the original constraint through by -1. The number of iterations required by the dual simplex method is usually less than that of the ordinary simplex approach since there are no artificial variables to be eliminated from the solution base.

The dual simplex method is quite similar to the ordinary simplex method with only a few minor alterations. In fact, once the initial solution is determined, the only difference is in the procedure for selecting the pivot row and pivot column. In order to begin the dual simplex method, all $z_j - c_j$ row values for a minimization problem must be zero or negative. The initial solution would be infeasible because the right-hand-side values (b_i^*) of some or all of the basic variables are negative. Given these conditions, the dual simplex method continues to increase the value of the objective function while maintaining nonpositive $z_j - c_j$ row values. When all basic variables have nonnegative b_i^* values, the solution becomes feasible and optimal.

The dual simplex method consists of the following steps:

1. Specify the initial solution at the origin such that the $z_j - c_j$ row values are negative for nonbasic variables.
2. If all b_i^* values are positive, the solution is feasible and optimal. If the solution is infeasible, continue to step 3.
3. Determine the pivot row (before the pivot column). The pivot row has the largest negative b_i^* value.

4. Determine the pivot column. The pivot column is determined by dividing each $z_j - c_j$ value in the nonbasic variable columns by the *negative* coefficient in the pivot row and corresponding column (and ignoring the columns with zero or positive coefficients). The minimum value indicates the pivot column.
5. Determine the new tableau values by the normal simplex method and return to step 2.

To illustrate the steps of the dual simplex method consider the following example:

Minimize $Z = 4x_1 + 3x_2$
subject to

$$2x_1 + 4x_2 \geqslant 16$$
$$3x_1 + 2x_2 \geqslant 12$$
$$x_1, x_2 \geqslant 0$$

Normally, to transform this problem into proper simplex form it would be necessary to subtract surplus variables and add artificials. However, in the dual simplex method the constraints are multiplied by -1, which converts them to $\leqslant$ inequalities and then slack variables are added.

$$-2x_1 - 4x_2 + s_1 = -16$$
$$-3x_1 - 2x_2 + s_2 = -12$$

The initial simplex tableau for this problem is shown in table 4.5.

Table 4.5 Initial dual simplex tableau

c_b \ c_j	basis	b_i^*	4 x_1	3 x_2	0 s_1	0 s_2
0	s_1	−16	−2	−4	1	0
0	s_2	−12	−3	−2	0	1
	z_j	0	0	0	0	0
	$z_j - c_j$		−4	−3	0	0

Notice that the problem meets the necessary conditions for the dual simplex method—the negative b_i^* values indicate an infeasible solution and the $z_j - c_j$ row values are negative for nonbasic variables, which indicates optimality.

First, the pivot row is determined by observing the largest negative b_i^* value. Therefore, s_1 is the pivot row. Second, the pivot column is determined from the following computations:

Nonbasic Variable	$z_j - c_j$	÷	Coefficient in Pivot Row	=	Ratio
x_1 column	−4		−2		2
x_2 column	−3		−4		3/4 ← pivot column

Since x_2 has the minimum ratio it is selected as the pivot column. All tableau cell values are now determined in the same manner as in a regular simplex problem, which results in the second tableau (table 4.6).

Table 4.6 Second dual simplex tableau

c_b \ c_j	basis	b_i^*	4 x_1	3 x_2	0 s_1	0 s_2
3	x_2	4	1/2	1	−1/4	0
0	s_2	−4	−2	0	−1/2	1
	z_j	12	3/2	3	−3/4	0
	$z_j - c_j$		−5/2	0	−3/4	0

The second tableau is still infeasible. The pivot row for the second tableau is s_2 since it is the only remaining negative b_i^* value. The pivot column is x_1 (with a selection ratio of 5/4). The resulting third and final dual simplex tableau is shown in table 4.7.

Table 4.7 Optimal dual simplex solution

c_b \ c_j	basis	b_i^*	4 x_1	3 x_2	0 s_1	0 s_2
3	x_2	3	0	1	−3/8	1/4
4	x_1	2	1	0	1/4	−1/2
	z_j	17	4	3	−1/8	−5/4
	$z_j - c_j$		0	0	−1/8	−5/4

The third dual simplex tableau is optimal because it is now both feasible (all b_i^* values are positive) and optimal (all $z_j - c_j$ row values are negative or zero). The identical solution could have been obtained using the normal simplex method (and in this case, the same number of tableaus).

The dual simplex method is not applied directly to a maximization problem since $c_j - z_j$ for a maximization problem will always yield an initial soution that is not optimal. Thus the presence of a negative b_i^* value would result in an initial solution that is neither optimal nor feasible, a violation of the conditions necessary to apply the dual simplex method. (This can be verified by observing a graphic analysis of a minimization and a maximization problem. The solution at the origin for a minimization problem is always better than optimal (i.e., it is zero), while the solution at the origin is never optimal for a maximization problem.) However, the dual simplex method is extremely useful in performing sensitivity analysis on a maximization problem as well as a minimization problem since sensitivity analysis is typically performed on the final optimal tableau. In the case of applying the dual simplex method to the optimal solution of a maximization problem the steps of the dual simplex method remain the same as shown previously except that $c_j - z_j$ is used (as will be demonstrated in the section in this chapter on sensitivity analysis).

Sensitivity Analysis

It is rare that a manager can determine the model parameters of a linear programming problem (c_j, b_i, a_{ij}) with absolute certainty. In reality the model parameters are usually simply estimates and, as such, subject to some uncertainty. As a result, it may often be desirable for a manager/decision maker to observe the effects of parameter changes (which would reflect uncertainty) on the optimal solution of the problem. The analysis of parameter changes and their effect on linear programming solutions is referred to as **sensitivity,** or **postoptimality, analysis.** In other words, it is the study of parameter changes and the sensitivity of the optimal solution to these changes.

The most obvious means for analyzing parameter changes is to make the change in the original problem formulation, solve the problem again via the simplex method and compare the new solution with the old. However, this is both time consuming and computationally inefficient. Alternatively, it is generally possible to perform sensitivity analysis by manipulating the final simplex tableau.

The different categories of parameter changes that will be the subjects of this section include:

1. Changes in right-hand-side values, b_i
2. Changes in the objective function coefficients, c_j
3. Changes in the constraint coefficients, a_{ij}
4. Addition of a new variable
5. Addition of a new constraint

Changes in b_i Values

Recall the production example from the previous section on duality.

$$\text{Maximize } Z = 4x_1 + 5x_2 \qquad \text{(profit)}$$

subject to

$$x_1 + 2x_2 \leq 10 \text{ hr.} \qquad \text{(labor)}$$
$$6x_1 + 6x_2 \leq 36 \text{ lb.} \qquad \text{(material)}$$
$$8x_1 + 4x_2 \leq 40 \text{ ft}^2. \qquad \text{(space)}$$
$$x_1, x_2 \leq 0$$

Now consider the effect of increasing one of the b_i values ($b_1 = 10$, $b_2 = 36$, $b_3 = 40$) by an amount, Δ. For example, observe how a change in the labor constraint from 10 hours to 12 hours ($\Delta = 2$) is represented graphically in figure 4.2. Increasing b_1 by two hours (from 10 to 12) has the effect of moving the constraint equation, $x_1 + 2x_2 = b_1$, out from the origin to a new position parallel to the old constraint. This is an obvious occurrence since the slope of the constraint line has not changed but the axis intercepts have. Note that this change redefines the feasible solution space from area *OABCD* to *OA′CD*. This example demonstrates that a change in a b_i value can affect the final solution. In other words, the feasible solution space may change to the point where the optimal solution basis also changes.

Figure 4.2 Change in the b_1 parameter.

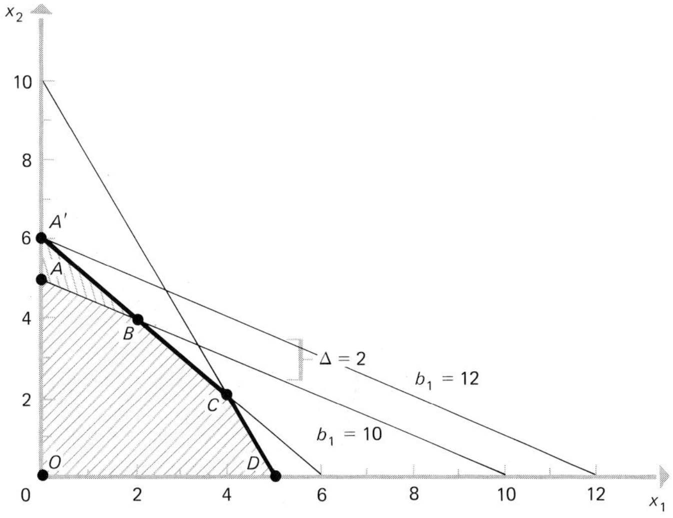

It is possible to develop a general approach for determining a range for b_i over which the variables in the solution basis will remain optimal. In order to demonstrate this approach our production example will again be employed. Consider a general increase in the labor constraint of Δ hours. The problem constraints become

$$x_1 + 2x_2 \leq 10 + 1\Delta$$
$$6x_1 + 6x_2 \leq 36 + 0\Delta$$
$$8x_1 + 4x_2 \leq 40 + 0\Delta.$$

Substituting these constraints into the simplex process results in the initial tableau in table 4.8.

Observe that in table 4.8 the *coefficients of* Δ in the b_i^* column are the same as the values in the s_1 column. The effect of this similarity becomes apparent in the final optimal tableau (table 4.9).

Table 4.8 Initial simplex tableau

c_j / c_b	basis	b_i^*	4 x_1	5 x_2	0 s_1	0 s_2	0 s_3
0	s_1	$10 + 1\Delta$	1	2	1	0	0
0	s_2	$36 + 0\Delta$	6	6	0	1	0
0	s_3	$40 + 0\Delta$	8	4	0	0	1
	z_j	0	0	0	0	0	0
	$c_j - z_j$		4	5	0	0	0

Table 4.9 Optimal simplex tableau

c_j / c_b	basis	b_i^*	4 x_1	5 x_2	0 s_1	0 s_2	0 s_3
5	x_2	$4 + 1\Delta$	0	1	1	$-1/6$	0
4	x_1	$2 - 1\Delta$	1	0	-1	1/3	0
0	s_3	$8 + 4\Delta$	0	0	4	-2	1
	z_j	$28 + \Delta$	4	5	1	1/2	0
	$c_j - z_j$		0	0	-1	$-1/2$	0

The final optimal tableau shows that the coefficients of Δ in the b_i^* column have remained the same as the s_1 column values. In effect, the Δ coefficients can be considered as an additional tableau column exactly like the s_1 column. Thus, the Δ coefficients in the b_i^* column in the final tableau would always be the same as the values in the s_1 column. This means that it is unnecessary to go through all the simplex tableaus to determine the general effects of Δ on the final solution. As a general rule it is only necessary to increase (or decrease) the final b_i^* values by a multiple of Δ, where the multiple is given by the column coefficients of the slack variable (s_i) for b_i. Thus, for this example, if the final tableau b_i^* values are

b_i^*
4
2
8

and a change in b_1 is prescribed, then the s_1 column values

s_1
1
−1
4

are added to the b_i^* values as Δ multiples

$$x_2 = 4 + 1\Delta$$
$$x_1 = 2 - 1\Delta$$
$$s_3 = 8 + 4\Delta.$$

From the prior discussion of the simplex method we know that these solution values will remain feasible as long as they are positive. Thus, in order to determine the range of feasibility for b_1, the following inequalities are solved for Δ:

$$x_2\text{: } 4 + \Delta \geq 0$$
$$\Delta \geq -4$$
$$x_1\text{: } 2 - \Delta \geq 0$$
$$-\Delta \geq -2$$
$$\Delta \leq 2$$
$$s_3\text{: } 8 + 4\Delta \geq 0$$
$$4\Delta \geq -8$$
$$\Delta \geq -2$$

It can now be stated that the solution basis will remain positive and, thus, feasible as long as

$$-4 \leqslant -2 \leqslant \Delta \leqslant 2.$$

Since -2 is more constraining than -4, the latter value is discarded (e.g., if -4 were used then s_3 could become negative, but if -2 is used as the endpoint then neither x_2 or s_3 will become negative). The range for Δ is, therefore,

$$-2 \leqslant \Delta \leqslant 2.$$

Recalling that $b_1 = 10 + \Delta$ (or $\Delta = b_1 - 10$) and substituting this amount in the Δ range inequality yields

$$-2 \leqslant b_1 - 10 \leqslant 2$$

or

$$8 \leqslant b_1 \leqslant 12.$$

This range means that the *variables* in the optimal solution basis will remain feasible as long as b_1 is between 8 and 12 hours. However, it does not mean that the solution *values* will remain the same. For example, suppose $\Delta = 2$ and, thus, $b_1 = 12$. This results in the following solution values for x_2, x_1, and s_3:

$x_2 = 4 + \Delta$	$x_1 = 2 - \Delta$	$s_3 = 8 + 4\Delta$
$x_2 = 6$	$x_1 = 0$	$s_3 = 16$

To check the general approach and the range values, let $\Delta = 4$ and $b_1 = 14$. In this case, $x_1 = -2$, which renders the solution basis infeasible.

An additional property, which can be examined within the framework of a b_i change, relates to the value of model resources and, thus, the dual form of the problem. Consider a case where the manager might desire to increase the available resources (b_i values). Which resources should be increased in order to realize the best marginal increase in the value of the objective function? To answer this question observe the dual solution to the example previously highlighted in tables 4.2 and 4.3:

$$Z_d = 28$$
$$y_1 = 1$$
$$y_2 = 1/2$$
$$y_3 = 0$$

Labor hours should be increased since it contributes the greatest amount ($y_1 = 1$) to the value of the objective function. The resource b_1 (labor hours) should be increased, if possible, up to the maximum amount—12 hours. To increase b_1 beyond this amount renders the basis infeasible.

Changes in Objective Function Coefficients

Changes in the profit or cost contributions (c_j) in the objective function can occur for a basic or a nonbasic variable. The sensitivity ranges for each are determined differently; thus, these two distinct cases will be studied separately.

Changes in c_j When x_j Is a Nonbasic Variable

In order to demonstrate sensitivity analysis for c_j parameters for nonbasic variables, an altered version of the previous production example (p. 139) will be employed. This example, the formulation of which follows this paragraph, consists of two products, x_1 and x_2, and two constraint equations. The first constraint is for labor and reflects the hours per unit of labor required for each product and the total hours available (12). The second constraint is for material and shows the pounds per unit required for each product and total pounds available (16).

$$\text{Maximize } Z = 6x_1 + 4x_2$$

subject to

$$2x_1 + 6x_2 \leq 12$$
$$4x_1 + 4x_2 \leq 16$$
$$x_1, x_2 \geq 0$$

This problem is demonstrated graphically in figure 4.3. The function objective, Z, indicated by the dashed line has as its optimal point, C. At this point, $x_1 = 4$, $x_2 = 0$, and $s_1 = 4$. However, notice that if we increase c_2 from 4 to 8, the objective function slope becomes less steep as shown by Z' in figure 4.3. This reduction in slope also results in a new optimal solution point, B, at which $x_1 = 3$ and $x_2 = 1$. This demonstrates the effect of a c_j change; the slope of the objective function changes, which, in turn, can affect the optimality of the original solution. As such, in performing sensitivity analysis of a c_j parameter, we are interested in determining a range for c_j over which the present solution will remain optimal.

Figure 4.3 Change in c_2 causes change in slope of objective function.

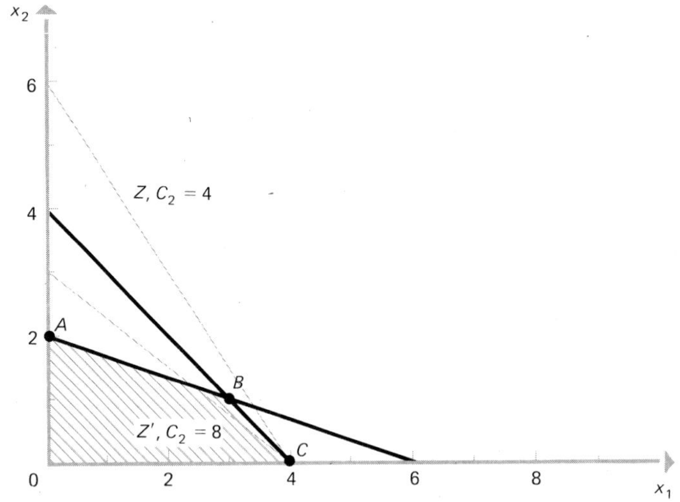

It is necessary to observe only the final simplex tableau to determine the range values for c_j when x_j is a nonbasic variable. Table 4.10 is the optimal solution tableau for the example problem.

Table 4.10 Final optimal solution

c_b \ c_j	basis	b_i^*	6 x_1	4 x_2	0 s_1	0 s_2
0	s_1	4	0	4	1	$-1/2$
6	x_1	4	1	1	0	$1/4$
	z_j	24	6	6	0	$3/2$
	$c_j - z_j$		0	-2	0	$-3/2$

Now consider the effect of a Δ change in c_2, the objective function contribution coefficient for the *nonbasic* variable x_2. Since x_2 is nonbasic and therefore c_2 is not included in the c_b column, the only rows affected by a change in c_2 are the c_j and $c_j - z_j$ rows. Thus, a Δ change in c_2 results in the modified tableau in table 4.11:

Table 4.11 Final tableau with a Δ change in c_2

c_b \ c_j	basis	b_i^*	6 x_1	4 + Δ x_2	0 s_1	0 s_2
0	s_1	4	0	4	1	−1/2
6	x_1	4	1	1	0	1/4
	z_j	24	6	6	0	3/2
	$c_j - z_j$		0	−2 + Δ	0	−3/2

The $c_j - z_j$ row value in the x_2 column is computed by subtracting $z_j = 6$ from $c_j = 4 + \Delta$, which yields $-2 + \Delta$. This solution will remain optimal only if $c_j - z_j$ remains negative. Thus, to determine Δ the following computation is made:

$$-2 + \Delta \leq 0$$
$$\Delta \leq 2$$

Recalling that $c_2 = 4 + \Delta$, or $\Delta = c_2 - 4$, and substituting this amount in the Δ inequality yields

$$c_2 - 4 \leq 2$$
$$c_2 \leq 6.$$

As long as c_2 is less than 6, the present basic solution will remain optimal. This not only means that the variables x_1 and s_1 remain in the solution basis, but also the values for these variables ($x_1 = 4$, $s_1 = 4$) and the Z value ($z_j = 24$) will remain the same.

The fact that c_2 has a single-ended range can be seen in figure 4.3. As c_2 increases (becomes ≥ 4) the objective function line becomes "flatter." As c_2 gets larger and the slope changes, the optimal solution changes from point C to point B, when $c_2 > 6$, thus, changing the optimal solution. On the other hand, if c_2 gets smaller, the slope of the objective function gets steeper and steeper but the solution at point C will remain optimal, since the objective function will not pass through any other feasible solution point.

Changes in c_j When x_j Is a Basic Variable

The determination of a range for c_j over which the basic simplex solution remains optimal when x_j is a basic variable is somewhat more complex than the case when x_j is nonbasic. The primary difficulty results from the fact that since x_j is a basic variable and therefore c_j is included in the c_b column, the z_j row values will be multiples of c_j. Consider the example employed in the previous section, except that the Δ change is now for c_1 (table 4.12).

Table 4.12 Initial simplex tableau

c_b \ c_j	basis	b_i^*	$6+\Delta$ x_1	4 x_2	0 s_1	0 s_2
0	s_1	12	2	6	1	0
0	s_2	16	4	4	0	1
	z_j	0	0	0	0	0
	$c_j - z_j$		$6+\Delta$	4	0	0

Performing the simplex operations results in the final simplex tableau (table 4.13).

Table 4.13 Final simplex tableau

c_b \ c_j	basis	b_i^*	$6+\Delta$ x_1	4 x_2	0 s_1	0 s_2
0	s_1	4	0	4	1	$-1/2$
$6+\Delta$	x_1	4	1	1	0	$1/4$
	z_j	$24+4\Delta$	$6+\Delta$	$6+\Delta$	0	$3/2+\Delta/4$
	$c_j - z_j$		0	$-2-\Delta$	0	$-3/2-\Delta/4$

In the final simplex tableau, notice that since x_1 is a basic variable, the c_1 value $(6 + \Delta)$ is included in the c_b column. As a result, $c_1 = 6 + \Delta$ becomes a multiple of the z_j row values. Therefore, the effect of the Δ change in the final tableau can be determined (without including the Δ change in all simplex iterations) by simply inserting $c_j + \Delta$ in place of c_j in the c_b column in the final tableau and calculating the $c_j - z_j$ values normally. This results in $c_j - z_j$ row values for both nonbasic variables, which include Δ values. If one of these variables enters the solution, then the present solution is no longer optimal. In order for the present basic solution to remain optimal, these $c_j - z_j$ values must remain negative or zero. Thus, we will solve for the following inequalities for the x_2 and s_2 column $c_j - z_j$ values.

$$-2 - \Delta \leq 0$$
$$-\Delta \leq 2$$
$$\Delta \geq -2$$

and

$$-3/2 - \Delta/4 \leq 0$$
$$-\Delta/4 \leq 3/2$$
$$\Delta \geq -6$$

Substituting the original c_1 value $(6 + \Delta)$ in these inequalities yields

$$\Delta \geq -2$$
$$c_1 - 6 \geq -2$$
$$c_1 \geq 4$$

$c_1 = 6 + \Delta$
$\therefore \Delta = c_1 - 6$

and

$$\Delta \geq -6$$
$$c_1 - 6 \geq -6$$
$$c_1 \geq 0.$$

The range $c_1 \geq 0$, which was derived from the calculations for the s_2 column, indicates that s_2 would not enter the basis as long as c_1 is positive. However, the range calculated from the x_2 column indicates that x_2 would enter the solution if c_1 fell to \$4.00 or less. Thus, by process of elimination, it is apparent that the present basic solution will remain optimal only as long as $c_1 \geq 4$.

Now let us observe the development of the range of sensitivity for c_j when *both* decision variables are basic. Our example can be adjusted to yield such a solution by changing the objective function to $Z = 4x_1 + 6x_2$. A Δ change in the c_1 coefficient results in the following final optimal solution (table 4.14).

Table 4.14 Final simplex tableau

c_j / c_b	basis	b_i^\star	$4 + \Delta$ x_1	6 x_2	0 s_1	0 s_2
6	x_2	1	0	1	1/4	$-1/8$
$4 + \Delta$	x_1	3	1	0	$-1/4$	3/8
	z_j	$18 + 3\Delta$	$4 + \Delta$	6	$1/2 - \Delta/4$	$3/4 + 3\Delta/8$
	$c_j - z_j$		0	0	$-1/2 + \Delta/4$	$-3/4 - 3\Delta/8$

For the two nonbasic variables (s_1 and s_2) the $c_j - z_j$ row values must remain negative for the basic solution to remain optimal. Thus,

$$-1/2 + \Delta/4 \leq 0$$
$$\Delta/4 \leq 1/2$$
$$\Delta \leq 2$$

$c_1 = 4 + \Delta$
$\therefore \Delta = c_1 - 4$
$\therefore c_1 - 4 \leq 2$
$\therefore c_1 \leq 6$

and

$$-3/4 - 3\Delta/8 \leq 0$$
$$-3\Delta/8 \leq 3/4$$
$$\Delta \geq -2.$$

$\therefore c_1 - 4 \geq -2$
$\therefore c_1 \geq 2$

Substituting the c_1 value $(4 + \Delta)$ in these inequalities yields the range for c_1.

$$\begin{aligned} \Delta &\leq 2 \\ c_1 - 4 &\leq 2 \\ c_1 &\leq 6 \end{aligned}$$

and

$$\begin{aligned} \Delta &\geq -2 \\ c_1 - 4 &\geq -2 \\ c_1 &\geq 2 \end{aligned}$$

or

$$2 \leq c_1 \leq 6.$$

Figure 4.4 reflects this example and the c_1 range, which is bounded on both ends. Notice that the objective function will encounter new feasible solution points, *A* or *C*, as it becomes flatter or steeper.

To summarize, in determining the sensitivity range for c_j over which the present basic solution will remain optimal, it is only necessary to analyze the final tableau. First the z_j values for the *nonbasic* variables are increased by a multiple of Δ and then subtracted from the nonbasic values. The new $c_j - z_j$ values are then solved as $\leq$ inequalities to determine Δ, the change in c_j.

Figure 4.4 Graphic analysis of c_1 range.

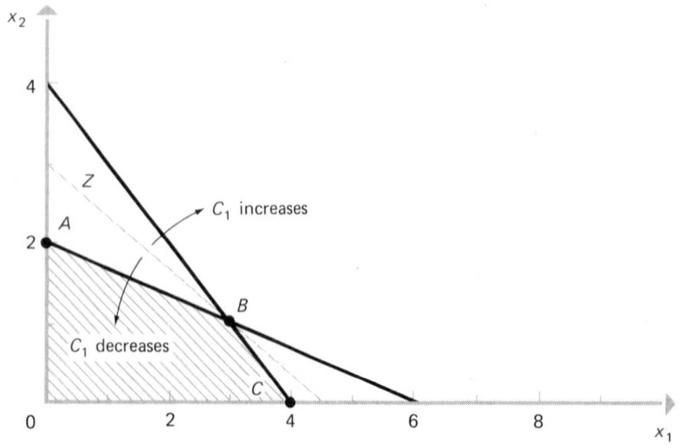

Changes in Constraint Coefficients

As with the b_i and c_j parameters, the sensitivity of solution optimality to changes in a_{ij} parameters must be considered for *nonbasic* and *basic* variables separately.

Changes in a_{ij} When x_j Is a Nonbasic Variable

Following the solution of a linear programming problem, it may become necessary to change the unit resource requirements for a particular product (i.e., the a_{ij} coefficients). When the a_{ij} coefficient of a nonbasic variable is changed, the range of a_{ij} over which the optimality of the basic solution will not be affected is determined in a manner similar to the b_i range determination. Again the following production example will be employed:

$$\text{Maximize } Z = 6x_1 + 4x_2 \quad \text{(profit)}$$

subject to

$$2x_1 + 6x_2 \leq 12 \quad \text{(labor)}$$
$$4x_1 + 4x_2 \leq 16 \quad \text{(material)}$$
$$x_1, x_2 \geq 0$$

From previous analysis of this problem we know that x_2 is a nonbasic variable (see table 4.10). Thus, we will first consider a Δ change in the labor requirement for product 2 (i.e., a_{12}). This results in the following new labor constraint:

$$2x_1 + (6 + \Delta)x_2 \leq 12$$

Substituting this new constraint equation into the initial simplex tableau (table 4.15) yields:

Table 4.15 Initial simplex tableau

c_b \ c_j	basis	b_i^*	6 x_1	4 x_2	0 s_1	0 s_2
0	s_1	12	2	$6 + 1\Delta$	1	0
0	s_2	16	4	$4 + 0\Delta$	0	1
	z_j	0	0	0	0	0
	$c_j - z_j$		6	4	0	0

The Δ coefficients in the x_2 column and the coefficients in the s_1 column are identical. As a result, in the final tableau the Δ coefficients in the x_2 column will be the same as the s_1 column values (table 4.16).

Table 4.16 Final simplex tableau

c_b \ c_j	basis	b_i^*	6 x_1	4 x_2	0 s_1	0 s_2
0	s_1	4	0	4 + Δ	1	0
6	x_1	4	1	1	0	1/4
	z_j	24	6	6	0	3/2
	$c_j - z_j$		0	−2	0	−3/2

In the final tableau, it can be seen that a change in a_{12} has no effect on the final basic solution since Δ is not present in the $c_j - z_j$ row. This is due to the fact that labor is not a binding constraint in the optimal solution. However, now consider a change in a_{22}, the material requirement for product 2.

$$4x_1 + (4 + \Delta)x_2 \leq 16$$

This will result in the following optimal tableau (table 4.17):

Table 4.17 Final simplex tableau

c_b \ c_j	basis	b_i^*	6 x_1	4 x_2	0 s_1	0 s_2
0	s_1	4	0	4 + 0Δ	1	0
6	x_1	4	1	1 + Δ/4	0	1/4
	z_j	24	6	6 + 3Δ/2	0	3/2
	$c_j - z_j$		0	−2 − 3Δ/2	0	−3/2

Note that the Δ coefficients in the final tableau correspond to the appropriate slack column coefficients—in this case s_2. Observing table 4.17, it is clear that a change in a_{22} can affect the optimality of the final solution. To determine the a_{22} range over which the present basic solution will remain optimal, the following $c_j - z_j \leq 0$ inequality is solved:

$$-2 - 3\Delta/2 \leq 0$$
$$-3\Delta/2 \leq 2$$
$$\Delta \geq -4/3$$

when change in a_{ij} of a non basic
- add to the matrix columns a Δ of the value of its slack column in the final tableau
- iterate
- ab $c_j - z_j \leq 0$ or ≥ 0
- see if the Δ is w/i range - if it doesn't - a new variable will enter range.

and since

$$a_{22} = \Delta + 4$$
$$a_{22} - 4 > -4/3$$
$$a_{22} \geqslant 8/3$$

Interpreting this range, if a_{22} becomes less than 8/3, the present solution will no longer be optimal. In other words, a new variable will enter the solution basis. If a_{22} does remain greater than 8/3, then the present basis will remain optimal and the solution values will remain the same.

Changes in a_{ij} When x_j Is a Basic Variable

Changes in the a_{ij} coefficient of a basic variable can result in numerous changes in the final simplex tableau. This should be apparent since the initial tableau pivot number could contain a Δ value and, as a result, could transmit multiples of Δ throughout the tableau in subsequent iterations. As such, it is possible for the final tableau to become infeasible as well as nonoptimal. Because of the profound effects caused by an a_{ij} change, when x_j is a basic variable, it is difficult to prescribe a systematic means for sensitivity analysis. Methods have been developed to reflect the sensitivity of the optimal solution to a_{ij} changes for basic variables. However, these methods are only applicable to special cases and even then the results cannot be obtained directly from the final tableau. Subsequent tableau iterations are generally required. Given these conditions the best means to perform sensitivity analysis on a_{ij} parameter changes is to simply solve the problem again with the a_{ij} changes included.

Addition of a New Constraint

After solution of a linear programming problem it may occur to the manager that a particular resource constraint was overlooked in the model formulation, or perhaps the manager may want to know the effect of adding a new resource to enhance a product. However, if the new constraint is added to the problem the original solution can become infeasible. This will only be true though if the constraint is actively involved in the basic solution. As such, the new constraint should first be tested to see if it does indeed affect the solution. To accomplish this, the manager will test original optimal solution values in the new constraint to see if the constraint is satisfied.

Consider the previous production problem with the following additional constraint for storage space:

$$4x_1 + 2x_2 \leqslant 20$$

The solution values indicated in table 4.10 (for the two constraint problems) are $x_1 = 4$, $x_2 = 0$, and $s_1 = 4$. Substituting these values in the new constraint, we find that this constraint is not violated, $4(4) + 2(0) \leq 20$. As such, the optimal solution does not change and nothing additional needs to be done in terms of sensitivity analysis. However, consider the following new constraint:

$$4x_1 + 2x_2 \leq 12$$

The optimal solution values *do not* satisfy this constraint. Therefore, the new constraint in the form $4x_1 + 2x_2 + s_3 = 12$ is added to the final simplex tableau as shown in table 4.18.

Table 4.18 Final simplex tableau with the new constraint added

c_b \ c_j	basis	b_i^*	6 x_1	4 x_2	0 s_1	0 s_2	0 s_3
0	s_1	4	0	4	1	−1/2	0
6	x_1	4	1	1	0	1/4	0
0	s_3	12	4	2	0	0	1
	c_j	24	6	6	0	3/2	0
	$c_j - z_j$		0	−2	0	−3/2	0

In the table 4.18 the a_{31} coefficient (4) is inappropriate. Since x_1 is a basic variable, this cell value should be zero. (Recall from chapter 3 and Appendix *A* that an identity matrix always exists in the tableau for variables in the solution basis. Thus, to achieve the identity matrix for this tableau, a_{31} must become zero.) The a_{31} coefficient can be changed to zero by multiplying the x_1 row by 4 (i.e., 4 times all x_1 row values) and then subtracting this row from the s_3 row. This results in the altered tableau in table 4.19.

This last tableau is now infeasible but in proper form for solution via the dual simplex method. Since s_3 is the only negative b_i^* value, it is the pivot row. The pivot column is x_2. Performing the normal simplex operations results in the tableaus and the optimal solution in tables 4.20 and 4.21.

The final tableau in table 4.21 results in a new solution that is both optimal and feasible.

Table 4.19 Altered final simplex tableau

c_b \ c_j	basis	b_i^*	6 x_1	4 x_2	0 s_1	0 s_2	0 s_3
0	s_1	4	0	4	1	−1/2	0
6	x_1	4	1	1	0	1/4	0
0	s_3	−4	0	−2	0	−1	1
	z_j	24	6	6	0	3/2	0
	$c_j - z_j$		0	−2	0	−3/2	0

Table 4.20 Second simplex tableau

c_b \ c_j	basis	b_i^*	6 x_1	4 x_2	0 s_1	0 s_2	0 s_3
0	s_1	−4	0	0	1	−5/2	2
6	x_1	2	1	0	0	−1/4	1/2
4	x_2	2	0	1	0	1/2	−1/2
	z_j	24	6	4	0	1/2	1
	$c_j - z_j$		0	0	0	−1/2	−1

Table 4.21 Final simplex tableau

c_b \ c_j	basis	b_i^*	6 x_1	4 x_2	0 s_1	0 s_2	0 s_3
0	s_2	8/5	0	0	−2/5	1	−4/5
6	x_1	12/5	1	0	−1/10	0	3/10
4	x_2	6/5	0	1	1/5	0	−1/10
	z_j	82/5	6	4	1/5	0	7/5
	$c_j - z_j$		0	0	−1/5	0	−7/5

Addition of a New Decision Variable

The addition of a new model variable can be handled in much the same way as the addition of a new constraint. However, it must be accomplished through the dual of the problem as opposed to the primal. Consider the addition of a new variable, x_3, to the previous example with corresponding c_j and a_{ij} coefficients.

$$\text{Maximize } Z_p = 6x_1 + 4x_2 + 3x_3$$

subject to

$$2x_1 + 6x_2 + x_3 \leq 12$$
$$4x_1 + 4x_2 + 2x_3 \leq 16$$
$$x_1, x_2, x_3 \geq 0$$

The dual form of this problem is

$$\text{Minimize } Z_d = 12y_1 + 16y_2$$

subject to

$$2y_1 + 4y_2 \geq 6$$
$$6y_1 + 4y_2 \geq 4$$
$$y_1 + 2y_2 \geq 3$$
$$y_1, y_2 \geq 0.$$

The final constraint, $y_1 + 2y_2 \geq 3$, which reflects the new variable addition in the primal, must be tested to determine if it is satisfied for the dual solution values, $y_1 = 0$, $y_2 = 3/2$. Substituting these dual solution values in the final dual constraint does indeed satisfy the constraint. Thus, the dual remains feasible and the primal remains optimal. (Positive dual basic solution values become negative $c_j - z_j$ values in the primal. Thus, a feasible dual solution results in an optimal primal solution and vice versa.)

However, if the added variable (x_3) had, for example, a c_3 coefficient of 5 in the primal objective function, then the corresponding dual constraint would be $y_1 + 2y_2 \geq 5$. The dual solution values no longer satisfy this constraint. Given this condition, this new constraint must be added to the final tableau (of the dual problem) and the altered tableau solved via the dual simplex method. When an optimal feasible solution is reached, the $z_j - c_j$ row values of the dual yield the new primal optimal solution.

ENGLISH MUFFINS IN A LOAF. You'll love how simple this loaf is to make. There's no need to knead. Your family will love how delicious it tastes. Just cut a slice and there's a homemade English Muffin ready to toast for breakfasts, lunches or snacks.

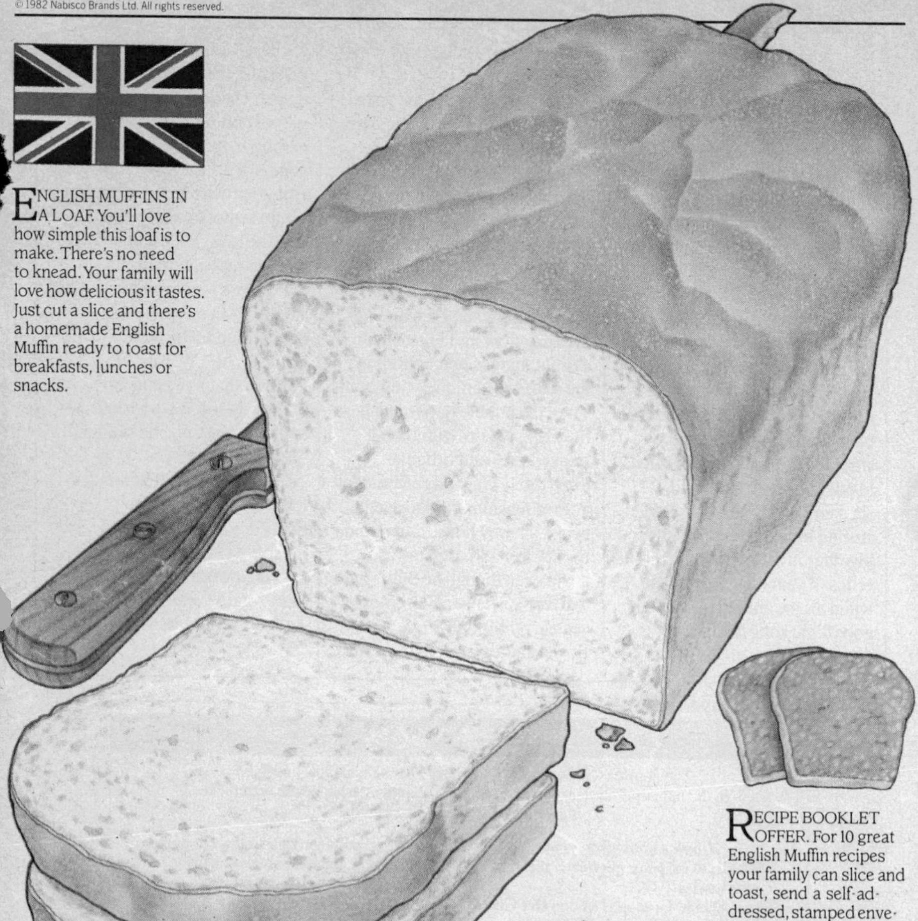

RECIPE BOOKLET OFFER. For 10 great English Muffin recipes your family can slice and toast, send a self-addressed, stamped envelope to: Fleischmann's® English Muffin Recipes, 1075 Ellesmere Road, Scarborough, Ontario. M1P 2X2.

NO KNEADING NEEDED.

ENGLISH MUFFINS IN A LOAF

1 tbsp. (15 mL) sugar • 1/2 cup (125 mL) warm water 110°F (40°C) • 2 envelopes Fleischmann's Fast Rising Active Dry Yeast • 2 cups (500 mL) milk • 2 tsp. (10 mL) salt • 1/4 tsp. (1 mL) baking soda • 6 cups (1500 mL) all-purpose flour (measure by spooning lightly into cup) • cornmeal.

Dissolve sugar in warm water • Add yeast and let stand 10 minutes then stir well • Combine milk and salt in saucepan • Heat over low heat until lukewarm only • Add milk mixture to dissolved yeast • Add 3 cups flour (750 mL) combined with baking soda • Mix until smooth • Stir in enough of the remaining 3 cups flour (750 mL) to make a stiff batter • Divide batter in half and press into two 8 1/2 x 4 1/2 x 2 1/2-inch (1.5 L) loaf pans that have been greased and sprinkled with cornmeal • Sprinkle tops with cornmeal and cover • Let rise in a warm place 45 minutes or until centre of loaf is about 1 1/2-inches (4 cm) above edge of the pan • Bake at 400°F (200°C) for 25 minutes. Remove from pans and cool • Slice and toast • Makes 2 loaves.

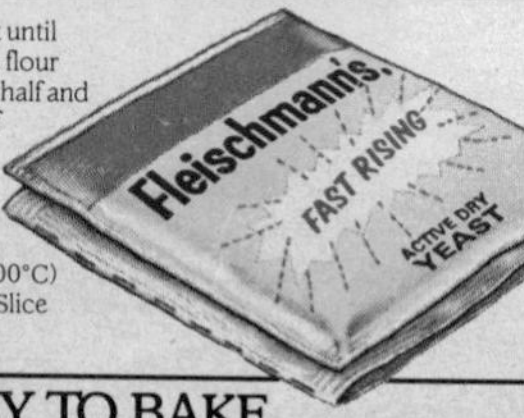

FLEISCHMANN'S MAKES IT EASY TO BAKE.

MY LIFE/ THESE TIMES

I kicked him out of my home. Even now, in a quiet room, I hate to hear the sound of a furnace chugging away. It reminds me of the day he left and the muttered obscenities he tossed into the room before the final slam of the door.

When he had gone I went into his room and stood in his cave of *Penthouse* centrefolds. The furnace vent reeked of cigarette butts being toasted, and pot-smoking apparatus was stuffed inside the mattress he had slashed for this purpose. Large stuffed toy animals were lumped together in a corner of the room, relics of years not so long ago when all the animals sang their goodnight song to him.

What would I do now with no one to care for?

That was almost three years ago and a new relationship has yet to be established. Tentatively, stretched at times like an overburdened spring, we've groped our way to a limited understanding. He moved in with his father when he left, and still lives there. Sometimes when I see him his eyes are clear and I listen with delight that his perceptions of the world are uniquely his own. Then the bubble bursts and he is hostile as he sits with blood-flecked eyes and ridicules everything I say. I went away for a trip a few months ago and he broke into my house and found my car key and used my car again even though he didn't have a driver's licence. He comes to see me on Mother's Day with flowers and a card saying, "To the best Mum in the world," and gives me a hug that is warm and tender. He has gone back to school part time, he's worked part time, he has voluntarily gone to a drug-abuse clinic. Apparently he has plans for the future so not to worry about him, he says. It all seems so tenuous and uncertain.

Princess Margaret was quoted as saying, in response to a question about her son, "What can I say, he's 17, isn't he?" Perhaps that's as good an answer as any. It sure beats smiles of pink plastic saying, "Just fine, thank you."

I do not dream of winning a lottery, a trip for two to Barbados or an automobile, but if I could rub Aladdin's Lamp, my voice would say, "Could I Start Again Please?"

Audrey Richter ■

SUMMER RECIPE BOOKLET

Detach and use this booklet containing quick and easy recipes. Look for Volume II next month.

Summary

In this chapter, two of the most important concepts in linear programming, duality and sensitivity analysis, have been presented. The economic information provided by these two forms of analysis is often more useful and important to a manager or firm than the original problem and solution. In addition, the study of duality and sensitivity analysis engenders a thorough and complete understanding of linear programming in general. As such, the reader should not treat these topics lightly.

In the chapters that follow on mathematical programming, the topics will basically be variations of the general linear programming model discussed in chapters 2, 3, and 4. As a result, the reader who has thoroughly studied these three chapters should be well prepared for these advanced topics.

References

Baumol, W. J. *Economic Theory and Operations Analysis*. Englewood Cliffs, New Jersey: Prentice-Hall, 1961.

Dantzig, G. B. *Linear Programming and Extensions*. Princeton, New Jersey: Princeton University Press, 1963.

Hadley, G. *Linear Programming*. Reading, Massachusetts: Addison-Wesley Publishing Co., 1962.

Loomba, N. P. *Linear Programming: A Managerial Perspective*. 2d ed. New York: MacMillan, 1976.

Pfaffenberger, R. C., and Walker, D. A. *Mathematical Programming for Economic and Business*. Ames, Iowa: Iowa State University Press, 1976.

Phillips, D. T.; Ravindran, A.; and Solberg, J. J. *Operations Research: Principles and Practice*. New York: John Wiley & Sons, 1976.

Spivey, W. A., and Thrall, R. M. *Linear Optimization*. New York: Holt, Rinehart and Winston, 1970.

Taha, H. A. *Operation Research: An Introduction*. 2d ed. New York: MacMillan, 1976.

Problems

1. A manufacturer produces two products, x_1 and x_2, from which the profits are respectively \$9 and \$12. Each product must go through two production processes for which there are labor constraints. There is also a material constraint and a storage limitation. The problem is formulated as a linear programming model as follows:

$$\text{Maximize } Z = 9x_1 + 12x_2 \quad \text{(profit, \$)}$$

subject to

$$\begin{aligned}
4x_1 + 8x_2 &\leq 64 && \text{(process 1, labor hr.)} \\
5x_1 + 5x_2 &\leq 50 && \text{(process 2, labor hr.)} \\
15x_1 + 8x_2 &\leq 120 && \text{(material, lb.)} \\
x_1 &\leq 7 && \text{(storage space, units)} \\
x_2 &\leq 7 && \text{(storage space, units)} \\
x_1, x_2 &\geq 0
\end{aligned}$$

The final optimal simplex tableau for this problem is:

c_b \ c_j	basis	b_i^*	9 x_1	12 x_2	0 s_1	0 s_2	0 s_3	0 s_4	0 s_5
9	x_1	4	1	0	−1/4	2/5	0	0	0
0	s_5	1	0	0	−1/4	1/5	0	0	1
0	s_3	12	0	0	7/4	−22/5	1	0	0
0	s_4	3	0	0	1/2	−2/5	0	1	0
12	x_2	6	0	1	1/4	−1/5	0	0	0
	z_j	108	9	12	3/4	6/5	0	0	0
	$c_j - z_j$		0	0	−3/4	−6/5	0	0	0

a. Interpret the $c_j - z_j$ values (shadow prices) for this tableau.
b. Determine the total value of each resource in achieving the $108 profit.
c. Formulate the dual to this problem.
d. Define the dual variables.

2. A fertilizer company produces two kinds of fertilizer spreaders, regular and cyclone. Each spreader must go through two processes in which parts are made and then assembled. Letting x_1 = the quantity of regular spreaders produced and x_2 = the quantity of cyclone spreaders produced, the problem is formulated as

Maximize $Z = 9x_1 + 7x_2$ (profit, $)

subject to

$12x_1 + 4x_2 \leq 60$ (process 1, production hr.)

$4x_1 + 8x_2 \leq 40$ (process 2, production hr.)

$x_1, x_2 \geq 0.$

The final optimal simplex tableau for this problem is:

c_b \ c_j	basis	b_i^*	9 x_1	7 x_2	0 s_1	0 s_2
9	x_1	4	1	0	1/10	−1/20
7	x_2	3	0	1	−1/20	3/20
	z_j	57	9	7	11/20	12/20
	$c_j - z_j$		0	0	−11/20	−12/20

a. Interpret the $c_j - z_j$ values (shadow prices) for this tableau.
b. Determine the total value of each resource in achieving the \$57 profit.
c. Formulate the dual to this problem.
d. Define the dual variables.

3. A furniture manufacturer makes two kinds off tables, end tables (x_1) and coffee tables (x_2). The manufacturer is restricted by material and labor constraints. The linear programming formulation of the manufacturer's problem is

$$\text{Maximize } Z = 200x_1 + 300x_2 \quad \text{(profit, \$)}$$

subject to

$$2x_1 + 5x_2 \leq 180 \quad \text{(labor, hr.)}$$
$$3x_1 + 3x_2 \leq 135 \quad \text{(wood, lb.)}$$
$$x_1, x_2 \geq 0.$$

The final optimal simplex tableau for this problem is:

c_b \ c_j	basis	b_i^*	200 x_1	300 x_2	0 s_1	0 s_2
300	x_2	30	0	1	1/3	−2/9
200	x_1	15	1	0	−1/3	5/9
	z_j	12,000	200	300	100/3	400/9
	$c_j - z_j$		0	0	−100/3	−400/9

a. Interpret the $c_j - z_j$ values (shadow prices) for this tableau.
b. Determine the total value of each resource in achieving the \$12,000 profit.
c. Formulate the dual to this problem.
d. Define the dual variables.

4. A chemical company makes bags of insecticide from two compounds, x_1 and x_2. Each pound of x_1 costs \$.06 while each pound of x_2 cost \$.10. Each compound contains ingredients A, B, and C, and each bag of insecticide must contain at least minimum amounts of these ingredients. The linear programming formulation of this problem is

Minimize $Z = \$.06x_1 + .10x_2$ (cost, \$)

subject to

$$4x_1 + 3x_2 \geqslant 12 \quad \text{(ingredient } A\text{, units)}$$
$$3x_1 + 6x_2 \geqslant 12 \quad \text{(ingredient } B\text{, units)}$$
$$5x_1 + 2x_2 \geqslant 10 \quad \text{(ingredient } C\text{, units)}$$
$$x_1, x_2 \geqslant 0.$$

The final optimal simplex tableau for this problem is:

c_b \ c_j	basis	b_i^*	.06 x_1	.10 x_2	0 s_1	0 s_2	0 s_3
0	s_3	1.2	0	0	−8/5	7/15	1
.10	x_2	0.8	0	1	1/5	−4/15	0
.06	x_1	2.4	1	0	−2/5	1/5	0
	z_j	.22	.06	.10	−.004	−.014	0
	$c_j - z_j$		0	0	−.004	−.014	0

a. Interpret the $c_j - z_j$ values (shadow prices) for this tableau.
b. Determine the total value associated with each ingredient requirement in achieving the minimum cost of \$.22.
c. Formulate the dual to this problem.
d. Define the dual variables.

5. An electronics firm produces electric motors for washing machines (x_1) and dryers (x_2). The firm has resource constraints for production time, steel, and wire. The linear programming model has been formulated as

Maximize $Z = 70x_1 + 80x_2$ (profit, \$)

subject to

$$2x_1 + x_2 \leqslant 19 \quad \text{(production, hr.)}$$
$$x_1 + x_2 \leqslant 14 \quad \text{(steel, lb.)}$$
$$x_1 + 2x_2 \leqslant 20 \quad \text{(wire, ft.)}$$
$$x_1, x_2 \geqslant 0.$$

The final optimal simplex tableau for this model is:

c_b \ c_j	basis	b_i^*	70 x_1	80 x_2	0 s_1	0 s_2	0 s_3
70	x_1	6	1	0	2/3	0	−1/3
0	s_2	1	0	0	−1/3	1	−1/3
80	x_2	7	0	1	−1/3	0	2/3
	z_j	980	70	80	20	0	30
	$c_j - z_j$		0	0	−20	0	−30

a. Interpret the $c_j - z_j$ values (shadow prices) for this tableau.
b. Determine the total value of each resoure in achieving the $980 profit.
c. Formulate the dual to this problem.
d. Define the dual variables.

6. A school dietician is attempting to determine a lunch menu that will minimize cost and meet certain minimum dietary requirements. The two main staples in the meal are meat and potatoes, which provide protein, iron, and carbohydrates. The problem has been formulated as follows:

x_1 = meat, oz.

x_2 = potatoes, oz.

Minimize $Z = \$.03x_1 + .02x_2$ (cost, $)

subject to

$$4x_1 + 5x_2 \geqslant 20 \quad \text{(protein, mg)}$$
$$12x_1 + 3x_2 \geqslant 30 \quad \text{(iron, mg)}$$
$$3x_1 + 2x_2 \geqslant 12 \quad \text{(carbohydrates, mg)}$$
$$x_1, x_2 \geqslant 0$$

The final optimal simplex tableau for this problem is:

c_b \ c_j	basis	b_i^*	.03 x_1	.02 x_2	0 s_1	0 s_2	0 s_3
.02	x_2	3.6	0	1	0	.20	−.80
.03	x_1	1.6	1	0	0	−.133	.20
0	s_1	4.4	0	0	1	.47	−3.20
	z_j	.120	.03	.02	0	0	−.010
	$z_j - c_j$		0	0	0	0	−.010

a. Interpret the $z_j - c_j$ values (shadow prices) for this tableau.
b. Determine the total value associated with each dietary requirement in achieving the minimum cost of \$.111.
c. Formulate the dual to this problem.
d. Define the dual variables.

7. A manufacturer produces three products daily, x_1, x_2, and x_3. The three products are each processed through three production operations with time constraints and then stored. The problem has been formulated as

$$\text{Maximize } Z = 40x_1 + 35x_2 + 45x_3 \quad \text{(profit, \$)}$$

subject to

$$\begin{aligned}
2x_1 + 3x_2 + 2x_3 &\leq 120 \quad \text{(operation 1, hr.)}\\
4x_1 + 3x_2 + x_3 &\leq 160 \quad \text{(operation 2, hr.)}\\
3x_1 + 2x_2 + 4x_3 &\leq 100 \quad \text{(operation 3, hr.)}\\
x_1 + x_2 + x_3 &\leq 40 \quad \text{(storage, ft.}^2\text{)}\\
x_1, x_2, x_3 &\geq 0.
\end{aligned}$$

The final optimal simplex tableau for this model is:

c_b \ c_j	basis	b_i^*	40 x_1	35 x_2	45 x_3	0 s_1	0 s_2	0 s_3	0 s_4
0	s_1	10	−1/2	0	0	1	0	1/2	−4
0	s_2	60	2	0	0	0	1	1	−5
45	x_3	10	1/2	0	0	0	0	1/2	−1
35	x_2	30	1/2	1	1	0	0	−1/2	2
	z_j	1,500	40	35	45	0	0	5	25
	$c_j - z_j$		0	0	0	0	0	−5	−25

a. Interpret the $c_j - z_j$ values (shadow prices) for this tableau.
b. Determine the total value of each resource in achieving the \$1,500 profit.
c. Formulate the dual to this problem.
d. Define the dual variables.
e. How does the fact that this is a multiple optimal solution affect the interpretation of the dual values?

8. Given the linear programming problem,

$$\text{Maximize } Z = 9x_1 + 12x_2$$

subject to

$$\begin{aligned} 4x_1 + 8x_2 &\leq 64 \\ 5x_1 + 5x_2 &\leq 50 \\ 15x_1 + 8x_2 &\leq 120 \\ x_1 &\leq 7 \\ x_2 &\leq 7 \\ x_1, x_2 &\geq 0. \end{aligned}$$

a. Formulate the dual to this problem.
b. Solve the dual problem using the simplex method.

9. Given the linear programming problem,

$$\text{Minimize } Z = 20x_1 + 16x_2$$

subject to

$$\begin{aligned} 3x_1 + x_2 &\geq 6 \\ x_1 + x_2 &\geq 4 \\ 2x_1 + 6x_2 &\geq 12 \\ x_1, x_2 &\geq 0. \end{aligned}$$

a. Formulate the dual to this problem.
b. Solve the dual problem using the simplex method.

10. Given problem 5,

$$\text{Maximize } Z = 70x_1 + 80x_2$$

subject to

$$\begin{aligned} 2x_1 + x_2 &\leq 19 \\ x_1 + x_2 &\leq 14 \\ x_1 + 2x_2 &\leq 20 \\ x_1, x_2 &\geq 0. \end{aligned}$$

Formulate the dual to this problem and solve using the simplex method.

11. Formulate the dual for the following linear programming problem:

$$\text{Maximize } Z = 10x_1 + 5x_2 + 8x_3$$

subject to

$$\begin{aligned}
6x_1 + 12x_2 + 4x_3 &\leq 1{,}600 \\
x_1 + 3x_2 + 2x_3 &\leq 400 \\
x_1 + x_2 + x_3 &\leq 300 \\
x_1 &\leq 150 \\
x_2 &\leq 200 \\
x_3 &\leq 100 \\
x_1, x_2, x_3 &\geq 0
\end{aligned}$$

12. Formulate the dual for the following linear programming problem:

$$\text{Maximize } Z = 25x_1 + 20x_2 + 10x_3 + 30x_4$$

subject to

$$\begin{aligned}
x_1 + x_2 &\leq 400 \\
x_3 + x_4 &\leq 600 \\
50x_1 + 45x_2 &\leq 16{,}000 \\
40x_3 + 30x_4 &\leq 25{,}000 \\
2x_1 + 3x_3 &\leq 800 \\
4x_2 + x_4 &\leq 900 \\
x_1, x_2, x_3, x_4 &\geq 0
\end{aligned}$$

13. Formulate the dual for the following linear programming problem:

$$\text{Minimize } Z = x_1 + x_2 + x_3 + x_4$$

subject to

$$\begin{aligned}
10x_1 + 12x_2 + 7x_3 + 8x_4 &\geq 300 \\
50x_3 + 25x_4 &\geq 600 \\
20x_2 + 30x_4 &\geq 800 \\
x_1 &\geq 10 \\
x_2 &\geq 8 \\
x_3 &\geq 10 \\
x_4 &\geq 20 \\
x_1, x_2, x_3, x_4 &\geq 0
\end{aligned}$$

14. Given the following linear programming problem:

Maximize $Z = 5x_1 + x_2$

subject to

$$
\begin{aligned}
4x_1 + 3x_2 &= 24 \\
x_1 &\leq 6 \\
x_1 + 3x_2 &\leq 12 \\
x_1, x_2 &\geq 0
\end{aligned}
$$

Formulate the dual for this problem.

15. Given the following linear programming problem:

Maximize $Z = 2x_1 + 2x_2 - x_3$

subject to

$$
\begin{aligned}
x_1 + x_2 - 2x_3 &\leq 6 \\
-2x_1 - x_2 + x_3 &\leq 5 \\
2x_1 + 6x_2 &= 10 \\
x_1, x_2, x_3 &\geq 0
\end{aligned}
$$

Formulate the dual for this problem.

16. Given the following linear programming problem:

Minimize $Z = x_1 + 2x_2 + x_3$

subject to

$$
\begin{aligned}
2x_1 - 3x_2 + x_3 &= 6 \\
2x_1 - 3x_2 - x_3 &\geq 1 \\
x_1, x_2 &\geq 0 \\
x_3 &\sim \text{unrestricted}
\end{aligned}
$$

Formulate the dual for this problem.

17. Given the following linear programming problem:

Maximize $Z = 4x_1 + 10x_2 + 6x_3$
subject to

$$\begin{aligned} x_1 + 3x_2 + 4x_3 &\leq 40 \\ 2x_2 + x_3 &\leq 20 \\ 10x_1 + 6x_2 + 20x_3 &= 100 \\ x_1 + 2x_2 &= 60 \\ x_1, x_2, x_3 &\geq 0 \end{aligned}$$

Formulate the dual for this problem.

18. Given the following linear programming problem:

Minimize $Z = 2x_1 + x_2 + x_3 + 2x_4$

subject to

$$\begin{aligned} x_1 + x_3 &\geq 200 \\ x_3 + x_4 &\geq 400 \\ -.6x_1 + .4x_2 &\geq 0 \\ x_1 + x_2 + x_3 + x_4 &\geq 1{,}000 \\ x_2, x_3, x_4 &\geq 0 \\ x_1 &\sim \text{unrestricted} \end{aligned}$$

Formulate the dual for this problem.

19. Given the following linear programming problem:

Minimize $Z = 2x_1 + 4x_2 + 3x_3$

subject to

$$\begin{aligned} x_1 + 2x_2 - 3x_3 &\geq 30 \\ x_1 + 2x_2 &\geq 40 \\ -x_1 + x_2 + x_3 &\geq 30 \\ x_1, x_2 &\geq 0 \\ x_3 &\sim \text{unrestricted} \end{aligned}$$

Formulate the dual for this problem.

20. Given the following linear programming problem:

$$\text{Minimize } Z = 10x_1 + 16x_2 + 8x_3 + 20x_4$$

subject to

$$\begin{aligned} 4x_1 + 2x_2 + 3x_3 + 4x_4 &\geq 100 \\ x_2 + x_4 &\geq 40 \\ 2x_3 + 3x_4 &\geq 60 \\ x_1 + x_3 &\geq 30 \\ x_1, x_2, x_3, x_4 &\geq 0 \end{aligned}$$

Formulate the dual for this problem.

21. Given the following linear programming problem:

$$\text{Maximize } Z = x_1 + 2x_2 + 2x_3$$

subject to

$$\begin{aligned} x_1 + x_2 + 2x_3 &\leq 12 \\ 2x_1 + x_2 + 5x_3 &= 20 \\ x_1 + x_2 - x_3 &\geq 8 \\ x_1, x_2, x_3 &\geq 0 \end{aligned}$$

Formulate the dual for this problem.

22. Given the following linear programming problem:

$$\text{Maximize } Z = 4x_1 + 2x_2$$

subject to

$$\begin{aligned} x_1 + x_2 &\geq 1 \\ -4x_1 + x_2 &\leq 0 \\ -x_1 + 4x_2 &\geq 0 \\ -x_1 + x_2 &\leq 1 \\ x_1 + x_2 &\leq 6 \\ x_1 &\leq 3 \\ x_1, x_2 &\geq 0 \end{aligned}$$

a. Formulate the dual for this problem.
b. Solve the dual of this problem via the simplex method.

23. Given the following linear programming problem:

Maximize $Z = x_1 + 2x_2 + x_3$

subject to

$$
\begin{aligned}
x_1 + x_2 + x_3 &= 200 \\
x_1 &\leq 150 \\
x_2 &\leq 40 \\
x_3 &\leq 70 \\
-x_1 - 1.6x_2 - 1.2x_3 &\geq -300 \\
x_1, x_2, x_3 &\geq 0
\end{aligned}
$$

Formulate the dual for this problem.

24. Given the followng linear programming problem:

Minimize $Z = 2x_1 - x_2 + 3x_3$

subject to

$$
\begin{aligned}
x_1 + 2x_2 + x_3 &\geq 12 \\
x_2 - 2x_3 &\geq -6 \\
6 \leq x_1 + 2x_2 + 4x_3 &\leq 24 \\
x_1, x_2 &\geq 0 \\
x_3 &\sim \text{unrestricted}
\end{aligned}
$$

Formulate the dual for this problem.

25. Given the following linear programming problem:

Maximize $Z = 3x_1 + 2x_2 + 5x_3$

subject to

$$
\begin{aligned}
3x_1 - 2x_2 + 10x_3 &\leq 200 \\
x_2 - 3x_3 &\leq 100 \\
x_1 + x_2 &\geq 45 \\
x_1 + x_2 + x_3 &= 75 \\
x_1, x_3 &\geq 0 \\
x_2 &\sim \text{unrestricted}
\end{aligned}
$$

Formulate the dual for this problem.

26. Given the following linear programming problem:

Minimize $Z = 4x_1 + 6x_2$

subject to

$$x_1 + x_2 \geqslant 8$$
$$2x_1 + x_2 \geqslant 12$$
$$x_1, x_2 \geqslant 0$$

Solve using the dual simplex method.

27. Given the following linear programming problem:

Minimize $Z = 3x_1 + 5x_2 + 2x_3$

subject to

$$x_1 + x_2 - 3x_3 \geqslant 35$$
$$x_1 + 2x_2 \geqslant 50$$
$$x_1, x_2, x_3 \geqslant 0$$

Solve using the dual simplex method.

28. Given the following linear programming problem:

Minimize $Z = 4x_1 + 3x_2$

subject to

$$2x_1 + x_2 \geqslant 10$$
$$-3x_1 + 2x_2 \leqslant 6$$
$$x_1 + x_2 \geqslant 6$$
$$x_1, x_2 \geqslant 0$$

Solve using the dual simplex method.

29. Given the following linear programming problem:

Maximize $Z = 6x_1 + 2x_2 + 12x_3$

subject to

$$4x_1 + x_2 + 3x_3 \leq 24$$
$$2x_1 + 6x_2 + 3x_3 \leq 30$$
$$x_1, x_2, x_3 \geq 0$$

The optimal simplex tableau for this problem is:

c_b \ c_j	basis	b_i^*	6 x_1	2 x_2	12 x_3	0 s_1	0 s_2
12	x_3	8	4/3	1/3	1	1/3	0
0	s_2	6	−2	5	0	−1	1
	z_j	96	16	4	12	4	0
	$c_j - z_j$		−10	−2	0	−4	0

a. Find the ranges for all b_i values for which the solution will remain feasible.
b. Find the ranges for all c_j values for which the solution will remain optimal.
c. Find the range for a_{12} for which the solution will remain optimal.
d. What effect will the addition of the following constraint have on the solution?

$$x_1 + 2x_2 + 2x_3 \leq 12$$

30. Given the following linear programming problem:

Maximize $Z = 10x_1 + 8x_2$

subject to

$$x_1 + 3x_2 \leq 30$$
$$6x_1 + 3x_2 \leq 120$$
$$x_1, x_2 \geq 0$$

The optimal simplex tableau for this problem is:

c_b \ c_j	basis	b_i^*	10 x_1	8 x_2	0 s_1	0 s_2
8	x_2	4	0	1	2/5	−1/15
10	x_1	18	1	0	−1/5	1/5
	z_j	212	10	8	6/5	22/15
	$c_j - z_j$		0	0	−6/5	−22/15

a. Find the feasible ranges for all b_i values.
b. Find the optimal ranges for all c_j values.
c. What effect does the addition of the following constraint have on the solution?

$$2x_1 + x_2 \leq 40$$

d. What effect does the addition of the following constraint have on the solution?

$$x_1 + x_2 \leq 20$$

e. What effect will the addition of a decision variable (x_3) to the model have on the solution?

Maximize $Z = 10x_1 + 8x_2 + 6x_3$

subject to

$$x_1 + 3x_2 + 2x_3 \leq 30$$
$$6x_1 + 3x_2 + 4x_3 \leq 120$$
$$x_1, x_2, x_3 \geq 0$$

31. Given the following linear programming problem:

$$\text{Minimize } Z = 3x_1 + 5x_2 + 2x_3$$

subject to

$$\begin{aligned} x_1 + x_2 - 3x_3 &\geqslant 35 \\ x_1 + 2x_2 &\geqslant 50 \\ -x_1 + x_2 + x_3 &\geqslant 25 \\ x_1, x_2, x_3 &\geqslant 0 \end{aligned}$$

The optimal simplex tableau for this problem is:

c_b \ c_j	basis	b_i^*	3 x_1	5 x_2	2 x_3	0 s_1	0 s_2	0 s_3
0	s_2	15	0	0	−4	−3/2	1	−1/2
3	x_1	5	1	0	−2	−1/2	0	1/2
5	x_2	30	0	1	−1	−1/2	0	−1/2
	z_j	165	3	5	−11	−4	0	−1
	$z_j - c_j$		0	0	−13	−4	0	−1

a. Explain how the feasible ranges for all b_i values would be determined.
b. Find the optimal ranges for all c_j values.
c. Explain the requirements for a change in a_{23}.
d. What effect does the addition of the following constraint have on the solution?

$$2x_1 + x_2 + x_3 \geqslant 30.$$

e. What effect does the addition of the following constraint have on the solution?

$$x_2 + x_3 \geqslant 40.$$

f. What effect will the addition of a fourth decision variable (x_4) to the model have on the solution?

$$\text{Minimize } Z = 3x_1 + 5x_2 + 2x_3 + 3x_4$$

subject to

$$\begin{aligned} x_1 + x_2 - 3x_3 + 2x_4 &\geq 35 \\ x_1 + 2x_2 + \quad\quad x_4 &\geq 50 \\ -x_1 + x_2 + x_3 + 2x_4 &\geq 25 \\ x_1, x_2, x_3 &\geq 0 \end{aligned}$$

32. Given the following linear programming problem:

$$\text{Maximize } Z = 5x_1 + 7x_2 + 8x_3$$

subject to

$$\begin{aligned} x_1 + x_2 + x_3 &\leq 32 \\ x_1 &\leq 20 \\ x_2 &\leq 15 \\ x_3 &\leq 18 \\ x_1, x_2, x_3 &\geq 0 \end{aligned}$$

The optimal simplex tableau for this problem is:

c_b \ c_j	basis	b_i^*	5 x_1	7 x_2	8 x_3	0 s_1	0 s_2	0 s_3	0 s_4
7	x_2	14	1	1	0	1	0	0	−1
0	s_2	20	1	0	0	0	1	0	0
0	s_3	1	−1	0	0	−1	0	1	1
8	x_3	18	0	0	1	0	0	0	1
	z_j	242	7	7	8	7	0	0	1
	$c_j - z_j$		−2	0	0	−7	0	0	−1

a. Find the feasible ranges for all b_i values.
b. Find the optimal ranges for all c_j values.
c. Find the optimal ranges for a_{11}.
d. What effect does the addition of the following constraint have on the solution?

$$2x_1 + 3x_2 + x_3 \leq 30$$

e. What effect will the addition of a fourth decision variable have on the solution?

Maximize $Z = 5x_1 + 7x_2 + 8x_3 + 6x_4$
subject to

$$x_1 + x_2 + x_3 + x_4 \leq 32$$
$$x_1 \leq 20$$
$$x_2 \leq 15$$
$$x_3 \leq 18$$
$$x_1, x_2, x_3 \geq 0$$

33. A food processing company produces three canned fruit products; mixed fruit, fruit cocktail, and fruit delight. The main ingredients in each product are pears and peaches. Each product is produced in lots and must go through three processes: mixing, canning, and packaging. The resource requirements for each product and each process are shown in the following linear programming formulation:

Maximize $Z = 10x_1 + 6x_2 + 8x_3$ (profit, \$)

subject to

$$20x_1 + 10x_2 + 16x_3 \leq 320 \quad \text{(pears, lb.)}$$
$$10x_1 + 20x_2 + 16x_3 \leq 400 \quad \text{(peaches, lb.)}$$
$$x_1 + 2x_2 + 2x_3 \leq 43 \quad \text{(mixing, hr.)}$$
$$x_1 + x_2 + x_3 \leq 60 \quad \text{(canning, hr.)}$$
$$2x_1 + x_2 + x_3 \leq 40 \quad \text{(packaging, hr.)}$$
$$x_1, x_2, x_3 \geq 0$$

The optimal simplex tableau is:

c_b \ c_j	basis	b_i^*	10 x_1	6 x_2	8 x_3	0 s_1	0 s_2	0 s_3	0 s_4	0 s_5
10	x_1	8	1	0	8/15	1/15	1/30	0	0	0
6	x_2	16	0	1	8/15	−1/30	1/15	0	0	0
0	s_3	3	0	0	2/5	−1/40	−1/10	1	0	0
0	s_4	36	0	0	−1/15	−1/30	−1/30	0	1	0
0	s_5	8	0	0	−3/5	−1/10	0	0	0	1
	z_j	176	10	6	128/15	7/15	1/15	0	0	0
	$c_j - z_j$		0	0	−8/15	−7/15	−1/15	0	0	0

a. What is the maximum price the company would be willing to pay for additional pears? How much would be purchased at that price?
b. What is the marginal value of peaches? Over what range of peaches is this price valid?
c. The company can purchase a new machine for mixing that can increase the hours available for mixing from 40 to 60. Will this affect the optimal solution?
d. The company can also purchase a new machine for packaging that can increase the hours available for packaging from 40 to 50. Will this affect the optimal solution?
e. If the manager should attempt to secure additional units of only one of the resources, which should it be and how much should be secured?
f. The company is considering adding a third fruit, oranges, to the mix to increase demand. The requirements for oranges and their availability is given as $2x_1 + 3x_2 + 2x_3 \leq 100$ oranges. What effect will this have on the solution?
g. The company is considering a new product, fancy fruit. Profit is \$6 per lot. Each lot will contain 12 pounds of pears, 14 pounds of peaches, and will require 2 hours to mix, 1 hour to can, and 2 hours to package. How will this affect the product mix given in the solution?

34. A lumber products firm produces three types of pressed paneling from pine and spruce. The three types of paneling are Western, Old English, and Colonial. Each sheet must be cut and pressed. The resource requirements are given in the following linear programming formulation:

$$\text{Maximize } Z = 4x_1 + 10x_2 + 8x_3 \quad \text{(profit, \$)}$$

subject to

$$\begin{aligned} 5x_1 + 4x_2 + 4x_3 &\leq 200 \quad \text{(pine, lb.)} \\ 2x_1 + 5x_2 + 2x_3 &\leq 160 \quad \text{(spruce, lb.)} \\ x_1 + x_2 + 2x_3 &\leq 50 \quad \text{(cutting, hr.)} \\ 2x_1 + 4x_2 + 2x_3 &\leq 80 \quad \text{(pressing, hr.)} \\ x_1, x_2, x_3 &\geq 0 \end{aligned}$$

The optimal simplex tableau is:

c_b \ c_j	basis	b_i^*	4 x_1	10 x_2	8 x_3	0 s_1	0 s_2	0 s_3	0 s_4
0	s_1	80	−7/3	0	0	1	0	−4/3	−2/3
0	s_2	70	−1/3	0	0	0	1	1/3	−4/3
8	x_3	20	1/3	0	1	0	0	2/3	−1/6
10	x_2	10	1/3	1	0	0	0	−1/3	1/3
	z_j	260	6	10	8	0	0	2	2
	$c_j - z_j$		−2	0	0	0	0	−2	−2

a. What is the marginal value of an additional pound of spruce? Over what range of available spruce is this value valid?
b. What is the marginal value of an additional hour of cutting? Over what range is this value valid?
c. Given a choice between securing more cutting hours and more pressing hours, which should management select? Why?
d. If the amount of spruce available to the firm decreases from 160 to 100 pounds, will it affect the solution?
e. What unit profit would have to be made from western paneling before management would consider producing it?
f. Management is considering changing the profit of colonial paneling from \$8 to \$13. Would this affect the solution?
g. The firm is considering production of a new type of paneling, mediterranean. It would yield a profit of \$6, require 3 pounds of pine, 4 pounds of spruce, and it would take 1 hour to cut and 4 hours to press. Will the production of this new paneling affect the present solution?

35. A manufacturing firm produces four products, x_1, x_2, x_3, and x_4. Each product requires material and machine processing. The linear programming model is formulated as:

$$\text{Maximize } Z = 2x_1 + 8x_2 + 10x_3 + 6x_4 \quad \text{(profit, \$)}$$

subject to

$$2x_1 + x_2 + 4x_3 + 2x_4 \leq 200 \quad \text{(material, lb.)}$$
$$x_1 + 2x_2 + 2x_3 + x_4 \leq 160 \quad \text{(machine processing, hr.)}$$
$$x_1, x_2, x_3, x_4 \geq 0$$

The optimal simplex tableau is:

c_b \ c_j	basis	b_i^*	2 x_1	8 x_2	10 x_3	6 x_4	0 s_1	0 s_2
6	x_4	80	1	0	2	1	2/3	−1/3
8	x_2	40	0	1	0	0	−1/3	2/3
	z_j	800	6	8	12	6	4/3	10/3
	$c_j - z_j$		−4	0	−2	0	−4/3	−10/3

a. What is the marginal value of an additional pound of material? Over what range of material is this value valid?
b. What is the marginal value of additional hours of processing time? Over what range of hours is this value valid?
c. How much would the contribution to profit of x_1 have to increase before x_1 would be produced? Before x_4 would be produced?
d. Suppose new consumer standards require additional processing. The new process requires 2 hours for x_1 and x_4 and 4 hours for x_2 and x_3. A total of 200 hours are available. Does this affect the solution?

Part 3

Network and Inventory Models

5 Transportation and Assignment Problems

This chapter is concerned with two special types of linear programming applications, transportation and assignment **network models**. While all linear programming problems can be solved by the simplex method, these special cases can be solved by special network flow techniques that are generally more efficient than the simplex method. Many of the modeling concepts and solution procedures for these network models are actually extensions of the linear programming concepts and procedures presented in the previous chapters.

The Transportation Problem

In general, the transportation problem deals with the transportation of a product from a number of sources, with limited supplies, to a number of destinations, with specified demands, at the minimum total transportation cost. For example, a product produced at three factories (sources) must be distributed to three stores (destinations), as shown in figure 5.1.

Each factory has a specified weekly productive capacity, and each store has a specified weekly demand for the product. Given a unique unit cost of transporting the product from each factory to each store, the problem is to determine the number of units to ship from each factory to each store, with the objective of minimizing total transportation costs. The requirements (or constraints) of the problem are that demand at each store must be met without exceeding productive capacity at each factory. The problem is illustrated as a generalized transportation network model in figure 5.2.

Figure 5.1 A transportation problem involving three factories and three stores.

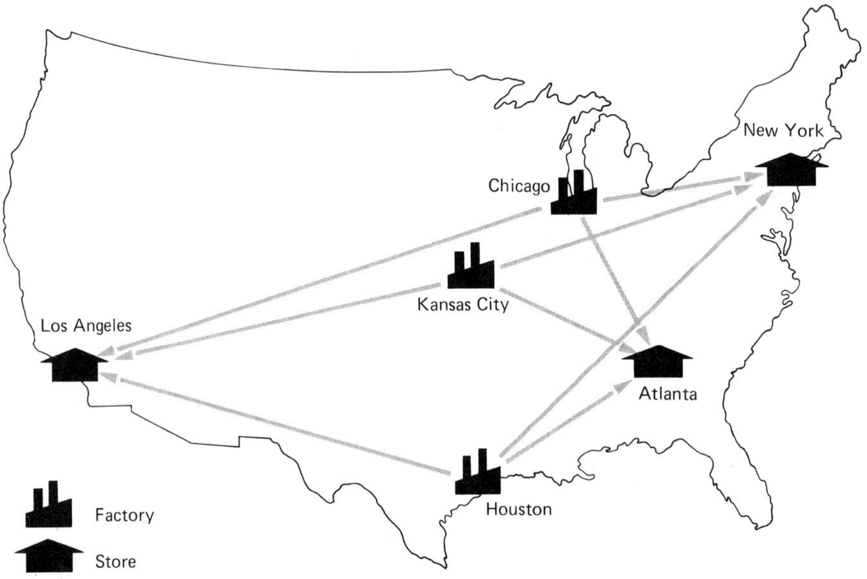

Figure 5.2 Transportation network model for three factories and three stores.

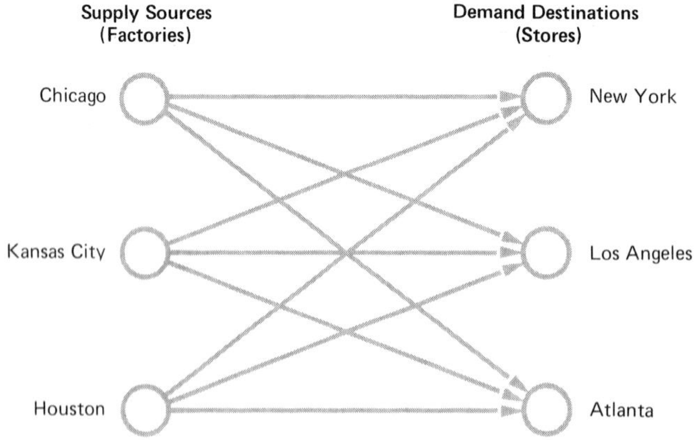

The Balanced Transportation Problem

To illustrate the transportation problem, an example will be presented in which total supply from all sources exactly equals total demand at all destinations. This type of problem is referred to as a **balanced transportation problem.**

A concrete company transports concrete from three plants to three construction sites. The supply capacities of the three plants, the demand requirements at the three sites, and the transportation costs ($/ton) are as follows:

From Plant	To Construction Site 1	2	3	Supply (tons)
1	$8	5	6	120
2	15	10	12	80
3	3	9	10	80
Demand (tons)	150	70	60	280

This transportation problem is illustrated as a network model in figure 5.3. Each of the three plants ($i = 1, 2, 3$) can supply concrete to each of the three construction sites ($j = 1, 2, 3$). The problem is "balanced" since the total concrete demanded is equal to the total supply, 280 tons of concrete. It is rare to observe a balanced transportation problem in reality; however, the analysis of a balanced problem is a good starting point to understanding the transportation solution processes to be presented.

Figure 5.3 Network model for concrete transportation problem.

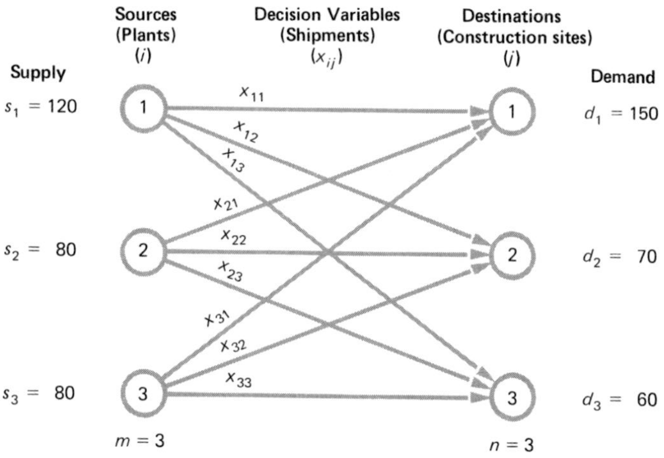

This example problem can be formulated as a linear programming problem as follows:

Let

x_{ij} = the number of tons of concrete shipped from plant i ($i = 1,2,3$) to site j ($j = 1,2,3$).

$$\text{Minimize } Z = \$8x_{11} + 5x_{12} + 6x_{13} + 15x_{21} + 10x_{22} + 12x_{23} + 3x_{31} + 9x_{32} + 10x_{33}$$

subject to

$$\begin{aligned}
x_{11} + x_{12} + x_{13} &= 120 \text{ (supply, plant 1)} \\
x_{21} + x_{22} + x_{23} &= 80 \text{ (supply, plant 2)} \\
x_{31} + x_{32} + x_{33} &= 80 \text{ (supply, plant 3)} \\
x_{11} + x_{21} + x_{31} &= 150 \text{ (demand, site 1)} \\
x_{12} + x_{22} + x_{32} &= 70 \text{ (demand, site 2)} \\
x_{13} + x_{23} + x_{33} &= 60 \text{ (demand, site 3)} \\
\text{all } x_{ij} &\geqslant 0
\end{aligned}$$

The model constraints represent the total amount that can be supplied by each plant and the total amount demanded at each construction site as sums of the individual shipping alternatives (i.e., routes). The constraints are represented as equalities because the problem is balanced (all units supplied will be distributed and all demand will be met). The objective function represents the total cost where each c_{ij} value is the per ton transporting cost from plant i to site j.

The general formulation of a transportation problem with m sources and n destinations is

$$\text{Minimize } = \sum_{i=1}^{m} \sum_{j=1}^{n} c_{ij} x_{ij}$$

subject to

$$\sum_{j=1}^{n} x_{ij} = s_i \text{ (supply, } s_i\text{, at source } i,\ i = 1, 2, \ldots, m)$$

$$\sum_{i=1}^{m} x_{ij} = d_j \text{ (demand, } d_j\text{, at destination } j,\ j = 1, 2, \ldots, n)$$

$$\text{all } x_{ij} \geqslant 0.$$

The balanced condition of the transportation problem is expressed as

$$\sum_{i=1}^{m} s_i = \sum_{i=1}^{m} \left(\sum_{j=1}^{n} x_{ij} \right) = \sum_{j=1}^{n} \left(\sum_{i=1}^{m} x_{ij} \right) = \sum_{j=1}^{n} d_j.$$

This problem could be solved using the simplex method, as were linear programming problems in previous chapters; however, even a relatively small problem, such as our example with three sources and three destinations, can mushroom into a rather large simplex tableau with six constraints, nine decision variables, and six artificial variables. Inspection of the transportation problem reveals, however, that all the coefficients, a_{ij}, in the constraint equations are ones. This model feature leads to the use of special solution methods that are computationally more efficient than the simplex method.

The Transportation Tableau

Because of the special structure of the transportation problem it can be put in a unique tabular form called the **transportation tableau.** This tableau has the general form shown in table 5.1.

Table 5.1 General transportation tableau

		Destinations						
To / From		1	2	. . .	j	. . .	n	Supply
Sources	1	c_{11} x_{11}	c_{12} x_{12}	. . .	c_{1j} x_{1j}	. . .	c_{1n} x_{1n}	s_1
	2	c_{21} x_{21}	c_{22} x_{22}	. . .	c_{2j} x_{2j}	. . .	c_{2n} x_{2n}	s_2
	⋮	⋮	⋮		⋮		⋮	⋮
	i	c_{i1} x_{i1}	c_{i2} x_{i2}	. . .	c_{ij} x_{ij}	. . .	c_{in} x_{in}	s_i
	⋮	⋮	⋮		⋮		⋮	⋮
	m	c_{m1} x_{m1}	c_{m2} x_{m2}	. . .	c_{mj} x_{mj}	. . .	c_{mn} x_{mn}	s_m
Demand		d_1	d_2	. . .	d_j	. . .	d_n	$\Sigma s_i = \Sigma d_j$

The sources are listed as rows and the destinations as columns. The tableau has $m \times n$ cells. The unit transportation cost (c_{ij}) is recorded in the small box in the upper-right-hand corner of each cell. The demand at each destination is recorded in the bottom row, while the supply from each source is listed in the right-hand column. The lower-right-hand corner box reflects the fact that supply and demand are equal. The x_{ij} variable in each cell represents the number of units transported from source i to destination j (which is to be solved for).

The transportation tableau for the concrete transportation problem is shown in table 5.2.

Table 5.2 Transportation tableau for concrete transportation problem

From \ To	1	2	3	Supply
1	[8]	[5]	[6]	120
2	[15]	[10]	[12]	80
3	[3]	[9]	[10]	80
Demand	150	70	60	280

Given the problem in tableau form, it can now be solved via one of several transportation solution techniques. However, in order to begin the solution process an initial basic feasible solution must be determined.

The Initial Solution

Referring to the general formulation of the transportation problem, it can be seen that there are m supply constraints and n demand constraints, which translates into $m + n$ total constraints. In a typical linear programming problem the number of basic variables in the simplex tableau (b_i*) is equal to the number of constraints. However, in a transportation problem, one of the constraints is redundant. The balance conditions,

$$\sum_{i=1}^{m} s_i = \sum_{j=1}^{n} d_j,$$

result in the fact that if $m+n-1$ constraints are met then the $m+n$ equation will also be met. As such, only $m+n-1$ *independent* equations exist. Thus, the initial solution will have only $m+n-1$ basic variables.

There are several methods available to develop an initial basic feasible solution. Three of the more popular methods for developing an initial solution will be examined: the **northwest corner method, the least-cost method,** and **Vogel's approximation method (VAM).**

Northwest Corner Method

The northwest corner method is the simplest of the three methods to develop an initial solution. The northwest corner method can be summarized as follows:

1. Start at the northwest corner (upper-left-hand corner) of the tableau and allocate as much as possible to x_{11} without violating the supply or demand constraints (i.e., x_{11} is set equal to the minimum of the values of s_1 or d_1).
2. This will exhaust the supply at source 1 and/or the demand for destination 1. As a result, no more units can be allocated to the exhausted row or column, and it is eliminated. Next allocate as much as possible to the adjacent cell in the row or column that has not been eliminated. If both row and column are exhausted, move diagonally to the next cell.
3. Continue in the same manner until all supply has been exhausted and demand requirements have been met.

For the transportation example in which tons of concrete are transported, the initial solution by the northwest corner method is shown in table 5.3.

Table 5.3 Initial solution by the northwest corner method

From \ To	1	2	3	Supply
1	[8] 120	[5]	[6]	120
2	[15] 30	[10] 50	[12]	80
3	[3]	[9] 20	[10] 60	80
Demand	150	70	60	280

The initial solution is obtained as follows: (1) As many tons as possible are allocated to x_{11} according to $x_{11} = \min(120, 150) = 120$. This exhausts the supply for plant 1 and as a result eliminates row 1 from further consideration. (2) Since $x_{11} = 120$, all but 30 tons demanded at site 1 have been supplied. The next adjacent cell, x_{21}, is allocated as much as possible according to $x_{21} = \min(30, 80) = 30$. This eliminates column 1 from further consideration. (3) Next, $x_{22} = \min(50, 70) = 50$, which eliminates row 2. (4) $x_{32} = \min(20, 80) = 20$. (5) $x_{33} = \min(60, 60) = 60$.

Notice that this stair-step process results in an initial solution with 5 $(m+n-1)$ basic variables and 4 nonbasic variables (i.e., zero allocation). For this solution, total cost is

$$Z = (\$8 \times 120) + (\$15 \times 30) + (\$10 \times 50) + (\$9 \times 20) + (\$10 \times 60)$$

$$= \$2{,}690.$$

Remember that this is only an *initial* solution and, thus, not necessarily optimal. In fact, of the three methods for obtaining an initial solution, the northwest corner is the least efficient since it does not consider the unit transportation costs in making allocations. As a result, it is likely that several additional solution iterations will be required before the optimal solution is obtained.

Least-Cost Method

The least-cost method attempts to reflect the objective of cost minimization by systematically allocating to cells according to the magnitude of their unit costs. The general procedure for the least-cost method can be summarized as follows:

1. Select the x_{ij} variable (cell) with the minimum unit transportation cost (c_{ij}) and allocate as much as possible. For the minimum c_{ij}, x_{ij} = minimum (s_i, d_j). This will exhaust either row i or column j.
2. From the remaining cells that are feasible (i.e., have not been filled or their row or column eliminated), select the minimum c_{ij} value and allocate as much as possible.
3. Continue this process until all supply and demand requirements are satisfied.

Again consider the transportation example of transporting tons of concrete. Table 5.4 gives the initial cell allocation by the least-cost method.

Table 5.4 Initial allocation by the least-cost method

From \ To	1	2	3	Supply
1	[8]	[5]	[6]	120
2	[15]	[10]	[12]	80
3	[3] 80	[9]	[10]	80
Demand	150	70	60	280

The first step in the least-cost method results in an allocation to x_{31}, since c_{31} = \$3 is the minimum cell cost. The amount allocated is x_{31} = minimum (150,80) = 80. Since this allocation exhausts source 3 supply, row 3 is eliminated, and x_{32} and x_{33} are no longer feasible. Also, the demand for 150 tons at site 1 is reduced by the 80 allocated tons so that the demand now equals 70 tons.

The next cell allocation is selected from the remaining six cells. The minimum c_{ij} is c_{12} = \$5, and x_{12} = minimum (70,120) = 70. This allocation is shown in table 5.5.

Table 5.5 Second allocation by the least-cost method

From \ To	1	2	3	Supply
1	[8]	[5] 70	[6]	120
2	[15]	[10]	[12]	80
3	[3] 80	[9]	[10]	80
Demand	150	70	60	280

The remaining cell allocations are made in the same manner. The initial solution by the least-cost method is shown in table 5.6.

In case of ties between the minimum c_{ij} values, simply select between the tied cells arbitrarily. Because this is only an initial solution it has no effect on the eventual optimal solution, except possibly to require more iterations to obtain it.

Table 5.6 Initial solution by the least-cost method

From \ To	1	2	3	Supply
1	[8]	[5] 70	[6] 50	120
2	[15] 70	[10]	[12] 10	80
3	[3] 80	[9]	[10]	80
Demand	150	70	60	280

The initial solution by the least-cost method as shown in table 5.6 ($x_{12} = 70$, $x_{13} = 50$, $x_{21} = 70$, $x_{23} = 10$, and $x_{31} = 80$) results in the following total transportation cost:

$$Z = (\$5 \times 70) + (6 \times 50) + (15 \times 70) + (12 \times 10) + (3 \times 80)$$
$$= \$2{,}060$$

Comparing the total initial cost derived from the least-cost method with the northwest corner method shows a reduction of $630 with the least-cost method. In general, the least-cost method will usually result in a better (lower cost) initial solution than the northwest corner method. This should be apparent since the least-cost method employs cost as a criterion for allocation and the northwest corner method does not. As a result the number of additional iterations required to find an optimal solution will be less. However, cases can infrequently occur in which the same or a better initial solution is achieved from the northwest corner method.

Vogel's Approximation Method

Vogel's approximation method (VAM) typically provides a better initial solution than the northwest corner method and often better than the least-cost method. In fact, in many cases the initial solution obtained by VAM will be optimal. VAM consists of making allocations in a manner that will minimize the penalty (i.e., regret or opportunity) cost for selecting the wrong cell for an allocation. The VAM process can be summarized as:

1. Calculate the **penalty cost** for each row and column. The penalty costs for each row i are computed by subtracting the smallest c_{ij} value in the row from the next largest c_{ij} value in the same row. Column penalty costs are obtained the same way, by subtracting the smallest c_{ij} value in each column from the next largest column c_{ij} value. These costs are the penalty for not selecting the minimum cell cost.
2. Select the row or column with the greatest penalty cost (breaking any ties arbitrarily). Allocate as much as possible to the cell with the minimum c_{ij} value in the indicated row or column; that is, for minimum c_{ij}, x_{ij} = minimum (s_i, d_j). As a result the largest penalties are avoided.
3. Adjust the supply and demand requirements to reflect the allocation(s) already made. Eliminate any rows and columns in which supply and demand have been exhausted.
4. If all supply and demand requirements have not been satisfied, go to the first step and recalculate new penalty costs. If all row and column values have been satisfied, the initial solution has been obtained.

Applying these steps to our example results in an initial VAM allocation in the transportation tableau as shown in table 5.7.

As an example of the calculation of penalty costs, consider the first row. The smallest c_{ij} value is 5 for c_{12}. The next largest is $c_{13} = 6$. Thus, the penalty cost is the difference between these two values, $6 - 5 = \$1$. All remaining row and column penalty costs are computed the same way.

Table 5.7 Initial VAM allocation

From \ To	1	2	3	Supply	Row Penalty Costs
1	[8]	[5]	[6]	120	1
2	[15]	[10]	[12]	80	2
3	[3] 80	[9]	[10]	80	6
Demand	150	70	60	280	
Column Penalty Costs	5	4	4		

The greatest penalty cost for this tableau is \$6 for row 3. The allocation in this row is made to the cell with the minimum c_{ij} value, in this case x_{31}. The amount allocated to x_{31} = minimum (80,150) = 80. Now the tableau must be adjusted to reflect the exhaustion of source 3 supply and the elimination of row 3. In addition, the remaining demand at site 1 now becomes 70 tons rather than 150. The adjusted tableau with the newly calculated penalty costs and the second allocation is shown in table 5.8.

Table 5.8 Transportation tableau adjusted for the second VAM allocation

From \ To	1	2	3	Supply	Row Penalty Costs
1	[8] 70	[5]	[6]	120	1
2	[15]	[10]	[12]	80	2
3	[3] 80	[9]	[10]	80	–
Demand	150	70	60	280	
Column Penalty Costs	7	5	6		

Column 1 is selected for the second allocation since it has the greatest revised penalty cost, $7. The allocation in this column is made to cell x_{11} since it has the minimum c_{ij} value of $8. The amount allocated to x_{11} = minimum (70,120) = 70. This allocation results in the elimination of column 1 and the reduction of row 1 supply to 50 tons. This process of allocation and recomputing penalty costs continues until all supply and demand requirements are met. The solution for this example obtained by VAM is shown in table 5.9.

Table 5.9 VAM solution

From \ To	1	2	3	Supply
1	[8] 70	[5]	[6] 50	120
2	[15]	[10] 70	[12] 10	80
3	[3] 80	[9]	[10]	80
Demand	150	70	60	280

The total cost of this solution is

$$Z = (\$8 \times 70) + (6 \times 50) + (10 \times 70) + (12 \times 10) + (3 \times 80)$$
$$= \$1{,}920.$$

The total cost for this initial solution, $1,920, is the lowest initial cost obtained from all three of the initial solution methods. In fact, this solution is also optimal, a condition that will be shown in following discussion of solution methods. In general, VAM reduces the subsequent number of iterations required to reach the optimal solution since it usually provides a better initial solution than the other two methods.

Determining an Optimal Solution

Two methods are presented for determining an optimal solution once an initial basic feasible solution has been obtained. These methods are the **stepping-stone method** and the **modified distribution method.**

Stepping-Stone Method

Once an initial basic feasible solution is obtained for the transportation problem, the next step is to determine if the total transportation cost can be further reduced by entering a nonbasic variable (i.e., allocating units to an empty cell) into the solution. The process of evaluating the nonbasic variables to determine if improvement is possible and then reallocating units is called the **stepping-stone method.**

The stepping-stone method derives its name from the fact that a closed loop of occupied cells is used to evaluate each empty cell (nonbasic variable). These occupied cells are thought of as stepping-stones in a pond—the pond being the entire tableau.

Employing the initial solution obtained by the northwest corner method (table 5.10), which we know is not optimal, we will demonstrate the evaluation of each nonbasic variable via the stepping-stone method.

Table 5.10 Initial northwest corner solution

From \ To	1	2	3	Supply
1	[8] 120	[5]	[6]	120
2	[15] 30	[10] 50	[12]	80
3	[3]	[9] 20	[10] 60	80
Demand	150	70	60	280

Each empty cell represents a nonbasic variable. For the nonbasic variable to enter the solution it must contribute to a reduction in the value of the objective function. The variable x_{12} is arbitrarily considered as a possible entering variable. Suppose that we decide to allocate one unit to that cell. By doing so there are now 71 units in the second column of table 5.10, which is a violation of the demand constraint. As a result, one unit must be subtracted from either 50 (x_{22}) or 20 (x_{32}) in column 2. Subtract 1 unit from x_{22}, yielding 49, and therefore column 2 has 70 units again. But row 2 now has 79 units, which violates the supply requirement. As a result, one unit must be added to x_{21}, which again conforms row 2 to the supply requirement of 80 units. However, column 1 now has 151 allocated units. Thus, one unit must be subtracted from x_{11} so that column 1 now meets the demand constraint of 150 units. Row 1 is now completely satisfied even though one unit was subtracted from x_{11} because originally one unit was added to x_{12}, the empty cell. This closed path process is the stepping-stone procedure. This path for x_{12} is shown in table 5.11.

Empty Cell	Closed Loop
x_{12}	$x_{12} \rightarrow x_{22} \rightarrow x_{21} \rightarrow x_{11} \rightarrow x_{12}$
	(+1) (−1) (+1) (−1)

Table 5.11 Evaluation of cell x_{12} according to the stepping-stone method

From \ To	1	2	3	Supply
1	−1 [8] 120	+1 [5]	[6]	120
2	+1 [15] 30	−1 [10] 50	[12]	80
3	[3]	[9] 20	[10] 60	80
Demand	150	70	60	280

Several important conditions regarding the construction of stepping-stone paths should be mentioned at this point.

1. The direction taken, either clockwise or counterclockwise, is immaterial in determining the closed path. The same path will result regardless of direction.
2. There is only one unique closed path for each empty cell.

3. The path must follow only (change direction at) occupied cells; the exception being the nonbasic variable being evaluated.
4. However, both empty and occupied cells can be skipped over in the construction of a closed path. Consider the following arbitrarily constructed example:

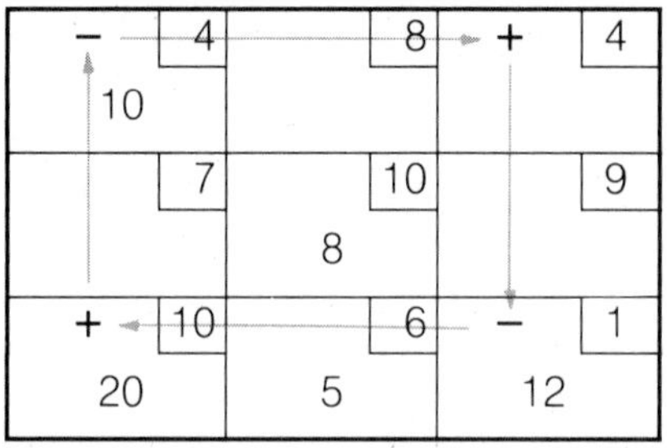

5. A path can cross over itself. Consider the following arbitrarily constructed example, where the nonbasic variable, x_{31}, is being evaluated:

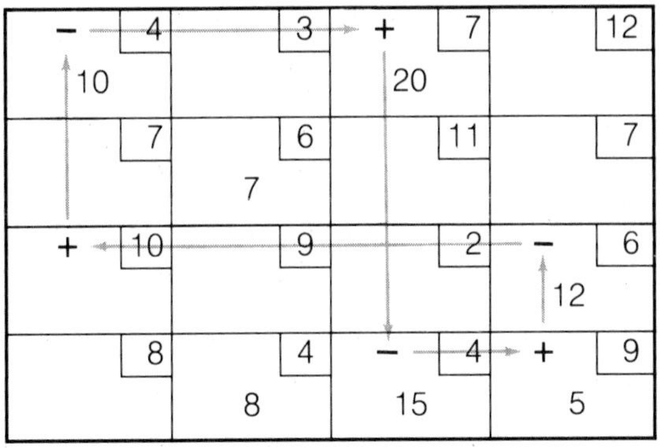

− 4 3 + 7 12
10 20
7 6 11 7
7
+ 10 9 2 − 6
12
8 4 − 4 + 9
8 15 5

6. Exactly one addition and one subtraction must appear in each row and column on the path.

The purpose of the path is to maintain the supply and demand constraints while reallocating units to an empty cell.

Now we must consider the cost of this reallocation. This is done by evaluating the costs along the closed path. Referring to table 5.11, if one unit is added to x_{12}, a cost of \$5 (the unit transportation cost for x_{12}) will be incurred. However, the subsequent subtraction of a unit from x_{22} will reduce cost by \$10. Similarly, the addition of a unit to x_{21} will increase cost by \$15 while the subtraction of a unit from x_{11} will reduce cost by \$8. These cost additions and reductions are summarized as follows (where c_{ij}^* is the net cost change for allocating one unit to x_{ij}):

$$c_{12}^* = +\, c_{12} - c_{22} + c_{21} - c_{11}$$

$$c_{12}^* = \$5 - 10 + 15 - 8$$

$$c_{12}^* = +\$2$$

Thus, if one unit is reallocated to x_{12}, a net increase of \$2 in total transportation cost would result. Therefore, x_{12} should not be chosen as an entering variable since it increases cost rather than reducing it.

All nonbasic variables (empty cells) are evaluated in the same manner to determine if any of them result in a net cost decrease and would therefore be a candidate for the entering nonbasic variable. If no candidate exists (i.e., all empty cells have positive c_{ij}^* values), then the solution is optimal. This is not the case for this example. Table 5.12 summarizes the various stepping-stone paths for all empty cells while table 5.13 summarizes the corresponding net cost changes resulting from each path.

Table 5.12 Stepping-stone paths for all nonbasic variables

Empty Cell	Closed Path
x_{12}	$x_{12} \rightarrow x_{22} \rightarrow x_{21} \rightarrow x_{11} \rightarrow x_{12}$
x_{13}	$x_{13} \rightarrow x_{33} \rightarrow x_{32} \rightarrow x_{22} \rightarrow x_{21} \rightarrow x_{11} \rightarrow x_{13}$
x_{23}	$x_{23} \rightarrow x_{33} \rightarrow x_{32} \rightarrow x_{22} \rightarrow x_{23}$
x_{31}	$x_{31} \rightarrow x_{21} \rightarrow x_{22} \rightarrow x_{32} \rightarrow x_{31}$

Table 5.13 Cell cost summary for all nonbasic variables

c_{ij}^*	Path Cost Reductions and Additions		Net Cost Change
c_{12}^*	\$ 5 − 10 + 15 − 8	=	+\$2
c_{13}^*	\$ 6 − 10 + 9 − 10 + 15 − 8	=	+\$2
c_{23}^*	\$12 − 10 + 9 − 10	=	+\$1
c_{31}^*	\$ 3 − 15 + 10 − 9	=	−\$11

From the cost analysis of all nonbasic variable stepping-stone paths in the example, only x_{31} has a negative net cost change ($c_{31}^* = -\$11$). Thus, x_{31} is the only nonbasic variable, which, if entered in the solution basis, will reduce cost. If there had been two or more nonbasic variables with negative c_{ij}^* values, then the one with the greatest net cost decrease would be selected. In case of a tie, selection of the entering nonbasic variable is arbitrary.

Since it has been determined that x_{31} is the entering nonbasic variable, next it must be decided how much will be allocated to the x_{31} cell. Given that each unit allocated to x_{31} will decrease cost by \$11 we naturally desire to allocate as many units as possible to x_{31}. However, each unit allocated is taken from other occupied cells in the tableau. Thus, in order to maintain the supply and demand constraints, the allocation must be made according to the already determined stepping-stone path for x_{31} (see tables 5.12 and 5.14).

Table 5.14 Stepping-stone path for the entering nonbasic variable, x_{31}

From \ To	1	2	3	Supply
1	[8] 120	[5]	[6]	120
2	− [15] 30	+ [10] 50	[12]	80
3	+ [3]	− [9] 20	[10] 60	80
Demand	150	70	60	280

The amount allocated to x_{31} is restricted by the supply of 80 units and demand of 150 units. However, the amount allocated is also restricted by the amount that can feasibly be transferred along the closed path. Notice that for every unit allocated to x_{31}, a unit is subtracted from x_{21} and x_{32}.

If more than 20 units are allocated to x_{31}, then x_{32} will become negative, resulting in an infeasible condition. Thus, the amount allocated to the nonbasic entering variable is restricted to the minimum amount in a cell to be subtracted from ($x_{\bar{ij}}$) in the closed path. For this example,

$$x_{31} = \text{minimum } (x_{\bar{21}}, x_{\bar{32}})$$

and, in general,

$$\text{reallocated } x_{ij} = \text{minimum } (x_{\bar{ij}} \text{ on the closed path}).$$

A reallocation of 20 units to x_{31}, the entering nonbasic variable, results in the following new tableau with x_{32} as the leaving variable (table 5.15).

Table 5.15 Transportation tableau with initial reallocation

From \ To	1	2	3	Supply
1	[8] 120	[5]	[6]	120
2	[15] 10	[10] 70	[12]	80
3	[3] 20	[9]	[10] 60	80
Demand	150	70	60	280

The same stepping-stone process of evaluating each empty cell must be repeated for table 5.15 to determine if the solution is optimal or if there is a new candidate for the entering nonbasic variable. This results in two more iterations of the stepping-stone method before the optimal solution is achieved (tables 5.16 and 5.17).

Table 5.16 Second iteration: x_{23} enters, x_{21} leaves

From \ To	1	2	3	Supply
1	[8] 120	[5]	[6]	120
2	[15]	[10] 70	[12] 10	80
3	[3] 30	[9]	[10] 50	80
Demand	150	70	60	280

Table 5.17 Third iteration (optimal): x_{13} enters, x_{33} leaves

From \ To	1	2	3	Supply
1	[8] 70	[5]	[6] 50	120
2	[15]	[10] 70	[12] 10	80
3	[3] 80	[9]	[10]	80
Demand	150	70	60	280

The optimal solution, shown in table 5.17, is indicated by the fact that all empty cells have positive c_{ij}^* values. Thus, the solution can no longer be improved. The value of the objective function for the optimal solution is

$$Z = (\$8 \times 70) + (\$6 \times 50) + (\$10 \times 70) + (\$12 \times 10) + (\$3 \times 80)$$
$$Z = \$1{,}920.$$

It should be noted that this solution is the same as the initial solution obtained by VAM (table 5.9). The minimum cost shipping network for the concrete transportation problem is illustrated in figure 5.4.

Figure 5.4 Minimum cost shipping network for concrete transportation problem.

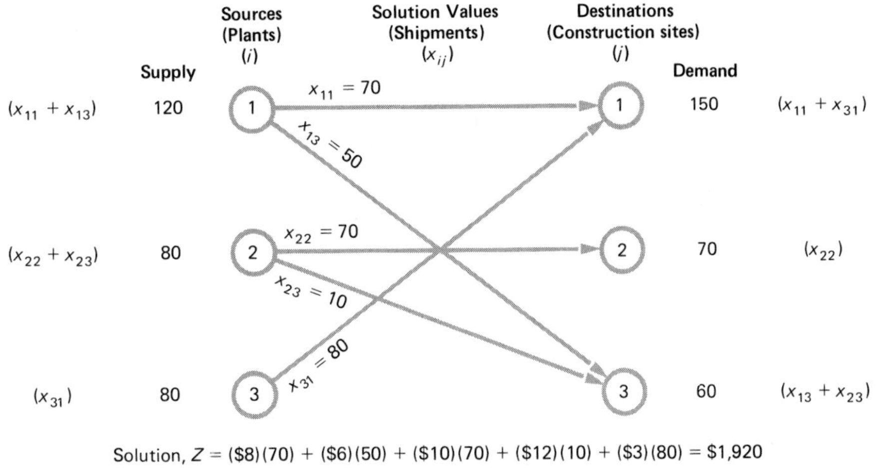

Modified Distribution Method

The modified distribution method (MODI) of solution is a variation of the stepping-stone method based on the dual formulation. It differs from the stepping-stone method in that with MODI it is unnecessary to determine all the closed paths for nonbasic variables. Instead, the $c_{ij}*$ values are determined simultaneously and the closed path is identified only for the entering nonbasic variable. This eliminates the cumbersome task of identifying all the stepping-stone paths.

In the MODI method, a value, u_i, is defined for each row (i) and a value, v_j, is defined for each column (j) in the transportation tableau. For each basic variable (i.e., occupied cell), x_{ij}, the following relationship exists:

$$u_i + v_j = c_{ij},$$

where c_{ij} is the unit cost of transportation.

To demonstrate the MODI technique, we will refer back to the northwest corner initial solution of the concrete transportation example, which is shown again in table 5.18. Table 5.18 shows the u_i and v_j designations for each row and column.

Table 5.18 Initial northwest corner solution

		$v_1 = 8$	$v_2 = 3$	$v_3 = 4$	
	From \ To	1	2	3	Supply
$u_1 = 0$	1	[8] 120	[5]	[6]	120
$u_2 = 7$	2	[15] 30	[10] 50	[12]	80
$u_3 = 6$	3	[3]	[9] 20	[10] 60	80
	Demand	150	70	60	280

Applying the relationship for u_i, v_j, and c_{ij} for each basic variable results in the following equations:

$$x_{11} : u_1 + v_1 = c_{11} = 8$$
$$x_{21} : u_2 + v_1 = c_{21} = 15$$
$$x_{22} : u_2 + v_2 = c_{22} = 10$$
$$x_{32} : u_3 + v_2 = c_{32} = 9$$
$$x_{33} : u_3 + v_3 = c_{33} = 10$$

As can be observed, five equations $(m + n - 1)$ with six unknowns $(m + n)$ now exist. To solve this set of equations, it is only necessary to assign any of the unknowns (u_i or v_j) an arbitrary value. Usually, u_1 is assigned a value of zero. With $u_1 = 0$ it is an easy task to determine the value of the remaining variables as follows:

$$u_1 = 0$$
$$0 + v_1 = 8, \quad v_1 = 8$$
$$u_2 + 8 = 15, \quad u_2 = 7$$
$$7 + v_2 = 10, \quad v_2 = 3$$
$$u_3 + 3 = 9, \quad u_3 = 6$$
$$6 + v_3 = 10, \quad v_3 = 4$$

All the u_i and v_j values have now been determined (note that it is also possible to have negative u_i and v_j values). The value of each nonbasic variable net cost change, $c_{ij}*$, is now determined by the following relationship:

$$c_{ij}* = c_{ij} - u_i - v_j$$

This formula for nonbasic variables results in $c_{ij}*$ values identical to those determined by the stepping-stone method.

$$c_{12}* = c_{12} - u_1 - v_2 = 5 - 0 - 3 = +2$$
$$c_{13}* = c_{13} - u_1 - v_3 = 6 - 0 - 4 = +2$$
$$c_{23}* = c_{23} - u_2 - v_3 = 12 - 7 - 4 = +1$$
$$c_{31}* = c_{31} - u_3 - v_1 = 3 - 6 - 8 = -11$$

As in the stepping-stone method, the negative value for $c_{31}*$ $(-\$11)$ indicates that the present solution is not optimal and x_{31} is the entering nonbasic variable. The amount allocated to x_{31} must now be determined *according to the stepping-stone procedure*. Thus, 20 units are allocated to x_{31}, resulting in the new tableau in table 5.19.

Table 5.19 First iteration determined by MODI

From \ To	1	2	3	Supply
1	[8] 120	[5]	[6]	120
2	[15] 10	[10] 70	[12]	80
3	[3] 20	[9]	[10] 60	80
Demand	150	70	60	280

At this stage the u_i, v_j, and c_{ij}^* values must be recomputed for this new tableau in order to test for optimality and determine the entering nonbasic variable.

The optimal solution for this example requires the same number of iterations as in the stepping-stone method, and the same allocation will be made at each iteration.

The MODI method can be summarized in the following steps:

1. Determine u_i values for each row and v_j values for each column by using the relationship $c_{ij} = u_i + v_j$ for all basic variables and assigning a value of zero to u_1.
2. Compute the net cost change, c_{ij}^*, for each nonbasic variable using the formula

$$c_{ij}^* = c_{ij} - u_i - v_j.$$

3. If a negative c_{ij}^* value exists, the solution is not optimal. Select the x_{ij} variable with the greatest negative c_{ij}^* value as the entering nonbasic variable.
4. Allocate units to the entering nonbasic variable, x_{ij}, according to the stepping-stone process. Return to step 1.

Relationship of MODI to the Dual

The MODI method of evaluating nonbasic variables in the transportation tableau is directly related to the dual of the transportation primal. Consider the general formulation of a transportation problem with $m = 3$ rows and $n = 3$ columns:

$$\text{Minimize } Z_p = c_{11}x_{11} + c_{12}x_{12} + c_{13}x_{13} + c_{21}x_{21} + c_{22}x_{22} + c_{23}x_{23} + c_{31}x_{31} + c_{32}x_{32} + c_{33}x_{33}$$

subject to

$$\begin{aligned}
x_{11} + x_{12} + x_{13} &= s_1 \\
x_{21} + x_{22} + x_{23} &= s_2 \\
x_{31} + x_{32} + x_{33} &= s_3 \\
x_{11} + x_{21} + x_{31} &= d_1 \\
x_{12} + x_{22} + x_{32} &= d_2 \\
x_{13} + x_{23} + x_{33} &= d_3 \\
x_{ij} &\geq 0
\end{aligned}$$

where s_i = supply requirements, and d_j = demand requirements.

Defining u_1 as the dual variable for the source (supply) constraints and v_j as the dual variable for the destination (demand) constraints results in the following dual formulation:

$$\text{Maximize } Z_d = (s_1u_1 + s_2u_2 + s_3u_3) + (d_1v_1 + d_2v_2 + d_3v_3)$$

subject to

$$\begin{aligned}
u_1 + v_1 &\leq c_{11} \\
u_1 + v_2 &\leq c_{12} \\
u_1 + v_3 &\leq c_{13} \\
u_2 + v_1 &\leq c_{21} \\
u_2 + v_2 &\leq c_{22} \\
u_2 + v_3 &\leq c_{23} \\
u_3 + v_1 &\leq c_{31} \\
u_3 + v_2 &\leq c_{32} \\
u_3 + v_3 &\leq c_{33} \\
u_i, v_j &\sim \text{unrestricted}
\end{aligned}$$

Now recall the dual property (from chapter 4), which holds that the constraints of the dual reflect the value of resources involved in the contribution to cost (or profit) of each product. As such, each dual constraint representing a primal basic variable must exactly equal the contribution to profit, c_{ij}. In other words the resources must return at least the contribution to profit and no more. This means that the dual constraints for primal basic variables are equations.

$$u_i + v_j = c_{ij}, \text{ for all basic variables } x_{ij}$$

This results in $m + n - 1$ equations with $m + n$ unknowns, the identical condition obtained in the MODI method. Now if we consider the dual variables in terms of the primal form, the entering nonbasic variable is the largest positive c_{ij}^* value, where

$$u_i + v_j - c_{ij} = c_{ij}^*.$$

To verify this, turn the dual on its side as if it were the primal. The first column would contain u_1, v_1, and c_{11}. The sum of u_1 and v_1 corresponds to the z_{ij} value in the simplex tableau. Thus, for the primal minimization problem,

$$z_{ij} - c_{ij} = u_i + v_j - c_{ij}.$$

If we let $z_{ij} - c_{ij} = c_{ij}^*$ and multiply this equation through by -1, the relationship used to select the entering nonbasic variable in MODI results in

$$-c_{ij}^* = -(u_i + v_j - c_{ij})$$
$$-c_{ij}^* = c_{ij} - u_i - v_j.$$

Also note that u_i and v_j are unrestricted variables (allowing them to be positive or negative) since the primal constraints are equalities.

The Unbalanced Transportation Problem

Thus far only a balanced transportation problem, where supply equals demand, has been considered. However, in most realistic situations balanced cases are the exception. In general, most problems are **unbalanced** problems—supply exceeds demand or vice versa. In the case of an unbalanced problem, the transportation solution method requires a slight modification.

The first case to be considered results when demand exceeds supply. To demonstrate this unbalanced condition consider a modified version of the concrete transporting example used in the previous section. Assume that demand at site 3 has been increased from 60 truckloads to 90 truckloads. Total demand is now 310 units while supply remains 280 units. The problem is now reformulated as

$$\text{Minimize } Z = 8x_{11} + 5x_{12} + 6x_{13} + 15x_{21} + 10x_{22} + 12x_{23} + 3x_{31} + 9x_{32} + 10x_{33}$$

subject to

$$x_{11} + x_{12} + x_{13} = 120$$
$$x_{21} + x_{22} + x_{23} = 80$$
$$x_{31} + x_{32} + x_{33} = 80$$
$$x_{11} + x_{21} + x_{31} \leqslant 150$$
$$x_{12} + x_{22} + x_{23} \leqslant 70$$
$$x_{13} + x_{23} + x_{33} \leqslant 90$$
$$x_{ij} \geqslant 0$$

The $\leqslant$ demand constraints indicate that all units available will be supplied; however, one or more of the demand constraints will not be met. To reflect this condition in the transportation tableau, a "dummy" row is added to which all the units demanded, for which supply is not available, will be allocated. The modified tableau is shown in table 5.20.

Table 5.20 Unbalanced transportation tableau with a dummy row added (demand > supply)

From \ To	1	2	3	Supply
1	8	5	6	120
2	15	10	12	80
3	3	9	10	80
Dummy	0	0	0	30
Demand	150	70	90	310

In effect, an imaginary source has been added that balances supply and demand. The unit transportation costs of the three new destination cells are zero since allocations to those cells do not affect the solution. Actually, these dummy cells are analogous to slack variables, which, you will recall, have c_{ij} values of zero in the objective function.

The addition of the dummy source does not affect the methods for obtaining an initial solution or the stepping-stone and MODI methods for determining an optimal solution. The normal procedure should be followed in each case. The northwest corner method retains its same form. In the least-cost method, the dummy cells with c_{ij} values equal to zero are all tied for the minimum cost; thus, one of the cells is selected arbitrarily. (Alternatively, the dummy row can be ignored and allocations made according to the minimum positive cell. Then after all allocations have been made, the excess is allocated to the appropriate feasible dummy variable.) In the VAM method, the dummy c_{ij} values are used as the lowest column cost values when computing penalty costs. In the stepping-stone and MODI methods, the dummy cells are treated exactly the same as regular cells.

In the case where supply exceeds demand, the opposite modification of the tableau is required—a dummy *column* is added (see table 5.21). For example, in our original concrete transportation problem, if demand at destination 1 is 100 tons instead of the original 150, total demand becomes 230 and total supply remains at 280 units. Again, the methods of solution remain unchanged.

Table 5.21 Unbalanced problem, supply exceeds demand

From \ To	1	2	3	Dummy	Supply
1	8	5	6	0	120
2	15	10	12	0	80
3	3	9	10	0	80
Demand	100	70	60	50	280

Degeneracy

In order to evaluate all empty cells in determining the entering nonbasic variable, the number of occupied cells (i.e., basic variables) must be equal to $m + n - 1$. If a transportation tableau has less than $m + n - 1$ occupied cells it is degenerate. Degeneracy can occur either at the initial solution or during subsequent iterations.

Application of the stepping-stone or MODI solution methods is prohibited if degeneracy exists. Without $m + n - 1$ basic variables it is impossible to determine all the closed paths or solve the $m + n - 1$ MODI equations ($u_i + v_j = c_{ij}$).

Consider the sample transportation tableau in table 5.22 and the initial solution obtained by the northwest corner method.

Table 5.22 A degenerate case initial solution

From \ To	1	2	3	Supply
1	[8] 100	[5]	[6]	100
2	[15]	[10] 100	[12] 20	120
3	[3]	[9]	[10] 80	80
Demand	100	100	100	300

Because the demand at destination 1 is identical to the supply at source 1 (100 units), the chain of adjacent occupied cells is broken. As a result, there are only four basic variables when there should be five (i.e., $m + n - 1 = 5$). Thus, a degenerate solution exists.

To compensate for this deficiency, a fictitious allocation must be made to one of the empty cells to reestablish the $m + n - 1$ condition. Thus, 0 is allocated to one of two candidates, x_{12} or x_{21}. The allocation of 0 indicates that there are no actual units in that cell but it is treated as an occupied cell for solution purposes. It is, in effect, a dummy allocation that enables the identification of all closed paths. Possible candidates for the 0 allocation are x_{12} and x_{21} since they are the two variables that normally would have an allocation in the northwest corner method. (However, there are several other possible dummy candidates.) Selecting x_{12} as the dummy basic variable results in the following tableau (table 5.23), which can be evaluated in the usual manner.

Table 5.23 Tableau with x_{12} as a dummy basic variable

From \ To	1	2	3	Supply
1	[8] 100	[5] 0	[6]	100
2	[15]	[10] 100	[12] 20	120
3	[3]	[9]	[10] 80	80
Demand	100	100	100	300

Now consider the case where the solution becomes degenerate during one of the iterations of the solution process. Table 5.24 is an initial solution obtained via the northwest corner method.

Table 5.24 Initial solution via the northwest corner method

From \ To	1	2	3	Supply
1	[8] 120	[5]	[6]	120
2	[15] 30	[10] 50	[12]	80
3	[3]	[9] 30	[10] 50	80
Demand	150	80	50	280

Evaluation of the nonbasic variables for this tableau indicates that x_{31} should enter the solution basis. Allocating the maximum feasible amount of 30 units results in the tableau shown in table 5.25.

Table 5.25 First iteration of the tableau

From \ To	1	2	3	Supply
1	[8] 120	[5]	[6]	120
2	[15]	[10] 80	[12]	80
3	[3] 30	[9]	[10] 50	80
Demand	150	80	50	280

When the allocation of 30 units is made to x_{31}, the solution becomes degenerate since both x_{21} and x_{32} equal 30 units. In other words, two variables left the basis when x_{31} entered, rather than the normal exit of one variable. To proceed to the solution of this problem, 0 must be allocated to one of the two leaving variables, x_{21} or x_{32}. Doing so enables the further evaluation of the solution. Consider the example in table 5.26 with the 0 allocation made to x_{32}.

Table 5.26 Tableau with x_{32} as a dummy basic variable

From \ To	1	2	3	Supply
1	[8] 120	[5]	[6]	120
2	[15]	[10] 80	[12]	80
3	[3] 30	[9] 0	[10] 50	80
Demand	150	80	50	280

Evaluation of this tableau by the stepping-stone process identifies x_{12} as the entering nonbasic variable ($c^*_{12} = -\$9$). However, the stepping-stone path for this cell ($x_{12} \rightarrow x_{32} \rightarrow x_{31} \rightarrow x_{11}$) contains the 0 in x_{32} as the minimum amount to be subtracted. As such, the stepping-stone process results only in a transfer of the 0 from x_{32} to x_{12} (table 5.27). The solution process than continues in the normal manner.

Table 5.27 Transfer of dummy basic variable from x_{32} to x_{12}

From \ To	1	2	3	Supply
1	[8] 120	[5] 0	[6]	120
2	[15]	[10] 80	[12]	80
3	[3] 30	[9]	[10] 50	80
Demand	150	80	50	280

Multiple Optimal Solutions

The optimal solution to a transportation problem exists when the net cost change, c_{ij}^*, for all nonbasic variables is positive. However, as in the simplex tableau, when a nonbasic variable has a net cost change of zero (i.e., $c_{ij}^* = 0$), an alternative optimal solution is implied. The total cost value remains the same but a different solution mix (i.e., an alternative allocation pattern) exists.

Consider the optimal solution to the concrete transportation example shown again in table 5.28.

Table 5.28 Optimal transportation tableau

From \ To	1	2	3	Supply
1	[8] 70	[5]	[6] 50	120
2	[14]	[10] 70	[12] 10	80
3	[3] 80	[9]	[10]	80
Demand	150	70	60	280

Evaluation of the nonbasic variables in this tableau shows that the solution is optimal with a minimum total cost of \$1,920. However, the nonbasic variable x_{21} has a net cost change, c^*_{21}, of zero. Thus, a multiple optimal solution exists that can be identified by allocating as much as feasible to x_{21} according to the stepping-stone path—in this case 10 units. This results in a different allocation pattern (table 5.29) with a total cost of \$1,920.

Table 5.29 Alternative optimal solution

From \ To	1	2	3	Supply
1	[8] 60	[5]	[6] 60	120
2	[14] 10	[10] 70	[12]	80
3	[3] 80	[9]	[10]	80
Demand	150	70	60	280

Prohibited Routes

In many real-world problems, it is not possible to transport units over certain routes. A transportation problem with prohibited routes can be reflected by assigning a large c_{ij} value, M, to the x_{ij}, which is prohibited. The normal solution process is then conducted with the M value treated as any other c_{ij} value. As in a simplex tableau, the variable with $c_{ij} = M$ will eventually be forced out of the solution. (The same result can be obtained by blocking out the prohibited cell and ignoring it in the solution process.)

The Transshipment Problem

An important extension of the transportation formulation is the **transshipment problem,** in which each source and destination can also be an intermediate point of shipment from other sources or destinations. The transshipment problem can be solved with a few minor adjustments to the problem formulation of the transportation solution methods.

Consider the transportation problem example in tableau form in table 5.30.

Table 5.30 Transportation tableau

From (*i*) \ To (*j*)	1	2	3	Supply
1	12	11	7	70
2	8	6	14	80
3	9	10	12	50
Demand	60	100	40	200

If each of the i sources and j destinations can also be intermediate points of transshipment to another source or destination, the modified tableau in table 5.31 results.

Table 5.31 Transshipment problem in expanded tableau format

From \ To	$i=1$	$i=2$	$i=3$	$j=1$	$j=2$	$j=3$	Supply
$i=1$				12	11	7	70
$i=2$				8	6	14	80
$i=3$				9	10	12	50
$j=1$							
$j=2$							
$j=3$							
Demand				60	100	40	200

The original problem is located in the upper-right-hand quadrant. The other new cells represent the possibility of intermediate transshipments. For example, cell $i=1$ to cell $i=3$ indicates that units can be shipped from source 1 to source 3 before being shipped to a final destination, j. However, the transshipment tableau is incomplete in its present form.

The supply and demand requirements for these new rows and columns must reflect the fact that each source and destination can now equal *all* units supplied and demanded. In other words, while only 60 units are demanded at destination 1, the remaining 140 units can be shipped through this intermediate point before reaching the final destination. Therefore, 200 units can actually be routed through destination 1. Thus, the supply and demand requirements must be increased by an amount that is at least as large as the total demand (which also equals supply). In this problem, the total amount of 200 units is therefore added to each initial row supply value and each column demand value. Also, 200 units of supply are inserted in each newly added row, and 200 units of demand are inserted in each newly added column. These are currently zero, as shown in table 5.31. The resulting supply and demand values are given in table 5.32.

Table 5.32 Complete transshipment tableau

From \ To	$i=1$	$i=2$	$i=3$	$j=1$	$j=2$	$j=3$	Supply
$i=1$	[0] 200	[14]	[8]	[12]	[11]	[7] (70)	270
$i=2$	[3]	[0] 200	[5]	[8]	[6] (80)	[14]	280
$i=3$	[7]	[10]	[0] 200	[9] (50)	[10]	[12]	250
$j=1$	[2]	[1]	[11]	[0] 200	[8]	[3]	200
$j=2$	[6]	[5]	[3]	[1] (10)	[0] 190	[2]	200
$j=3$	[10]	[9]	[11]	[7]	[2] (30)	[0] 170	200
Demand	200	200	200	260	300	240	

The c_{ij} values for the new cells are the transshipment costs as determined by management. The costs are often different for shipment in opposite directions because of alternative modes of transportation and route conditions. For example, the cell representing the route from $i = 1$ to $j = 3$ is \$7 per unit, while the cost of going from $j = 3$ to $i = 1$ is \$10 per unit.

All c_{ij} values for this example are shown in table 5.32. The c_{ij} values are zero on the diagonal from upper left to lower right since there is no shipping from a source to itself ($i = i$) or from a destination to itself ($j = j$).

Table 5.32 also shows the optimal solution for this example obtained by using the VAM and stepping-stone methods. Interpreting the optimal solution, all the values on the zero cost diagonal can be ignored since they are meaningless. The remaining circled values yield the optimal solution. The transshipment network given by the optimal solution is presented in figure 5.5.

Figure 5.5 Transshipment solution network.

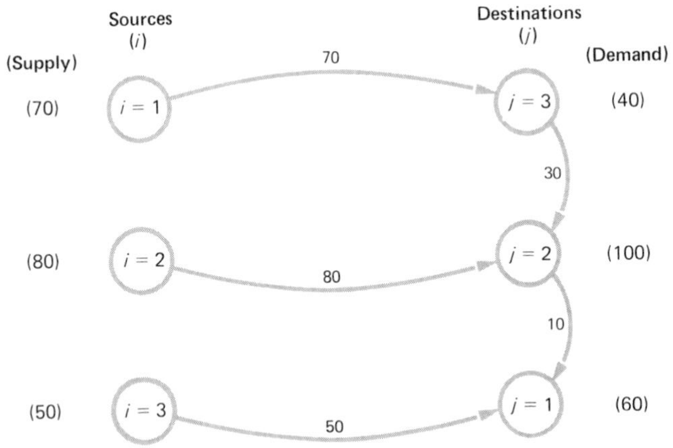

To demonstrate the intermediate-point shipping of the transshipment problem, observe that 70 units are shipped directly from source 1 ($i=1$) to destination 3 ($j=3$). However, 30 of those units are subsequently transshipped from destination 3 ($j=3$) to destination 2 ($j=2$), leaving a net total of 40 units at destination 3, the amount demanded. The 30 units transshipped from destination 3 to destination 2 are combined with 80 units shipped directly from source 2 ($i=2$) to destination 2 for a total of 110 units. However, 10 of these units are transshipped from destination 2 to destination 1, leaving a net total of the 100 units demanded at destination 2. The 10 units transshipped from destination 2 are combined with 50 units shipped from source 3, resulting in 60 total units at destination 1. The total minimum cost of the transshipment problem is \$1,490.

The Assignment Problem

An important variation of the transportation problem is the assignment problem, where there are an equal number of sources and destinations and each source supply and destination demand equals *one*. Consequently, the quantity allocated, or assigned, must be either zero or one. Because of its simple structure, the assignment problem can be solved most efficiently by its own unique method rather than by the previously described transportation methods. The assignment method is based on a theorem first proved by a Hungarian mathematician, Dr. Konig, and is, therefore, sometimes referred to as the **Hungarian method of assignment.**

To demonstrate the assignment problem and its solution, the following example will be employed. Three operators are available to be assigned to work on three machines in a manner that will minimize total cost. The cost of each operator, *i*, working on machine, *j*, is given as follows:

Operator *i*	Machine *j* 1	2	3	Supply
1	$7	3	5	1
2	8	9	2	1
3	9	6	8	1
Demand	1	1	1	3

If this problem is solved using standard transportation solution methods, the initial solution will be degenerate. (This can be easily verified by setting up the problem in the transportation tableau and determining the initial solution by any of the three methods.) However, the special characteristics of the assignment problem enable it to be solved in a more efficient manner.

The first step in the assignment method of solution is to develop an **opportunity cost table.** An opportunity cost is analogous to the penalty cost discussed in the VAM method. In other words, if the wrong course of action is taken, a lost opportunity (or cost) results. This table is constructed by first subtracting the minimum value in each row from all other values in the same row. For the example problem, the assignment tableau with row reductions made by subtracting 3 in row 1, 2 in row 2, and 6 in row 3 is shown in table 5.33. (Note that since supply and demand are always one, the demand row and supply column are deleted from assignment tableaus). The fact that constant values are subtracted from each row has no effect on the optimal solution. Since the whole row is reduced by the same amount, the relationship between variables (i.e., their relative magnitude) is not changed. Thus, the derivation of a zero in a row or column cell signifies the best course of action relative to other cells.

Table 5.33 Assignment tableau with row reductions

Operator \ Machine	1	2	3
1	4	0	2
2	6	7	0
3	3	0	2

This same procedure is repeated for each column by subtracting the minimum column value. Subtracting 3 from column 1, 0 from column 2, and 0 from column 3 results in the completed opportunity cost table (table 5.34).

Table 5.34 Completed opportunity cost table

Operator \ Machine	1	2	3
1	1	0	2
2	3	7	0
3	0	0	2

The zero elements in table 5.34 represent the lowest opportunity costs of assignment. Thus, to minimize total cost, assignments are made to those cells with 0 values. As such, the optimal assignment is:

Operator	Machine	Cost
1	2	$ 3
2	3	2
3	1	9
		$14

This problem is constructed in such a manner that the optimal solution was achieved after the completion of the opportunity cost table. That is, three unique assignments could be made. Next consider a case where such a condition does not exist. When this situation arises, an iterative solution process must be employed.

Consider the example cost table in table 5.35 for the assignment of four operators to four machines.

Table 5.35 Initial assignment tableau

Operator \ Machine	1	2	3	4
1	10	15	16	18
2	14	13	16	10
3	11	9	8	18
4	13	13	11	9

Row and column reductions for this cost schedule result in the opportunity cost table in table 5.36.

Table 5.36 Assignment tableau with row and column reductions

Operator \ Machine	1	2	3	4
1	0	4	6	8
2	4	2	6	0
3	3	0	0	10
4	4	3	2	0

For an optimal assignment to exist, table 5.36 must result in four unique assignments. Upon inspection it can be seen that this is not the case. Both operators 2 and 4 have an assignment to machine 4 *only*; thus, there is only one unique assignment between these two operators. A convenient way of determining if the appropriate number of unique assignments exist is to draw the minimum number of lines, horizontally and/or vertically, required to cross out all zeros. If the minimum number of lines drawn is equal to the number of rows (m) or columns (n), then an optimal assignment is present. Performing this operation on the opportunity cost table (table 5.36) results in table 5.37.

Table 5.37 Assignment tableau with line tests for independent zeros

Operator \ Machine	1	2	3	4
1	0	4	6	8
2	4	2	6	0
3	3	0	0	10
4	4	3	2	0

As can be seen, only three lines are required to cross out all zeros (although these three lines could have been drawn in different positions); thus, the required four unique assignments do not exist. To progress towards optimality, the next step is to subtract the smallest uncrossed cell value from all other uncrossed cell values. This same minimum value is also added to every value at the intersection of two lines. Thus, 2 is subtracted from the first three values in rows 2 and 4, and also added to 8 at the intersection of row 1 and column 4, and to 10 at the intersection of row 3 and column 4, as shown in table 5.38. By adding the value 2 to the intersected values we maintain the same relative difference between cell values.

Table 5.38 Adjusted assignment tableau

Operator \ Machine	1	2	3	4
1	0	4	6	10
2	2	0	4	0
3	3	0	0	12
4	2	1	0	0

The test for four unique assignments must be repeated. In this case, it now requires a minimum of four lines to cross out all zeros, regardless of how they are drawn. Analyzing table 5.38, the optimal assignments are as follows:

Operator	Machine	Cost
1	1	$10
2	4	10
3	2	9
4	3	11
		$40

However, there is also a second feasible optimal assignment to this problem (i.e., multiple optimal solutions):

Operator	Machine	Cost
1	1	$10
2	2	13
3	3	8
4	4	9
		$40

The solution procedure for the assignment method can be summarized as follows:

1. Develop the opportunity cost table through row and column reductions.
2. Draw the minimum number of horizontal and/or vertical lines necessary to cross out all zeros. If the number of lines satisfies the condition $m = n$, the optimal assignment has been determined. If not, perform step 3.
3. Subtract the minimum uncrossed value from all uncrossed cell values and add this same amount to all values at the intersection of lines.
4. Repeat the test for $m = n$ unique assignments.

Prohibited Assignments

It may occur that an assignment of an operator to a facility is prohibited—perhaps due to a physical impairment. In such cases a value of M should be assigned to the cell representing the prohibited assignment and the solution method continued normally.

Unequal Supply and Demand

An important requirement of the assignment problem is that the number of rows, m, equal the number of columns, n. However, in realistic situations this condition may not occur naturally. Often the number of available operators will exceed the number of machines, or vice versa. In such cases, a dummy row or column is added to balance the requirements. The procedure is the same as that utilized for the unbalanced transportation problem. The unit assignment costs for the dummy row or column will all be zero.

The cost table in table 5.39 represents a situation where there are 4 operators and 3 machines. In the optimal solution, one of the operators will be assigned to the dummy machine.

Table 5.39 An unbalanced assignment tableau (supply > demand)

Operator \ Machine	1	2	3	Dummy
1	7	10	4	0
2	9	8	6	0
3	11	3	2	0
4	7	6	3	0

Summary

In this chapter, some of the more interesting and useful variations of the general linear programming problem have been analyzed: the transportation, transshipment, and assignment problems. While these variations have been discussed within a limited range of examples, they have many useful applications in the real world.

This chapter completes the presentation and analysis of *linear* programming; however, the field of mathematical programming contains several more advanced and useful techniques, some of which will be discussed in subsequent chapters.

References

Ackoff, R. L., and Sasieni, M. W. *Fundamentals of Operations Research.* New York: John Wiley & Sons, 1968.

Charnes, A., and Cooper, W. W. *Management Models and Industrial Applications of Linear Programming.* New York: John Wiley & Sons, 1961.

Churchman, C. W.; Ackoff, R. L.; and Arnoff, E. L. *Introduction to Operations Research.* New York: John Wiley & Sons, 1957.

Hillier, F. S., and Lieberman, G. J. *Introduction to Operations Research.* 2d ed. San Francisco: Holden-Day, 1974.

Hitchcock, F. L. "The Distribution of a Product from Several Sources to Numerous Localities." *Journal of Mathematics and Physics* 20 (1941): 224–30.

Hoffmann, T. R. *Production: Management and Manufacturing Systems.* Belmont, Calif.: Wadsworth Publishing Co., 1967.

Koopmans, T. C., ed. *Activity Analysis of Production and Allocation.* Cowles Commission Monograph No. 13, New York: John Wiley & Sons, 1951.

Kwak, N. K. *Mathematical Programming with Business Applications.* New York: McGraw-Hill, 1973.

Levin, R. I., and Lamone, R. *Linear Programming for Management Decisions,* Homewood, Ill.: Richard D. Irwin, 1969.

Llewellyn, R. W. *Linear Programming.* New York: Holt, Rinehart and Winston, 1964.

Orchard-Hays, W. *Advanced Linear Programming Computing Techniques.* New York: McGraw-Hill, 1968.

Taha, H. A. *Operations Research.* 2d ed. New York: Macmillan, 1976.

Problems

1. A given transportation problem has the following costs and supply and demand requirements:

From \ To	1	2	3	4	Supply
1	$ 7	6	2	12	70
2	3	9	8	7	40
3	10	4	11	5	100
Demand	30	60	90	30	210

a. Find the initial solution using the northwest corner method, the least-cost method, and Vogel's approximation method. Compute total cost for each.
b. Using the VAM initial solution, find the optimal solution using the stepping-stone method. Compute total minimum cost for the solution.

2. A given transportation problem has the following costs and supply and demand requirements:

From \ To	1	2	3	4	Supply
1	$500	750	300	450	12
2	650	800	400	600	17
3	400	700	500	550	11
Demand	10	10	10	10	40

a. Find the initial solution using the northwest corner method, the least-cost method, and Vogel's approximation method. Compute total cost for each.
b. Using the VAM initial solution, find the optimal solution using the modified distribution method (MODI).

3. Solve the following transportation problem:

From \ To	1	2	3	Supply
1	$40	10	20	800
2	15	20	10	500
3	20	25	30	600
Demand	1,050	500	650	

4. A given transportation problem has the following costs and supply and demand requirements:

From \ To	1	2	3	Supply
A	\$6	7	4	100
B	5	3	6	180
C	8	5	7	200
Demand	135	175	170	

Find the initial solution using the least-cost method and Vogel's approximation method. Is the VAM solution optimal? Explain.

5. Given the following transportation problem:

From \ To	1	2	3	Supply
A	\$ 6	9	M	130
B	12	3	5	70
C	4	8	11	100
Demand	80	110	60	

a. Find the initial solution using VAM and solve using the stepping-stone method.
b. Formulate this problem as a general linear programming model.

6. Solve the following linear programming problem:

$$\text{Minimize } Z = 3x_{11} + 12x_{12} + 8x_{13} + 10x_{21} + 5x_{22} + 6x_{23} + 6x_{31} + 7x_{32} + 10x_{33}$$

subject to

$$x_{11} + x_{12} + x_{13} = 90$$
$$x_{21} + x_{22} + x_{23} = 30$$
$$x_{31} + x_{32} + x_{33} = 100$$
$$x_{11} + x_{21} + x_{31} \leq 70$$
$$x_{12} + x_{22} + x_{32} \leq 110$$
$$x_{13} + x_{23} + x_{33} \leq 80$$
$$x_{ij} \geq 0$$

7. Given the following transportation problem:

From \ To	A	B	C	D	Supply
1	$ 5	12	7	10	50
2	4	6	7	6	50
3	2	8	5	3	60
Demand	40	20	30	70	

a. Find the initial solution using the northwest corner method, the least-cost method, and VAM. Compute the cost for each method.
b. Solve using MODI.

8. Given the following transportation problem:

From \ To	1	2	3	Supply
A	$ 6	9	7	130
B	12	3	5	70
C	4	8	11	100
Demand	80	110	60	

a. Find the initial solution using the least-cost method.
b. Solve using the stepping-stone method.

9. Steel is produced and then stored in warehouses in three cities.

Warehouse Location	Weekly Production (tons)
A. Pittsburgh	150
B. Birmingham	210
C. Gary	320
	680

These plants supply steel to markets in four cities, which have the following demand:

Market Location	Weekly Demand (tons)
1. Detroit	130
2. St. Louis	70
3. Chicago	180
4. Norfolk	240
	620

The following shipping costs per ton have been determined:

From \ To	1	2	3	4
A	$14	9	16	18
B	11	8	7	16
C	16	12	10	22

However, due to a trucker's strike, shipments are presently prohibited from Birmingham to Chicago.

a. Set up a transportation tableau for this problem and determine the initial solution. Identify the method used to find the initial solution.
b. Solve this problem using MODI.
c. Are there multiple optimal solutions? Explain. If there are alternative solutions, identify them.
d. Formulate this problem as a general linear programming model.

10. Given the following linear programming problem:

$$\text{Minimize } Z = 24x_{11} + 9x_{12} + 6x_{13} + 18x_{14} + 10x_{21} + 18x_{22} + 14x_{23} + 12x_{24} + 17x_{31} + 21x_{32} + 20x_{33} + Mx_{34}$$

subject to

$$x_{11} + x_{12} + x_{13} + x_{14} \leq 100$$
$$x_{21} + x_{22} + x_{23} + x_{24} \leq 180$$
$$x_{31} + x_{32} + x_{33} + x_{34} \leq 200$$
$$x_{11} + x_{21} + x_{31} = 120$$
$$x_{12} + x_{22} + x_{32} = 100$$
$$x_{13} + x_{23} + x_{33} = 90$$
$$x_{14} + x_{24} + x_{34} = 140$$
$$x_{ij} \geq 0$$

a. Set up the transportation tableau for this problem and determine the initial solution. Identify the method used to find the initial solution.
b. Solve this problem using MODI. Compute total minimum cost.
c. Are there multiple optimal solutions? Explain. If there are alternative solutions, identify them.

11. Tobacco is purchased and stored in warehouses in four cities at the end of each growing season.

Location	Capacity (tons)
A. Charlotte	90
B. Raleigh	50
C. Lexington	80
D. Danville	60
	280

These warehouses supply tobacco to companies in three cities, which have the following demand:

Plant	Demand (tons)
1. Richmond	120
2. Winston-Salem	100
3. Durham	110
	330

The following railroad shipping costs per ton have been determined:

From \ To	1	2	3
A	$ 7	10	5
B	12	9	4
C	7	3	11
D	9	5	7

However, due to railroad construction, shipments are presently prohibited from Charlotte to Richmond.

a. Set up the transportation tableau for this problem and determine the initial solution using VAM and compute total cost.
b. Solve using MODI.
c. Are there multiple optimal solutions? Explain. If there are alternative solutions, identify them.
d. Formulate this problem as a linear programming model.

12. Given the following linear programming problem:

$$\text{Minimize } Z = 17x_{11} + 10x_{12} + 15x_{13} + 11x_{21} + 14x_{22} + 10x_{23} + 9x_{31} + 13x_{32} + 11x_{33} + 19x_{41} + 8x_{42} + 12x_{43}$$

subject to

$$x_{11} + x_{12} + x_{13} = 120$$
$$x_{21} + x_{22} + x_{23} = 70$$
$$x_{31} + x_{32} + x_{33} = 180$$
$$x_{41} + x_{42} + x_{43} = 30$$
$$x_{11} + x_{21} + x_{31} + x_{41} = 200$$
$$x_{12} + x_{22} + x_{32} + x_{42} = 120$$
$$x_{13} + x_{23} + x_{33} + x_{43} = 80$$

a. Set up the transportation tableau for this problem and determine the initial solution using VAM.
b. Solve using the stepping-stone method.

13. Oranges are grown, picked, and then stored in warehouses in Tampa, Miami, and Fresno. These warehouses supply oranges to markets in New York, Philadelphia, Chicago, and Boston. The following shipping costs per ton and supply and demand requirements exist:

From \ To	New York	Philadelphia	Chicago	Boston	Supply
Tampa	$ 9	14	12	17	200
Miami	11	10	6	10	200
Fresno	12	8	15	7	200
Demand	130	170	100	150	

Due to a distributor's agreement, shipments are prohibited from Miami to Chicago.

a. Set up the transportation tableau for this problem and determine the initial solution using the least-cost method.
b. Solve using MODI.
c. Are there multiple optimal solutions? Explain. If there are alternative solutions, identify them.
d. Formulate this problem as a linear programming model.

14. Given the following transportation problem:

From \ To	A	B	C	Supply
1	$7	10	6	300
2	4	9	8	150
3	5	7	5	400
Demand	200	400	350	

a. Set up the transportation tableau for this problem and find the initial solution by the northwest corner method, least-cost method, and VAM. Compute the cost for each method.

b. Using the VAM initial solution, solve the problem using the stepping-stone method.

15. A manufacturing firm produces diesel engines in four cities, Phoenix, Seattle, Omaha, and St. Paul. The company is able to produce the following engines per month:

Plant	Production
1. Phoenix	5
2. Seattle	25
3. Omaha	20
4. St. Paul	25
	75

Three trucking firms that purchase the engines have the following demand in their plants in three cities:

Firm	Demand
A. Greensboro	10
B. Columbus	20
C. Louisville	15
	45

The transportation costs from source to destination per engine are given in hundreds of dollars.

From \ To	A	B	C
1	$ 7	8	5
2	6	10	6
3	10	4	5
4	3	9	11

However, the Columbus firm will not accept engines made in Seattle and the Louisville firm will not accept engines from St. Paul; therefore, these routes are prohibited.

a. Set up the transportation tableau for this problem. Find the initial solution using VAM.
b. Solve for the optimal solution using the stepping-stone method. Compute the total minimum cost.
c. Formulate this problem as a linear programming model.

16. Given the following transportation problem:

From \ To	A	B	C	D	Supply
1	$12	10	9	15	36
2	10	8	2	10	25
3	9	5	13	8	30
Demand	26	40	25	30	

a. Find the initial solution using the northwest corner method.
b. Solve using the stepping-stone method.

17. Given the following transportation problem:

From \ To	A	B	C	D	E	Supply
1	$21	12	28	17	9	50
2	15	13	20	50	12	60
3	18	17	22	10	8	40
4	M	2	10	5	1	70
5	33	29	35	27	23	30
Demand	40	30	50	60	50	

a. Find the initial solution using VAM.
b. Solve using MODI.

18. Given the following transportation problem:

From \ To	A	B	C	D	Supply
1	$20	M	17	19	60
2	15	M	10	14	10
3	8	11	M	9	30
4	12	17	20	16	20
Demand	30	20	40	50	

a. Find the initial solution using VAM.
b. Solve using the stepping-stone method.

19. A distribution firm has three sources of supply, A, B, and C and three destinations 1, 2, and 3 that demand units. The shipping cost per unit as well as supply and demand are given as follows:

From \ To	1	2	3	Supply
A	$5	4	4	600
B	7	5	2	300
C	3	4	6	500
Demand	200	800	400	1,400

However, in addition to shipping directly from source to destination, units can be shipped between sources, between destinations, and from destinations to sources. The unit shipping costs for these routes are:

From \ To	A	B	C
A	$0	8	7
B	9	0	4
C	8	3	0

From \ To	1	2	3
1	$0	6	8
2	7	0	5
3	6	7	0

From \ To	A	B	C
1	$6	5	4
2	6	3	5
3	7	4	5

a. Formulate this problem as a transshipment model and solve.
b. Diagram the solution in network form.

20. A company produces units in three cities for outlets in three other cities. The shipping costs per unit as well as supply and demand are:

From \ To	Atlanta	Richmond	Newark	Supply
Dallas	$ 4	6	10	1,000
St. Louis	7	5	4	300
Chicago	8	7	6	100
Demand	200	400	800	

The company can also ship between sources and between destinations if it provides cheaper transportation. The unit shipping costs for these routes are:

From \ To	Dallas	St. Louis	Chicago
Dallas	$0	5	7
St. Louis	4	0	3
Chicago	6	2	0

From \ To	Atlanta	Richmond	Newark
Atlanta	$0	3	5
Richmond	2	0	4
Newark	6	6	0

Shipping costs from the original destinations to the original sources are the same as the shipping costs from sources to destinations.

a. Solve this problem as a transshipment model.
b. Diagram the solution in network form.

21. A manufacturing firm produces a product, which it stores in three different warehouses. The firm supplies its product to four retailers. Units can be shipped between warehouses and between retailers as well as from warehouses to retailers; however, units cannot be shipped from retailers back to warehouses. The amount supplied by each warehouse and the amount demanded by each retailer and shipping costs per unit are:

From \ To	R_1	R_2	R_3	R_4	Supply
W_1	\$10	14	10	5	80
W_2	12	9	6	7	120
W_3	7	11	8	13	110
Demand	50	100	100	60	

From \ To	W_1	W_2	W_3
W_1	\$0	4	10
W_2	5	0	9
W_3	7	3	0

From \ To	R_1	R_2	R_3	R_4
R_1	\$0	7	5	8
R_2	7	0	6	5
R_3	4	5	0	7
R_4	9	6	4	0

a. Formulate this problem as a transshipment model and solve.
b. Diagram this solution in network form.

22. Given the following shipping network:

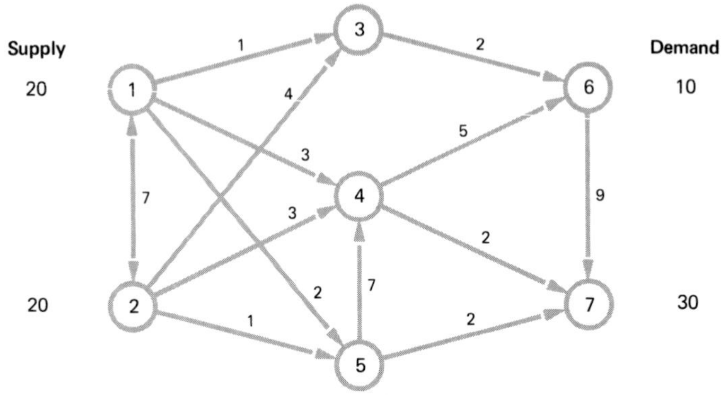

The values on the arrows are unit shipping costs. Nodes 1 and 2 represent sources that supply 20 units each while nodes 6 and 7 represent destinations where 10 and 30 units are demanded, respectively.

Formulate this network as a transshipment problem and solve to determine the optimal shipping routes that will minimize total cost.

23. A firm produces a product at three factories and sells the product at three retail stores. The firm has four warehouses to which all products are shipped for distribution to retail stores. Units are never shipped directly from one factory to another, nor are units shipped from one retail outlet to another. Likewise, units are never shipped directly from the factory to the retail store. However, units can be shipped from one warehouse to another. The firm wants to determine the shipping pattern from factories to warehouses to retail stores that will minimize cost. The various unit shipping costs are:

From \ To	W_1	W_2	W_3	W_4
F_1	\$ 5	8	4	7
F_2	3	12	6	2
F_3	10	4	9	5

From \ To	R_1	R_2	R_3
W_1	\$ 7	12	6
W_2	13	8	2
W_3	5	3	11
W_4	9	10	4

From \ To	W_1	W_2	W_3	W_4
W_1	\$ 0	4	8	3
W_2	9	0	7	10
W_3	6	2	0	5
W_4	12	11	4	0

The production capacities at the factories and the demand at the retail stores are:

Factory	Retail Store
F_1: 1,400	R_1: 1,100
F_2: 1,000	R_2: 2,200
F_3: 1,200	R_3: 500

a. Formulate this problem as a transshipment model and solve.
b. Diagram the shipping pattern in network form.

24. A plant has four workers to be assigned to four machines. The time (in minutes) required to produce a product by each worker on each machine is:

Worker \ Machine	A	B	C	D
1	10	12	9	11
2	5	10	7	8
3	12	14	13	11
4	8	15	11	9

Determine the optimal assignment and compute total minimum time.

25. A job shop has four machinists to be assigned to four machines. The hourly cost required to operate each machine by each machinist is:

Machinist \ Machine	A	B	C	D
1	\$12	11	8	14
2	10	9	10	8
3	14	8	7	11
4	6	8	10	9

However, due to a lack of experience, machinist 3 cannot operate machine B.

a. Determine the optimal assignment and compute total minimum cost.
b. Formulate this problem as a general linear programming model.

26. A pharmaceutical firm has five salespersons that the firm wants to assign to five sales regions. Because of previously acquired contacts, the salespersons are able to cover the regions in different amounts of time. The amount of time (in days) required by each salesperson to cover each region is:

Salesperson \ Region	A	B	C	D	E
1	17	10	15	16	20
2	12	9	16	9	14
3	11	16	14	15	12
4	14	10	10	18	17
5	13	12	9	15	11

Which salesperson should be assigned to each region in order to minimize total time? Identify the optimal assignments and compute total minimum time.

27. A manufacturing firm has five employees and six machines. The firm desires to assign the employees to the machines in a manner that will minimize cost. A cost table showing the cost incurred by each employee on each machine is:

Employee \ Machine	A	B	C	D	E	F
1	$12	7	20	14	8	10
2	10	14	13	20	9	11
3	5	3	6	9	7	10
4	9	11	7	16	9	10
5	10	6	14	8	10	12

However, due to union rules regarding departmental transfers, employee 3 cannot be assigned to machine E and employee 4 cannot be assigned to machine B.

a. Solve this problem, indicating the optimal assignment and computing total minimum cost.
b. Formulate this problem as a general linear programming model.

28. Given the following cost table for an assignment problem:

Worker \ Machine	A	B	C	D
1	$10	2	8	6
2	9	5	11	9
3	12	7	14	14
4	3	1	4	2

Determine the optimal assignment for this problem and compute total minimum cost. Identify all alternative solutions if multiple optimal solutions exist.

29. An electronics firm produces electronic components that it supplies to various electrical manufacturers. Past quality-control records indicate that the number of defective items produced were different for each employee. The average number of defects produced by each employee per month for each of six components is given in the following table:

Employee \ Component	A	B	C	D	E	F
1	30	24	16	26	30	22
2	22	28	14	30	20	13
3	18	16	25	14	12	22
4	14	22	18	23	21	30
5	25	18	14	16	16	28
6	32	14	10	14	18	20

Determine the optimal assignment that will minimize the total average monthly defects.

30. A dispatcher presently has six taxicabs at different locations and five customers who have called for service. The mileage from each taxi's present location to each customer is:

Cab \ Customer	1	2	3	4	5
A	7	2	4	10	7
B	5	1	5	6	6
C	8	7	6	5	5
D	2	5	2	4	5
E	3	3	5	8	4
F	6	2	4	3	4

Determine the optimal assignment(s) that will minimize the total mileage traveled.

31. A college athletic conference has six basketball officials it must assign to three conference games. Two officials must be assigned to each game. The conference office desires to assign the officials such that the total distance traveled by all six officials will be minimized. The distances each official would have to travel to each game are given in the following table:

Official \ Game	A	B	C
1	20	45	10
2	40	90	70
3	60	70	30
4	30	60	40
5	70	15	50
6	80	25	35

However, the conference office has decided not to assign official 4 to game A because of previous conflicts with one of the coaches.

a. Should this problem be solved by the transportation method or the assignment method? Explain.
b. Determine the optimal assignment(s) for this problem that will minimize the total distance traveled by the officials.

32. A university department head has five instructors to be assigned to four different courses. In the past all of the instructors have taught the courses and have been evaluated by the students. The rating for each instructor for each course is given in the following table (a perfect score is 100):

Instructor \ Course	A	B	C	D
1	80	75	90	85
2	95	90	90	97
3	85	95	88	91
4	93	91	80	84
5	91	92	93	88

The department head wants to know the optimal assignment of instructors to courses that will maximize the overall average evaluation. The instructor not assigned will be made a grader.

Solve this problem using the assignment method.

33. Solve the following linear programming problem:

$$\begin{aligned}\text{Minimize } Z = {} & 18x_{11} + 30x_{12} + 20x_{13} + 18x_{14} + 25x_{21} + 27x_{22} \\ & + 22x_{23} + 16x_{24} + 30x_{31} + 26x_{32} + 19x_{33} + 32x_{34} \\ & + 40x_{41} + 36x_{42} + 27x_{43} + 29x_{44} + 30x_{51} + 26x_{52} \\ & + 18x_{53} + 24x_{54}\end{aligned}$$

subject to

$$\begin{aligned}x_{11} + x_{12} + x_{13} + x_{14} &\leq 1 \\ x_{21} + x_{22} + x_{23} + x_{24} &\leq 1 \\ x_{31} + x_{32} + x_{33} + x_{34} &\leq 1 \\ x_{41} + x_{42} + x_{43} + x_{44} &\leq 1 \\ x_{51} + x_{52} + x_{53} + x_{54} &\leq 1 \\ x_{11} + x_{21} + x_{31} + x_{41} + x_{51} &= 1 \\ x_{12} + x_{22} + x_{32} + x_{42} + x_{52} &= 1 \\ x_{13} + x_{23} + x_{33} + x_{43} + x_{53} &= 1 \\ x_{14} + x_{24} + x_{34} + x_{44} + x_{54} &= 1 \\ x_{ij} &\geq 0\end{aligned}$$

6 Network Models, Including CPM/PERT

Network models have played an increasingly important role in management science for at least two major reasons: first, models of real-world systems are relatively easy to conceive and construct in network form and, second, network models can be communicated effectively to management as visual facsimiles of the real-world systems under consideration. Therefore, the concepts of network analysis, commonly referred to as network flow theory, represent important topics in the study of management science.

Applications of network analysis have been made in areas such as information and product flows, cybernetics, transportation, distribution, and travel systems, and planning and control of one-time projects. The transportation and assignment models in chapter 5, which were solved by special modifications of the linear programming solution algorithm, also represent network-oriented problems.

The network topics to be presented in this chapter include (1) the **shortest-route problem,** (2) the **minimal spanning-tree problem,** (3) the **maximal flow problem,** and (4) **CPM/PERT** for project planning and control.

The shortest-route problem involves finding the shortest route from an origin to a destination through a **network** of alternative routes. For example, this model can determine the travel route from one city to another, over a network of possible roads, that will minimize total travel distance, time, or cost.

The minimal spanning-tree problem involves determining the route of connections between *all points* of a network, with the objective of minimizing the total length of these connections. For example, this model can determine the routes for cable connections to all points, which are defined as cable television customers, while minimizing the amount of cable used.

The maximal flow problem involves allocation of flows in a capacitated network in order to maximize the total flow through the network, from a specified source to a destination. For example, this model can determine the maximum flow of oil from a refinery to a tank farm through a pipeline network with various specified flow capacities for each connecting pipeline.

The last network problem presented involves the analysis for planning and control of one-time projects. The project activities are analyzed with respect to time, which results in time-dimensional networks. Project planning and control problems are usually modeled and analyzed by the well-known network techniques CPM (Critical Path Method) and PERT (Program Evaluation and Review Technique). One of the most important functions of these techniques is to determine the longest time path through the network. This path is referred to as the **critical path** because it includes the project activities that require the most careful control in order to complete the project on time.

Network Terminology and Notation

Network models in management science have evolved from the more general **theory of graphs.** A graph model consists of two main components, nodes and branches. A **node** is one of a set of junction points, commonly denoted by a circle; certain pairs of the nodes are joined by connecting lines called **branches** (or arcs, links, or edges). When the branches of a graph are assumed to represent a flow of some sort, it is referred to as a *network*.

Figure 6.1 shows a network model consisting of six nodes and nine branches. Nodes are typically identified by numbers or letters within circles. Branches, the connecting lines (or arrows) between nodes, establish the model relationships. Figure 6.1 shows, for example, that since there is no connecting branch, there cannot be any flow or travel between nodes 2 and 3.

Figure 6.1 A sample network model.

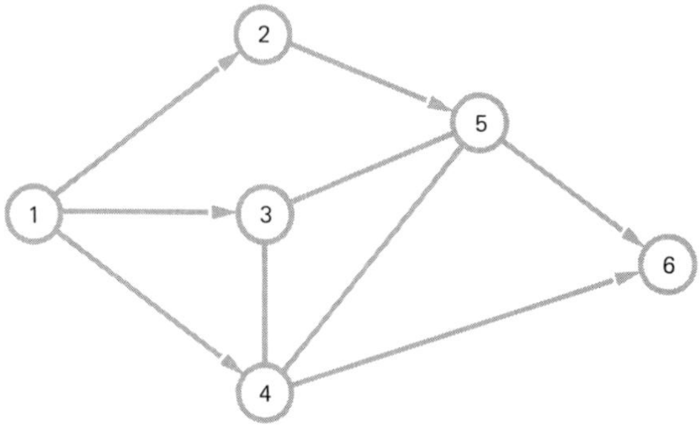

Nodes typically represent locations, such as cities, pumping stations, switching centers, and air terminals. Branches can represent connecting roads, pipelines, cables, air travel routes, etc., with associated quantities, such as distance, time, costs, and capacity.

Given that any pair of nodes may be referred to, in general, as i and j, a branch may be identified as branch (i,j) or branch (j,i). For example, the network in figure 6.1 consists of branches including (1,3), (3,4), and (4,6) but does not include branches (2,3) or (3,2). Note, that the (i,j) branch identification does not *necessarily* imply flow direction; that is, branch (3,4) is the same as branch (4,3), where flow may go in either direction between nodes 3 and 4.

A branch with a specified direction is referred to as a **directed branch,** which is oftentimes indicated graphically by a connecting line with an arrow showing the direction of required flow, such as branches (1,2), (1,3), and (1,4) in figure 6.1.

The flow times for an undirected branch may be different depending upon the direction of flow; that is, flow may go in either direction, but at different rates. In such a case, the flow values are indicated separately for the different directions of flow from i to j (i,j) and from j to i (j,i).

When the flow direction has been determined for a particular branch, the branch identification will denote the flow direction by $(i \rightarrow j)$, showing that the flow is from node i to node j. For example, if the flow from node 1 to node 6 is determined to be from 1 to 3 to 5 to 4 to 6, the undirected branches (3,5) and (4,5) are then given as $(3 \rightarrow 5)$ and $(5 \rightarrow 4)$. Of course, branches (1,3) and (4,6) are *directed* and must flow as indicated from $(1 \rightarrow 3)$ and $(4 \rightarrow 6)$.

A sequence of connecting branches between any two nodes i and j is referred to as a **chain** from i to j. For example, in figure 6.1, the sequence of branches including (1,3), (3,4), and (4,6) is one possible chain between nodes 1 and 6. If direction is specified along the chain, it is called a **path.** For example, if the flow between nodes 3 and 4 is from 3 to 4, then $(1 \rightarrow 3)$, $(3 \rightarrow 4)$, $(4 \rightarrow 6)$ is also a path (which can be stated as $1 \rightarrow 3 \rightarrow 4 \rightarrow 6$). A **cycle** is a chain connecting a node to itself—(3,4), (4,5), (5,3) is a cycle.

The origin in a network is usually referred to as the **source node,** and the destination is frequently called the **sink node.** Thus, flow or travel in a network is usually from the source to the sink node. In the figure 6.1 network, node 1 is the source and node 6 is the sink.

Shortest-Route Problem

The shortest-route problem is concerned with determining the shortest route from an origin to a destination through a connected network, given the distance associated with each branch of the network. For example, the nodes of the network may represent cities considered for travel from an origin city to a destination city, and the network branches may represent the roads with associated distances from one city to another. The problem is to determine the route to follow through the network of cities and connecting roads (nodes and connecting branches) in order to minimize total travel distance. Note that the objective could also be to minimize the total travel time or total travel cost. Also, the branches could be directed or undirected.

Various solution procedures have been proposed for the shortest-route problem, including linear programming. However, the following procedure is generally considered to be the simplest and quickest. The essence of the procedure is that it fans out from the origin node, successively identifying the next node that has the shortest route from the origin. Thus, the procedure not only finds the shortest route from the origin to the destination, but also, as a by-product of the solution procedure, finds the shortest route from the origin to every other node in the network.

This procedure can be illustrated by the network in figure 6.2. Based on this network we wish to determine the shortest route from the origin, 1, to the destination, 8. The nodes represent cities, and the branches represent roads with associated travel distances in hundreds of miles. Note that all branches are *undirected* so that travel may occur in either direction from node *i* to *j* or *j* to *i*, and the travel distance is the same in either case. However, there is a restriction in that travel cannot return from nodes 2, 3, or 4 to the origin node, 1, and it also cannot return from the destination node, 8, to nodes 5, 6, or 7.

Figure 6.2 Shortest-route network.

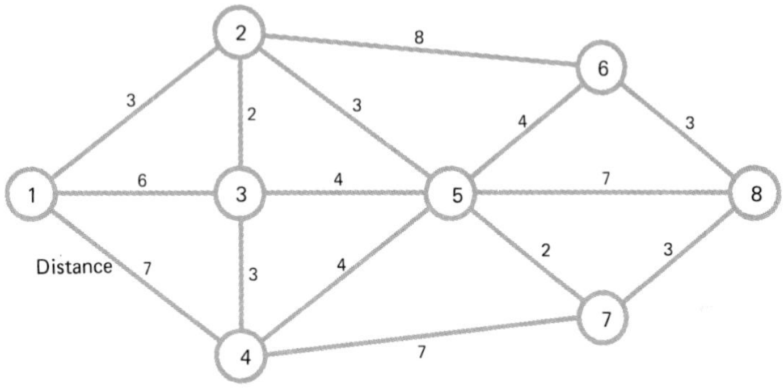

Solution Approach

The basic approach is to identify two sets of nodes, the **permanent set** and the **adjacent set.** Initially, only node 1, the origin, is placed in the permanent set. The nodes in the adjacent set are the nodes directly connected to the permanent set by connecting branches. Initially, in the figure 6.2 network, only node 1 is in the permanent set, and the adjacent set includes nodes 2, 3, and 4, which are connected to node 1 by branches (1,2), (1,3), and (1,4).

The basic steps of the procedure are as follows:

1. Designate the origin as the permanent set, and identify the adjacent set of nodes.
2. Identify the node in the adjacent set with the shortest distance from the origin.
3. *Store* the connecting branch (and its associated direction), which leads to the selected adjacent node. *Delete* from further consideration any other branches that lead from the permanent set to the selected adjacent set node.
4. Add the selected adjacent node to the permanent set.
5. Identify the new adjacent set of nodes, and repeat from step 2.

For example, *first* start with node 1 in the permanent set and nodes 2, 3, and 4 in the adjacent set (fig. 6.3). *Second,* select node 2 in the adjacent set as the node with the shortest distance from the origin; *third,* store branch (1→2); *fourth,* add node 2 to the permanent set, resulting in a permanent set consisting of nodes 1 and 2; and *fifth,* identify the new adjacent set consisting of nodes 3, 4, 5, and 6.

The initial case (*A*) and the first iteration (*B*) of the shortest-route solution procedure are shown in figure 6.3. Shown are the nodes in the permanent set (indicated by dashed lines) and the nodes in the connecting adjacent set. In addition, only the branches connecting the nodes in the permanent set to the adjacent set are shown. Note that after one iteration, node 3 is now connected to the permanent set (nodes 1 and 2) by both the branches (1,3) and (2,3). Note also that the *stored* branch (1→2) is denoted by the bold line from node 1 to 2.

Figure 6.3 (*A*) The initial permanent set. (*B*) Permanent set after one iteration.

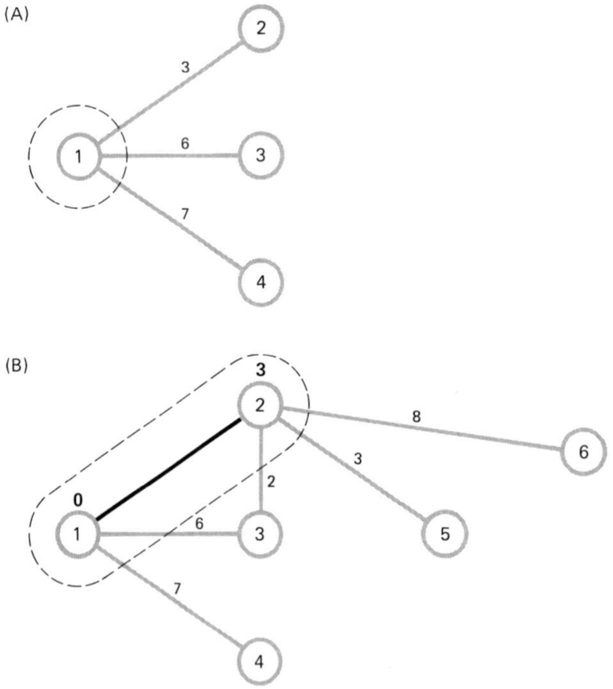

In order to select the next node for entry into the permanent set, return to step 2, which requires that the node in the newly defined adjacent set with the shortest route to the origin be identified. The computational procedure for this step is facilitated by assigning **labels** to nodes as they are put into the permanent set. The label value assigned to a node in the permanent set is defined as the shortest distance from that node to the origin (thus, the origin node, 1, has a label value of zero). In figure 6.3*B*, the label value of zero for node 1 and the label value of three for node 2 are each shown in boldface above the permanent set nodes.

To determine which node from the connecting adjacent set to enter into the permanent set (i.e., which node has the shortest route to the origin), simply compute the sum of the label value (for the node in the permanent set) and the connecting branch distance for each connecting node, and select the node that results in the minimum value.

The second iteration of the procedure for the selection of one of the nodes from the adjacent set is described in table 6.1. (Also refer to fig. 6.3*B*.)

Table 6.1 Second iteration for selection of adjacent set node

Permanent Set Node	Adjacent Set Node	Label Value	+	Connecting Branch Distance	=	Total Distance to Source
1	3	0	+	6	=	6
1	4	0	+	7	=	7
2	6	3	+	8	=	11
2	5	3	+	3	=	6
2	3	3	+	2	=	5 (minimum)

Thus, the node in the adjacent set with the shortest route to the origin is node 3 with a distance of 5 and with connecting branch (2→3). According to procedure, store branch (2→3) along with its associated flow direction. Note that branch (1,3) must also be deleted from further consideration, since we cannot have two optimal routes from the source to node 3. The new permanent set consists of nodes 1, 2, and 3, and a new adjacent set may now be identified.

Figure 6.4 shows the permanent set and the adjacent set after the second iteration. The adjacent set consists of nodes 4, 5, and 6. Note that the only difference between figure 6.3*B* and figure 6.4 is that the connecting branches (3,4) and (3,5) have now been added due to the redefinition of the permanent set (addition of node 3); and branch (1,3) has been deleted (shown as a dotted line) since branch (2→3) has been identified as part of the shortest route from node 1 to node 3.

Figure 6.4 Permanent set after two iterations.

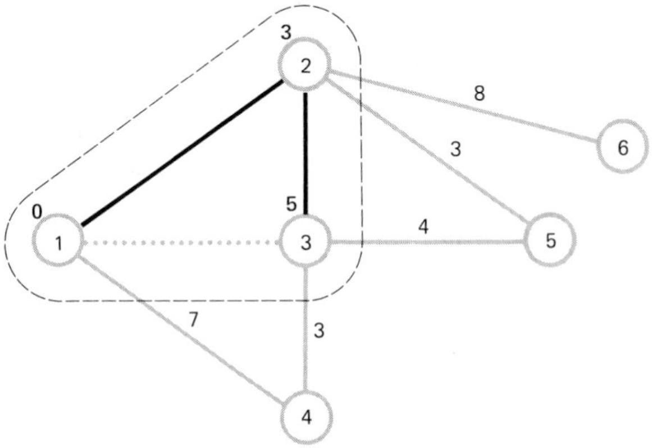

We are now ready to proceed with the third iteration in the solution procedure. The first three iterations are summarized in table 6.2. Note that the adjacent set node with the minimum total distance to the source is identified for each iteration. The branch to be stored is indicated, and any branches to be deleted are denoted by an X to the right of the connecting branch (i,j) identification. Table 6.2 also shows the action taken after each iteration.

Table 6.2 Iterations 1, 2, and 3 of shortest-route problem solution procedure

	Nodes								
Iteration	Permanent Set	Adjacent Set	Connecting Branch	Permanent Set Label		Connecting Branch Distance		Total Distance to Source
1	{1}	{2,3,4}	(1,2)	0	+	3	=	3 (minimum)
			(1,3)	0	+	6	=	6
			(1,4)	0	+	7	=	7
Action: Store Branch (1 → 2) Add Node 2 to Permanent Set								
2	{1,2}	{3,4,5,6}	(1,3)X	0	+	6	=	6
			(1,4)	0	+	7	=	7
			(2,6)	3	+	8	=	11
			(2,5)	3	+	3	=	6
			(2,3)	3	+	2	=	5 (minimum)
Action: Store Branch (2 → 3) Delete Branch (1,3) Add Node 3 to Permanent Set								
3	{1,2,3}	{4,5,6}	(1,4)	0	+	7	=	7
			(2,6)	3	+	8	=	11
			(2,5)	3	+	3	=	6 (minimum)
			(3,5)X	5	+	4	=	9
			(3,4)	5	+	3	=	8
Action: Store Branch (2 → 5) Delete Branch (3,5) Add Node 5 to Permanent Set								

After the third iteration, the permanent set consists of nodes 1, 2, 3, and 5, as shown in figure 6.5. The connecting branch (2→5) has been stored, and the connecting branch (3,5) has been deleted.

To summarize the first three iterations: nodes 2, 3, and 5 have been added to the permanent set (with node 1 initialized in the permanent set). Branches (1→2), (2→3), and (2→5) have been stored, showing the shortest route from the source node to nodes 2, 3, and 5 in the permanent set. Branches (1,3) and (3,5) have been deleted from further consideration (as shown by the dotted lines in fig. 6.5).

Figure 6.5 Permanent set after three iterations.

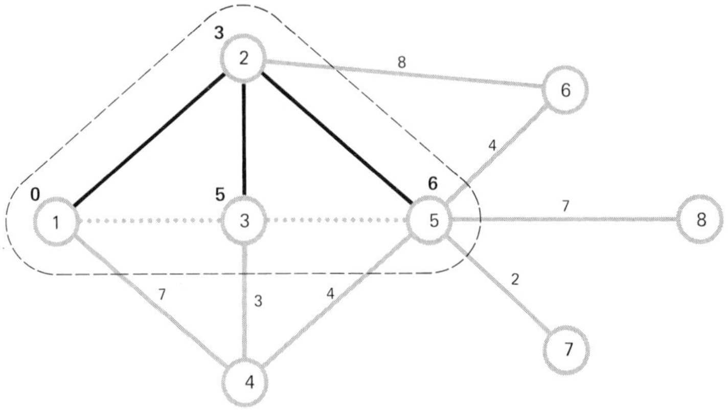

The permanent set now has one or more connecting branches to every other node in the network (fig. 6.5). Thus, the adjacent set consists of nodes 4, 6, 7, and 8. Note that node 4 now has three connecting branches from the permanent set, (1,4), (3,4), and (5,4), and node 6 has two connecting branches, (2,6) and (5,6). The label values are shown above each node in the permanent set indicating the shortest route distance from that node to the source.

Table 6.3 shows the remaining iterations required to obtain the shortest route from the source to the destination, node 8. Figure 6.6 shows the permanent and adjacent sets, with connecting branches, after iterations 4, 5, and 6. The seventh iteration yields the final solution, as shown in figure 6.7. This figure shows all network branches, with bold optimal route branches to indicate the shortest route from the source to every other network node. The label values give the shortest distance from the origin to each node.

Thus, the shortest route from the source to node 8, the destination, is given by branches (1 → 2), (2 → 5), (5 → 7), and (7 → 8), or path 1 → 2 → 5 → 7 → 8, with a distance of 1,100 miles.

Table 6.3 Iterations 4–7 of shortest-route problem solution procedure

Iteration	Nodes: Permanent Set	Nodes: Adjacent Set	Connecting Branch	Permanent Set Label		Connecting Branch Distance		Total Distance to Source
4	{1,2,3,5}	{4,6,7,8}	(1,4)	0	+	7	=	7 (minimum)
			(2,6)	3	+	8	=	11
			(3,4)X	5	+	3	=	8
			(5,6)	6	+	4	=	10
			(5,8)	6	+	7	=	13
			(5,7)	6	+	2	=	8
			(5,4)X	6	+	4	=	10
Action: Store Branch (1 → 4) Delete Branches (3,4) and (5,4) Add Node 4 to Permanent Set								
5	{1,2,3,4,5}	{6,7,8}	(2,6)	3	+	8	=	11
			(5,6)	6	+	4	=	10
			(5,8)	6	+	7	=	13
			(5,7)	6	+	2	=	8 (minimum)
			(4,7)X	7	+	7	=	14
Action: Store Branch (5 → 7) Delete Branch (4,7) Add Node 7 to Permanent Set								
6	{1,2,3,4,5,7}	{6,8}	(2,6)X	3	+	8	=	11
			(5,6)	6	+	4	=	10 (minimum)
			(5,8)X	6	+	7	=	13
			(7,8)	8	+	3	=	11
Action: Store Branch (5 → 6) Delete Branch (2,6) Add Node 6 to Permanent Set								
7	{1,2,3,4,5,6,7}	{8}	(5,8)X	6	+	7	=	13
			(7,8)	8	+	3	=	11 (minimum)
			(6,8)X	10	+	3	=	13
Action: Store Branch (7 → 8) Delete Branches (5,8) and (6,8) Add Node 8 to Permanent Set (Since Node 8 is the Destination; Stop; Optimal Solution Obtained)								

Figure 6.6 (*A*) Permanent set after four iterations. (*B*) Permanent set after five iterations. (*C*) Permanent set after six iterations.

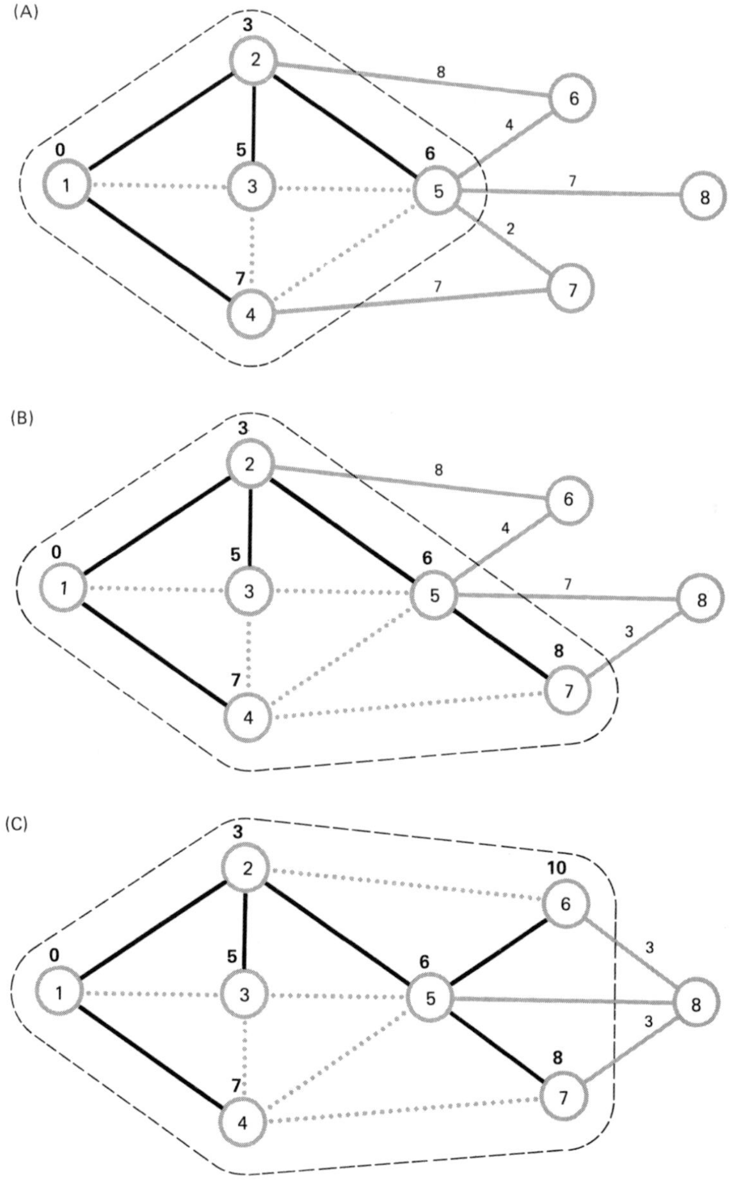

Figure 6.7 Final solution after seven iterations.

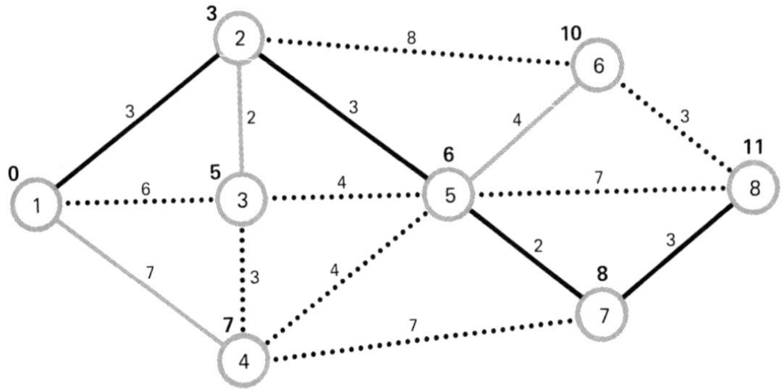

Minimal Spanning-Tree Problem

The minimal spanning-tree problem is a variation of the shortest-route problem. However, the minimal spanning-tree problem is easier to solve and the interpretation of the problem objective is different. Whereas the objective of the shortest-route problem is to determine the minimum distance (time or cost) *route* from a specified origin to a specified destination, the objective of the minimal spanning-tree problem is to *connect* all the network nodes such that the total branch lengths required are minimum (distance, time, or cost). The resulting solution forms a *tree* that "spans" (connects) all designated points (e.g., cities, terminals, street intersections, retail outlets).

There are numerous practical applications of the minimal spanning-tree problem—for example, determination of the minimum length of cable needed to connect a given set of homes to cable television, transmission wire to connect a given set of cities to electricity, pipeline to connect a given set of terminals, track to connect rail service to a set of on/off loading stations, bus routes to connect to specified stops. In general, it is applicable to transportation, distribution, and communication networks where all specified nodes (intersections, terminals, etc.) must be connected.

Solution Approach

The minimal spanning-tree problem can be solved rather easily by arbitrarily selecting any node and connecting it to the closest node. This is followed by selecting the node closest to *either* of the two nodes already connected and connecting this third node to the closest node in the initial set. This process is repeated until all nodes have been connected. The procedure is summarized as follows:

1. Arbitrarily select any node of the network and connect it to the nearest node (in terms of a specified measurement, such as distance, time, or cost).

2. Identify the unconnected node that is nearest to a connected node, and connect these two nodes. If there is a tie, arbitrarily choose between them.
3. Repeat step 2 until all nodes have been connected. The resulting spanning tree of connected nodes results in minimum total branch length.

The solution procedure is demonstrated for the same network given in figure 6.2, which is reproduced in figure 6.8. It should be pointed out that it is assumed that the branches in figure 6.8 represent the feasible connections between the nodes. For example, a high-voltage power transmission line must be connected to a designated set of businesses (nodes) via underground cable, and the lines must follow existing streets (such as the branches shown in fig. 6.8). The values given along the branches represent the street distances (in miles) between buildings to be connected.

Figure 6.8 Minimal spanning-tree network.

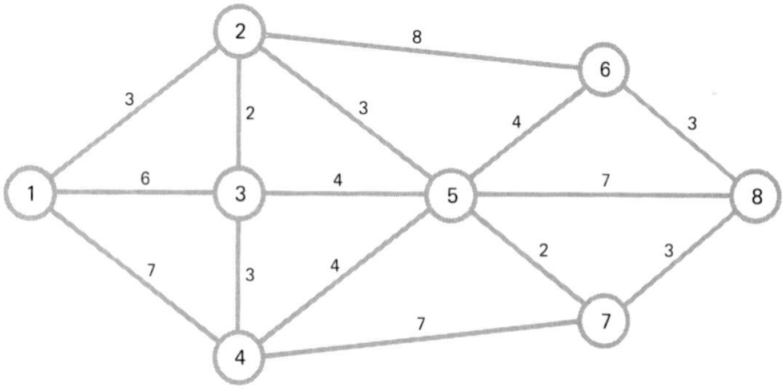

We could arbitrarily begin with *any* node in the network, however, node 1 will be selected to facilitate comparison with the shortest-route problem. The unconnected node closest to node 1 is node 2, with a distance of three miles. Therefore, node 2 is connected to node 1 (as shown by the bold line in fig. 6.9).

Figure 6.9 Connection of node 1 and node 2.

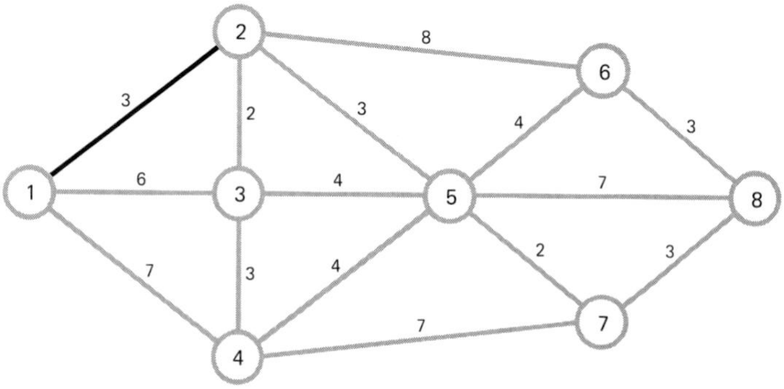

The unconnected node closest to either node 1 or node 2 is node 3, via branch (2,3) with a distance of two. Thus, node 3 is connected to node 2, as shown by the bold line in figure 6.10.

Figure 6.10 Selection of node 3 as closest unconnected node.

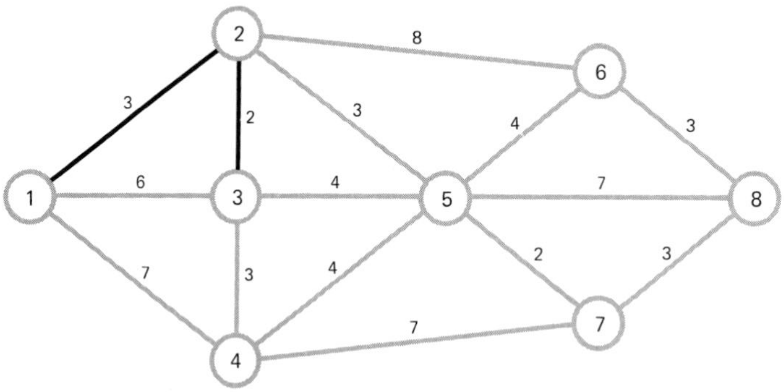

There is a tie for closest unconnected node to any of the connected nodes 1, 2, or 3. Node 4 is a distance of three from node 3, and node 5 is also a distance of three from node 2. We can, therefore, arbitrarily select either candidate. Node 4 is selected to connect to node 3, as shown in figure 6.11.

Figure 6.11 Arbitrary selection of node 4 as closest unconnected node.

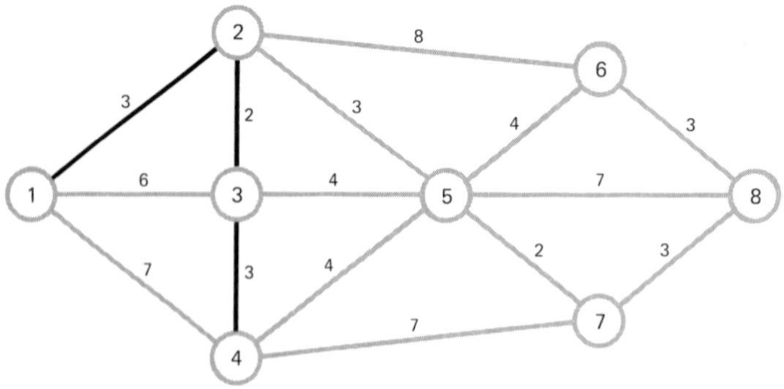

Node 5 is now the closest unconnected node, with a distance of three from node 2. According to procedure, node 5 is connected to node 2, as shown by the bold line in figure 6.12.

Node 7 is now the closest unconnected node, with a distance of two to node 5. It is connected as shown in figure 6.13.

The unconnected node closest to any connected node is now node 8, a distance of three from node 7. Node 8 is connected to node 7 (fig. 6.14).

Figure 6.12 Selection of node 5 as closest unconnected node.

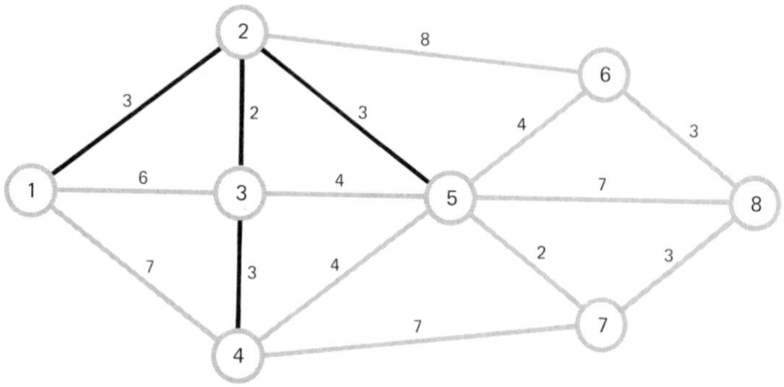

Figure 6.13 Selection of node 7 as closest unconnected node.

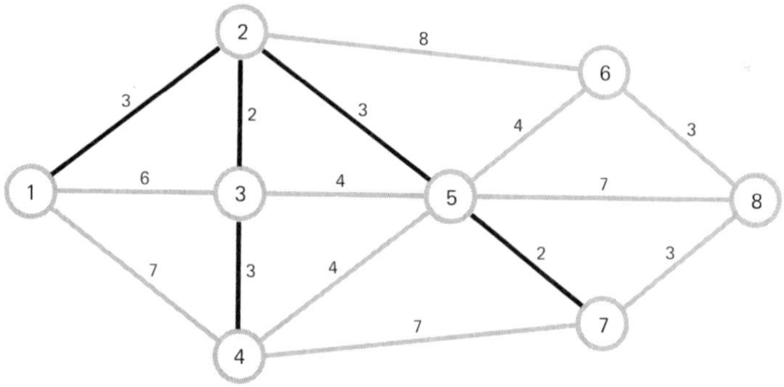

Figure 6.14 Selection of node 8 as closest unconnected node.

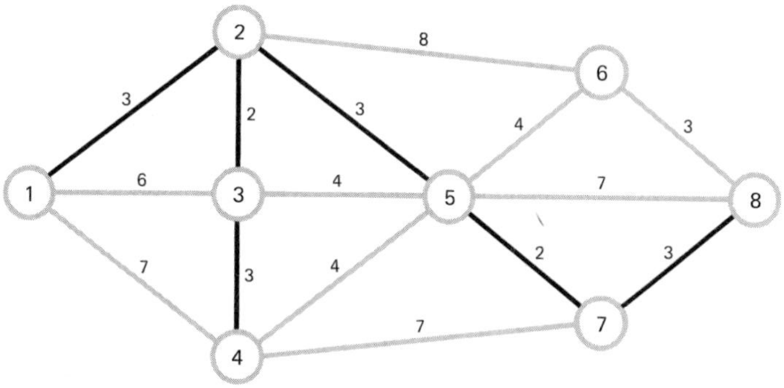

Finally, the only unconnected node remaining is 6, and it is closest to node 8. Node 6 is connected to node 8 as shown in figure 6.15.

Figure 6.15 Final solution. Selection of node 6 as closest unconnected node.

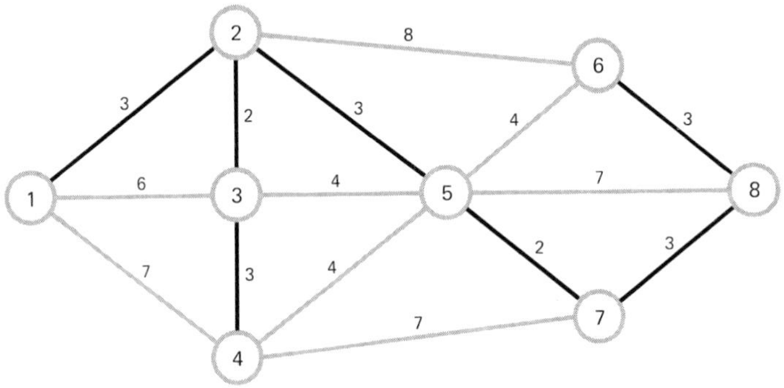

All nodes are now connected, resulting in the minimal spanning tree of connections and a total length of nineteen miles of underground cable. As stated earlier, any node may be initially selected to begin the solution process without affecting the final results. This can be verified by choosing a node other than node 1 and repeating the solution procedure for this example.

Finally, the solution for the minimal spanning-tree problem, shown in figure 6.15, may be contrasted to the solution for the shortest-route problem, which was shown in figure 6.7. Note that different solutions have been obtained for the two different problem definitions.

Figure 6.15 shows the minimum length of cable required to connect all buildings (nodes) in the network. On the other hand, figure 6.7 shows the shortest travel route from the node 1 origin to a *specified* destination, where designation of one node in the network versus another node as the destination represents, in effect, a *different trip*. This is why route (1→4) is shown in figure 6.7 as the shortest route from node 1 to node 4; node 4 has been identified as the destination for that particular trip. Similarly, branch (5→6) is identified in figure 6.7 as part of the shortest-route path if the objective is to get from node 1 to the destination designated as node 6.

As a concluding note, it should be pointed out that neither the shortest-route problem nor the minimal spanning-tree problem addresses the problem of routing a traveler through a sequence of cities (nodes), where all cities must be visited at least once. This represents the so-called **traveling salesman problem,** where the objective is to determine the sequence in which the cities should be visited in order to minimize the total distance traveled. The traveling salesman problem represents a class of problems known as combinatorial problems, which usually require solution by the **branch-and-bound method** presented in chapter 15.

Maximal Flow Problem

The maximal flow problem involves routing flows through a network in order to maximize the total flow from a specified source to a specified destination. Examples include product flow through a network of pipelines, message flow through a communication network, and vehicle flow over a network of roads.

The flow network consists of nodes connected by branches, where nodes might represent street intersections and branches represent the streets. In the case of a pipeline network, the nodes might represent junction points at valves or pumping stations, and the branches the connecting pipelines. The objective is to determine the maximum achievable flow from the source or origin of the network to the sink or destination, where each branch has a specified capacity restriction associated with it (i.e., street vehicle-flow capacity, pipeline product-flow capacity, and transmission wire message-flow capacity).

Prior to presentation of the solution procedure for the maximal flow problem, several key concepts will first be presented.

Concepts and Assumptions of the Maximal Flow Problem

An essential assumption of the maximal flow problem is **conservation of flow.** This assumption states that total flow into a node must be exactly equal to total flow out of the node. Figure 6.16 illustrates this concept, where the values along the arrows represent the flow quantities into and out of node *i*. Note that the total flow of 14 into node *i* is equal to the total flow out of node *i*.

Figure 6.16 Conservation of flow at node *i*.

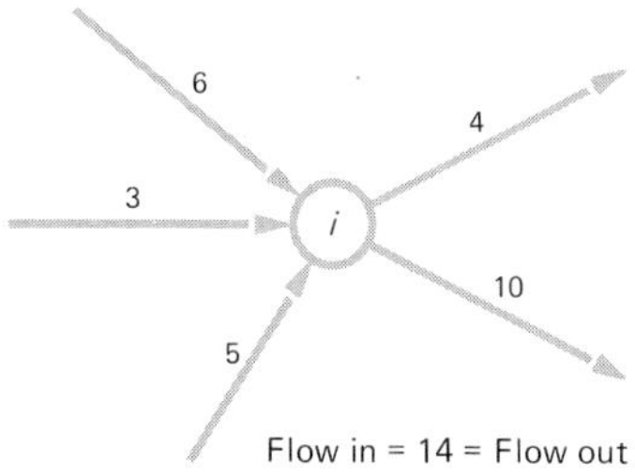

The maximal flow problem may be applied to networks consisting of directed or undirected branches. Generally, the physical interpretation for directed versus undirected branches is relatively straightforward. For example, a network of natural gas pipelines, connecting at valves, represents a network of *undirected* branches—gas may flow in either direction through a pipeline of specified capacity regardless of flow direction. An example of a network of *directed* branches is an irrigation canal network where flow is controlled by gravity—the water must flow one direction only, downhill, along a canal of specified capacity. Another example of a directed branch is a one-way street in a traffic network with an associated one-way vehicle flow capacity.

It is apparent that when the flow is directed, or restricted, to one direction, the only meaningful capacity restriction is in the flow direction. However, in the case of undirected branches where flow may go in either direction, it is not necessarily true that the branch is also *capacity undirected*. The natural gas pipeline represents an undirected capacity; the capacity of each pipeline remains the same regardless of the direction of gas flow. On the other hand, while a two-way street represents an undirected flow branch (flow can go in both directions), it may be *capacity directed* if it has one lane in one direction and three lanes in the opposite direction.

Anytime a real-world maximal flow problem involves a possible *simultaneous* two-way flow with directed capacities, it is usually most convenient to treat this as two separate directed branches with associated capacities.

The final topic of interest in maximal flow problems involves the concept of **net flow** along a branch. For example, in the case of the two-way street, it will be the **net flow** in one direction or the other that will be of interest in a maximal flow problem. Thus, if x_{ij} represents the traffic flow from intersection i to intersection j, and x_{ji} the flow from j to i, the net flow will be the larger value minus the smaller value. This solution will also yield the direction of net flow.

This concept is of special interest since the solution method of the maximal flow problem requires that we temporarily allow flows in *either direction* along a directed branch during the process of determining the solution, and then calculate the net flow (in the restricted direction) at the end of the solution procedure.

This particular feature of the maximal flow problem solution procedure is illustrated in figure 6.17. Represented is a network of five natural gas pipelines, connected at points identified as junctions C and D. There are two input valves, A and B, and two output valves, E and F. The natural gas can flow through the pipelines under pressure at the capacity rates shown.

Figure 6.17 Natural gas pipeline diagram.

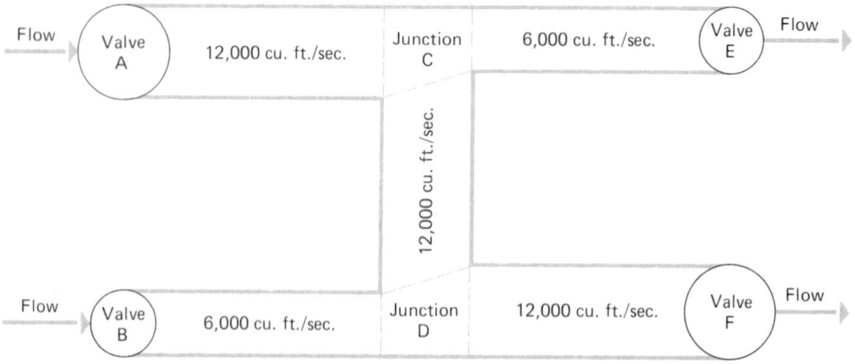

In network terminology, the nodes are identified as A, B, C, D, E, and F. The branches (pipelines) are denoted as (A,C), (B,D), (C,D), (C,E), and (D,F). Note that natural gas flows in at valves A and B, and out at valves E and F. The pipeline capacities are given as 12,000 cubic feet per second for branches (A,C), (C,D), and (D,F) and as 6,000 cubic feet per second for branches (B,D) and (C,E). Junctions C and D simply represent interconnecting points of the pipelines, but not valves.

Suppose that initially only valves A and F are opened (valves B and E remain closed). Natural gas would flow at the rate of 12,000 cubic feet per second along the path $A \rightarrow C \rightarrow D \rightarrow F$, as soon as pipes (C,E) and (B,D) have filled. Note especially that the flow from node C to D is 12,000 cubic feet per second. Now, suppose that valves B and E are also opened. Almost instantaneously, the gas flow becomes as follows:

Branch (pipe)	Flow (cu. ft./sec.)
(A→C)	12,000
(C→E)	6,000
(B→D)	6,000
(D→F)	12,000
(C→D)	6,000

The net flow from node C to D is now reduced from 12,000 cubic feet per second to 6,000 cubic feet per second. The change that has taken place is that 6,000 of the 12,000 cubic feet per second of gas that had been flowing along the path $A \rightarrow C \rightarrow D \rightarrow F$ has been diverted (redirected) to $(C \rightarrow E)$. The 12,000 cubic feet per second of gas now flowing through $(D \rightarrow F)$ is made up of 6,000 cubic feet per second from $(B \rightarrow D)$, the newly opened valve, and 6,000 cubic feet per second still coming from $A \rightarrow C \rightarrow D$.

It is interesting to note that if we had simply retained the initial flow of 12,000 cubic feet per second along the path $A \rightarrow C \rightarrow D \rightarrow F$, we could think of the new 6,000 cubic feet per second flow as following path $B \rightarrow D \rightarrow C \rightarrow E$. This would yield a fictitious two-way flow for (C,D) of:

Branch (pipe)	Flow (cu. ft./sec.)
(C→D)	12,000
(D→C)	6,000

By subtracting the smaller flow from the larger, we obtain the direction and quantity of the actual flow through $(C \rightarrow D)$ of 6,000 cubic feet per second.

The solution method for the maximal flow problem employs the approach of temporarily assigning fictional flows in the wrong direction along a branch—in this instance, the assignment of a flow of 6,000 cubic feet per second along $(D \rightarrow C)$—in order to represent the real effect of redirecting part of the previously assigned flow—redirection of 6,000 cubic feet per second from $(C \rightarrow D)$ to $(C \rightarrow E)$.

Solution Approach

For each *iteration* of the solution procedure for the maximal flow method, perform the following steps:

1. Find any path through the network, from the source node to the sink node with *some* available flow capacity on each branch of the selected path. (If no such path exists, the optimal solution has been reached).
2. Determine, on the path selected, the branch with the smallest flow capacity currently available. Call this capacity C, and allocate a *flow* of C to each branch on the selected path.
3. *Decrease* the currently available flow capacity of each branch on the selected path by amount C.
4. *Increase* by amount C the flow capacity, *in the reverse direction*, for each branch of the selected path. (Note: this step is performed in order to keep track of the potential flow redirection possible for each branch on the selected path, as was described for the natural gas example.) Return to step 1.

The solution procedure will first be applied to the very simple network shown in figure 6.18. The flow direction is from left to right, from source node 1 to sink node 4. The branch flow capacities are given as the numbers just above or to the right of each branch—next to the node from which the flow emanates. For example, the flow capacity for branch (1,2) is 12 in the direction from node 1 to node 2. The flow capacity for that same branch in the reverse direction, from node 2 to node 1, is zero. Branch (1,2) is a directed branch, in the direction from node 1 to node 2.

Figure 6.18 Maximal flow network.

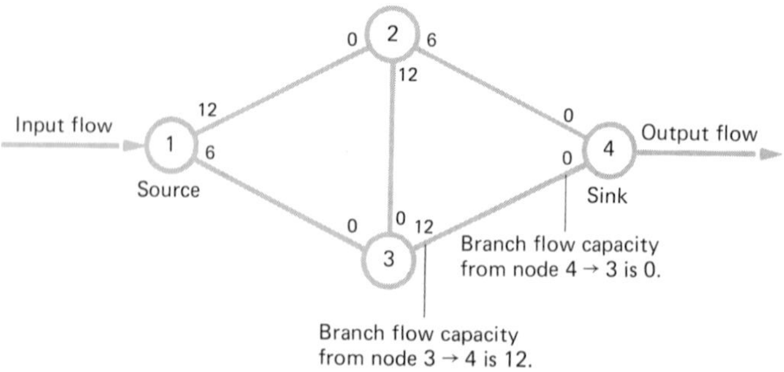

Inspection of the specified capacities for all the branches of the network reveals that all branches are directed, as indicated by positive flow capacities at one end of the branch (next to the node from which the flow emanates) and by zero flow capacities at the other end of the branch.

It is apparent that this network is quite similar to the natural gas example, except that we now have a single source and a single sink. It is also apparent by inspection that the optimal solution will be flows of 12 for (1→2), 6 for (1→3),

6 for (2→3), 6 for (2→4), and 12 for (3→4). However, in order to illustrate the concept of temporary assignment of a fictional flow in the wrong direction along a branch, we will go through the steps of the solution procedure as follows.

1. Find any path through the network with positive flow capacity on each branch. Assume that path 1→2→3→4 is selected because we can see that this will allow us to assign the maximum flow of 12 on the first try.
2. Determine, on the path selected, the branch with the smallest flow capacity. Call this capacity C and allocate a flow of C to each branch selected. Allocate a flow of $C = 12$ to each of the branches (1→2), (2→3), and (3→4).
3. Decrease by amount C the currently available flow capacity of each branch on the selected path. Decrease each flow capacity number shown on the 1→2 →3→4 path branches by crossing out the current capacity (12 in each case) and replacing it with the remaining capacity (zero in each case). This step is shown in figure 6.19. This shows that there are no remaining flow capacities on those branches.

Figure 6.19 Decrease by flow capacity 12.

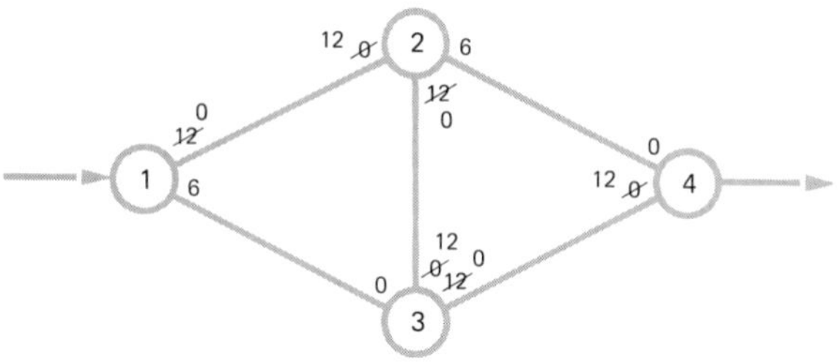

4. Increase by amount C the flow capacity in the reverse direction for each branch of the selected path. Increase each flow capacity number along the path 4→3→2→1 by crossing out the current capacities (zero in each case) and replace with the value added (12). This step is also shown in figure 6.19.

Note that the network in figure 6.19, with revised flow capacities, now shows possible flows of 6 from (1→3) and (2→4) and a possible flow of 12 from (3→2), even though branch (2,3) was originally defined as a directed branch in the direction of (2→3). Thus, we are going to allow a temporary assignment of flow in the wrong direction in order to redirect a portion of the current flow from node 2 to node 3 to a different path. If we did not do this, we would have to stop at this point, because there is no place for flow from (1→3) to go, since the capacity along (3→4) is used up.

Therefore, return to step 1 of the solution procedure and identify path 1→ 3→2→4 in figure 6.19 with a potential maximal flow capacity of 6 units, as dictated by the flow capacities on both branches (1→3) and (2→4). We, therefore, allocate a flow of 6 to branches (1→3), (3→2), and (2→4).

Next reduce the branch flow capacities by the amount of assigned flow on the 1→3→2→4 path; and *increase* the reverse-direction capacities for the same branches—the 4→2→3→1 path. This procedure is shown in figure 6.20 where the old numbers have been crossed out and replaced by the new values. Note that branch (2,3) has now had its capacities revised twice. The six on branch (2,3) next to node 2 indicates that the actual remaining capacity for branch (2→3) is 6 units. The six next to node 3 indicates a flow of 6 units from node 2 to node 3, which leaves us with a remaining flow of 6 that could potentially be redirected and thought of as a potential flow of 6 from node 3 to node 2.

Figure 6.20 Decrease by assigned flow 6.

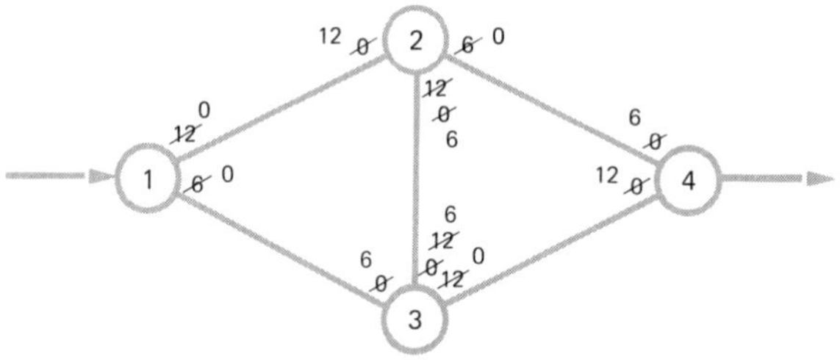

Since there are no remaining positive capacity paths from the source to the sink, the optimal solution has been obtained. The solution is as follows:

Iteration	Path	Assigned Flow
Iteration 1	1 → 2 → 3 → 4	12
Iteration 2	1 → 3 → 2 → 4	6

As a final step, inspect each branch assignment to identify any flow allocations in both directions. Branch (2,3) has the following two-way flow assignments:

Branch	Flow Assignment
(2 → 3)	12
(3 → 2)	6

Therefore, simply deduct the smaller flow assignment from the larger, which yields the true net flow assignment of 6 for branch (2→3). Thus, the maximum flow for the network is 18 units summarized as follows:

	Branch		Flow	
Flow In	(1 → 2)		12	18
	(1 → 3)		6	
	(2 → 3)		6	
	(2 → 4)	Flow Out	6	18
	(3 → 4)		12	

The network for a more complex example is shown in figure 6.21. Recall that paths with positive flow capacities may be chosen arbitrarily, so the number of iterations required to reach a solution can vary depending upon the order of the selection of paths.

Figure 6.21 Maximal flow network.

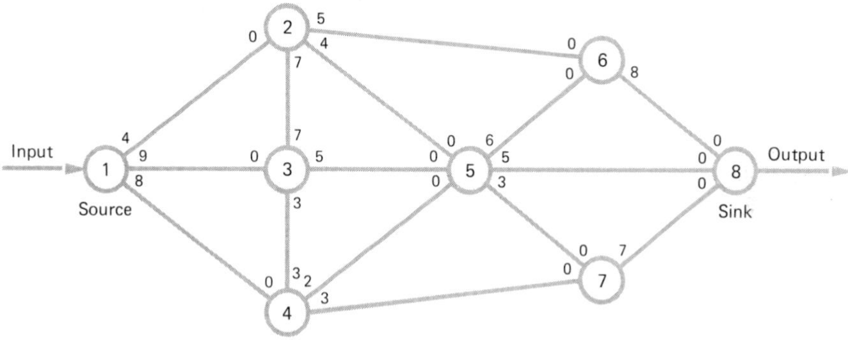

Iteration 1 Path 1→2→6→8 is arbitrarily selected and a maximum possible flow allocation of 4 units is assigned. The maximum flow for this path is due to the capacity of branch (1,2). Figure 6.22 shows the revision of flow capacities on the selected path for iteration 1.

Figure 6.22 Flow capacities after one iteration.

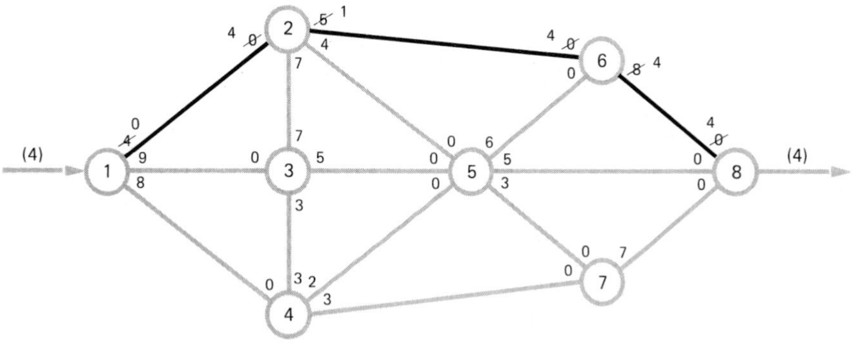

Iteration 2 Path 1→3→5→8 is arbitrarily selected with a flow allocation of 5 units. Figure 6.23 shows the branch capacity revisions for this iteration.

Iteration 3 Path 1→4→7→8 is arbitrarily selected with a flow allocation of 3 units. The maximum flow for this path is determined by the capacity of branch (4,7). Figure 6.24 shows this iteration.

Iteration 4 Path 1→3→2→5→6→8 is next selected as a path with remaining available flow capacity. The maximum possible flow allocation of 4 units is assigned to this path. See figure 6.25.

Iteration 5 Path 1→4→5→7→8 is selected with a flow allocation of 2 units. Figure 6.26 shows this iteration.

6.26

Iteration 6 Path 1→4→3→2→6→5→7→8 is selected as the only remaining path with positive flow capacity. A maximum flow allocation of 1 is assigned. Figure 6.27 shows this iteration.

Figure 6.23 Flow capacities after two iterations.

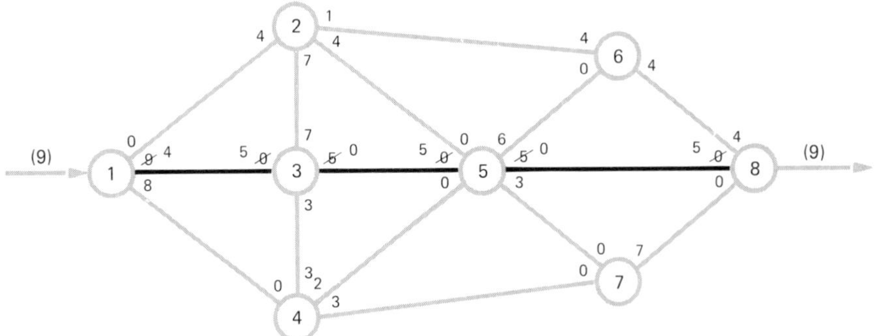

Figure 6.24 Flow capacities after three iterations.

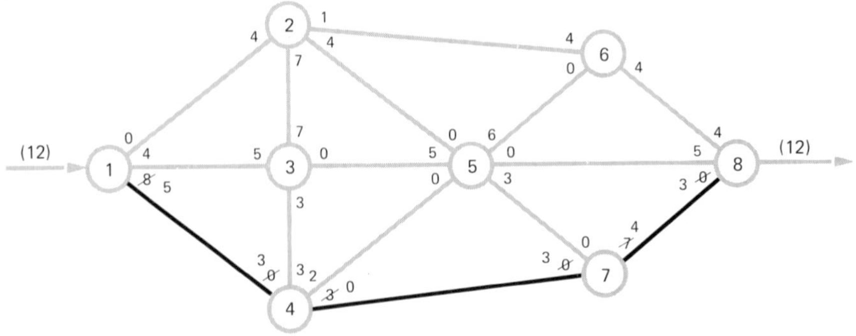

Figure 6.25 Flow capacities after four iterations.

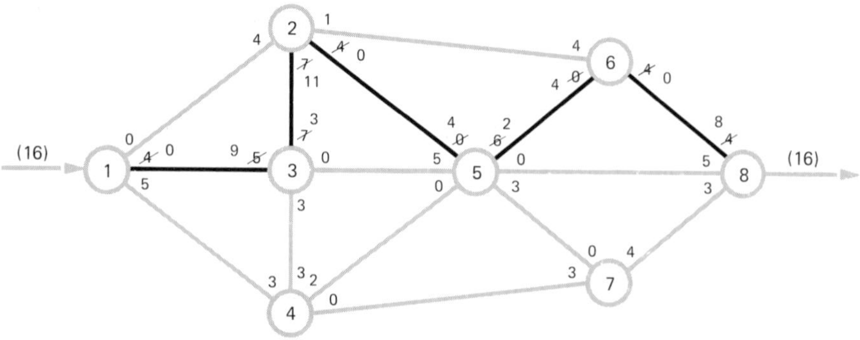

Figure 6.26 Flow capacities after five iterations.

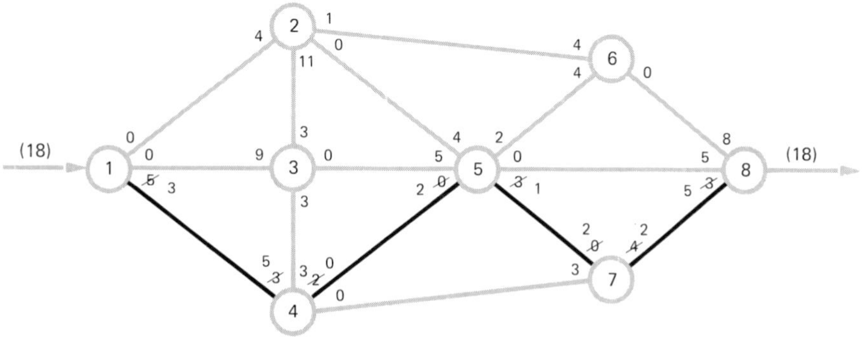

Figure 6.27 Flow capacities after six iterations.

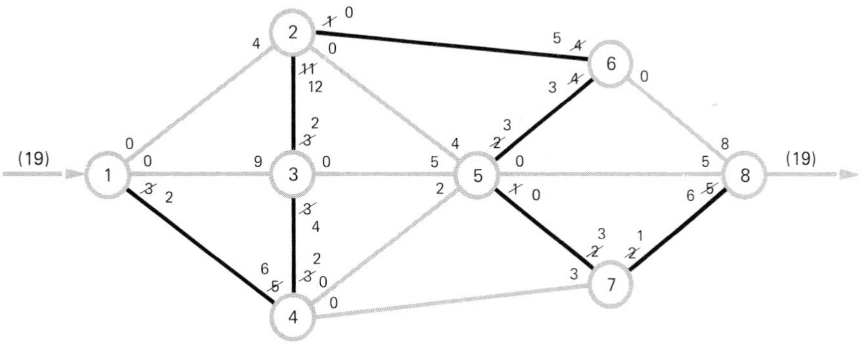

Note that in iteration 6 an allocation of 1 has been assigned to branch (5,6) in the "wrong" direction (since this branch was shown in fig. 6.21 to be directed from node 5 to node 6). The net flow for branch (5,6) may now be determined as:

Iteration	Flow Allocation Branch	Flow
Iteration 4	(5 → 6)	4
Iteration 6	(6 → 5)	1

Therefore, the actual net flow for branch (5→6) will be 3 units. The effect will be to reroute one unit of the 4-unit flow that had been assigned to (5→6) and route it to (5→7) instead. Likewise, the one unit of flow rerouted away from (5→6) will be replaced at node 6 with the last unit of flow coming from (2→6) and it will, in turn, be sent to (6→8). The final network after all iterations is shown in figure 6.28. The assigned flow amount is shown in parentheses for each branch, along with the direction of flow, which is indicated by arrows.

Figure 6.28 Final solution after all iterations.

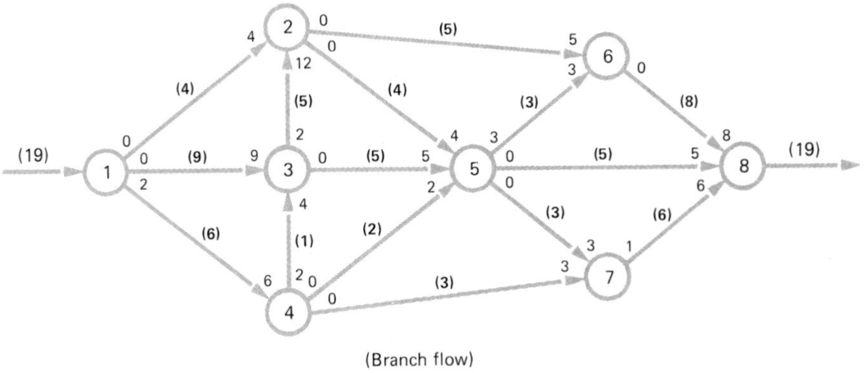

The allocated flow for each branch is summarized in table 6.4. The individual allocations to each branch are shown for each iteration, and the total branch allocations are given at the bottom. Also shown is the branch capacity and the remaining branch capacity after the last iteration. These values may be verified by comparing them to figure 6.28. Note that the reverse direction flow allocation for branch (5→6) is given as a minus 1 in table 6.4, yielding the net flow allocation in the total allocation row.

Table 6.4 Iterations and allocated flows of maximal flow problem solution procedure

	Branch																
Iteration	1→2	1→3	1→4	2→3	2→5	2→6	3→2	3→4	3→5	4→3	4→5	4→7	5→6	5→7	5→8	6→8	7→8
1	4					4										4	
2		5							5						5		
3			3									3					3
4		4			4		4						4			4	
5			2								2			2			2
6			1			1	1			1			−1	1			1
Total Allocation	4	9	6	0	4	5	5	0	5	1	2	3	3	3	5	8	6
Capacity	4	9	8	7	4	5	7	3	5	3	2	3	6	3	5	8	7
Unused Capacity	0	0	2	7	0	0	2	3	0	2	0	0	3	0	0	0	1

CPM/PERT for Project Planning, Scheduling, and Control

CPM and PERT are two of the best-known network modeling techniques of management science. CPM **(Critical Path Method)** and PERT **(Program Evaluation and Review Technique)** were each developed to aid in the planning, scheduling, and control of large, complex projects.

PERT was developed in 1958 to aid in the planning and scheduling of the U.S. Navy's Polaris missile project, which involved over three thousand different contracting organizations. The outstanding success of the Polaris project is largely responsible for the popular acceptance of PERT as a planning and control device by government and business. CPM was developed independently and simultaneously by the DuPont Company to provide a technique for control of the maintenance of DuPont chemical plants.

The two techniques are almost identical with regard to their basic concepts, which focus on **activities, events, predecessors,** and a **critical path.** Thus, they are frequently referred to jointly as CPM/PERT. Both techniques are used as tools in the planning, scheduling, and control of projects that consist of numerous activities, which although independent of one another must be completed in a prescribed order or sequence.

Historically, the PERT technique emphasized the uncertainties associated with activity completion times, and fundamental to PERT is the concept of an event, or the reaching of a certain milestone in the completion of a project. CPM, on the other hand, has historically assumed certainty with regard to activity time estimates, and more emphasis has been placed on the trade-off between project cost and completion time. PERT has been emphasized as a tool for planning and control of research and development projects, while CPM has been more frequently used in large construction projects. CPM/PERT analysis has been applied to numerous projects, including shipbuilding, highway construction, oil refinery maintenance projects, major building construction, missile countdown procedures, auditing projects, and many others.

CPM/PERT Network Components and Precedence Relationships

CPM/PERT networks consist of two major components, *activities* and *events*. Activities of the network represent the project operations or tasks to be conducted. As such, activities consume time and resources and incur costs. Events of the network represent project milestones and occur at points in time, such as the start or the completion of an activity. A prerequisite for CPM/PERT network modeling includes breaking down the project to be analyzed into independent jobs, or activities, and specifying the precedence relationships for the activities.

CPM/PERT activities are commonly represented graphically as arrows (directed branches) and events are represented by circles (nodes) of the network. Figure 6.29, for example, illustrates the network activities, events, and precedence relationship for the construction of a new sidewalk, which includes (*a*) construction of concrete forms followed by (*b*) pouring of the concrete. The sidewalk construction project is summarized as follows:

Activity Identification	Activity Start and Finish Nodes (i, j)	Activity Description	Activity Predecessor	Activity Duration Estimate
a	(1, 2)	Construct Forms	—	5 hours
b	(2, 3)	Pour Concrete	a	1 hour

Figure 6.29 CPM/PERT network for sidewalk construction.

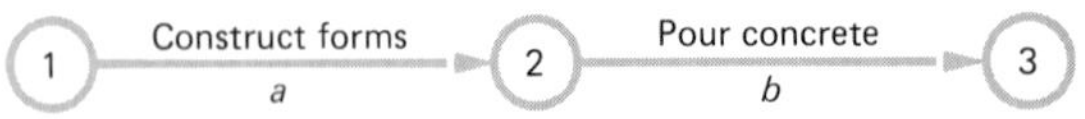

The network diagram in figure 6.29 illustrates the precedence relationship of the two project activities—activity *b* (pouring of concrete) cannot begin until activity *a* (construction of forms) has been completed. Specification of the precedence relationships among project activities is a fundamental requirement of CPM/PERT modeling and analysis.

Node 1 in the network diagram is the event (start construction of concrete forms) that represents the start of the project. Node 2 represents both the events, completion of forms construction and start the pouring of concrete. Node 3 represents the event completion of pouring the concrete, as well as completion of the project.

A project node is said to have *occurred* (or to have been *realized*) when all activities terminating at the node have been completed. Only upon realization of a node can the activity or activities emanating from the node be started. For example, node 2 in figure 6.29 is realized upon completion of activity a, the only activity terminating at node 2. Node 2 is realized at the end of five hours, the time required to construct the concrete forms. At this point in time, activity b (start the pouring of concrete) emanating from node 2 may begin. The project is completed upon realization of node 3, complete pouring of concrete. For the example shown, project completion will occur at the end of six hours.

Concurrent and Dummy Activities

The sidewalk construction example will be expanded slightly to demonstrate a case where two activities are conducted concurrently. In this example the activities include (a) construction of concrete forms and (a') preparation of the concrete (mixing of the cement, gravel, and water to yield concrete ready for pouring). Both activities a and a' are predecessors to activity b (pouring of the concrete). The redefined sidewalk construction project is shown graphically as a network in figure 6.30*A* and is summarized as follows:

Activity Identification	Activity Start and Finish Nodes (i, j)	Activity Description	Activity Predecessor	Activity Duration Estimate
a'	(1, 2)	Prepare Concrete	—	2 hours
a	(1, 2)	Construct Forms	—	5 hours
b	(2, 3)	Pour Concrete	a, a'	1 hour

Figure 6.30 Refined network models. (*A*) Incorrect network representation. (*B*) Correct network representation.

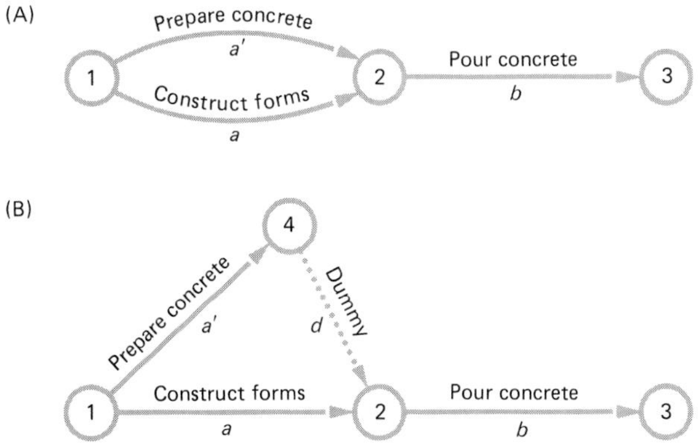

The figure 6.30*A* network, however, represents an incorrect modeling procedure for CPM/PERT networks. This network violates a basic rule of CPM/PERT modeling: *two or more network activities cannot simultaneously share the same start and finish nodes*. This rule has been violated in figure 6.30*A* since both activities *a* and *a'* emanate from node 1 and end at node 2.

This problem is resolved with the introduction of a **dummy activity.** The correct network model for the redefined example is shown in figure 6.30*B* and is summarized as follows:

Activity Identification	Activity Start and Finish Nodes (*i*, *j*)	Activity Description	Activity Predecessor	Activity Duration Estimate
a'	(1, 4)	Prepare Concrete	—	2 hours
a	(1, 2)	Construct Forms	—	5 hours
d	(4, 2)	Dummy Activity	*a'*	0 hours
b	(2, 3)	Pour Concrete	*a*, *d*	1 hour

The network has been correctly revised to include a new node, 4, and a new dummy activity, *d*, that emanates from node 4 and ends at node 2.[1] A dummy activity is illustrated graphically by a dashed line and an arrowhead to indicate direction. A dummy activity does not consume time or resources, but it does preserve the required precedence relationship among project activities. Thus, the time duration associated with dummy activity *d* is zero.

Note that the numbers assigned to network nodes have no meaning in regard to activity precedence relationships. Rather, the precedence relationships are shown by the *arrangement* of the network of connected arrows and nodes. The predecessor for activity *d* is activity *a'*, and the predecessors for activity *b* are activity *a* and activity *d*, which, therefore, ensures the completion of activity *a'* prior to start of activity *b*.

Project Critical Path

After a project has been decomposed (broken down) into its activities and events, and estimates of the activity durations have been obtained, a primary objective of CPM/PERT analysis is to determine the minimum time required for completion of the entire project. The minimum time required for project completion is equal to the **longest time path,** or sequence of connected activities, through the network, which describes the precedence relationships of all project activities. The longest time path is also referred to as the **critical path.**

To illustrate the concept of the critical path, we will return to the sidewalk construction example shown again in figure 6.31. The estimated activity time durations are shown above each network activity.

1. It would have been equally correct to reverse the arrangement of activities *a* and *a'* in figure 6.30*B*—to have represented activity *a* by branch (1, 4) and *a'* by branch (1, 2). Either approach would correct the problem of having both activities *a* and *a'* emanating from node 1 and ending at node 2.

Figure 6.31 Project network critical path.

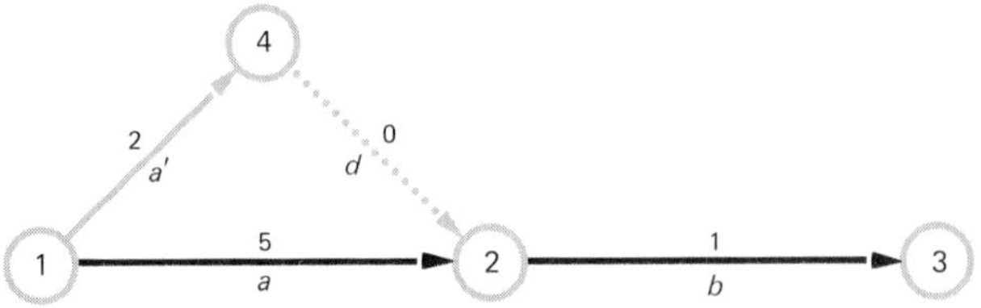

Since activity a' (preparation of concrete) is completed at the end of two hours, node 4 is *realized* at that point in time. The dummy activity, d, is then simultaneously started and completed within this same amount of time (two hours), since it consumes zero time. However, node 2 is not yet realized at time 2 (at the end of two hours), since activity b (pouring of concrete) cannot begin until *both* its predecessors, a and d, have been completed. Activity a (construction of forms) is not completed until time 5—at the end of five hours. Thus, node 2 is said to be realized at time 5, which is equal to *the latter of the two completion times* for activities a and d terminating at node 2.

Upon the completion of both predecessors to activity b (realization of node 2), activity b is started at time 5. Since the duration for activity b is one hour, it will be completed at time 6, event 3 will be realized, and the project completed.

The project is not considered complete until activity b is finished. Since activity b is the only activity following node 2, it obviously belongs to the *critical path* for determining project duration. However, from node 1 to node 2 there are two paths that are candidates for the critical path: path 1–4–2 and path 1–2. The path from node 1 to node 2 has been determined as the longest duration path. Thus, the project critical path is 1–2–3, which yields a minimum possible project duration of six hours. Activities a and b are defined as **critical activities,** which determine overall project duration. The critical path is shown on the figure 6.31 network by bold arrows.

In summary, the critical path is the longest path, or sequence of connected activities, through the network, which determines the minimum time required to complete the project. Activities on the critical path are referred to as **critical activities.** These activities, or jobs, are critical in determining the project's duration. In order to shorten the project completion time, it is necessary to shorten one or more of the activities on the critical path.

As a final point regarding figure 6.31, note that activity a' (preparation of concrete) is completed after two hours, whereas activity b (pouring of the concrete) cannot begin until after the five hours required to complete activity a (construction of concrete forms). Thus, a **slack,** or **float,** period of three hours is associated with activity a'. This means that the preparation of the concrete may be delayed by up to three hours without delaying the overall project. On the other hand, activities a and b have zero slack; these activities cannot be delayed without delaying the entire project. Further computational methods for determining the project critical path and computing activity slacks will be presented in the following section on activity scheduling.

Activity Scheduling

A primary objective of CPM/PERT analysis is the determination of an **activity schedule,** which gives the start and finish times for each project activity. Preparation of such a schedule also provides a rigorous framework for determining the project critical path (and simultaneously the project duration) and computing the slack associated with each project activity.

Preparation of an activity schedule will be presented within the context of the following project example. The B & B National Bank wishes to plan and schedule the development and installation of a new computerized check-processing system. The changeover in check-processing procedures requires employment of additional personnel to operate the new system, development of new systems (computer software), and modification of existing check-sorting equipment. The activities required to complete the project and the precedence relationships among the activities have been determined by bank management and are given in the following table:

Activity	Description	Activity Predecessor
a	Position Recruiting	—
b	System Development	—
c	System Training	a
d	Equipment Training	a
e	Manual System Test	b, c
f	Preliminary System Changeover	b, c
g	Computer-Personnel Interface	d, e
h	Equipment Modification	d, e
i	Equipment Testing	h
j	System Debugging and Installation	f, g
k	Equipment Changeover	g, i

The next step is to obtain estimates of the project activity times and construct the network diagram for the project. The following table gives a summary of the project activities showing the activity time (duration) estimates. Also shown are the start and end nodes (i, j) for each activity of the project network, which is illustrated in figure 6.32. Note that in the table and figure 6.32 it is necessary to include two dummy activities since activity g, in conjunction with activity i, is a predecessor to activity k; and, also, activity g, in conjunction with activity f, is a predecessor to activity j. Examination of the project network reveals that the activity precedence relationships can be achieved only by the inclusion of the dummy activities D_1 and D_2. Inclusion of the two dummy activities reflects the additional CPM/PERT rule that a single activity cannot be shown as two different branches of the network. Without dummy activities D_1 and D_2, it would be necessary to show activity g as both the branches (4,8) and (4,6) in order to preserve the required precedence relationship. This is resolved by showing activity g as branch (4,5) and connecting node 5 to nodes 6 and 8 with dummy activities.

Activity	Activity Start and End Nodes (i, j)	Activity Predecessor	Activity Duration (in days)
a	(1, 2)	—	9
b	(1, 3)	—	11
c	(2, 3)	*a*	7
d	(2, 4)	*a*	10
e	(3, 4)	*b, c*	1
f	(3, 6)	*b, c*	5
g	(4, 5)	*d, e*	6
h	(4, 7)	*d, e*	3
i	(7, 8)	*h*	1
D_1	(5, 8)	*g*	0
D_2	(5, 6)	*g*	0
j	(6, 9)	f, D_2	2
k	(8, 9)	i, D_1	8

Figure 6.32 Project network for new check-processing system.

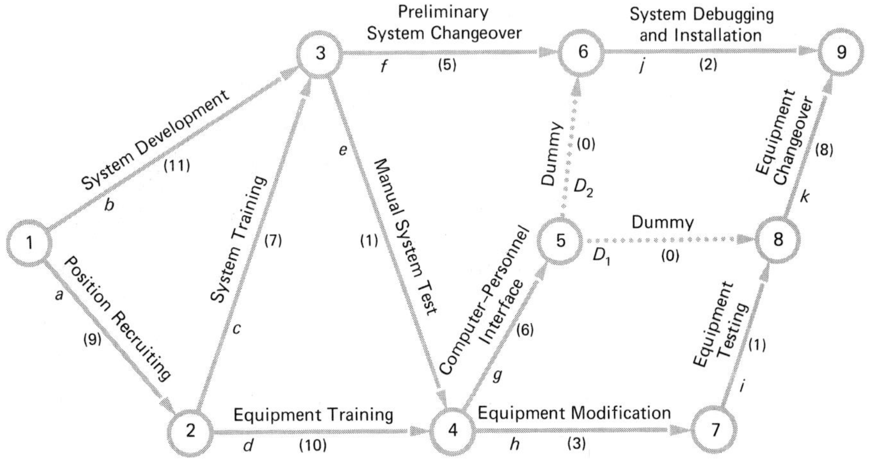

The following discussion will present the CPM/PERT concepts of **earliest time** and **latest time.** In order to present these concepts, network activities will be referred to by their start and end nodes, using the (i, j) notation given in the previous table. It should be noted that the terms *event* and *node* will be used interchangeably throughout the subsequent discussion.

Earliest Time

The earliest time (ET) is the point in time at which *all* activities leading to a node have been completed. In other words, the earliest time is the time of node realization. ET for a node is determined as the *latest* activity completion time for all activities ending at the node. ET_i (where i denotes node i) is, therefore, the earliest starting time for all activities emanating from node i.

ET values for each event are calculated by a *forward* pass through the network, progressing from the project start node to project completion node. Since node 1 is the initial project event in figure 6.32, it follows that $ET_1 = 0$. The earliest time for event 2 is equal to the completion time for activity (1,2), since this activity is the only activity terminating at event 2. Thus, $ET_2 = 9$, or the end of nine days.

The earliest time for node 3 is determined as the latest activity completion time for either activity (1,3) or (2,3). The completion time for activity (1,3) is eleven days. Activity (2,3) is started at the end of nine days (ET_2), conducted for a period of seven days, and completed at the end of sixteen days ($9 + 7 = 16$). Since the activity completion time of sixteen days for (2,3) is later than the completion time of eleven days for (1,3), the earliest time for node 3 is at the end of sixteen days ($ET_3 = 16$). Also, activities (3, 4) and (3, 6) emanating from node 3 cannot be started until the occurrence or realization of node 3 at time 16. This requirement preserves the stipulated precedence relationship of project activity starts given initially for this example.

The calculation procedure for determining the earliest time for each network node, j, is given as follows:

$$\text{Determine: } ET_j = \text{Max } \{ET_i + t_{ij}\}$$

for all activities (i, j) ending at node j, where t_{ij} is the estimated time duration for activity (i, j), and ET_i is the earliest time that activity (i, j) can be started.

For example, the earliest time for node 3 is computed as

$$\begin{aligned} ET_3 &= \text{Max } \{ET_1 + t_{13}, ET_2 + t_{23}\} \\ &= \text{Max } \{0 + 11, 9 + 7\} \\ &= \text{Max } \{11, 16\} \\ &= 16. \end{aligned}$$

Calculations of the earliest times for all network nodes are summarized in table 6.5. Notice that node 9, the project completion node, is realized at time 33 (at the end of thirty-three days). Therefore, the project duration is thirty-three days.

Latest Time

The next step in completing the activity-scheduling analysis and determining the project critical path is to compute the event latest times. The event latest time (LT) is the latest time an event can occur without delaying completion of the project

Table 6.5 Calculation of earliest times (forward pass)

Activity Ending Node (j)	Activity Start Node (i)	Earliest Time + Activity Time ($ET_i + t_{ij}$)	Maximum* = Earliest Time at Node j (ET_j)
1	—	—	0*
2	1	0 + 9	9*
3	1	0 + 11	11
	2	9 + 7	16*
4	2	9 + 10	19*
	3	16 + 1	17
5	4	19 + 6	25*
6	3	16 + 5	21
	5	25 + 0	25*
7	4	19 + 3	22*
8	5	25 + 0	25*
	7	22 + 1	23
9	6	25 + 2	27
	8	25 + 8	33*

beyond the time frame established in the forward pass. Recall that the forward pass determined the earliest project completion time to be thirty-three days. The objective of the latest time calculations is to determine to what extent each project activity can be delayed and still complete the project within thirty-three days.

LT values for each event are calculated by a *backward* pass through the network, starting at node 9 and ending at node 1. Since the objective is to complete the project by the earliest time ($ET_9 = 33$), it follows that LT_9 also equals 33. The latest time for event 6 is equal to $33 - 2 = 31$, or $LT_9 - t_{69} = LT_6$. Since the time required to complete activity (6,9) is two days, node 6 must be realized by no later than time 31 in order to complete the project at time 33. The latest time for node 8 is given as $LT_9 - t_{89} = 33 - 8 = 25$.

Since activity (4,5) precedes both activities (6,9) and (8,9), the dummy activities (5,6) and (5,8) have been included in the network to preserve this relationship. The duration for a dummy activity is always zero. The latest *allowable* time for realization of node 5 is calculated as the *earlier* of the times $LT_6 - t_{56}$ and $LT_8 - t_{58}$. Since both t_{56} and t_{58} equal zero, we have $31 - 0$ versus $25 - 0$. Thus, LT_5 must equal 25, the earlier time, in order to complete the project by time 33.

In general, the calculation procedure for determining the latest time for each network node, i, is given by the following:

Determine: $LT_i = \underset{j}{\text{Min}} \{LT_j - t_{ij}\}$

for all activities (i, j) emanating from node i.

For example, the latest time at node 5 is computed as

$$\begin{aligned} LT_5 &= \text{Min} \{LT_6 - t_{56}, LT_8 - t_{58}\} \\ &= \text{Min} \{31 - 0, 25 - 0\} \\ &= \text{Min} \{31, 25\} \\ &= 25. \end{aligned}$$

Calculations of the latest times for all network nodes are summarized in table 6.6. By definition, $LT_n = ET_n$, where n is the project termination (or sink) node, and $LT_1 = ET_1 = 0$ for the project start (or source) node.

Table 6.6 Calculation of latest times (backward pass)

Activity Start Node (i)	Activity End Node (j)	Latest Time − Activity Time ($LT_j - t_{ij}$)	Minimum* = Latest Time at Node i (LT_i)
9	—	—	33*
8	9	33 − 8	25*
7	8	25 − 1	24*
6	9	33 − 2	31*
5	6	31 − 0	31
	8	25 − 0	25*
4	5	25 − 6	19*
	7	24 − 3	21
3	4	19 − 1	18*
	6	31 − 5	26
2	3	18 − 7	11
	4	19 − 10	9*
1	2	9 − 9	0*
	3	18 − 11	7

The project network is shown in figure 6.33, giving the values for *ET* and *LT* alongside each network node. (The reader may ignore, for the time being, the *TS* and *FS* values alongside each network activity.) Note that the earliest times and latest times are equal for nodes along the path 1–2–4–5–8–9. Since the latest *allowable* node realization times, in order to complete the project at time 33, are exactly equal to the earliest *possible* node realization times, the sequence of connected activities along the 1–2–4–5–8–9 path constitute the critical path. The bold arrows along this path denote critical activities. No activity along the critical path may be delayed if the project is to be completed at the end of thirty-three days. Thus, the schedule for these activities is rigid, without any allowance for variation.

Figure 6.33 Project network showing event times, activity slacks, and critical path.

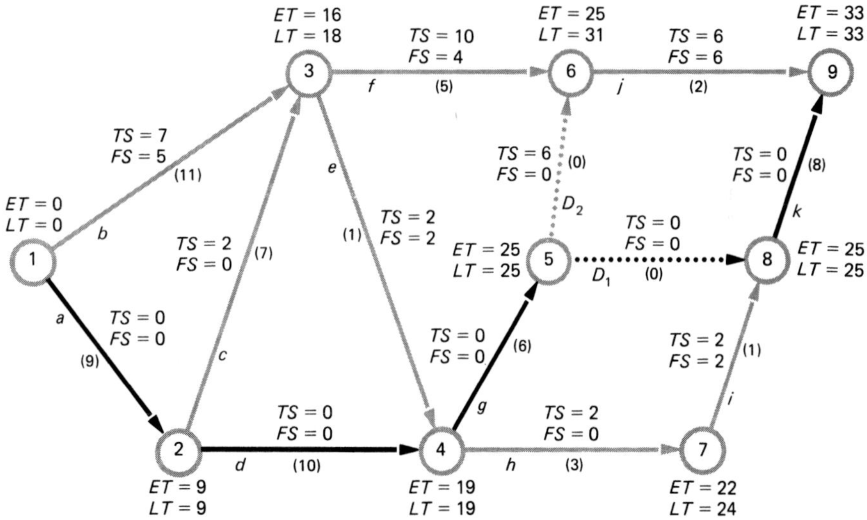

Activity Slack

Activities not on the critical path, however, may be delayed to some extent without delaying completion of the project beyond the thirty-three day time period. Activity slacks provide a measure of the extent to which noncritical activities may be extended or delayed. These are the *TS* and *FS* values shown next to each activity in figure 6.33.

Two types of slack are defined for each activity of the project. **Total slack** (TS_{ij}) for activity (i, j) is the maximum time period available to schedule the activity minus the estimated duration of the activity. The times within which an activity must be scheduled are computed from the *ET* and *LT* values for each network activity's start node and end node. Thus, the allowable scheduling time for activity (i, j) is determined from the computed values of ET_i and LT_j. For example, activity (3, 6) must be scheduled to begin no earlier than time 16 ($ET_3 = 16$) and to end no later than time 31 ($LT_6 = 31$). The maximum time period available for completion of activity (3, 6) is $LT_6 - ET_3 = 31 - 16 = 15$ days. Since activity (3, 6) requires only five days for completion, it may be delayed or extended by as much as ten days without delaying completion of the project.

Total slack values for each network activity are computed by:

$$TS_{ij} = LT_j - ET_i - t_{ij}$$
$$= \text{latest time at } j - \text{earliest time at } i - \text{activity } (i, j) \text{ duration.}$$

For example, the total slack values for activities (3,6) and (6,9) are

$$TS_{36} = LT_6 - ET_3 - t_{36}$$
$$= 31 - 16 - 5$$
$$= 10$$
$$TS_{69} = LT_9 - ET_6 - t_{69}$$
$$= 33 - 25 - 2$$
$$= 6.$$

The total slack values for each network activity are shown alongside each activity in figure 6.33.

Note that the total slack for activity (6,9) is given as six days and the total slack for activity (3,6) is ten days. However, the total slack computation for activity (6,9) includes the assumption that node 6 will be realized by time 25 ($ET_6 = 25$), whereas the total slack computation for activity (3,6) includes the assumption that node 6 will not be realized until time 31 ($LT_6 = 31$). This leads to the concept of **shared slack** among activities in a given sequence. Activity (3,6) has ten days total slack. If activity (3,6) is delayed by only four days (completion at time 25), then activity (6,9) will have six days slack. On the other hand, if activity (3,6) is delayed by ten days (completion at time 31), then activity (6,9) will have zero slack available. Any delay in activity (3,6) beyond four days will reduce the slack for activity (6,9). Thus, both activities (3,6) and (6,9) jointly share six days slack. That is, activity (3,6) may be delayed by four days, and, in addition, the *sequence of activities* on the path 3–6–9 may be delayed by up to a total of six days without delaying the project.

Since activity (3, 6) has total slack of ten days, of which six days are shared with activity (6, 9), activity (3, 6) also has **free slack** (FS_{ij}) of four days. This is because activity (3, 6) may be delayed by up to four days without any effect on the earliest possible starting time of activity (6, 9). If activity (3, 6) starts at time 16 ($ET_3 = 16$), it will be completed at time 21 ($ET_3 + t_{36} = 16 + 5 = 21$), leaving four days of free slack prior to the earliest possible start time for activity (6, 9).

In general, free slack for an activity is defined as the amount by which an activity may be delayed without causing *any* delay in its *immediate successor* activities. The computation procedure for free slack for activity (i,j) is given as follows:

$$FS_{ij} = ET_j - ET_i - t_{ij}$$
$$= \text{earliest time at } j - \text{earliest time at } i - \text{activity } (i,j) \text{ duration.}$$

For example, the free slack values for activities (3,6) and (6,9) are

$$FS_{36} = ET_6 - ET_3 - t_{36}$$
$$= 25 - 16 - 5$$
$$= 4.$$
$$FS_{69} = ET_9 - ET_6 - t_{69}$$
$$= 33 - 25 - 2$$
$$= 6$$

The values for free slack are also shown alongside each activity in figure 6.33, and the entire project including all previously computed values is summarized in table 6.7. The values of both total slack and free slack always equal zero for each activity on the critical path. In some cases, total activity slack is positive while free slack is equal to zero, since any delay in the activity would delay its successor activity(s) beyond its earliest start date. Also, in several cases, free slack equals total slack. This is because the activity does not share any slack with its successor activity(s). In all cases, $FS \leq TS$.

Table 6.7 Time values for the bank check-processing project

Activity	Alternate Activity Designation (i, j)	Activity Duration (t_{ij})	Earliest Time at Node i ET_i	Latest Time at Node j LT_j	For Activity (i, j) Total Slack TS_{ij}	For Activity (i, j) Free Slack FS_{ij}
a^*	(1, 2)	9	0	9	0	0
b	(1, 3)	11	0	18	7	5
c	(2, 3)	7	9	18	2	0
d^*	(2, 4)	10	9	19	0	0
e	(3, 4)	1	16	19	2	2
f	(3, 6)	5	16	31	10	4
g^*	(4, 5)	6	19	25	0	0
h	(4, 7)	3	19	24	2	0
i	(7, 8)	1	22	25	2	2
D_1^*	(5, 8)	0	25	25	0	0
D_2	(5, 6)	0	25	31	6	0
j	(6, 9)	2	25	33	6	6
k^*	(8, 9)	8	25	33	0	0

*Critical path activities

Probabilistic Activity Times

Up to this point, activity times have been presented as constant values. This treatment of time estimates as known constants, which yields a deterministic model, assumes certainty when specifying activity times. It is reasonable to expect that considerable uncertainty will often be associated with the estimation of project activity times.

The original version of PERT assumed that project activity times were random variables (probabilistic). It was further assumed that the random variable, activity duration, could be associated with the beta distribution, which is a versatile probability distribution that can assume a variety of shapes.

The PERT method for project analysis assumes that three estimates of the activity duration will be obtained for each project activity. The activity duration estimates required are as follows:

1. *Optimistic time* (a_{ij})*:* the shortest possible time required for the completion of activity (i, j). The probability that the activity could be completed in a shorter time period is extremely small (approximately .01).
2. *Most likely time* (m_{ij})*:* the most likely (modal) time required to complete activity (i, j). If the activity were repeated many times, this is the duration that would occur most frequently.
3. *Pessimistic time* (b_{ij})*:* the longest possible time required for completion of activity (i, j). The probability that completion of the activity would take longer than this time estimate is extremely small (approximately .01).

Given the a_{ij}, m_{ij}, b_{ij} time estimates for each project activity and the assumption that the activity time follows a beta distribution, formulas have been derived for calculating the mean ($\hat{t}_{ij}$) and variance (v_{ij}) for each activity time distribution. These formulas are assumed to provide reasonable approximations of the parameters for the beta-distributed activity times. The formulas are given as follows:

$$\text{Mean, or average time: } \hat{t}_{ij} = \frac{a_{ij} + 4m_{ij} + b_{ij}}{6}$$

$$\text{Variance: } v_{ij} = \left(\frac{b_{ij} - a_{ij}}{6}\right)^2$$

Three examples of the beta distribution, showing the relative locations of a_{ij}, m_{ij}, b_{ij}, and $\hat{t}_{ij}$, are illustrated in figure 6.34. It is shown that the distribution is unimodal (has only one highest point), continuous, and has finite limits. The distribution may be symmetrical (fig. 6.34*C*) or skewed in either direction (fig. 6.34*A* and *B*).

Figure 6.34 Beta distributions for activity times. (*A*) Skewed to right. (*B*) Skewed to left. (*C*) Symmetrical.

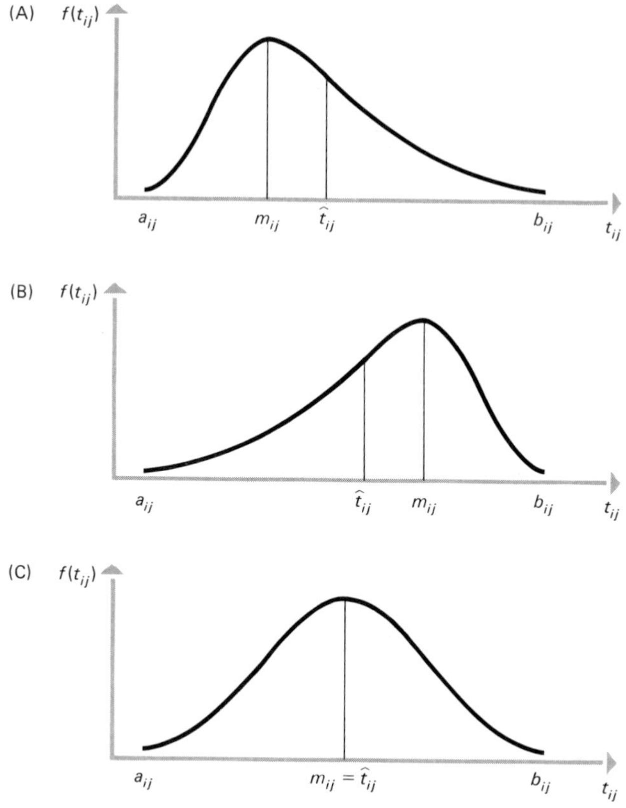

The project network is analyzed after obtaining three time estimates for each activity and converting them to the two parameter values, $\hat{t}_{ij}$ and v_{ij}. The following table gives the time estimates for the previous check-processing changeover example. The values of the three time estimates provided have been contrived to facilitate easy verification of the beta formula calculations and to yield mean activity times equal to the single-value estimates originally provided for the example. In this way, the network analysis using mean activity times ($\hat{t}_{ij}$) to determine *ET*, *LT*, *TS*, *FS*, and the critical path yields the same results as those obtained previously using the single-value estimates (t_{ij}) for activity times.

Activity	Activity Nodes (i, j)	Time Estimates: Optimistic a_{ij}	Most Likely m_{ij}	Pessimistic b_{ij}	Beta Distribution Parameters: Mean $\hat{t}_{ij}$	Variance v_{ij}
a*	(1, 2)	5	8	17	9	4
b	(1, 3)	3	12	15	11	4
c	(2, 3)	4	7	10	7	1
d*	(2, 4)	5	8	23	10	9
e	(3, 4)	1	1	1	1	0
f	(3, 6)	1	4	13	5	4
g*	(4, 5)	3	6	9	6	1
h	(4, 7)	1	2.5	7	3	1
i	(7, 8)	1	1	1	1	0
j	(6, 9)	2	2	2	2	0
k*	(8, 9)	5	8	11	8	1

*Critical path activities
Note: Dummy activities are excluded since they have zero times

Probability Statements about Project Completion Times

The PERT method assumes that activity times are statistically independent and identically distributed (beta); therefore, the means and variances for activity times may be added to yield total project mean time and variance along a network path. The PERT method further assumes that there will be sufficient activities involved such that the summed totals will be *normally distributed,* according to the **central limit theorem** of probability theory.

If the preceding assumptions are met, it is then possible to make probability statements about the expected (average) completion time for the project. Likewise, it should also be possible to make probability statements about the time required to reach various milestones within the project.

The probability statements in PERT are based on the earliest times (ET) for reaching various events in the network. Therefore, the sum of the activity mean and variance times always refer to the activities on the *longest (time) path* to the node for which probability statements are to be made.

In the bank check-processing example, the sum of the mean activity times on the critical path is thirty-three days. This is the expected, or mean, project time, which is assumed to be normally distributed. The sum of the variances for activity times on the critical path is fifteen days. The calculations for determining the mean and variance of project time are summarized as follows:

$$\text{Mean project time:} \quad E(t) = \hat{t}_{12} + \hat{t}_{24} + \hat{t}_{45} + \hat{t}_{89}$$
$$= 9 + 10 + 6 + 8$$
$$= 33 \text{ days}$$

$$\text{Variance, project time: } V(t) = v_{12} + v_{24} + v_{45} + v_{89}$$
$$= 4 + 9 + 1 + 1$$
$$= 15 \text{ days}$$

Given the mean and variance for the total project time and the assumption of normality, probability statements about project completion time can be made. In order to read probability values from a table for the normal curve, the value of the **standardized random variate (Z)** must first be determined. For the example project, it is calculated as follows:

$$Z = \frac{t' - E(t)}{\sqrt{V(t)}}$$

where

$E(t)$ = mean of normal distribution (mean project time)

$V(t)$ = variance of normal distribution (variance, project time)

t' = the project completion time for which a probability statement is to be made.

For example, suppose the bank wishes to know the probability of completing the project within forty days or less ($t' = 40$). The computation is summarized as follows:

$$P(t \leqslant t') = P(t \leqslant 40) = P\left(Z \leqslant \frac{40 - 33}{\sqrt{15}}\right)$$
$$= P\left(Z \leqslant \frac{7}{3.873}\right)$$
$$= P(Z \leqslant 1.8)$$
$$= .9641$$

In other words, the probability value found in a normal distribution table (see Appendix D, table D.3) for a Z value of 1.8 is .9641. This is illustrated in figure 6.35, with the area under the curve to the left of 40 shown as .9641. Thus, there is a 96% chance of completion within forty days and a 4% chance that project completion will require more than forty days.

In a similar manner, probability statements can be made about earliest completion times at each node of the project network by summing the $\hat{t}_{ij}$ and v_{ij} values for activities on the longest path to each node. This procedure provided by PERT for assessing project completion uncertainties is often attacked as not being rigorous in a probabilistic sense; however, it is often used in actual practice as a workable approach.[2]

2. For further discussion, see J. W. Pocock, "PERT as an Analytical Aid for Program Planning—Its Payoff and Problems." *Operations Research* 10 (1962): 893–903.

Figure 6.35 Probability of project completion in forty days or less.

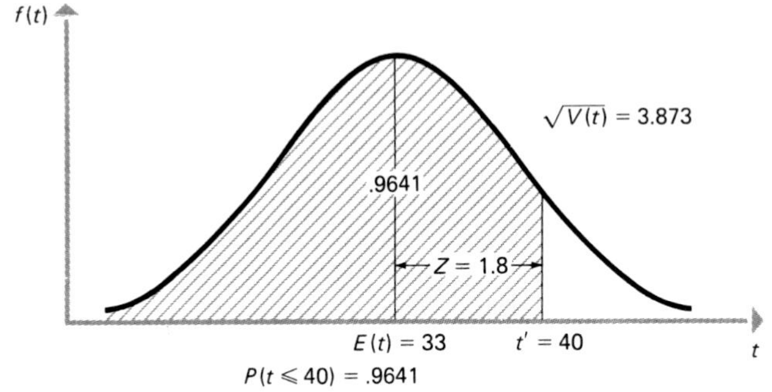

Activity Costs and Project Crashing

Extensions of project time analysis are project **time/cost analysis** and project **crashing.** The term *crashing* refers to the shortening of project duration by ''rushing'' or ''crashing'' one or more of the critical project activities to completion in less than normal time. This is achieved by devoting more resources (i.e., material, equipment, and labor) to the activity to be crashed. One example is working overtime on a project, which speeds up the completion of the activity but also adds to the cost in the form of overtime wages.

Network cost analysis has historically been associated with CPM; however, it can be applied to either PERT or CPM networks. The purpose of project cost analysis is to determine which activities in the network to crash and by how much.

In network cost analysis, the two types of costs associated with each activity are also estimated: **normal-time cost** and **crash-time cost.** These costs are also associated with two time estimates for each activity: **normal time** and **crash time.** In the case of CPM networks, this requires that a crash-time estimate be provided in addition to the normal expected time previously described. For PERT networks, the crash-time estimate is usually the most optimistic time estimate, a_{ij}. The normal-time estimate for PERT networks can be either the estimated most likely time, m_{ij}, or the computed expected time, $\hat{t}_{ij}$.

For purposes of simplicity, the relationship between normal-time cost and crash-time cost for an activity is generally assumed to be linear. Such a relationship for one activity is illustrated in figure 6.36. Thus, the crash cost per unit of time can be estimated by computing the relative change in cost per unit change in time. For the example illustrated in figure 6.36, the crash cost is \$100 per week, computed as follows:

$$\frac{\text{Crash Cost} - \text{Normal Cost}}{\text{Normal time} - \text{Crash time}} = \frac{400 - 100}{5 - 2} = \frac{300}{3} = \$100$$

Figure 6.36 Activity time-cost relationship.

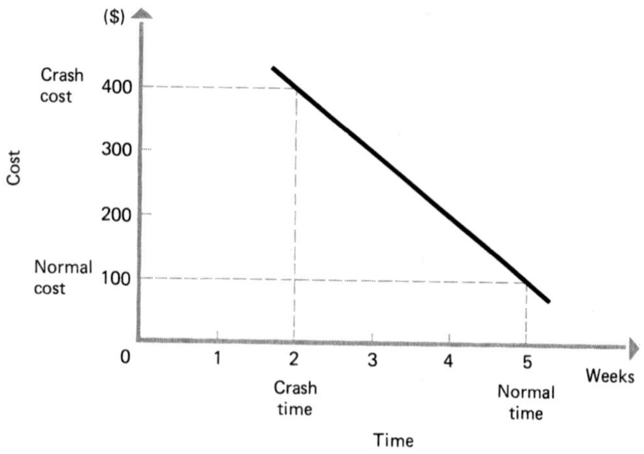

The objective of crash-cost analysis is to reduce the total project completion time while minimizing the cost of crashing. Since the project completion time can be shortened only by crashing critical activities, it follows that not all project activities should be crashed. However, as activities are crashed, the critical path may change, requiring further crashing of previously noncritical activities in order to further reduce the project completion time.

The general procedure for crashing project activities while minimizing cost is given as follows:

Step 0 Determine the minimum project time and associated critical path for the two cases: (a) if all activities are completed in normal time and (b) if all activities are crashed. The normal-time critical path is the point of departure for the crashing analysis. Determination of the minimum project time when all activities are crashed provides the stopping point for the crashing analysis. Begin with the normal-time critical path.

Step 1 Identify and crash the activity on the critical path with the minimum crash cost per unit of time. If there is more than one critical path, identify and crash the activity(s) on the critical path(s) with the minimum joint crash cost per unit of time.

Step 2 Revise the network, adjusting for the time and cost assigned to the crashed activity(s). Determine the critical path(s), using normal activity times for noncrashed activities, and crash times for crashed activities. If the project time equals the crashing time computed in Step 0, stop; otherwise, return to Step 1.

The following example will illustrate an application of these steps to a specific project. The example project is described in the following table, which gives normal and crash times and normal and crash costs for each activity. Also, the computed values of crash cost per week are given. The total project cost if all activities are completed in normal time is $6,400. If all activities are crashed, the total cost is $9,800.

		Time (weeks)		Cost ($)		
Activity	(*i*, *j*)	Normal	Crashed	Normal	Crashed	Crash Cost Per Week
a	(1, 2)	14	6	1,400	2,200	100
b	(1, 3)	12	8	1,000	1,800	200
c	(2, 5)	18	14	1,600	2,000	100
d	(2, 4)	6	4	800	1,200	200
e	(3, 4)	4	2	400	800	200
f	(4, 5)	8	6	400	600	100
g	(5, 6)	12	8	800	1,200	100
				6,400	9,800	

The project network is illustrated in figure 6.37. Activity crash costs per week are shown alongside each activity, and under each cost value are the values for normal time and crash time (in parentheses). For example, the normal time for activity (1, 2) is 14, the crash time is 6, and the cost per week of crashing is $100.

Figure 6.37 Project network.

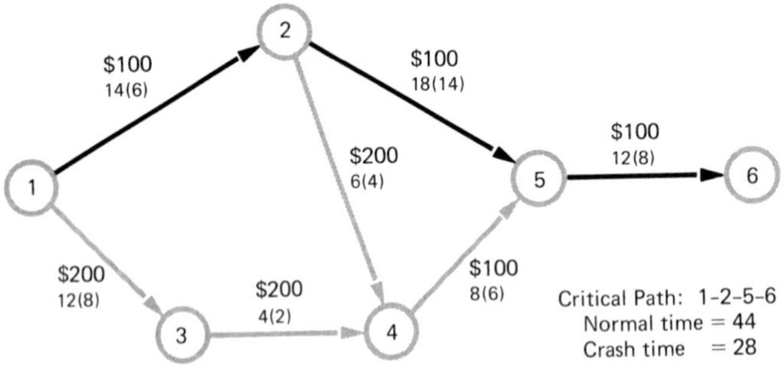

Figure 6.37 shows that in Step 0 the critical path is 1–2–5–6 for both normal and crash activity times. The project time, assuming normal activity times, is forty-four weeks at a total cost of $6,400. If all activities are crashed, the project time is twenty-eight weeks at a total cost of $9,800.

The normal-time critical path is the point of departure for the next step, and twenty-eight weeks is the stopping point for the crashing analysis (the objective is to complete the project within twenty-eight weeks at the least cost beyond $6,400).

Iteration 1

Step 1 Identify the activity on the critical path with the minimum crash cost per week. Since it is the same for each activity on the critical path, arbitrarily select activity (1, 2) to crash. It is crashed by eight weeks to its lower limit, six weeks. The associated crashing cost is \$800 (\$100 × 8), yielding a total project cost of \$7,200 (6,400 + 800).

Step 2 Revise the network, adjusting for the time and cost assigned to activity (1,2), as shown by the network in figure 6.38. There are now two critical paths, 1–2–5–6 and 1–3–4–5–6. Note that the activity times used for the computation are the time values *not* in parentheses. Return to Step 1.

Figure 6.38 Project network with activity (1,2) crashed.

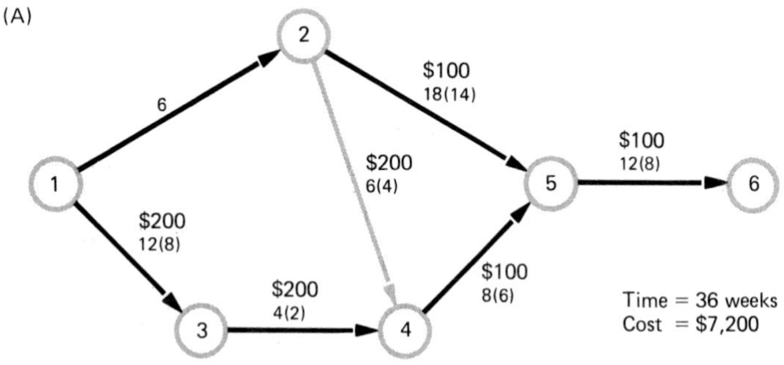

Iteration 2

Step 1 Select the activity(s) on the critical path(s) with the minimum crashing cost(s) that will reduce the total project time. Only by crashing activity (5, 6) can project time be reduced without crashing more than one activity. If project time could be reduced at less cost by crashing two activities (in one or both of the two critical paths), this would be done. However, in this case, the least-cost option is to crash activity (5, 6). Activity (5, 6) is crashed by four weeks to its lower limit of eight weeks. The associated crashing cost is \$400, resulting in a total project cost of \$7,600.

Step 2 Revise the network, adjusting for crashed activity (5, 6), as shown by the network in figure 6.39*A*. Project time has been reduced to thirty-two weeks; however, the critical paths remain as 1–2–5–6 and 1–3–4–5–6. Return to Step 1.

Iteration 3

Step 1 Select the activity(s) that can be crashed at minimum crashing cost and that result in a reduction in project time. Since there is no single activity shared by both critical paths that has not been crashed, select two activities (one from each critical path) to be crashed at minimum crashing cost. If only a single activity has been crashed on one of the critical paths, the other critical path remains critical (unshortened), and the total project time remains unchanged. Therefore, select two activities (one from each critical path) that result in the minimum *aggregate* weekly crashing cost.

Activity (2, 5) must be selected from path 1–2–5–6 as it is the only remaining activity not crashed. Select activity (4, 5) on path 1–3–4–5–6 since it has the least weekly crashing cost. Determine which of the two activities selected for crashing can be crashed by the least amount, and crash each activity by that amount. Although activity (2, 5) can be crashed by four weeks, activity (4, 5) can be crashed by only two weeks. Therefore, activity (4, 5) is crashed by two weeks to its lower limit of six weeks, and activity (2, 5) is crashed by two weeks to a duration of sixteen weeks. Note, it makes no sense to crash (2, 5) further since it would not shorten the overall project time, due to critical path 1–3–4–5–6. The costs of crashing activities (2, 5) and (4, 5) are $200 each, yielding a total crashing cost of $400 and a total project cost of $8,000.

Step 2 Revise the network, reflecting crashed activities, as shown by the network in figure 6.39*B*. Total project time has been reduced to thirty weeks, and the same two critical paths exist. Return to Step 1.

Iteration 4

Step 1 Two weeks crashing capability remains for activity (2,5) since it was crashed by only two weeks in Iteration 3. On the other critical path (1–3–4–5–6), activities (1, 3) and (3, 4) both have the same crashing cost, and both activities can be crashed by two weeks. Therefore, arbitrarily select activity (3, 4) to crash by two weeks to its lower limit of two weeks. Crash activity (2, 5) by its remaining two weeks capability, to its lower limit of fourteen weeks. The cost of crashing activity (2, 5) is $200 while the cost of crashing activity (3, 4) is $400, yielding a total crashing cost of $600, and a project cost of $8,600.

Step 2 Revise the network, reflecting crashed activities, as shown by the network in figure 6.39*C*. Total project time has been reduced to twenty-eight weeks, which is equal to the minimum time if all activities were crashed. Also, one of the critical paths consists of entirely crashed activities; therefore, no further reduction in project duration can be achieved.

The minimum possible project time has been obtained without crashing all project activities. The table on page 284 provides a summary of the solution results. Five of the seven project activities were crashed, with the resulting activity times shown. Total activity cost is shown to be $8,600, including $6,400 normal costs and $2,200 crashing costs.

Figure 6.39 Project network with (*A*) activities (1,2) and (5,6) crashed; (*B*) activities (1,2), (5,6), (2,5), and (4,5) crashed; (*C*) activities (1,2), (5,6), (2,5), (4,5), and (3,4) crashed.

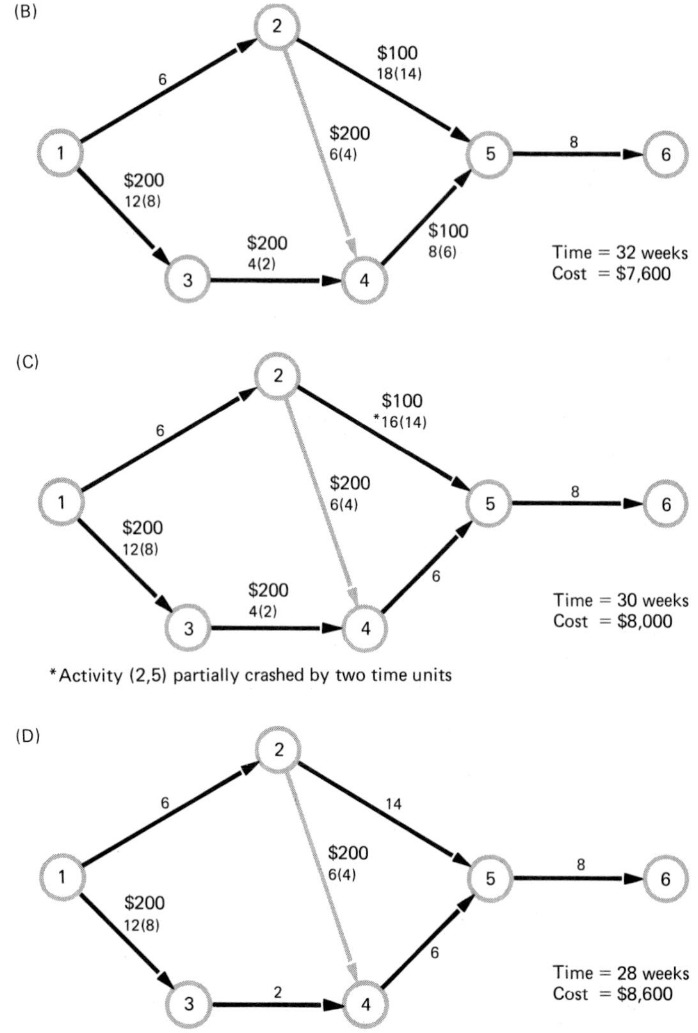

Activity	(*i*, *j*)	Decision	Results: Crashing Cost ($)	Activity Time (weeks)	Activity Cost ($)
a	(1, 2)	Crash by 8	800	6	2,200
b	(1, 3)	Normal	—	12	1,000
c	(2, 5)	Crash by 4	400	14	2,000
d	(2, 4)	Normal	—	6	800
e	(3, 4)	Crash by 2	400	2	800
f	(4, 5)	Crash by 2	200	6	600
g	(5, 6)	Crash by 4	400	8	1,200
			2,200		8,600

The **trade-off** between project time and cost is summarized in the following table and illustrated in figure 6.40. Shown are the total project times and costs, beginning with normal activity completion times and ranging through the successive steps of the crashing procedure.

Iteration	Result	Project Time (weeks)	Project Cost ($)
0	No crashings	44	6,400
1	Activity (1, 2) crashed by 8 weeks	36	7,200
2	Activity (5, 6) crashed by 4 weeks	32	7,600
3	Activity (2, 5) initially crashed by 2 weeks and activity (4, 5) crashed by 2 weeks	30	8,000
4	Activity (2, 5) further crashed by 2 weeks and activity (3, 4) crashed by 2 weeks	28	8,600

If the project must be completed within a less-than-normal time, figure 6.40 shows the associated project direct cost within the feasible range of forty-four weeks to twenty-eight weeks. However, the appropriate decision structure for the crashing decision should include not only the direct costs considered thus far (such as direct materials, equipment, and labor costs) but also should include indirect costs (such as salaried personnel, facilities, interest charges, utilities, and other overhead costs), as well as any contractual penalties associated with project completion time.

Figure 6.40 Time-cost trade-off relationship.

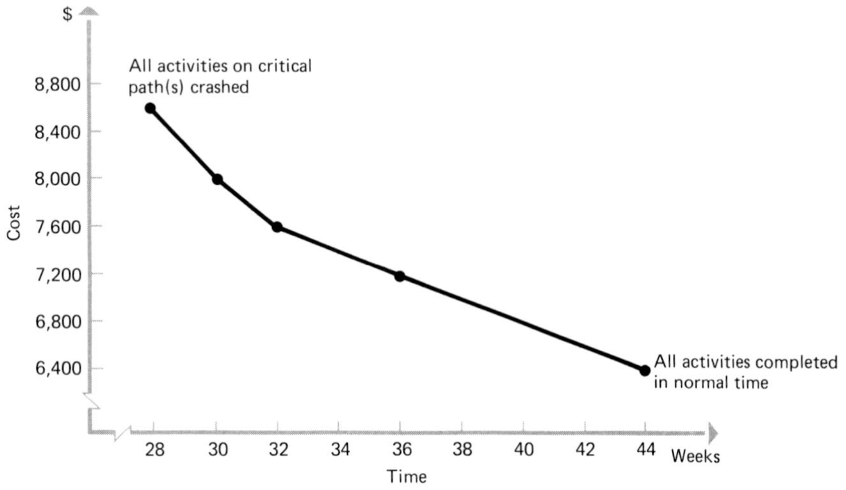

Whereas direct costs are greatest when crashing the project to the least possible time, indirect costs and penalties increase as a function of project time. Figure 6.41 illustrates a hypothetical example showing both direct and indirect project cost curves, as well as the total cost curve, as functions of different project completion times. The optimal project duration is the time associated with the minimum point on the total cost curve, as shown in figure 6.41.

Figure 6.41 Direct, indirect, and total cost curves.

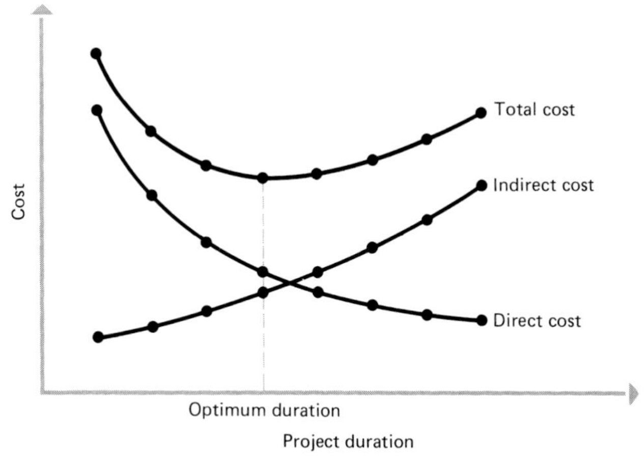

Summary

In this chapter several of the more important topics in network modeling have been presented, including the shortest-route problem, the minimal spanning-tree problem, the maximal flow problem, and the CPM/PERT technique for project planning and control. Network modeling has become increasingly popular as a management science technique because of the communication value of visual network models to managers. This has been especially true of the last topic in this chapter, CPM/PERT, which has become one of the most frequently employed management planning tools. In fact, management scientists frequently use CPM/PERT for planning management science model development and implementation.

References

Ford, L. R., Jr., and Fulkerson, D. R. *Flows in Networks*. Princeton, N.J.: Princeton University Press, 1962.

Hillier, F. S., and Lieberman, G. J. *Operations Research*. 2d ed. San Francisco: Holden-Day, 1974.

Moder, J., and Phillips, C. R. *Project Management with CPM and PERT*. 2d ed. New York: Van Nostrand Reinhold Co., 1970.

Trueman, R. E. *An Introduction to Quantitative Methods for Decision Making*. 2d ed. New York: Holt, Rinehart and Winston, 1977.

Wiest, J. D., and Levy, F. K. *A Management Guide to PERT/CPM*. 2d ed. Englewood Cliffs, N.J.: Prentice-Hall, 1977.

Problems

1. Solve the following shortest-route network problem where node 1 is the origin and node 5 is the destination. The distances in miles are shown along the network branches.

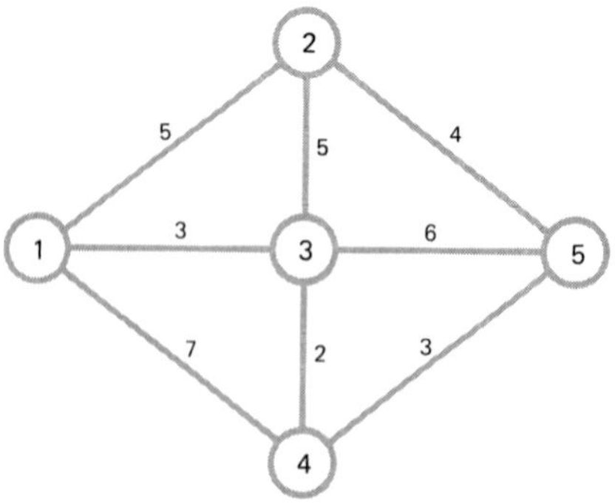

2. The following figure represents a highway network, where distances are shown in hundreds of miles along each branch of the network. A trucking company wishes to know the shortest route from location 1 to location 7 (node 1 to node 7). Determine the shortest-route solution.

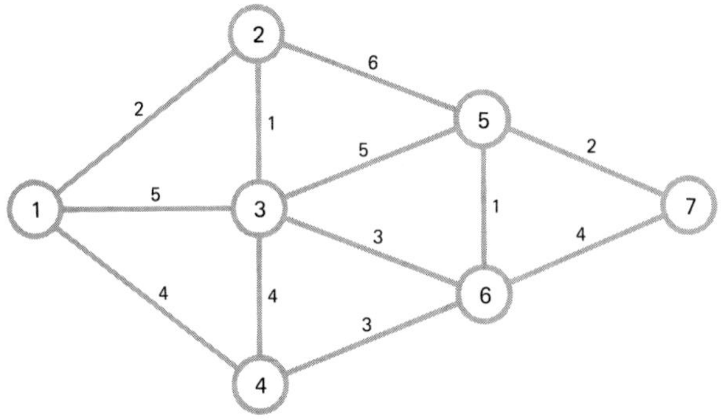

3. Given the problem 2 network, assume that node 3 represents a central storage facility from which truckloads of materials are transported to each of the various endpoint locations denoted by nodes 1, 2, 4, 5, 6, and 7. (a) Each individual shipment from the central storage facility is transported to only one of the alternative endpoint destinations. Determine the shortest routes from the central storage facility to each of the delivery endpoints. (b) In which cases could fractional truckload deliveries be made (i.e., a portion of a truckload delivered to one location and the remainder to another location), without altering the shortest-route solutions obtained in part *a*? Provide a detailed statement.

4. Given the problem 2 network, assume that a trucking company wishes to know the route requiring the least *time* to travel from node 1 to node 7. Trucks can average 50 miles per hour over each branch of the highway network with the following exceptions; the subroutes from nodes 2 to 3 and from 6 to 5 are steep upgrades. Trucks can only average speeds of 25 miles per hour from 2 to 3 and from 6 to 5. On the other hand, trucks can average the normal 50 miles per hour on the downgrades, from 3 to 2 and from 5 to 6. (a) Illustrate the network with the appropriate *directed* branches and associated values for evaluation of the minimum time route. (b) Determine the shortest time route from node 1 to node 7. (c) Assume that the destination is redefined as node 6 rather than node 7. Identify the alternate optimal routes from node 1. (d) Given that a truck is at the node 7 destination, determine the shortest time route(s) for the return trip to node 1.

5. Determine the shortest route from origin to destination for the following transportation network, where distances are given along the network branches in hundreds of miles.

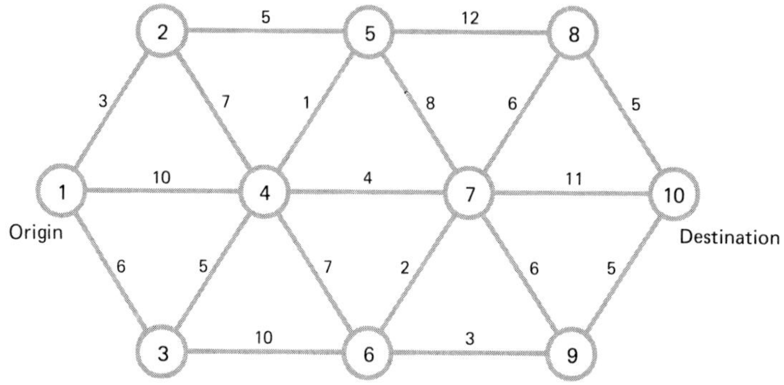

6. Operators of aircraft charter services must determine in advance what route will be taken from origin to destination. The aircraft normally navigates from one VOR (very-high-frequency omnirange) station to another during the flight from home field to another airport. The following network represents the possible flight paths considered, where the intermediate nodes represent VOR stations and the values along the network branches represent flight hours. Determine the shortest route (in flight hours) for the charter service from the origin to destination.

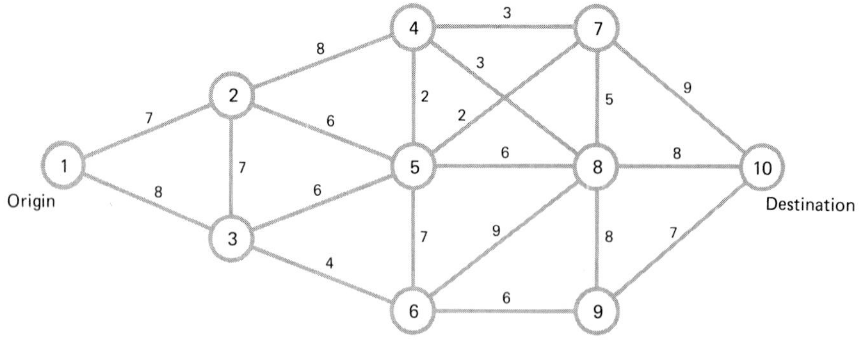

7. Assume that the values along the directed branches of the following network represent the *costs* associated with beginning at node i and ending at node j. The costs in hundreds of dollars are summarized as follows:

Beginning at Node i	Ending at Node j $j = 1$	2	3	4
$i = 0$	$4	5	9	11
1	—	2	5	7
2	—	—	3	5
3	—	—	—	4

Determine the minimum cost route from node 0 to node 4.

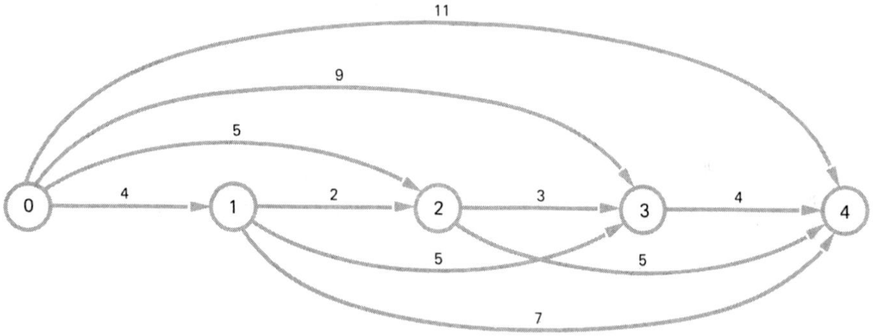

8. A railroad company is purchasing a new diesel unit to be used in the company's switching yard operations of coal cars. At the end of five years, the company is planning to replace all current coal cars with new, larger cars, so the diesel unit will have to be replaced with a new, larger unit at that time. However, the current diesel switching unit receives heavy use resulting in rapidly increasing operating and maintenance costs as it ages. Therefore, it may be economical to replace it one or more times during the coming five-year planning period. The following table summarizes the company's estimated total net discounted costs associated with operation and replacement of the diesel unit (purchase price for new unit minus sale price for old unit, plus operating and maintenance costs of owned unit) assuming purchase at the end of year i and sale at the end of year j. Year 0 represents the current point in time, year 1 represents the end of year 1, etc. Dollar values are given in hundreds of thousands.

Total Net Discounted Costs					
Year	Year Sold (j)				
Purchased (i)	1	2	3	4	5
0	$5	6	8	14	20
1	—	5	7	11	15
2	—	—	5	9	13
3	—	—	—	5	11
4	—	—	—	—	5

Formulate and solve the problem as a shortest-route network problem. Determine at what times the diesel unit should be replaced during the five-year planning period in order to minimize total net discounted costs. (Hint: Examine the problem 7 network structure.)

9. Given the problem 1 network, assume that each node represents a telephone location and the objective is to connect all telephone locations using the minimum amount of telephone line. Determine the minimal spanning-tree solution.

10. Given the problem 2 network, assume that the network represents potential water main routes to connect homes in a new subdivision (where nodes represent home locations and branch values represent distances in hundreds of yards). Determine the minimal spanning-tree solution for the minimum pipeline required to connect all new homes.

11. Given the problem 5 network, assume that the network represents potential electrical transmission line routes to connect all cities (nodes) in the network. Determine the minimal spanning-tree solution to minimize the transmission line required.

12. Given the problem 6 network, assume that the network nodes represent homes to which underground television cable is to be connected. The network branches represent streets along which the cable may be buried, and the values shown along the network branches represent distance in hundreds of feet. Determine the minimal spanning-tree solution to connect all homes to the television cable while minimizing the total length of television cable used.

13. Given the following message transmission network, determine the maximum flow of messages from the input source to the output sink. The message flow capacity from node i to node j (in messages per minute) is given along branch (i, j) nearest node i. Specify the solution quantity and direction of message flow for each branch of the network.

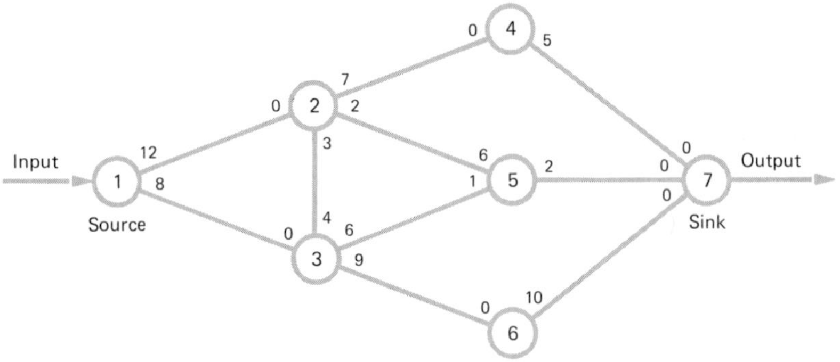

14. Given the following oil pipeline network, determine the maximum flow of oil from the input source to the output sink. The oil flow capacity from node i to node j (in barrels per minute) is given along branch (i,j) nearest node i. Specify the solution quantity and direction of flow for each branch of the pipeline network.

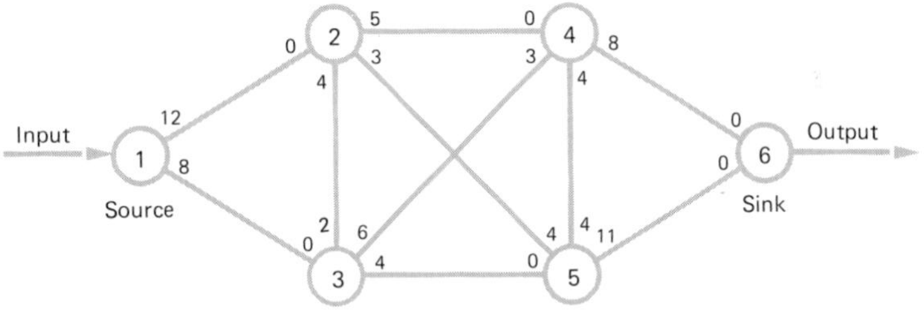

15. Given the following highway network, determine the maximum vehicle flow from the source to the sink. The vehicle flow capacity from node i to node j (in hundreds of vehicles per hour) is given along branch (i,j) nearest node i. Specify the solution quantity and direction of flow for each branch of the highway network.

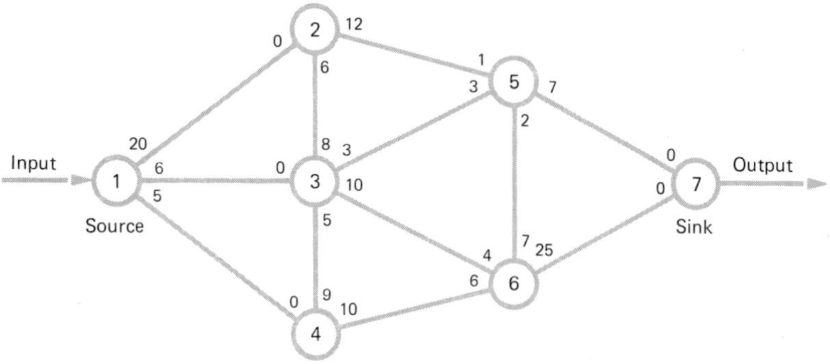

16. Given the following natural gas pipeline network, determine the maximum gas flow from the source to the sink. The flow capacity from node i to node j (in hundreds of cu. ft./sec.) is given along branch (i,j) nearest node i. Specify the solution quantity and direction of flow for each branch of the pipeline network.

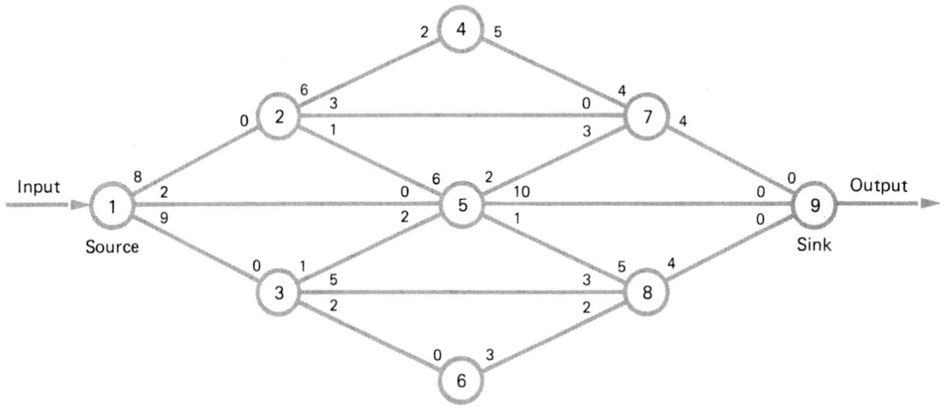

17. An equipment maintenance building is to be erected near a large construction site. Also, an electric generator and a large water storage tank are to be installed a short distance away and connected to the building. The activity descriptions and estimated durations are given in the following table, along with the required activity precedence relationships for the project.

Activity	Activity Description	Activity Predecessor	Activity Duration (weeks)
a	Clear and level site	—	2
b	Erect building	*a*	6
c	Install generator	*a*	4
d	Install water tank	*a*	2
e	Install maintenance equipment	*b*	4
f	Connect generator and tank to building	*b,c,d*	5
g	Paint and finish work on building	*b*	3
h	Facility test and checkout	*e,f*	2

Complete the following:

a. Construct the network figure for the project.
b. Determine the earliest time (ET) and latest time (LT) for each network node.
c. Determine total slack (TS) and free slack (FS) for each project activity.
d. Identify the project critical path and interpret its meaning.
e. Prepare a table summarizing the project activity schedule.

18. Given the project in problem 17, assume that management has decided that activity *h* (test and checkout) requires only the completion of activity *e* (installation of maintenance equipment). Complete the following:

   a. Construct the project network.
   b. Determine the *ET* and *LT* values for each network node.
   c. Determine the *TS* and *FS* values for each project activity.
   d. Identify the critical path.
   e. Prepare a summary activity schedule for the project.

19. Given the following project network, where activity durations (in days) are shown alongside each network arrow, complete the following:

   a. Determine the *ET* and *LT* values for each node.
   b. Determine the *TS* and *FS* values for each activity.
   c. Identify the project critical path.
   d. Excluding dummy activities, identify those activities that share slack with another activity. Also identify which activity the slack is shared with and by what amount.

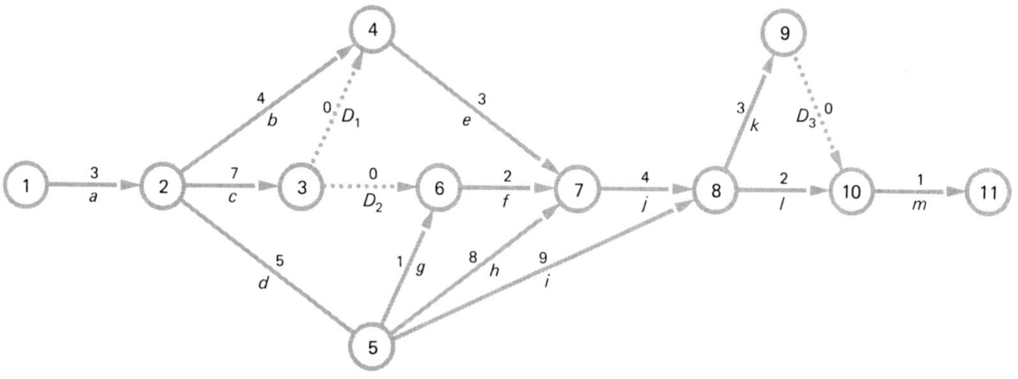

20. Given the project network in problem 19, assume that an additional activity, *n*, must be added. Its predecessors are activities *b* and *c* and its only successor is activity *m*. Given that the estimated duration for activity *n* is fourteen days, complete the following:

   a. Determine *ET* and *LT* for each network node.
   b. Determine *TS* and *FS* for each project activity.
   c. Identify the project critical path.
   d. Identify the network path (sequence of activities) that determines the earliest time for each project node.

21. Given the project in problem 17, assume that three time estimates are obtained for each activity:

	Time Estimates (weeks)		
Activity	*a* Optimistic	*m* Most Likely	*b* Pessimistic
a	1	2	3
b	4	6	14
c	2	4	6
d	1	2	5
e	3	4	11
f	1	5	6
g	1	3	5
h	2	2	2

Complete the following:

a. Compute the mean ($\hat{t}_{ij}$) and variance (v_{ij}) times for each activity.
b. Using the computed $\hat{t}_{ij}$ values, determine the earliest time and latest time for each network node.
c. Determine the *TS* and *FS* values for each project activity.
d. Identify the project critical path.
e. Compare the results for parts *a*, *b*, and *c* to results obtained in problem 17. Has the critical path changed? If so, what caused the change in the critical path? Has the project completion time changed? If so, what caused the change?
f. What is the probability the project will be completed in sixteen weeks or less?
g. Determine the probability that the project will be completed in nineteen weeks or less.
h. Determine the probability that the project will require fifteen or more weeks for completion.

22. Given the project network in problem 19, assume that three time estimates are obtained for each activity:

	Time Estimates (days)		
Activity	*a* Optimistic	*m* Most Likely	*b* Pessimistic
a	1	3	5
b	3	4	5
c	4	6	10
d	3	5	7
e	1	2	5
f	2	2	2
g	1	1	1
h	4	7	16
i	6	8	16
j	1	4	7
k	2	3	4
l	1	2	3
m	1	1	1

Complete the following:

a. Compute the values of the mean and variance for each activity time.
b. Using the values computed in *a*, determine the values of *ET* and *LT* for each network node.
c. Determine the *TS* and *FS* values for each project activity.
d. Identify the project critical path.
e. Compare the results to the results for problem 19. Has the critical path changed?
f. Which project activities have the greatest amount of uncertainty with regard to duration? Are any of these activities on the critical path? What are the implications of this uncertainty with regard to project critical path?
g. Illustrate graphically the distribution of project completion time with associated mean and variance.
h. Determine the 95 percent confidence interval estimate of project completion time.
i. Determine the probability of project completion within twenty-seven or less days.

23. The following project description provides estimates of both activity durations and associated direct costs. Two estimates are provided for each activity—estimated normal time (and associated cost) and estimated crash time (and associated cost):

			Time Estimates (weeks)		Direct Cost Estimates (thousands of dollars)	
Activity	(*i*, *j*)	Predecessor	Normal	Crash	Normal	Crash
a	(1, 2)	—	20	8	100	148
b	(1, 4)	—	24	20	120	140
c	(1, 3)	—	14	7	70	119
d	(2, 4)	*a*	10	6	50	82
e	(3, 4)	*c*	11	5	55	73

Given the preceding information, complete the following:

a. Determine the crashing cost per week for each activity.
b. Determine the minimum cost project-crashing solution.
c. What are the crashing cost savings for the part *b* solution in comparison with crashing all project activities?
d. Identify the project critical path(s) for the crashing solution.
e. Illustrate with a table and a graph the time-cost trade-off for the problem.

24. The following project description provides estimates of normal activity times (and associated costs) and crash activity times (and associated costs) as follows:

			Time Estimates (days)		Direct Cost Estimates (thousands of dollars)	
Activity	(*i*, *j*)	Predecessor	Normal	Crash	Normal	Crash
a	(1, 2)	—	16	8	200	440
b	(1, 3)	—	14	9	100	180
c	(2, 4)	*a*	8	6	50	70
d	(2, 5)	*a*	5	4	60	130
e	(3, 5)	*b*	4	2	150	300
f	(3, 6)	*b*	6	4	80	160
g	(4, 6)	*c*	10	7	300	450
h	(5, 6)	*d*, *e*	15	10	500	800

Given the preceding information, complete the following:

a. Determine the crashing cost per day for each activity.
b. Determine the minimum cost project-crashing solution.
c. What are the crashing cost savings for the part *b* solution in comparison with crashing all project activities?
d. Identify the project critical path(s) for the crashing solution.
e. Illustrate with a table and a graph the time-cost trade-off curve for the problem.

7 Inventory Models

The study of inventory models in this chapter represents a slight departure from the focus of the rest of the text. While the preceding chapters have dealt predominantly with the description of management science techniques, this chapter presents an application of management science principles to a business function, inventory control. To include a study of inventory models at this point, however, is not inappropriate or unusual for several reasons.

Inventory analysis was one of the initial areas of application of quantitative methods and techniques first studied as early as 1915. Since then it has become one of the most popular areas of analysis, appearing in the majority of management science texts as well as comprising a substantial portion of the literature in operations research and production management. It is not surprising that inventory analysis has held such a position of prominence in all forms of quantitative business methods since inventory often represents as much as 40 percent of the total invested capital of industrial organizations. In addition to being a major portion of the total current assets of many businesses, inventory represents an important decision variable at all stages of product manufacturing, distribution, and sales. As such, changes in inventory policy can have a significant effect throughout an organization.

However, beyond these "practical" business reasons, inventory analysis is also an excellent vehicle for exposing the student of management science to the general classic modeling concepts. The methodology and logic employed in developing and analyzing inventory models provide a basic groundwork for management science modeling that can be transferred to other areas of application. In fact, the fundamental classic inventory model is so widely reproduced as an example of quantitative methods in business that the reader may already be familiar with basic inventory modeling.

The study of inventory in this chapter concentrates on the presentation of several of the more popular inventory models. These inventory models can be subdivided into two fundamental forms. The first form is the classic **deterministic EOQ model** and its several variations. The analysis of this classic model will provide the groundwork for the second model form, **stochastic inventory models.**

Inventory Functions

Inventory is broadly defined as any stock of economic resources that are idle at a given point in time. This can include raw materials awaiting use in manufacturing operations, semifinished goods temporarily stored during the manufacturing process, finished goods awaiting distribution, and finished goods awaiting sale in wholesale or retail outlets. Inventories may also include nonphysical assets such as cash, accounts receivable, and human resources.

Although inventory is generally considered to be a nonearning asset, the optimal managerial decision is not simply to reduce inventory to the lowest possible level. Inventories are necessary to achieve workable systems of production, distribution, and marketing of physical goods. For example, raw materials must be accumulated in inventory for further processing into finished goods. Also, raw material inventories are often accumulated as a hedge against price inflation or labor strikes in industries supplying or using these materials. During the process of production, inventory serves the function of decoupling successive stages of manufacturing. This allows the various production departments to operate more independently, without direct reliance on the schedule of output of prior departments in the production process. The distribution of finished goods almost always requires certain quantities of inventory in transit and accumulations at intermediate delivery points.

It may also be more economical to carry a certain amount of inventory in order to produce or purchase in large lots so as to achieve reduced production setup costs or quantity discounts on items purchased. Inventories may be accumulated in order to smooth out the level of production operations so that employees do not have to be temporarily laid off and later rehired and retrained.

The most visible function of inventory is at the retail store level, where inventory is carried to absorb random fluctuations in demand. The objective of inventory at the retail level is to meet demand as it occurs and avoid out-of-stock situations, which can result in lost sales. Additionally, inventory on display serves as a promotional device.

Thus, although inventories are nonearning assets, it is apparent that inventories serve many functions that are vital to the overall production-distribution-marketing system. The important point is that since inventories are found throughout the system and constitute a major segment of total investment, it is crucial that good inventory management be practiced.

Basic Inventory Decisions

The basic inventory decisions concern what quantity to order and when to order. Thus, when attempting to model inventory systems, these are the important decision variables. Throughout the chapter it will be shown that in many cases it is possible to consider each of these decisions separately. However, in some cases the two decisions are interdependent, and the optimal values for the two decision variables must be obtained simultaneously. The rationale for considering these variables separately or jointly depends on the individual models, which will be discussed later in this chapter.

Evaluation Criteria—Inventory Costs

The most common criteria considered in inventory analysis are inventory-related costs, which can be categorized as (1) ordering costs, (2) carrying costs, and (3) shortage costs. Each of these will be discussed separately in detail.

Ordering Costs

Ordering costs are those costs associated with replenishing the stock of inventory on hand. These are costs that vary with the number of orders made and are expressed in terms of dollar cost per order. The following are sample costs incurred each time an order is made:

Requisitioning
Purchase order
Transportation
Receiving
Inspection
Placing in storage
Accounting and auditing
Payment to supplier

Carrying Costs

Carrying costs are those costs associated with holding a certain stock of inventory on hand. Carrying costs are often referred to as holding costs. These costs vary with the level of inventory held and sometimes vary with the time the item is held, as in the case of perishable goods. The longer goods are held in inventory, the longer money is tied up in those goods, which causes higher inventory costs. There are several components of carrying cost and the relative impact of each depends upon the type of inventory goods considered. The following are commonly considered components of carrying cost:

Foregone profit on investment tied up in inventory
Direct storage costs (rent, heat, lights, refrigeration, record keeping, security, etc.)
Product obsolescence or deterioration
Depreciation, taxes, and insurance

Carrying costs may be specified in several ways. The most general form is the dollar cost of carrying one unit in inventory per unit time. The time horizon commonly considered is one year; that is, the carrying cost is the cost of carrying one unit in inventory for one year. Another common approach is to specify carrying cost per year as a percentage of average inventory value; for example, carrying cost may equal 15% to 20% of average inventory value.

Shortage Costs

Shortage costs are often referred to as stockout costs. Inventory shortages occur when demand exceeds the supply of inventory on hand. Shortages may either be accidental or a planned policy of the company.

If inventory shortages result in the permanent loss of sales for items demanded but not filled, the shortage cost then includes lost profits due to unsatisfied demand. Additionally, shortages can result in an "ill-will" cost due to permanently lost customers and the associated long-term lost profits of future sales.

On the other hand, the firm may simply back order demands not filled when shortages occur. This is common practice in most mail-order houses. Thus, the relevant cost of shortage then becomes the clerical and paperwork costs associated with back orders. However, back-ordered shortages may also result in some lost customers, creating some ill-will costs.

Deterministic Inventory Models

The classic model often referred to as the EOQ (economic order quantity) model is the simplest of the inventory models. Although it is generally too simplified to reflect most real-world situations, it is nevertheless a good base from which to launch a study of inventory models. The presentation of the classic EOQ model is organized into a series of steps, each describing a different model form. Actually the first step describes the basic, or classic, inventory model and succeeding steps simply reflect one or more changes in the basic assumptions of the initial model. Also, the set of models represents a logical development of deterministic inventory models, from the simplest case to the more complex cases.

Assumptions of the Classic EOQ Model

The objective of the classic EOQ model is the minimization of total inventory costs typically achieved by the determination of an optimal order quantity (Q). Additional assumptions of the deterministic EOQ model are as follows:

1. Inventory usage rate (demand) is constant over time.
2. Inventory demand is known with certainty.
3. The entire order quantity is received at once.
4. Inventory is replenished when inventory is exactly zero (no excess stock is carried and no shortages are allowed).
5. Reorder lead time is zero (order is received at the same instant it is placed).

The last assumption is unnecessary, since we could assume a constant, known reorder lead time without affecting our model results; however, in order to simplify the initial presentation we will include this assumption.

The assumptions of the classic inventory model are illustrated graphically in figure 7.1, which is referred to as the **inventory level model.** This distinction in model title is made since inventory models are illustrated graphically in two ways: (1) graphic model of inventory level and (2) graphic model of inventory costs.

Figure 7.1 Classic inventory level model.

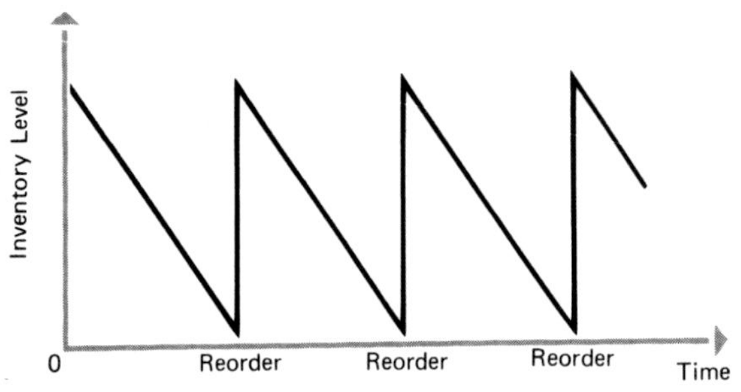

Note in figure 7.1 that the downward sloping line shows the level of inventory being reduced at a constant rate over time (constant and known demand). Also, since demand is constant and known and since receipt of goods ordered is instantaneous, the reorder point occurs when the inventory level falls to exactly zero.

Formulation of the Classic EOQ Model

The objective of inventory analysis is to determine the optimal order quantity that will minimize total inventory costs. The two classes of costs included in the inventory model are ordering costs and carrying costs, and the objective is to minimize the sum of these two costs. Since it has been assumed at this point that shortages never occur, shortage costs are not considered.

Figure 7.2 illustrates inventory costs graphically. Note that as the quantity per order increases, fewer orders are necessary and, therefore, ordering costs decrease. However, as order sizes increase there will be more time between orders and inventory carried will increase, resulting in increased carrying costs. Total inventory costs first decrease as the order size increases but begin to rise again after a point. The objective of inventory analysis is to solve for the optimal value of order quantity that corresponds to minimum total inventory costs. This point labeled Q_{opt} is shown graphically in figure 7.2

Model Symbols

The first step in constructing the inventory model is to define the variables and parameters (generally constants) of the model. Initially, the parameters of the model are given as symbols. The approach of inventory analysis is to define model parameters as symbols, when possible, and solve for the general case. Thus, one can substitute the values of the parameters into the solution for the general case model and obtain an optimal solution for a specific problem, without having to solve the entire model for each new set of parameter values. The model symbols are defined following figure 7.2.

Figure 7.2 Classic inventory decision model.

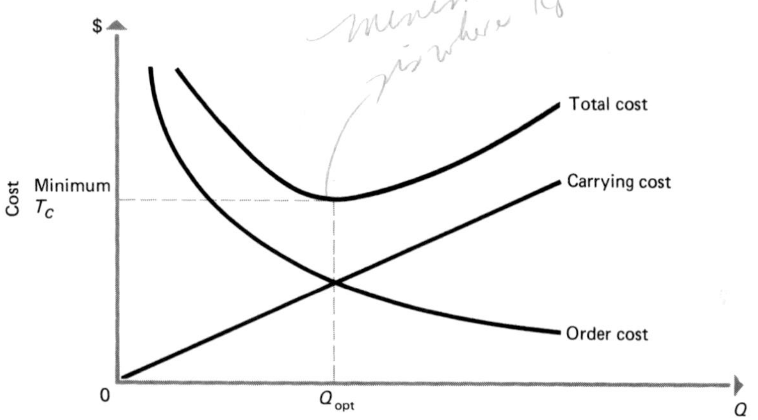

TC = total annual inventory cost
C_o = ordering costs per order
C_c = carrying cost per unit per year
Q = quantity ordered, per order
D = demand (usage) for goods in inventory, expressed on an annual basis

Now that we have developed the inventory model components, the next step is to mold them into a mathematical model for minimizing total inventory cost. However, prior to construction of the mathematical model, the concept of **average inventory** will be examined. Note that the usage rate (demand) for goods in inventory is assumed to be constant; thus, the average inventory held will be $Q/2$, where Q (quantity ordered) is the maximum level of inventory held at the time of each order receipt. The average inventory level is illustrated graphically in figure 7.3.

Figure 7.3 Average inventory model.

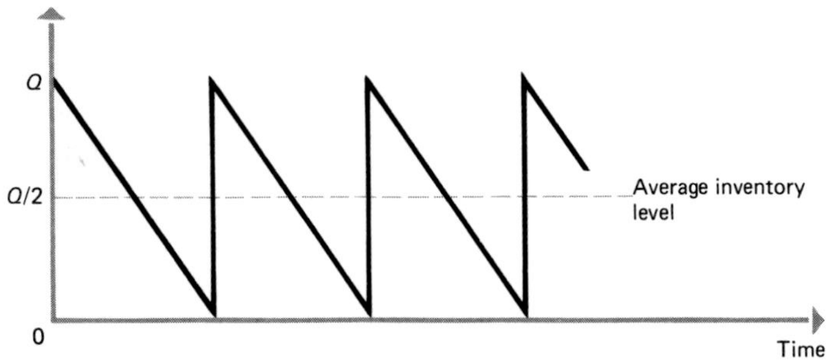

The EOQ Model

The inventory model is constructed by analyzing each of the cost categories separately.

Total ordering cost per year is simply the cost per order, C_o, multiplied by the number of orders per year. (A time period of one year will always be assumed, however, any time frame could be used.) Since total usage or demand is known to be D, then the number of orders per year will be $\frac{D}{Q}$.

$$\text{total ordering cost} = C_o \cdot \frac{D}{Q}$$

Total carrying cost is the carrying cost per unit held per year, C_c, times the average number of units held $\left(\frac{Q}{2} \text{ from fig. 7.3}\right)$.

$$\text{total carrying cost} = C_c \cdot \frac{Q}{2}$$

Total inventory cost is the sum of ordering and carrying costs as follows:

$$\text{total annual cost} = \text{total ordering cost} + \text{total carrying cost}$$

$$TC = C_o \cdot \frac{D}{Q} + C_c \cdot \frac{Q}{2}$$

Note that a third cost component in the total inventory cost equation, total purchase cost, is not considered. This cost, represented as $D \cdot P$ (where P is the purchase price per unit), is generally not included in the inventory function since it is not strictly an inventory cost. That is, purchase cost is not a decision variable and, as such, does not enter into the determination of an optimal order quantity, Q. However, in a strict technical sense, total annual inventory cost could be written as

$$TC = C_o \cdot \frac{D}{Q} + C_c \cdot \frac{Q}{2} + D \cdot P.$$

The model can now be solved for the optimal order quantity. For this model this can be accomplished by equating total carrying cost to total ordering cost and solving for Q. This corresponds to the point in figure 7.2 where the curves for carrying cost and ordering cost intersect. (This approach will not work for all types of inventory models but, in general, holds true for equations of the form $y = ax^{-1} + bx$.) Thus, total ordering cost is set equal to total carrying cost.

$$C_o\frac{D}{Q} = C_c\frac{Q}{2}$$

Solving this equation for Q yields

$$Q^2 = \frac{2C_oD}{C_c}$$

and

$$Q_{opt} = \sqrt{\frac{2C_oD}{C_c}}.$$

The optimal value of Q can also be determined as the lowest point on the total cost curve in figure 7.2. This approach requires that the derivative of the total cost equation with respect to Q be computed.

$$TC = C_o\frac{D}{Q} + C_c\frac{Q}{2}$$

$$\frac{dTC}{dQ} = \frac{-C_oD}{Q^2} + \frac{C_c}{2}$$

Since this derivative represents the slope of the total cost curve, by setting the equation equal to zero and solving for Q, we will be solving for Q at the minimum cost point of the curve (i.e., where the slope = 0). Thus,

$$0 = \frac{-C_oD}{Q^2} + \frac{C_c}{2}$$

$$Q_{opt} = \sqrt{\frac{2C_oD}{C_c}}.$$

As has been demonstrated, for this simple EOQ model the algebraic approach will suffice; however, for more complex models it will be necessary to employ differential calculus.

In order to solve for any specific inventory problem that satisfies the assumptions of the basic EOQ model, simply insert the values of C_o, C_c, and D into the general solution model. For example, assume that the values of the model parameters are determined to be

C_o =	\$ 50	Cost per order
C_c =	\$100	Cost per unit held in inventory on an annual basis
D =	4,900	Demand for goods in inventory on an annual basis.

Then, the solution for the optimal order quantity is

$$
\begin{aligned}
Q_{opt} &= \sqrt{\frac{2C_oD}{C_c}} \\
&= \sqrt{\frac{(2)(50)(4,900)}{100}} \\
&= \sqrt{4,900} \\
Q_{opt} &= 70 \text{ units.}
\end{aligned}
$$

The order quantity that minimizes total inventory cost is 70 units.

Several additional types of information may be desired regarding the inventory model, including the value of the minimum total inventory cost, how often to order per year, and the length of time between orders. The nature of the classic inventory model is such that once the value of Q has been determined, these other values are also directly available. These values are defined as

N = number of orders per year
T_b = time between orders
T = total time (in this case one year).

In the development of the EOQ model it was shown that the number of orders per year equals annual demand divided by order size, or $N = \frac{D}{Q}$. Thus, for our example the solution value for N_{opt} will be

$$N_{opt} = \frac{D}{Q_{opt}} = \frac{4,900}{70} = 70 \text{ orders.}$$

Also, the solution value for time between orders is simply the total time horizon divided by the number of orders, or $T_b = \frac{T}{N}$. Thus,

$$(T_b)_{opt} = \frac{T}{N_{opt}} = \frac{365}{70} = 5.214 \cong 5 \text{ days.}$$

The value used for T may be 1 for one year, or it could be in months, weeks, or days, depending upon the form of solution desired.

Finally, the minimum total inventory cost for the optimal value of Q may be derived by referring to the original model.

$$TC_{opt} = C_o\frac{D}{Q_{opt}} + C_c\frac{Q_{opt}}{2}$$

$$TC_{opt} = 50 \cdot \frac{4,900}{70} + 100 \cdot \frac{70}{2}$$

$$= \$7,000$$

It is interesting to note that the determination of TC is analogous to the general form of the solution for Q, as follows:

$$TC_{opt} = C_o\frac{D}{Q_{opt}} + C_c\frac{Q_{opt}}{2}$$

Substituting for Q, the optimal solution in terms of model parameters,

$$TC_{opt} = \frac{C_oD}{\sqrt{\frac{2C_oD}{C_c}}} + \frac{C_c\sqrt{\frac{2C_oD}{C_c}}}{2}$$

and combining terms and several mathematical manipulations, yields

$$TC_{opt} = \sqrt{2C_oC_cD}.$$

Thus, simply substitute the parameter values for the model into this equation to obtain the minimum total inventory cost. For the example solution, this would yield

$$TC = \sqrt{(2)(50)(100)(4,900)}$$

$$TC = \$7,000.$$

Reorder Point

The second step in our discussion of inventory models actually does not involve a new model at all. However, one assumption of the previous model is modified and a new assumption is added. The assumption that goods ordered are received at the same instant as ordered (assumption 5) is now discarded. The other assumptions of the initial model remain the same, and it is now assumed that the time between placing and receiving an order is known and constant.

By modifying the last assumption of the initial model, the concept of reorder lead time is introduced. Thus, an additional consideration for model analysis is added, but the basic cost model previously presented is unchanged.

The inventory level model is again illustrated graphically in figure 7.4. However, in this case it is assumed that there is some time lag from the time the goods are ordered to the time the order is received. This is generally called **lead time.** Figure 7.4 illustrates the lead time for each order. Note that in this case, goods are now ordered before the level of inventory falls to zero. The inventory level at which an order is placed is termed the **reorder point.**

Figure 7.4 Inventory model with reorder point.

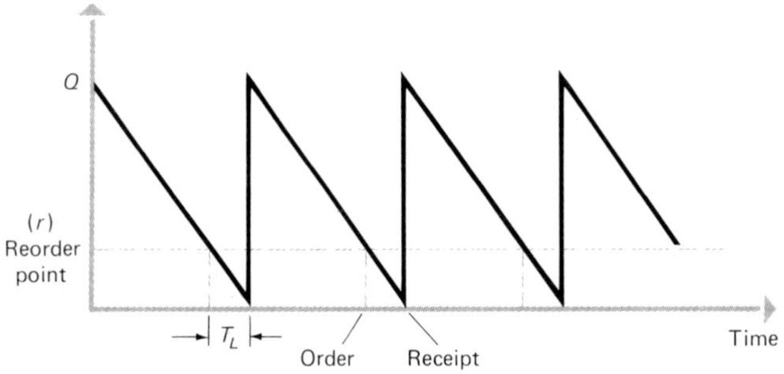

With the assumptions of this model—constant and known demand and constant and known lead time—it is a simple matter to compute the reorder point. The reorder point is the product of the demand (in units per day) during lead time multiplied by the lead time (in days). These values are defined as

r = reorder point (inventory level in units)

T_L = lead time (days).

If the demand per day (assuming a 365-day-a-year operation) is $\frac{D}{365}$, then the reorder point is simply

$$r = T_L \frac{D}{365}.$$

Suppose the demand per day is 15 units and the lead time is 5 days. The reorder point would be 75 units, or $r = 75$, which means that an order would be placed when the inventory level falls to 75 units. It is important to point out that the solution value for Q (the optimal order quantity) is not affected by the assumption that there is lead time involved in receipt of goods. Therefore, the classic model may include the requirement that Q be computed by the method illustrated initially and also that r be determined.

Variations in the Classic EOQ Model

Two modifications in the EOQ model that result in different inventory model forms will now be discussed: carrying cost as a percentage and time as a model variable.

Carrying cost may be expressed as a percentage of average dollar value of inventory held rather than a dollar carrying cost per unit held. If the percentage approach is used, the unit price (or value) of inventory in stock must also be specified, in order to determine the average value of inventory held.

The variables for the carrying-cost portion of the model are now as follows:

K_c = carrying cost as a percentage of average dollar value of inventory on an annual basis

P = price (or value) per unit of inventory held in inventory

Therefore, we can see that the equation for total annual carrying cost may now be expressed as

$$\text{total carrying cost} = K_c P \frac{Q}{2}.$$

That is, the annual carrying cost equals the percentage carrying cost times the average inventory value.

The inventory model now becomes

$$TC = C_o \frac{D}{Q} + K_c P \frac{Q}{2}.$$

The same solution procedure is used for this modified model as was followed for the initial model; that is, equate the two types of inventory cost and solve for Q. Thus, we obtain

$$C_o \cdot \frac{D}{Q} = K_c \cdot P \cdot \frac{Q}{2}$$

and

$$Q_{opt} = \sqrt{\frac{2C_o D}{K_c P}}.$$

The resulting model approach introduces a new parameter, price of goods in stock, and changes the definition of C_c to a percentage value, K_c, versus the dollar value definition of the initial model.

Suppose, for example, that the values of the model parameters were found to be the following:

C_o =	\$50	Cost per order
K_c =	20%	Carrying cost as a percent of average inventory value on an annual basis
D =	4,900	Annual demand for goods in inventory
P =	\$500	Price or value per unit of goods in inventory

The solution value for Q would be

$$Q = \sqrt{\frac{2C_oD}{K_cP}}$$

$$= \sqrt{\frac{(2)(50)(4,900)}{(0.20)(500)}}$$

$$Q_{opt} = 70.$$

Another fairly common practice in inventory models is to specify the time horizon over which the inventory analysis is to apply as a variable. The symbol commonly used to denote the time horizon is T. In this case it is often found that the demand for goods in inventory is specified as demand during time T. Also, the holding or carrying cost in this case is often specified as the cost of holding one unit in inventory "per unit time" (such as days). Thus, for this case, it is necessary to include the variable T in the construction of the inventory model.

The inventory model will now be specified, where the total time horizon is simply identified as T, and the following definitions apply:

D = demand during time T (e.g. time horizon in days)
C_c = carrying cost per unit of inventory per unit time (e.g., per day)

Thus, the model is as follows:

$$\text{ordering cost} = C_o \cdot \frac{D}{Q}$$

$$\text{carrying cost} = C_c \cdot \frac{Q}{2} \cdot T$$

$$TC = C_o \frac{D}{Q} + C_c \frac{Q}{2} T$$

The solution to the preceding model is determined in a manner similar to the initial model, yielding

$$C_o \frac{D}{Q} = C_c \frac{Q}{2} T$$

and

$$Q_{opt} = \sqrt{\frac{2C_oD}{C_cT}}.$$

Q_{opt} is the optimal inventory order quantity for the system evaluated over the time horizon T (where C_c is specified in terms of the same time units as T).

Suppose we modify the previous example so that the time horizon is six months (or 182.5 days). For this example, the demand over that period would be 2,450 units. The cost of carrying inventory, per day, would be 27.4¢ per unit day. Recall that ordering cost equals \$50. Thus, the model solution would yield

$$Q = \sqrt{\frac{2C_oD}{C_cT}}$$

$$= \sqrt{\frac{(2)(50)(2,450)}{(0.274)(182.5)}}$$

$$Q_{opt} = 70 \text{ units.}$$

As expected, we obtain the same solution as previously obtained.

Noninstantaneous Receipt Model

The next step in the development of inventory models is the case in which goods are received in a constant stream over time, rather than at one point in time. This is analogous to a situation where items are produced for inventory and simultaneously used internally but not at the same rate. All other assumptions of the initial model remain unchanged—only assumption 3 is changed.

The parameters unique to this model are defined as follows:

R = rate at which goods are received over time on an annual basis; also known as the manufacturing rate or production rate

D = rate at which goods are demanded over time on an annual basis

All other model symbols are unchanged from the original model.

Attention must first be given to the average inventory for this model. First, recall from the initial *EOQ* model that average inventory was half the maximum inventory level, which in that case was Q, the reorder quantity. In this model, the maximum inventory level must be adjusted for the fact that the goods are steadily received and used over time. This is achieved as follows:

$\frac{Q}{R}$ = period required to receive one entire order (order receipt period) as a proportion of a year

$\frac{Q}{R} \cdot D$ = number of units in inventory demanded (usage rate) during order receipt period

$Q - \left(\frac{Q}{R} \cdot D\right)$ = maximum level of inventory for any given order

$\frac{1}{2}\left[Q - \left(\frac{Q}{R} \cdot D\right)\right]$ = average inventory level

This expression for average inventory can be modified to read

$$\frac{Q}{2}\left(1 - \frac{D}{R}\right).$$

Note that in this relationship the ratio $\left(\frac{D}{R}\right)$ represents the proportion of production that goes to meet demand while $\left(1 - \frac{D}{R}\right)$ reflects the proportion of production allocated to inventory.

The inventory level model for this case is illustrated graphically in figure 7.5. Note that it is assumed that the rate at which an order is received is greater than its usage rate ($R > D$). Thus, immediately after an order is placed, the inventory level rises at a constant rate, $R - D$, up to the point, $Q - \left(\frac{Q}{R} \cdot D\right)$, and then falls at the constant demand rate, D.

Figure 7.5 Inventory model with noninstantaneous receipt.

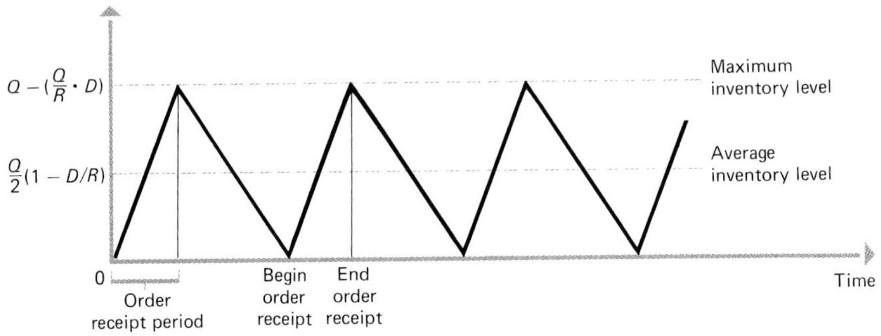

The inventory model is now developed as follows:

$$\text{ordering cost} = C_o \cdot \frac{D}{Q}$$

$$\text{carrying cost} = C_c \cdot \frac{Q}{2}\left(1 - \frac{D}{R}\right)$$

$$TC = C_o\frac{D}{Q} + C_c\frac{Q}{2}\left(1 - \frac{D}{R}\right)$$

The solution is obtained in a manner similar to the initial model.

$$C_o\frac{D}{Q} = C_c\frac{Q}{2}\left(1 - \frac{D}{R}\right)$$

Solving for Q,

$$Q^2 = \frac{2C_oD}{C_c\left(1 - \frac{D}{R}\right)}$$

and

$$Q_{opt} = \sqrt{\frac{2C_oD}{C_c\left(1 - \frac{D}{R}\right)}}.$$

The solution is the same as that obtained for the classic EOQ model except that C_c must be multiplied by the factor $\left(1 - \frac{D}{R}\right)$ to include the fact that goods ordered are received over time, as opposed to receipt at a single point in time.

For example, assume the values for the model parameters are as follows:

$C_o = \$\ 50$	Ordering cost per order
$C_c = \$100$	Carrying cost per unit inventory per year
$D = 4{,}900$ units	Annual demand
$R = 9{,}800$ units	Annual production rate

Thus, the solution yielded by the preceding model is

$$Q = \sqrt{\frac{2C_oD}{C_c\left(1 - \frac{D}{R}\right)}}$$

$$= \sqrt{\frac{(2)(50)(4{,}900)}{100\left(1 - \frac{4{,}900}{9{,}800}\right)}}$$

$$Q_{opt} = \sqrt{9{,}800} \cong 99 \text{ units}.$$

Note that since the goods ordered are received over time, there will be no carrying cost associated with those goods received and used immediately during that time. In the case of the example, exactly half of the goods received are used during the order receipt period. Thus, the total carrying costs will be reduced for this model. Therefore, it becomes economical to order in larger quantities for this case than for the initial model.

Production Lot-Size Model

This variation of the inventory model modifies the noninstantaneous receipt model by considering it within a different framework of application. Suppose the firm under consideration manufactures its own goods for inventory rather than ordering from outside the firm. Thus, if we consider the production lot size as the order quantity, we can cast this problem within the framework of the preceding model.

Consider the following example. Suppose a firm has an annual demand for goods produced of 6,500 units. The set-up cost for each production run is assumed to be $200. Inventory carrying cost per unit per year is $3.20. The production rate is 12,500 units per year. (Assume 250 operating days per year.)

The optimal production lot size is determined as follows:

$$Q = \sqrt{\frac{2C_oD}{C_c\left(1 - \frac{D}{R}\right)}}$$

$$= \sqrt{\frac{(2)(200)(6{,}500)}{(3.20)\left(1 - \frac{6{,}500}{12{,}500}\right)}}$$

$$Q_{opt} = \sqrt{1{,}692{,}708} \cong 1{,}300 \text{ units per production run}$$

The optimal number of production runs may be determined as follows:

$$N = \frac{D}{Q_{opt}}$$

$$N_{opt} = \frac{6{,}500}{1{,}300} = 5 \text{ production runs per year}$$

The length (in days) between the start of each production run will be

$$(T_b)_{opt} = \frac{T}{N_{opt}}, \text{ where } T = 250$$

$$\cong 50 \text{ working days between run starts.}$$

Thus, the optimal solution to this production-inventory problem is to produce 1,300 units per production run, with 5 production runs per year, starting every 50 working days. Note that since the production rate is 50 units per day, it will take $\frac{1{,}300}{50} = 26$ days to complete a run. Thus, 24 working days will remain before the start of the next production run for this product. During this time other goods can be produced. Also, the maximum inventory level reached will be $Q\left(1 - \frac{D}{R}\right)$, or $1{,}300\left(1 - \frac{6{,}500}{12{,}500}\right) = 1{,}300(.48) = 624$ units.

By using the same approach used in the initial model to develop the general model for total cost, it can be seen that the minimum total production-inventory cost will be

$$TC = \sqrt{2C_oC_cD\left(1 - \frac{D}{R}\right)}$$

$$TC_{opt} \cong \$1{,}998.00.$$

Inventory Model with Shortages

It was assumed in all previous model variations that an order was received (or that production began) at the precise instant the level of inventory reached zero. Thus, shortages were not allowed to occur, and shortage cost was ignored in the inventory analysis.

We will now modify this assumption by allowing inventory shortages to occur. However, it will be assumed that all demand not met due to an inventory shortage will be back ordered. Thus, all demand will eventually be met.

The assumptions of the original classic inventory model are retained here except for assumption 4, which precluded shortages. We continue to assume constant and known demand, instantaneous replenishment (entire order is received simultaneously), and zero reorder lead time (receipt of goods at the instant an order is placed).

The inventory level model with shortages is illustrated in figure 7.6. Since back orders (shortages) are filled when an order is placed (and received), the maximum inventory level does not reach the level of Q (the order quantity). Rather shortages (S) are filled immediately upon receipt of an order, and the inventory level returns to a level of V, which is equal to $Q - S$. Since the maximum inventory level is lowered, the inventory carrying cost is likewise reduced. An extreme example of this case would occur if the entire demand for products is back ordered, resulting in no inventory and carrying costs of zero. However, the reduction of carrying costs must be balanced against the shortage costs associated with back orders.

Figure 7.6 Inventory model with shortages.

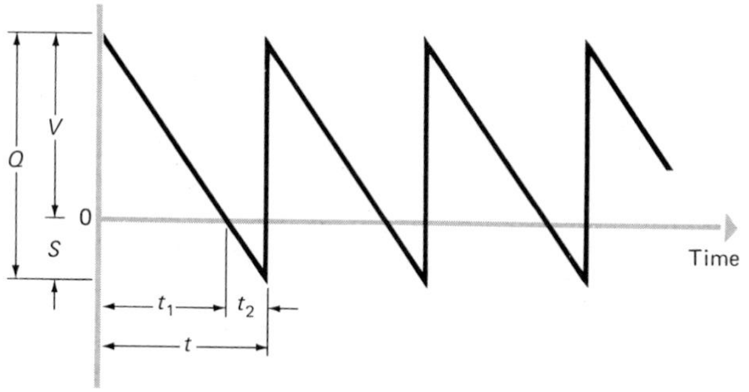

The same description for the previously defined model variables will be used with some additions, as follows:

TC = total annual inventory cost
Q = quantity ordered per order
N = number of orders per year
S = back order quantity (shortages) per order
V = maximum inventory volume $(Q - S)$
D = demand, on annual basis
C_o = ordering cost per order
C_c = carrying cost per unit of inventory per year
C_s = shortage cost per unit of shortage per year
t_1 = time period during which inventory is on hand in an order cycle
t_2 = time period during which there is a shortage in an order cycle
t = order cycle time—time between receipt of orders $(t_1 + t_2)$

The time units used for t, t_1, and t_2 are in terms of fractions of a year. For example, if the order cycle time is 73 days, the value t would be .20 years (73 days ÷ 365 days = .20 years).

The overall cost function for the inventory model with shortages is

Total Cost = Ordering Cost + Carrying Cost + Shortage Cost.

The various components of this total cost model can be derived from inspection of the geometric properties of figure 7.6. Carrying cost is computed as follows. First note that since the maximum inventory level is given as V, the average inventory level during the period inventory is available (i.e., during t_1) is $\frac{V}{2}$. Thus, the carrying cost during the period from the receipt of one order to the next (t) is

$$C_c \cdot t_1 \cdot \frac{V}{2}.$$

(Also note that this quantity is the area of the triangle in fig. 7.6 formed by these values and multiplied by C_c. Thus, the area reflects the amount of inventory on hand.)

The key to converting this carrying-cost relationship to an annual basis is to recognize that the geometrical relationship of t_1 to V is equal to the relationship of t to Q (i.e., similar triangles). Given that $\frac{t_1}{V} = \frac{t}{Q}$, then

$$t_1 = t \cdot \frac{V}{Q}.$$

Substituting this term into the previously defined carrying-cost relationship yields

$$\text{carrying cost per period} = \frac{C_c t V^2}{2Q}.$$

Because $tN = 1$ year, which can be restated as $N = \frac{1}{t}$, we can multiply the carrying-cost equation by $\frac{1}{t}$ and obtain the annual carrying cost as follows:

$$\text{annual carrying cost} = \frac{C_c V^2}{2Q}$$

The shortage cost is determined in a similar manner. Since S is the maximum level of shortages, the average shortage level during the period t_2 is $\frac{S}{2}$. Thus, the shortage cost during one order cycle (t) is

$$C_s \cdot t_2 \cdot \frac{S}{2}$$

The geometrical relationship of t_2 to S is equal to the relationship of t to Q. Thus, $\frac{t_2}{S} = \frac{t}{Q}$ can be converted to

$$t_2 = t \cdot \frac{S}{Q}$$

By substituting this term into the previously defined shortage cost equation we obtain

$$\text{shortage cost per order period} = \frac{C_s\, tS^2}{2Q}.$$

Multiplying this equation by $\frac{1}{t}$ results in the annual shortage cost,

$$\text{annual shortage cost} = \frac{C_s S^2}{2Q}.$$

Since $S = Q - V$, shortage cost can also be defined as

$$\frac{C_s(Q - V)^2}{2Q}.$$

Ordering cost is unaffected by the allowance of shortages.

$$\text{annual order cost} = \frac{C_oD}{Q}$$

The total cost model can now be written as

$$TC = \frac{C_oD}{Q} + \frac{C_cV^2}{2Q} + \frac{C_s(Q - V)^2}{2Q}.$$

In order to determine the optimal values for Q and V, the total cost equation (TC) is differentiated with respect to Q and V, respectively. Each partial derivative is then set equal to zero and solved simultaneously for Q_{opt} and V_{opt}. To elaborate, the minimum point on the total cost curve has a slope of zero; thus, by determining the derivative, which defines the slope, and setting it equal to zero, the value of Q corresponding to the minimum cost can be determined.

$$\frac{\partial TC}{\partial Q} = 0 = -\frac{C_oD}{Q^2} + \frac{C_s}{2} - \frac{V^2}{2Q^2}(C_c + C_s)$$

$$\frac{\partial TC}{\partial V} = 0 = -C_s + \frac{C_cV}{Q} + \frac{C_sV}{Q}$$

and solving simultaneously yields

$$Q_{opt} = \sqrt{\frac{2C_oD}{C_c}} \cdot \sqrt{\frac{C_c + C_s}{C_s}}$$

$$V_{opt} = \sqrt{\frac{2C_oD}{C_c}} \cdot \sqrt{\frac{C_s}{C_c + C_s}}$$

$$S_{opt} = Q_{opt} - V_{opt}.$$

Also, the optimal solutions for t and TC are

$$t_{opt} = \sqrt{\frac{2C_o}{C_cD}} \cdot \sqrt{\frac{C_c + C_s}{C_s}}$$

$$TC_{opt} = \sqrt{2C_oC_cD} \cdot \sqrt{\frac{C_s}{C_c + C_s}}.$$

As a sample problem, return to the original classic EOQ model, but now assume that shortages are allowed, which can be back ordered, with a unit shortage cost of \$200. The model parameter values are given as

$C_o = \$\ 50$ Order cost per order
$C_c = \$100$ Carrying cost per unit per year
$C_s = \$200$ Shortage cost per unit per year
$D = 4{,}900$ Annual demand.

The optimal solution for the problem is

$$Q = \sqrt{\frac{2C_oD}{C_c}} \cdot \sqrt{\frac{C_c + C_s}{C_s}}$$

$$= \sqrt{\frac{(2)(50)(4{,}900)}{(100)}} \cdot \sqrt{\frac{100 + 200}{200}}$$

$$Q_{opt} \cong 85 \text{ units.}$$

Note that the solution for Q in the shortage model is simply the classic EOQ solution multiplied by $\sqrt{\frac{C_c + C_s}{C_s}}$. Further solution results are as follows:

$$V = \sqrt{\frac{2C_oD}{C_c}} \cdot \sqrt{\frac{C_s}{C_c + C_s}}$$

$$= 70(0.82) = 57.4$$

$$V_{opt} \cong 57 \text{ units}$$

and

$$S_{opt} = Q_{opt} - V_{opt} = 85 - 57$$

$$S_{opt} \cong 28 \text{ units}$$

Thus, the optimal decision is to allow shortages of 28 units to accumulate before ordering 85 units, raising the inventory level to 57 units. The optimal time, in years, between orders is

$$t = \sqrt{\frac{2C_o}{C_cD}} \cdot \sqrt{\frac{C_c + C_s}{C_s}} = \sqrt{\frac{(2)(50)}{(100)(4{,}900)}} \cdot (1.22)$$

$$= \sqrt{\frac{1}{4{,}900}} \cdot (1.22) = (0.014)(1.22)$$

$$t_{opt} = 0.017 \text{ year.}$$

By multiplying 0.017 by 365, we find that the optimal time between order receipts is approximately 6 days. The optimal total inventory cost associated with the preceding solution values is

$$TC = \sqrt{2C_oC_cD} \cdot \sqrt{\frac{C_s}{C_c + C_s}}$$

$$= \sqrt{(2)(50)(100)(4{,}900)} \cdot \sqrt{\frac{200}{100 + 200}}$$

$$TC_{opt} = \$5{,}715.50.$$

Note the following comparison between the results of the original classic EOQ model in which shortages were not allowed and the same model where shortages are allowed:

	Classic EOQ Model No Shortages	Shortage Model
Q (order quantity)	70 units	85 units
V (maximum inventory volume)	70 units	57 units
S (shortage back orders)	0	28 units
TC (total inventory cost)	$7,000	$5,715.50
t (time between orders)	5 days	6 days

It is apparent that under certain circumstances it is economical to allow shortages. It should be pointed out that if shortage cost (C_s) were assigned the value of infinity in the shortage model, the solution results would be identical to the original classic EOQ model.

Noninstantaneous Receipt Model with Shortages

The variation of the EOQ model that will be discussed next is the most general and complex of the deterministic EOQ models. This model expands on the noninstantaneous receipt model in that shortages are allowed. All other assumptions of the initial model remain the same. Figure 7.7 graphically illustrates the conditions surrounding this inventory model. Variables and parameters are defined the same as in previous model cases with the following exceptions:

t_1 = time period during which inventory increases in an order cycle

t_2 = time period during which inventory is reduced in an order cycle

t_3 = time period during which the shortage increases in an order cycle

t_4 = time period during which the shortage is reduced in an order cycle

t = order cycle time ($t_1 + t_2 + t_3 + t_4$)

Note that all times are on a yearly basis (i.e., fraction of a year).

Figure 7.7 Inventory model with shortages and noninstantaneous receipt.

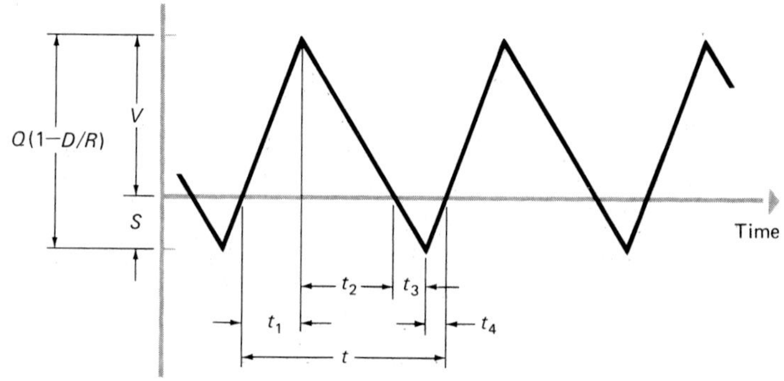

Total annual cost for this model is

$$TC = \text{Ordering Cost} + \text{Carrying Cost} + \text{Shortage Cost}$$

and, in variable terms,

$$TC = \frac{D}{Q} \cdot \left[C_o + C_c \cdot (t_1 + t_2) \cdot \frac{V}{2} + C_s \cdot (t_3 + t_4) \cdot \frac{S}{2} \right].$$

The individual cost components comprising this equation are derived analytically from figure 7.7. Notice that the carrying cost and the shortage cost terms are both derived in the same manner as in the previous shortage model. That is, carrying cost per cycle is the average inventory ($V/2$) during the period in which inventory exists ($t_1 + t_2$) multiplied by the carrying cost per unit (C_c). Shortage cost is developed similarly.

The total cost equation must now be modified such that the values of t_1, t_2, t_3, t_4, and V are expressed in terms of Q and S, the solution variables. By again observing figure 7.7, relationships between these values and Q and S can be identified as follows. First, the various time values (t_1, t_2, t_3, and t_4) can be defined as follows:

$$t_1 = \frac{V}{R-D} \qquad t_3 = \frac{S}{D}$$

$$t_2 = \frac{V}{D} \qquad t_4 = \frac{S}{R-D}$$

(Note that these four relationships are formulated by applying the simple formula, rise ÷ run = slope, to fig. 7.7.)

The terms $(t_1 + t_2)$ and $(t_3 + t_4)$ in the total cost equation can be redefined as

$$t_1 + t_2 = \frac{V}{R-D} + \frac{V}{D}$$

$$t_3 + t_4 = \frac{S}{D} + \frac{S}{R-D}.$$

The term V in the $t_1 + t_2$ equation remains to be expressed in terms of Q and S. Recall from the derivation of the noninstantaneous receipt model that the maximum amount of inventory for any period is $Q\left(1 - \frac{D}{R}\right)$. However, it can be seen from figure 7.7 that in this model the corresponding change in inventory level, from lowest level to highest level, is equal to $V + S$.

$$V + S = Q\left(1 - \frac{D}{R}\right)$$

and

$$V = Q\left(1 - \frac{D}{R}\right) - S$$

Since it has been determined that $t_1 + t_2 = V\left(\frac{1}{R - D} + \frac{1}{D}\right)$, the value for V can be substituted in this equation to yield

$$t_1 + t_2 = \left[Q\left(1 - \frac{D}{R}\right) - S\right]\left(\frac{1}{R-D} + \frac{1}{D}\right).$$

Also, recall that

$$t_3 + t_4 = S\left(\frac{1}{R-D} + \frac{1}{D}\right).$$

Substituting these quantities for $t_1 + t_2$ and $t_3 + t_4$ plus the formulated value for V in the total cost equation presented on page 321 results in the following:

$$TC = \frac{D}{Q}\left\{C_o + C_c\left[Q\left(1 - \frac{D}{R}\right) - S\right]\left(\frac{1}{R-D} + \frac{1}{D}\right)\left[\frac{Q\left(1 - \frac{D}{R}\right) - S}{2}\right] + C_s\left[S\left(\frac{1}{R-D} + \frac{1}{D}\right)\right]\frac{S}{2}\right\}.$$

Simplifying,

$$TC = \frac{D}{Q}\left\{C_o + \frac{C_c\left[Q\left(1 - \frac{D}{R}\right) - S\right]^2}{2D\left(1 - \frac{D}{R}\right)} + \frac{C_s S^2}{2D\left(1 - \frac{D}{R}\right)}\right\}$$

and

$$TC = \frac{C_o D}{Q} + \frac{C_c\left[Q\left(1 - \frac{D}{R}\right) - S\right]^2}{2Q\left(1 - \frac{D}{R}\right)} + \frac{C_s S^2}{2Q\left(1 - \frac{D}{R}\right)}.$$

In order to determine the optimal values of Q and S, this equation must be differentiated with respect to Q and S.

$$\frac{\partial TC}{\partial Q} = 0$$

$$= -\frac{C_o D}{Q^2} + \frac{C_c\left(1 - \frac{D}{R}\right)}{2} - \frac{C_c S^2}{2Q^2\left(1 - \frac{D}{R}\right)} - \frac{C_s S^2}{2Q^2\left(1 - \frac{D}{R}\right)}$$

and

$$\frac{\partial TC}{\partial S} = 0 = -C_c + \frac{C_c S}{Q\left(1 - \frac{D}{R}\right)} + \frac{C_s S}{Q\left(1 - \frac{D}{R}\right)}$$

The two resulting equations must be solved simultaneously for the optimal values of Q and S. Performing these mathematical operations yields

$$Q_{opt} = \sqrt{\frac{2C_o D}{C_c\left(1 - \frac{D}{R}\right)}} \cdot \sqrt{\frac{C_c + C_s}{C_s}}$$

and

$$S_{opt} = \sqrt{\frac{2C_o D}{C_s}} \cdot \sqrt{1 - \frac{D}{R}} \cdot \sqrt{\frac{C_c}{C_c + C_s}}.$$

The following example will demonstrate the inventory policy that can be derived from the formulation of this noninstantaneous receipt model with shortages.

The values for the model parameters are as follows:

C_o =	$100	Ordering cost per order
C_c =	$ 20	Carrying cost per unit of inventory per year
C_s =	$ 50	Shortage cost per unit of shortage per year
D =	6,000	Annual demand
R =	12,000	Annual production rate

The optimal values of Q and S according to the previously developed formulas are

$$Q = \sqrt{\frac{2C_oD}{C_c\left(1 - \frac{D}{R}\right)}} \cdot \sqrt{\frac{C_c + C_s}{C_s}}$$

$$= \sqrt{\frac{2(100)(6,000)}{20\left(1 - \frac{6,000}{12,000}\right)}} \cdot \sqrt{\frac{20 + 50}{50}}$$

$$Q_{opt} = 410 \text{ units}$$

$$S = \sqrt{\frac{2C_oD}{C_s}} \cdot \sqrt{1 - \frac{D}{R}} \cdot \sqrt{\frac{C_c}{C_c + C_s}}$$

$$= \sqrt{\frac{2(100)(6,000)}{50}} \cdot \sqrt{1 - \frac{6,000}{12,000}} \cdot \sqrt{\frac{20}{20 + 50}}$$

$$S_{opt} = 59 \text{ units.}$$

Given these optimal values for Q and S, total cost is computed as follows:

$$TC = \frac{C_o D}{Q} + \frac{C_c\left[Q\left(1 - \frac{D}{R}\right) - S\right]^2}{2Q\left(1 - \frac{D}{R}\right)} + \frac{C_s S^2}{2Q\left(1 - \frac{D}{R}\right)}$$

$$TC = \frac{100(6{,}000)}{410} + \frac{(20)\left[410\left(1 - \frac{6{,}000}{12{,}000}\right) - 59\right]^2}{2(410)\left(1 - \frac{6{,}000}{12{,}000}\right)}$$

$$+ \frac{(50)(59)^2}{2(410)\left(1 - \frac{6{,}000}{12{,}000}\right)}$$

$$TC = \$2{,}927$$

The maximum inventory level, V, is

$$V = Q\left(1 - \frac{D}{R}\right) - S$$

$$= 410\left(1 - \frac{6{,}000}{12{,}000}\right) - 59$$

$$V = 146 \text{ units.}$$

The time between receipt of orders, t, is

$$t = t_1 + t_2 + t_3 + t_4 = \frac{Q}{D}$$

$$= \frac{410}{6{,}000}$$

$$t = .068 \text{ years} \simeq 25 \text{ days.}$$

Quantity Discount Model

This stage in the development of inventory models describes the case where there is a price discount for goods purchased to replenish inventory if purchased in sufficient quantity. For example, the normal price for goods is \$50, however, if purchased in order sizes of at least 100 units, the quantity discount price becomes \$48. This model is formulated in the same manner as the modified classic model in which carrying cost (K_c) was specified as a percentage of average dollar value of inventory held. Thus, the price is also included in the carrying cost equation in order to yield the dollar value of inventory. If price breaks are allowed for large quantity orders, the inventory model must consider not only ordering cost and carrying cost but also the cost of goods purchased.

Therefore, the model for the quantity discount case would be:

$$TC = \text{total ordering cost} + \text{total carrying cost} + \text{total cost of goods}$$

$$TC = C_o \frac{D}{Q} + K_c P \frac{Q}{2} + PD$$

Note that there are no new variables introduced in this model. However, the definition of *TC* now includes the total value of goods purchased per year, which is indicated in the model by the term *PD*.

The model is solved in the following manner. First, *TC* is computed with a quantity discount, then without the discount. The two total cost cases are then compared and the order quantity, *Q*, is the one that results in the minimum total cost.

This modeling situation is illustrated graphically in figure 7.8. The *TC* curve for the nondiscount case is higher than for the discount case, since a higher product price is included if no discount is assumed. The minimum order quantity required to receive the price discount is indicated by the solid vertical line.

Figure 7.8 Inventory model with quantity discount.

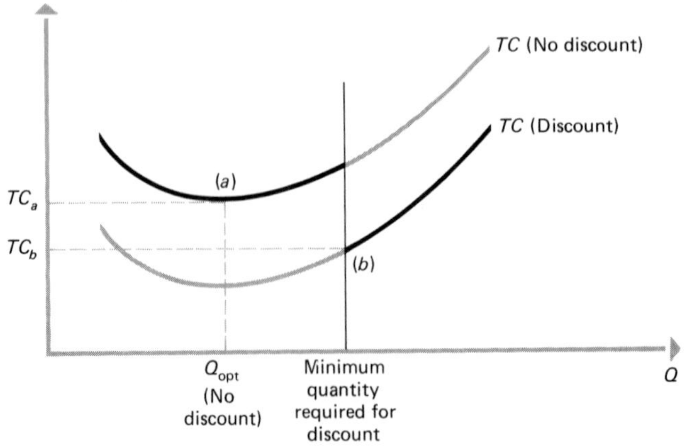

Note that only the darkened portions of the two curves are relevant to the analysis of the quantity discount model. That is, if Q is less than the discount quantity, the higher price is charged and the upper cost curve is relevant. If Q is equal to or greater than the discount quantity, the lower price is charged and the lower cost curve is relevant.

The objective is to determine whether the lowest point on the upper curve is less than the lowest *allowable* point on the lower curve. Since point b is lower than point a, taking advantage of the quantity discount results in the minimum total cost.

The following example illustrates the quantity discount problem. Assume that a firm is faced with determining the optimal ordering policy for the following situation:

C_o	= \$20	Order cost per order
K_c	= 20%	Carrying cost as a percentage of average inventory per year
D	= 300 units	Total annual demand for goods
P	= \$50	Price per unit, without a quantity discount
P'	= \$48	Price per unit, with a quantity discount

In order to receive the quantity discount price, order sizes must equal or exceed 50 units.

First determine Q_{opt} with the discount received.

$$Q_{opt} = \sqrt{\frac{2C_oD}{K_cP'}}$$

$$Q_{opt} = \sqrt{\frac{(2)(20)(300)}{(0.20)(48)}}$$

$$Q_{opt} = \sqrt{1{,}250} \cong 35$$

If the value of Q_{opt} is less than the minimum quantity required to receive the discount price, we must set Q equal to the required order quantity to receive the discount; thus, set Q equal to 50. Computing the value of TC for Q = 50 and P' = 48.

$$TC = C_o\frac{D}{Q} + K_cP'\frac{Q}{2} + P'D$$

$$= (20)\left(\frac{300}{50}\right) + (0.20)(48)\left(\frac{50}{2}\right) + (48)(300)$$

$$TC = 14{,}760$$

Now determine Q_{opt} without the quantity discount.

$$Q_{opt} = \sqrt{\frac{2C_oD}{K_cP}}$$

$$Q_{opt} = \sqrt{\frac{(2)(20)(300)}{(0.20)(50)}}$$

$$Q_{opt} = \sqrt{1{,}200} \cong 35$$

Computing the value of TC for $Q = 35$ and $P = 50$,

$$TC = C_o\frac{D}{Q} + K_cP\frac{Q}{2} + PD$$

$$= (20)\left(\frac{300}{35}\right) + (0.20)\left(\frac{35}{2}\right) + (50)(300)$$

$$TC \simeq 15{,}346.$$

The results are summarized as follows:

	Order Size = 50 Discount	Order Size = 35 No Discount
Ordering Cost	$ 120	$ 171
Carrying Cost	240	175
Cost of Goods	14,400	15,000
Total Cost	$14,760	$15,346

When the discount is received, the order size is larger and, thus, fewer orders are placed and the ordering costs are less. Also, since the price is lower for the quantity discount case, the cost of goods is less. Carrying costs are more since fewer orders mean that the average level of inventory is higher. This is somewhat offset by the lower price, which tends to reduce the average value of inventory held. The total inventory and goods cost is less when the discount is taken; therefore, the order quantity decided upon is 50.

Probabilistic Inventory Models

In the previous models many of the model components were treated as constants that were known with certainty; however, in real world situations these components are often uncertain. One of the inventory elements that is most commonly a random variable is demand. In most cases the firm is uncertain about when demand for an item will occur and the amount that will be demanded. In such cases, demand is typically defined by a probability distribution.

Other elements subject to uncertainty include lead time and customer back ordering. Often the firm does not know with certainty how long it will take to receive an order from a supplier and if the amount requested will be received. Thus, lead time can be considered a random variable. If enough inventory is not on hand, the firm cannot always be sure that a customer will back order, and if the customer does back order, that the same amount will be requested.

Many of the costs associated with inventory models can also be subject to uncertainty. Carrying costs and ordering costs can both be random variables in cases where the firm has no control over them. If customer back ordering is subject to uncertainty then shortage costs to the firm are also subject to uncertainty.

There are a variety of models and techniques available to reflect conditions of uncertainty in inventory analysis ranging from analytical approaches to such techniques as simulation. Some of these approaches are relatively simple and straightforward while others are highly sophisticated and quite complex. In this section, several of the more straightforward approaches to reflecting uncertainty in inventory models will be presented. For a more in-depth study of probabilistic inventory models, the interested reader is directed to any of the numerous excellent texts listed in the references.

Uncertain Demand

All variations of the classic inventory model presented so far have been based on the assumption that demand is constant and known with certainty (assumptions 1 and 2 of the classic EOQ model). The alternative case occurs when the demand rate is stochastic, or probabilistic. However, the assumption that lead time is constant and known with certainty is maintained. The order quantity can still be computed according to the classic EOQ formula, either by assuming that demand is constant and that no stockouts will occur or by using average demand ($\overline{D}$). In either case, the order quantity is not optimal but only an *approximated* optimal solution.

However, since demand is actually a random variable, the computation of the reorder point is not so simple. One approach is to determine the *expected* (average) demand during lead time and reorder when that inventory level is reached. This is analogous to assuming that demand during lead time is also known and constant. This approach invariably leads to stockouts (shortages) at various intervals of time.

As an alternative, firms often maintain **safety stocks,** or buffers, of inventory to avoid inventory shortages when the demand during order lead time is not known with certainty. The problem then becomes the determination of optimal safety stock to hold in order to avoid inventory stockouts.

Inventory Model with Safety Stocks

An illustration of the inventory level model with shortages is shown in figure 7.9. In the first and third cycles of the model, inventory shortages would have occurred if no safety stock were carried. In the second cycle of the model, a surplus of inventory would have occurred even without a safety stock. An implicit assumption of this model is that these surpluses and deficits balance out over a year, so that on the average the excess inventory held is represented by the shaded area (safety-stock level).

Figure 7.9 Inventory model with safety stock.

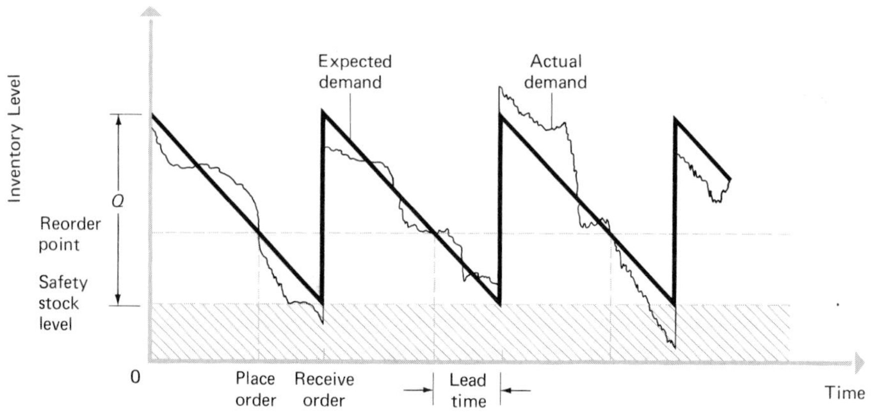

Most often it is the case that inventory safety stocks are never entirely depleted; therefore the unit carrying cost for safety stock is multiplied by the entire safety-stock level. If annual safety-stock cost is denoted as TC_{ss} and the safety-stock inventory level as I_s, the annual safety-stock carrying costs are determined as follows:

$$TC_{ss} = C_c I_s$$

where

C_c = carrying cost per unit held per year

The safety-stock costs must be balanced against the stockout costs, which are a function of the probabilistic demand and the safety stock held. In other words, a cost trade-off between carrying costs for inventory safety stocks and inventory stockout costs must be considered.

It is assumed that although the demand during lead time is not known with certainty, it can be described by a probability distribution. As an example, consider a firm that has kept records of the relative frequency of the levels of demand during lead time and developed a probability distribution of demand during lead time as follows:

Demand During Lead Time	Probability (Relative Frequency)
80	0.10
90	0.20
100	0.40
110	0.20
120	0.10
	1.00

From this probability distribution of demand during lead time, it can be seen that if a reorder point of 120 units is used, the firm would never expect a stockout. Thus, stockout costs would be zero for this case. However, if 110 units is used as the reorder point, a demand of 120 units would be expected 10% of the time, resulting in stockouts 10% of the time. If 100 units is specified as the reorder point, stockouts of 10 units could be expected 20% of the time and stockouts of 20 units 10% of the time.

The expected average demand during lead time is computed as follows:[1]

$$E(\text{demand}) = .10(80) + .20(90) + .40(100) + .20(110) + .10(120)$$
$$E(\text{demand}) = 100 \text{ units}$$

If a reorder point of over 100 units is selected, the excess is considered the safety stock. The expected number of shortages for reorder points of 100, 110, and 120 (and associated safety stocks of 0, 10, and 20) are summarized as follows:

Reorder Point	Safety Stock	Actual Lead Time Demand	x Resulting Shortage	p_i Probability of Demand (Shortage)	xp_i	$E[x]$ Expected Shortage ($\Sigma\, xp_i$)
100	0	100	0	0.4	0	
		110	10	0.2	2	4
		120	20	0.1	2	
110	10	110	0	0.2	0	1
		120	10	0.1	1	
120	20	120	0	0.1	0	0

Thus, the expected number of shortages incurred when no safety stock is allowed is 4. If a safety stock of 10 units is provided, the expected shortage is 1. Of course, if the reorder point is set at 120, providing a safety stock of 20 units, no shortages are incurred.

1. Refer to Appendix C in which the concept of expected value is discussed in detail.

Since these computations yield the expected shortages per inventory order, the total expected shortages per year would simply be that figure multiplied by the number of orders.

We saw previously that when Q_{opt} is determined by the classic EOQ formula, we also can determine N, the optimal number of orders, as $\frac{D}{Q_{opt}}$. Thus, we can obtain the total expected shortage costs.

$$TC_s = C_s \cdot N \cdot E[x]$$

where

TC_s = total annual shortage cost
C_s = cost per unit shortage
N = number of orders per year
$E[x]$ = expected number of shortages per order

As an example, assume that the inventory carrying cost has been determined to be \$10 per unit per year ($C_c = 10$). Further assume that shortage costs have been estimated at \$3 per unit shortage ($C_s = 3$). The classic EOQ model is used to determine Q_{opt} using *expected* annual demand. Using the formula $\frac{D}{Q} = N$, the number of orders per year can be determined. For this example, assume that $N = 12$ (orders per year).

Safety-stock inventory carrying cost is computed by simply multiplying the safety-stock level times the unit carrying cost (\$10). Assuming that the previously given probability distribution of demand is appropriate, the cost analysis is as follows:

I_s Safety Stock	C_c Inventory Level Carrying Cost	$TC_{SS} = I_s C_c$ Total Annual Safety Stock Carrying Cost
0	\$10	\$ 0
10	10	100
20	10	200

Expected shortage costs are computed as the combined product of the cost per unit shortage, the number of orders per year, and the expected shortage per order period.

Safety Stock Level	C_s Cost Per Unit Shortage	N Number of Orders Per Year	$E[x]$ Expected Shortages Per Order Period	$TC_s = C_s N\, E[x]$ Expected Annual Shortage Cost
0	\$3	12	4	\$144
10	3	12	1	36
20	3	12	0	0

The appropriate safety-stock level is determined by comparing the various safety-stock levels and associated total carrying and shortage costs summarized as follows:

Safety Stock Level I_s	Safety Stock Inventory Carrying Cost TC_{ss}	Expected Shortage Cost TC_s	Total Expected Costs $TC_{ss} + TC_s$
0	\$ 0	\$144	\$144
10	100	36	136
20	200	0	200

Thus, total expected safety-stock inventory carrying and shortage costs are minimized when a safety stock of 10 units is carried (reorder point of 110 units). It should be pointed out that the optimal solution is now based on an *expected* cost value. This requires that this policy be carried out over a long period of time in order to balance out variations in actual costs.

Determining Safety Stocks According to Service Levels

A somewhat different approach to the determination of safety stocks is the use of customer service levels. In this case, the goal is to satisfy some specified percentage of total customers on a regular basis. To achieve this prescribed service level a safety stock is added to the average maximum inventory level. In this approach, the reorder point, r, is defined as

$$r = \overline{D}_L + Z\sigma_{D_L}$$

where

$\overline{D}_L$ = average demand during lead time

Z = number of standard deviations required for a specified service level (using a normal distribution)

σ_{D_L} = the standard deviation of demand during lead time.

As such, the safety stock, SS, for this approach is

$$SS = Z\sigma_{D_L}.$$

This approach is analogous to the development of the upper limit of a confidence interval.

The following example will demonstrate this approach. A firm desires to establish an inventory policy (i.e., an order quantity, reorder point, and safety stock) that will maintain a 95% service level. That is, 95% of all customers demanding the product during the lead time will be serviced. The daily demand for the product is normally distributed with a mean of 50 units and a standard deviation of 6 units. Lead time is constant and equals 5 days. Thus, average demand during lead time, $\overline{D}_L$, is 250 units (i.e., 50 units/day · 5 days) with a standard deviation, σ_{D_L}, of 13.5 units. (Since demand is independent, the variance of demand during lead time is equal to the sum of the variances of demand (i.e., $\sigma_{D_L}{}^2 = 5 \times 36 = 180$; thus, $\sigma_{D_L} = \sqrt{180} = 13.4$). Order cost, C_o, equals \$20 and carrying cost, C_c, equals \$0.20 per unit.

The optimal order quantity, Q, is computed by using the classic EOQ formula except that average annual demand is used in place of constant demand (i.e., $\overline{D} = 50 \times 365$).

$$Q_{opt} = \sqrt{\frac{2C_o\overline{D}}{C_c}}$$

$$= \sqrt{\frac{2(20)(50)(365)}{0.20}}$$

$$Q_{opt} = 1{,}910$$

The reorder point is calculated separately and reflects the desired service level.

$$r = \overline{D}_L + Z\sigma_{D_L}$$

Since a 95% service level corresponds to a Z value of 1.645 standard deviations, then

$$r = 250 + (1.645)(13.5)$$

$$r = 250 + 22$$

$$r = 272 \text{ units.}$$

Based on these computations, the firm's inventory policy requires that an order quantity of 1,910 units be ordered every time inventory falls to 272 units. This includes a safety stock of 22 units.

Alternative Approaches to Stochastic Inventory Models

The examples of probabilistic inventory models presented in this section are somewhat simplified. Often times in reality, such model parameters as order quantity, orders per year, reorder point, and safety stock are *interdependent* as well as uncertain. In such cases, alternative approaches that are often quite complex are required. Some of these alternatives include Markov analysis (chapter 9), simulation (chapter 11), dynamic programming (chapter 12), as well as advanced analytical methods employing calculus and statistics. The reader interested in pursuing the more advanced topics in inventory theory should consult the texts listed in the references.

Summary

In this chapter, one of the more popular and traditional areas of management science, inventory modeling, has been presented. In fact, it is one of the oldest examples of the application of mathematical modeling to a business function. Inventory is a problem area of concern for almost every type of organization. As such, it provides an area of application and study for the student of management science that he or she is usually familiar with at least in general terms. Thus, it is an excellent vehicle for demonstrating the basic concepts of model building that can be applied to other management science model forms. However, beyond these reasons for studying inventory models, it also is a potentially lucrative area for management science application since it often represents a substantial portion of the total costs of a firm. In numerous instances, substantial reductions in total costs have been realized by developing more efficient inventory policies. Because of the pervasive nature of inventory in organizations many of the models and techniques, such as simulation, mathematical programming, and dynamic programming, presented in other chapters in this text are often applied to the problems of inventory.

References

Buchan, J., and Koenigsberg, E. *Scientific Inventory Management*. Englewood Cliffs, N.J.: Prentice-Hall, 1963.

Buffa, E. S., and Taubert, W. H. *Production-Inventory Systems: Planning and Control*. Rev. ed. Homewood, Ill.: Richard D. Irwin, 1972.

Churchman, C. W.; Ackoff, R. L.; and Arnoff, E. L. *Introduction to Operations Research*. New York: John Wiley & Sons, 1957.

Hadley, G., and Whitin, T. M. *Analysis of Inventory Systems*. Englewood Cliffs, N.J.: Prentice-Hall, 1963.

Magee, J. F., and Boodman, D. M. *Production Planning and Inventory Control*. 2d ed. New York: McGraw-Hill, 1967.

Starr, M. K., and Miller, D. W. *Inventory Control: Theory and Practice*. Englewood Cliffs, N.J.: Prentice-Hall, 1962.

Problems

1. Given the following inventory information:

   Ordering cost = \$70 per order

   Carrying cost = \$3 per unit per year

   Demand = 5,000 units per year

   Determine the optimal order quantity, the minimum total cost, the number of orders per year, and the time between orders (assuming a 365 day year).

2. A firm is faced with the attractive situation in which it can obtain immediate delivery of an item it stocks for retail sale. The firm has therefore not bothered to order the item in any systematic way. It has recently hired a management consultant to study their inventory control. The consultant has determined that the various costs associated with making an order are approximately \$30 per order. In addition, she has determined that the costs of carrying one unit of the item in inventory for one year amount to approximately \$20 (primarily direct storage cost and foregone profit on investment in inventory). The demand forecast for the item is 19,200 units per year and is reasonably constant over time. When an order is placed for the item, the entire order is immediately delivered to the firm from the supplier. The firm operates six days a week plus a few Sundays, or approximately 320 days per year. Determine the following:

   a. Optimal order quantity per order
   b. Total annual inventory ordering and carrying costs associated with the optimal order size policy
   c. Optimal number of orders to place per year
   d. Number of operating days between orders, based on the optimal ordering policy

   Illustrate the inventory level model for this problem. Show the answers to *a* and *d* on the graph.

3. Referring to problem 2, assume that the consultant hired by the firm wishes to illustrate to the firm's management the nature of the decision analysis employed for the solution to the inventory ordering policy. Illustrate graphically the inventory decision model by including along the horizontal axis several order quantities below and above the optimal quantity, and plot the associated ordering and carrying costs. Show graphically that the optimal order quantity is the value computed in problem 2.

4. Given the following inventory information:

$$C_o = \$1{,}200 \text{ per order}$$
$$C_c = \$50 \text{ per unit per year}$$
$$D = 2{,}000 \text{ units per year}$$
$$T_L = 10 \text{ days}$$
$$\text{year} = 310 \text{ days}$$

a. Compute the optimal order quantity and total minimum cost.
b. Determine the reorder point.

5. Again referring to problem 2, assume that rather than receiving immediate delivery of an order the firm must wait two days for the order to arrive. (a) At what inventory level (reorder point) should the firm reorder? (b) Illustrate on the inventory level model the point in time and the inventory level point at which a reorder should be made. (c) Since the firm has to wait two days for the order, should it recalculate the optimal order quantity? (d) Suppose the lead time required to receive an order was twelve days; how many orders would the firm have outstanding at any given point in time? (e) Shouldn't the firm simply lump these orders together and receive them all at once? Why or why not? (f) Complete a table showing the annual ordering costs, annual carrying costs, and total inventory related costs for the following two cases: (1) order every twelve days and (2) order at the interval determined in the solution to problem 2.

6. The purchasing manager for a large steel firm must determine the ordering policy for coal to operate 12 converters. Each converter requires exactly 5 tons of coal per day to operate, and the firm operates 360 days per year. The purchasing manager has determined that the ordering cost is $80 per order, and the cost of holding coal is 20% of the average level held. The purchasing manager has negotiated a contract to obtain the coal for $12 per ton for the coming year.

a. Determine the optimal quantity of coal to receive in each order.
b. Determine the total inventory-related costs associated with the optimal ordering policy (do not include the cost of the coal).
c. If 5 days lead time are required to receive an order of coal, how much coal should be on hand when an order is placed?

7. Given the following inventory information for a noninstantaneous model:

$$C_o = \$200 \text{ per order}$$

$$C_c = \$8 \text{ per unit per year}$$

$$D = 10{,}000 \text{ units demanded annually}$$

$$R = 15{,}000 \text{ units produced annually}$$

Compute the optimal order size, minimum total cost, and maximum inventory level.

8. A lumber mill processes 10,000 logs annually, operating 250 days per year. Immediately upon order, the logging company supplier begins delivery to the lumber mill at the rate of 60 logs per day. The lumber mill has determined that the ordering cost per order is $62.50 and the cost of carrying logs in inventory, awaiting processing, is $15 per log on an annual basis. Determine the following:

   a. The optimal number of log orders
   b. The total inventory cost associated with the optimal order quantity
   c. The number of lumber mill operating days between orders
   d. The number of lumber mill operating days required to receive an order

   Illustrate the inventory level model graphically. Show the answers to *c* and *d* and the maximum inventory level.

9. An aluminum company has predicted the demand for aluminum rivets for the coming year to be 20,000 cases. The average demand rate based on past data is reasonably constant. The company produces at the rate of 160 cases of rivets per day, operating 250 working days annually. The production setup cost for each production run is $144. The annual carrying cost of rivets produced for inventory is $32 per case. Determine the following:

   a. Optimal quantity to produce for each production run
   b. Length (in working days) of each production run
   c. Time (in days) between production run start-ups
   d. Total production setup and inventory carrying costs
   e. Days per year that are used for production of rivets

10. A large grocery chain is faced with the following decision. The cost of ordering a particular item is $40 per order. The carrying cost is 25% of the average inventory level on an annual basis. Yearly demand for the item is 20,000 cases at a constant rate. The grocery firm currently pays $40 per case for the item. However, they have been offered a $1 per case discount if they order in minimum lots of 1,000 cases. Should the firm take the discount? Show a comparative analysis of all costs involved for the two alternatives.

11. Given the following inventory information for a shortage model:

C_o = \$150 per order
C_c = \$12 per unit per year
C_s = \$20 per unit
D = 1,500 units demanded annually
year = 365 days

a. Compute the optimal order quantity and the optimal maximum inventory level.
b. Compute total minimum cost.
c. Determine the maximum shortage allowed.
d. Determined the optimal time between orders.

12. Refer again to problem 2. The firm is considering reducing their inventory level further by simply allowing some shortages to occur. They would back order demand not met and fill the demand when the stock was replenished. It is estimated that the cost of shortages is \$30 per unit on an annual basis. All other relevant data is given in problem 2. Determine the following:

a. The new optimal order quantity
b. The total inventory ordering, carrying, and shortage costs associated with the optimal order quantity
c. The back order quantity, per order

Perform a comparative analysis of the solution to problem 2 and the current solution, showing all the various costs involved.

13. Develop the graph of the classic inventory decision model with shortages similar to the graphic analysis shown in figure 7.2. Indicate the optimal value of Q that corresponds to total minimum cost.

14. A firm produces its own inventory from its manufacturing facility and maintains an inventory policy that allows for shortages. Annual demand is 8,000 units, and annual production is 10,000 units. The cost of ordering is \$200 per order while the cost of holding one item in storage is \$5. The firm has estimated that each unit they are unable to supply and must back order costs \$15. Develop an inventory policy for the firm that contains the following:

a. Optimal order size, Q
b. Optimal shortage, S
c. Total minimum cost
d. The maximum inventory level, V
e. t_1, t_2, t_3, t_4, and t (Explain each of these times.)

Develop a graphical analysis of this policy (similar to fig. 7.7) that includes these values.

15. A carpet company produces a particular brand of shag carpet in its mill, which it then sells in its own outlet store adjacent to the mill. The demand for the shag carpet at the outlet is 70,000 yards per year. The mill is able to produce carpet at a rate of 120,000 yards per year. The cost of holding one yard of carpet in inventory is $0.30. It costs the mill $120 to start a production run for the shag carpet. The present company policy is to not allow shortages.

    a. Determine the optimal order quantity and total minimum cost for the company.
    b. Assume the company changes their present policy and decides to allow shortages. They estimate that if the outlet is not able to fill a customer order it will cost the company $0.20 per yard. Determine the optimal order quantity, maximum shortage level, and total minimum cost.
    c. Compare the results of both inventory policies. Which policy should the carpet company adopt?

16. Solve problem 9 assuming that the aluminum company allows shortages to exist and the shortage cost is $20 per unit. Compare the results of this model with the results for problem 9. Which policy results in the lowest inventory cost?

17. Given the following inventory data:

    C_o = $300/order
    C_c = $15/unit
    C_s = $40/unit
    D = 20,000/year
    P = 30,000/year

    Determine optimal Q, S, V, and total minimum cost.

18. A firm has developed a probability distribution of demand during lead time as follows:

Demand During Lead Time	Probability
500	.10
600	.20
700	.40
800	.20
900	.10
	1.10

Inventory carrying costs equal $0.75 per unit per year, the cost per order is $150, the shortage cost has been estimated as $2 per unit, and the optimal number of orders per year is 10.

Determine the appropriate safety stock level that will minimize safety stock carrying and shortage costs.

19. The production foreman for a large mill has encountered a problem of stockouts. On the other hand, he is under pressure from top management to keep the level of inventory down. He faces the difficult problem of fluctuating demand for the product in inventory. The foreman knows that he must keep some safety stock on hand to guard against higher than average demands, but he is unable to determine the optimal level to hold. Assume that you have been employed as a consultant to analyze the problem. It will be assumed that the firm has contracted for 20 orders of 300 units per order. The inventory carrying cost is $5 per unit per year, and the estimated shortage cost is $4 per unit shortage. Past records show that the relative frequency of various demand levels during the lead time to receive an order are as follows:

Demand During Lead Time (units)	Relative Frequency
240	0.05
260	0.10
280	0.20
300	0.30
320	0.20
340	0.10
360	0.05

Determine the following for the production foreman:

a. The optimal reorder level
b. The optimal safety stock to hold
c. The total safety-stock inventory carrying and shortage cost associated with the optimal reorder policy
d. The inventory carrying cost for the safety stock alone

Illustrate the decision model for this problem graphically.

20. Assume that the classic EOQ model was used to determine the order sizes in problem 19. What was the assumed ordering cost per order?

21. A lawn products store has determined the following information regarding its demand for fertilizer:

$$\begin{aligned} \text{Average daily product demand} &= 120 \text{ pounds (normally distributed)} \\ \text{Standard deviation} &= 30 \text{ pounds} \\ \text{Lead time} &= 10 \text{ days} \\ C_o &= \$300 \text{ per order} \\ C_c &= \$0.08 \text{ per pound} \end{aligned}$$

a. Compute the optimal order quantity.
b. Determine the safety stock and reorder point that will maintain a 95% service level.

22. A company desires to establish an inventory policy that will maintain a 90% service level. The daily demand for the company's product is normally distributed with a mean of 120 units and a standard deviation of 20 units. Lead time is constant and equals 7 days. Ordering costs equal $60 and carrying costs equal $.40 per unit.

a. Determine the average demand during lead time and the standard deviation.
b. Compute the optimal order quantity.
c. Determine the reorder point that will reflect the desired service level.

23. A firm has established an inventory reorder point of 520 units under conditions of uncertain demand, which encompasses an average demand during lead time of 400 units with a standard deviation of 80 and a safety stock of 120 units. What service level will be maintained by this reorder point?

Part

4

Probabilistic Models

8

Decision Theory and Games

The environment within which decisions are made is often categorized into four states: **certainty, risk, uncertainty,** and **conflict.** Decision theory, one of the subjects of this chapter, is primarily concerned with decision making under the conditions of risk and uncertainty. The theory of games is concerned with decision making under conflict. Both decision theory and game theory assist the decision maker in analyzing problems with numerous alternative courses of action and consequences. A basic objective of decision and game theories is to provide a structure wherein information concerning the relative likelihood of different occurrences may be evaluated to enable the decision maker to identify the best course of action.

A state of *certainty* exists when all the information required to make a decision is known and available (i.e., **perfect information**). In many of the previous chapters in this text, models were formulated and solved under conditions of assumed certainty. For example, in the analysis of linear programming problems, the exact amount of resources required to produce a product, the available resources, and unit profit were all assumed to be known with certainty. A similar condition of certainty was also assumed in the presentation of transportation, assignment, and most of the network and inventory models. Assuming certainty for a problem where information is not known with certainty often provides a reasonable approximation of the optimal solution.

The condition of *risk* exists when perfect information is not available but the probabilities that certain outcomes will occur can be estimated. Thus, for decision problems under risk, probability theory is an important component. Various stochastic methods such as chance-constrained programming, queueing theory, Markov analysis, simulation, and probabilistic inventory control have been developed for decision analysis under risk.

A state of *uncertainty* refers to a condition where the probabilities of occurrences in a decision situation are not known. Under risk the outcomes of a decision situation are defined by a probability distribution, while under uncertainty no probability function can be determined. As such, *certainty* and *uncertainty* represent the two extremes of a continuum representing available information while *risk* is a point in between.

The fourth decision state, *conflict,* exists when the interests of two or more decision makers are in competition. In other words, if decision maker *A* benefits from a selected course of action, it is only possible because decision maker *B* has also taken a certain course of action. Hence, decision makers are not only interested in their own courses of action but also in the actions of others in the decision situation.

Decision Making Under Risk

For decision making under risk, the various *courses of action* that are available and feasible must be identified first. Next, the *possible events* and their *associated probabilities* of occurrence must be estimated. (Events are also referred to as *states of nature*). Thirdly, the *conditional payoff* for a given course of action under a given event is determined. It is not always a simple matter to identify the exact monetary payoffs for the action-event combination. However, accumulated experience and/or past records often provide relatively accurate estimated payoffs for many decisions. To demonstrate these steps in decision making under risk, several examples will be considered.

Example 8.1 Concession Problem

A concessions firm handles all the concessions for a professional football team. The manager of the firm is attempting to ascertain whether to stock the concession stands with cola or coffee. A local agreement among beverage dealers prohibits any one concessionaire from selling more than one beverage at a game. The payoff is primarily dependent upon the weather conditions. If the weather is cold, selling coffee results in a greater payoff. On the other hand, if the weather is relatively warm, cola brings in a greater payoff. The courses of action, states of nature, (events), probabilities of occurrence of the alternative states of nature, and the payoffs associated with the different combinations of actions and states of nature are given in the following table:

Alternatives	States of Nature	
Action (a_i)	$p_1 = 0.3$ Cold Weather	$p_2 = 0.7$ Warm Weather
Sell Cola (a_1)	\$1,500	\$5,000
Sell Coffee (a_2)	\$4,000	\$1,000

The conditions necessary for a decision problem under risk exist in this example. First, alternative courses of action are available and a choice must be made between them. The occurrence of the states of nature (events) are not known with certainty, but the probabilities of their occurrence are determined from historical experience.

The most widely used criterion for decision making under risk is the **expected value,** which is discussed in detail in Appendix C. The expected value for a given course of action is simply the weighted average payoff, which is the sum of the payoffs for each action multiplied by the probabilities associated with each state of nature. For this example, the expected value for a_1, denoted by $E(a_1)$, is

$$E(a_1) = (\$1{,}500 \times 0.3) + (\$5{,}000 \times 0.7) = \$3{,}950.$$

The expected value for a_2 is

$$E(a_2) = (\$4{,}000 \times 0.3) + (\$1{,}000 \times 0.7) = \$1{,}900.$$

Comparing the expected values associated with each course of action indicates that a_1 (selling cola) is the logical alternative since it has the higher expected payoff—\$3,950 compared to an expected payoff of \$1,900 for a_2 (selling coffee).

Now consider the condition where the probability distribution of events is not known. In the previous example, this would mean that the probabilities for cold and warm weather are not available. Given this situation, the decision maker might desire to know the probability that would equalize the effects of the two courses of action. In order to establish indifference toward the two courses of action, the expected values must be identical. Since p_1 is defined as the probability of cold weather, then p_2, the probability of warm weather, is also defined as $1 - p_1$.

The expected values of a_1 and a_2 are now

$$E(a_1) = 1{,}500p_1 + 5{,}000(1 - p_1)$$

$$E(a_2) = 4{,}000p_1 + 1{,}000(1 - p_1).$$

Since indifference requires that the expected values be equal,

$$E(a_1) = E(a_2)$$

$$1{,}500p_1 + 5{,}000(1 - p_1) = 4{,}000p_1 + 1{,}000(1 - p_1).$$

Solving this equation we find that $p_1 = .615$. Now, if the probability of cold weather is .615 (and thus the probability of warm weather is .385), the decision maker is indifferent about selling cola or coffee. However, if the probability of cold weather is greater than .615, the concessionaire should sell coffee since the expected value of selling coffee would be greater.

While the expected value is employed as the decision criterion in this problem, it does not mean that if a_1 is chosen a payoff of exactly \$3,950 will result. On the contrary, the eventual payoff of an action is rarely equal to the expected value. For example, if cola is sold and the weather is warm, \$5,000 will be made. The expected value is used in problems involving risk because it maximizes the payoff over a given period of time. If the decision problem is repetitive, this same problem will occur a large number of times. Because the expected value is the same as the average payoff when the decision problem is repeated a number of times, it is a valid criterion for decision making.

When a decision problem under conditions of risk is not repetitive, the expected value as a decision criterion may be inappropriate. In real-world situations, a decision maker may avoid a course of action that has a very large conditional loss, or negative payoff, even when its expected value is greater than the alternative courses of action. This type of situation is considered in the following example.

Example 8.2 Investment Problem

A firm is contemplating two investment alternatives, *A* and *B*, involving two different financial conditions. Each condition has an equal probability of occurrence (i.e., $p_1 = 0.5$, $p_2 = 0.5$). The payoff matrix for this problem is shown in the following table:

Alternatives	States of Nature	
Investment	$p_1 = 0.5$ Condition 1	$p_2 = 0.5$ Condition 2
A	−$1,000,000	$1,060,000
B	20,000	30,000

The expected values for the two plans are

$$E(A) = -\$1{,}000{,}000\ (0.5) + \$1{,}060{,}000\ (0.5) = \$30{,}000$$

$$E(B) = \$20{,}000\ (0.5) + \$30{,}000\ (0.5) = \$25{,}000.$$

Although the expected value of plan *A* is $5,000 greater than plan *B*, the decision maker is unlikely to choose *A* over *B*. In this case, the decision maker might put a higher priority on avoiding the potential loss associated with condition 1 and investment *A* than on the long-run average payoff. If, however, the firm involved has sufficient liquid assets to absorb the possibility of a large negative payoff, the expected value may well be justified as the decision criterion. (This concept of risk avoidance will be discussed in greater detail in the section on utility, p. 350.)

Expected Opportunity Loss

An alternative criterion for evaluating decisions under risk is known as the **expected opportunity loss** (EOL). The fundamental principle behind EOL is the minimization of *expected regret* experienced due to the selection of a particular decision alternative. The concept of expected opportunity loss is demonstrated in the following example.

Consider a firm that has three investment alternatives, *A*, *B*, *C*, and two states of nature reflecting varying market conditions. The basic components of this decision situation are given in the following table:

Alternatives	States of Nature	
Investment	$p_1 = 0.4$ Market Condition 1	$p_2 = 0.6$ Market Condition 2
A	\$ 50,000	−\$10,000
B	\$ 15,000	\$60,000
C	\$100,000	\$10,000

The opportunity losses (or regrets) are computed for each state of nature by first identifying the best course of action for each state of nature. For market condition 1, investment *C* is the best decision. The opportunity loss realized by selecting either investment *A* or *B* is computed by subtracting their payoffs from the investment *C* payoff. Thus, the regret (opportunity loss) for investment *A* is 100,000 − 50,000 = \$50,000 and for investment *B*, 100,000 − 15,000 = \$85,000. If market condition 2 is said to be known with certainty, the regret for each alternative action can be computed in the same manner as for market condition 1. In this case, investment *B* is the best alternative. The opportunity losses for all investment alternatives, given the states of nature, are summarized in the following table:

Alternatives	States of Nature	
Investment	$p_1 = 0.4$ Market Condition 1	$p_2 = 0.6$ Market Condition 2
A	\$50,000	\$70,000
B	\$85,000	0
C	0	\$50,000

The expected opportunity loss, which includes the probability of each market condition, is computed by determining the expected value for each action. Thus,

$$EOL_A = 0.4(50{,}000) + 0.6(70{,}000) = \$62{,}000$$

$$EOL_B = 0.4(85{,}000) + 0.6(0) = \$34{,}000$$

$$EOL_C = 0.4(0) + 0.6(50{,}000) = \$30{,}000.$$

It can be seen that the best alternative is investment *C*, because it *minimizes* the expected regret, or opportunity loss, that can be suffered by the decision maker. However, while EOL is an alternative decision criterion for decision making under conditions of risk, the results will always be the same as those obtained by the expected value criterion previously presented. Thus, only one of the two methods need be applied to reach a decision.

Expected Value of Perfect Information

An additional extension of the criteria of expected value and expected opportunity loss is the **expected value of perfect information.** When making a decision under conditions of risk, less information is available than under conditions of certainty. Within the context of decision theory, this is interpreted as the difference between stated outcomes with associated probabilities (i.e., risk) and knowing with certainty which outcome will occur. If information could be acquired by the decision maker that would change the decision conditions from risk to certainty, it is said to be perfect information. Again, consider the investment example used in the previous EOL analysis.

The expected values for each investment alternative are computed as

$$E(A) = 0.4(50{,}000) + 0.6(-10{,}000) = \$14{,}000$$

$$E(B) = 0.4(15{,}000) + 0.6(60{,}000) = \$42{,}000$$

$$E(C) = 0.4(100{,}000) + 0.6(10{,}000) = \$46{,}000.$$

These amounts represent the payoffs that could be expected by the investor given imperfect (partial) information. The best decision is investment C based on its higher expected value of \$46,000. If conditions of certainty existed, the decision maker would know in advance which event would occur (either market condition 1 or 2) and what action should be taken. If market condition 1 exists with certainty, then investment C should be made with a return of \$100,000. If condition 2 exists, then investment B should be selected with a \$60,000 return. Since the first condition occurs 40% of the time and the second occurs 60% of the time, the expected value under conditions of certainty would be

$$EV = 0.4(100{,}000) + 0.6(60{,}000) = \$76{,}000.$$

Comparing the expected investment return with perfect information (\$76,000) to the expected return without it (\$46,000) yields the expected value of perfect information,

$$EVPI = 76{,}000 - 46{,}000 = \$30{,}000.$$

The EVPI, \$30,000, is now the maximum amount the decision maker might pay (possibly to an investment counseling service or a research firm) to obtain perfect information. Perfect information, in this case, translates to knowing with certainty what state of nature will occur in the future. It should be noted that the EVPI is also equal to the EOL of the best alternative, C. This is always the case since the EOL is a measure of the difference between the expected values of decisions under conditions of risk and certainty.

Utility

Decision makers do not always select alternatives that maximize expected value (i.e., dollars) in a decision situation. This occurs for several reasons. First, people are not always willing to accept potential losses in the present in order to realize potential gains in the long run. These people can be described as *risk avoiders*. On the other hand, there are *risk takers* who are willing to gamble greater amounts of money than the current expected return would warrant.

The following brief examples demonstrate the human tendency of risk aversion. Consider a decision situation with two alternatives: (1) Flip a coin and if it comes up heads, you receive \$100,000, but if it comes up tails, you receive nothing; or you can receive (2) a gift of \$20,000 with certainty. The expected value of the first alternative is \$50,000, which, when compared to the second alternative, would be the selected alternative under the previously discussed decision criterion. However, rarely would a decision maker choose the first alternative over the second. In other words, the risk of receiving nothing (versus the certainty of receiving \$20,000) offsets the potential large gain of \$100,000 with a probability of .5. Most decision makers would prefer the security of the second alternative rather than gamble on the risk inherent in the first alternative.

A second situation concerns the common procedure of purchasing insurance. Almost everyone buys insurance coverage for their home, car, and/or life. However, the expected value of a return is negative since insurance companies set rates that insure them a profit. Yet people buy insurance to avoid the possibility of a large potential loss. Both of these examples indicate that people often make decisions that result in less expected payoff with less risk rather than decisions that result in greater payoff with increased risk. Every individual's attitude toward risk is heavily influenced by the magnitude of the potential payoffs (or losses) relative to personal wealth.

This behavior can be explained by the concept of **utility,** which is defined as a measure of an individual decision maker's preference for monetary return (as opposed to avoiding risk). Von Neumann and Morgenstern developed a decision criterion whereby utility can be measured. According to their theory of utility, in a decision situation, a person will choose the alternative that maximizes his or her expected utility.

The Von Neumann and Morgenstern concept of utility is measured on a cardinal scale in units referred to as **utiles.** Utility is measured by observing a decision maker's pattern of decisions in risk situations.

For example, consider a homeowner who is attempting to decide whether or not to insure her house, which is valued at \$50,000. The annual insurance premium is \$300. There is a .0002 probability that the house will be destroyed by fire in the upcoming year. What should this individual do? The following payoff matrix for the *cost* of insurance can be developed:

	States of Nature	
Alternatives	$p_1 = .0002$ Fire	$p_2 = .9998$ No Fire
Insurance (a_1)	\$ 300	\$300
No Insurance (a_2)	\$50,000	0

The expected costs for the alternatives are

$$E(a_1) = \$300$$

$$E(a_2) = .0002(50{,}000) + .9998(0) = \$10.$$

The obvious choice according to the expected value criterion would be to select alternative 2, no insurance, since it has a much lower expected cost. However, if the decision situation is reformulated in terms of utility, a different outcome occurs. If the insurance premium of \$300 is valued at only -1 utile in relationship to the disastrous loss of \$50,000, which is valued at $-100{,}000$ utiles, the utility matrix is presented as follows:

	States of Nature	
Alternatives	$p_1 = .0002$ Fire	$p_2 = .9998$ No Fire
Insurance (u_1)	-1	-1
No Insurance (u_2)	$-100{,}000$	0

The expected utility for each alternative is given as follows:

$$E(u_1) = -1$$

$$E(u_2) = -100{,}000\ (.0002) = -20$$

In this case, the expected utility is higher (less negative) for alternative 1 than for alternative 2, indicating that insurance should be purchased, the logical choice of most homeowners.

The difficulty with employing utility as a decision criterion is the determination of utility values. The mechanics of utility are similar to those involved in determining expected value. Typically, a **utility curve** that relates utility values to dollar values is constructed. The basis for obtaining such a curve usually consists of placing the decision maker in various hypothetical decision situations and plotting the decision maker's pattern of choices in terms of risk and utility. Figure 8.1 shows several utility curves and the risk preference associated with each.

Subjective Probabilities

An additional decision concept relevant to this discussion is the use of **subjective probabilities.** Subjective probabilities are measures of one's degree of belief in future outcomes. Experiments conducted in the area of subjective probabilities suggest that decision making under conditions of risk is influenced by the decision maker's belief regarding the outcomes of future events. This reinforces the assumption that the individual decision maker is capable of assessing value and probability in a decision situation. Consequently, the study of subjective probability is relevant to decision theory.

Figure 8.1 Utility curves and associated risk preferences.

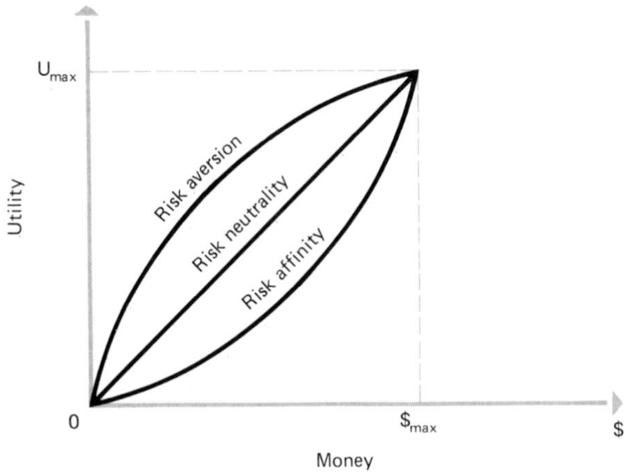

Often included in the study of subjective probability is **Bayesian decision analysis,** or Bayes rule. Bayes rule is an orderly and systematic procedure of revising probabilities of potential states of nature based on additional information, experiments, and personal judgments. Thus, Bayesian analysis is an important tool in the decision-making process. Both topics of subjective probability and Bayes rule are discussed in more detail in Appendix C.

Decision Making Under Uncertainty

Decision making under uncertainty refers to decision situations in which the probabilities of potential outcomes are not known (or estimated). In a situation of uncertainty the decision maker is cognizant of the alternative outcomes under varying states of nature as in the decision situation under risk. However, the decision maker is unable to assign probabilities to the states of nature.

As an example, consider a decision maker who has $100,000 to invest in one of three alternative investment plans: stocks, bonds, or a savings account. It is assumed that the decision maker wishes to invest all of the funds in one plan. The conditional payoffs of the investments are based on three potential economic conditions: accelerated, normal, or slow growth. The payoff matrix for this decision situation is constructed the same way as a risk situation.

Alternatives	Economic Conditions		
Investment	Accelerated Growth	Normal Growth	Slow Growth
Stocks	$10,000	$6,500	−$4,000
Bonds	8,000	6,000	1,000
Savings	5,000	5,000	5,000

The payoff matrix reflects the fact that investments in stocks or bonds yield different returns depending on the economic conditions. Investment in the savings plan guarantees a \$5,000 return, regardless of the economic conditions. Since a condition of uncertainty exists, there are no probabilities associated with the alternative states of nature (economic conditions). There are several criteria available for decision making under uncertainty. Some of the more prominent of these criteria will be examined via this investment example.

Laplace Criterion

The **Laplace criterion** suggests that since the probabilities of future states of nature are unknown, it should be assumed that all states of nature are equally likely to occur. In other words, each state of nature is assigned the same probability. Thus, in the investment example, a probability of 1/3 is assigned to each of the three economic conditions. As such, the expected values for the three investment alternatives are

$$E(\text{stocks}) = 1/3(10{,}000) + 1/3(6{,}500) + 1/3(-4{,}000) = \$4{,}167$$

$$E(\text{bonds}) = 1/3(8{,}000) + 1/3(6{,}000) + 1/3(1{,}000) = \$5{,}000$$

$$E(\text{savings}) = \$5{,}000.$$

Using normal decision-making criteria, the decision maker would select the best alternative, which, in this case, would exclude stocks and be indifferent to the selection of either the savings plan or bond plan.

Maximin Criterion

The **maximin criterion,** which is sometimes referred to as the Wald criterion after its originator, Abraham Wald, is based on the assumption that the decision maker is pessimistic, or conservative, about the future. According to this criterion, the minimum returns for each alternative are compared and the alternative that yields the maximum of the minimum returns is selected. In our investment example, the minimum payoffs for each investment alternative are as follows:

Investment	Minimum Payoff
Stocks	−\$4,000
Bonds	1,000
Savings	5,000

Employing the maximin criterion, the savings plan would be selected because it results in the maximum of the minimum returns, \$5,000.

The maximin criterion is obviously designed for the decision maker who is conservative about the future (i.e., a risk avoider). However, one flaw in this criterion is the exclusion of a large portion of the information available since only the minimum returns for each alternative are used. Typically, in real-world situations, all available information is employed.

Maximax Criterion

The reverse approach to the maximin criterion is the **maximax criterion.** The maximax criterion is based on the assumption of an optimistic decision maker. According to this criterion the decision maker selects the alternative that represents the maximum of the maximum payoffs.

For our investment example, the maximum payoff for each of the three investment plans is as follows:

Investment	Maximum Payoff
Stocks	$10,000
Bonds	8,000
Savings	5,000

Employing the maximax criteria, the stock plan is selected because it results in the maximum of the maximum payoffs, $10,000.

The maximax criterion is an appropriate criterion for the decision maker who is optimistic about the future (i.e., a risk taker). However, as with the maximin criterion, this method ignores much of the available information, an atypical occurrence in most realistic situations.

Hurwicz Criterion

The criterion suggested by Leonid Hurwicz represents a compromise between the maximin and maximax criteria. Decision makers in reality are rarely completely pessimistic or completely optimistic. In fact, the most accurate decision makers usually display a mixture of pessimism and optimism. As a result, Hurwicz devised a **coefficient of optimism** to measure the decision maker's degree of optimism. The scale of the coefficient of optimism, α, is from 0 to 1, where 0 reflects complete pessimism and 1 reflects complete optimism. (If $\alpha = 0$, the decision maker is said to have zero optimism, while if $\alpha = 1$, the decision maker is totally optimistic.) Since the coefficient of optimism is α, the coefficient of pessimism can be defined as $1 - \alpha$.

The Hurwicz approach requires that for each alternative the maximum payoff should be multiplied by α and the minimum payoff multiplied by $1 - \alpha$. This results in weighted values, the highest of which represents the best alternative.

In our investment example, the maximum and minimum payoffs are:

Investment	Maximum Payoff	Minimum Payoff
Stocks	$10,000	−$4,000
Bonds	8,000	1,000
Savings	5,000	5,000

If the coefficient of optimism is $\alpha = 0.6$, the weighted value for each alternative is

Stocks:

$$\$10{,}000(0.6) + [-4{,}000(0.4)] = \$4{,}400$$

Bonds:

$$8{,}000(0.6) + 1{,}000(0.4) = \$5{,}200$$

Savings:

$$5{,}000(0.6) + 5{,}000(0.4) = \$5{,}000.$$

Since the bond plan has the highest weighted value it is selected as the best alternative. When $\alpha = 0$, the Hurwicz criterion becomes the maximin criterion and when $\alpha = 1$, it becomes the maximax criterion.

A fundamental problem with the Hurwicz criterion is the determination of α. Often several α values have to be experimented with before a realistic estimation of the decision maker's degree of optimism can be determined. A further problem with this decision criterion is that it also excludes some available information (in this case, economic condition of normal growth).

Regret Criterion

The **regret,** or **minimax,** criterion originated by L. J. Savage is based on the concept of opportunity loss introduced in the previous section on decision making under risk. The basic principle underlying this approach is that the decision maker experiences regret when a state of nature occurs that causes the selected alternative to realize less than the maximum payoff. The amount of regret or opportunity loss is determined by subtracting the alternative payoffs for particular states of nature from the maximum payoff. The regret criterion requires that the minimum of the maximum regrets be selected (i.e., a minimax criterion).

For our investment example, the following regret matrix can be developed:

Alternatives	Economic Conditions		
Investment	Accelerated Growth	Normal Growth	Slow Growth
Stocks	$ 0	$ 0	$9,000
Bonds	2,000	500	4,000
Savings	5,000	1,500	0

In order to demonstrate the computation of the values in this table, consider the first state of nature, accelerated growth. Within this state of nature the stock plan is the best, thus, the opportunity loss resulting from the selection of the bond plan is $10,000 − 8,000 = $2,000, and, from the selection of the savings plan, $10,000 − 5,000 = $5,000.

The maximum regret for each alternative is:

Investment	Maximum Regret
Stocks	$9,000
Bonds	4,000
Savings	5,000

Since the regret criterion requires the selection of the alternative that is the minimum of maximum regrets, the bond plan ($4,000) is selected.

Summary of Decision Criteria

The decisions made in the example for each decision criterion are summarized as follows:

Criterion	Decision (Investment selected)
Laplace	Savings or Bonds
Maximin	Savings
Maximax	Stocks
Hurwicz (α = .6)	Bonds
Regret	Bonds

This summary does not indicate a consensus decision. What results is a mix of possible decisions. The criterion and decision that are finally selected depends upon the characteristics and philosophy of the decision maker. For example, the extremely optimistic decision maker might ignore the fact that only one criterion recommends the stock decision and select this investment simply because the maximax criterion most closely reflects this decision maker's view of the decision situation.

Decision Trees

The decision criteria that have been presented are applicable to situations within a static framework, such as a single time period. However, if the decision problem requires a series of related decisions, a **decision tree** can be useful. A decision tree is a schematic diagram of a sequence of alternative decisions and the results of those decisions. A decision tree is beneficial for several reasons. First, it provides a pictorial representation of the sequential decision process, which facilitates understanding of the process. Second, it makes the expected value computations easier as they can be performed directly on the tree diagram. Third, the actions of more than one decision maker can be considered.

Consider the following example, which demonstrates the use of a decision tree. A firm is attempting to decide whether or not to introduce a new product. Profit from the new product depends on three things—

1. whether the competitive firm introduces a similar product;
2. the type of promotional campaign the firm launches;
3. the type of promotional campaign the competitor develops.

If the competitor does not introduce a similar product, the firm can launch a major promotional campaign and maximize profit. If the competitor introduces a product, the profit will depend on the promotional campaigns of both the firm and the competitor. There are three basic types of promotional campaigns based on cost: major, normal, and minor. The sequence of decisions and their consequences are shown as a decision tree in figure 8.2.

Figure 8.2 Decision tree for promotion of new product.

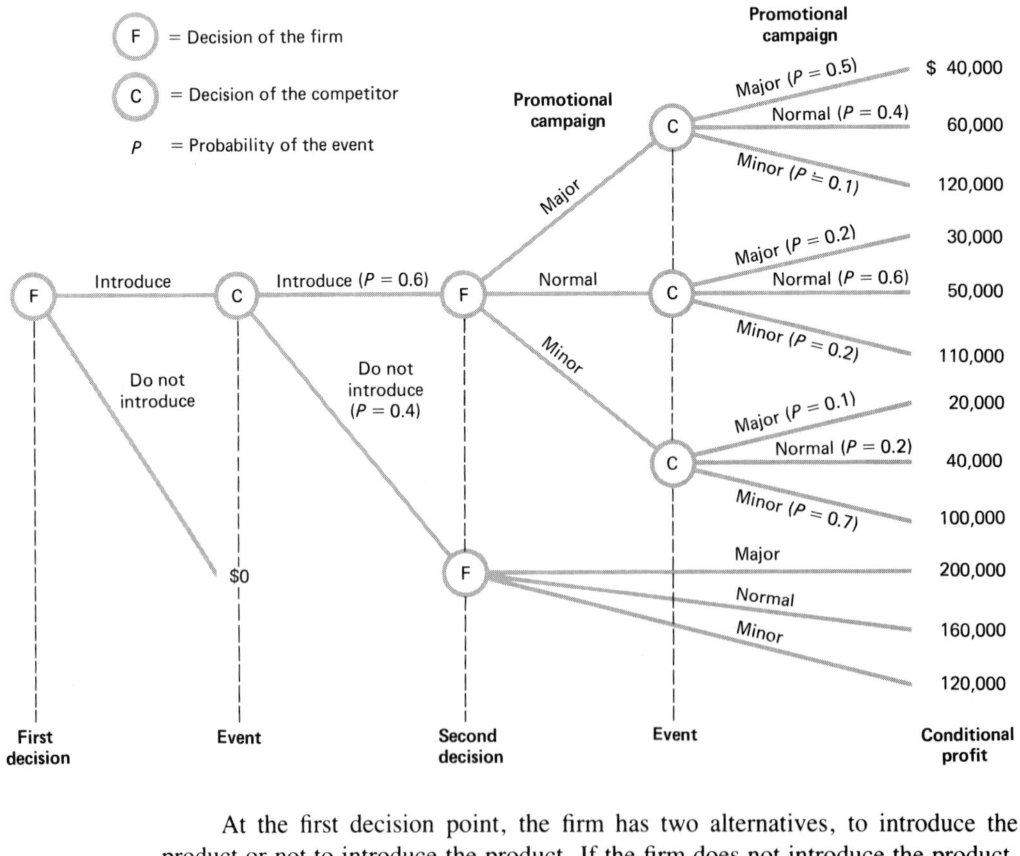

At the first decision point, the firm has two alternatives, to introduce the product or not to introduce the product. If the firm does not introduce the product, the conditional profit will be, of course, zero. If the firm introduces the product, the competitor has two alternatives, to introduce or not to introduce a similar product. The probability of the competitor introducing a product is 0.6 and for not introducing the product it is 0.4. At the second decision point, the firm has three promotional strategies: a major, normal, or minor campaign. If the competitor does not introduce a similar product, the firm's promotional effort will not bring any response from the competitor. However, if the competitor introduces a similar product, the response to the firm's promotional campaign will be the identical three types of promotional strategies. For example, if the firm employs a major promotional campaign, the competitor's responses and their probabilities are 0.5 for a major campaign, 0.4 for a normal campaign, and 0.1 for a minor campaign. If the response to the firm's major campaign is a major campaign from the competitor, the conditional profit will be \$40,000. The major campaign-normal campaign combination results in \$60,000, and the major-minor combination brings \$120,000 conditional profit to the firm. These profit figures do not include the research and development costs of \$70,000. Other combinations of campaigns, probabilities, and conditional profits are also shown in figure 8.2.

The best way to analyze this kind of sequential decision problem is to work from the end of the decision tree and calculate the expected profit for each sequence of decisions. For example, the expected profit for the combination of decisions of the firm to introduce the product, of the competitor to introduce a similar product, and of the firm to use a major promotional campaign is

$$\$40{,}000(0.5) + \$60{,}000(0.4) + \$120{,}000(0.1) = \$56{,}000.$$

Figure 8.3 presents the decision tree with the expected profits for various decision points and events. The expected profits are shown in the rectangular boxes.

When the competitor introduces a similar product, the three promotional strategies result in the following expected profits: major campaign = \$56,000, normal campaign = \$58,000, minor campaign = \$80,000. Since the greatest expected profit is associated with the minor campaign, we can eliminate the other two strategies (as indicated by the sign ||). Thus, when the competitor introduces a similar product and the firm uses a minor promotional strategy, the optimal expected profit is \$80,000.

If the competitor does not introduce a similar product, the highest conditional profit is \$200,000 when the firm adopts a major campaign strategy. Therefore, we can eliminate the other two strategies (indicated by || again). Now the expected profit of the firm's introduction of a new product can be calculated. This expected profit is the sum of the expected profit for the event that the competitor introduces a similar product (\$80,000) multiplied by its probability (0.6) and the expected profit of the event that the competitor does not introduce a similar product (\$200,000) multiplied by its probability (0.4). Thus,

$$\text{expected profit} = \$80{,}000(0.6) + \$200{,}000(0.4) = \$128{,}000.$$

The research and development cost for the new product is \$70,000. Since the expected net profit of introducing the new product is \$58,000, the decision to introduce the product should be made.

Figure 8.3 Decision tree with expected values.

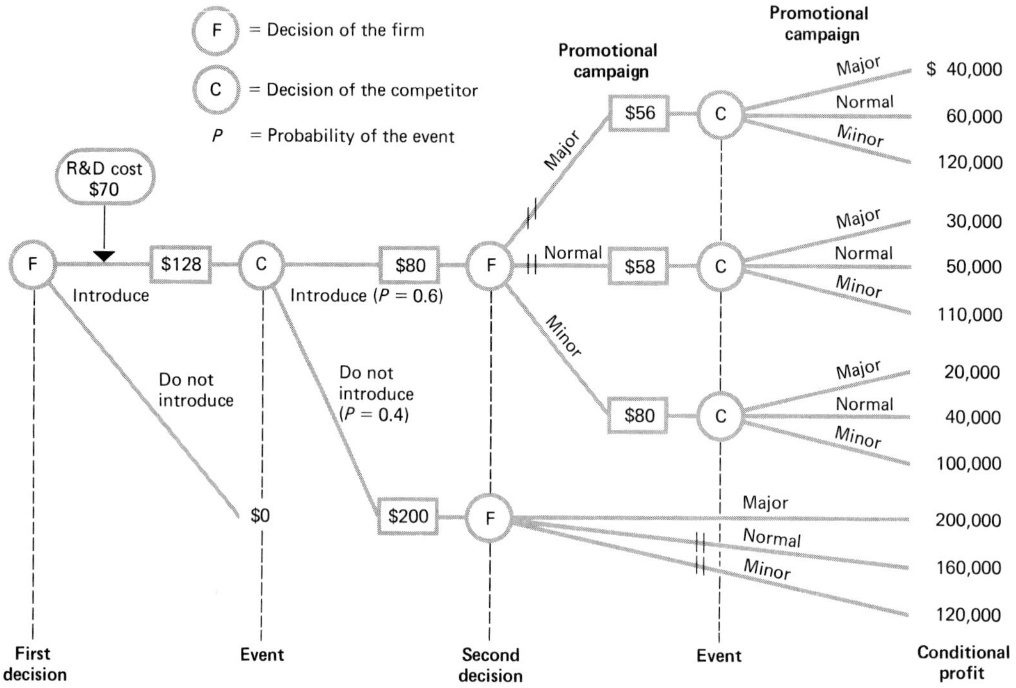

Game Theory

The fundamental characteristic of game theory that differentiates it from decision theory is that it is assumed in game theory that the decision maker competes with other rational, intelligent, goal-seeking opponents. In decision theory, a passive opponent existed, such as the states of nature. Thus, the word *game* is used to denote decisions under conditions of conflict or competition.

Game theory was introduced in 1944 by von Neumann and Morgenstern in their classic work, *Theory of Games and Economic Behavior*. Although the book received praise as a landmark in decision theory, practical application of game theory to decisions involving conflict has been limited.

For our purposes, the most important contribution of game theory is its conceptual framework, which proves useful in understanding general decision problems. Game theory provides a framework for analyzing competitive situations in which the competitors (players) make use of logical thought processes and mathematical techniques to determine optimal strategies for winning. Thus, by studying game theory, the decision maker may ultimately make more intelligent decisions.

Two-Person, Zero-Sum Games

Game theory is generally classified according to the number of opponents (or players). The usual distinction is between two-person games and games involving three or more persons. Game theory is largely undeveloped for games involving three or more persons, and it is this limitation that has restricted its applicability to real-world situations. However, the study of two-person games has enough theoretical merit to warrant its presentation.

Game theory is also categorized according to the total payoff available to the players, with zero-sum and constant-sum games distinguished from nonzero-sum and nonconstant-sum games. The theory of nonzero-sum games is also relatively undeveloped. Therefore, the presentation in this section will be limited to two-person, zero-sum games.

Formulation of the Two-Person, Zero-Sum Game

Consider a game situation in which there are two opponents identified as player *A* and player *B*. Player *A* must select from alternative strategies while considering the concurrent strategy selections of player *B*. This is analogous to the conditions of decision theory except that states of nature are replaced by the various strategies available to the opponent.

The combined payoff to both players is a constant sum. In other words, the portion obtained by player *A* is lost by player *B*, who receives the remaining portion of the constant sum. For example, if two firms are competing for 100% of the market, the portion obtained by firm *A* is exactly the portion lost by firm *B*. Since no more than 100% of the market can be obtained, the constant sum is 100. The term zero-sum refers to the fact that the sum of *A*'s positive payoff (gain) and *B*'s negative payoff (loss) is zero.

Payoff Matrix

It is assumed that each player knows the exact payoffs for every possible combination of strategies available to each player. Also, the payoffs are in a form that is transferable to either player with the same value to each; that is, the players' utilities regarding payoff are the same.

The following table is a sample payoff matrix showing the payoffs for player *A* that result from all combinations of strategies for each player. The payoff matrix represents only the gains of player *A*. However, any gain by player *A* is subsequently a loss for player *B*, and the sum of the two is zero. For example, if *A* selects strategy 1 and *B* selects strategy *x*, then *A* wins 80% of the market and *B* loses 80% of the market, yielding a sum of zero. Expressed as a constant sum, if *A* gains 80%, then player *B* receives 20%, which results in the constant sum of 100%. It is traditional to express the payoff matrix in terms of gains for the player on the side and losses for the player on top.

		Player B Strategies x	y	z
Player A Strategies	1	80	40	75
	2	70	35	30

By evaluating the alternative strategies of player *B*, it can be seen that if player *A* selects strategy 1 and *B* selects strategy *x*, player *B* would lose 80% of the market; if *B* selects *y*, 40% would be lost; and if *B* selects *z*, 75% would be lost. If player *B* is a cautious decision maker, strategy *y* would be selected in order to minimize the possible loss to 40%. This selection is shown in the following table. The value 40 is referred to as the **value** of the game.

		Player B Strategies x	y	z	
Player A Strategies	1	80	(40)	75	← Player A Selection
	2	70	35	30	
			↑ Player B Selection		

Maximin and Minimax Principles

The maximin principle for gains and the minimax principle for losses are basically the same as the criteria presented in the discussion of decision theory. According to the maximin principle, decision maker *A* is pessimistic and, as such, selects a strategy that maximizes gains from among the minimum possible outcomes. At the same time, player *B* attempts to minimize losses from among the maximum anticipated losses (minimax).

For example, player *A* identifies the minimum gain from both available strategies (1 and 2) and selects the strategy that will return the maximum gain from among these minimum values. It can be seen in the following table that 40 is the minimum gain for strategy 1, and 30 is the minimum gain for strategy 2. Since the maximum of these two values is 40, strategy 1 is selected by player *A*. For player *B*, 80 is the maximum loss for strategy *x*. The maximum loss for *y* is 40, and the maximum loss for *z* is 75. The minimum of these losses is 40, thus, strategy *y* is selected by player *B*.

		Player B Strategies x	y	z	Minimum of A's row gains	
Player A Strategies	1	80	(40)	75	(40)	(max)
	2	70	35	30	30	
Maximum of B's column losses		80	(40) (min)	75		

This analysis of strategy selection by players *A* and *B* results in a solution that satisfies both players. In other words, if *A* assumes that *B* is attempting to minimize *A*'s gains and if *B* assumes that *A* is attempting to maximize *B*'s losses, then the players have no incentive to change their strategy selections.

Since neither player would risk changing his or her strategy from the one selected, this type of result is referred to as **pure strategy.** Pure strategies exist only when the solution has reached a point of equilibrium or steady state, which is referred to in game theory as a **saddle point.** The saddle point exists when neither player desires to change strategies, based on observation of the opponent's selection of a strategy. If *A* knows that *B* has selected strategy *y*, *A*'s maximum gain is obtained by selecting strategy 1. Likewise, if *B* knows that *A* has selected strategy 1, *B*'s losses can be minimized by selecting strategy *y*. Thus, neither player has any incentive to move to a different strategy.

It is important to note that, in general, the maximin (minimax) principle leads to the optimal solution for each player as long as each opponent follows this principle. However, if one of the players does not use this principle, the solution will not be optimal.

Role of Dominance

Referring again to the previous example, it can be seen that strategy 1 results in the maximum gain for player *A*, regardless of which strategy *B* selects. Thus, strategy 1 is said to **dominate** strategy 2. For cases in which a particular strategy is completely dominated by another strategy, the dominated strategy can be removed from the payoff matrix since the player would never consider selecting it.

For player *B*, strategy *x* is dominated by strategy *y* since the loss for strategy *x* is always greater than the loss for *y* regardless of which strategy player *A* selects. (For that matter, strategy *x* is also dominated by strategy *z*.) Therefore, strategy *x* can be removed from consideration.

The following table illustrates the resulting payoff matrix with the dominated strategies shaded. The resulting payoff matrix is easily evaluated. Player *A* can select only strategy 1, which means that player *B* will select *y* in order to minimize losses to 40 rather than 75. Note that the solution is the same as that previously obtained.

		Player B Strategies		
		x	y	z
Player A Strategies	1	80	40	75
	2	70	35	30

The concept of dominance is useful for a payoff matrix of large size. The rule of dominance can be employed to reduce the size of the matrix considerably prior to final analysis for determining the optimal solution. Consider the example given in the following table in which each player has four strategies. For player *A*, strategies 1 and 4 are dominated by strategy 2; therefore, they can be removed from the payoff matrix.

		Player B Strategies			
		w	x	y	z
Player A Strategies	1	40	80	35	60
	2	65	90	55	70
	3	55	40	45	75
	4	45	25	50	50

Examining the remaining rows, 2 and 3, it can be seen that, for player *B*, strategies *w* and *z* are dominated by *y*. Therefore, these columns can be removed as shown in the following table:

		Player B Strategies			
		w	x	y	z
Player A Strategies	2	65	90	55	70
	3	55	40	45	75

Finally, by examining the remaining 2-by-2 payoff matrix, it can be seen that row 2 now dominates row 3. Thus, the final payoff matrix consists of a single strategy for *A* and two strategies for *B* as shown in the following table. To minimize loss, player *B* will select strategy *y*. Thus, the saddle point solution yields pure strategy 2 for *A* and pure strategy *y* for *B* with the value of the game at 55.

		Player *B* Strategies	
		x	*y*
Player *A* Strategy	2	90	(55)

Two-Person, Zero-Sum Games with Mixed Strategies

Many times a two-person, zero-sum game will not result in the selection of pure strategies. This is because no point of equilibrium can be reached. For this type of game situation, it is possible to obtain a steady-state solution by assuming that the players will select mixed strategies.

As an example of a mixed strategy situation, consider a firm whose management and employee's union are engaged in contract negotiations. The payoff matrix for the two groups is shown in the following table. The payoffs are in cents per hour and represent the overall value of the salary and benefits increases per employee. The matrix represents gains to the union and losses to management.

		Management Strategies			
		w	*x*	*y*	*z*
Union Strategies	1	75	105	65	45
	2	70	60	55	40
	3	80	90	35	50
	4	95	100	50	55

The union obviously wishes to maximize the employees' gains while management desires to minimize its losses. Assuming both groups are prudent, the maximin (minimax) principle can be used to analyze the game. The maximin game results are shown in the following table:

		Management Strategies				
		w	x	y	z	Minimum of row gains
Union Strategies	1	75	105	65 →	45	45
	2	70	60	55	40	40
	3	80	90	35	50	35
	4	95	100	(50)	← [55]	(50) (max)
Maximum of column losses		95	105	65	[55] (min)	

The selected strategies indicated in this table reflect the fact that there is no saddle point (i.e., common payoff value). Assuming that the union selects strategy 4, management would quickly switch their strategy from z to y in order to reduce their losses. Now given that management has moved to strategy y, the union would select strategy 1 resulting in a gain, 65. This move by the union will be followed by a change in strategy by management to z in order to again reduce losses. The union would then move to strategy 4 and the process would begin again. Thus the game ends up in an infinite loop as shown by the arrows. The maximin (minimax) approach results in an indeterminable solution where one of the players will always be dissatisfied.

Mixed Strategies

From the loop created in the previous table, it is apparent that only strategies 1 and 4 for the union and y and z for management are relevant. (This can be verified by reducing the payoff matrix by the dominance rule). The following table reflects the reduced payoff matrix:

		Management Strategies	
		y	z
Union Strategies	1	65	45
	4	50	55

The method of mixed strategies assumes that since neither player knows what strategy the other will select, each player will attempt to formulate a strategy that is indifferent to the opponent's strategy selection. This can be accomplished by randomly selecting among several strategies according to a predefined plan. The random selection plan involves selecting each strategy a certain percent of the time such that the player's gains (or losses) are equal regardless of the opponent's selection of strategies. Selection of a strategy a given percent of the time is analogous to selecting a strategy with a given probability on a one-time basis.

In order to determine this probability (percentage), let the union select strategy 1 or 4 according to probabilities such that the expected gains are the same regardless of management's selection of strategies y or z.

If management selects strategy y, the possible payoffs to the union are 65 and 50. If the union selects strategy 1 with a probability of p (and therefore selects strategy 4 with a probability of $(1-p)$), the union's expected gains are

$$(p)(65) + (1-p)(50).$$

On the other hand, if management selects z, then the union's expected gains would be

$$(p)(45) + (1-p)(55).$$

Now in order for the union to be indifferent to the strategy management selects, the expected gains of the union for each of management's possible selections must be equal. Thus, setting the two equations for the union's expected gains equal yields p as follows:

$$\begin{aligned} (p)(65) + (1-p)(50) &= (p)(45) + (1-p)(55) \\ 25p &= 5 \\ p &= 1/5 = 0.2 \\ 1-p &= 1-0.2 = 0.8 \end{aligned}$$

Therefore, the union would select strategy 1 20% of the time and strategy 4 80% of the time, which results in the expected gains being equal regardless of management's strategies.

Management would likewise determine probabilities in the same manner for strategies y and z by equating expected losses if the union selects 1 to the expected losses if the union selects 4:

$$\begin{aligned} (p)(65) + (1-p)(45) &= (p)(50) + (1-p)(55) \\ 25p &= 10 \\ p &= 2/5 = 0.4 \\ 1-p &= 1 - 0.4 = 0.6 \end{aligned}$$

Therefore, management would select strategy y with a probability of 0.4 and z with a probability of 0.6.

It now becomes apparent that a common value in terms of *expected value* exists:

Union's expected gains

If management selects y, $(0.2)(65) + (0.8)(50) = 53.0$

If management selects z, $(0.2)(45) + (0.8)(55) = 53.0$

Management's expected losses

If the union selects 1, $(0.4)(65) + (0.6)(45) = 53.0$

If the union selects 4, $(0.4)(50) + (0.6)(55) = 53.0$

Thus, an equilibrium of sorts has been gained. The mixed strategy solution results in an expected game value of 53. It should be noted that if the negotiation process were repeated many times the average would tend toward the expected value of 53. However, if there was only a single negotiation session, the actual result would be a single pure strategy for each player. Thus, one of the players, union or management, would be dissatisfied.

Linear Programming and Game Theory

Linear programming can be applied to the two-person, zero-sum game to solve for the probabilities associated with mixed strategies. The major advantage of linear programming is that it can be applied to games with more than two strategies per player (e.g., 2-by-4, 3-by-3).

To illustrate the linear programming formulation of a game situation, consider the sample payoff matrix for a 2-by-4 game in the following table:

		Player *B* Strategies			
		w	*x*	*y*	*z*
Player *A* Strategies	1	80	35	55	50
	2	20	70	40	60

First, the game for player *A* will be formulated. The probabilities of selecting strategies 1 and 2 for player *A* are indicated by P_1 and P_2, respectively. If player *B* selects strategy w, then the expected mixed-strategy payoff to player *A* is $80P_1 + 20P_2$. Player *A* desires to select a mixed strategy of strategies 1 and 2, such that the expected payoff is the same regardless of *B*'s action. In addition, player *A*'s objective is to select the mixed strategy in such a way as to maximize the minimum expected payoffs.

The value of the game to A is determined by the strategy selected regardless of whether the selection is optimal. Since A will attempt to maximize the expected payoff for the strategies B might select, the payoffs must be equal to or greater than the value of the game. (Then by maximizing the value of the game, A will maximize expected payoffs).

If the value of the game is denoted by V, then the expected payoffs to A for different strategies of B can be written as

$$80P_1 + 20P_2 \geqslant V \quad \text{Player } B \text{ selects strategy } w$$

$$35P_1 + 70P_2 \geqslant V \quad \text{Player } B \text{ selects strategy } x$$

$$55P_1 + 40P_2 \geqslant V \quad \text{Player } B \text{ selects strategy } y$$

$$50P_1 + 60P_2 \geqslant V \quad \text{Player } B \text{ selects strategy } z$$

where

P_1 = probability that A will select strategy 1

P_2 = probability that A will select strategy 2.

Since P_1 and P_2 are the probabilities with which A will select strategies 1 and 2, respectively, their sum must equal 1.0.

$$P_1 + P_2 = 1.0$$

Player A's objective is to maximize expected payoffs that can be achieved by maximizing the value of the game (V). Note that V has been defined as the criterion variable and P_1 and P_2 as the decision variables.

By dividing the preceding constraints by V, the desired linear programming form can be obtained:

$$\frac{80P_1}{V} + \frac{20P_2}{V} \geqslant 1$$

$$\frac{35P_1}{V} + \frac{70P_2}{V} \geqslant 1$$

$$\frac{55P_1}{V} + \frac{40P_2}{V} \geqslant 1$$

$$\frac{50P_1}{V} + \frac{60P_2}{V} \geqslant 1$$

$$\frac{P_1}{V} + \frac{P_2}{V} = \frac{1}{V}$$

In order to simplify the model, let $P_1/V = p_1'$ and $P_2/V = p_2'$. The objective of player A is to maximize V, which can be achieved by minimizing $1/V$ (since as V becomes larger, $1/V$ becomes smaller). To simplify, let $1/V = v'$. The resulting linear programming model is now stated as

Minimize $v' = p_1' + p_2'$

subject to

$$80p_1' + 20p_2' \geq 1$$
$$35p_1' + 70p_2' \geq 1$$
$$55p_1' + 40p_2' \geq 1$$
$$50p_1' + 60p_2' \geq 1$$
$$p_1', p_2' \geq 0.$$

The simplex solution to this model yields the following optimal solution:

$$p_1' = \frac{3}{245}, p_2' = \frac{2}{245} \text{ and } v' = \frac{1}{49}$$

Substituting p_1', p_2', and v' into the original variable relationships (i.e., $p_1' = P_1/V$, $p_2' = P_2/V$, $v' = 1/V$) yields the following:

$$P_1 = 0.6, P_2 = 0.4, \text{ and } V = 49$$

The value of the game applys only to strategies x and y for player B, which can be verified by applying the minimax principle to the payoff table (p. 368).

The linear programming formulation for player B is developed in a similar manner. Let the probabilities of selecting strategies w, x, y, or z be P_w, P_x, P_y, and P_z, respectively.

Player B wishes to minimize the maximum expected losses while facing the possibility that A might select strategy 1 or 2. The expected losses to B, for each of A's alternatives, are

$$80P_w + 35P_x + 55P_y + 50P_z$$
$$20P_w + 70P_x + 40P_y + 60P_z.$$

If the value of the game is again denoted by V, B's objective will be to minimize V, such that

$$80P_w + 35P_x + 55P_y + 50P_z \leq V$$
$$20P_w + 70P_x + 40P_y + 60P_z \leq V.$$

Also,

$$P_w + P_x + P_y + P_z = 1.$$

Dividing each constraint by V yields

$$\frac{80P_w}{V} + \frac{35P_x}{V} + \frac{55P_y}{V} + \frac{50P_z}{V} \leqslant 1$$

$$\frac{20P_w}{V} + \frac{70P_x}{V} + \frac{55P_y}{V} + \frac{60P_z}{V} \leqslant 1$$

$$\frac{P_w}{V} + \frac{P_x}{V} + \frac{P_y}{V} + \frac{P_z}{V} = \frac{1}{V}.$$

Substituting the following new variables,

$$p_w' = \frac{P_w}{V}, p_x' = \frac{P_x}{V}, p_y' = \frac{P_y}{V}, p_z' = \frac{P_z}{V}.$$

Player B desires to minimize V and maximize $1/V$, which is again denoted by v'. Thus, the following linear programming formulation for B results:

Maximize $v' = p_w' + p_x' + p_y' + p_z'$

subject to

$$80p_w' + 35p_x' + 55p_y' + 50p_z' \leqslant 1$$
$$20p_w' + 70p_x' + 40p_y' + 60p_z' \leqslant 1$$
$$p_w', p_x', p_y', p_z' \geqslant 0$$

The simplex solution is

$$p_x' = \frac{3}{490}, p_y' = \frac{1}{70} \text{ and } v' = \frac{1}{49}.$$

Thus,

$$P_x = 0.3, P_y = 0.7, \text{ and } V = 49.$$

P_w and P_z will have solution values of zero; therefore, strategies w and z will not be employed by player B in the mixed-strategy solution.

An additional point of interest regarding the simplex solution to the game problem is the fact that the dual solution for player A is player B's solution. In other words, the linear programming formulation for B is the dual of the formulation for A. Thus, it is only necessary to formulate and solve the linear programming problem for one of the players to yield the solution for both.

Summary

In the previous chapters, models have been developed in decision environments that assume conditions of certainty. However, in many cases, certainty does not exist and, instead, risk, uncertainty, and even conflict are present in the decision environment. In such cases, decision theory and the theory of games, the topics presented in this chapter, provide information to aid the decision maker in making efficient decisions. Although real-life applications of decision theory and the theory of games are somewhat rare (or at least rarer than many of the other model forms presented in this text), the study of these topics provides the decision maker with insight into the logic of decision making under conditions where certainty does not exist. This includes the types of data that must be gathered and the ways in which this data must be analyzed in order to make well-informed decisions.

References

Baumol, W. J. *Economic Theory and Operations Analysis*. Englewood Cliffs, N.J.: Prentice-Hall, 1961.

Dorfman, R.; Samuelson, P. A.; and Solow, R. M. *Linear Programming and Economic Analysis*. New York: McGraw-Hill, 1958.

Kwak, N. K. *Mathematical Programming with Business Applications*. New York: McGraw-Hill, 1973.

Luce, R. D., and Raiffa, H. *Games and Decisions*. New York: John Wiley & Sons, 1957.

Von Neumann, J., and Morgenstern, O. *Theory of Games and Economic Behavior*. Princeton, N.J.: Princeton University Press, 1944.

Williams, J. D. *The Compleat Strategyst*. rev. ed. New York: McGraw-Hill, 1966.

Problems

1. Given the following payoff matrix:

	States of Nature		
Alternatives	$p_1 = 0.3$ 1	$p_2 = 0.5$ 2	$p_3 = 0.2$ 3
A	\$1,000	\$2,000	\$500
B	800	1,200	900
C	700	700	700

a. Compute the expected value of each of the alternatives and select the best alternative.
b. Develop the opportunity loss table and compute the expected opportunity loss for each alternative.
c. Determine the expected value of perfect information (EVPI).

2. An investor must decide between two alternative investments, stocks or bonds. The returns for each investment under two possible economic conditions are as follows:

	States of Nature	
Investment Alternatives	$p_1 = 0.8$ Condition 1	$p_2 = 0.2$ Condition 2
Stocks	\$10,000	−\$4,000
Bonds	7,000	2,000

a. Compute the expected value of each investment alternative and select the best alternative.

b. What probabilities for conditions 1 and 2 would have to exist before the investor would be indifferent toward stocks and bonds?

3. The financial success of a ski resort in the Blue Ridge Mountains is dependent upon the amount of snow during the winter months. If the snowfall averages more than 40 inches, the resort will be successful; if the snowfall is between 30 and 40 inches, a moderate return is expected; and if the snowfall averages less than 30 inches, financial losses will accrue. Probabilities for each snowfall amount have been developed by a weather service. The financial return for each snowfall level is

	States of Nature		
	$p_1 = 0.4$ More than 40 in.	$p_2 = 0.2$ Between 30 and 40 in.	$p_3 = 0.4$ Less than 30 in.
Financial Return	\$120,000	\$40,000	−\$40,000

A large hotel chain has offered to lease the resort during the winter months for \$40,000. Compute the expected value to determine whether the resort should operate or lease. Explain your answer.

4. A meat market purchases steak from a local meat packing house. The meat is purchased on Monday at a price of $2.00 per pound, and the meat market sells the steak for $3.00 per pound. Any steak left over at the end of the week is sold to a local zoo for $0.50 per pound. The demand for steak and the probabilities of occurrence are as follows:

Demand (lb.)	Probability
20	.10
21	.20
22	.30
23	.30
24	.10
	1.00

For this type of problem the alternative actions are the amounts (between 20 and 24 pounds) to stock and the states of nature are the demands.

a. Construct the payoff matrix for this problem and determine the amount that should be stocked.
b. Construct the opportunity loss table and determine the amount to stock based on the expected opportunity loss of each alternative.
c. Compute the EVPI.

5. A grocer must decide how many cases of milk to stock each week in order to meet demand. The probability distribution of demand is

Demand (cases)	Probability
15	.20
16	.25
17	.40
18	.15
	1.00

Each case costs the grocer $10, who, in turn, sells it for $12. Unsold cases are sold to a local farmer (who mixes it with feed for livestock) for $2 per case. If a shortage exists, the grocer considers the profit of $2 per case to be a cost. In addition, customer ill will costs are $2 per case. Thus, a shortage cost of $4 per case is incurred.

a. Construct the payoff matrix for this problem.
b. Compute the expected value of each alternative amount stocked and select the best alternative.
c. Construct the opportunity loss table and determine the best alternative.
d. Compute the expected value of perfect information.

6. A newsstand purchases magazines from a publisher for $1.00 per copy and sells them for $1.50 per copy. Any copies not sold are returned to the publisher for $.20 per copy. The probability distribution for demand is

Demand	Probability
10	.05
11	.15
12	.20
13	.30
14	.15
15	.10
16	.05
	1.00

a. Construct the payoff matrix and determine the number of magazines to stock.
b. Construct the opportunity loss table and determine the number of magazines to stock.
c. Compute EVPI.

7. A greenhouse specializes in raising carnations that are sold to florists. Carnations are sold for $3.00 per dozen and cost $2.00 per dozen to grow and distribute to the florists. Unsold carnations left at the end of the day are sold to local restaurants and hotels for $0.75 per dozen. If demand is not met, a customer ill will cost of $1.00 per dozen is incurred. The daily demand for the carnations is

Daily Demand	Probability
20	.05
22	.10
24	.25
26	.30
28	.20
30	.10
	1.00

a. Develop the payoff matrix for this problem.
b. Compute the expected value for each alternative number of carnations to stock and select the best alternative.
c. Develop the opportunity cost table for this problem.
d. Compute the EVPI.

8. A person is considering investing in one of three alternative investment plans, A, B, and C, under uncertain economic conditions. The payoff matrix for this decision situation is

	Economic Conditions		
Alternatives	1	2	3
A	$5,000	$ 7,000	$3,000
B	−2,000	10,000	6,000
C	4,000	4,000	4,000

Determine the best investment plan using each of the following criteria:

a. Laplace
b. maximin
c. maximax
d. Hurwicz ($\alpha = 0.3$)
e. regret (minimax)

9. A local investor is considering three alternative real estate investments, a motel, a theater, and a restaurant. The motel and theater will be adversely or favorably affected depending on the availability of gasoline, while the restaurant will be relatively stable for any condition. The payoff matrix under uncertainty for this decision framework is

	Gasoline Availability		
Investment Alternatives	Shortage	Stable	Surplus
Motel	−$8,000	$10,000	$25,000
Theater	−12,000	8,000	4,000
Restaurant	6,000	6,000	5,000

Determine the best investment under conditions of uncertainty using each of the following criteria:

a. Laplace
b. maximin
c. maximax
d. Hurwicz ($\alpha = 0.4$)
e. regret (minimax)

10. A manufacturer is considering several capital investment proposals. The manufacturer can either expand the physical plant, maintain its present size, or sell part of the physical plant. Of course, the success of each course of action depends on the future demand for the product. The payoff matrix under conditions of uncertainty for this decision problem is

	Demand		
Investment Alternatives	Increase	Stable	Decrease
Expand	$20,000	$4,000	−$10,000
Same	11,000	8,000	− 2,000
Sell	− 5,000	−2,000	15,000

Determine the best investment alternative under conditions of uncertainty using each of the following criteria:

a. Laplace
b. maximin
c. maximax
d. Hurwicz ($\alpha = 0.6$)
e. regret (minimax)

11. Compute the payoff matrix for problem 5 assuming conditions of uncertainty (i.e., probabilities for demand are not known.) Determine the best amount to stock using each of the following criteria:

a. Laplace
b. maximin
c. maximax
d. Hurwicz ($\alpha = 0.2$)
e. regret (minimax)

12. An oil company is considering making a bid on a shale oil development contract to be awarded by the federal government. The company has decided to bid $210 million. They estimate that they have a 70% chance of winning the contract at this bid. If the firm wins the contract, management has three alternatives for processing the shale. It can develop a new method for extracting the oil, use the present process, or ship the shale overseas for processing. The development cost of a new process is $30 million. The outcomes and probabilities associated with developing the new method are as follows:

Event	Probability	Financial Outcome ($ millions)
Extremely successful	0.7	$450
Moderately successful	0.2	200
Failure	0.1	20

The present method costs \$7 million, and the outcomes and probabilities for this alternative are given as follows:

Event	Probability	Financial Outcome (\$ millions)
Extremely successful	0.6	\$300
Moderately successful	0.2	200
Failure	0.2	40

The cost of processing the shale overseas is \$5 million. If the shale is shipped overseas, a return of \$230 million is guaranteed.

Construct a decision tree for this problem and determine the optimal decision strategy.

13. Given the following payoff matrix for a two-person, zero-sum game, solve the game using the maximin (minimax) principle. Include in your answer: (*a*) the strategy selection for each player, and (*b*) the value of the game to player *A* and to player *B*. Can any strategies be eliminated by the rule of dominance? Does the game have a saddle point?

		Player *B* Strategies		
		x	*y*	*z*
Player *A* Strategies	1	−500	−100	700
	2	100	0	200
	3	500	−200	−700

14. Solve the following two-person, zero-sum game using the maximin (minimax) principle. Determine the pure strategies for each player. What is the value of the game?

		Player *B* Strategies					
		u	*v*	*w*	*x*	*y*	*z*
Player *A* Strategies	1	1	1	2	4	5	−5
	2	3	−3	4	3	2	4
	3	6	2	3	5	7	5
	4	2	1	3	4	6	0

15. Show that by using the rule of dominance, the payoff matrix of problem 14 can be reduced to either a single row or a single column. Further show that the solution to the game, obtained from the reduced payoff matrix, is the same as was obtained in problem 14.

16. Determine algebraically the mixed strategies for each player, given the following payoff matrix. What is the expected gain for player *A* and the expected loss for player *B*?

		Player *B* Strategies	
		x	*y*
Player *A* Strategies	1	60	50
	2	45	55

17. Consider the following two-person, zero-sum game:

		Player *B* Strategies		
		x	*y*	*z*
Player *A* Strategies	1	500	600	300
	2	100	325	250
	3	200	550	450

a. Use the maximin (minimax) principle to determine if pure strategies exist.
b. Identify the cycling path that will result.
c. Using the rule of dominance, reduce the payoff matrix to a 2-by-2 matrix. Discuss the payoff cells remaining by referring to the cycling path.
d. Solve algebraically for the mixed-strategy probabilities for players *A* and *B*.
e. Determine the expected gain for player *A* and the expected loss for player *B*. Discuss the meaning of this solution value.

18. Formulate the following game as a linear programming problem, and solve for the mixed-strategy probabilities for player *B*. Solve by the simplex method. Show that the mixed-strategy solution for player *A* is also given by the dual solution in the final simplex tableau.

		Player *B* Strategies	
		x	*y*
Player *A* Strategies	1	85	15
	2	45	60
	3	75	35
	4	20	70

19. Assume that two firms are competing for a market share of the sales for a particular product. Each firm is considering what promotional strategy to employ for the coming sales period. Assume that the following payoff matrix describes the increase in market share for firm *A* and the decrease in market share for firm *B*. Determine the optimal strategies for each firm.

		Firm *B* Strategies		
		No Promotion	Moderate Promotion	Extensive Promotion
Firm *A* Strategies	No Promotion	5	0	−10
	Moderate Promotion	10	6	2
	Extensive Promotion	20	15	10

a. Which firm would be the winner in terms of market share?
b. Would the solution strategies necessarily maximize profits for either of the firms?
c. What might the two firms do to maximize their joint profits?

20. Formulate the union-management game on page 366 as a linear programming problem. Using the simplex method, solve for management's mixed-strategy probabilities. Determine the union's mixed-strategy probabilities from the dual solution.

9

Markov Analysis

Markov chains, named after the Russian probability theorist A. A. Markov, are a particular class of probabilistic models that are often applicable to decision-making problems in business and industry. Actually, Markov chains are a special case of the more general probabilistic models known as **stochastic processes** in which the current state of a system depends upon all previous states. A Markov process is a stochastic process distinguishable by the fact that the current state of the system depends only upon the immediately preceding state of the system. For example, a student who has completed two quarters of a three-quarter statistics sequence desires not to have the same professor for the third quarter as the second. If there are four professors who teach the sequence, the student's decision process should first eliminate the second-quarter professor and randomly select from the remaining three professors. Thus, the decision is dependent only upon the conditions in the immediately preceding state—the second quarter. The decision is probabilistic since there is a one-third probability of selecting any one of the remaining three professors.

Some problems to which Markov analysis has been applied include consumer brand switching, customer accounts receivable behavior, machine maintenance and operating characteristics, certain classes of inventory and queueing problems, inspection and replacement analysis, and water resource analysis. The properties of Markov analysis and several examples of its application are presented in this chapter. Further information related to Markov chains can be found in Appendixes *A* and *C*.

Properties of Markov Processes

There are two elements that must be determined in the process of constructing a Markov model of a system. These elements include determining the possible **states** of the system and the probabilities of moving between states (also called **transition probabilities**). A system state is the status of the system at a point in time, such as whether or not a machine is operating, which professor is taken, whether an account is paid or not paid, how many customers use each of several different brands of product, and whether a delivery truck is servicing store A or B. Transition probabilities represent the probability of the system moving from one state to another during a specified period. The transition probabilities are dependent only upon the current state of the system. These components are expressed mathematically as

$$P\{X_t = j_t | X_{t-1} = j_{t-1}, X_{t-2} = j_{t-2}, \ldots, X_o = j_o\}$$

$$P\{X_t = j_t | X_{t-1} = j_{t-1}\},$$

$$\text{for } t = 0, 1, 2, \ldots n.$$

Thus, if t represents points in time, the family of random variables, X, represents a stochastic process with discrete states at discrete points in time. This formulation is a Markov chain, which states that the conditional value of X_t (which defines the state of the system at time t), given all past states, is equal to the conditional value of X_t, given only the state in the previous time period, X_{t-1}. (This is simply a restatement of the property noted earlier—that the probability of the system moving from one state to another is uniquely determined by the immediately preceding state.) Thus, the probability

$$P\{X_t = j_t | X_{t-1} = j_{t-1}\}$$

is called the one-step (or first order) transition probability. (In general, an nth order Markov process is one in which the current state depends upon the n preceding states. Only first-order Markov processes will be considered in this chapter.)

An additional property of a Markov chain is that the probability of going from one state i to another state j does not change with time.

$$P\{X_t = j | X_{t-1} = i\} = P\{X_{t+n} = j | X_{t+n-1} = i\}$$

Given these conditions, the one-step transition probability of going from state i to j, can be defined as

$$p_{ij} = P\{X_1 = j | X_o = i\}$$

and P_{ij} is the same in any time period.

Given also that the set of possible states in a Markov chain is finite, a square matrix, $\boldsymbol{P}$, made up of all p_{ij}'s of the Markov chain can be formed.

$$\mathbf{P} = \begin{array}{c} \\ 1 \\ 2 \\ \vdots \\ i \\ \vdots \\ n \end{array} \begin{array}{c} \begin{array}{cccccccc} 1 & 2 & \cdots & j & \cdots & n \end{array} \\ \begin{bmatrix} p_{11} & p_{12} & \cdots & p_{1j} & \cdots & p_{1m} \\ p_{21} & p_{22} & \cdots & p_{2j} & \cdots & p_{2m} \\ \vdots & \vdots & & \vdots & & \vdots \\ p_{i1} & p_{i2} & \cdots & p_{ij} & \cdots & p_{im} \\ \vdots & \vdots & & \vdots & & \vdots \\ p_{m1} & p_{m2} & \cdots & p_{mj} & \cdots & p_{mm} \end{bmatrix} \end{array}$$

Example 9.1 Urn Problem

To illustrate this point, let us turn briefly to an example commonly used in introductory probability and statistics classes. Assume that there are two urns each containing four balls. Urn x contains one red and three black balls while urn y contains two red and two black balls. If one ball is drawn (and subsequently replaced) from either of the urns, the probabilities can be summarized as follows:

Urn x	*Urn y*
$P(R\|x) = 1/4$	$P(R\|y) = 2/4$
$P(B\|x) = 3/4$	$P(B\|y) = 2/4$

where $P(\text{color}|\text{urn})$ = the probability of selecting a specific color ball, given that the ball is drawn from a specific urn.

The probability of selecting a red or black ball depends only upon which urn the ball is drawn from.

Assume that if a red ball is drawn, the next draw will be from urn x; if a black ball is drawn, the next draw will be from urn y. Thus, the *state* of the system will be defined as the urn from which the ball is drawn. Movement from one state to another (from one urn to another) is defined by the preceding probabilities. The probability of drawing a red or a black ball and the resulting movement from one urn to another form the basis of a Markov chain process. This process is summarized in the following table:

From State	To State *x*	*y*
x	1/4	3/4
y	1/2	1/2

The states in the table are abbreviated x and y, which denote the urn being sampled. The probabilities of moving from one state (urn) to another are also given. Therefore, if we are at urn x, the probability of drawing a red ball and remaining at urn x for the next draw is 1/4. The probability of drawing a black ball from urn x and moving to urn y for the next draw is 3/4. If we are at urn y, the probability of moving to state x or state y (urn x or urn y) is 1/2. Note that the probabilities in the matrix would not change for subsequent draws, since we are assuming that each ball removed from the urns is replaced.

In summary, the probabilities of moving from one state to the other at any given point depend upon two things: the state (urn) we are currently sampling and the nature of the process in question that determines the transition probabilities (in this case, the number of red and black balls in each of the two urns). Note that the transition probabilities sum to 1.0 for each *row*, indicating that we must either stay at urn x (draw a red ball) or move to urn y (draw a black ball).

This table represents the commonly used transition probability matrix which is described in the preceding section. The states *from* which the system moves are listed along the left, and the states *to* which the system moves are listed across the top. The transition probabilities (p_{ij}) of system movement from one of the states on the left, i, to one of the states on the top, j, complete the Markov process description.

Another commonly used approach for describing a Markov process is a transition probability diagram (see fig. 9.1). The circled letters represent the states of the system, and the arrows represent the possible movement of the system with the transition probabilities of movement listed along each arrow.

Figure 9.1 Markov transition probability diagram.

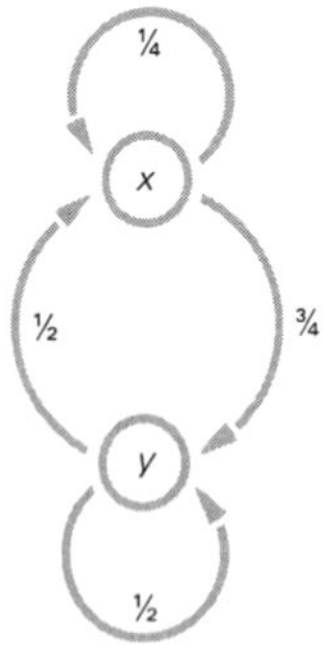

Developing the Transition Probabilities

To understand Markov processes it is essential that the fundamental basis of the transition probability matrix be clearly understood. Although the drawing of balls from urns is a convenient mathematical model, it is not immediately obvious what the real-world applications might be. One of the most popular illustrations of Markov chains is the so-called **brand-switching model.** We will use this process of consumer behavior to demonstrate the development of the transition probabilities.

Customer Brand Switching

Assume that the market under consideration is located in a small, rather isolated town. Due to the long traveling distance for shopping outside this town, virtually all shopping for certain consumer items is done in the town. The reasons for these assumptions will become clear as the discussion develops. The product under consideration is women's hosiery, of which there are three brands sold in the town. If we assume that there are 7,000 women in the town and each woman purchases only one of the three available brands, then the total market for hosiery must be divided in some way among the three brands. No specific consideration will be given to the various styles, sizes, and shapes of hose within each brand. The three hosiery brands are Sport Look, Sheer Touch, and Super Support.

Now, let us assume that an extensive market research study has been conducted on hosiery purchases in the town. The study has yielded the number of women who classified themselves as customers of one of the three brands at two given points in time. The status of brand customers at the two points in time is given in the following table:

	Time 1	Time 2
Sport Look	2,000	2,100
Sheer Touch	4,000	3,300
Super Support	1,000	1,600

At first glance, it would appear that there has been a significant shift in brand preference from one point in time to the next. The Super Support brand experienced a net increase of 600 customers, while Sport Look gained 100 and Sheer Touch lost 700. However, this analysis is superficial. A thorough analysis requires consideration of the underlying features of the process.

The market research study also yielded the actual gains and losses of customers for each brand. The movements of customers from one brand to another is shown in the following table. For convenience, the brands will now be referred to as *A* (Sport Look), *B* (Sheer Touch), and *C* (Super Support).

		To Brand		
		2,100	3,300	1,600
	From Brand	*A*	*B*	*C*
2,000	*A*	1,600	200	200
4,000	*B*	400	2,800	800
1,000	*C*	100	300	600

The table illustrates that although brand B lost a net of 700 customers, it also gained 200 new customers from brand A and 300 new customers from brand C. However, this gain in new customers was offset by losses of 400 customers to A and 800 to C. Note that for brand B the retention of old customers is shown at the intersection of row B and column B, while the gain of new customers is shown in the remaining cells of *column B*. The loss of customers is shown in the remaining cells of *row B*. The same format follows for brands A and C. Figure 9.2 illustrates by means of a tree diagram the movement of customers among brands.

Figure 9.2 Customer movement among brands.

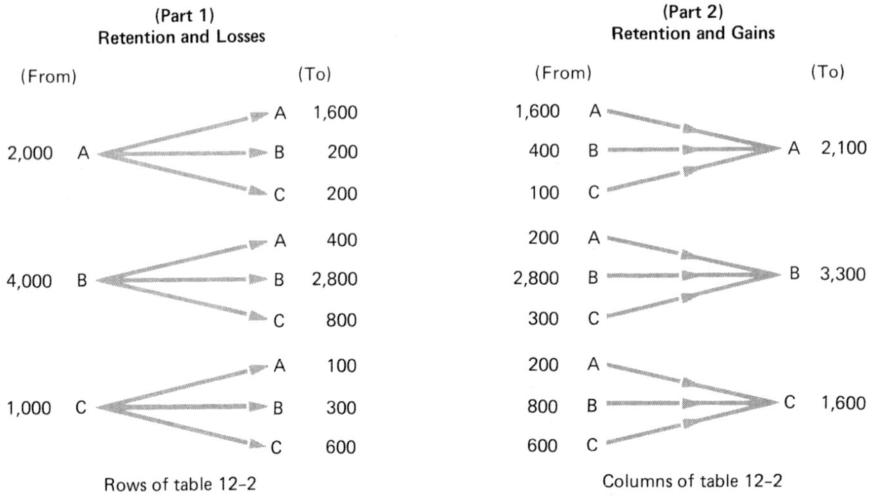

Note that part 1 of figure 9.2 relates to the rows of the customer movement matrix, while part 2 relates to the columns. In part 1, the number of customers that switched from brand A to B, from B to B, and from C to B corresponds to the movement of customers *to* brand B in part 2.

If we assume that the observed movement of customers among brands is *stable* (the same relative movement will continue), we can develop from these figures the probability transition matrix. The probability that brand A will retain current customers is 1,600/2,000 = .8. The probability that brand A will lose customers to B is 200/2,000 = .1, and the same for losses to brand C. Putting it another way, brand B loses 400/4,000 = 10% of its customers to A, retains 2,800/4,000 = 70%, and loses 800/4,000 = 20% to C. The same approach is used for brand C. The resulting probability transition matrix is given in the following table:

From Brand	To Brand A	B	C
A	.8	.1	.1
B	.1	.7	.2
C	.1	.3	.6

The transition probability matrix is also illustrated graphically in figure 9.3. Note that the transition probability matrix can be reduced to the assumption that only one customer is involved. Thus, if the system is in state *A* (the customer is a brand *A* customer), the probability of moving to state *A* (retaining the customer) is .8, the probability of moving to state *B* (becoming a brand *B* customer) is .1, and so forth. In order to convert states into numbers of customers, we simply multiply the initial number of customers by the resulting transition probabilities. (This will be illustrated in the next section).

Figure 9.3 Transition probabilities among brands.

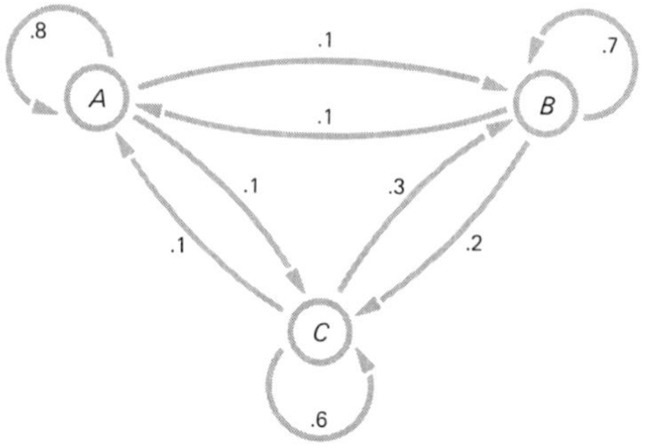

The assumption that the complete flow of customers from each brand to all others is known with certainty is an important consideration in developing the probability transition matrix. For purposes of using such probabilities, it must also be assumed that the same relative flow will continue (the process is stable) and that the transitions will be considered over the same length of time as in the initial study.

Predicting Future States

The value of obtaining the transition probability matrix in a Markov process is that it allows us to predict future states. Referring again to the previous example, what is the predicted market share of each brand in future time periods? The prediction of future states requires only that the initial state of the system be specified and that the transition probabilities be known. The successive future states of the Markov process are referred to as *chains*; hence the name Markov chains.

Since many systems being analyzed by the Markov method are such that the system is "in" one state and not in any of the remaining states, we will first approach the problem in this manner. That is, we will initially assume that there is only one customer in the system and that the customer is in one of the states (a customer of one of the three brands). We will then show how this is easily expanded to the previously discussed brand-switching example.

First, assume that the two points in time used in the marketing research study are labeled as time 0 and time 1. We now wish to predict the number of customers for each brand at time 2. We will first do this by determining the probability of one customer being in one of the three states at time 2.

Tree Diagrams

Tree diagrams are a convenient technique by which to illustrate a limited number of transitions of a Markov process. Figures 9.4, 9.5, and 9.6 illustrate the probabilities of the system states for the cases in which the system was initially in states *A*, *B*, and *C*, respectively. An examination of figure 9.4 indicates that if the system was in state *A* at time 0, the probabilities of being in states *A*, *B*, and *C* at time 2 are .66, .18, and .16, respectively (as shown in the first row of the transition probability table on p. 390.) The derivation of the second and third rows of the transition probability table are illustrated in figures 9.5 and 9.6, respectively.

Figure 9.4 Two-period transition from state *A*.

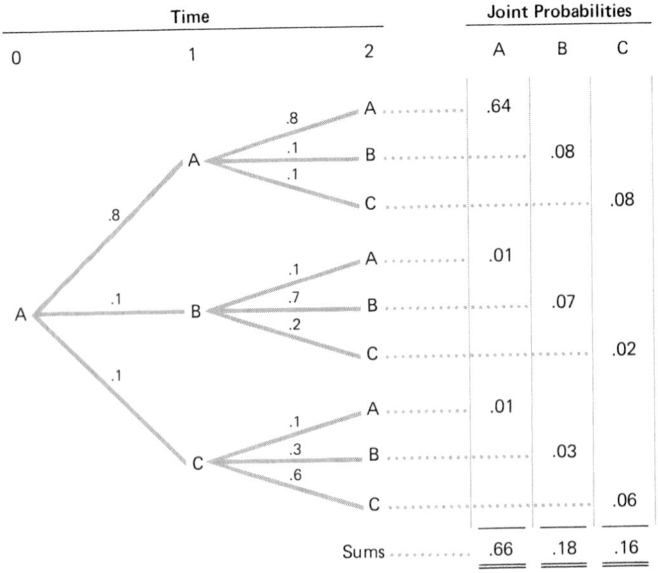

Figure 9.5 Two-period transition from state *B*.

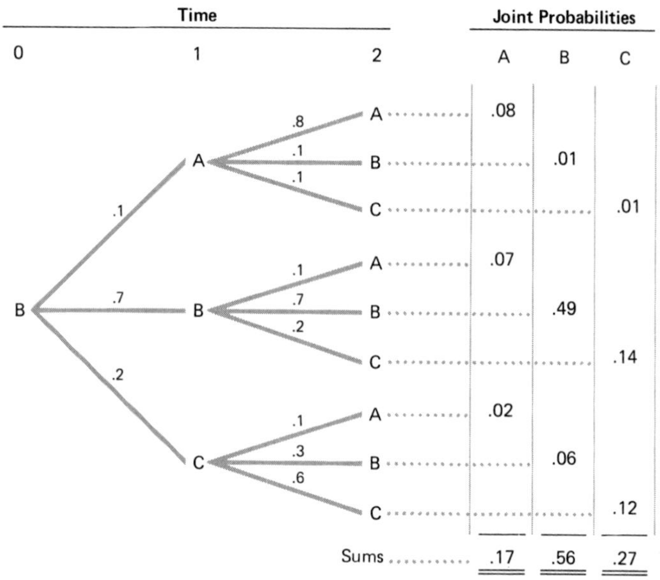

Figure 9.6 Two-period transition from state *C*.

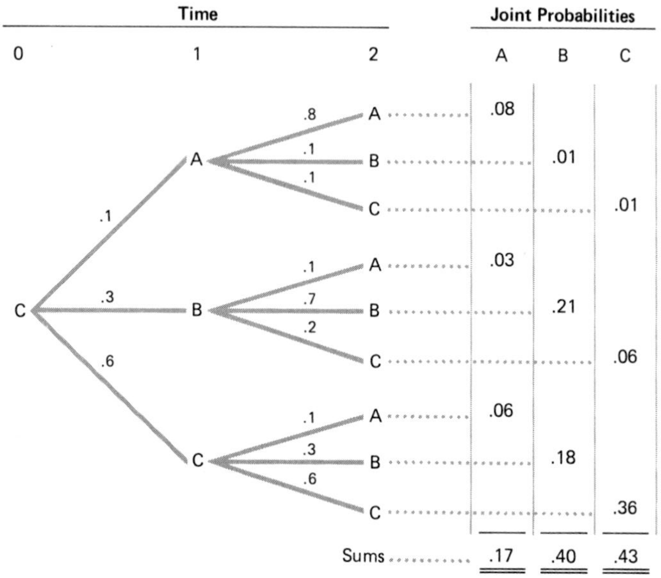

		To State Time 2		
	From State	*A*	*B*	*C*
	A	.66	.18	.16
Time 0	*B*	.17	.56	.27
	C	.17	.40	.43

Note that the above table probabilities relate to the transition over two time periods; thus, they are referred to as two-step transition probabilities.

In order to convert our one-customer case back to the original example, recall that initially the numbers of customers for each brand were $A = 2{,}000$, $B = 4{,}000$, and $C = 1{,}000$. Thus, the predicted number of customers for brand A at time 2 includes retained customers plus customers gained from brands B and C (the column of probabilities under A).

$$2{,}000\,(.66) + 4{,}000\,(.17) + 1{,}000\,(.17) = 1{,}320 + 680 + 170 = 2{,}170$$

Likewise, the numbers of predicted customers for brands B and C at time 2 are $2{,}000(.18) + 4{,}000(.56) + 1{,}000(.40) = 3{,}000$, and $2{,}000(.16) + 4{,}000(.27) + 1{,}000(.43) = 1{,}830$ respectively.

Matrix Approach

It is impossible to proceed much further in the analysis of Markov chains without introducing the methods of matrix algebra. For those requiring a review of matrix methods, see Appendix A.

Matrix multiplication provides a convenient vehicle for predicting the state of a Markovian system at some time period beyond a reference time. Given the previous example, matrix multiplication can be used to predict the state of the system at time n.

System State

We first describe the state of the system at time 0 by a one dimensional matrix, called a **vector.** The state of the system at time 0 is given by

$$p(0) = [p_1(0), p_2(0), p_3(0)]$$

where

$p(0)$ = a vector of $p_i(0)$ values

$p_1(0)$ = probability of being in state 1 at time 0

$p_2(0)$ = probability of being in state 2 at time 0

$p_3(0)$ = probability of being in state 3 at time 0.

If we assume that the system is in state 1 at time 0, then $p(0) = [1.0, 0, 0]$. Likewise, for states 2 and 3 at time 0, we would have [0, 1.0, 0] and [0, 0, 1.0], respectively.

Transition Probability Matrix

We next describe the transition probability matrix by

		To State		
	From State	1	2	3
P =	1	p_{11}	p_{12}	p_{13}
	2	p_{21}	p_{22}	p_{23}
	3	p_{31}	p_{32}	p_{33}

where

$\boldsymbol{P}$ = the matrix of transition probabilities

p_{ij} = the probability of going from state i to state j (for example, p_{13} is the probability of going from state 1 to state 3).

Future State Prediction

In order to compute the probability of being in state j at time 1 (when we are currently at time 0), perform the following operation:

$$p(1) = p(0)\boldsymbol{P}$$

where

$p(1)$ = vector of state probabilities at time 1

$p(0)$ = vector of state probabilities at time 0

$\boldsymbol{P}$ = transition probability matrix

This equation can also be written as

$$[p_1(1), p_2(1), p_3(1)] = [p_1(0), p_2(0), p_3(0)] \cdot \begin{bmatrix} p_{11} & p_{12} & p_{13} \\ p_{21} & p_{22} & p_{23} \\ p_{31} & p_{32} & p_{33} \end{bmatrix}$$

Let us return to our previous brand-switching example and assume that we are in state 1 at time 0 (we will now refer to brand A as 1, B as 2, and C as 3). The probabilities of being in each of the three states after one time period (from time 0 to time 1) are given as follows:

$$[1.0, 0, 0] \cdot \begin{bmatrix} .8 & .1 & .1 \\ .1 & .7 & .2 \\ .1 & .3 & .6 \end{bmatrix} = [.8, .1, .1]$$

and if we were in state 2 (brand B) at time 0, we would have for time 1

$$[0, 1.0, 0] \cdot \begin{bmatrix} .8 & .1 & .1 \\ .1 & .7 & .2 \\ .1 & .3 & .6 \end{bmatrix} = [.1, .7, .2].$$

Finally, if we were in state 3 at time 0, we would have

$$[0, 0, 1.0] \cdot \begin{bmatrix} .8 & .1 & .1 \\ .1 & .7 & .2 \\ .1 & .3 & .6 \end{bmatrix} = [.1, .3, .6].$$

Now, if we wish to know the probabilities of being in the various states at time 2, we simply compute

$$p(2) = p(1)\boldsymbol{P}.$$

These probabilities are developed as follows:

$$[.8, .1, .1] \cdot \begin{bmatrix} .8 & .1 & .1 \\ .1 & .7 & .2 \\ .1 & .3 & .6 \end{bmatrix} = [.66, .18, .16]$$

$$[.1, .7, .2] \cdot \begin{bmatrix} .8 & .1 & .1 \\ .1 & .7 & .2 \\ .1 & .3 & .6 \end{bmatrix} = [.17, .56, .27]$$

$$[.1, .3, .6] \cdot \begin{bmatrix} .8 & .1 & .1 \\ .1 & .7 & .2 \\ .1 & .3 & .6 \end{bmatrix} = [.17, .40, .43].$$

Note that these are exactly the same results as were obtained in figures 9.4, 9.5, and 9.6 of the tree diagrams. However, to expand the tree diagrams to one more stage would be tedious indeed. If we wish the state probabilities for time 3, we compute

$$p(3) = p(2)\boldsymbol{P}$$

$$[.66, .18, .16] \cdot \begin{bmatrix} .8 & .1 & .1 \\ .1 & .7 & .2 \\ .1 & .3 & .6 \end{bmatrix} = [.562, .240, .198]$$

$$[.17, .56, .27] \cdot \begin{bmatrix} .8 & .1 & .1 \\ .1 & .7 & .2 \\ .1 & .3 & .6 \end{bmatrix} = [.219, .490, .291]$$

$$[.17, .40, .43] \cdot \begin{bmatrix} .8 & .1 & .1 \\ .1 & .7 & .2 \\ .1 & .3 & .6 \end{bmatrix} = [.219, .426, .355]$$

Thus, given that we started at time 0 with 2,000, 4,000, and 1,000 customers for each of the respective brands, the prediction of the number of customers using each brand at time 3 is computed as follows:

$$[2{,}000, 4{,}000, 1{,}000] \cdot \begin{bmatrix} .562 & .240 & .198 \\ .219 & .490 & .291 \\ .219 & .426 & .355 \end{bmatrix} = [2{,}219, 2{,}866, 1{,}915]$$

The customers using each brand after three periods are listed in the following table:

Brand		Number of Customers
1. *A*		2,219
2. *B*		2,866
3. *C*		1,915
	Total	7,000

Initial State Specification

It should be pointed out that the initial states of the Markov process can be specified in any one of several ways. Since in many Markovian systems the system is only in one of the states, this was the manner in which the example was first illustrated. Since $p_1(0)$ is the probability of being in state 1, and $p_2(0)$ is the probability of being in state 2, and $p_3(0)$ is the probability of being in state 3 (at time 0), we then represented the possible states by the initial state vector $[p_1(0), p_2(0), p_3(0)]$ as

State	Initial State Probability Vector
1	[1, 0, 0]
2	[0, 1, 0]
3	[0, 0, 1]

However, it does not necessarily have to be the case that the system is in only one of the possible states with a probability of 1.0 (and zero probabilities of being in all other states). Rather the state of the system might be such that there is some probability that the system is in each of the states. For example, the initial state vector might be given as [.3, .6, .1]. Thus, there is a probability of less than one that the system is in each state (with the probabilities summing to 1.0). Actually, if [.3, .6, .1] is the state vector at time 0, this is simply referred to as the *state* of the system at that time.

In fact, the initial state vector need not even be specified as probabilities. We could have simply specified the initial state vector as the number of customers of each brand, as follows [2,000, 4,000, 1,000]. Likewise, we also could have specified the initial state vector as the fraction of market shares of each brand as [2/7, 4/7, 1/7], or as the decimal portion of market shares of each brand as [.286, .571, .143].

Multiperiod Transition Probabilities

We have seen that in order to predict the system state at time 1, we multiplied the system state at time 0 by the transition matrix. Then, to get the prediction for time 2, we multiplied the state vector for time 1 by the transition matrix. We repeated this process again to get our prediction for time 3. We can now show that there is a more efficient approach for predicting the state at time n than the previously described successive multiplication.

Note that we got $p(1)$ by computing $p(0)P$, then we got $p(2)$ by multiplying $p(1)$ by $\boldsymbol{P}$, and, finally, $p(3) = p(2)\boldsymbol{P}$. Now, it can be seen that if $p(1) = p(0)\boldsymbol{P}$ and $p(2) = p(1)\boldsymbol{P}$, then also, $p(2) = p(0)\boldsymbol{PP}$. Likewise, if $p(3) = p(2)\boldsymbol{P}$, then also, $p(3) = p(0)\boldsymbol{PPP}$, which is $p(0)\boldsymbol{P}^3$. Thus, in general, $p(n) = p(0)\boldsymbol{P}^n$. Carefully observe that $\boldsymbol{P}^n$ is the nth power of $\boldsymbol{P}$. This reads, the state vector at time n, $p(n)$, is equal to the state vector at time zero, $p(0)$, multiplied by the nth power of the transition matrix, $\boldsymbol{P}^n$. In terms of the individual elements of the state vector and transition matrix, we can write

$$[p_1(n), p_2(n), \ldots, p_m(n)] = [p_1(0), p_2(0), \ldots, p_m(0)] \cdot \begin{bmatrix} p_{11} & p_{12} & \cdots & p_{1m} \\ p_{21} & p_{22} & \cdots & p_{2m} \\ \cdot & & & \cdot \\ \cdot & & & \cdot \\ \cdot & & & \cdot \\ p_{m1} & p_{m2} & \cdots & p_{mm} \end{bmatrix}^n$$

where

n = the number of time periods hence for which a prediction is desired

0 = the initial point in time, for which the state is known

m = the number of possible states for the system (note that the transition matrix is always $m \times m$).

Thus, in order to derive the state conditions at time 3, for the brand-switching example, we can simply perform the following:

$$[2{,}000,\ 4{,}000,\ 1{,}000] \cdot \begin{bmatrix} .8 & .1 & .1 \\ .1 & .7 & .2 \\ .1 & .3 & .6 \end{bmatrix}^3 = [2{,}219,\ 2{,}866,\ 1{,}915]$$

Steady-State Conditions

In many cases, the Markov chain process will converge to a *steady-state* condition. This is shown for the customer brand-switching example in the following table. The predicted future states are also illustrated graphically in figure 9.7.

Number of Customers at End of Period	Brand		
	A	*B*	*C*
0	2,000	4,000	1,000
1	2,100	3,300	1,600
2	2,170	3,000	1,830
3	2,219	2,866	1,915
4	2,253	2,803	1,944
5	2,277	2,770	1,953
6	2,294	2,753	1,953
7	2,306	2,742	1,952
8	2,314	2,736	1,950
9	2,320	2,731	1,949
10	2,324	2,729	1,947
11	2,327	2,727	1,946
12	2,329	2,725	1,946
13	2,330	2,724	1,946
14	2,331	2,724	1,945
15	2,332	2,723	1,945
16	2,332	2,723	1,945

Figure 9.7 Predicted Markov states for sixteen periods.

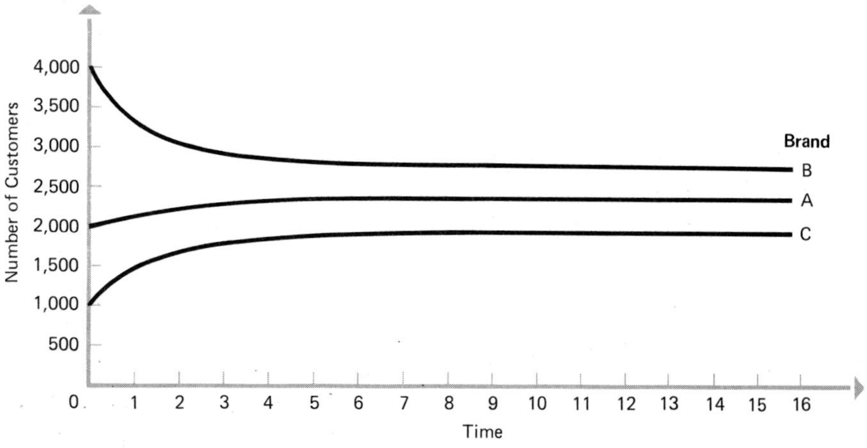

Note that the number of customers for each brand converges to a steady-state after the fifteenth future period. The steady-state conditions are summarized in terms of numbers of customers and proportions in the following table:

States	*A*	*B*	*C*	Total
Number of Customers	2,332	2,723	1,945	7,000
Proportions	.333	.389	.278	1.000

In general, as n grows larger the state values tend to stabilize at a steady state. This is a logical occurrence since the present state tends to lose significance for future states at time periods in the distant future. In other words, if a customer is using brand B now, the probability that the customer will be using brand A or C twenty periods from now would probably be the same as for twenty-one periods. By the same token, it is also logical to presume that the fact that a customer is now using brand B holds no significance for determining which brand the customer will be using twenty periods from now. Thus, regardless of which state a system begins in, after a number of periods the probability vector for A, B, and C will be the same.

Computation of Steady-State Conditions

The steady-state conditions can be computed by observing that as steady-state is reached, multiplication of a state condition by the transition probabilities does not change the state condition. That is,

$$p(n) = p(n-1)\boldsymbol{P}$$

for any value of n after steady-state is reached. For example, if we multiply the state condition of the brand-switching example at the end of period 16 by the transition matrix,

$$[2{,}332,\ 2{,}723,\ 1{,}945] \cdot \begin{bmatrix} .8 & .1 & .1 \\ .1 & .7 & .2 \\ .1 & .3 & .6 \end{bmatrix},$$

we obtain the same state values, [2,332, 2,723, 1,945], as our previous results. Thus, a steady state has been reached.

Steady-State Vector

There is an alternative to the previously demonstrated methods for determining the steady-state values. The steady-state values can also be determined algebraically as follows. We will first represent the state values, at steady state, by the symbol π. Thus, at steady state the state vector is given, in terms of decimal proportions, as

$$\pi = [\pi_1, \pi_2, \pi_3] = [.333, .389, .278]$$

where

π = vector of state probabilities (relative proportions)

π_1 = value of state condition 1

π_2 = value of state condition 2

π_3 = value of state condition 3.

Note, that the time period is not given here since, as steady-state, these values are independent of time.

Since multiplication of a state condition by the transition matrix yields the same condition at steady state, we can write

$$\pi = \pi \cdot \boldsymbol{P}$$

or

$$[\pi_1, \pi_2, \pi_3] = [\pi_1, \pi_2, \pi_3] \cdot \begin{bmatrix} p_{11} & p_{12} & p_{13} \\ p_{21} & p_{22} & p_{23} \\ p_{31} & p_{32} & p_{33} \end{bmatrix}.$$

This assumes that there are three possible state conditions, as there were in the brand-switching example. For the brand-switching example, we would have

$$[\pi_1, \pi_2, \pi_3] = [\pi_1, \pi_2, \pi_3] \cdot \begin{bmatrix} .8 & .1 & .1 \\ .1 & .7 & .2 \\ .1 & .3 & .6 \end{bmatrix},$$

which yields

$$\pi_1 = .8\pi_1 + .1\pi_2 + .1\pi_3$$

$$\pi_2 = .1\pi_1 + .7\pi_2 + .3\pi_3$$

$$\pi_3 = .1\pi_1 + .2\pi_2 + .6\pi_3.$$

We further include the fact that the sum of the state probabilities must sum to 1.0.

$$\pi_1 + \pi_2 + \pi_3 = 1.0$$

We now have four equations with three unknowns, which can be solved simultaneously to determine the steady-state values of π_1, π_2, and π_3. Noting that one of the initial three equations is redundant, we can eliminate any one of the three (for example, eliminate the third equation). That is, if we solve for π_1 and π_2, then π_3 is automatically known since $\pi_1 + \pi_2 + \pi_3 = 1.0$. As such, the third equation, which also solves for π_3, is redundant and need not be included. The three remaining equations to be solved simultaneously can be written as

$$-.2\pi_1 + .1\pi_2 + .1\pi_3 = 0$$

$$.1\pi_1 - .3\pi_2 + .3\pi_3 = 0$$

$$1.0\pi_1 + 1.0\pi_2 + 1.0\pi_3 = 1.0.$$

Solving these equations simultaneously yields

$$\pi_1 = .333 \qquad \pi_2 = .389 \qquad \pi_3 = .278,$$

which are the steady-state conditions.

As noted earlier, as n grows larger, the matrix of transition probabilities to the power n (i.e. $\boldsymbol{P}^n$) approaches a limiting form in which all rows are identical and equal to the steady-state vector. Thus, for the preceding example, the transition matrix, for a very large value of n, would be

$$\boldsymbol{P}^n = \begin{bmatrix} .333 & .389 & .278 \\ .333 & .389 & .278 \\ .333 & .389 & .278 \end{bmatrix}$$

If we return to the sixteenth period of the table on page 395, we find that we obtain exactly the same values for π_1, π_2, and π_3.

In our simultaneous solution of the equations to obtain π_1, π_2, and π_3, we actually solved for the steady-state *proportions* of market share, or the *probabilities* of one customer being in any one of the states. If we had desired to get the *number* of customers for each brand directly, we would have simply set the following equation equal to 7,000:

$$\pi_1 + \pi_2 + \pi_3 = 7{,}000 \text{ (total number of customers)},$$

which yields

$$\pi_1 = 2{,}332$$

$$\pi_2 = 2{,}723$$

$$\pi_3 = 1{,}945.$$

For relatively small problems, such as the brand-switching example, the equations can be solved simultaneously by elementary algebraic substitution. For problems that involve more states, matrix algebra is recommended. Solution of systems of linear equations by matrix algebra is discussed in Appendix A.

Steady State for the Urn Example

Let us return briefly to the initial example in which we were drawing (and replacing) a ball from one of two urns. Recall that urn x contained one red and three black balls, while urn y contained two red and two black balls. If we draw a red ball, we draw the next ball from urn x. If we draw a black ball, the next ball is drawn from urn y. With the specified quantities of red and black balls for each urn, the transition probability matrix was determined to be as follows:

	To State	
From State	x	y
x	1/4	3/4
y	1/2	1/2

The states are defined to be the urn that we are drawing from. We now wish to determine the steady-state conditions, (i.e., the proportion of the time we would draw from each urn over the long run).

We again define the state conditions at steady-state as π. Since we have two possible state conditions for this example (urn x or urn y), $\pi = (\pi_1, \pi_2)$. If we are at steady state, we know that

$$[\pi_1, \pi_2] = [\pi_1, \pi_2] \cdot \begin{bmatrix} 1/4 & 3/4 \\ 1/2 & 1/2 \end{bmatrix},$$

which yields

$$\pi_1 = \tfrac{1}{4}\pi_1 + \tfrac{1}{2}\pi_2$$

$$\pi_2 = \tfrac{3}{4}\pi_1 + \tfrac{1}{2}\pi_2$$

and, further, we know that the state vector must sum to one,

$$\pi_1 + \pi_2 = 1.0.$$

Since one of the initial equations (not including the state vector summed to one) is always redundant, we can eliminate the second equation, yielding the following equations for simultaneous solution:

$$-\tfrac{3}{4}\pi_1 + \tfrac{1}{2}\pi_2 = 0$$

$$\pi_1 + \pi_2 = 1.0$$

Solving these equations simultaneously yields

$$\pi_1 = \tfrac{2}{5} \text{ and } \pi_2 = \tfrac{3}{5}.$$

Thus, our steady-state vector is given as $\pi = [2/5, 3/5] = [.4, .6]$. We expect that over the long run we will be drawing from urn x 40% of the time and from urn y 60% of the time.

Note that our analysis of this Markovian process is dependent upon two things: (1) the rule by which we move from one urn to the other does not change and (2) the mix of red to black balls in each urn does not change. This is a well-defined structure for our problem. However, an analogous sort of structure must also hold for any Markov chain process. This is why, for our brand-switching example, we assumed that all customers would be divided up among the three brands and none would shop elsewhere (i.e., leave the system). This is also why we assumed that the transition probabilities for switching from one brand to another were constant, or stable. If customers switch in and out of the system (shop in another town) or if the transition probabilities change over time, then the steady-state conditions do not exist. It is these factors that often limit the applicability of Markov analysis.

Doubly Stochastic Transition Matrix

It has already been shown that the sum of the transition probabilities in each row of the transition matrix is 1.0. However, if the *columns* also sum to 1.0, the transition matrix is referred to as **doubly stochastic.**

For any doubly stochastic transition matrix, in which the number of states is m, the steady-state vector of probabilities is given as

$$\pi_1, \pi_2, \pi_3, \ldots, \pi_m = \frac{1}{m}.$$

For example, given the following transition matrix,

$$\boldsymbol{P} = \begin{bmatrix} 1/2 & 1/4 & 1/4 \\ 1/4 & 1/2 & 1/4 \\ 1/4 & 1/4 & 1/2 \end{bmatrix}, \text{ where } m = 3,$$

the steady-state vector is immediately given by

$$\pi = (\pi_1, \pi_2, \pi_3) = \left(\frac{1}{m}, \frac{1}{m}, \frac{1}{m}\right) = \left(\frac{1}{3}, \frac{1}{3}, \frac{1}{3}\right).$$

Existence of Steady-State Conditions

A Markov chain process may not always reach steady state. However, it is possible to determine if the process will go to steady state. If there is some n for which every element of $\boldsymbol{P}^n$ is greater than zero, then steady-state conditions exist. For example, consider the following transition matrix:

$$\boldsymbol{P} = \begin{bmatrix} 0 & 1/2 & 2/3 \\ 2/3 & 0 & 1/3 \\ 1/3 & 1/3 & 1/3 \end{bmatrix}$$

Squaring $\boldsymbol{P}$, we get

$$\boldsymbol{P}^2 = \begin{bmatrix} 4/9 & 2/9 & 3/9 \\ 1/9 & 3/9 & 5/9 \\ 3/9 & 2/9 & 4/9 \end{bmatrix}$$

Since every element of P^n for $n = 2$ is positive, we have determined that steady-state conditions do exist. When P^n, for some n, has all positive elements, this is oftentimes referred to as a *regular* transition matrix.

Special Cases of Markov Processes

Absorbing States

A state is referred to as an **absorbing,** or **trapping, state** if it is impossible to leave that state. This will occur if any p_{ii} is equal to 1.0; that is, if any transition probability in the retention diagonal, from upper left to lower right, is equal to 1.0.

Further, a Markov chain is said to be absorbing if *any* state is absorbing, and it is possible to go from each state to an absorbing state in a finite number of steps. Consider, for example, the following transition probability matrix:

	States	A	B	C
	A	1	0	0
P =	B	1/2	1/4	1/4
	C	1/3	1/3	1/3

Since $p_{11} = 1.0$, state A is an absorbing state. Also, the probabilities of going from B and C to A in a finite number of steps is positive. Therefore, the Markov chain is absorbing, and the steady-state conditions are $\pi = (1.0, 0, 0)$. Note that the steady-state conditions are not determined by the usual method in the case of the absorbing Markov chain. Rather, $\pi_i = 1.0$ for the i in which there is a trapping state, and all other $\pi_i = 0$. If there is more than one trapping state, then a steady-state condition independent of initial state conditions does not exist.

A well-known example of Markov chains with absorbing states is the "accounts receivable" or "bad debt" example, which we will briefly review. In this example, a firm has developed the following transition probability matrix, where the states are the months of outstanding accounts (i.e., debts):

$$P = \begin{array}{c} \\ a \\ 1 \\ 2 \\ 3 \\ b \end{array} \begin{bmatrix} a & 1 & 2 & 3 & b \\ 1 & 0 & 0 & 0 & 0 \\ .60 & 0 & .40 & 0 & 0 \\ .75 & 0 & 0 & .25 & 0 \\ .50 & 0 & 0 & 0 & .50 \\ 0 & 0 & 0 & 0 & 1 \end{bmatrix}$$

where, a = an account paid and b = a bad debt.

A bad debt is labeled as such only after three months have passed and the account has not been paid. For example, if an account receivable is in month 2, there is a 0.75 probability it will be paid off in the next period and 0.25 probability it will still be unpaid in month 3. Since it is impossible for a bad debt to occur until three months have elapsed, there is a 0.0 probability of state *b* occurring in the first and second months.

Much useful information can be obtained from this type of matrix configuration through several relatively simple matrix manipulations. (However, these manipulations do require a familiarity with matrix algebra, which is presented in Appendix A). The first step is to change the matrix into general form as follows:

$$\boldsymbol{P} = \begin{array}{c} \\ a \\ b \\ 1 \\ 2 \\ 3 \end{array} \left[\begin{array}{cc|ccc} a & b & 1 & 2 & 3 \\ 1 & 0 & 0 & 0 & 0 \\ 0 & 1 & 0 & 0 & 0 \\ \hline .60 & 0 & 0 & .40 & 0 \\ .75 & 0 & 0 & 0 & .25 \\ .50 & .50 & 0 & 0 & 0 \end{array}\right]$$

Now four submatrices exist that are in the following general form:

$$\boldsymbol{P} = \left[\begin{array}{c|c} \boldsymbol{I} & \boldsymbol{O} \\ \hline \boldsymbol{R} & \boldsymbol{Q} \end{array}\right],$$

where

$\boldsymbol{I}$ = an identity matrix

$\boldsymbol{O}$ = a matrix of zeros

$\boldsymbol{R}$ = a matrix containing the transition probabilities of being absorbed in the next period

$\boldsymbol{Q}$ = a square matrix containing transition probabilities for movement between all nonabsorbing states.

The first matrix operation determines the **fundamental matrix, *F*,** which gives the expected number of times the system would be in any of the nonabsorbing states before absorption occurs (i.e., before the debt is paid off or becomes bad). The fundamental matrix is computed by taking the inverse of the difference between an identity matrix and $\boldsymbol{Q}$.

$$\boldsymbol{F} = (\boldsymbol{I} - \boldsymbol{Q})^{-1}$$

where $\boldsymbol{I}$ is an identity matrix of the same magnitude as $\boldsymbol{Q}$. For this example,

$$\boldsymbol{F} = \left(\begin{bmatrix} 1 & 0 & 0 \\ 0 & 1 & 0 \\ 0 & 0 & 1 \end{bmatrix} - \begin{bmatrix} 0 & .40 & 0 \\ 0 & 0 & .25 \\ 0 & 0 & 0 \end{bmatrix} \right)^{-1}$$

$$F = \begin{array}{c} \\ 1 \\ 2 \\ 3 \end{array} \begin{array}{c} \begin{array}{ccc} 1 & 2 & 3 \end{array} \\ \begin{bmatrix} 1 & .40 & .10 \\ 0 & 1 & .25 \\ 0 & 0 & 1 \end{bmatrix} \end{array}.$$

Thus, according to the F matrix, if you are in state 1, the expected number of times you would occupy state 2 would be 0.4 before the debt is paid off or becomes bad.

The next matrix operation requires the multiplication of F and R.

$$F \cdot R = \begin{array}{c} \\ 1 \\ 2 \\ 3 \end{array} \begin{array}{c} \begin{array}{ccc} 1 & 2 & 3 \end{array} \\ \begin{bmatrix} 1 & .40 & .10 \\ 0 & 1 & .25 \\ 0 & 0 & 1 \end{bmatrix} \end{array} \cdot \begin{array}{c} \\ 1 \\ 2 \\ 3 \end{array} \begin{array}{c} \begin{array}{cc} a & b \end{array} \\ \begin{bmatrix} .60 & 0 \\ .75 & 0 \\ .50 & .50 \end{bmatrix} \end{array} = \begin{array}{c} \\ 1 \\ 2 \\ 3 \end{array} \begin{array}{c} \begin{array}{cc} a & b \end{array} \\ \begin{bmatrix} .95 & .05 \\ .875 & .125 \\ .50 & .50 \end{bmatrix} \end{array}$$

The $F \cdot R$ matrix reflects the probability of eventually being absorbed given any starting state. For example, if the account is presently in the second month there is a .875 probability that it will eventually be paid and a .125 probability that it will result in a bad debt.

If the original P matrix is carried to the second and third power, further information can be obtained.

$$P^2 = \begin{array}{c} \\ a \\ b \\ 1 \\ 2 \\ 3 \end{array} \begin{array}{c} \begin{array}{ccccc} a & b & 1 & 2 & 3 \end{array} \\ \begin{bmatrix} 1 & 0 & 0 & 0 & 0 \\ 0 & 1 & 0 & 0 & 0 \\ .90 & 0 & 0 & 0 & .10 \\ .875 & .125 & 0 & 0 & 0 \\ .50 & .50 & 0 & 0 & 0 \end{bmatrix} \end{array}, \quad P^3 = \begin{array}{c} \\ a \\ b \\ 1 \\ 2 \\ 3 \end{array} \begin{array}{c} \begin{array}{ccccc} a & b & 1 & 2 & 3 \end{array} \\ \begin{bmatrix} 1 & 0 & 0 & 0 & 0 \\ 0 & 1 & 0 & 0 & 0 \\ .95 & .05 & 0 & 0 & 0 \\ .875 & .125 & 0 & 0 & 0 \\ .50 & .50 & 0 & 0 & 0 \end{bmatrix} \end{array}$$

Notice that the R matrix changes at each step from P^1 to P^3. This change represents the change in flow of funds from month to month. Thus, the flow of funds (the percentage of paid accounts or of bad debts) in each month can be determined by subtracting the R matrices for each period as follows:

$$\Delta R1 = R1 - R0 = \begin{bmatrix} .60 & 0 \\ .75 & 0 \\ .50 & .50 \end{bmatrix} - \begin{bmatrix} 0 & 0 \\ 0 & 0 \\ 0 & 0 \end{bmatrix} = \begin{bmatrix} .60 & 0 \\ .75 & 0 \\ .50 & .50 \end{bmatrix}$$

$$\Delta R2 = R2 - R1 = \begin{bmatrix} .90 & 0 \\ .875 & .125 \\ .50 & .50 \end{bmatrix} - \begin{bmatrix} .60 & 0 \\ .75 & 0 \\ .50 & .50 \end{bmatrix} = \begin{bmatrix} .30 & 0 \\ .125 & .125 \\ 0 & 0 \end{bmatrix}$$

$$\Delta R3 = R3 - R2 = \begin{bmatrix} .95 & .05 \\ .875 & .125 \\ .50 & .50 \end{bmatrix} - \begin{bmatrix} .90 & 0 \\ .875 & .125 \\ .50 & .50 \end{bmatrix} = \begin{bmatrix} .05 & .05 \\ 0 & 0 \\ 0 & 0 \end{bmatrix}$$

Each of these $\Delta \boldsymbol{R}$ matrices represent the change in cash flow from period to period. For example, observing $\Delta \boldsymbol{R}2$, if the account is in month 2 then .125 of the funds will be paid and .125 will become bad debts. If we assume that the account books show accounts receivables as

one month	\$1,000
two months	800
three months	200

and transform this data into a **status vector,** *s*,

$$s = [1{,}000 \;\; 800 \;\; 200],$$

we can determine that portion of the \$2,000 total flowing in during each of the three months. This is achieved by multiplying the status vector by each $\Delta \boldsymbol{R}$ matrix as follows:

$$s\Delta \boldsymbol{R}1 = [1{,}000 \;\; 800 \;\; 200] \begin{bmatrix} .60 & 0 \\ .75 & 0 \\ .50 & .50 \end{bmatrix} = \overset{\quad a \qquad\; b}{[1{,}300 \;\; 100]}$$

$$s\Delta \boldsymbol{R}2 = [1{,}000 \;\; 800 \;\; 200] \begin{bmatrix} .30 & 0 \\ .125 & .125 \\ 0 & 0 \end{bmatrix} = \overset{\quad a \qquad\; b}{[400 \;\; 100]}$$

$$s\Delta \boldsymbol{R}3 = [1{,}000 \;\; 800 \;\; 200] \begin{bmatrix} .05 & .05 \\ 0 & 0 \\ 0 & 0 \end{bmatrix} = \overset{\quad a \qquad\; b}{[50 \;\; 50]}$$

This information provides an accounts schedule for the three-month period, showing in each period the amount paid and the amount becoming bad debts. For example, of the \$2,000 total on the books, \$1,300 is paid in month 1 while \$100 becomes a bad debt, \$400 is paid in month 2 while \$100 becomes a bad debt, and \$50 is paid in month 3 while \$50 becomes a bad debt.

Transient State

A state is referred to as **transient** if it is impossible to move to that state from any other state except itself. For example, in the following transition matrix, state *B* is a transient state.

	States	*A*	*B*	*C*
	A	3/4	0	1/4
P =	*B*	1/5	3/5	1/5
	C	1/3	0	2/3

Eventually all movement will be away from state *B*, and π_2 will equal 0.

For the case in which there is a transient state, the steady-state probabilities can be computed by the usual method, after first eliminating from consideration the zero value state (i.e., $\pi_2 = 0$ in this case). Thus, for the example given, the steady-state probabilities can be computed by simultaneously solving the following equations:

$$\pi_1 = \tfrac{3}{4}\pi_1 + \tfrac{1}{3}\pi_3$$

$$\pi_3 = \tfrac{1}{4}\pi_1 + \tfrac{2}{3}\pi_3$$

$$\pi_1 + \pi_2 + \pi_3 = 1.0$$

The reader may verify that the steady-state conditions are $\pi = [4/7, 0, 3/7]$.

In the accounts receivable example for absorbing states, all nonabsorbing states (i.e., states 1, 2 and 3) are transient states since eventually all movement will be toward absorption and away from these states.

Cycling Processes

A **cycling,** or **periodic,** Markov process is characterized by all zeros in retention cells (retention cells are in the diagonal from upper left to lower right), and all ones or zeros in nonretention cells of the transition matrix. For example, the following transition matrices exhibit cycling behavior.

$$\mathbf{P}_x = \begin{array}{c} A \\ B \end{array}\overset{\begin{array}{cc} A & B \end{array}}{\begin{bmatrix} 0 & 1 \\ 1 & 0 \end{bmatrix}} \quad \mathbf{P}_y = \begin{array}{c} A \\ B \\ C \end{array}\overset{\begin{array}{ccc} A & B & C \end{array}}{\begin{bmatrix} 0 & 1 & 0 \\ 0 & 0 & 1 \\ 1 & 0 & 0 \end{bmatrix}} \quad \mathbf{P} = \begin{array}{c} A \\ B \\ C \\ D \end{array}\overset{\begin{array}{cccc} A & B & C & D \end{array}}{\begin{bmatrix} 0 & 1 & 0 & 0 \\ 0 & 0 & 1 & 0 \\ 0 & 0 & 0 & 1 \\ 1 & 0 & 0 & 0 \end{bmatrix}}$$

If we consider $\mathbf{P}_y$, it is apparent that the system will move sequentially from *A* to *B* to *C* to *A* and so on. Thus, there can be no steady-state conditions for a cycling Markov process.

It is important to note that the process is not cycling unless all nonretention cells of the transition matrix are 1.0 or 0. Stated another way, if any one of the retention cells of the transition matrix is positive, it is not a cycling process. For example, the following transition matrix is not cycling:

	State	A	B	C
P =	A	0	1	0
	B	0	0	1
	C	1/3	1/3	1/3

Using the standard process, we can determine the steady-state conditions as $\pi = [1/6, 1/3, 1/2]$.

Recurrent Sets

A Markov chain may trap the process within a *set* of states. The concept is similar to the preceding absorbing state, except that the trap involves more than one state. A recurrent set containing several states is oftentimes referred to as a **generalized trapping state.**

Consider the following transition matrix:

	States	A	B	C	D
P =	A	3/4	1/4	0	0
	B	1/2	1/2	0	0
	C	0	0	2/3	1/3
	D	0	0	1/5	4/5

It is apparent that the system is trapped in either states *A* or *B* or it is trapped in states *C* or *D*. Thus, the system has two recurrent sets. Since the long-term behavior of the system is dependent on the starting point, there can be no steady-state solution.

Consider the following system with one recurrent set:

	States	A	B	C	D
P =	A	3/4	1/4	0	0
	B	1/2	1/2	0	0
	C	0	1/3	1/3	1/3
	D	0	0	1/5	4/5

Once the system reaches either state A or B, it remains in one or the other of those states. However, since the system can reach state A or B in a finite number of steps (note that $p_{32} = 1/3$), there is only one recurrent set and the steady-state solution can be obtained. This is accomplished by observing that in the long run π_3 and π_4 must eventually go to zero. (Note the 1/5 probability that D goes to C and the 1/3 probability that C goes to B, from which there is no return to C or D.) Thus, the steady-state conditions are $\pi_1 = 2/3$, $\pi_2 = 1/3$, $\pi_3 = 0$, $\pi_4 = 0$, where π_1 and π_2 are computed by the usual method.

As a final example, consider the following transition matrix:

	States	A	B	C
	A	0	1	0
P =	B	1	0	0
	C	0	0	1

Here we have two recurrent sets, where the system is trapped in A or B, or it is trapped in C. Since C is a single absorbing state, the Markov process is an absorbing system. Also, note that the recurrent set, which includes A and B, is also a cycling set. Thus, the system outcome is completely dependent upon the starting conditions. If the starting condition is state C, the system is trapped in C. If the starting condition is A or B, the system is trapped in A or B and cycles between the two states.

Summary

In this chapter, a special class of stochastic processes called Markov chains, has been presented. The fundamental concepts and properties of Markov analysis were discussed, and several examples of the types of problems to which Markov analysis can be applied were presented. The study of Markov models provides valuable insight into the analysis of problems that have several potential outcomes after the passage of periods of time. It should be emphasized that Markov models are *descriptive* models, as opposed to optimization models or methods, and, as such, they are used to predict the system status at future points in time and the expected steady state.

References

Feller, W. *An Introduction to Probability Theory and Its Applications*. Vol. 1, 3rd ed. New York: John Wiley & Sons, 1968.

Howard, R. A. *Dynamic Programming and Markov Processes*. Cambridge: M.I.T. Press, 1960.

Kemeny, J. G., and Snell, J. L. *Finite Markov Chains*. Princeton, N.J.: D. Van Nostrand Company, 1960.

Parzen, E. *Stochastic Processes*. San Francisco: Holden-Day, 1962.

Searle, S. R., and Hausman, W. H. *Matrix Algebra for Business and Economics*. New York: John Wiley & Sons, 1970.

Problems

1. Would you classify Markov chain models as deterministic or probabilistic models? Discuss the basis for your answer.

2. A Markov process is dependent on how many previous states?

3. What are the major elements of a Markov process model? Describe each component.

4. Two firms share the market for a particular product. Firm *A* is an old and well-established firm, while firm *B* is a new and aggressive competitor. Firm *A* is alarmed at the progress being made by firm *B* and has asked its market research department for a forecast of future market shares for the two firms, assuming that the same market conditions prevail. The current market shares held by the two firms are as follows:

Firm	Market Share
A	80%
B	20%

The market research department has determined that customers switch among the two firms according to the following probabilities:

	To Firm	
From Firm	*A*	*B*
A	.5	.5
B	.6	.4

a. Determine the market research department's market-share forecast for one period in the future, two periods in the future, three periods in the future.
b. Based on the results of (*a*), estimate the equilibrium market share for each firm (rounded to the nearest whole percentage).
c. Illustrate customer switching among the two firms as a Markov transition probability diagram (see fig. 9.1).

5. Refer to problem 4. Beginning with firm *A*, illustrate the three-period transition as a tree diagram (see fig. 9.4). Prepare the same illustration beginning with firm *B*. Compute the sums of the joint probabilities of ending at *A* for each of the two tree diagrams. Perform the same computation for the case in which the tree branching ends at *B* for each of the tree diagrams. Four probability values are thus obtained.

a. Describe the four probability values.
b. Insert the four probabilities in the appropriate cells of the following matrix:

	Ending Firm	
Beginning Firm	*A*	*B*
A		
B		

c. Show that by multiplying the two probabilities in column *A* by the original market share of firm *A* (80%) and summing these products, the market-share forecast for three periods in the future is obtained. Also, show that by multiplying the two probabilities in column *B* by the original market share for firm *B* (20%) and summing these products, the market-share forecast for three periods in the future is obtained. Compare these results with the results obtained in problem 4(*a*).

6. What is meant by *steady state*, or *equilibrium*, in Markov analysis?

7. Assume that a manufacturing firm wishes to predict the status of machine operations in the future. Through historical records, the firm has determined that if a machine breaks down in a particular week, the probability of breakdown in the following week, after repair, is only .2. However, if a machine has not broken down in a particular week, the probability of breakdown in the following week is .6. The firm has therefore developed the following probability table of machine breakdowns:

	Week *n* + 1 Status	
Week *n* Status	No Breakdown	Breakdown
No Breakdown	.4	.6
Breakdown	.8	.2

a. Assuming that the machine is not broken down in week n, what are the probabilities that the machine will break down in week $n+1$, $n+2$, $n+3$, $n+4$, $n+5$?
b. Determine the steady-state condition (i.e., forecast the percentage of future weeks in which the machine will break down).

8. A department store is interested in predicting the behavior of customers for which accounts receivable are outstanding. Their credit department has been asked to analyze their records and predict payment probabilities. Historical records have yielded the following payment patterns of credit customers:

	Month $n+1$	
Month n	Paid Bill	Did Not Pay Bill
Paid Bill	.90	.10
Did Not Pay Bill	.80	.20

Assume that these probabilities are used to predict the behavior of a credit customer with regard to bill payment.

a. If a credit customer did not pay his bill in month n, what is the probability he will not pay it in any of the next three months?
b. If a customer did not pay his bill in month n, what are the probabilities he will pay his bill in month $n + 1$, in month $n + 2$, in month $n + 3$? (Note, assume that monthly bills include purchases made in that month plus any outstanding balance from previously unpaid bills).
c. Determine the steady-state conditions (i.e., the probability the customer will pay a bill or not pay a bill in month $n + 1$ regardless of whether he paid in month n).

9. Describe and illustrate a state vector of Markov analysis.

10. Describe and illustrate a transition matrix of Markov analysis.

11. Given the following transition matrix for a three state system, algebraically determine the steady-state conditions.

	1	2	3
1	.6	.2	.2
2	.4	.3	.3
3	.1	.5	.4

12. Students switch among the various colleges of a university according to the following probability transition matrix:

	To		
From	Engineering	Liberal Arts	Business
Engineering	.5	.3	.2
Liberal Arts	.1	.7	.2
Business	.1	.1	.8

Assume that the number of students in each college of the university at the beginning of the fall quarter is as follows:

Engineering	3,000
Liberal Arts	5,000
Business	2,000

a. Forecast the number of students in each college after the end of the third quarter, based on a four-quarter system. Determine by first computing P^n.
b. Determine the steady-state conditions for the university.

13. It has been said that stock market prices have a tendency to move in opposite directions from day to day. Assume that a stock market analyst has determined from historical data that a particular stock price will move up or down according to the following probabilities:

	Day $n+1$	
Day n	Increase	Decrease
Increase	.3	.7
Decrease	.8	.2

Determine the steady-state conditions.

14. Describe the meaning of absorbing, or trapping, states in Markov chains. Give an example.

15. What is meant by transient states in Markov chains? Give an example.

16. Refer to the brand-switching example on page 387 of this chapter. Assume instead that the transition probability matrix is the following:

	To Brand		
From Brand	*A*	*B*	*C*
A	.7	.2	.1
B	.1	.5	.4
C	.2	.3	.5

The steady-state probabilities can be immediately determined. What are the steady-state probabilities, and why can they be easily determined?

17. Suppose the transition matrix for the brand-switching example is as follows:

	To Brand		
From Brand	*A*	*B*	*C*
A	.8	.1	.1
B	0	1.0	0
C	.1	.3	.6

What will happen in this case? What type of process is represented?

18. Assume that the transition matrix for the brand-switching example is as follows:

	To Brand		
From Brand	*A*	*B*	*C*
A	.8	.2	0
B	.1	.7	.2
C	.4	.6	0

Determine the steady-state solution. What general type of process is illustrated?

19. The weather service has determined the following transition probabilities for air pollution movement:

	Day $n + 1$		
Day n	Clean	Average	Polluted
Clean	.3	.6	.1
Average	.3	.5	.2
Polluted	.1	.7	.2

a. Determine the steady-state probabilities for each pollution state.
b. During a year, how many days will the air remain in code state?

20. A firm has developed the following transition probability matrix for their accounts receivables. The states in this matrix are the months of an outstanding debt. *P* is a state indicating a debt is paid, while *B* is a state indicating the debt has been classified as bad.

	P	1	2	3	*B*
P	1	0	0	0	0
1	.3	0	.7	0	0
2	.5	0	0	.5	0
3	.6	0	0	0	.4
B	0	0	0	0	1

a. Determine the probability that a debt will eventually be paid or be classified as bad for each starting state in month 1.
b. If the firm's books presently have accounts receivables defined by the following status vector, s = \$5,000, \$3,000, \$2,000, determine the cash flow that will result in each month.

21. Would you classify Markov chain models as optimization models? Discuss your answer.

10

Queueing Theory

Waiting lines are one of the most common occurrences of everyday life. No doubt, you can recall having waited in line during college registration, to checkout at a grocery store, to make a deposit or withdrawal at a bank, for service at a hamburger stand, to pay at a toll bridge, for service at a gas station, and numerous other situations. Waiting lines, often referred to as **queues,** can consist of people, automobiles, equipment, or other units awaiting service.

The study of waiting lines, known as *queueing theory,* is far from new. Queueing theory can be traced back to the classic work of A. K. Erlang, a Danish mathematician, who studied the fluctuating demands on telephone facilities and associated service delays. Erlang's work was first published in 1913 under the title *Solution of Some Problems in the Theory of Probabilities of Significance in Automatic Telephone Exchanges*. Thus, waiting line analysis represents one of the oldest of the various topical areas considered in management science.

Waiting lines may exist in the form of an observable line of individuals or objects waiting for service or they may occur in a more abstract sense, as when machines break down in a factory and form a queue to wait for repair. Often customers enter a shoe store or ice cream parlor and take a number, indicating their turn for service, and then browse around the store to inspect the items for sale. This, nevertheless, represents a queueing process. Table 10.1 summarizes several instances of commonly recognized queueing situations.

Table 10.1 Commonly recognized waiting line situations

Situation	Arrivals	Servers	Service Process
School registration	Students	Registration desk	Course assigned and forms signed
Grocery store	Customers	Checkout counter	Bill computation and payment
Bank	Customers	Teller	Deposit, withdrawal, check cashed
Traffic intersection	Automobiles	Traffic light	Controlled passage through intersection
Doctor's office	Patients	Doctor and staff	Treatment
Machine maintenance	Machine breakdown	Repairmen	Repair machine
Shipping terminal	Trucks	Docks	Unloading and loading
Assembly line	Product components	Assembly workers	Assemble product
Mail-order store	Mail orders	Mail-order clerks	Process and mail products ordered
Telephone exchange	Calls	Electronic switching equipment	Complete connection
Air terminal	Airplanes	Runways	Airplanes landing and taking off
Tool crib	Workers	Tool attendants	Check out or check in tools

Basic Components of a Waiting Line Process

The basic components of a waiting line process are **arrivals, servers,** and **waiting lines** (queues). These components are illustrated graphically in figure 10.1.

Figure 10.1 Basic components of a waiting line process.

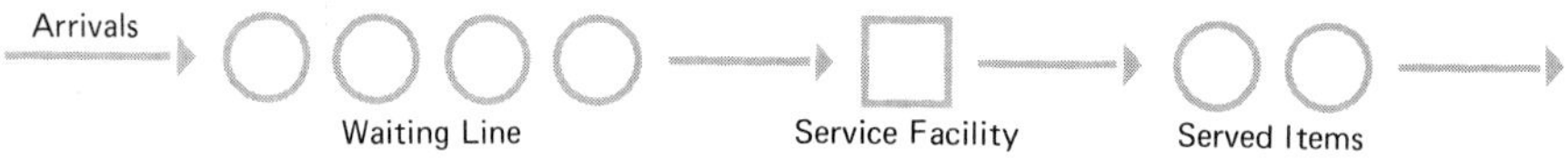

Arrivals

Every queueing problem involves the arrival of items, such as customers, equipment, and telephone calls, for service. This element of the queueing process is often referred to as the **input process.** The input process includes the **source** of arrivals, commonly referred to as the **calling population,** and the **manner** in which arrivals occur, which is generally a random process. As we will see at a later point in this chapter, a precise description of the input process is required in order to analyze the overall queueing problem.

Servers

Equally important in the description of a queueing process are the servers, otherwise referred to as the **service mechanism.** The service mechanism may involve one or more servers, or one or more service facilities. For example, a shoe store may have several sales personnel or a toll road may have several toll gates. The service mechanism may simply consist of a single server in a single facility, such as the ticket sales person selling seats for a movie. In addition to a precise description of the service mechanism in terms of the number and configuration of servers, there must be a description of the manner in which services are completed, which is often a random process.

Queues

The focal point of waiting line analysis is, of course, the waiting line itself. The extent to which queues exist depends primarily upon the nature of the arrival and service processes. However, another important determinant of the nature of the waiting line is the **queue discipline.** The queue discipline is the decision rule that prescribes the order in which items in the queue will be served (i.e., first-come, first-served; last-come, first-served; or some other priority rule). Of course, if waiting lines do not exist, this also has important implications for the queueing analysis since it implies idle servers or excess service capacity.

Basic Structures of Waiting Line Processes

Waiting line processes are generally categorized into four basic structures, according to the nature of the service facilities: (1) single-channel, single-phase; (2) multiple-channel, single-phase; (3) single-channel, multiple-phase; and (4) multiple-channel, multiple-phase. Each of the four categories of queueing processes is illustrated graphically in figure 10.2.

Figure 10.2 Basic waiting line structures. (*A*) Single-channel, single phase. (*B*) Multiple-channel, single-phase. (*C*) Single-channel, multiple-phase. (*D*) Multiple-channel, multiple-phase.

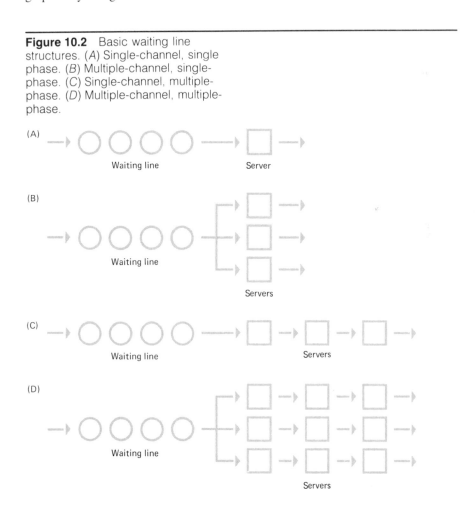

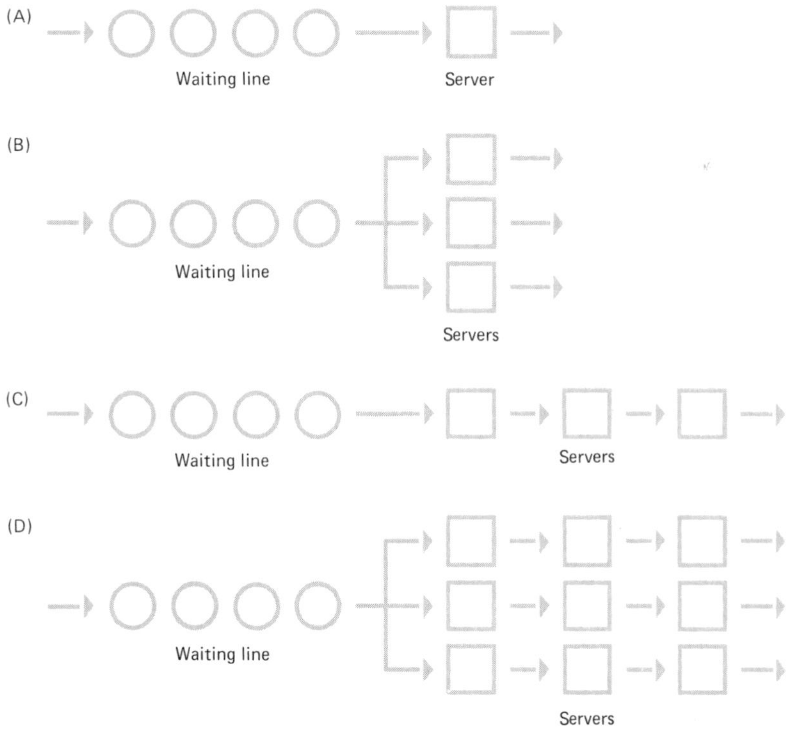

The number of channels in a queueing process is simply the number of parallel servers available for servicing arrivals. The number of phases, on the other hand, indicates the number of sequential service steps each individual arrival must go through. An example of a single-channel, single-phase queueing process would be a drive-in bank teller with only one teller facility. On the other hand, many banks have several drive-in teller windows, which is an example of a multiple-channel, single-phase operation.

When patients go to a doctor for treatment, they often wait in a reception room prior to entering the treatment facilities. Then, upon being seated in the treatment room, the patient often receives an initial checkup or treatment from the hygienist followed by treatment from the doctor. This sort of situation constitutes a single-channel, multiple-phase queueing process. If there are several doctors and assistants, it is a multiple-channel, multiple-phase process.

The reader may immediately visualize a familiar waiting situation that fits none of the previous categories of waiting line processes. This is reasonable and expected. The four presented categories of queueing processes are simply the four *basic* categories. Numerous queueing variations can be described. For example, rather than a single queue preceding the multiple-channel, single-phase case, there might often be separate queues preceding each server. This occurs, for example, in grocery stores, banks, and department stores. Also, in the multiple-phase cases, queues may or may not build up prior to each of the secondary server locations, such as in a manufacturing job shop operation. In the multiple-channel, multiple-phase case, items might switch back and forth from one channel to the other, between each of the various service phases. It becomes readily apparent that queueing models can become quite complex. However, the fundamentals of basic queueing theory are relevant to the analysis of all queueing problems, regardless of complexity. As such, these fundamentals will be the subject of this chapter.

Example 10.1 A Bank's Queueing Problem

The following example of a waiting line situation is presented to highlight the basic process involved. A bank has one drive-in teller window, at which customers may make deposits, cash checks, and conduct other miscellaneous bank business. The bank opens for service at 9:00 A.M. Customers arrive in their automobiles for service at random intervals. The time required to service each customer is also a random variable. Of course, customers are served on a first-come, first-served basis. The process is reflected in the table on the following page for the first hour of operation at the bank drive-in window.

The table indicates that service begins upon each customer's arrival only if no earlier customer is currently being serviced. Otherwise, a waiting line forms and later customers must wait for service. This example suggests some immediate questions for consideration. Is a customer waiting time of eleven minutes acceptable? Such an extensive waiting time at a bank drive-in window could result in highly dissatisfied customers and possibly the loss of their business. Is a queue length of up to four customers acceptable? The driveway preceding the service window can accommodate only a few automobiles. Customers may balk at seeing a long waiting line and simply refuse to enter the service queue. This may also result in temporarily or permanently lost business. Does the small amount of server idle time imply that the teller is overworked and another drive-in teller is needed, or is the teller simply too slow due to inexperience?

Time of Customer Arrival	Time Service Begins	Service Time Required	Time Service Ends	Customer Waiting Time	Server Idle Time	Number of Customers Waiting
9:05 A.M.	9:05 A.M.	4 min.	9:09 A.M.	0 min.	5 min.	2
9:06	9:09	3	9:12	3	0	1
9:08	9:12	5	9:17	4	0	0
9:20	9:20	4	9:24	0	3	2
9:22	9:24	2	9:26	2	0	1
9:23	9:26	1	9:27	3	0	0
9:30	9:30	8	9:38	0	3	3
9:32	9:38	3	9:41	6	0	3
9:33	9:41	4	9:45	8	0	3
9:37	9:45	2	9:47	8	0	4
9:40	9:47	1	9:48	7	0	2
9:41	9:48	7	9:55	7	0	1
9:44	9:55	4	9:59	11	0	0
9:59	9:59	2	10:01	0	0	0

Questions such as these require a formal framework for analysis. The following section presents a general decision framework for waiting line problems.

Decision Framework for Waiting Line Problems

In contrast with linear programming or inventory theory, there is no unified body of knowledge regarding the optimization of waiting line problems. Thus, most texts on queueing theory simply emphasize the development of the queueing system's **operating characteristics.** Operating characteristics describe the performance of the system in the form of such measures as expected customer waiting time and percent server idle time. However, the measures of the system's performance are actually only inputs into a broader conceptual framework, within which most waiting line problems can be analyzed.

Most analyses of waiting line problems eventually reduce to the question of what level of service should be provided—what service capacity should be provided or how many servers are needed? If the decision variable is to be level of service, then the model must formally identify the relationship of level of service to other relevant parameters and variables. The criterion by which this decision model is evaluated is total expected cost.

The general relationship of the decision variable, level of service, to the evaluation criterion, total expected cost, is shown graphically in figure 10.3. It can be seen that total expected cost is the sum of two separate costs: (1) service costs and (2) waiting costs.

Figure 10.3 Decision model for waiting line analysis.

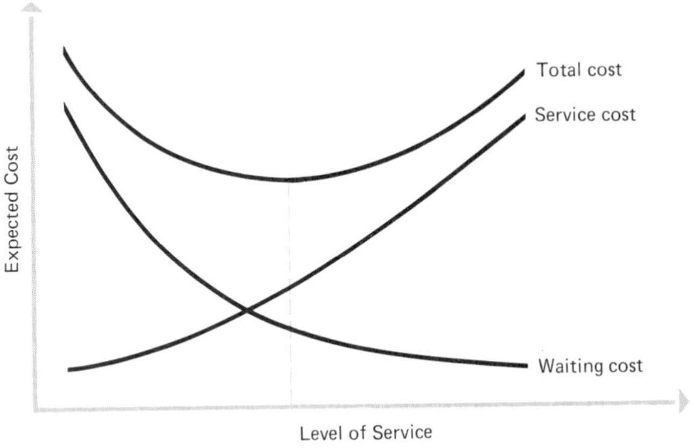

Service Costs

As the level of service is increased, the related service costs will increase. For example, if two dock workers unload trucks at a warehouse depot, instead of one, costs are increased by the amount of the second worker's wages. The exact shape of the function relating service level to service costs must be determined for each individual case being analyzed.

Another way in which service costs are often included in the analysis of waiting line problems is to include only server idle time costs. As the level of service is increased, the server idle time is also expected to increase. Either approach for including service-related costs should normally yield the same results. The decision maker might desire to include some value other than the server's wages to measure the unit cost of increased service level. By considering server idle time, the opportunity cost of not allocating the server to alternative productive activities can be used, rather than server wages. Cases can be made for considering service-related costs in either of the two ways discussed.

Waiting Costs

There is generally an inverse relationship between service level and expected customer waiting time. It is, however, much more difficult to arrive at some explicit statement of waiting costs per unit waiting time. As such, this question is often ignored in the literature of queueing theory, and the system's operating characteristics are simply presented with the ultimate decision analysis left up to the individual manager. However, since the decision must ultimately rest upon relating waiting time to service level, even if no waiting cost is specified, it is implicitly included in the analysis.

Waiting cost can be simply an estimate of the cost of lost business (i.e., customers become impatient and leave the place of service due to excessive waiting times). This type of cost may include the cost of lost profit on a one-time basis, or it may reflect the long-term cost of permanently lost customers. If the waiting situation occurs internally in an organization, such as manufacturing workers waiting for parts at a parts department, the cost of waiting should reflect the cost of lost productivity of the worker during the waiting time.

Thus, the decision problem becomes one of customer waiting time costs versus service level costs. A general decision model for a waiting line problem can be specified as follows:

$$\text{Minimize} \quad E(C|S) = IC_I + WC_W$$

where

$E(C|S)$ = total expected cost for a given service level S

I = total expected server idle time for a specified period (e.g., one day)

C_I = cost per unit time of server idle time

W = total expected waiting time for all arrivals for a specified period (e.g., one day)

C_W = cost per unit time of customer waiting time

Although the level of service, S, is not explicitly identified in the above functional relationship as a variable, it should be recognized that service level is the decision variable, and the model is evaluated for each level of service under consideration.

Consider the following example in which this analysis could be used. A bank has two drive-in teller windows and wishes to select one of two alternative staffing levels for a particular day (i.e., to operate either one or two drive-in teller windows). It is important to note that since arrival rates of customers fluctuate according to the hour of the day and the day of the week, this analysis should logically be performed for each hour of operation during the week's operation.

Assume that the waiting line analysis yields the following information:

Number of Servers (s)	One Teller	Two Tellers
Total server idle time (I)	30 minutes	340 minutes
Total customer waiting time (W)	130	25

The estimated cost per unit of server idle time (C_I) is \$ .10, and the estimated cost per unit of customer waiting time is (C_W) \$3.00. Substituting these cost values into the previously defined cost model results in the total expected cost for each level of service.

$$E(C|S = 1) = (30)(0.10) + (130)(3.00)$$
$$= 3.00 + 390.00$$
$$= \$393.00$$
$$E(C|S = 2) = (340)(0.10) + (25)(3.00)$$
$$= 34.00 + 75.00$$
$$= \$109.00$$

It is apparent from this analysis that the cost of customer waiting time far outweighs the cost of server idle time. Therefore, even though the addition of a second teller results in excessive idle time for the two tellers, the bank should provide two tellers for the day under consideration.

It will again be pointed out that no general optimization theory exists regarding the decision analysis of queueing problems. The purpose of the preceding model is to place the queueing problem within the bounds of a decision-making framework.

The generally accepted components of decision analysis for queueing problems have been identified. However, the actual analysis of queueing problems may require any one of a large variety of forms, depending upon the actual situation under study. For this reason, queueing theory has been developed to provide a wide variety of descriptive measures of the queueing system's performance, previously referred to as operating characteristics. The manner and conditions under which these values are obtained for input into the decision framework is the traditional subject of queueing theory.

Inputs for the Queueing Analysis

Cost Inputs

It is assumed in queueing analysis, as well as in all other management science models, that certain parameters will be provided by the decision maker. For the case of the model of waiting-line analysis, it is assumed that management can provide reasonably accurate estimates of the values of C_I (cost per unit time of server idle time) and C_W (cost per unit time of customer waiting time). The actual process by which such managerial estimates are derived constitutes a field of study in itself and will not be pursued further here.

Server Idle Time and Customer Waiting Time Estimates

Queueing theory provides such operating characteristics as expected server idle time and expected customer waiting time. The following discussion of queueing theory will present the development of these inputs. Queueing theory provides models (formulas) by which to compute the expected waiting time and the expected server idle time, under specified assumptions regarding the nature of the queueing process.

As was previously pointed out, due to the wide range of potential approaches to queueing problems, queueing theory provides many measures of the waiting line system's performance. The decision maker must select the measures relevant to the problem. In addition to the two measures of performance included in the model, management might also specify that the expected (average) number of customers in the waiting line should not exceed four. Management might alternatively specify that the maximum number of customers waiting plus the customer in service (*the number in the system*) should never exceed five, with a 90% degree of certainty. By setting up these stipulations, management has added certain desired service conditions to the decision analysis model. Answers concerning whether these conditions are met or violated can be obtained from queueing theory in the form of operating characteristics.

The operating characteristics commonly obtained in the analysis of waiting lines are summarized as follows:

Probability of any specified number in the system
Mean (expected) waiting time per customer
Mean (expected) queue length
Mean time in the system per customer
Mean number of units in the system
Probability of the service facility being idle

Queueing Theory Assumptions

Queueing theory has been developed by making a number of assumptions about the several basic components of a waiting line process. For each change in an assumption, a different theoretical model evolves. As has been implied in the previous discussions, an almost infinite variety of waiting line situations exists. Although we will consider only a few of the basic theoretical models here, the overall conceptual basis for queueing analysis in general should become clear.

Distribution of Arrivals

Queueing models belong to the class of management science models known as probabilistic (stochastic) models. This is because certain elements of the process are included in the model as random variables (as opposed to constant-valued parameters). These random variables are most often described by some associated probability distribution.

Both the arrivals and service times in a queueing process are generally represented as random variables. For example, the number of customers arriving per unit time (e.g., per five-minute period) at a drive-in teller window may vary randomly but according to some definable probability distribution.

The *number of arrivals* per unit time at a service location may vary randomly according to any one of many probability distributions. However, the most commonly *assumed* distribution relating to customer arrivals is the Poisson distribution.

This assumption about the distribution of arrivals is not without empirical basis. Many statistical studies have resulted in the conclusion that arrivals are Poisson distributed for many queueing processes.

The general model (formula) for the Poisson probability distribution is

$$P(r) = \frac{e^{-\lambda}(\lambda)^r}{r!}$$

where

$$\begin{aligned} r &= \text{number of arrivals} \\ P(r) &= \text{probability of } r \text{ arrivals} \\ \lambda &= \text{mean arrival rate} \\ e &= 2.71828. \text{ (the base of natural logarithms)} \\ r! &= r(r-1)(r-2)\cdots 3\cdot 2\cdot 1 \quad (r \text{ factorial}). \end{aligned}$$

The Poisson distribution corresponds to the assumption of random arrivals, since each arrival is assumed to be independent of other arrivals and also independent of the state of the system. One interesting characteristic of a Poisson distribution, which makes it easier to work with than some other distributions, is that the mean is equal to the variance. Thus, by specifying the mean of a Poisson distribution, the entire distribution is defined.

The Poisson distribution is a *discrete* probability distribution since it relates to the *number* of arrivals per unit time. Figure 10.4 portrays the Poisson distribution graphically for several different values of the mean, λ. It can be seen that as the mean becomes larger, the distribution becomes flatter and more symmetrical. For example, if the mean arrival rate λ at a drive-in teller window per five-minute period is 2, the probabilities associated with different numbers of arrivals are as follows:[1]

r Number of Arrivals	$P(r)$ Probability
0	0.1358
1	0.2707
2	0.2707
3	0.1805
4	0.0902
5	0.0361
6	0.0120
7	0.0034
8	0.0009

1. A table of Poisson probability values for various values of r and λ is given in Appendix D.

Figure 10.4 Poisson distribution.

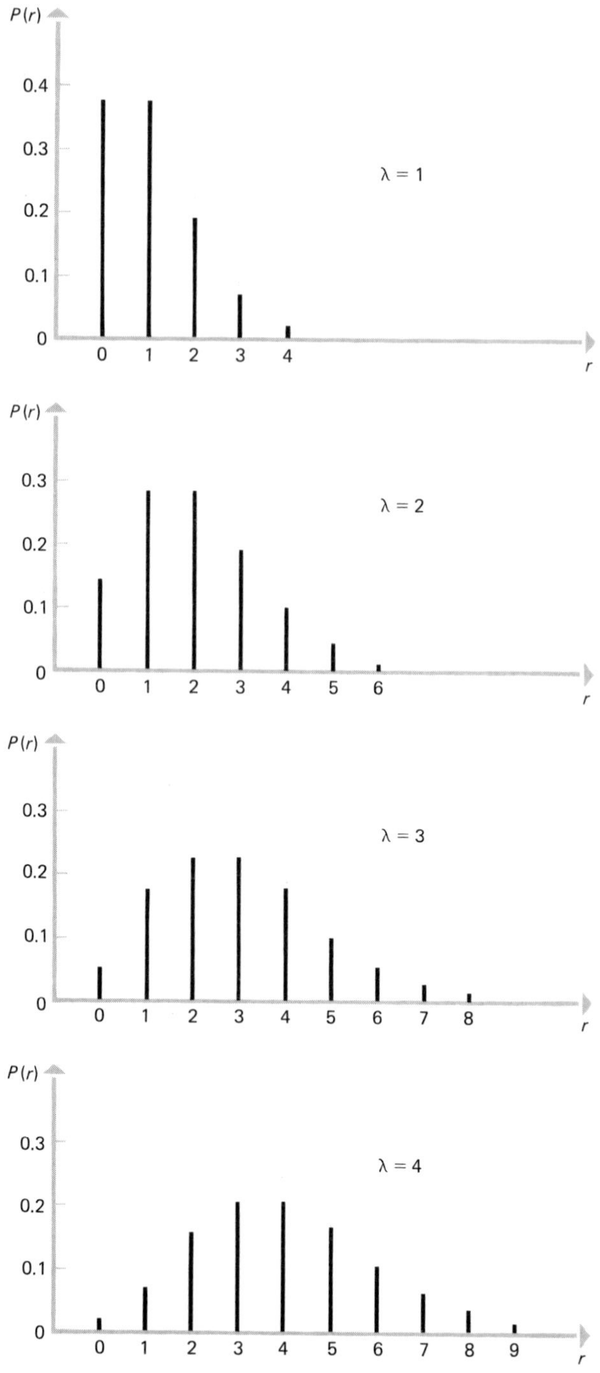

An interesting feature of the Poisson process is that if the number of arrivals per unit time is Poisson distributed with a mean rate of λ, then the *time between arrivals (interarrival time)* is distributed as a *negative exponential* probability distribution with mean of $1/\lambda$. Thus, if the mean arrival *rate* per five-minute period is 2, then the mean *time between arrivals* is 2.5 minutes (5 minutes/2 arrivals = 2.5 minutes per arrival). This relationship is summarized as follows:

Arrival Rate	Time Between Arrivals
Poisson Mean = λ λ = 2 arrivals per 5-minute period	Negative exponential Mean = $1/\lambda$ $1/\lambda = (1/2)(5 \text{ minutes}) = 2.5$ minutes.

Distribution of Service Times

Service times in a queueing process may also fit any one of a large number of different probability distributions. The most commonly assumed distribution for service times is the negative exponential distribution. Thus, from the preceding discussion of the relationship between the Poisson and negative exponential distributions, if service times follow a negative exponential distribution, then the service rate follows a Poisson distribution.

The description of arrivals in terms of arrival *rate* (Poisson) and services in terms of service *times* (negative exponential) is a matter of convention that has developed in the literature of queueing theory.

Empirical research has shown that the assumption of negative exponentially distributed service times is not valid nearly as often as is the assumption of Poisson-distributed arrivals. Therefore, for actual applications of queueing analysis, this assumption would have to be carefully checked before attempting to use such a model. Other possible distributions of service times will be presented at a later point in the chapter.

The general model (formula) for the negative exponential probability density function is

$$f(t) = \mu e^{-\mu t}$$

where

t = service time

$f(t)$ = probability density associated with t

μ = mean service rate

$1/\mu$ = mean service time

e = 2.71828, . . . (base of natural logarithms).

As in the case of the Poisson arrival rate, the negative exponential service time corresponds to the assumption that service times are completely random. The probability of completing a service for a customer in any subsequent time period after service is begun is independent of how much time has already elapsed on the service for that customer.

The negative exponential distribution is a *continuous* probability distribution, since it relates to time of service. Figure 10.5 illustrates graphically the negative exponential distribution. It can be seen that short service times have the highest probability of occurrence. As service time increases, the probability function ''tails off'' (exponentially) toward zero probability. The area under the curve in figure 10.5 for the negative exponential distribution is determined from its cumulative distribution function, which is computed through integration as follows:

$$F(T) = \int_0^T \mu e^{-\mu t}\, dt = -e^{-\mu t}\Big|_0^T = -e^{-\mu T} + e^0 = 1 - e^{-\mu T}$$

This may be further described as

$$F(T) = f(t \leqslant T) = 1 - e^{-\mu T}$$

where $F(T)$ is the area under the curve to the left of T. Also,

$$1 - F(T) = f(t \geqslant T) = e^{-\mu T}$$

where $1 - F(T)$ is the area under the curve to the right of T.

Figure 10.5 Negative exponential probability density distribution.

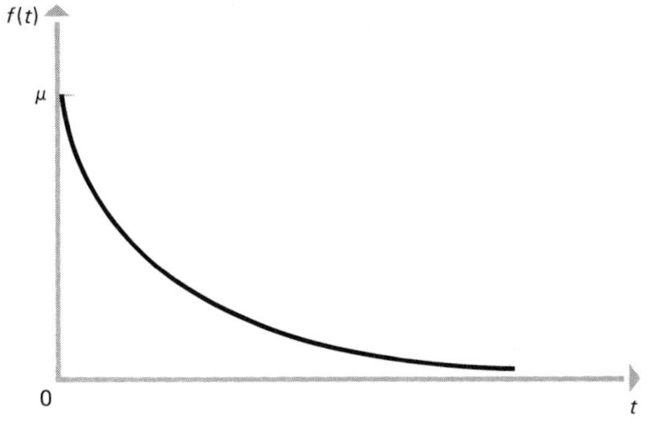

For example, if the mean service time ($1/\mu$) at a drive-in teller window is two minutes, the probabilities that service will take T or more minutes, for various values of T, are:[2]

Service Times of at Least T	Probability $f(t \geq T)$
0 minutes	1.000
1	0.607
2	0.368
3	0.223
4	0.135
5	0.082
6	0.050
7	0.030
8	0.018
9	0.011
10	0.007
11	0.004
12	0.003
13	0.002
14	0.001

Queue Discipline

As discussed previously, the queue discipline is a decision rule that determines the order in which waiting customers will be selected for service. In queueing theory models, it is generally assumed that customers are serviced on a first-come, first-served basis. If this assumption is not appropriate for the queueing system under study, a different model must be developed.

A feature of customer behavior that can affect the service order is the customer who becomes impatient and decides to leave the system before being served. This is known in the literature of queueing theory as **reneging.**

Infinite Versus Finite Calling Population

The calling population in queueing theory is the source of arrivals to be serviced. When considering a waiting line problem, such as a bank drive-in teller operation, it is reasonable to assume that the calling population is, for all practical purposes, infinite. However, if the source of arrivals for service is ten machines in a machine shop, which must be serviced when they break down, this is obviously a finite calling population.

The key consideration in this case is whether the probability of customer arrivals is affected by the removal of one customer from the population (by entry

2. A table of values of e^x and e^{-x} is given in Appendix D.

into the service system). This question is analogous to the traditional probability example of drawing balls from an urn *without replacement*. If there are five balls in an urn, the probability of drawing a ball of a certain characteristic on the second draw is certainly different than it was on the first draw. However, if there are 500,000 balls in the urn initially, the probabilities would be virtually unaffected by the first draw.

Basic queueing theory models generally include the initial assumption of an infinite calling population (source). However, the finite source case is sufficiently abundant in real life that models including this assumption are often developed. Both situations will be presented in this chapter.

Infinite Versus Finite Queue Length

Although queueing theory models generally begin with the assumption that waiting lines could theoretically build up to an unlimited length, this is often not the case in reality. There may be limited space prior to the service facility in which queues can build up. For example, the driveway preceding a drive-in teller window can accommodate only a limited number of vehicles, and there may be a city ordinance against queueing up on the adjacent street. On the other hand, customers may simply refuse to enter a long line, even if space is available. This is often referred to as **balking** in the literature of queueing theory. Although the assumption of infinite queues is more attractive from a mathematical solution standpoint, queues of a finite length (sometimes referred to as **truncated** queues) are often a more realistic assumption.

Steady State Versus Transient Queueing Systems

A very important assumption of queueing theory is concerned with whether the system reaches an equilibrium, or steady-state condition. That is, it is assumed that operating characteristics, such as queue length and average waiting time, will assume constant average values after the system has been in operation for a period of time. Almost all basic models of queueing theory assume a steady-state condition. However, some waiting line systems can never be expected to operate long enough to achieve a steady state. Some advanced queueing theory models have been developed in which the solution depends directly on the elapsed time since the system began operation (transient queueing systems analysis). The emphasis, however, in this chapter will be on steady-state models.

Arrival Rate Versus Service Rate

It is logical to assume that the rate at which services are completed must exceed the arrival rate of customers. If this is not the case, the queues would simply continue to grow, and there would be no steady-state solution. It is generally assumed that the service rate does exceed the arrival rate.

An interesting relationship between arrival rates, service rates, and expected queue lengths can be illustrated. If the arrival rate must be less than the service rate, then the ratio of arrival rate to service rate will be less than 1. As that ratio approaches 1, the expected queue length will approach infinity (in the steady-state solution, with certain assumptions). This relationship is illustrated graphically in figure 10.6.

Figure 10.6 Relationship of queue length to arrival/service rate ratio.

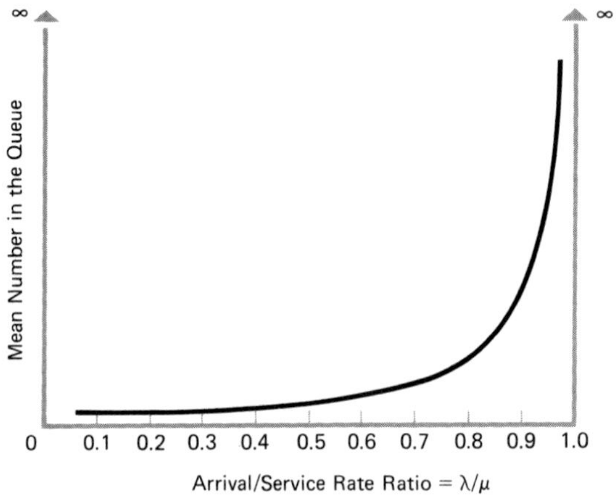

In figure 10.6, λ represents the mean arrival rate and μ represents the mean service rate. It can be seen that as the ratio of λ to μ exceeds 0.7 the expected queue length increases very rapidly. The relationship of queue length to arrival rate and service rate does assume infinite (or at least very large) possible queue lengths. However, if finite (or truncated) queues are assumed, the figure would not be accurate. Thus, if customers balk (do not enter the queue) or if they renege (become impatient and leave), it would, in fact, be possible for the arrival rate to exceed the service rate and still obtain a steady-state solution.

Queueing Theory Models

Several queueing theory models and their related assumptions will now be presented. Each of the different models will actually be presented in the form of several submodels (equations) that yield the aforementioned operating characteristics for the queueing process.

Single-Channel, Single-Phase Models

The derivation of the most common case of the single-channel, single-phase queueing process will be presented first, followed by several variations. This first model assumes Poisson arrivals and exponential service times. (The negative exponential density function will henceforth be referred to as simply the exponential distribution.)

In all subsequent cases, the following assumptions will be made, unless otherwise stated within the specific model discussion:

1. Infinite calling population (unlimited arrival source)
2. Infinite queue (unlimited or nontruncated queue)
3. First-come, first-served queue discipline
4. Steady-state solution (equilibrium over time)
5. Service rate exceeds arrival rate ($\mu > \lambda$)

Several approaches can be used in showing this derivation. The approach taken here attempts to maximize your intuitive understanding rather than performing elaborate mathematical computations. Although the intuitive approach is not as attractive from a theoretical point of view, it is hoped that an increase in understandability compensates for this lack of mathematical rigor.

As stated previously, it is assumed that we have steady-state conditions. Therefore, although many derivations of the queueing probabilities are initially developed as a function of time, and then later adjusted to reflect time independence, we shall simply begin our development of the equations with the assumption that the various probabilities considered are not dependent on how long the system has been operating.

The first point to be considered is the probability of an arrival or an end of service during some increment of time. If the expected number of arrivals per hour (λ) is one, what is the probability of an arrival during some very short increment of time? First we will assume that we divide the time period (one hour) into enough increments such that no more than one arrival could occur during any one time increment. If we divide the hour into minutes, we have sixty time increments. If no more than one arrival could occur during any one of the sixty time increments and we expect a total of one arrival during the hour, then the probability of one arrival during one time increment is 1/60. This is determined by multiplying the expected number of arrivals in one hour by the time increment, 1/60 of an hour. If we expect five arrivals during an hour ($\lambda = 5$), the probability of one arrival during one of the sixty increments would be $5 \times 1/60$ of an hour $= 5/60 = 1/12$. If we draw one ball from an urn containing sixty balls, of which five are red balls, the probability of drawing a red ball is the number of red balls (5) times the probability of drawing any one of the sixty balls (1/60), yielding 5/60 or a probability of 1/12.

Minutes may not actually be very small time increments for some systems being considered, such as a queue for a computer system. Certainly more than one arrival may occur in one minute in many systems. We, therefore, simply divide our time period into smaller time increments. Suppose we divide an hour into seconds, so that each time increment is 1/3,600 of an hour. Therefore, if we expect one arrival in an hour, the probability of an arrival during some time increment is $1 \times 1/3{,}600 = 1/3{,}600$. If we expected five arrivals in an hour, the probability of one arrival during one time increment is $5 \times 1/3{,}600 = 5/3{,}600 = 1/720$. We could next divide the hour into microseconds and be reasonably sure that no more than one arrival will occur during one time increment.

If we assume that the fraction of an hour is represented by Δt, and that the mean (expected) arrival rate per hour is λ, then the probability of one arrival during Δt is equal to $\lambda(\Delta t)$. The same argument follows for the probability of one departure (end of service) during Δt, which is given by $\mu(\Delta t)$, where μ = mean (expected) service rate. Since we assume that no more than one arrival can occur during Δt and no more than one departure during Δt, we also assume that both an arrival and a departure will not occur simultaneously during Δt. Note that if $\lambda(\Delta t)$ is the probability of an arrival during Δt and $\mu(\Delta t)$ is the probability of a departure, then the joint probability of both occurring simultaneously is $\lambda(\Delta t)\mu(\Delta t) = \lambda\mu(\Delta t)^2$. If Δt is infinitesimally small, then $(\Delta t)^2$ will be virtually zero, and thus $\lambda(\Delta t)\mu(\Delta t) \cong 0$.

Thus, there are three possible events during Δt, an addition of one unit in the system, a reduction of one unit in the system, or no change in the system (no arrival and no departure). If $\lambda(\Delta t)$ is the probability of an arrival during Δt, then $1 - \lambda(\Delta t)$ is the probability of no arrival. Likewise, if $\mu(\Delta t)$ is the probability of a departure during Δt, then $1 - \mu(\Delta t)$ is the probability of no departure from the system. The joint probability of no arrival and no departure is given by the product of the two events.

$$[1 - \lambda(\Delta t)][1 - \mu(\Delta t)] = 1 - \lambda\Delta t - \mu\Delta t + \lambda\mu(\Delta t)^2$$

The last term is eliminated for the same argument given previously, $(\Delta t)^2 \cong 0$. Thus, we have as the probability of no change, $1 - (\lambda\Delta t + \mu\Delta t)$. The states of the system at time t and $t + \Delta t$, with the three possible events during Δt, are shown in figure 10.7 (where k is the number of units in the system).

Of course, when there are zero units in the system ($k = 0$) at time t, only two events can occur. Either there is no arrival, with probability $1 - \lambda\Delta t$, or there is an arrival, with probability $\lambda\Delta t$. When $k \geqslant 1$ at time t, all three events can occur, which is shown for the cases where $k = 1$, $k = 2$, and $k = n$ at time t. For example, for the general case where $k = n$ at time t, the probability of moving to $k = n-1$ at $t + \Delta t$ equals $\mu\Delta t$; the probability of moving to $k = n$ at $t + \Delta t$ equals $1 - (\lambda\Delta t + \mu\Delta t)$; and the probability of moving to $k = n + 1$ at $t + \Delta t$ equals $\lambda\Delta t$.

We will identify P as the probability of the number of units in the system (the state of the system), and denote by a subscript, n, to P the number in the system. Thus, P_n is the probability of n units in the system. Referring to figure 10.7, we see that there are two ways to have zero in the system at time $t + \Delta t$: when $k = 0$ at time t and no arrival occurs, and when $k = 1$ at time t and one departure occurs. The probability of zero in the system at time $t + \Delta t$ is then the probability of zero at time t times the probability of no arrival $[P_0(1 - \lambda\Delta t)]$, plus the probability of one at time t times the probability of one departure $[P_1(\mu\Delta t)]$, which yields

$$P_0 = P_0(1 - \lambda\Delta t) + P_1(\mu\Delta t). \tag{10.1}$$

Figure 10.7 Queueing system states.

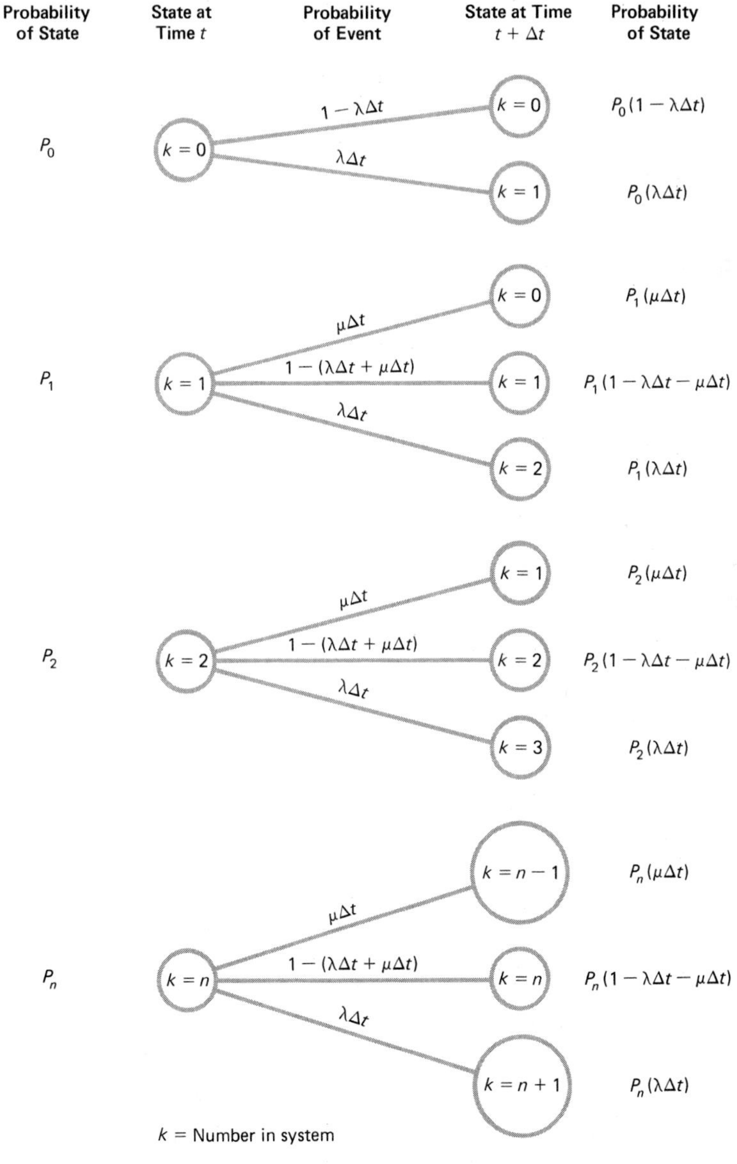

By referring again to figure 10.7, we see that there are three ways to have one in the system at time $t + \Delta t$: when $k = 0$ at time t and one arrival occurs during Δt; when $k = 1$ at time t and no arrival or departure occurs; and when $k = 2$ at time t and one departure occurs. Thus, the probability of one unit in the system is given by

$$P_1 = P_0(\lambda\Delta t) + P_1(1 - \lambda\Delta t - \mu\Delta t) + P_2(\mu\Delta t). \tag{10.2}$$

For the general case, the probability of n units in the system at time $t + \Delta t$, is given by

$$P_n = P_{n-1}(\lambda\Delta t) + P_n(1 - \lambda\Delta t - \mu\Delta t) + P_{n+1}(\mu\Delta t). \tag{10.3}$$

We next solve equation (10.1) for P_1 in terms of P_0, as follows:

$$\begin{aligned}
P_0 &= P_0(1 - \lambda\Delta t) + P_1(\mu\Delta t) \\
(\mu\Delta t)P_1 &= P_0 - P_0(1 - \lambda\Delta t) \\
(\mu\Delta t)P_1 &= P_0[1 - (1 - \lambda\Delta t)] \\
(\mu\Delta t)P_1 &= P_0(\lambda\Delta t) \\
P_1 &= P_0\frac{\lambda\Delta t}{\mu\Delta t}
\end{aligned}$$

The Δt's cancel, and we get

$$P_1 = P_0\left(\frac{\lambda}{\mu}\right). \tag{10.4}$$

We next solve equation (10.3) for P_{n+1} in terms of P_n and P_{n-1}, which yields

$$P_{n+1} = P_n\left(\frac{\lambda + \mu}{\mu}\right) - P_{n-1}\left(\frac{\lambda}{\mu}\right).$$

Substituting the value 1 for n, we get

$$P_2 = P_1\left(\frac{\lambda + \mu}{\mu}\right) - P_0\left(\frac{\lambda}{\mu}\right).$$

We can then substitute equation (10.4) for P_1, yielding

$$\begin{aligned}
P_2 &= P_0\left(\frac{\lambda}{\mu}\right)\left(\frac{\lambda + \mu}{\mu}\right) - P_0\left(\frac{\lambda}{\mu}\right) \\
&= P_0\left[\left(\frac{\lambda}{\mu}\right)\left(\frac{\lambda + \mu}{\mu}\right) - \left(\frac{\lambda}{\mu}\right)\right] \\
&= P_0\left[\frac{\lambda}{\mu}\left(\frac{\lambda + \mu}{\mu} - 1\right)\right] \\
&= P_0\frac{\lambda^2 + \lambda\mu - \lambda\mu}{\mu^2}
\end{aligned}$$

$$P_2 = P_0\left(\frac{\lambda}{\mu}\right)^2. \tag{10.5}$$

When we solve for P_3, we find that

$$P_3 = P_0\left(\frac{\lambda}{\mu}\right)^3. \tag{10.6}$$

Similarly,

$$P_4 = P_0\left(\frac{\lambda}{\mu}\right)^4 \tag{10.7}$$

thus, by induction, we can infer that

$$P_n = P_0\left(\frac{\lambda}{\mu}\right)^n. \tag{10.8}$$

From probability theory, we know that the sum of the probabilities for all possible outcomes must sum to one. Thus we have

$$\sum_{n=0}^{\infty} P_n = 1.0. \tag{10.9}$$

Substituting equation (10.8) for P_n, we have

$$\sum_{n=0}^{\infty} P_0\left(\frac{\lambda}{\mu}\right)^n = 1.0$$

or

$$P_0 = \frac{1}{\sum_{n=0}^{\infty} (\lambda/\mu)^n}.$$

The denominator of this expression is an infinite geometric series, which converges to

$$\sum_{n=0}^{\infty}\left(\frac{\lambda}{\mu}\right)^n = \frac{1}{1 - \lambda/\mu}.$$

Thus, we have

$$P_0 = \left(1\Big/\frac{1}{1 - \lambda/\mu}\right)$$

$$P_0 = 1 - \frac{\lambda}{\mu}. \tag{10.10}$$

Recalling from equation (10.8) that

$$P_n = P_0\left(\frac{\lambda}{\mu}\right)^n$$

and substituting equation (10.10) for P_0 in this equation, we get

$$P_n = \left(1 - \frac{\lambda}{\mu}\right)\left(\frac{\lambda}{\mu}\right)^n. \tag{10.11}$$

Thus, for steady-state conditions, equation (10.10) yields the probability of no units in the system, and equation (10.11) yields the probability of n units in the system. Note that equation (10.11) reduces to equation (10.10) when $n = 0$.

The average of some variable X is, by definition, $\sum_{\text{all } X} X \cdot P_X$; therefore, the average number in the system (denoted by L) is given by

$$L = \sum_{n=0}^{\infty} n \cdot P_n.$$

Thus, substituting equation (10.11) for P_n in the previous expression, we get

$$L = \sum_{n=0}^{\infty} n \cdot \left(1 - \frac{\lambda}{\mu}\right)\left(\frac{\lambda}{\mu}\right)^n$$

$$= \left(1 - \frac{\lambda}{\mu}\right) \sum_{n=0}^{\infty} n \cdot \left(\frac{\lambda}{\mu}\right)^n.$$

The term $\sum_{n=0}^{\infty} n(\lambda/\mu)^n$ is an infinite geometric series, which converges to

$$\sum_{n=0}^{\infty} n\left(\frac{\lambda}{\mu}\right)^n = \frac{\lambda/\mu}{(1 - \lambda/\mu)^2},$$

and therefore

$$L = \left(1 - \frac{\lambda}{\mu}\right)\left[\frac{\lambda/\mu}{(1 - \lambda/\mu)^2}\right],$$

which reduces to

$$L = \frac{\lambda}{\mu - \lambda}. \tag{10.12}$$

Our purpose here is to determine several measures of queueing system performance, described as follows: L, mean number in the system; L_q, mean number in the queue; W, mean time in the system; and W_q, mean time waiting in the queue. It is important to note that once any one of the values L, L_q, W, or W_q has been determined, the other three can be found directly.

If we expect λ arrivals per unit time and if each of these arrivals spends an average time in the system of W, then the total time in the system for λ arrivals is λW. For example, if two customers arrive, and each arrival spends three hours in the system, then the total customer hours in the system is six. This implies that there are six ($L = 6$) customers in the system on the average (i.e., customers 1 and 2 in their third hour in the system, customers 3 and 4 in their second hour, and customers 5 and 6 in their first hour). This gives us the relationship

$$L = \lambda W. \tag{10.13}$$

The same rationale can be given for the relationship of the number in the queue and the waiting time.

$$L_q = \lambda W_q \tag{10.14}$$

The expected time (W) in the system must be equal to the expected time in the queue (W_q) plus the expected time in the service facility. We already know that the expected time in service is $1/\mu$. Therefore, we have

$$W = W_q + \frac{1}{\mu}. \tag{10.15}$$

Therefore, once we have solved for L by equation (10.12),

$$L = \frac{\lambda}{\mu - \lambda}, \text{ mean number in the system.}$$

We then get W from equation (10.13)

$$W = \frac{L}{\lambda}, \text{ mean time in the system.}$$

W_q is given by equation (10.15)

$$W_q = W - \frac{1}{\mu}, \text{ mean waiting time.}$$

And finally L_q, from equation (10.14), is

$$L_q = \lambda W_q, \text{ mean number in the queue.}$$

The queueing equations for the other models presented in the chapter are in some cases developed by a similar process and in other cases by a much more complex process.

These model variables and relationships can be summarized as follows:

λ = mean arrival rate ($1/\lambda$ = mean time between arrivals)

μ = mean service rate ($1/\mu$ = mean service time)

n = number of customers (units) in the system (includes those waiting and in service)

The probability of no units in the system is

$$P_0 = 1 - \frac{\lambda}{\mu}.$$

The probability of n units in the system is

$$P_n = \left(\frac{\lambda}{\mu}\right)^n \left(1 - \frac{\lambda}{\mu}\right).$$

The probability of k or more units in the system is

$$P_{n \geqslant k} = \left(\frac{\lambda}{\mu}\right)^k.$$

Mean (expected) number of units in the system is

$$L = \frac{\lambda}{\mu - \lambda}.$$

Mean number of units in the queue is

$$L_q = \frac{\lambda^2}{\mu(\mu - \lambda)}.$$

Mean time in the system is

$$W = \frac{1}{\mu - \lambda}.$$

Mean waiting time is

$$W_q = \frac{\lambda}{\mu(\mu - \lambda)}.$$

Service facility utilization factor (ρ) is

$$\rho = \frac{\lambda}{\mu}.$$

Proportion server idle time is

$$I = 1 - \frac{\lambda}{\mu}.$$

It is also of interest to review the following relationships among the various operating characteristics:

$$P_n = P_0\left(\frac{\lambda}{\mu}\right)^n$$

$$L_q = L - \frac{\lambda}{\mu} = \lambda W_q$$

$$L = L_q + \frac{\lambda}{\mu} = \lambda W$$

$$W_q = W - \frac{1}{\mu} = \frac{L_q}{\lambda}$$

$$W = W_q + \frac{1}{\mu} = \frac{L}{\lambda}$$

$$I = 1 - \rho = P_0$$

Thus, when any one of the operating characteristics L_q, L, W_q, or W has been obtained, the other three measures of system performance can be determined directly. It should also be noted that the proportion idle time, I, and the probability of zero customers in the system, P_0, are the same.

Example 10.2 A Single-Channel, Single-Phase Problem

The preceding basic queueing equations will be illustrated in the following example problem. Assume that the system of interest is a drive-in bank teller window. Further assume that customers arrive in their cars at the average rate of twenty per hour (or one every three minutes) according to a Poisson distribution. Assume also that the bank teller spends an average of two minutes per customer to complete a service, and that the service time is exponentially distributed. Customers, who arrive from an infinite population, are served on a first-come, first-served basis, and there is no limit to possible queue length. From this description of the system, we can obtain the queueing system's operating characteristics for the steady-state condition.

The parameters of the arrival rate and service time distributions are as follows:

	Mean Rate	Mean Time
Arrivals	Poisson: $\lambda = 20/\text{hr.}$	Exponential: $\frac{1}{\lambda} = \frac{1\text{ hr}}{20} = 3\text{ min.}$
Services	Poisson: $\mu = 30/\text{hr.}$	Exponential: $\frac{1}{\mu} = \frac{1\text{ hr}}{30} = 2\text{ min.}$

Note that in the following computations since the parameters λ and μ are used, the time values yielded will be in terms of hours.

$$L = \frac{\lambda}{\mu - \lambda} = \frac{20}{30 - 20} = \frac{20}{10} = 2 \text{ persons}$$

There will be an average of two persons (cars) in the system (waiting or being served).

$$L_q = \frac{\lambda^2}{\mu(\mu - \lambda)} = \frac{(20)^2}{30(30 - 20)} = \frac{400}{30(10)} = \frac{400}{300} = 1.33 \text{ persons}$$

There will be an average of 1.33 cars waiting in line.

$$W = \frac{1}{\mu - \lambda} = \frac{1}{30 - 20} = \frac{1}{10} \text{ hour } (= 6 \text{ minutes})$$

The average time in the system per customer will be six minutes.

$$W_q = \frac{\lambda}{\mu(\mu - \lambda)} = \frac{20}{30(30 - 20)} = \frac{20}{30(10)} = \frac{20}{300}$$
$$= \frac{1}{15} \text{ hour } (= 4 \text{ minutes})$$

The average waiting time per customer will be four minutes.

Thus, on the average, each customer will spend six minutes in the process of waiting and being serviced, of which four minutes will be spent waiting in line. Note that the difference is two minutes, which is spent in service, and is equal to the original value specified for $1/\mu$, the mean service time. There will be an average of two cars in the system and an average of 1.33 cars waiting for service. Intuitively, it might seem that if there are an average of two customers in the system, that there would therefore be an average of one in service, and the number waiting would be only one. However, the expected number in service is actually .67, which is equal to $L - L_q$ or λ/μ. Recall that arrivals and service times are *random* over time, so that part of the time the drive-in teller is idle and part of the time more than one customer is waiting. The values obtained are simply the averages, over an *assumed* period of time.

An additional operating characteristic, the probability of zero customers in the system, is determined as follows:

$$P_0 = 1 - \frac{\lambda}{\mu}$$
$$= 1 - \frac{20}{30}$$
$$P_0 = 0.33$$

The probability of no customers in the system is 0.33. Since the proportion idle time of the server (I) is equal to P_0, the bank drive-in teller is idle 33% of the time. Of course, the teller is busy 67% of the time, which is the server utilization factor.

$$\rho = \lambda/\mu = 0.67$$

Probability distributions of the exact number in the system and of some number (or greater) in the system, are computed as follows:

	Probability of n Customers in System		Probability of k or More Customers in System
n	$P_n = \left(\frac{20}{30}\right)^n \left(1 - \frac{20}{30}\right)$	k	$P_{n \geq k} = \left(\frac{20}{30}\right)^k$
0	0.333	0	1.000
1	0.222	1	0.667
2	0.148	2	0.444
3	0.099	3	0.296
4	0.066	4	0.198
5	0.044	5	0.132
6	0.029	6	0.088
7	0.019	7	0.058
8	0.013	8	0.039
9	0.009	9	0.026
10	0.006	10	0.017

It is of considerable interest to note that 13.2% of the time there will be five or more customers in the system ($P_{n \geq 5} = 0.132$). Thus, if the driveway preceding the drive-in teller window has a capacity limit of three cars (a total capacity of four cars in the system), then the operating system would have sufficient capacity only 87% of the time. Customers would have to line up on the adjacent street 13% of the time. If we assume that customers are lost as a result of insufficient system capacity, a modified queueing model must be used, assuming a finite possible queue length.

Suppose that the bank's management has discovered that by replacing the present teller with a more skilled and experienced teller, the service time is reduced from an average of 2 minutes per customer to 1.5 minutes per customer (40 customers per hour). However, the experienced teller's salary is $6 per hour, which is double the $3-per-hour salary of the present teller. Management also estimates the cost of customer waiting time to be $5 per minute in terms of customer dissatisfaction. Should the bank replace the current teller with the more skilled and experienced teller?

The system operating characteristics required to analyze the problem are W_q and I, which are summarized below:

Case 1: Current teller ($1/\mu$ = 2 minutes per customer)

$$W_q = \frac{\lambda}{\mu(\mu - \lambda)} = 4 \text{ minutes, mean waiting time}$$

$I = 1 - \lambda/\mu = 33\%$, percent idle time

Case 2: more experienced teller ($1/\mu$ = 1.5 minutes per customer)

$$W_q = \frac{\lambda}{\mu(\mu - \lambda)} = 1.5 \text{ minutes, mean waiting time}$$

$I = 1 - \lambda/\mu = 50\%$, percent idle time

Since the mean arrival rate (λ) is twenty per hour and the drive-in teller operation is open eight hours per day, the expected number of customers is 160. Thus, the total expected waiting times are 640 minutes for case 1 and 240 minutes for case 2. The teller will be idle 2.64 hours and 4 hours for case 1 and case 2, respectively. The relative costs are summarized in the following table:

	Case 1 $1/\mu$ = 2 minutes	Case 2 $1/\mu$ = 1.5 minutes
Customer waiting time cost	(640)(\$5) = \$3,200	(240)(\$5) = \$1,200
Server idle time cost	(2.64)(\$3) = \$7.92	(4)(\$6) = \$24.00

Thus, the bank could expect to reduce customer waiting cost by \$2,000 at a cost of \$16.08 by replacing the current teller with the more experienced teller.

It should be noted that server idle time is the appropriate variable to consider regarding the service level cost only if it can be assumed that the value of lost productivity during idle time is equal to the teller's wage level in each case. If this is not the case, then the correct manner in which to analyze the problem is to compare the total cost of each service level. In this case it would be eight hours at \$3 per hour (\$24) versus eight hours at \$6 per hour (\$48). The cost of increased service level is therefore \$24. Although the value of lost productivity during idle time is the theoretically correct manner in which to analyze a queueing problem, it is usually as difficult to estimate as the cost of customer waiting time. Thus, simply comparing the total costs of service is generally the best approximation. In any event, the resulting decision is the same.

Poisson Arrivals, Undefined Service Times

In many cases, the service time cannot be assumed to fit an exponential distribution. However, if it can be assumed that the service times are independent, with some common probability distribution (*any* distribution, as long as it is the same for all services), whose mean ($1/\mu$) and standard deviation (σ) are known, then the following model equations define the system's operating characteristics:

$$\rho = \frac{\lambda}{\mu}$$

$$P_0 = 1 - \frac{\lambda}{\mu}$$

$$L_q = \frac{\lambda^2\sigma^2 + (\lambda/\mu)^2}{2(1 - \lambda/\mu)}$$

$$L = L_q + \frac{\lambda}{\mu}$$

$$W_q = \frac{L_q}{\lambda}$$

$$W = W_q + \frac{1}{\mu}$$

For the previous example of the drive-in bank teller operation, service time might be some undefined, nonexponential distribution with mean $1/\mu = 2$ minutes $= 1/30$ hour and standard deviation $\sigma = 4$ minutes $= 1/15$ hour. The following operating characteristics would therefore be obtained:

$$\rho = \frac{20}{30}$$

$$= 0.67, \text{ percent teller utilization}$$

$$P_0 = 1 - \frac{20}{30}$$

$$= 0.33, \text{ the probability of no cars}$$

$$L_q = \frac{(20)^2(1/15)^2 + (20/30)^2}{2(1 - 20/30)}$$

$$= \frac{(400)(1/225) + (400/900)}{2/3}$$

$$= \frac{(3{,}200 + 800)/1{,}800}{2/3}$$

$$= \frac{4{,}000}{1{,}800}\left(\frac{3}{2}\right) = \frac{2{,}000}{600}$$

$$= 3.33 \text{ customers waiting}$$

$$L = 3.33 + \left(\frac{20}{30}\right)$$

$$= 4.0 \text{ customers in the system}$$

$$W_q = \frac{3.33}{20} = 0.1665 \text{ hour}$$

$$\cong 10 \text{ minutes waiting}$$

$$W = 0.1665 + \left(\frac{1}{30}\right) = 0.1665 + 0.0333$$

$$= 0.1998 \text{ hours}$$

$$\cong 12 \text{ minutes in the system}$$

It is interesting to compare the results just obtained to those obtained for the exponential service time case. The comparative results are summarized as follows:

	L_q Customers Waiting	L Customers in the System	W_q Minutes Waiting	W Minutes in the System
Exponential service times	1.33	2	4	6
Undefined service times	3.33	4	10	12

Recall from the discussion of the exponential distribution that the standard deviation is equal to the mean. For the case of arbitrary service times, we have doubled the standard deviation from two minutes to four minutes.

Thus, the number in the system and the time in the system have both doubled. The number waiting and the waiting time have both increased by two and a half times. This indicates that, in addition to average service time, the variance of the services also has an important effect on the performance of the queueing system.

Poisson Arrivals, Constant Service Times

Although constant service times may not represent a large number of real situations, it may be the case for mechanically performed services. For this case, simply set $\sigma = 0$ and use the preceding model (undefined service times).

Poisson Arrivals, Erlang Service Times

The Erlang distribution is a very important distribution in queueing theory because it can be made to fit most empirically determined service times. The Erlang distribution (density function) is

$$f(t) = \frac{(\mu k)^k}{(k-1)!} t^{k-1} e^{-k\mu t},$$

where μ is the mean and k is the parameter that determines the dispersion of the distribution. The Erlang distribution is shown, for several values of k, in figure 10.8. Note that both the exponential distribution ($k = 1$) and constant times ($k = \infty$) are special cases of the Erlang distribution.

Figure 10.8 Erlang distribution for selected values of k.

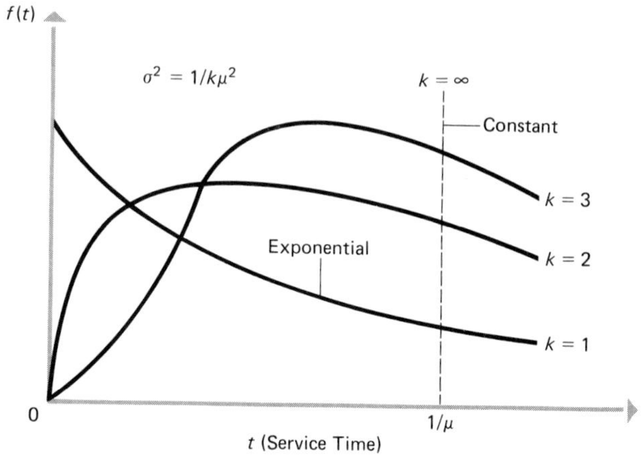

An intuitive interpretation for k can be given as follows. Suppose a single server performs several functions for a customer during one service operation. If the several respective functions (k) performed have identical exponential distributions with mean $1/k\mu$, then the aggregate service distribution is an Erlang distribution with parameters μ and k. The mean of the Erlang will be $1/\mu$ and the variance σ^2 will be $1/k\mu^2$. However, even if this is not the physical process, the Erlang distribution may fit the service time distribution. It is also of interest to note that k is assumed to be an integer value in the Erlang distribution and is therefore simply a special case of the *gamma* distribution, where k can be any real value.

In order to solve for the operating characteristics for the Erlang (or gamma) service time model, simply set $\sigma^2 = 1/k\mu^2$ and use the model for undefined service times. For example, assume that the bank drive-in teller performed two functions ($k = 2$) for each customer (in conjunction with the previous example data). Thus,

$$\rho = \frac{\lambda}{\mu} = \frac{20}{30} = .67$$

$$P_0 = 1 - \frac{2}{3} = .33$$

$$L_q = \frac{\lambda^2\sigma^2 + (\lambda/\mu)^2}{2(1 - \lambda/\mu)}$$

where

$$\sigma^2 = \frac{1}{k\mu^2} = \frac{1}{(2)(30)^2} = \frac{1}{1{,}800}.$$

Thus,

$$L_q = \frac{(400)(1/1{,}800) + (20/30)^2}{2(1 - 20/30)}$$

$$L_q = 1 \text{ customer waiting}$$

$$L = L_q + \frac{\lambda}{\mu}$$

$$= 1 + \frac{2}{3}$$

$$= 1.67 \text{ customers in the system}$$

$$W_q = \frac{L_q}{\lambda} = \frac{1}{20}$$

$$= .05 \text{ hours waiting (3 minutes)}$$

$$W = W_q + \frac{1}{\mu}$$

$$= .05 + \frac{1}{30}$$

$$= .083 \text{ hours} \cong 5 \text{ minutes in the system.}$$

Poisson Arrivals, Exponential Service Times, Finite Queue

For the bank drive-in teller example, suppose that the maximum number of cars the system can contain is four and that cars cannot line up on the adjacent street. This might be due to a city ordinance or customers might simply refuse to enter the queue.

In either event, the model must be modified to consider the truncated (finite) queueing system. It should be noted that for this case the service rate does *not* have to exceed the arrival rate ($\mu > \lambda$) in order to obtain steady-state conditions. The resultant operating characteristics, where M is the maximum number in the system, are as follows:

$$P_0 = \frac{1 - \lambda/\mu}{1 - (\lambda/\mu)^{M+1}}$$

$$P_n = (P_0)\left(\frac{\lambda}{\mu}\right)^n \text{ for } n \leq M$$

$$L = \frac{\lambda/\mu}{1 - \lambda/\mu} - \frac{(M + 1)(\lambda/\mu)^{M+1}}{1 - (\lambda/\mu)^{M+1}}$$

Since P_n is the probability of n units in the system, if we define M as the maximum number allowed in the system, then P_M (the value of P_n for $n = M$) is the probability that a customer will not join the system. The remaining equations are

$$L_q = L - \frac{\lambda(1 - P_M)}{\mu}$$

$$W = \frac{L}{\lambda(1 - P_M)}$$

$$W_q = W - \frac{1}{\mu}.$$

As an example, we will determine the system operating characteristics for the first model example (Poisson arrivals, exponential service times) if the maximum number in the system is four ($M = 4$). Given that $\lambda = 20$ arrivals/hour and $\mu = 30$ services/hour,

$$P_0 = \frac{1 - 20/30}{1 - (20/30)^5} = .38$$

$$P_M = (.38)\left(\frac{20}{30}\right)^4$$

$$\cong .076 \text{ probability of } M = 4 \text{ in the system}$$

$$L = \frac{20/30}{1 - 20/30} - \frac{(5)(20/30)^5}{1 - (20/30)^5}$$

$$\cong 1.24 \text{ customers in the system}$$

$$L_q = 1.24 - \frac{20(1 - .076)}{30}$$

$$\cong .62 \text{ customers waiting}$$

$$W = \frac{1.24}{20(1 - .076)} = .07 \text{ hours}$$

$$\cong 4.2 \text{ minutes in the system}$$

$$W_q = .07 - \frac{1}{30} = .04 \text{ hours}$$

$$\cong 2.4 \text{ minutes waiting.}$$

Finite Calling Population, Exponential Service Times

When considering the case of a finite number of machines that must be repaired when they break down, the *infinite* calling population model is not appropriate. As previously stated, this is because the probability of arrivals is affected by the number of arrivals that have already occurred. Recall that previously $1/\lambda$ was defined as the mean time between arrivals. However, in the case of the finite calling population, each machine alternates between being outside the queueing system (i.e., the machine is in operation) and the time the machine is inside the queueing system (i.e., the machine is being repaired or waiting to be repaired). As such, $1/\lambda$ is defined as the mean time between breakdowns of machines in operation.

Thus, if the time spent outside the system between failures and the service times are exponential distributions with means $1/\lambda$ and $1/\mu$, respectively, then the operating characteristics are given as follows:

$$P_0 = \frac{1}{\displaystyle\sum_{n=0}^{N} \frac{N!}{(N-n)!}\left(\frac{\lambda}{\mu}\right)^n}, \text{ where } N = \text{population size}$$

$$P_n = \frac{N!}{(N-n)!}\left(\frac{\lambda}{\mu}\right)^n P_0, \text{ where } n = 1, 2, \ldots, N$$

$$L_q = N - \frac{\lambda + \mu}{\lambda}(1 - P_0)$$

$$L = L_q + (1 - P_0)$$

$$W_q = \frac{L_q}{(N - L)\lambda}$$

$$W = W_q + \frac{1}{\mu}$$

The computations associated with the finite calling population model are somewhat cumbersome. Fortunately, tables have been developed that yield system operating characteristics for various combinations of input parameters. Thus, by referring to these tables the finite queueing process can be analyzed with relative ease.[3]

A number of additional single-server queueing models have been developed. Some examples include systems in which the server works faster as the queue becomes longer or the arrival rate is reduced as the queue lengthens. Models have also been developed for queue disciplines other than first-come, first-served, such as service in random order, or priority discipline models. These and other advanced single-server models are, however, beyond the scope of this chapter and will not be considered here.

Multiple-Channel, Single-Phase Models

Since a large number of real-world queueing systems include multiple servers, an introductory presentation of multiple-channel models will be given. Multiple-channel models, however, can become quite complex and therefore only a limited case will be considered.

Prior to its presentation, the multiple-channel model should be carefully distinguished from other similar queueing systems. The multiple-channel, single-phase model to be presented assumes that a single waiting line forms prior to the service facility. The service facility contains several servers, who serve customers from the single queue as the servers become available. Service is on a first-come, first-served basis. This case was illustrated in figure 10.2. Such a situation might

3. See L. G. Peck and R. N. Hazelwood, *Finite Queueing Tables* (New York: John Wiley & Sons, 1958).

exist, for example, if there are several attendants operating separate tool checkout counters, in which workmen wait for service in a single line.

This would not be the case for systems such as grocery store checkout counters, where separate queues form behind each counter. This type of system would actually represent several single-channel, single-phase facilities operating simultaneously. Since customers do not often move from one line to the other (jockey) in the grocery store example, this system could be studied by applying single-server models to each facility. However, when customers commonly jockey from one queue to another, such as from one teller line to another in a bank, neither the multiple-channel model (for all tellers) nor the single-channel model (for each teller independently) is appropriate for analysis of the system. For more complex queueing processes such as this, simulation can be used.

Poisson Arrivals, Exponential Service Times

The multiple-channel, single-phase model to be presented here assumes Poisson arrivals and exponential service times. Arrivals are assumed to come from an infinite population, and an unlimited (infinite) queue may build up. Service is on a first-come, first-served basis. The mean effective service rate for the overall system is $s \cdot \mu$ (where s equals the number of servers) and $s \cdot \mu$ exceeds the customer arrival rate (λ). It is further assumed that the service time distribution for each server is the same, regardless of which one of the servers performs the service for a customer.

The steady-state results for the previously described model are given as follows:

$$P_0 = \frac{1}{\left[\sum_{n=0}^{s-1} \frac{(\lambda/\mu)^n}{n!}\right] + \left[\frac{(\lambda/\mu)^s}{s!(1 - \lambda/s\mu)}\right]}$$

$$P_n = \frac{(\lambda/\mu)^n}{n!}P_0 \quad \text{if } n \leqslant s$$

$$P_n = \frac{(\lambda/\mu)^n}{s!s^{n-s}}P_0 \quad \text{if } n > s$$

$$\rho = \frac{\lambda}{s\mu}$$

$$L_q = \frac{P_0(\lambda/\mu)^s\rho}{s!(1 - \rho)^2}$$

$$L = L_q + \frac{\lambda}{\mu}$$

$$W_q = \frac{L_q}{\lambda}$$

$$W = W_q + \frac{1}{\mu}$$

Consider an example where trucks arrive at a shipping terminal to be unloaded and loaded. Assume that the terminal dock capacity is three trucks. As trucks enter the terminal, the drivers receive numbers, and when one of the three dock spaces becomes available, the truck with the lowest number enters the space. Put in terms of our queueing models, the system can be described as a three-channel, single-phase facility.

Further assume that truck arrivals are Poisson distributed and unloading and loading (service) times are exponentially distributed. The terminal grounds are sufficiently large that there is no significant limit to the number of trucks that can be waiting at any one time.

If the average truck arrival rate is five per hour and the average service rate per dock space is two per hour (thirty minutes per truck), the system's steady-state operating characteristics are computed after the following system inputs.

$$\lambda = 5$$

$$\mu = 2$$

$$s = 3$$

$$s\mu = 6$$

$$\rho = \frac{\lambda}{s\mu} = \frac{5}{(3)(2)} = \frac{5}{6} = 0.8333$$

To determine P_0, first compute the initial term in the denominator of the formula as follows:

$$\begin{aligned}\sum_{n=0}^{s-1} \frac{(\lambda/\mu)^n}{n!} &= \frac{(\lambda/\mu)^0}{0!} + \frac{(\lambda/\mu)^1}{1!} + \frac{(\lambda/\mu)^2}{2!}\\ &= \frac{(5/2)^0}{0!} + \frac{(5/2)^1}{1!} + \frac{(5/2)^2}{2!}\\ &= \frac{1}{1} + \frac{2.5}{1} + \frac{6.25}{2}\\ &= 1 + 2.5 + 3.125\\ &= 6.625\end{aligned}$$

The second term in the denominator of the P_0 formula is

$$\frac{(\lambda/\mu)^s}{s!(1 - \lambda/s\mu)} = \frac{(5/2)^3}{3!(1 - 5/6)} = \frac{125/8}{6(1/6)} = 15.625.$$

Therefore,

$$\begin{aligned}P_0 &= \frac{1}{6.625 + 15.625} = \frac{1}{22.25}\\ &= 0.0449.\end{aligned}$$

Since considerable computational effort is involved in calculating the value of P_0, a table of values for P_0 has been provided in appendix table D.4 for various combinations of $\lambda/\mu s$ (utilization factor) and s (number of channels).

The system's other operating characteristics are as follows:

$$L_q = \frac{P_0(\lambda/\mu)^s\rho}{s!(1 - \rho)^2}$$

$$= \frac{(0.0449)(5/2)^3(5/6)}{3!(1 - 5/6)^2} = \frac{(0.0449)(125/8)(5/6)}{(6)(1/36)}$$

$$= (0.0449)\left(\frac{625}{48}\right)\left(\frac{6}{1}\right) = (0.0449)\left(\frac{625}{8}\right)$$

$$\cong 3.5 \text{ trucks waiting}$$

$$L = L_q + \frac{\lambda}{\mu} = 3.5 + \frac{5}{2}$$

$$= 6.0 \text{ trucks in the system}$$

$$W_q = \frac{L_q}{\lambda} = \frac{3.5}{5}$$

$$= 0.7 \text{ hour (42 minutes) waiting time}$$

$$W = W_q + \frac{1}{\mu} = 0.7 + \frac{1}{2}$$

$$= 1.2 \text{ hours (72 minutes) in the system}$$

Thus, on the average, there will be 6 trucks in the system, with an average of 3.5 trucks waiting for service. The difference of 2.5 is the average number of trucks in service in the three service locations, which reflects the fact that a portion of the time one or more servers will be idle. In fact, the entire system will be idle almost 5% of the time ($P_0 = 0.0449$). The mean time in the system will be seventy-two minutes, of which forty-two minutes will be spent waiting for a dock space. The difference of thirty minutes is exactly the expected service time, $1/\mu$, originally specified.

It is also of considerable interest to know how many trucks can be expected to be in the system at any one time. Some probabilities of various numbers of trucks in the system are given as follows:

$$P_n = \frac{(\lambda/\mu)^n}{n!} P_0 \quad \text{if } n \leq s$$

$$P_n = \frac{(\lambda/\mu)^n}{s!s^{n-s}} P_0 \quad \text{if } n > s$$

For particular values of n,

$$P(n = 1) = \frac{(5/2)^1}{1!}(0.0449) = 0.11225$$

$$P(n = 2) = \frac{(5/2)^2}{2!}(0.0449) = 0.14031$$

$$P(n = 3) = \frac{(5/2)^3}{3!}(0.0449) = 0.11693$$

$$P(n = 4) = \frac{(5/2)^4}{3!3^{4-3}}(0.0449) = 0.09744$$

$$P(n = 5) = \frac{(5/2)^5}{3!3^{5-3}}(0.0449) = 0.08120.$$

The preceding values are included in a summary of the number in the system, along with associated individual probabilities and cumulative probabilities, in the following table:

n Number in the System	P_n Probability	N N or Less in the System	$P_n \leq N$ Cumulative Probability
0	0.045	0	0.045
1	0.112	1	0.157
2	0.140	2	0.297
3	0.117	3	0.414
4	0.097	4	0.511
5	0.081	5	0.592
6	0.068	6	0.660
7	0.056	7	0.716
8	0.047	8	0.763
9	0.038	9	0.801
10	0.033	10	0.834
11	0.027	11	0.861
12	0.023	12	0.884
13	0.019	13	0.903
14	0.016	14	0.919
15	0.013	15	0.932

This table shows that the probability distribution of the number in the system is rather flat and widely dispersed. Thus, even though the expected (mean) number in the system is six, management may wish to know the chances of having ten or more trucks in the system (or what is the probability that there will be seven or more trucks waiting to unload and load?). The probability of having ten or more trucks in the system is given as $P(n \geq 10) = 1 - P(n \leq 9)$, where $P(n \leq 9)$ is obtained from the table as 0.801. Therefore, there is about a 20% chance that there will be ten or more trucks in the system. In other words, 20% of the time there will be at least ten trucks in the system.

The sample problem raises some interesting questions regarding the various methods for changing the service level. Several possibilities exist. Management could consider increasing the number of service positions at the dock (increase the number of channels). They could also consider trying to increase the service rate with the existing capacity. This might be done by hiring more labor to unload and load trucks, or it might be achieved by installing faster and more efficient equipment. It should be noted that even though several persons might be employed at each individual dock position, this can still be thought of as one of the several channels, and μ can be varied by adding or subtracting personnel.

Several other multiple-channel, single-phase models have been developed, such as for the cases of truncated queues and finite calling populations. These, however, are beyond the scope of this chapter.

Multiple-Phase Models

Multiple-phase queueing models will not be analyzed in detail in this chapter, since they become extremely complex very quickly. However, one case should be discussed. If the multiple-phase system satisfies all the assumptions of Poisson arrivals, exponential service times, infinite calling population, infinite possible queues, and service rate(s) exceeds arrival rate(s), then the multiple-phase system can be analyzed rather easily.

The fundamental point here is that if a service facility has a Poisson input with parameter λ and exponential service time distribution with parameter μ (where $\mu > \lambda$), then the steady-state *output* of this service facility is also a Poisson process with parameter λ. Thus, each successive facility in a multiple-phase system will have a Poisson input with parameter λ. This condition will hold for the single-channel model and for the multiple-channel model just discussed (if $s\mu > \lambda$).

Thus, the individual phases may be evaluated independently of one another, and the aggregate operating characteristics can be obtained by summing the corresponding values obtained at the respective facilities. The operating characteristics referred to are total expected waiting time, total expected time in the system, total expected number in queues, and total expected number in the overall system. It is important to note here that the intermediate queues are also assumed to be allowed to build up to any length.

Figure 10.9 illustrates three examples of multiple-phase models that can be analyzed by this procedure, if the previously stated assumptions are met. The first case (fig. 10.9*A*) is simply a single-channel, multiple-phase model. The two phases are evaluated independently, and the individual phase characteristics summed. The second case (fig. 10.9*B*) is simply two stages of a multiple-channel, single-phase process. Thus, each stage is evaluated independently according to the multiple-channel, single-phase equations, and the resulting operating characteristics are summed. The third case (fig. 10.9*C*) represents an initial multiple-channel, single-phase stage with each of the three servers followed by a single-channel, single-phase stage. This system is evaluated by solving the multiple-channel, single-phase equations for the first stage and then solving one of the following stage phases as a single-channel, single-phase process, with $\lambda_i = \lambda/3$ (where λ_i = mean arrival rate at the second stage for channel i server). Recall that the multiple-channel, single-phase model assumed that the service rate is identical for each server, yielding the assumption that $\lambda_i = \lambda/3$. Since the results are the same for each of the three second-stage servers, only one of these needs to be evaluated.

Figure 10.9 Multiphase models. (*A*) Single-channel, multiple-phase. (*B*) Multiple-channel, multiple-phase (case 1). (*C*) Multiple-channel, multiple-phase (case 2).

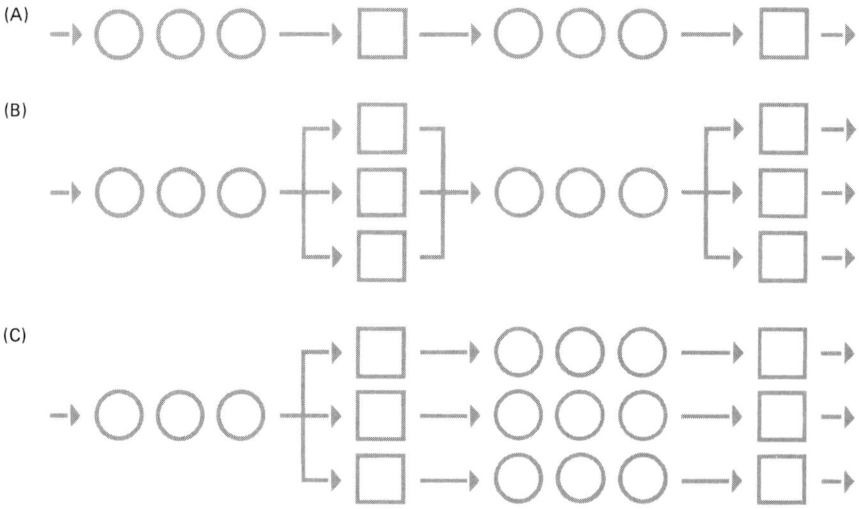

Summary

Several analytical models of queueing systems have been presented, along with the resulting equations for obtaining measures of the system's performance. However, the reader can quickly appreciate that the number of conceivable waiting line models is almost infinite.

The purpose of this chapter has been to give you a feel for the analysis of waiting line systems and the methods of obtaining at least rough approximations of the operating characteristics. The techniques of Markov analysis (chapter 9) and simulation (chapter 11) can also be employed to analyze queueing systems. The interested reader should explore these techniques with queueing possibilities in mind.

References

Buffa, E. S. *Operations Management: Problems and Models*. 3d ed. New York: John Wiley & Sons, 1972.

Feller, W. *An Introduction to Probability Theory and Its Applications*. Vol. 1, 3d ed. New York: John Wiley & Sons, 1968.

Hillier, F., and Lieberman, G. J. *Introduction to Operations Research*. 2d ed. San Francisco: Holden-Day, 1974.

Morse, P. M. *Queues, Inventories, and Maintenance*. New York: John Wiley & Sons, 1958.

Saaty, T. L. *Elements of Queueing Theory*. New York: McGraw-Hill, 1961.

Taha, H. A. *Operations Research: An Introduction*. New York: Macmillan, 1971.

Problems

1. Consider a waiting line process with the following characteristics:

   Infinite calling population
   Infinite possible queue
   First-come, first-served queue discipline
   Steady-state condition
   Service rate exceeds arrival rate
   Single-channel, single-phase system
   Poisson arrival rate, exponential service times

   Assume that the arrivals occur at a mean rate of three per hour ($\lambda = 3$) and the mean service rate is five per hour ($\mu = 5$).

   a. What is the probability of exactly one arrival during the first hour? two arrivals? three arrivals? four arrivals? What is the probability there will be four or more arrivals during the first hour?
   b. What is the probability that the first arrival will require a service time of at least six minutes (0.1 hour)? twelve minutes (0.2 hour)? thirty minutes (0.5 hour)?
   c. What percent of the time will the server be idle?
   d. What is the expected (mean) waiting time per arrival, in hours and in minutes?
   e. What is the mean number of arrivals waiting?
   f. What is the average time in the system (waiting and in service), in hours and in minutes?
   g. What is the average number of arrivals in the system?
   h. What value is the utilization factor?

2. For problem 1, construct a probability distribution for k or more units in the system, for values of k ranging from zero to six. Suppose it is highly undesirable to have a waiting line of three or more arrivals. What is the probability of this happening?

3. Referring again to problem 1, suppose the mean rate for arrivals increased to 4 per hour, 4.5 per hour, and 5 per hour. Plot the values of L_q versus values of λ/μ, for the arrival rates of 3, 4, 4.5, and 5 per hour. What happens as the arrival rate approaches the service rate?

4. Assume that all the conditions of problem 1 are met, except that the service distribution is unknown. The mean service time is known to be twelve minutes with a standard deviation of six minutes (in other words, the mean service rate, μ, equals five per hour, and the standard deviation of service times in hours, σ, is equal to 0.1). Determine the values for the following operating characteristics:

   a. Utilization factor
   b. P_0
   c. L_q
   d. L
   e. W_q
   f. W

   Compare these results with the results obtained in problem 1.

5. For problem 1, assume that it is possible to control the service rate (e.g., vary the available personnel in the service facility). Assume that the various service rates may be obtained according to the following schedule of associated costs:

Service Rate (μ)	Service Cost Per Hour
4 customers/hr.	\$ 3.00
4.5	6.00
5	9.00
5.5	12.00
6	15.00

   Further assume that the cost per hour for customers waiting is estimated to be \$10 per hour. Analyze the system over a period of eight hours. It is assumed that the system is in steady state at the beginning of the eight-hour period of analysis.

   a. Determine the optimal service level (service rate) and the associated expected total cost.
   b. Illustrate the decision analysis graphically, showing service cost, customer waiting cost, and total cost for the various service rates considered.

6. A single-server queueing system with an infinite calling population, a first-come, first-served queue discipline, poisson arrival rate, and exponential service times has the following mean arrival and service rates:

   λ = 16 customers per hour
   μ = 24 customers per hour

   Determine P_0, P_3, L, L_q, W, W_q, and the utilization factor.

7. The ticket booth on a university campus is operated by one person, who sells tickets for a football game on Saturday. The ticket seller can serve twelve customers per hour (exponentially distributed). An average of ten customers arrive to purchase tickets every hour (poisson distributed). Determine the average time a ticket buyer must wait in line to buy a ticket and the portion of time the ticket seller is busy.

8. A service station has one pump for selling unleaded gasoline. With this pump an attendant can service ten customers per hour (exponential service times). Customers arrive at the unleaded pump at a rate of six per hour (poisson distributed). Determine the average queue length, the average time in the system for a customer, and, the average time a customer must wait. If during a gasoline shortage the arrival rate increased to twelve customers per hour, what effect would it have on the average queue length?

9. A manufacturing firm produces a particular product in an assembly line operation. One of the machines on the line is a press that has a single line of in-process parts feeding into it. Units arrive at the press to be worked on according to an exponential distribution every 7.5 minutes (on the average). Operator processing times are Poisson distributed with a mean rate of ten parts per hour.

   a. Determine the average number of parts waiting to be worked on, the percentage of time the operator is working, and the percentage of time the machine is idle.
   b. The management of the firm desires to have their operators working 90% of the time. Determine the time between arrivals that will allow the press operator to meet this criterion.

10. A small airport that serves light aircraft has a single runway and one air traffic controller to land planes. It takes an airplane an average of twelve minutes to land and clear the runway (exponentially distributed). Planes arrive at the runway according to a poisson distribution at the rate of four per hour. Determine the following:

   a. The number of planes that will stack up (on the average) waiting to land.
   b. The average time a plane must circle before it can land.
   c. The average time it takes a plane to clear the runway once it notifies the airport it wants to land.
   d. The FAA has a rule that limits an air traffic controller to landing planes, on the average, a maximum of forty-five minutes out of every hour. (The controller must have an average of fifteen minutes idle time out of every hour to relieve tension). Will this airport have to hire an extra air traffic controller?

11. All trucks travelling on a particular stretch of interstate highway are required by law to stop at a weight station. Trucks arrive according to a poisson distribution with a mean rate of 200 per eight hour day. The weighing times are exponentially distributed with a mean rate of 220 trucks per day.

    a. Determine the average number of trucks waiting to be weighed, the average time each truck spends at the weigh station, and the average waiting time (before being weighed) for each truck.
    b. If the truck drivers find out that they have to remain at the weigh station longer than an average of fifteen minutes, they will start taking an alternative route or travel at night, thus depriving the state of taxes. For each minute more than fifteen minutes that trucks must be at the weigh station the state estimates it loses $10,000 in taxes per year. An extra set of scales would have the same service capacity as the existing set of scales, and it is assumed that arriving trucks would line up equally behind each set of scales. It will cost $50,000 per year to operate the new scales. Should the state install the new scales?
    c. Given the original conditions in this problem, suppose passing truck drivers look to see how many trucks are at the station. If drivers see four or more trucks are at the weigh station, they will pass the station by and risk being caught and ticketed by the state police. What is the probability that a truck will bypass the station?

12. Assume that a firm has ten machines that periodically break down and require service. The average time between breakdowns is three days, distributed according to an exponential distribution. The average time to repair a machine is two days, distributed according to an exponential distribution. One mechanic repairs the machines in the order in which they break down.

    a. Determine the probability of the mechanic being idle.
    b. Determine the mean number of machines waiting to be repaired.
    c. Determine the mean time machines wait to be repaired.
    d. Determine the probability that three machines are not operating (being repaired or waiting to be repaired).

13. Customers arrive at a service facility at the mean rate of eight per hour. The arrival rate is Poisson distributed. Service times are exponentially distributed with a mean of five minutes. The calling population is infinitely large; however, the maximum possible queue length is three customers. Determine the following:

    a. The probability of zero customers in the system
    b. The mean number of customers in the system
    c. The mean number of customers waiting
    d. The mean time a customer spends in the system
    e. The mean time a customer spends waiting
    f. The percent of arriving customers lost due to the queue length limitation

14. Assume the same conditions given in problem 1, with the following exceptions: mean arrival rate = eight per hour; mean service rate per server = five per hour; and number of servers = two (two-channel, single-phase system). Determine the following operating statistics:

   a. Probability of the system being empty
   b. Probability of exactly four in the system
   c. Utilization factor
   d. Mean length of the waiting line
   e. Mean time an arrival spends waiting

15. During registration at a university, students in the college of business must have their course schedule approved by the college advisor. The time it takes for the advisor to approve a schedule is exponentially distributed with a mean of two minutes. Students arrive at the advisor's office according to a poisson distribution with a mean rate of twenty-eight per hour.

   a. Compute L, L_q, W, W_q, and the utilization factor.
   b. The dean of the college has received numerous complaints from students about the length of time they must wait to have their schedules approved. The dean believes an average time of 10 minutes to wait and then get the schedule approved is reasonable. Each graduate assistant the dean assigns to the advisor's office will reduce the average time for *the advisor* to approve a schedule by .25 minutes, down to a minimum of 1.0 minutes to approve a schedule. How many assistants should the dean assign to the advisor?
   c. The dean is considering adding a second advisor rather than assigning assistants to serve the line of students at the office waiting to have their schedules approved. This new advisor can serve the same number of students per hour as the present advisor. Determine L, L_q, W, and W_q for this altered advisor system.
   d. As a student would you recommend adding the advisor?

16. A clinic has two general practitioners that see patients daily. Patients arrive at the clinic according to a poisson distribution with a mean rate of six per hour. The time a doctor spends with a patient is exponentially distributed with a mean of fifteen minutes. The patients wait in a waiting area until one of the two doctors is able to examine them. However, since patients typically do not feel well when they come to the clinic the doctors do not believe it is good practice to have the patients wait longer than an average of fifteen minutes. Should this clinic hire a third doctor and, if so, will this reduce the average waiting time to less than fifteen minutes?

17. Assume that an arriving customer must first be serviced in the facility described in problem 1 and then proceed directly to a second facility for a second phase of service. The second facility also meets all the assumptions of problem 1, but with a Poisson distributed service rate with a mean of four customers per hour. Thus, the overall system may be described as a single-channel, two-phase process. Determine P_0, L, L_q, W, and W_q for this system.

18. Trucks arrive at a firm's unloading facility according to a Poisson distribution, at the mean rate of twenty trucks per day. Only one truck at a time can be unloaded; however, unlimited space is available for trucks to wait for service. Assume an infinite population of trucks. The firm wishes to determine the optimal number of workers to employ for unloading the trucks. It is known that each worker can unload trucks at the mean rate of five trucks per working day without diminishing efficiency, up to a maximum of eight workers. The unloading rate varies according to a Poisson distribution. Workers are paid $25 per day, while the estimated cost of waiting trucks is $50 per day, per truck. The firm's management has observed the average number of arriving trucks (20) and the average rate at which workers can unload the trucks (5 per working day), and they have concluded that they should employ four workers (20/5 = 4). Determine whether the firm has arrived at a good decision. What number of workers would you recommend to management? Illustrate your decision analysis as a graphical decision model to present to the management of the firm.

11 Simulation

The subject of this chapter, simulation, represents a major divergence from the topics of previous chapters. Prior to this chapter, all topics have been concerned with the formulation of models that could be solved analytically. Linear programming and transportation problems were solved using algorithms (theoretically based step-by-step rules). In decision theory and game theory, various alternatives were analytically evaluated by using criteria such as expected value, maximin, and minimax. Thus, the approach of this text has been to first consider formulation and then develop analytical solutions to the model.

In many cases, the goal has been to determine optimal solutions. However, not all real-world problems lend themselves to mathematical modeling and solution in a manner that results in optimality. Some real-world situations cannot be represented in the concise model forms described in this text because of stochastic relationships, complexity, etc. In these cases, an alternative form of analysis is **simulation.**

A familiar form of simulation is analogue simulation, where an original physical system is replaced by an analogous physical system that is easier to manipulate. A typical example is the representation of a mechanical system by an equivalent electrical system. Much of the experimentation in the manned space flight program was conducted using physical simulation that recreated the conditions of space. However, the focus of this chapter will be computerized mathematical simulation. In this form, simulation can be defined, in general terms, as a means for deriving measures of performance about a complex system by conducting sampling experiments on a mathematical model of the system over periods of time. Presumably, the model of the system includes the relevant components of the system along with their mathematical relationships. The process of simulation normally involves ''running'' the model on a computer in order to obtain operational information.

The results, or output, of a simulation model are in the form of system **descriptors,** which describe the behavior of the simulated system. For example, the queueing equations in chapter 10 yielded solutions in the form of descriptors of system performance. (The model results were assumed to be input into a broader framework for the actual decision-making process.)

Since simulation of a model is closely akin to conducting sampling experiments on the real system, the results obtained are sample observations or sample statistics. For example, in a single-channel, single-phase queueing system, the analytically derived queueing equation for the mean number of customers waiting yields a value analogous to a population mean (μ), whereas simulation yields a value analogous to a sample mean ($\bar{x}$). Whether or not the sample mean approximates the steady-state mean of the queueing equation depends on the starting conditions of the simulation, the length of the period being simulated, and, of course, the accuracy of the model. In any event, the simulation results do contain sampling variance (error) just as in the case of direct sampling from the population. In cases where the simulation is conducted over time, covariance is included in the results.

Methods for dealing with such output are difficult at best. This points out a factor that should be considered when comparing the simulation models described in this chapter with the analytical models developed previously. While simulation provides flexibility as a tool of analysis, it may do so at the expense of accuracy of results. However, as previously noted, the problem under analysis may have no practical analytical approach, in which case simulation becomes the only alternative.

This chapter is organized in the following manner. First, an overview of the simulation process is presented. Next, the topic of stochastic simulation models, the focal point of the chapter, is described. These topics are followed by discussions of random number generation, model construction, optimization of results, model validation, alternative simulation computer languages, and applications of simulation.

The Simulation Process

The process of simulating a system consists of several distinct stages, which are summarized in figure 11.1. The initial stage of the process requires that for the system (or portion of the system) under analysis, the problem must be identified and formulated. For example, if an inventory system is being simulated, the problem may concern the number of units to order at certain reordering points. This step necessitates the specification of performance criteria, decision rules, and model parameters. Also, system variables must be identified as well as the relationship between the variables. In an inventory system, this stage might require the identification of cost as the performance criterion, decision rules for when to reorder, and variables such as demand, lead time, and buffer stock.

Once the model components have been identified, the model itself is developed and put into a form that can be analyzed on the computer. In many cases, the model can be written in a specific simulation language that is especially suited for the problem under analysis. When the model is developed, it must be validated to determine if it realistically represents the system being analyzed and if the results will be reliable. This is a critical problem area in simulation and usually a difficult task.

Figure 11.1 The simulation process.

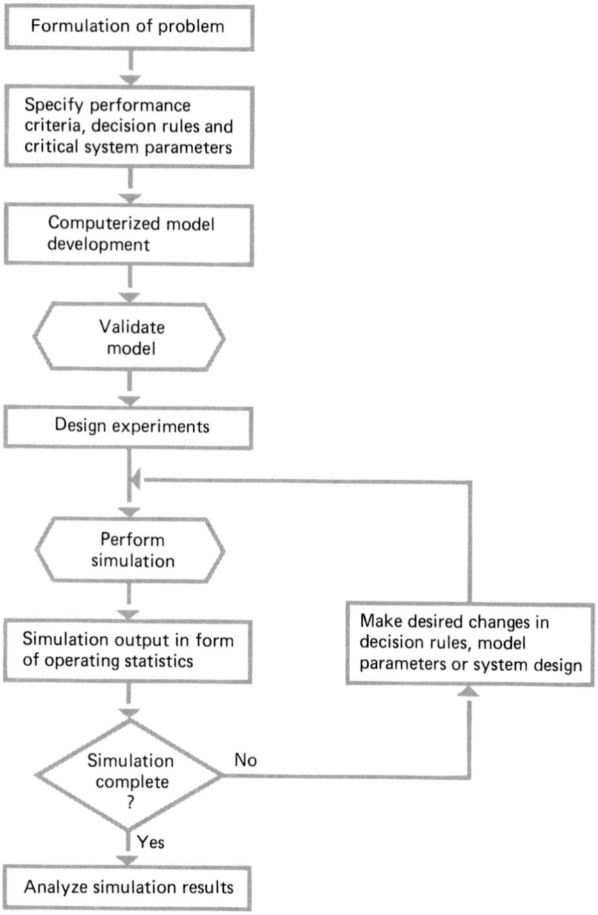

The next stage concerns the design of the experiments to be conducted with the simulation model. This is one of the most advantageous characteristics of simulation—the ability to experiment on the system. Following these preparatory events, the simulation model is run on the computer and the results obtained, usually in the form of operating statistics, such as the average carrying cost for an inventory system. Once the results are obtained, it must be determined if additional experiments are to be conducted. If not, the results are analyzed not only as a problem solution, but in terms of statistical reliability and correctness.

The remainder of this chapter is concerned primarily with model construction. As a result, many of the topics of the simulation process, such as problem formulation, identification of model components, and analysis of results, are treated only briefly. Nevertheless, these topics are important parts of the simulation process and are covered in detail in several of the references on simulation at the end of this chapter.

Stochastic Simulation

A characteristic of systems that often results in models too difficult to solve analytically is the inclusion of certain system components that must be represented as random variables. These random variables are represented in the simulation model by probability distributions, and the model is referred to as probabilistic, or stochastic. The majority of simulation models based on real-world problems are stochastic models. Because of the popularity of stochastic simulation, it is the primary focus of this chapter.

The Monte Carlo Sampling Process

The term **Monte Carlo sampling** has become synonymous with stochastic simulation in recent years. However, in reality, Monte Carlo sampling can be more narrowly defined as a technique for selecting numbers randomly from a probability distribution for use in a trial run of a simulation. As such, the Monte Carlo technique is not a simulation study or model in itself but a mathematical technique used within simulation.

The origin of modern stochastic simulation methods and the use of the Monte Carlo technique is attributed to Von Neumann and Ulan, who used the technique as a research tool in the development of the atomic bomb during World War II. This research involved a direct simulation of the probabilistic problems concerned with random neutron diffusion of fissionable material for nuclear shielding devices. Shortly thereafter, the possibility of applying these same Monte Carlo methods to nonprobabilistic problems was considered by these researchers and Fermi.

The name *Monte Carlo* is appropriate since the basic principle behind the technique is the same as the principle underlying many gambling devices, such as roulette wheels, dice, and playing cards. These devices produce random samples from well-defined populations—the same procedure employed in Monte Carlo methods.

As previously noted, the primary objective of stochastic simulation is to realistically reproduce the variability of the random variable(s) in the system being studied. In this section, the development of a random variable generator, also known as a **process generator,** will be discussed.

Consider the following simple example in which demand per day for a product is a discrete random variable defined by the probability distribution in the following table:

Demand per Day x	Probability of Demand $p(x)$
14	0.2
15	0.4
16	0.2
17	0.1
18	0.1

In the table, $p(x)$ is the probability that demand during any particular day will be x. The purpose of Monte Carlo simulation is to generate the random variable (demand) by "sampling" from the probability distribution. The demand per day could be randomly generated according to the probability distribution, $p(x)$, by spinning a roulette wheel that is segmented into portions corresponding to the probabilities, $p(x)$, as shown in figure 11.2.

Figure 11.2 The Monte Carlo process.

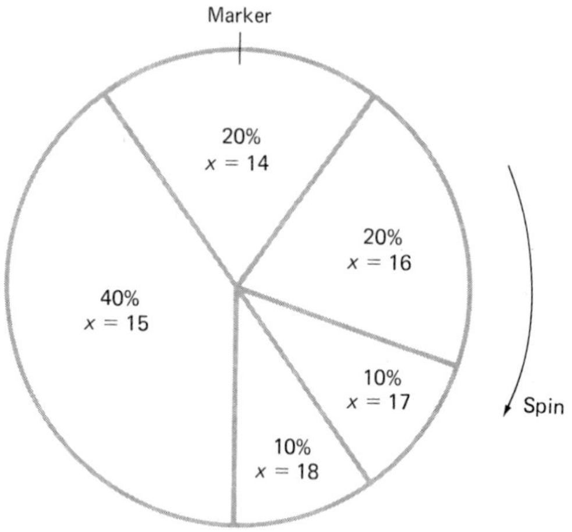

Given an unbiased spin of the wheel, a quantity for demand per day is generated depending on where the wheel stops. Over a period of days (many spins of the wheel), the relative frequency with which values are generated will approximate the probability distribution, $p(x)$. This process of generating values of x by randomly selecting from the probability distribution, $p(x)$, is an example of the Monte Carlo method.

The process of spinning the roulette wheel artificially reconstructs the system of demand occurring during a given day. In this reconstruction, a lengthy period of *real time* (i.e., a number of days) can be represented in a short period of *simulated time* (i.e., numerous spins of the wheel). Obviously though, it is not generally practical to generate the values of a random variable by spinning a wheel. Alternatively, the process of spinning the roulette wheel can be artificially constructed using random numbers.

A Random Process Generator

Spinning a roulette wheel to randomly generate demand according to a particular probability distribution is referred to as a random process generator. The random process generation technique employs the cumulative distribution function, $F(x)$, of the probability distribution under analysis to generate values of the random variable x. For our example, the cumulative distribution function, $F(x)$, is shown in the following table:

Demand per Day x	Probability of Demand $p(x)$	Cumulative Distribution $F(x)$
14	0.2	0.2
15	0.4	0.6
16	0.2	0.8
17	0.1	0.9
18	0.1	1.0
	1.0	

As shown in the preceding table, the cumulative distribution is defined over the interval (0, 1) and represents the probability that demand will be less than or equal to x, (i.e., $F(16) = P(x \leq 16) = .8$). $F(x)$ is shown graphically in figure 11.3. Note that the length of the vertical line in Figure 11.3 at each step corresponds exactly to the $p(x)$ probability value for each demand quantity. For example, starting at the top, the vertical line directly above the value 18 extends from 0.90 to 1.00.

Figure 11.3 Cumulative density function.

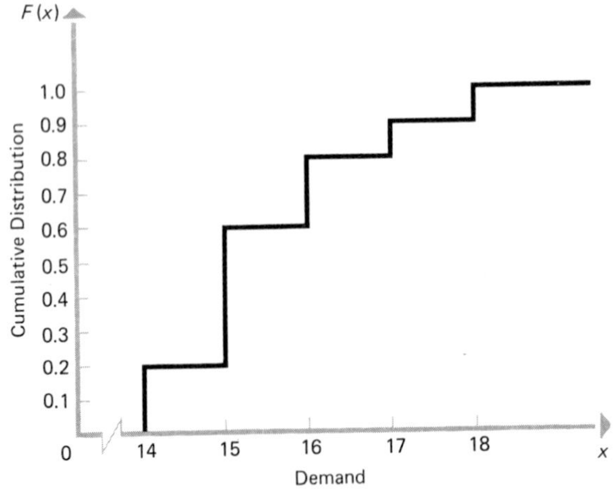

This range corresponds to the probability of a demand for eighteen units, $p(x) = 0.10$. The same condition is true for the vertical line above seventeen, reflecting a probability of 0.10 (.90 − .80 = 0.10). Likewise, the probability, $p(x)$, for $x = 16$ is given by the vertical line from 0.60 to 0.80, or $p(x) = 0.20$.

Thus, the cumulative distribution for x includes a series of ranges in which each range corresponds to a particular demand. If a number, r, between 0 and 1 can be generated randomly, then by determining which range the random number (r) falls in (i.e., the location of the random number along the vertical axis in Fig. 11.3), an associated value for demand, x, can be shown on the horizontal axis.

For example, a value of $r = .76$ falls on the vertical axis of figure 11.3, $F(x)$, within the range $.60 \leqslant F(x) \leqslant .80$. This, in turn, corresponds to a demand of sixteen units on the horizontal axis of figure 11.3. Thus, by randomly selecting values of r, values of x are randomly generated.

The process of generating values of the random variable using this Monte Carlo technique can be demonstrated manually although the process is normally computerized. The first step in the process is to generate a random number. In a computerized simulation model, subroutines exist that generate **pseudorandom numbers,** a process that will be discussed later in this chapter. However, for the purposes of this manual example, random numbers are obtained from the table of random numbers in Appendix D. From table D.5, the value $r = .39$ is selected. Observing the following table, which is a tabular representation of the $F(x)$ range of figure 11.3, it can be seen that $r = .39$ corresponds to a demand of fifteen.

Demand x	Probability of Demand $p(x)$	Ranges of Random Numbers* r	
14	0.2	0.0 → 0.19	
15 ←	0.4 ←	0.20 → 0.59 ←	
16	0.2	0.60 → 0.79	
17	0.1	0.80 → 0.89	$r = 0.39$
18	0.1	0.90 → 0.99	
	1.00		

*Note, for example, that the first range for r includes twenty possible values, from 0.0 to 0.19, which is the same as the probability of demand for $x = 14$.

In the following table, this process is repeated for fifteen consecutive demand periods (days). As before, the random numbers are selected from table D.5.

Demand Period	r	Demand (x)
1	.39	15
2	.73	16
3	.72	16
4	.75	16
5	.37	15
6	.02	14
7	.87	17
8	.98	18
9	.10	14
10	.47	15
11	.93	17
12	.21	15
13	.95	18
14	.97	18
15	.69	16
		$\Sigma = 240$

These tabular values simulate the daily demand of a product for fifteen periods. The average demand for the fifteen periods is sixteen units (240/15 = 16). This simulated average demand can be compared to the expected value of demand computed analytically from the probability distribution, using the following formula:

$$E(x) = \sum_{i=1}^{n} p_i x_i$$

where x_i = the demand i

p_i = the probability of demand i.

Then,

$$\begin{aligned} E(x) &= (.2)(14) + (.4)(15) + (.2)(16) + (.1)(17) + (.1)(18) \\ &= 15.5 \text{ units.} \end{aligned}$$

The average daily demand of sixteen units obtained from the simulation compares favorably with the analytical solution, $E(x) = 15.5$ units. The margin of difference between the simulated value and the analytical value is a result of the number of periods over which the simulation was conducted. Since the Monte Carlo method is actually a probabilistic sampling procedure, the results are subject to the size of the sample taken. Thus, the more periods for which the simulation is conducted, the more accurate the results (i.e., the simulated results approach steady-state conditions). For a more complex model with several stochastic variables, the interaction of the random variables might necessitate a large number of simulated periods.

Example 11.1 *Simulation of a Queueing System*

This example illustrates a more complex situation than the simulation of demand in the previous example in that a complete system will be simulated. Consider a service facility in which arrival intervals and service times are discrete random variables. The probability distributions for each random variable are as follows:

Arrival Interval x	Probability $p(x)$	Cumulative Probability $F(x)$	Range r_1
1.0 min.	.30	.30	$0.00 \rightarrow 0.29$
2.0	.50	.80	$0.30 \rightarrow 0.79$
3.0	.20	1.00	$0.80 \rightarrow 0.99$

Service Time y	Probability $p(y)$	Cumulative Probability $F(y)$	Range r_2
2.0 min.	.30	0.30	$0.00 \rightarrow 0.29$
3.0	.30	0.60	$0.30 \rightarrow 0.59$
4.0	.40	1.00	$0.60 \rightarrow 0.99$

Simulating this system requires the random generation of (1) the arrival intervals and (2) service times. The following table illustrates the simulation for ten customer arrivals.

Customer	r_1	Arrival Interval (x)	Arrival Clock	Enter Facility Clock	Waiting Time	Length of Queue at Entry	r_2	Service Time (y)	Departure Clock	Time in System
1	—	—	0	0	0	0	.39	3.0	3.0	3.0
2	.73	2.0	2.0	3.0	1.0	0	.72	4.0	7.0	5.0
3	.75	2.0	4.0	7.0	3.0	0	.37	3.0	10.0	6.0
4	.02	1.0	5.0	10.0	5.0	1	.87	4.0	14.0	9.0
5	.98	3.0	8.0	14.0	6.0	1	.10	2.0	16.0	8.0
6	.47	2.0	10.0	16.0	6.0	1	.93	4.0	20.0	10.0
7	.21	1.0	11.0	20.0	9.0	2	.95	4.0	24.0	13.0
8	.97	3.0	14.0	24.0	10.0	2	.69	4.0	28.0	14.0
9	.41	2.0	16.0	28.0	12.0	2	.91	4.0	32.0	16.0
10	.80	3.0	19.0	32.0	13.0	3	.67	4.0	36.0	17.0
					65.0	12				101.0

The following is a brief review of the manual simulation process employed to generate the values in the preceding table.

1. Customer 1 arrives at time 0, which is recorded on an arrival clock. The customer enters the service facility immediately (also time 0). As such, the waiting time and length of queue at entry are also 0. A random number, $r_2 = .39$, is selected from the table D.5, which results in a service time, y, of 3.0 minutes. After being serviced, the customer departs at simulated time 3, having been in the system for a total of three minutes.
2. Next, a random number, r_1, is selected for customer 2, which generates an arrival interval of 2.0 minutes between this customer and the previous one. Thus, customer 2 arrives at time 2 in the system. However, the customer will not enter the service facility until time 3, since that is the time customer 1 departed the facility. This results in a waiting time of one minute for customer 2. The queue was empty when customer 2 entered the system since customer 1 had entered at time 0. A second random variate, r_2, generates a service time, y, of four minutes. Since customer 2 entered the service facility at time 3.0 departure is at time 7, resulting in a total of five minutes in the system.
3. This process of selecting random numbers and generating arrival intervals and service times continues in the same manner for the remaining eight customers.

Several entries in the table require additional clarification. First, the length of queue at entry reflects the number of customers waiting in line viewed by the arriving customers. This number is determined by observing the arrival clock time for each customer and comparing it to the enter facility time for prior customers. Every customer whose facility entrance time is *greater than* the current customer's arrival time is in the queue. For example, customer 7 arrives at time 11. However, customer 5 did not enter the service facility until time 14. Thus, customers 5 and 6 were both in the queue when customer 7 arrived (i.e., length of queue at entry for customer 7 is 2).

Employing the simulated results, various statistical attributes of the system can be computed. For example, the average waiting time is 6.5 minutes, computed by dividing total waiting time by the number of customers. Similarly, the average length of the queue at entry is 1.2 customers, and the average total time in the system is 10.1 minutes. However, these results should be observed with caution. Notice that the waiting time, queue length, and time in system columns are increasing as the simulation ends. Thus, a steady state has not been reached. In fact, these values may simply continue to increase making the statistical results somewhat suspect and indicating several possibilities. First, ten observations are too few to base any conclusions on. The random numbers may simply not be uniformly distributed (see p. 481 for a discussion of testing the random numbers for uniformity). A longer simulation run may indeed show a steady-state solution. Second, the actual system could be inefficient, meaning that another server may be needed to avoid ever-increasing queues (assuming customers will not simply leave once a certain queue size is reached). In fact, the expected service time does exceed the expected interarrival times, which will result in an ever-increasing queue.

Stochastic Simulation with Continuous Probability Functions

The simulation illustrated in example 11.1 included discrete probability distributions for the random variables, arrival interval and service time. However, it is often more appropriate to represent time as a continuous random variable. The procedure for developing process generators for continuous random variables is different than in the discrete case.

Consider the following example of a continuous function reflecting a continuous probability distribution for the random variable x:

$$f(x) = \frac{x}{8}, \quad 0 \leq x \leq 4$$

Figure 11.4 is a graphic representation of this relationship.

Figure 11.4 A continuous probability function.

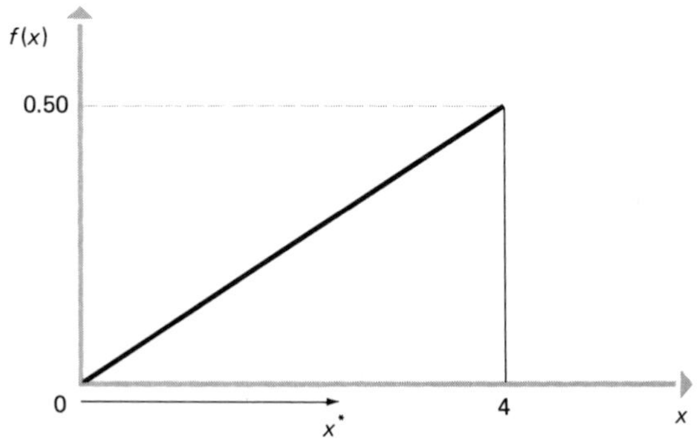

The area under the curve, $f(x) = x/8$ $(0 \leq x \leq 4)$, represents the probability of the occurrence of the random variable x. Therefore, the area under the curve must equal 1.0, since according to probability theory the sum of all probabilities of the occurrence of a random variable must equal one. By computing the area under the curve from 0 to any value of the random variable, x, the cumulative probability of that value of x can be determined. This is demonstrated for the previous example as follows:

$$F(x) = \int_0^x x/8 \; dx.$$

and thus,

$$F(x) = \frac{x^2}{16}.$$

Figure 11.5 is a graph of the cumulative distribution function.

Figure 11.5 Cumulative distribution function for a value of x.

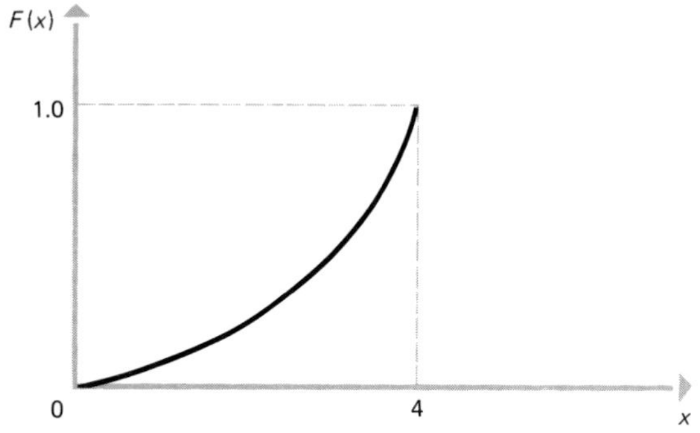

It can be seen that the range of values for the random variable x $(0 \leq x \leq 4)$ coincides with the cumulative probabilities $(0 \leq F(x) \leq 1.0)$. Thus, for any value $F(x)$ in the interval (0, 1), a corresponding value of x can be generated. Recall that in the previous discrete random variable case, we associated various values of x with discrete *ranges* of the cumulative distribution for x. However, in the case of the continuous random variable, the relationship between x and the cumulative distribution for x is described by a continuous function, $F(x)$. Therefore, each cumulative probability value corresponds to a unique value of x.

Therefore, any value of a random number, r, (between 0 and 1) can be translated directly into a value for x using the functional relationship for the cumulative distribution, $F(x)$. Since $F(x)$ is defined over the interval (0,1) and the random number is also defined over the interval (0,1), we can see that

$$r = F(x),$$

and therefore,

$$r = \frac{x^2}{16}$$

Since we wish to obtain a value of the random variable x, given a value for a random number, r, we must first solve the preceding equation for x, in terms of r, shown as follows:

$$x = 4\sqrt{r}$$

This solution for x in terms of r is known as taking the inverse of $F(x)$, denoted by $x = F^{-1}(r)$. Therefore, this approach is referred to as the **inverse transformation technique**.

By generating a random number, r, a value for x is determined by substitution of r into the equation $x = 4\sqrt{r}$. For example, if $r = .25$, $x = 2$. This is also shown on the cumulative distribution function in figure 11.6.

Figure 11.6 Cumulative distribution function for values of r and x.

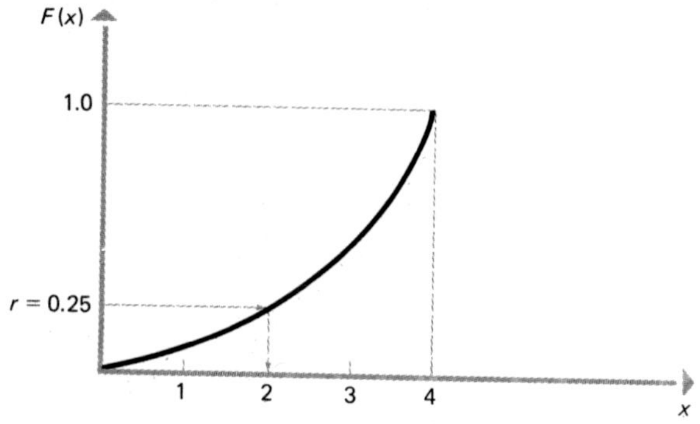

The process generator $x = 4\sqrt{r}$ performs the same function as the ranges for r in our previous discrete examples. The values of x are then used in the simulation model in the same manner as the previous examples.

Example 11.2 A Machine Breakdown Problem

This example is concerned with simulating machine breakdowns in a manufacturing plant. As an input into a model simulating the plant maintenance system, the time intervals between breakdowns must be generated. Based on past experience, it has been determined that a breakdown will occur sometime between four and nine months of operation, according to the distribution shown in figure 11.7.

Figure 11.7 Triangular distribution for machine breakdowns.

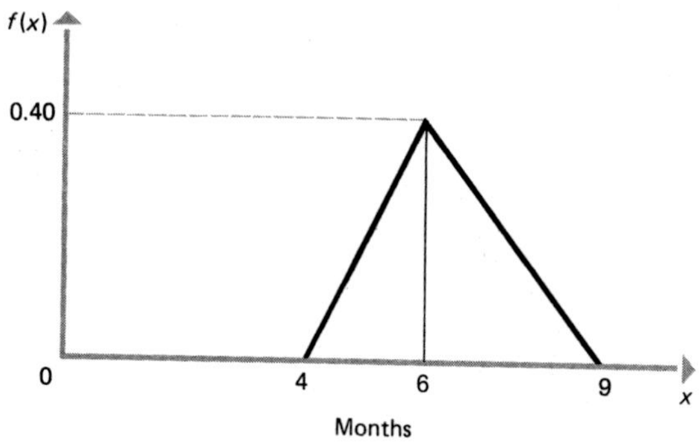

The problem is to develop a process generator to simulate the breakdown occurrences as given by the distribution in figure 11.7 for breakdown times. This distribution is defined by the following functions:

$$f_1(x) = -\frac{4}{5} + \frac{x}{5}, \qquad 4 \leqslant x \leqslant 6$$

$$f_2(x) = \frac{6}{5} - \frac{2x}{15}, \qquad 6 \leqslant x \leqslant 9.$$

Together $f_1(x)$ and $f_2(x)$ represent the probability of occurrence of the random variable x. The total area under the curve is 1.00, which represents the total probability. However, 40% of the area under the curve is defined by $f_1(x)$, while 60% of the area under the curve is defined by $f_2(x)$. (To verify those proportions, simply compute the area of the two triangles forming the distribution.)

The first step is to develop the cumulative distribution functions for $f_1(x)$ and $f_2(x)$.

$$F_1(x) = \int_4^x \left(-\frac{4}{5} + \frac{x}{5}\right) dx$$

$$= \frac{x^2}{10} - \frac{4x}{5} + \frac{8}{5}$$

and

$$F_2(x) = \frac{2}{5} + \int_6^x \left(\frac{6}{5} - \frac{2x}{15}\right) dx,$$

where 2/5, in $F_2(x)$, is the area of the first portion of the triangular distribution, that is the entire area under $F_1(x)$. Thus,

$$F_2(x) = -\frac{x^2}{5} + \frac{6x}{5} - \frac{22}{5}.$$

These two functions form the cumulative distribution illustrated in figure 11.8. Given the cumulative distribution functions $F_1(x)$ and $F_2(x)$, the next step is to set the random number, r, equal to $F(x)$ and then solve for x in terms of r (i.e., the inverse transformation technique). Thus, setting $F_1(x)$ and $F_2(x)$ equal to r, we obtain

$$r = \frac{x^2}{10} - \frac{4x}{5} + \frac{8}{5}, \; 4 \leqslant x \leqslant 6$$

and

$$r = -\frac{x^2}{15} + \frac{6x}{5} - \frac{22}{5}, \; 6 \leqslant x \leqslant 9.$$

Figure 11.8 Cumulative distribution function.

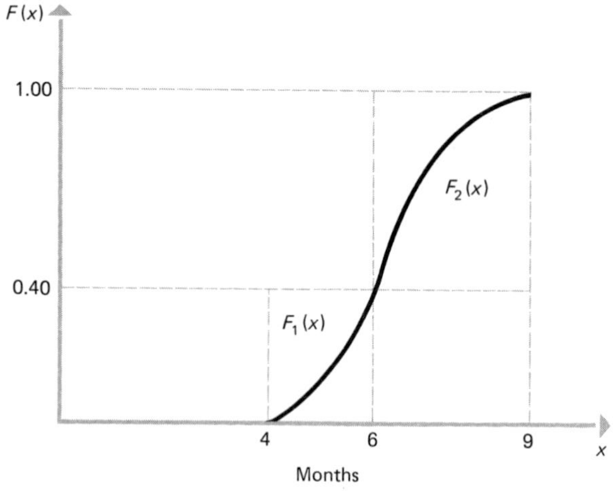

The next step is to solve these equations for x by using the quadratic formula for an equation of the following general form:

$$ax^2 + bx + c$$

and

$$x = \frac{-b \pm \sqrt{b^2 - 4ac}}{2a}$$

Putting the previously developed equations into quadratic form yields

$$0 = \frac{x^2}{10} - \frac{4x}{5} + \frac{8}{5} - r, \; 4 \leq x \leq 6$$

where

$$a = 1/10, \; b = -4/5, \text{ and } c = 8/5 - r,$$

and

$$0 = -\frac{x^2}{15} + \frac{6x}{5} - \frac{22}{5} - r, \; 6 \leq x \leq 9$$

where

$$a = -1/15, \; b = 6/5, \; c = -22/5 - r.$$

Substituting the appropriate values into the quadratic formula yields the inverse functions for x.

$$x = 4 \pm \sqrt{10r}\,, \; 4 \leq x \leq 6$$

and

$$x = 9 \pm \sqrt{15(1-r)}\,, \; 6 \leq x \leq 9$$

This results in four values for x. In the first equation, $x = 4 - \sqrt{10r}$ is infeasible because it represents a value of x less than four months, while in the second equation, $x = 9 + \sqrt{15(1-r)}$ is infeasible because it reflects a value greater than nine months. Thus, the process generators for x are

$$x = 4 + \sqrt{10r} \qquad 0.0 \leq r \leq 0.40, \quad 4 \leq x \leq 6$$

$$x = 9 - \sqrt{15(1-r)} \qquad 0.40 \leq r \leq 1.00, \quad 6 \leq x \leq 9.$$

In order to simulate the time of a breakdown, a random number, r, is selected and substituted into the appropriate equation for x. For example, a random number, $r = 0.30$, falls in the range $0 \leq r \leq 0.40$; so it is substituted into

$$x = 4 + \sqrt{10(.30)}$$

$$x = 5.7 \text{ months}.$$

This example is demonstrated graphically in figure 11.9.

Figure 11.9 Substitution of a random number.

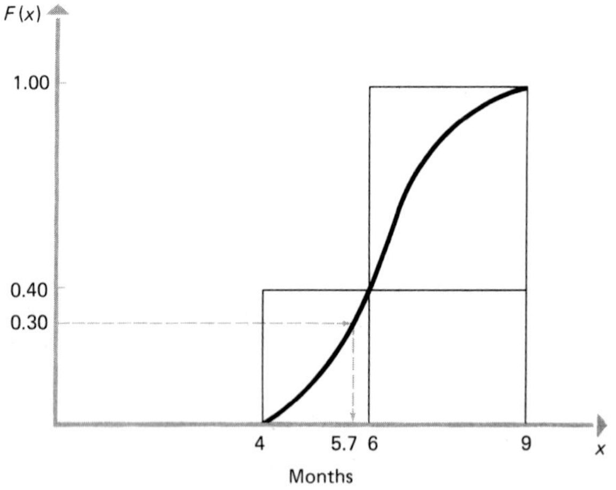

This process generator for determining the times between machine breakdowns can also be used within a larger simulation model; for example, the simulation of an entire plant breakdown and repair system. Once the time that a breakdown occurs is determined from the process generator, a similarly developed process generator for machine repair time can be used to reflect the actual breakdown and repair system. This simulation model could also generate the total annual breakdowns, the average time between breakdowns, the average repair time, the total annual breakdown cost, and the annual production time lost due to breakdowns. Of course, complex simulations such as this are usually performed on a computer.

Additional Inverse Transformations

In many problems that are analyzed via stochastic simulation, the random variables of the model are defined by well-known probability distributions. The inverse function for these distributions can often be developed with little difficulty. Examples of such distributions are the triangular, weibull, uniform, geometric, and exponential distributions. For example, the exponential distribution, often used in the simulation of queueing systems to generate interarrival times, has the following probability function

$$f(x) = \lambda e^{-\lambda x}$$

and the cumulative distribution

$$F(x) = 1 - e^{-\lambda x}.$$

Employing the inverse transformation technique,

$$r = 1 - e^{-\lambda x}$$

and

$$1 - r = e^{-\lambda x}.$$

Since r is uniformly distributed between (0,1), $1 - r$ is also uniformly distributed between (0,1); therefore, r can be substituted for $1 - r$.

$$r = e^{-\lambda x}$$

Solving for x results in the inverse function,

$$x = -\frac{\ln (r)}{\lambda}.$$

For many distributions, the inverse function does not exist or it is so complicated that it cannot be developed. For example, the cumulative function for the normal distribution cannot be developed directly from the probability function. Other distributions such as the often used beta (employed in PERT analysis) and gamma distributions are complex. In such cases, other methods besides the inverse transformation technique can be used. These include the **rejection method,** the **composition method,** and **approximation techniques**. These techniques, which are useful in dealing with more complex simulation models, are of a specialized nature. As such, they are best studied in specialized simulation texts (see references at the end of the chapter).

Random Number Generators

One of the important components of the simulation examples presented in this chapter is the generation of random numbers. Every example model has required random numbers to determine values of random variables. So far, the random numbers we have used have come from the random number table in Appendix D of this text. However, the generation of random numbers is not as simple as it may seem and can have a significant effect on the validity of the model results.

The random numbers in table D.5 were generated using a numerical technique. As such, they are not true random numbers but pseudorandom numbers. True random numbers can only be produced by a physical process such as spinning a roulette wheel. However, it is obvious that a physical process cannot be conveniently employed in a simulation model. Thus, the need exists for artificially created random numbers via a numerical technique.

In order to truly represent the random variables under analysis in the simulation model, the random numbers must have certain characteristics, as follows:

1. The random numbers should have a uniform distribution. This means that each random number in the interval (0, 1) has an equal chance of being selected. If this condition is not present (i.e., the values are not uniform), the simulation experiment will be biased and invalid.
2. The generation of the random numbers should be *efficient*. That is, the process for generating the random numbers should be inexpensive and quick, should recycle only after long periods, and should not degenerate into constant values.
3. The sequence of random numbers should be absent of any pattern. For example, although the sequence of numbers 0, 1, 2, 3, 4, 5, 6, 7, 8, 9, 0, 1, 2, 3, 4, 5, 6, 7, 8, 9, 0, 1, 2, 3, 4, 5, 6, 7, 8, 9, 0, is uniform, it is certainly not random.

In this section, several numerical techniques for generating random numbers will be examined. The first of these, the **mid-square** and **mid-product** methods, are examples of older techniques now considered less satisfactory than more recently developed methods. The last method, the **multiplicative congruential technique,** is considered to be representative of modern methods.

Mid-Square Method

The mid-square method employs a number referred to as a **seed value** to generate a series of random numbers. The seed value is squared, and selected middle digits are used as the random number. This number is then used as the seed value and squared to develop the next random number. For example, if the four-digit number 1,345 is used as the initial seed value, random numbers are generated as follows:

$$(1{,}345)^2 = 1809025, \quad r = 0902$$

$$(\ 0902)^2 = 813604, \quad r = 1{,}360$$

$$(1{,}360)^2 = \text{etc.}$$

The values generated would subsequently be employed as random numbers in the interval (0, 1) by transforming the number to a decimal value by dividing by 10,000. For example, 0902 would become .0902.

The mid-square method is generally unsatisfactory for use in a simulation model for several reasons. First, the method is inefficient because of the amount of time consumed by the many manipulations of the computer in developing the middle digits of the seed value. Second, this method will degenerate when a zero value comes up as the middle four digits. This results in a series of zeros. For these reasons this technique is rarely used at present.

Mid-Product Method

The mid-product method employs the following formula:

$$r_{n+1} = k(r_n)$$

where

r_n = a seed value

k = a constant

r_{n+1} = the middle digits of the product of $k(r_n)$.

For example, if $k = 100$, and $r_0 = 1{,}565$, then

$r_1 = 100(1{,}565) = 156500$

$r_1 = 5{,}650$

$r_2 = 100(565) = 56500$

$r_2 = 650$, etc.

However, this method is also unsatisfactory for the same reasons as the mid-square method (i.e., inefficiency and degeneration), although it does tend to be more uniformly distributed.

Multiplicative Congruential Method

Congruential techniques are the most widely used methods today for generating random numbers. These techniques generate random numbers that are more uniformly distributed than other techniques, and, in general, they are more efficient, requiring less computer time and cost. Also, the sequence of random numbers produced by a congruential technique is reproducible, although the sequence can be made to be quite long before cycling.

The multiplicative congruential method, which is indicative of several congruential techniques, has the following form:

$$r_{n+1} = ar_n (\text{mod } m)$$

In this relationship, a is a constant and r_0 (i.e., $n = 0$) is a seed number. The term *modulo m* (or mod m) means that the product of $a \times r_n$ is divided by m and the remainder is the random number r_{n+1}. For the best results, the parameters of this relationship should be selected according to the following conditions:

$$a = 8t \pm 3$$
$$t = \text{a positive integer}$$
$$r_0 = \text{an odd integer}$$
$$m = 2^b$$
$$a \simeq 2^{b/2}$$

Given these conditions, a series of 2^{b-2} random numbers will be generated before cycling.

Consider the following example employing the multiplicative congruential technique. The first step is to determine the values a and m. To compute m, a value, $b = 4$, is selected arbitrarily. Thus,

$$m = 2^b = 2^4$$

$$m = 16.$$

To compute a, t is arbitrarily assigned a value of 1.

$$a = 8t \pm 3$$

$$a = 8(1) \pm 3$$

$$a = 11, 5$$

However, $a \cong 2^{b/2}$, or $a \cong 4$. As such, the exact value of a is set at 5 since it is closer to the approximate value of 4 than the value $a = 11$. The period for this sequence is 2^{b-2}, or 4. This means that a sequence of four random numbers will be produced before the same sequence is repeated. Selecting $r_0 = 7$ (an odd positive integer) as the seed value produces the following sequence of random numbers,

$$r_{n+1} = ar_n(\text{mod } m)$$

$$\left.\begin{aligned} r_1 &= (5)(7)(\text{mod } 16) = 3 \\ r_2 &= (5)(3)(\text{mod } 16) = 15 \\ r_3 &= (5)(15)(\text{mod } 16) = 11 \\ r_4 &= (5)(11)(\text{mod } 16) = 7 \\ r_4 &= r_0 = 7 \end{aligned}\right\} \text{sequence of random numbers}$$

Notice that four random values were generated before the sequence started to repeat itself with the value of 7 again. This is obviously too short a sequence for use in a realistic simulation model. However, if the value of b is increased to 21, over a million random numbers can be produced prior to cycling.

The ability to exactly reproduce a random number sequence is not detrimental to simulation but is, in fact, useful. It enables a simulation experiment to be repeated with the same random numbers, which facilitates comparison of experimental results for several simulations.

Testing Random Numbers for Uniformity

The reliability of a simulation model in representing the system under analysis is at least partially dependent on whether the random numbers employed are, in fact, uniform. If the generated distribution of a model random variable is statistically incorrect, it could be a result of a deficiency in the technique used to generate random numbers. To ascertain whether the random numbers produced by a generator are uniform (i.e., statistically correct), several tests are available. One of the most popular techniques for testing the uniformity of random numbers, the chi-square test, will be presented here. However, it should be kept in mind that several other statistical tests are available for testing uniformity, as well as the other elements associated with the generation of random numbers.

The chi-square test statistic is

$$\chi^2 = \sum_{i=1}^{n} \frac{(O_i - E_i)^2}{E_i}$$

where

O_i = the observed values in the ith frequency class

E_i = the expected number of observations in each i class (i.e., the total number of observed values/n)

n = the total number of frequency class ranges.

The χ^2 test is conducted in the following manner. The total number of random numbers is divided into n equal frequency class ranges. The total number of observations within each range is then compared with the uniform expected number of values. For example, consider a batch of 200 random numbers. The random values are from 0 to 99 and are divided into ranges of interval 10 (i.e., 0–9, 10–19, 20–29, . . . , 90–99). Next, the random values are subdivided into the appropriate intervals. The number of generated values in each class i, O_i, is then compared to E_i, the expected number of observations in each class. If there are 200 total values and each value appears with equal frequency (i.e., they are uniform), then E_i = 200/10 = 20. These values are then substituted in the χ^2 test statistic. The following chi-square table demonstrates the computation of the χ^2 statistic for the hypothetical frequency of random numbers given under O_i:

Frequency Class Range i	Frequency (O_i)	E_i	$(O_i - E_i)$	$(O_i - E_i)^2$	$\frac{(O_i - E_i)^2}{E_i}$
0– 9	18	20	−2	4	.20
10–19	21	20	1	1	.05
20–29	19	20	−1	1	.05
30–39	20	20	0	0	0
40–49	22	20	2	4	.20
50–59	17	20	−3	9	.45
60–69	16	20	−4	16	.80
70–79	22	20	2	4	.20
80–89	21	20	1	1	.05
90–99	19	20	1	1	.05
					$\Sigma = 2.05$

Thus,

$$\chi^2 = \frac{\Sigma(O_i - E_i)^2}{E_i}$$

$$\chi^2 = 2.05.$$

This χ^2 computed statistic is compared to a critical value, $\chi^2_{\alpha,\ n-1}$ for a level of significance, α, and $n - 1$ degrees of freedom. For $\alpha = .05$ and nine degrees of freedom (i.e., $10 - 1 = 9$),

$$\chi^2_{.05,(9)} = 16.916 \text{ (from table D.6).}$$

Since $\chi^2_{.05,(9)} = 16.916 > \chi^2 = 2.05$, it can be concluded that the test reveals that the values are random at a level of significance of $\alpha = .05$. Other statistical tests for determining randomness include the Kolmogorov-Smirnov, gap, series, and poker tests.

Optimization in Simulation Models

Simulation is a management science tool that does not usually generate an optimal solution to a problem. Instead, a simulation model reflects the operation of a system in a compressed time frame. Although the results of the simulation represent the state of a system, the results should not be considered optimal in the same sense as the solution to a linear programming problem.

However, quasi-optimal solutions can be obtained for simulation models by employing **search techniques.** In other words, a set of different results to a simulation model are "searched" until the best result is found. Optimization in this manner requires a series of simulation runs, each with predetermined changes made in the decision variables.

As an example, consider the simulation of an inventory system. Management wishes to determine the optimal combination of order quantity, Q, and reorder point, R. Simulation is desirable as a mode of analysis because both lead time and demand per week are often random variables. The search process requires predefined values of Q and R to be set for each run and the results of the different runs compared. For example, in one particular simulation run, the inventory system was simulated with $Q = 5$ and $R = 3$. The results of the run yielded a total average inventory cost of $250. This value reflects one simulation run and is considered as one entry in the following lattice (or grid) of values.

		Q				
		1	2	3	4	5
R	1					
	2					
	3					$250
	4					

Nineteen other runs are required to complete the lattice for all combinations of R and Q. The minimum lattice entry is the quasi-optimal solution for the values of Q and R considered. The obvious difficulties with a search procedure like this is that for a complex problem with numerous variables, the lattice can become quite large and result in excessive computer time and cost. Also, the values for the decision variables considered may not include the optimal values.

Construction of the Simulation Model

The essential and probably most difficult aspects of Monte Carlo simulation have been presented. Beyond the generation of the process inputs to the model, it is a matter of developing the logical relationships for the model of the system. Most of the preceding chapters of this text have dealt with this topic to some extent.

However, since most simulation models are "run" on computers, the form of the model may consist of mathematically intractable statements or logical relationships that preclude a closed form analytical solution. The model may consist of submodels or components linked together by a logical relationship. The logical relationships are generally represented by the use of flowcharts or diagrams.

In order to demonstrate the development of a complete simulation model, consider the following drive-in teller window example. The model to be simulated is a single-channel, single-phase queueing system. Times between customer arrivals are randomly generated according to a negative exponential probability distribution, with a mean of 3 (minutes). Service times are also generated randomly according to a negative exponential probability distribution, with a mean of 2 (minutes). The analytical presentation of this queueing example is contained in chapter 10.

The logic for the model of this system is illustrated in the flow diagram of figure 11.10. The development of the model can be completed by defining all the system variables and parameters and specifying explicitly the relationships described in each block. For example, if time between arrivals is defined as the variable *TBA* and arrival time is defined as *ARIV*, then the relationship of the third block would be $ARIV_n = TBA + ARIV_{n-1}$.

Figure 11.10 Flow diagram for simulation model of drive-in bank problem.

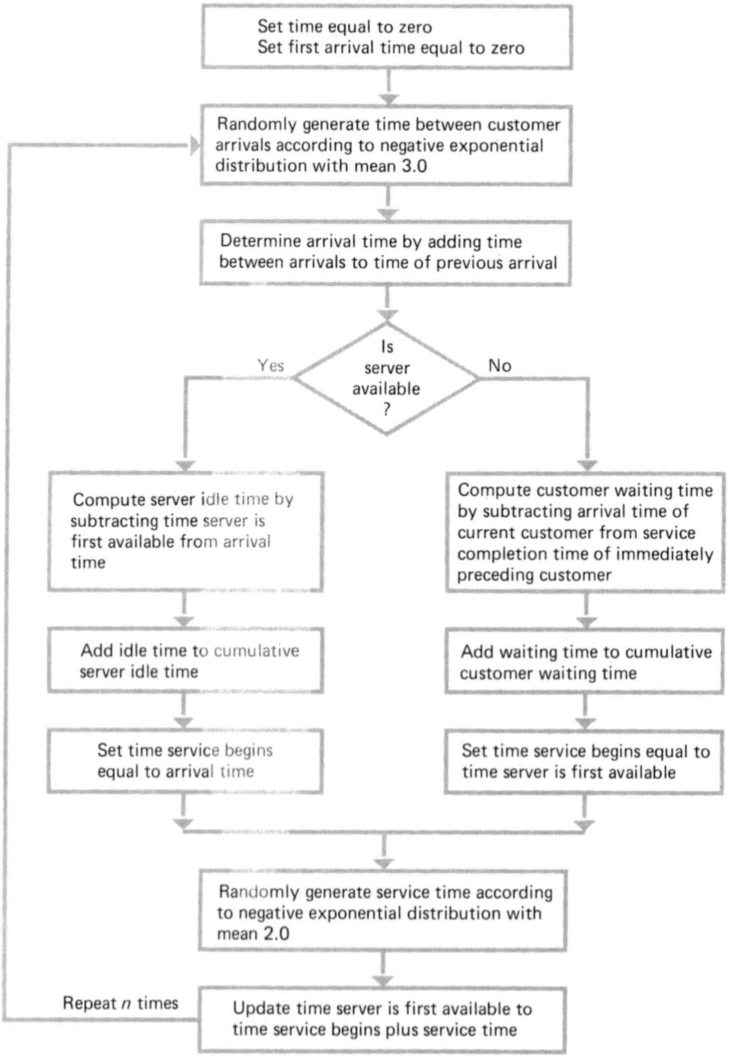

Most of the relationships to be developed for each diagram block are evident. The decision block (diamond) relationship is developed by comparing the customer arrival time to the time the server first becomes available. If the arrival (clock) time is prior to the (clock) time the server becomes available, the program branches to the right. Branching to the left occurs for the reverse time relationship. If the two times are equal, the program can be written to branch either way (the idle time and waiting time are zero).

After the relationships of each block are developed, the model is converted to computer code (a computer program). An advantage of computer simulation is the facility to include decision blocks (e.g., "Is server available?"). We also note that the relationships of each individual diagram block are relatively simple. However, the overall logic of the model may be quite complex when all the relationships are tied together. The individual relationships are tied together by the sequencing of the computer program statements.

Note that even though figure 11.10 represents a very simple simulation model, it includes the interaction of two probability distributions (time between customer arrivals and service times). When random variables are included in any model, regardless of the simplicity of the remaining model, the model becomes quite difficult to solve analytically.

Functions of the Constructed Simulation Model

The simulation model must perform several functions. The several functions are given as follows:

Random Variable Generation

The example shown in figure 11.10 includes two blocks in which the times between arrivals and the service times are randomly generated. In this case, they are generated from negative exponential probability distributions. The advantage of generating the random variable values from this theoretical probability distribution (versus an empirical distribution) is demonstrated by the fact that only a single statement is required in the program to perform this function.

Event Control

The flow diagram in figure 11.10 represents the flow of events. The logic of the program controls the sequence of events. Note that a key variable of the control feature is the time the server is first available. The program compares the arrival time to this control variable to determine the program branching and, thus, the flow of events.

System State Initialization

The status of the system must be defined initially. The first block of the flow diagram performs this function for our example.

System Performance Data Collection

Note that the diagram of figure 11.10 includes blocks that collect the cumulative server idle time and the cumulative customer waiting time. These are, of course, only two system descriptors that might be collected.

Statistical Computations and Report Generation

A final computation of the operational statistics is not shown in figure 11.10; however, this function occurs after the model has been simulated for the desired length of time (or alternatively for the desired number of customer arrivals). At the end of a simulation run of the simulation program, the program branches to the final portion of the program, which computes operating statistics and prints them out. For example, the cumulative idle time can be divided by the total time the system is simulated to yield the percentage server idle time, and the cumulative waiting time can be divided by the total number of customers to yield the mean waiting time per customer. Other statistics relating to system performance can also be collected and printed out, such as the standard deviation, range, median, and frequency distribution for the measured variable. A major advantage of simulation is its capability to collect and provide many different forms of statistical output.

Validation of the Model

A major difficulty of simulation is the validation of the model and the model results. The user of simulation generally wants to be certain that the model is internally correct in a programming sense—are the various operations performed in a logical and mathematically correct fashion? Does the model actually represent the real-world system being simulated? The old adage "garbage in, garbage out" is especially relevant for simulation. In order to gain some assurances about the validity of a simulation model, several testing procedures have been developed.

First, the model can be run several times for short periods of time or a few operations. This allows the simulation results to be compared with manually derived solutions for discrepancies. Another means of testing is to break the model into smaller components and run them separately. This reduces the complexity involved in seeking out errors in the model. In a similar vein, relationships in the model can be made less complex for testing purposes. For example, stochastic functions can be transformed to deterministic relationships and then tested.

In order to determine if the model reliably represents the system being simulated, the model results can be compared with real-world data. Several statistical tests exist for performing this type of statistical analysis. However, when a model is developed to simulate a new or unique system, there is no realistic way to insure that the results reflect the real system.

Other difficulties arising from the validation of simulation models concern the statistical properties of the results. As previously noted, simulation over time can yield output containing covariance. Techniques for analyzing the statistical properties of simulation results containing covariance are quite sophisticated. This highlights the fact that real-world simulation not only requires expertise in model construction but also a considerable degree of competence in statistical analysis.

Several tactical problems also exist in determining if the simulation model is a valid representation of the system being analyzed. One of these problems relates to starting conditions. Should the system be simulated by assuming the system is empty (i.e., starting a queueing facility with no customers in line) or should an attempt be made to establish the simulation so it will be as close as possible to normal operating conditions at the beginning of a run? Another tactical problem is the determination of how long the simulation should be run in order to reach a steady-state condition, if indeed a steady state exists. Studies have shown that simulation often requires a surprisingly long time to reach steady-state conditions. If steady state is not reached, simulation output in the form of averages will not be meaningful.

These factors represent only some of the difficulties that can be encountered in validating a simulation model. In most cases, a standard, foolproof procedure for validation is simply not possible. In the long run, the confidence placed in a simulation model often must be based on the insight and experience of the simulation user.

Simulation Languages

The computer programming aspects of simulation can be quite complex. Fortunately, generalized simulation languages have been developed to perform many of the functions of a simulation study. In fact, use of these languages requires only limited knowledge of a scientific or business-oriented programming language. In this section, several of the best known and most readily available simulation languages, **GPSS, DYNAMO, GASP IV,** and **SIMSCRIPT,** will be described.

GPSS

GPSS (General Purpose Systems Simulation) was originally developed in the early 1960s for the IBM Corporation by Gordon. GPSS III, the third version of the language, is a two-part program requiring the use of its own compiler. The first part is an assembly program that converts the system descriptors into input for the second part, which performs the actual simulation.

GPSS does not require program writing in the usual sense. The system model is constructed via block diagrams using GPSS-generated block commands that represent operational functions of the system. GPSS is oriented to transactions moving in time through a system made up primarily of facilities, queues, and storages. As such, GPSS is very compatible to queueing and network problems. The use of a GPSS program does not require any previous knowledge of computer programming.

DYNAMO

DYNAMO was created at M.I.T. in 1959 by Fox and Pugh as an outgrowth of the *Industrial Dynamics* modeling approach developed by Forrester for the analysis of the aggregate behavior of large-scale industrial systems. DYNAMO is a computer program that uses a model in the form of a set of equations describing the system as input. Then, the behavior of the system is simulated by evaluating the equations continuously for each time increment. DYNAMO emphasizes information feedback and delays in the large-scale system under analysis. It has been effectively employed in econometric modeling and simulating industrial complexes, in addition to urban, social, and world systems planning. Like GPSS, DYNAMO requires little or no prior programming knowledge for use.

GASP IV

GASP IV, developed by Pritsker and Hurst in 1973, is a successor to the GASP II language, which was an entirely discrete change (next event) language. The GASP II language was an outgrowth of the original work done by Kiviat at U.S. Steel Corporation. The primary difference between GASP II and GASP IV is the addition of the capability for continuous simulation combined with the original discrete capabilities.

Whereas GASP II is a discrete next event change language (i.e., the dependent variables of the model change discretely at simulated time points) and DYNAMO is a continuous change simulator (i.e., the dependent variables change continuously over time), GASP IV has the unique capability to perform a combination of both discrete and continuous changes in the same simulation. Thus, not only the more traditional discrete simulation of business problems, such as queueing, inventory, and production, but also the Forrester (systems dynamics) type models, may be simulated with GASP IV. This simulation language requires a knowledge of FORTRAN computer programming.

GASP IV is written entirely in FORTRAN IV and can be used on any computer with a FORTRAN compiler, a unique and attractive feature for a simulation language. Because GASP IV is made up of separate FORTRAN subroutines that perform each of the different simulation functions, GASP IV can be modified by a programmer to accommodate desired features not included in the program.

SIMSCRIPT

SIMSCRIPT was developed at the RAND Corporation in the early 1960s as a complete programming language. Although it was originally designed for simulation analysis, it can be used as a general purpose language. SIMSCRIPT requires its own special compiler and is available only on certain computer systems. Unlike GPSS and DYNAMO, SIMSCRIPT requires a knowledge of computer programming, particularly FORTRAN, on which SIMSCRIPT is based.

SIMSCRIPT defines the system to be simulated in terms of (1) *entities,* the components that make up the system; (2) *attributes* of the entities and the system, which are the properties associated with entities; and (3) *sets,* or groups of entities. In SIMSCRIPT, the status of the system is unchanged except at points in time called *event times*. As such, the system is described in terms of two types of events: *exogenous* events (those created outside the simulation framework) and *endogenous* events (those generated internally). Each event desired for the simulation model requires the construction of an event subroutine.

Recently the SIMSCRIPT language has been extended to include discrete continuous model capabilities as does GASP IV. SIMULA, a language that compiles in ALGOL and is widely used in Europe, is similar to SIMSCRIPT.

Applications of Simulation

Simulation can be applied to any problem too difficult to model and solve analytically. Some management scientists have noted that any complex real-world problem should first be modeled and solved analytically, even if simplifying assumptions must be introduced, in order to gain an intuitive feel for the model and system and to insure the validity of the model. This should be followed up by the formulation of a complete simulation model that includes all system complexities, to provide the final basis for analysis and decision making.

Simulation has been applied to an extremely wide range of problems. A few of the more prominent examples in the field of business are discussed in the following paragraphs.

Queueing

A major area of application for simulation has been in the analysis of waiting line problems. As indicated in chapter 10, the assumptions required for analytic solution of queueing problems are quite restrictive. With few exceptions, simulation is the only available approach for considering such problems as multiple-phase queueing systems.

Inventory Control

In chapter 7, the case was introduced where inventory demand per day, during a constant lead time, was described as a random variable. However, in the case where both demand per day and the lead time are random variables, the analysis becomes extremely difficult to accomplish by any means other than simulation. In addition, an inventory system might include the case where both the number of demands received per day and the size of each demand are random variables. This then creates a joint probability distribution for demand during lead time, a random variable, which is a function of three random variables, that could be analyzed only by simulation.

Networks

The PERT network includes the case where activity times are represented by the beta probability distribution. However, the analytical PERT solution does yield slightly biased results. This has been shown by simulating the network. Also, the PERT approach is limited to the beta probability distribution. If it is shown from empirical data that the activity times follow some other distribution, the network could be analyzed with simulation.

In PERT, all activities are assumed to occur with a probability of one. A completely self-contained computer program, called GERT IIIZ, has been developed that can simulate networks that include not only probabilistic activity times but also probabilistic branching—that is, the probability that an activity will occur may be less than one. The GERT IIIZ simulator also allows other non-PERT features, such as looping of activities back to intermediate events and multiple logic concerning event realization. Another self-contained computer program, called Q-GERT, which was developed by Pritsker, includes not only the GERT IIIZ capabilities but also special queue nodes that allow the user to analyze networks of queues.

Production

Various problems in production have been simulated, such as scheduling, sequencing, line balancing, plant layout, and plant location analysis. It is surprising how often various production problems can be viewed as queueing processes, and we have indicated the applicability of simulation to queueing problems. This is one reason for the popularity of using a queueing example to illustrate simulation.

Maintenance

Since machine breakdowns and facility failures typically occur according to some probability distribution, such problems are most generally analyzed by simulation. However, much analytical work has also been done in this area. Simulation, in conjunction with analytical methods, provides a powerful means for studying such problems.

Finance

Capital budgeting finance problems include estimates of cash flows. These cash flows are often composite results of many random variables. Simulation has been used to generate values of the various random variables in order to derive estimates of cash flows. A classic article by Hertz in 1964 illustrated the use of simulation for randomly generating the inputs into a rate of return calculation. The contributing inputs included such random variables as market size, selling price, growth rate, and market share.

Marketing

Marketing problems typically involve a great deal of uncertainty. Simulation provides the opportunity for a marketing strategist to experiment with alternative courses of action, when faced with a large number of interacting and widely varying random components. In addition, simulation can provide the marketing strategist with insights into the operation of the market under consideration. An example of a possible application of simulation in the marketing environment is contract bidding. Simulation allows the contractor to evaluate various alternative courses of action.

Public Service Operations

Recently the operations of police departments, fire departments, post offices, hospitals, court systems, airports, and other public systems have been analyzed by simulation. Typically, such operations are so complex that no other technique can be used to successfully analyze the overall system.

Environmental and Resource Conservation

Some of the more recent and innovative applications of simulation have been concerned with the effects of technology on the environment and natural resources. Highly complex models have been developed to ascertain the environmental effects of such projects as nuclear power plants, reservoirs, highways, and dams. In many cases, these simulation models include cost trade-offs to measure the financial feasibility of such projects. Similar models have been developed to simulate air, water, and noise pollution conditions. Other recent developments include the simulation of energy systems to determine the financial and environmental feasibility of capital projects. Such simulation models are quite important to the business community since these factors are becoming an increasing part of the business environment.

Summary

Simulation has become an increasingly important tool of analysis in recent years. Numerous surveys have shown simulation to be one of the most widely applied management science tools presently available. Evidence of this popularity is the number of specialized simulation languages that have been developed by industry and academia to deal with specific complex problem areas.

The popularity of simulation is due in large part to the flexibility it allows in analyzing systems, as opposed to more confining analytical methods. In other words, the problem does not have to fit the model or technique; instead, the model is developed to fit the problem. This inherent flexibility of simulation also makes it an excellent tool for experimenting on systems and problems in a laboratory-type atmosphere.

However, in spite of the versatility of the simulation technique, it must still be used with caution. The validation of the model and its subsequent results can be tedious and often impossible. The cost of model building and analysis can also be expensive and time consuming. This problem has become an area of such concern that output analysis of simulation results is developing into a new field in itself.

References

Forrester, J. *Industrial Dynamics*. Cambridge, Mass.: MIT Press, 1961.

Hammersly, J. M., and Handscomb, D. C. *Monte Carlo Methods*. New York: John Wiley & Sons, 1964.

Hertz, D. B. "Risk Analysis in Capital Investment," *Harvard Busines Review* 42 (1964): 95–106.

Markowitz, H. M.; Karr, H. W.; and Hausner, B. *SIMSCRIPT: A Simulation Programming Language*. Englewood Cliffs, New Jersey: Prentice-Hall, 1963.

Meier, R. C.; Newell, W. T.; and Pazer, H. L. *Simulation in Business and Economics*. Englewood Cliffs, New Jersey: Prentice-Hall, 1969.

Mize, J., and Cox, G. *Essentials of Simulation*. Englewood Cliffs, New Jersey: Prentice-Hall, 1968.

Moore, L. J., and Clayton, E. R. *GERT Modeling and Simulation: Fundamentals and Applications*. New York: Petrocelli/Charter, 1976.

Naylor, T. H.; Balintfy, J. L.; Burdick, D. S.; and Chu, K. *Computer Simulation Techniques*. New York: John Wiley & Sons, 1966.

Phillips, D. T.; Ravindran, A.; and Solberg, J. *Operations Research*. New York: John Wiley & Sons, 1976.

Pritsker, A. A. B. *Modeling and Analysis Using Q-GERT Networks*. 2d ed. New York: John Wiley & Sons, 1977.

Pritsker, A. A. B. *The GASP IV Simulation Language*. New York: John Wiley & Sons, 1974.

Pugh, A. L. *DYNAMO II User's Manual*. Cambridge, Mass.: MIT Press, 1970.

Schriber, T. S. *Simulation Using GPSS*. New York: John Wiley & Sons, 1974.

Tocher, K. D. "Review of Computer Simulation." *Operational Research Quarterly* 16 (1965): 189–217.

Van Horne, R. L. "Validation of Simulation Results." *Management Science* 17 (1971): 247–57.

Wyman, F. P. *Simulation Modeling: A Guide to Using SIMSCRIPT*. New York: John Wiley & Sons, 1970.

Problems

1. The time between arrivals at a service station pump is defined by the following probability distribution:

Time Between Arrivals (min.)	Probability
1	0.15
2	0.30
3	0.40
4	0.15
	1.00

Simulate the arrival of cars at the service station for twenty arrivals. Compute the mean time between arrivals and compare this with the expected value of the time between arrivals.

2. A retail firm has an inventory policy that requires an order size of five units and a reorder point of three units. Inventory-related costs include a holding cost of $4 per unit per period, an order cost of $10 per order, and a shortage (or stockout) cost of $40 for an unfilled order (i.e., partially filled). Units are not backordered. The following frequency distribution for demand was compiled for a fifty-week period.

Demand/week (units)	Frequency
0	2
1	4
2	14
3	20
4	8
5	1
6	1
	50

Lead time (the time until delivery of an order) has the following frequency distribution:

Lead Time (weeks)	Frequency
1	6
2	3
3	1
	10

The firm has a beginning inventory balance of five units. All orders are received at the beginning of the week.

a. Develop a simulation experiment to replicate this firm's inventory policy. Simulate for twenty weeks (using the random number table).
b. This simulation experiment reflects one order size and one reorder point. Explain how a simulation model could be designed to determine the optimal (lowest average cost) inventory policy.

3. A bank is attempting to determine if it should install one or two drive-in teller windows. The following probability distributions regarding arrival intervals and service times have been developed from historical data:

Time Between Arrivals (min.)	Probability
1	0.20
2	0.60
3	0.10
4	0.10
	1.00

Service Time (min.)	Probability
2	0.10
3	0.40
4	0.20
5	0.20
6	0.10
	1.00

In the two-server system, assume that a car will always join the shortest queue. When the queues are of equal length there is a .5 probability the driver will enter either queue.

a. Develop a simulation experiment based on a thirty-minute arrival period for both the one- and two-teller systems. Compute the average queue length, waiting time, and percentage utilization of each system.
b. Discuss the best system to install.

4. The time between arrivals of oil tankers at an unloading dock is given by the following probability distribution:

Time Between Ship Arrivals (days)	Probability
1	0.05
2	0.10
3	0.20
4	0.30
5	0.20
6	0.10
7	0.05
	1.00

a. Generate randomly the time between arrivals for the first twenty ships.
b. Compute the relative frequency of the times between arrivals in part (a). Compare these simulated results with the actual probability distribution. What is the difference between the two a result of?
c. Assume that the time to unload, clean, and prepare a ship for departure is five days. Develop a simulation experiment for the movement of ships to and away from the unloading dock. (Note, only one ship can be serviced at a time). Compute the mean time between arrivals, mean waiting time for unloading, mean number waiting to unload, mean time ships are waiting and unloading, mean number of ships waiting and being unloaded, proportion of arrivals entering an empty system, and the frequency distribution of number of ships waiting.
d. Now assume that the time required to unload, clean, and prepare ships is a random variable defined by the following distribution:

Time to Unload, Clean, Prepare (days)	Probability
3	0.10
4	0.20
5	0.40
6	0.30

e. Repeat part (c) for this condition.

5. An inventory manager for a firm wants to determine the mean demand for a particular product in stock during the reorder lead time. This information is needed to determine how far in advance to reorder before the stock level is reduced to zero. Both demand and lead time are random variables defined by the following probability distributions:

Lead Time (days)	Probability	Demand Per Day	Probability
1	0.5	1	0.1
2	0.3	2	0.3
3	0.2	3	0.4
		4	0.2

Simulate this problem for thirty reorders to estimate the mean demand during lead time.

6. Given the following continuous probability distribution,

$$f(x) = \frac{x}{6}, \ 0 \leq x \leq 8,$$

develop a process generator using the inverse transformation technique.

7. Given the following continuous triangular probability distribution, develop a process generator using the inverse transformation technique.

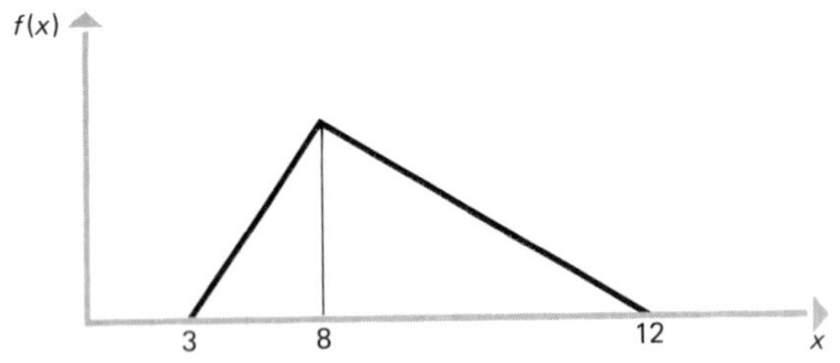

8. Given the following uniform distribution, develop a process generator using the inverse transformation technique.

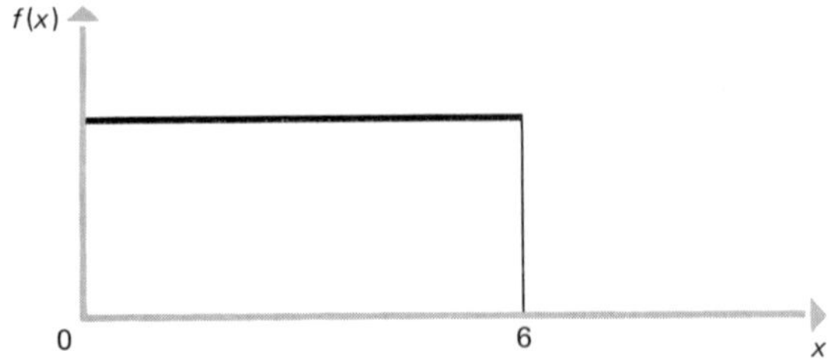

9. A job shop manager wants to develop a simulation model to schedule jobs through the shop. Part of the simulation model is a process generator for machine time for each job on each machine. The shop manager has estimated that the time for *one particular* job on one machine follows a triangular distribution.

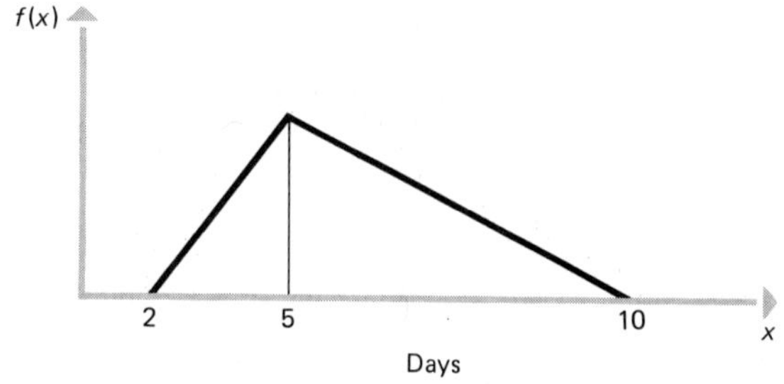

Develop a process generator for this machine time using the inverse transformation technique that could be used in the simulation model.

10. A manufacturing firm has determined that its maintenance schedule is reflected by the following probability distribution:

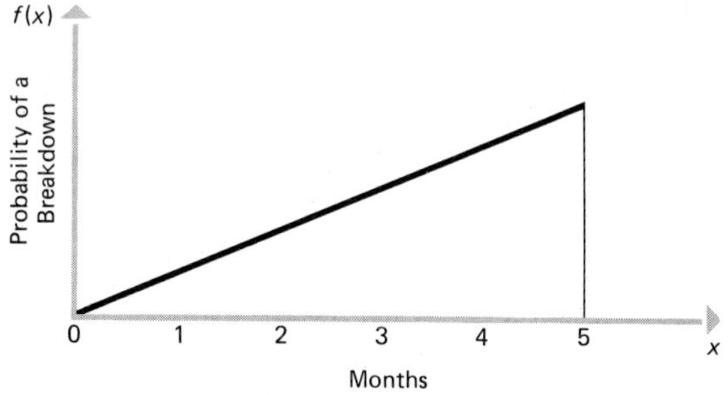

This distribution represents the time between breakdowns (i.e., machine run time). Every time a machine breaks down it requires time for repair according to the following probability distribution:

Repair Time (days)	Probability
1	.40
2	.30
3	.30
	1.00

Conduct a simulation experiment to replicate the firm's maintenance schedule for thirty-six months. Compute the average repair time and compare with the expected repair time.

11. Interarrival times of customers at a service facility are exponentially distributed with $\lambda = 20$/hour. Develop a process generator for this function and generate ten interarrival times.

12. Given a seed value of 1,776, compute a stream of five, four-digit random numbers using the mid-square method.

13. Given a seed value of 2,896 and a constant, $k = 100$, compute a stream of five random numbers using the mid-product method.

14. Given a seed value of 15, $b = 6$, and $t = 2$, develop a sequence of m random numbers using the multiplicative congruential method.

15. Perform a chi-square test on the random numbers developed in problem 14 to determine if they are uniform.

Part 5

Advanced Topics in Mathematical Programming

12

Dynamic Programming

Most of the topics presented in this text describe techniques in which the entire problem is solved with a *single* assault; that is, the variables of the problem are dealt with *simultaneously* or collectively. An exception is decision tree analysis in chapter 8 in which the branches and nodes of the network tree represent a sequence of decision alternatives, states of nature (with associated probabilities), and expected payoffs associated with the various combinations of decisions and states. **Dynamic programming** is closely akin to decision tree analysis in that problems are broken down (decomposed) into smaller components (subproblems or stages) where decisions are made sequentially. For this reason, dynamic programming is often referred to as a *multistage* decision process. Dynamic programming considers problems in which the outcome of a decision at one stage affects the subsequent decision and results at the next stage. Thus, each subproblem, which may change from stage to stage, is a function of prior stage decisions. Of course, if the stages are independent of one another, each stage can be solved separately and the results aggregated.

The innovator and person primarily responsible for popularizing dynamic programming is Richard Bellman. Bellman's work on dynamic programming dates back to the late 1940s and early 1950s, culminating in his classic text, *Dynamic Programming*. Unlike many of the previously presented techniques, dynamic programming does not involve a single problem-solving method (or algorithm), such as the simplex method for linear programming problems. Dynamic programming makes use of many available techniques, to solve stage subproblems.

As a concept, dynamic programming is more flexible than most mathematical models and methods in management science. Important applications of dynamic programming have been reported to solve problems in inventory control, network flows, job shop scheduling, production control, replacement and maintenance, sales planning, workforce scheduling, general resource allocation problems, and numerous others. This chapter will first present the fundamental concepts of dynamic programming, followed by a number of prototype problems and examples to illustrate model formulation and solution procedures.

Fundamental Concepts of Dynamic Programming

Dynamic programming includes several interrelated concepts that can be rather confusing when considered simultaneously. However, by studying each of the fundamental concepts individually, the overall modeling and solution approach to dynamic programming can be learned with a minimum of confusion. The purpose of this section is to present and illustrate each of the several concepts separately. It is interesting to note that the approach of studying the concepts of dynamic programming individually reflects the first basic concept of dynamic programming—**decomposition** of the problem into subcomponents for analysis.

Decomposition

The first concept fundamental to the dynamic programming approach to problem modeling and analysis is the subdivision of the problem into a sequence of smaller subproblems. Each subproblem is referred to as a stage or decision point. Because a problem can often be evaluated more easily and efficiently by stages explains why dynamic programming is frequently referred to as a multistage or sequential decision process.

The concept of problem decomposition into a sequence of stages, or subproblems, is illustrated abstractly in figure 12.1. In this illustration, it is assumed that a given problem can be subdivided into three stages. The basis for determining how to decompose a problem into stages will be presented later in this chapter.

Figure 12.1 Problem decomposition into a sequence of stages.

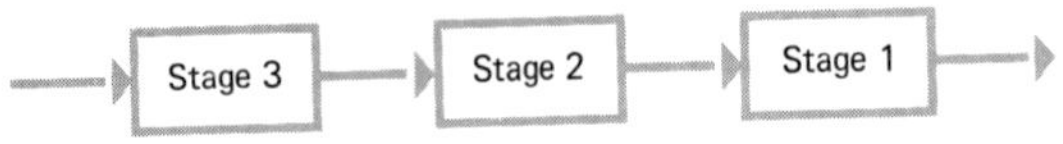

The reader should note that (1) the stages are connected by arrows flowing from left to right and that (2) the stages are numbered sequentially from right to left. Each of these features is related to separate concepts, to be presented shortly. For our present needs, it is sufficient to know that (1) the arrows are the *linkage*, or *connection*, between problem stages and they generally represent "information flow" about the current status of the system and that (2) the stages are numbered in reverse order, from right to left, to coincide with the problem solution sequence.

Suppose, for example, that a corporation owns plants in Atlanta, Baltimore, and Chicago (plants A, B, and C, respectively). The corporation has budgeted a total of $5 million for plant improvements to be allocated among the three plants during the coming fiscal year. The problem is to determine the portion of the $5 million capital to invest at each of the plants in order to maximize returns.

Dynamic programming will be used to solve this problem. The overall problem can be logically broken into three subproblems, or decision points, representing how much to invest in plant *A*, plant *B*, and plant *C*. Decomposition of the problem into three stages is shown in figure 12.2. It should be pointed out that the designation of the plant *A* investment problem as stage 3, plant *B* as stage 2, and plant *C* as stage 1 is arbitrary and that *any* assignment of the plants to the three stages is acceptable.

Figure 12.2 Decomposition of plant investment problem into three stages.

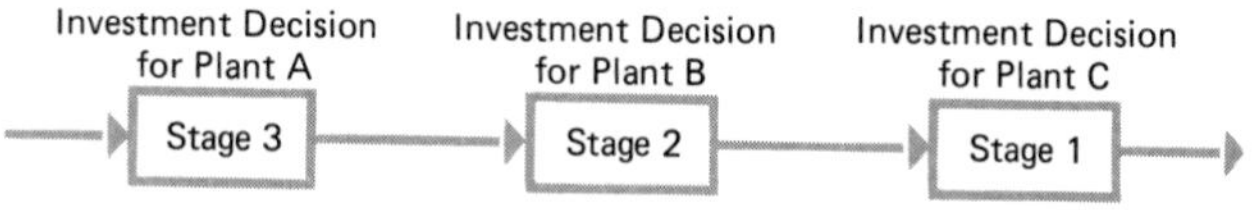

Suppose that the corporate problem is alternatively defined as how much to invest at a single plant over the three-year planning period of 1980, 1981, and 1982. The decomposition of this problem into stages is shown in figure 12.3. In this problem, the designation of years corresponding to stages should proceed from left to right, corresponding to the flow direction of the arrows. This is because the arrows represent information regarding the remaining amount of capital available for investment at each decision point (stage). Obviously, the first investment will be in 1980, and the second investment in 1981 will depend upon how much capital is left from the 1980 decision, and so on.

Figure 12.3 Decomposition of a single plant investment problem into three stages, based on a three-year planning period.

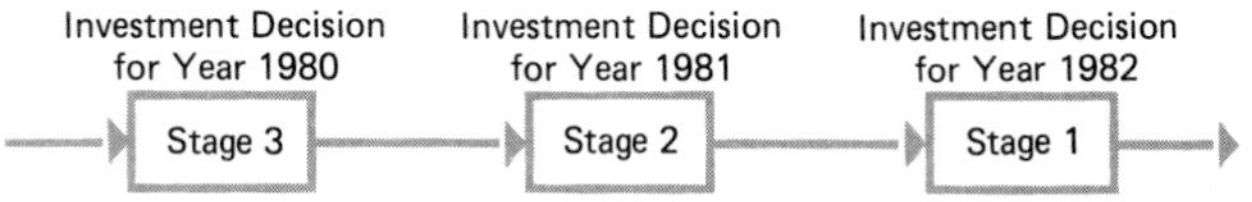

Although dynamic programming is often thought of as a technique for analysis over time, this is not *necessarily* the case. Dynamic programming has, however, been effectively applied to a large number of problems involving decisions over time and is frequently associated with time dependent problems.

Finally, dynamic programming, like all other management science techniques, employs certain symbolic notation necessary to present the modeling and solution procedure in a concise and generalized fashion. The symbol *n* is commonly used to denote the stage number. In general, problems that require the application of dynamic programming are decomposed into N stages. The stages range from N to 1 (i.e., for the *last* stage, $n = 1$). Thus,

$$n = \text{stage } n, \text{ where } n \in \{N, N-1, \ldots, n, n-1, n-2, \ldots, 2, 1\}.$$

The generalized stage numbering approach is illustrated in figure 12.4.

Figure 12.4 Generalized illustration of an N-stage dynamic programming problem.

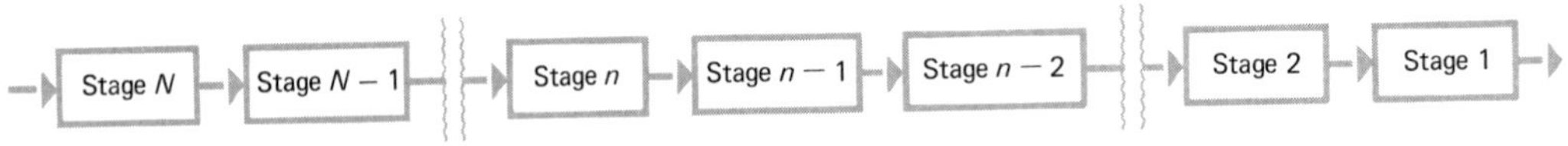

System Status

The concept of **system status,** or **states,** has already been implicitly introduced in the preceding discussion by the *arrows* in figures 12.1 through 12.4. As previously noted, the arrows provide the connection or linkage from one subproblem to the next subproblem and generally represent information flow about the status of the system from stage n to stage $n-1$, etc. It is obvious that this information flow is essential in the problem illustrated in figure 12.3. Management must know the remaining amount of capital available from the investment decision at stage 3 in order to effectively determine the course of action to take at stage 2. This is equally true for the stage 1 decision analysis. This concept is illustrated in figure 12.5.

Figure 12.5 System status shown as the output from stage n and the input into the adjacent stage $n-1$.

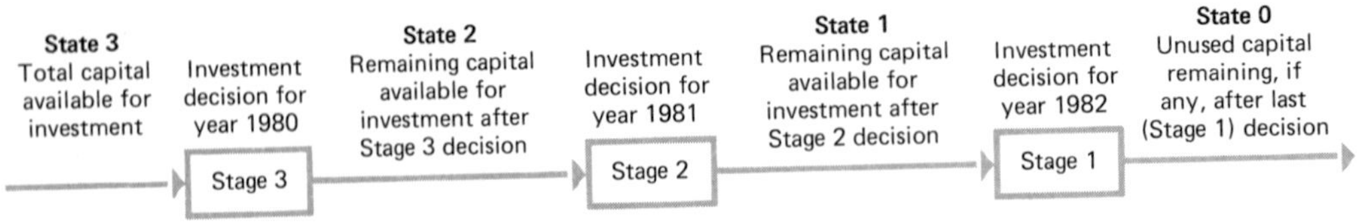

Another way of illustrating the concept of input states and stages is shown in figure 12.6, which shows only two of three stages of a hypothetical problem. It is assumed that five units of a particular resource (for example, an inventory of five available trucks for shipping) are available initially as input to stage 3. It is further assumed that, given the decision analysis at stage 3, the result will be an increase in the resource by one unit, no change, or a decrease in the resource by one unit. The resulting input (state) to the stage 2 decision problem is therefore six units of resource, five units of resource, or four units of resource.

Figure 12.6 Alternative inputs to stage 2 depend on the input state to stage 3 and the decision at stage 3.

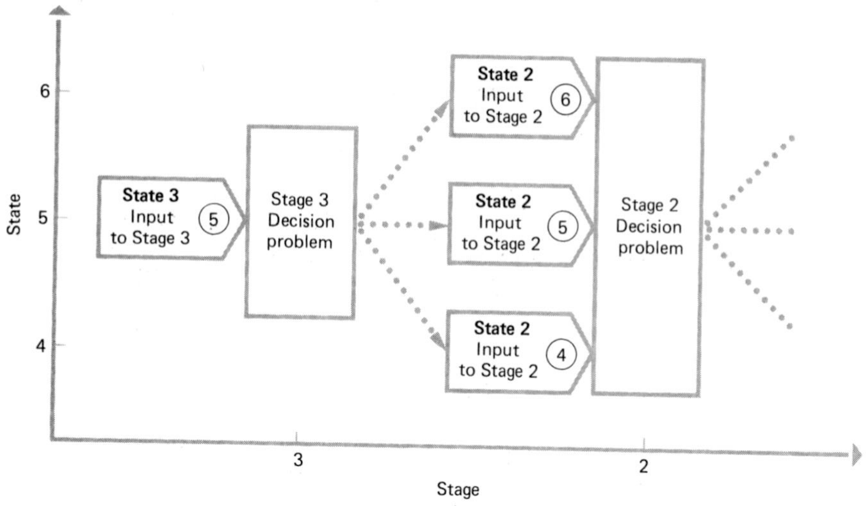

The decision options available at stage 2 are therefore dependent upon (or constrained by) the state input from stage 3 to stage 2, which has resulted from the combination of state input to stage 3 and the decision at stage 3. For example, there might be a maximum resource capacity of six units. If the state input to stage 2 is six units, this eliminates the option of increasing the resource by one unit at stage 2. If the state input to stage 2 is five or four units, the decision alternatives are still add one, no change, or decrease by one. Similarly, if there is a requirement to keep no less than four units on hand at all times, a state input of four units to stage 2 would limit the decision alternatives to no change or add one unit.

The illustration in figure 12.6 demonstrates that the range of possible decision alternatives at a particular stage is a function of the state input to the stage. The state input to a stage is the output from the *previous* (larger number) stage, and the previous stage output is a function of the state input to itself in combination with the decision at that stage. This concept is again illustrated in figure 12.7.

Figure 12.7 Information transfer between stages is a function of the system status.

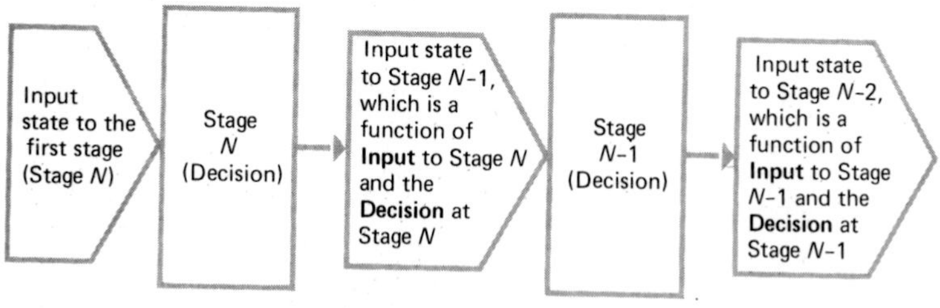

Figure 12.7 illustrates an additional point of importance—the total information requirements for making a decision at each stage are contained in the stage itself, including the return associated with various alternative decisions and the input to the stage. That is, to perform the decision analysis at stage n, the decision maker needs only to know the values of the stage n input and the decision alternatives and their associated returns at stage n. Thus, the overall problem may be decomposed into N stages, where each stage (subproblem) is evaluated separately, based on the stage input.

The symbol used to denote the state input, which is referred to as the **state variable,** is

$$S_n = \text{state input to stage } n.$$

The value of the state variable, S_n, is the status of the system resulting from the previous $(n + 1)$ stage decision.

Decision Variables

The decision variable, which has already been implicitly discussed in the previous section, represents the possible alternative actions and is denoted by

$$D_n = \text{decision variable at stage } n.$$

D_n represents the range of alternatives that can be selected from when making a decision at stage n.

Given the symbolic definitions for stage, input state, and decisions (n, S_n, and D_n), the general dynamic programming problem is illustrated in figure 12.8. Figure 12.8 completely defines the dynamic programming model of a problem in terms of the concepts presented thus far but does not yet include the return (profit, cost, utility, etc.) associated with the decisions. The return function will be presented shortly. Note that, in general, each state input variable for stage n is the output of the previous stage, $n + 1$.

Figure 12.8 The dynamic programming model illustrated in terms of stages, state variables, and decision variables.

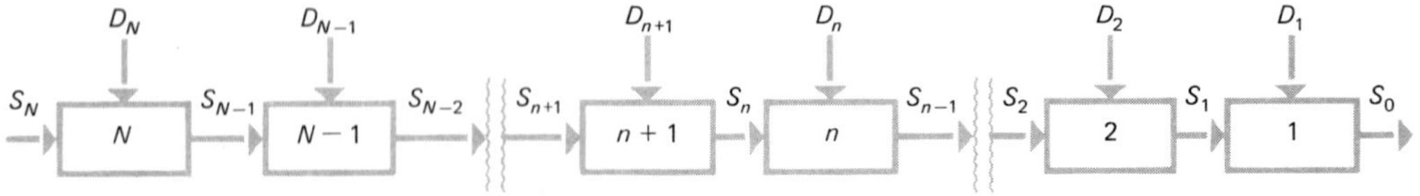

S_0 is a function of S_1 and D_1; S_1 is a function of S_2 and D_2; and, in general, S_n is a function of S_{n+1} and D_{n+1} (except S_N, which is usually given, for an example, as an initial quantity of resource available). Also, S_0 is frequently required to equal zero; that is, the entire quantity of resource should be used.

It was previously pointed out that the possible range of values for D_n is often a function of the input state, S_n. At this point in the discussion of decision variables, it should also be noted that D_n may be further constrained by additional requirements imposed by the *problem structure*. This feature will be illustrated by examples later in the chapter.

Transition Function

Although not specifically identified as such, the concept of a **transition function,** or **transform,** has already been incorporated into our discussion of dynamic programming. This concept is extremely important in dynamic programming and is discussed in greater detail here.

The transition function describes precisely how the stages of a dynamic programming model are interconnected. It defines, as a functional relationship, the value the state variable will have at each stage. For example, returning to the example in which a firm plans to invest in three plants (A, B, and C), the transition function is simply $S_{n-1} = S_n - D_n$, or $S_2 = S_3 - D_3$, which denotes that the capital available at stage 2 is equal to the capital available at stage 3 less the amount invested at stage 3. Likewise, $S_1 = S_2 - D_2$ and $S_0 = S_1 - D_1$. If all of the capital is to be invested in the three plants, then S_0 must equal zero and $D_1 = S_1$, yielding $S_1 - D_1 = 0$.

The transition function is generally illustrated by the graphical illustration of the dynamic programming problem. An example of a capital investment problem is shown, with the transition function described for each stage, in figure 12.9.

Figure 12.9 The transition function $S_{n-1} = S_n - D_n$ describes the relationship of the stages in the capital investment problem.

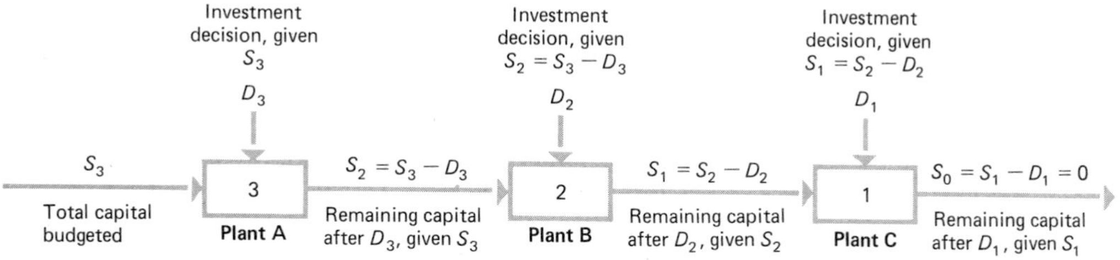

Figure 12.10 further illustrates this concept for two stages by relating it to the same example problem, assuming that \$3 million is the amount initially available and the capital must be invested in \$1 million amounts. Note that four alternative decisions are possible at stage N (invest 0, \$1, \$2, or \$3 million) as shown by the branches from (\$3) (the state input to stage N). Thus, the transition function is shown for each alternative decision as \$3 million less the decision amount, yielding the input state (circled amounts) to stage $N - 1$. Further note that the possible decision alternatives at stage $N - 1$ are a function of the value of the input state variable (S_{N-1}). Thus, if the value of $S_N - D_n = S_{N-1}$ is \$3 million, the range of alternatives for D_{N-1} are investments of 0, \$1, \$2, or \$3 million. On the other hand, if the value of the input state is \$1, the range of decision values at stage $N - 1$ is limited to 0 or \$1 million.

Figure 12.10 The transition function from stage N to stage $N-1$ for the \$3 million capital investment problem.

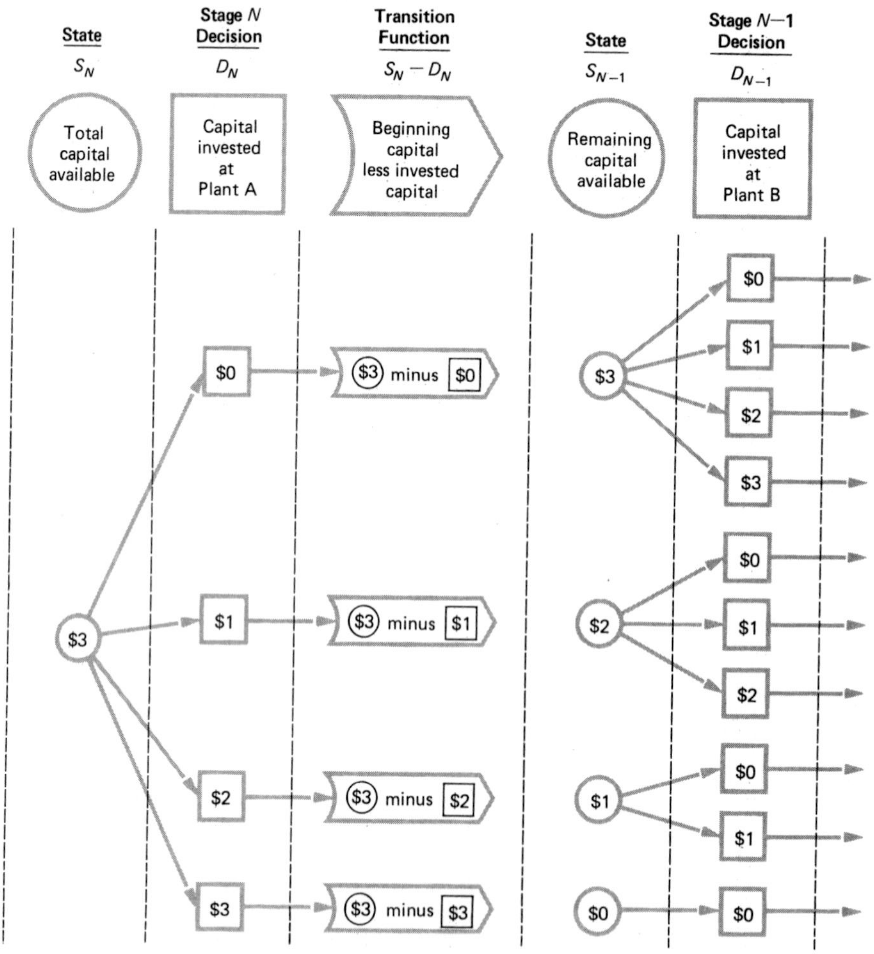

An important element of the model formulation (specification) in dynamic programming is to correctly specify the transition function. In general, the transition function is often described by one of the following forms:

$$S_{n-1} = S_n - D_n$$

$$S_{n-1} = S_n + D_n$$

$$S_{n-1} = S_n \cdot D_n$$

$$S_{n-1} = D_n$$

To correctly specify a transition function for a given problem may involve incorporating other problem parameters into the function, such as $S_{n-1} = a_n S_n + b_n D_n - c_n$, where a_n, b_n, and c_n are specified parameters of the problem. For example, if S_n is the input inventory level at stage n, D_n is the quantity purchased at stage n, and c_n is the quantity consumed in stage n; then the transition function can be specified as $S_{n-1} = S_n + D_n - c_n$ (i.e., resulting inventory level = beginning inventory + amount purchased − amount consumed), where c_n represents a forecast of monthly consumption of the resource.

The transition function plays a key role in the analysis of any dynamic programming problem. Part of the "art" of formulating dynamic programming models is to correctly perceive and specify the transition function for the problem being considered.

Stage Returns

The final element in the symbolic representation of a dynamic programming model is the return (profit, cost, utility, etc.) at each stage. The **stage return variable** is denoted by

$$R_n = \text{return at stage } n.$$

The return at stage n is shown here simply as R_n; a more thorough representation is given by

$$\text{Return at stage } n = R_n(S_n, D_n),$$

where $R_n(S_n, D_n)$ is read as the return at stage n, which is a function of the state input, S_n, and the decision, D_n. The fact that the return at each stage is a function of both the input status and the stage decision has been stated previously. Henceforth, R_n will be used, rather than $R_n(S_n, D_n)$, with the understanding that R_n is a function of both S_n and D_n.

A complete illustration, with all relevant model components, for any stage of a dynamic programming problem is given, first in figure 12.11 and symbolically in figure 12.12.

Figure 12.11 The model components for any stage of a dynamic programming problem.

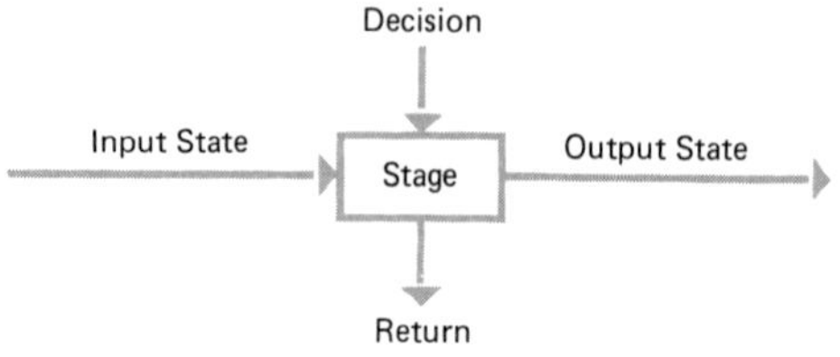

Figure 12.12 Symbolic representation of the model components for stage *n* of a dynamic programming problem.

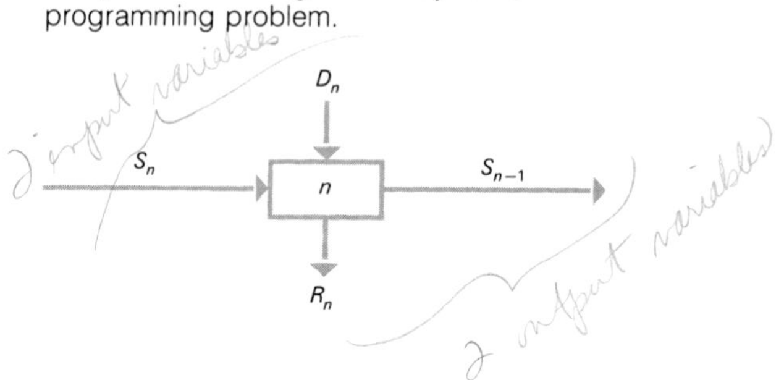

R_n is also generally given as representative of the stage n return *function*. Since R_n is a function of the state variable, S_n, and the decision variable, D_n, it is properly defined as the return function. Although the precise functional relationship denoted by R_n might be in the form of a mathematical equation such as $R_n = a_nS_n - b_nD_n$, where a_n and b_n are model parameters, the relationship of R_n to S_n and D_n is more frequently described in tabular form. An example for one stage, n, is given as follows:

Stage n		
State (S_n)	Decision (D_n)	Return (R_n)
0	0	0
1	0	0
	1	5
2	0	0
	1	5
	2	9

For the example, the input state variable to stage n, S_n, may be one of the integer values 0, 1, or 2 (e.g., a quantity of inventory units available at stage n). The decision variable, D_n, may take on one of the integer values 0, 1, or 2. Thus, the decision alternatives range from 0 to 2 (e.g., the amount of inventory used). However, note that the possible decisions are limited by the amount of inventory available (the input state variable). When $S_n = 0$, D_n is limited to 0. When $S_n = 1$, D_n is limited to 0 or 1. When $S_n = 2$, D_n may be 0, 1, or 2. Thus, the value of D_n is constrained by the input value of S_n. The tabular values for S_n and the corresponding range of possible values for D_n gives the functional relationship of D_n to S_n.

The values for R_n represent the return (e.g., profit) associated with each possible decision. Of course, the return, R_n, is directly defined by associated values of the decision, D_n. The functional relationship of R_n to D_n for the example is as follows:

$$
\begin{aligned}
\text{if } D_n &= 0 \qquad \text{then } R_n = 0 \\
D_n &= 1 \qquad \qquad R_n = 5 \\
D_n &= 2 \qquad \qquad R_n = 9
\end{aligned}
$$

Since the values of D_n depend upon the value of S_n, and R_n is a function of D_n, R_n is therefore a function of both S_n and D_n. Another way to illustrate this point is

$$
R_n = \begin{cases} 9, \text{ if } D_n = 2 \\ 5, \text{ if } D_n = 1 \\ 0, \text{ if } D_n = 0 \end{cases}, \text{ and if } S_n = 2
$$

$$
R_n = \begin{cases} 5, \text{ if } D_n = 1 \\ 0, \text{ if } D_n = 0 \end{cases}, \text{ and if } S_n = 1
$$

$$
R_n = \{ 0, \text{ if } D_n = 0, \text{ and if } S_n = 0.
$$

Refer back to figure 12.12, which shows that R_n is an output variable of stage n and is a function of the input variables S_n and D_n. It also shows that S_{n-1} is also an output variable of stage n as a function of S_n and D_n. Therefore, there are two input variables (S_n and D_n) and two output variables (R_n and S_{n-1}) at each stage of a dynamic programming model.

Figure 12.13 summarizes the relationship between state, decision, and return variables. For example, the term $(D_n|S_n = 1) = \{0, 1\}$ is read as the values that D_n may take on, given that $S_n = 1$, are either of the values in the set 0 or 1. Likewise, the term $(R_n|D_n = 1) = 5$ is read as the value of R_n, given the value of $D_n = 1$, is equal to 5. This discussion further demonstrates why the return function is often written as $R_n(S_n, D_n)$, since R_n is indeed a function of both S_n and D_n.

Figure 12.13 The output variables R_n and S_{n-1} are a function of the input variables S_n and D_n.

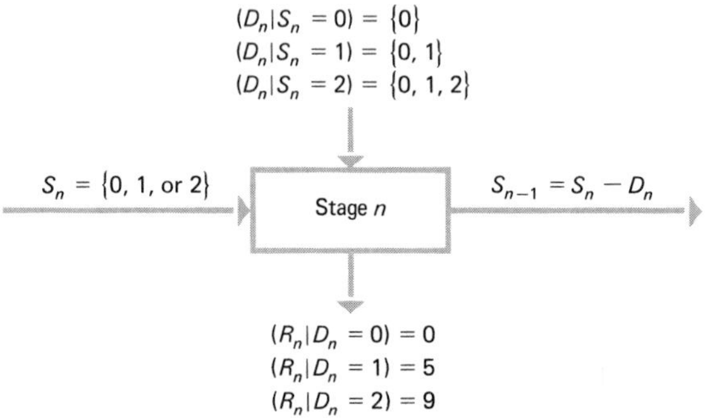

Stage Optimization

The dynamic programming approach to **stage optimization** is to determine the optimal decision at each stage, *for each possible input state value*. Thus, for the previous example, assuming we wish to maximize R_n, the optimal decision for each state value is shown as follows:

Stage n		
State (S_n)	Decision (D_n)	Return (R_n)
0	0*	0*
1	0	0
	1*	5*
2	0	0
	1	5
	2*	9*

The optimal decisions at stage n, for each state value, are

Input		*Decision*	*Return*
If $S_n = 0$,	then	$D_n^* = 0$,	$R_n^* = 0$
If $S_n = 1$,	then	$D_n^* = 1$,	$R_n^* = 5$
If $S_n = 2$,	then	$D_n^* = 2$,	$R_n^* = 9$

where D_n^* denotes the optimal value of D_n, and R_n^* denotes the associated optimal value of R_n, *for each of the three possible state inputs*. In general, at each stage, the optimal solutions must be determined *for each of the possible input values of the state variable*. This concept is illustrated in figure 12.14. Note that the optimal solution values for D_n and R_n are given for each possible value of input, S_n. As in figure 12.13, the vertical line between D_n^* and S_n and between R_n^* and S_n denotes the word *given*.

Figure 12.14 The optimal values of D_n and R_n, given the input value S_n.

$$(D_n^* | S_n = 0) = 0$$
$$(D_n^* | S_n = 1) = 1$$
$$(D_n^* | S_n = 2) = 2$$

$$S_n = \{0, 1, \text{ or } 2\}$$

Stage n

$$S_{n-1} = S_n - D_n$$

$$(R_n^* | S_n = 0) = 0$$
$$(R_n^* | S_n = 1) = 5$$
$$(R_n^* | S_n = 2) = 9$$

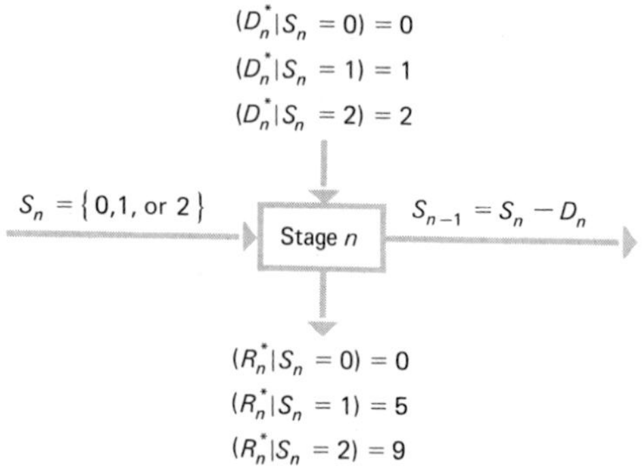

The symbolic notation of the optimal return for each possible state input is defined as follows:

$$f_n(S_n, D_n) = \text{the return at stage } n \text{ for the input value of the state variable, } S_n, \text{ and the decision, } D_n$$

and

$$f_n^*(S_n) = \text{the } \textit{optimal} \text{ return at stage } n \text{ for the input value of the state variable, } S_n$$

Actually, the definition for $f_n(S_n, D_n)$ is complete only for the case where $n = 1$; however, we will return to the definition of $f_n(S_n, D_n)$ later to elaborate on a more complete definition within the framework of multistage optimization analysis. For the present, using the preceding example, we can say that

$$f_n^*(S_n = 0) = 0, \text{ i.e., the optimal return when } S_n = 0 \text{ is } 0$$

$$f_n^*(S_n = 1) = 5, \text{ i.e., the optimal return when } S_n = 1 \text{ is } 5$$

$$f_n^*(S_n = 2) = 9, \text{ i.e., the optimal return when } S_n = 2 \text{ is } 9.$$

In summary, the optimization procedure of dynamic programming requires that, at each stage, the optimal solution be determined for each possible input state value. Furthermore, the optimal return at stage n, for each value of S_n, must be retained (recorded and stored for future use). This value is denoted in general by

$$f_n^*(S_n) = \underset{D_n}{\text{opt}}\{f_n(S_n, D_n)\}, \text{ for each value of } S_n, D_n,$$

which is read as the optimal return *for the value of* S_n equals the optimal value from among the returns associated with each of the possible decision alternatives, D_n, for this particular input state. Thus, for our example, $f_n^*(S_n)$ would be determined three times, for $S_n = 0$, $S_n = 1$, and $S_n = 2$. Given the problem data, this can be illustrated as follows:

State	*Alternative Decisions*	*Associated Returns*
$S_n = 0$	$D_n = 0$	$f_n(S_n, D_n) = 0$
$S_n = 1$	$D_n = 0$	$f_n(S_n, D_n) = 0$
	$D_n = 1$	$f_n(S_n, D_n) = 5$
$S_n = 2$	$D_n = 0$	$f_n(S_n, D_n) = 0$
	$D_n = 1$	$f_n(S_n, D_n) = 5$
	$D_n = 2$	$f_n(S_n, D_n) = 9$

Determine $f_n^*(S_n)$, for $S_n = 0$, which is $f_n^*(S_n) = 0$.

Determine $f_n^*(S_n)$, for $S_n = 1$, which is $\underset{D_n}{\text{opt}}\begin{Bmatrix} f_n(S_n, D_n) = 0 \\ f_n(S_n, D_n) = 5 \end{Bmatrix}$

Thus, $f_n^*(S_n) = 5$, for $S_n = 1$

Determine $f_n^*(S_n)$, for $S_n = 2$, which is $\underset{D_n}{\text{opt}}\begin{Bmatrix} f_n(S_n, D_n) = 0 \\ f_n(S_n, D_n) = 5 \\ f_n(S_n, D_n) = 9 \end{Bmatrix}$

Thus, $f_n^*(S_n) = 9$, for $S_n = 2$

You will note two things: (1) we have simply replaced R_n with $f_n(S_n, D_n)$ and (2) the optimal solution procedure is straightforward. However, as previously stated, the definition for $f_n(S_n, D_n)$ is complete only for the case where $n = 1$ (the last stage of the problem). The definition of $f_n(S_n, D_n)$ is significantly expanded for the case in which $n = 2, 3$, etc. This, however, is the next concept to be presented.

Recursion and the Recursive Return Function

The concept of **recursion** is commonly used by computer programmers. For example, a common FORTRAN statement is

$$X = X + 5.$$

This statement represents the concept of recursion. A program statement is recursive when each time it is executed in the program, the current value of X is redefined as the past value of X added to the value 5. Using subscript notation $X_n = X_{n-1} + 5$, if the initial value stored in X_0 is zero and the program looped back through the statement five times, the results would be $X_0 = 0$, $X_1 = 5$, $X_2 = 10$, $X_3 = 15$, $X_4 = 20$, and $X_5 = 25$.

The concept of recursion is extremely useful since only the value stored in X_{n-1} is necessary to update the value for X_n. Dynamic programming makes use of the same concept by simply keeping track of the return at stage $n-1$ to update the accumulated return at stage n.

Furthermore, dynamic programming also reduces the information storage requirements by concentrating only on *selected* returns from stage $n-1$. The returns retained are the *optimal returns* for each possible value of S_{n-1}. For the previous example, the only returns retained (stored) would be $f_n^*(S_n = 0) = 0$, $f_n^*(S_n = 1) = 5$, and $f_n^*(S_n = 2) = 9$. Thus, only three returns are retained from among the six returns computed (for all possible combinations of S_n and D_n).

In general, we can state the recursive return function of dynamic programming as follows:

$$f_n(S_n, D_n) = R_n + f_{n-1}(S_{n-1}, D_{n-1}),$$

which is read as the total accumulated return at (and including) stage n (given the input state to stage n and the decision at stage n) is equal to the stage n return *plus* the return at stage $n-1$, given the input state to stage $n-1$ and the decision at stage $n-1$. However, as previously stated, it is only necessary to retain the returns associated with the optimal decision at stage $n-1$ for each possible state input to stage $n-1$. Thus, the recursive equation, as it is used in dynamic programming, is written as follows:

$$f_n(S_n, D_n) = R_n + f_{n-1}^*(S_{n-1})$$

Returning to the previous example and designating it as the stage 1 subproblem, we have

$$f_1^*(S_1 = 0) = 0$$

$$f_1^*(S_1 = 1) = 5$$

$$f_1^*(S_1 = 2) = 9.$$

At stage 2, the decision analysis makes use of not only the return at stage 2 but also the optimal returns from stage 1 to determine the overall two-stage optimal decision. The decision analysis at stage 2 utilizes the recursion equation, which is written as

$$f_2(S_2, D_2) = R_2 + f_1^*(S_1),$$

where

$$f_1^*(S_1 = 0) = 0, \ f_1^*(S_1 = 1) = 5, \text{ and } f_1^*(S_1 = 2) = 9.$$

The recursive return function is somewhat similar to the transition function, in that it can take on a variety of forms depending upon the requirements of the problem structure at hand. Commonly encountered forms for the recursive return function are

$$f_n(S_n, D_n) = R_n + f_{n-1}^*(S_{n-1})$$

$$f_n(S_n, D_n) = R_n - f_{n-1}^*(S_{n-1})$$

$$f_n(S_n, D_n) = R_n \cdot f_{n-1}^*(S_{n-1}).$$

As in the case of the transition function, it may be necessary to formulate the recursive return function in a form such as $f_n(S_n, D_n) = a_nR_n + b_nf_{n-1}^*(S_{n-1}) - c_n$, where a_n, b_n, and c_n are specified parameters of the problem.

Example problems, which will be presented later, will illustrate some of the forms required for the return function to correctly represent the problem.

Multistage Sequential Optimization

Multistage sequential optimization could also be called *cumulative optimization analysis*. Multistage optimization, at a particular stage, includes all previously evaluated stages and incorporates those previously determined optimal solution values into the cumulative return value at the stage under consideration. This concept is illustrated graphically in figure 12.15.

In general, the optimizing procedure, which makes use of the recursion equation, is given by

$$f_n^*(S_n) = \underset{D_n}{\text{opt}} \{R_n + f_{n-1}^*(S_{n-1})\}.$$

Recall that S_n in $f_n^*(S_n)$ indicates that the optimal value of D_n must be found for the function contained in brackets, { }, for each possible input state value to stage n. R_n is the set of returns at stage n associated with possible solution values of D_n, and $f_{n-1}^*(S_{n-1})$ is the set of optimal returns for each possible input state to stage $n-1$.

Figure 12.15 Multistage sequential optimization of a dynamic programming problem.

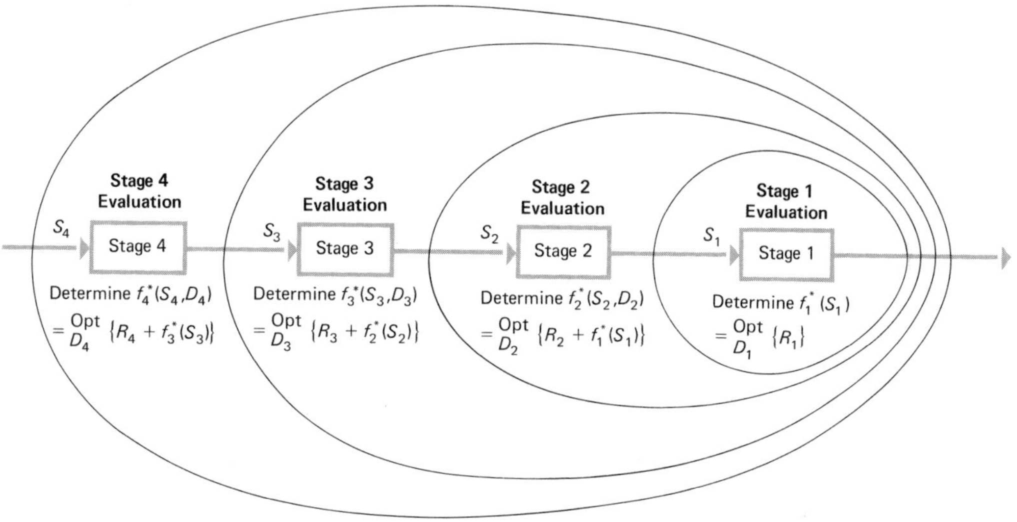

The only remaining problem in the recursive optimization procedure is the specification of the previously determined cumulative optimal return function (at stage $n-1$) in terms of the input state at stage n, the current stage under evaluation. This is accomplished by making use of the transition function. Recall that the transition function specifies the input to stage $n-1$ in terms of the input state at stage n and the decision at stage n. We will continue to employ the transition function used in the previous example, $S_{n-1} = S_n - D_n$, where the input resource at stage $n-1$ is equal to the input resource at stage n minus the amount of resource consumed at stage n.

We can, therefore, restate $f_{n-1}^*(S_{n-1})$ as

$$f_{n-1}^*(S_{n-1}) = f_{n-1}^*(S_n - D_n).$$

Thus, the previously determined cumulative optimal return function (at stage $n-1$) is now specified in terms of the input state, S_n, and decision, D_n, at stage n, by making use of the transition function.

The previously given recursive optimizing procedure is now restated in terms of stage n variables, as follows:

$$f_n^*(S_n) = \underset{D_n}{\text{opt}} \{R_n + f_{n-1}^*(S_n - D_n)\},$$

where f_{n-1}^* is the cumulative optimal set of returns determined previously at stage $n-1$ and $S_n - D_n$ is the transition function describing the output from stage n, which is the input to stage $n-1$ (in terms of the current stage S_n and D_n variables).

The multistage optimization procedure of dynamic programming begins by evaluating stage 1 as follows:

$$\text{Determine } f_1^*(S_1) = \underset{D_1}{\text{opt}} \{R_1\}, \text{ for each } S_1 \text{ input.}$$

The next subproblem solved is at stage 2.

$$\text{Determine } f_2^*(S_2) = \underset{D_2}{\text{opt}} \{R_2 + f_1^*(S_1)\}, \text{ for each } S_2 \text{ input,}$$

$$\text{where} \qquad S_1 = S_2 - D_2.$$

$$\text{Thus,} \qquad f_2^*(S_2) = \underset{D_2}{\text{opt}} \{R_2 + f_1^*(S_2 - D_2)\}, \text{ for each } S_2 \text{ input.}$$

The third stage decision analysis is given by

$$\text{Determine } f_3^*(S_3) = \underset{D_3}{\text{opt}} \{R_3 + f_2^*(S_2)\},$$

$$\text{where} \qquad S_2 = S_3 - D_3.$$

$$\text{Thus,} \qquad f_3^*(S_3) = \underset{D_3}{\text{opt}} \{R_3 + f_2^*(S_3 - D_3)\}.$$

This sequential stage solution procedure is continued through stage N. Note that in each case, the only decision variable under consideration at stage n is D_n. Likewise, note that at each stage the only return information needed to evaluate the problem is the current stage return and the previous stage set of cumulative optimal returns for all possible values of S_{n-1} (e.g., $S_n - D_n$).

Given the sequential optimization of the recursive return function for three stages, as follows:

Stage 1:

$$f_1^*(S_1) = \underset{D_1}{\text{opt}} (R_1)$$

Stage 2:

$$f_2^*(S_2) = \underset{D_2}{\text{opt}} \{R_2 + f_1^*(S_1)\}$$

Stage 3:

$$f_3^*(S_3) = \underset{D_3}{\text{opt}} \{R_3 + f_2^*(S_2)\},$$

where each stage can be optimized individually by making use of the transition function, such as $S_1 = S_2 - D_2$ and $S_2 = S_3 - D_3$. It can be shown that the overall system is optimized at stage 3 by a *sequential imbedded optimization function* of the following form:

$$f_3^*(S_3) = \underbrace{\operatorname*{opt}_{D_3} \left\{ R_3 + \underbrace{\operatorname*{opt}_{D_2} [R_2 + \underbrace{\operatorname*{opt}_{D_1} (R_1)}_{\text{stage 1}}]}_{\text{stage 2}} \right\}}_{\text{stage 3}}$$

In general, these recursive optimizing functions can be developed by the following steps:

Step A-1 Specify the decision alternatives, D_n, (i.e., the alternative values of D_n).

Step A-2 Determine the associated returns, R_n, at stage n for each decision alternative.

Step A-3 Determine the resulting output state, S_{n-1}, for each decision alternative, D_n, considered in step A-1.

Step B Determine the *sum* of the return, R_n, from step A-2 plus the cumulative optimal return from the previous stage, $f_{n-1}^*(S_{n-1})$, *given the values of* S_{n-1} from step A-3.

These four steps result in

$R_n + f_{n-1}^*(S_{n-1})$, for each possible state (S_n) and decision (D_n).

Step C Finally, determine the following *for each value of* S_n:

$$\operatorname*{opt}_{D_n} \{R_n + f_{n-1}^*(S_{n-1})\}$$

Step *C* provides the value of $f_n^*(S_n)$ for each S_n, which will then be used in the next stage, $n+1$, evaluation procedure.

Take special note of the fact that each stage involves the computation of the optimal decision for *any* possible input state. It is appropriate, at this point, to quote Bellman's principle of optimality.

> An optimal policy has the property that, whatever the initial state and the initial decision are, the remaining decisions must constitute an optimal policy with regard to the state resulting from the first decision.[1]

1. Richard E. Bellman and Stuart E. Dreyfus, *Applied Dynamic Programming*, p. 15.

Thus, Bellman's principle of optimality, which provides the foundation for dynamic programming, ensures that the solution procedure will provide the best course of action for *all future decisions*, regardless of how the current state was arrived at. Putting this in terms of stages, given the current state at stage n, the solution procedure provides the optimal solutions for stages n, $n-1$, . . . , 3, 2, 1, regardless of whether the decisions made at stages $N, N-1, \ldots, n+1$ were optimal.

Figure 12.16 illustrates, by use of a network tree diagram, the principle of optimality and the recursive optimization procedure, beginning at the last stage, and sequentially solving back to stage 3. The example in figure 12.16 assumes that stage 3 offers three alternatives (possible decisions), stage 2 offers two alternatives, and stage 1 offers three alternatives. No attempt is made to explicitly specify the transition function; rather, the tree diagram shows that given that one begins at state 3 in stage 3 and given each of the three alternative D_3 decisions, the arrows show the resulting movement to the state 2 locations (illustrating different states). Likewise, given the state 2 location, the arrows of the diagram show the resulting movement to state 1 associated with each possible D_2 action. A similar explanation is applicable to S_1, D_1, and the resulting S_0 locations.

Thus, figure 12.16 is an exhaustive enumeration of all possible states and decisions at stage 3, and resulting possible states and decisions at stage 2, and possible states and decisions at stage 1. Furthermore, figure 12.16 also portrays the returns associated with each possible alternative decision for each state at each stage (in squares).

Beginning at stage 1, the optimal decision (maximum return) is indicated by an asterisk *for each state* (S_1). This is further denoted by the darkened arrows from each S_1 to one of the three alternative S_0 locations. Thus, for each state we have determined

$$f_1^*(S_1) = \max_{D_1} R_1.$$

Moving to stage 2, we determine for each S_2 the optimal decision (maximum cumulative return), where for each S_2 and D_2 the return (R_2) is given in the right-hand box on the arrow from S_2 to S_1. In the left-hand box, on the arrow from S_2 to S_1, is the value

$$f_2(S_2, D_2) = R_2 + f_1^*(S_1).$$

We know the value of $f_1^*(S_1)$ for each alternative because it was retained from the stage 1 analysis, for each S_1 value.

We next determine the optimal solution value for D_2, for each S_2, as

$$f_2^*(S_2) = \max_{D_2} \{R_2 + f_1^*(S_1)\}.$$

Figure 12.16 All possible decisions, states, and associated returns for the sequential optimization of the dynamic programming problem beginning at stage 1.

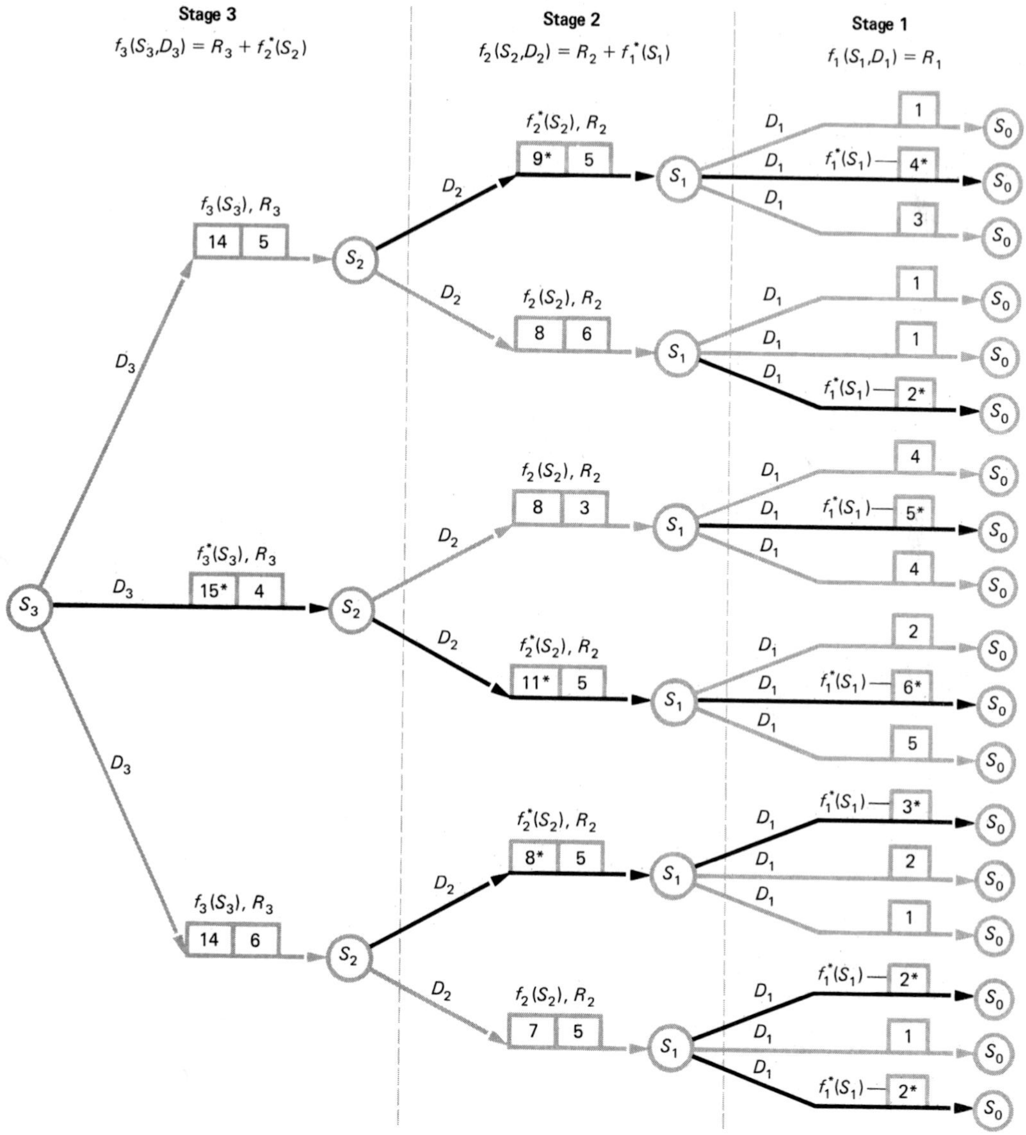

In the figure 12.16 example, the values of $f_2^*(S_2)$ are

$$f_2^*(S_2) = 9$$

$$f_2^*(S_2) = 11$$

$$f_2^*(S_2) = 8.$$

Finally, the optimal solution at stage 3 is computed as

$$f_3^*(S_3) = \max_{D_3} \{R_3 + f_2^*(S_2)\}$$

$$f_3^*(S_3) = 15.$$

Note that for each stage in figure 12.16, after the optimal decision has been determined, it is not necessary to retain information related to other alternatives. For example, after evaluating all eighteen alternatives at stage 1, one-third of the returns are retained for the stage 2 analysis. At stage 2, after evaluating the six alternatives (three states with two alternative decisions for each state), only one-half of the returns are retained for the stage 3 analysis. Thus, in this simple three-stage example, 67% of the returns are eliminated after the stage 1 analysis and 50% of the returns are eliminated after the stage 2 analysis.

To evaluate every combination of alternatives requires $3 \times 2 \times 3 = 18$ sets of computations; whereas using the dynamic programming approach, only nine sets of computations are required (i.e., at stage 1 we observed the max R_1 for each possible alternative that required no computation, stage 2 required six sets of computations, and stage 3 required three computations).

The savings in computation (and information storage) can be quite dramatic in larger problems. As a general rule of thumb, computations increase exponentially with the number of stages (subproblems) using exhaustive enumeration, but only linearly using dynamic programming. For example, in a problem with ten decision alternatives at each of N stages, exhaustive enumeration would require 10^N computations. Thus, for a problem with three stages, the total number of computations would be $10^3 = 1{,}000$, with five stages we would have $10^5 = 100{,}000$, and with ten stages, 10 billion computations. Because of the manner in which dynamic programming discards decision alternatives that are not feasible given the input state variable, it is not possible to predict precisely the number of computations required for any given problem; however, the computational effort for dynamic programming is generally described as increasing at an *additive* rate as the number of stages is increased, whereas exhaustive enumeration increases at an exponential rate.

The basic concepts of dynamic programming have been presented. The remainder of the chapter will present prototype examples of dynamic programming applications.

Dynamic Programming Applications

This section presents examples of several of the better-known applications of dynamic programming. Each example presents a different modeling structure in terms of the formulation of the recursive return function and/or the transition function of the problem. It should be recognized that each example is a prototype that can be applied to a wide range of problems with similar structures, the only difference being the description of the problem itself. Likewise, given the diversity of potential applications for dynamic programming, the examples presented are only some of the most commonly reported types of applications.

Allocation Problem

One of the most common examples of dynamic programming application is the allocation of a scarce resource, such as land, workforce, investment capital, or space, to several competing activities, such as types of land use, labor projects, or investment projects. The general formulation of this type of problem will be given first, followed by a capital budgeting example.

The problem variables are defined as follows:

K = amount of resource available

N = number of alternative activities (projects)

n = index denoting activity n

D_n = amount of resource allocated to activity n

R_n = return (profit, cost, utility) associated with activity n, given D_n

Also, it is assumed that the problem is such that the solution values for D_n must be integers and the total return can be obtained as the sum of the individual returns, R_n. The problem is formulated as

$$\text{Maximize} \sum_{n=1}^{N} R_n = R_1 + R_2 + \ldots + R_N$$

subject to

$$\sum_{n=1}^{N} D_n \leq K$$

$$= D_1 + D_2 + \ldots + D_N \leq K$$

where the D_n values are nonnegative integers.

(Note that, in general, *maximize* could be replaced by *minimize* for a cost function in the objective function, and the *inequality* could be replaced by an *equality* in the constraint.) The objective here is to maximize the sum of the returns associated with each of the activities, subject to the constraint that the sum of the resource allocations to each of the N activities must be equal to or less than the total amount of resource available, K.

Example 12.1 Capital Budgeting Problem

The ABC Company has budgeted \$5 million for the coming fiscal year to be allocated among three plants in Atlanta, Baltimore, and Chicago (plants A, B, and C) for capital improvements. The firm has decided to allocate the capital in block amounts of \$1 million. Furthermore, based upon the improvements proposed by plant managers, the minimum amount needed at each of the plants A and B is \$2 million; however, plant C could use as little as \$1 million. Also, the maximum investment amounts requested are \$4 million at plants A and B and \$3 million at plant C. Each of the plant managers has provided the expected returns (discounted present value of increase in cash flow) associated with each of the proposed levels of capital investment, as follows:

Decision Alternatives	Evaluation Criteria		
Amount Invested (in \$ millions)	Return Associated With Investment (in \$ millions)		
	Plant A	Plant B	Plant C
1	—	—	4
2	6	5	7
3	8	7	10
4	9	9	—

The company may, of course, decide to invest nothing at one or more of the plants, in which case the return is assumed to be zero. (Note that in some cases a negative return might be associated with investing nothing at a plant.) Furthermore, it is assumed that the ABC Company wants to invest all of the \$5 million budgeted for plant improvements. The problem will be formulated and solved as a dynamic programming problem, where the investment decision for each plant is analogous to a stage in the dynamic programming model.

The dynamic programming representation of the plant investment problem is shown in figure 12.17. Note that the assignment of plants to stages is, in this case, arbitrary. The problem will be solved sequentially, starting with stage 1 and working backward to stage 3.

Figure 12.17 The dynamic programming representation of the plant investment problem.

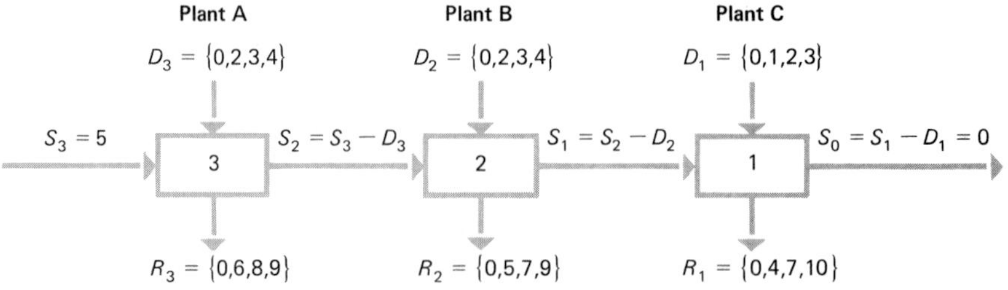

First, the stage 1 decisions (possible values of D_1) and associated returns are listed for each possible value of the state input variable, S_1. In this problem, S_1 is defined as the capital available for investment at stage 1. For example, if all $5 million were allocated to plants *A* and *B* (stages 3 and 2), the input value of S_1 would be zero, yielding the only possible value for D_1 as zero with an associated return of zero. As the possible values of S_1 increase, the range of alternative values for D_1, and associated returns increases accordingly. The stage 1 subproblem and decision analysis is summarized in the following table.

Stage 1 (Plant *C*)			
Input States S_1	Decisions D_1	Returns R_1	
0	0	0	$f_1^*(S_1=0)$
1	0	0	
	1	4	$f_1^*(S_1=1)$
2	0	0	
	1	4	
	2	7	$f_1^*(S_1=2)$
3	0	0	
	1	4	
	2	7	
	3	10	$f_1^*(S_1=3)$
4	0	0	
	1	4	
	2	7	
	3	10	$f_1^*(S_1=4)$
5	0	0	
	1	4	
	2	7	
	3	10	$f_1^*(S_1=5)$

Note that the table includes state input values of 4 and 5. For this particular problem this is not actually necessary because (1) the maximum amount that can be invested at stage 1 (plant *C*) is $3 million and (2) the firm has initially decided to invest all $5 million available. Therefore, the *maximum* amount of capital that would be remaining after the plant *A* and *B* decisions would be $3 million. However, if the return functions (R_n values associated with D_n values) at plants *A* and *B* are characterized by diminishing returns to scale after a point (i.e., a nonlinear return function) and if the firm had not specified that all $5 million would be invested, the state input to stage 1 might exceed the amount that could be invested at plant C. The full range of investment capital available is therefore shown for S_1 as a generalization of the allocation problem.

You will further note that the identification of optimal solutions for R_1 and associated D_1 for each possible input state value is trivial. This is generally true for the stage 1 subproblem in most dynamic programming problems. Oftentimes, the stage 1 optimal solutions can be identified by simple inspection.

The optimal solution values for D_1 and R_1 for each possible input state value (0, 1, 2, 3, 4, and 5) are also identified in the table by the shaded values, for each S_1 input. Recalling that the solution procedure of dynamic programming requires that we retain the optimal return for each state input, these values are identified in the table as $f_1^*(S_1 = \cdot)$ for each S_1 input. Having completed the stage 1 analysis, we move to the stage 2 analysis.

The values of all variables required for the stage 2 decision analysis are given in the following table.

Stage 2 (Plant B)

(1) Input States S_2	(2) Decisions D_2	(3) Returns R_2	(4) Output States S_1	(5) Optimal Returns, Prior Stages $f_1^*(S_1)$	(6) Total Returns $R_2 + f_1^*(S_1)$	
0	0	0	0	0	0	$f_2^*(S_2=0)$
1	0	0	1	4	4	$f_2^*(S_2=1)$
2	0	0	2	7	7	$f_2^*(S_2=2)$
	2	5	0	0	5	
3	0	0	3	10	10	$f_2^*(S_2=3)$
	2	5	1	4	9	
	3	7	0	0	7	
4	0	0	4	10	10	
	2	5	2	7	12	$f_2^*(S_2=4)$
	3	7	1	4	11	
	4	9	0	0	9	
5	0	0	5	10	10	
	2	5	3	10	15	$f_2^*(S_2=5)$
	3	7	2	7	14	
	4	9	1	4	13	

Transition Function: $S_1 = S_2 - D_2$

Recursion Function: $f_2(S_2) = R_2 + f_1^*(S_1)$

Moving from left to right, each column of values is described as follows:

1. *Input States*. Each possible value of S_2, the input state to stage 2, is given in this column. For example, if no capital is allocated to plant A (stage 3), the input value to stage 2 would be \$5 million. If \$4 million is allocated to stage 3, the input to stage 2 would be \$1 million, and so on.
2. *Stage 2 Decisions*. The range of possible investment decisions at stage 2 is given for each possible input value of S_2 in this column. Note that an investment amount of \$1 million is not feasible at stage 2 (plant B) as previously stated; thus, if the input value for S_2 is \$1 million, the only possible value for D_2 is 0.
3. *Stage 2 Returns*. The plant B returns associated with each possible decision (at stage 2) are given in this column.
4. *Output States*. The fourth column gives the amount of remaining capital, given the combination of input state to stage 2 and the investment decision at stage 2. The output state from stage 2 is the input state to stage 1 (i.e., S_1), and it is defined for this problem as $S_2 - D_2 = S_1$.
5. *Optimal Returns for Prior Stages*. This column gives the return for the optimal decision at stage 1, given the state input to stage 1 resulting from the combination of input state and decision at stage 2. Thus, the fourth column gives each possible value of S_1 and the fifth column gives the optimal return at stage 1 associated with that value of S_1. This is why the values of $f_1^*(S_1)$ are retained from the stage 1 analysis.
6. *Total Cumulative Returns*. The final column of values gives, for each combination of S_2 and D_2, the sum of the stage 2 return associated with D_2 (from the third column) plus the optimal return at stage 1 associated with the combination of S_2 and D_2 values (from the fifth column). This is, again, described functionally as for each combination of S_2 and D_2. The total return is

$$f_2(S_2) = R_2 + f_1^*(S_1),$$

where S_1 is defined by the transition function as $S_2 - D_2$. Note that $f_2(S_2)$ is completely defined in terms of the stage 2 state and decision variables, S_2 and D_2, and the return function at stage 2 can also be written as

$$f_2(S_2) = R_2 + f_1^*(S_2 - D_2).$$

The last step of the decision analysis at stage 2 is to identify (by inspection for this example) the optimal values of the total return, for each value of the input state—for each value of S_2, determine

$$\underset{D_2}{\text{Max}} \{R_2 + f_1^*(S_1)\}$$

and save this information in $f_2^*(S_2)$. The optimal return values for each S_2 value are identified in the previous table by $f_2^*(S_2 = \cdot)$. The optimal set of values for D_2, R_2, S_1, $f_1^*(S_1)$, and $f_2(S_2)$ are again identified, for each S_2 input, by the shaded values.

The reason for shading the optimal set of values, for each state input, will become apparent in the last stage of overall solution analysis.

The third and final stage of the dynamic programming problem is given in the next table. For this stage, there is only one input state value, the $5 million total capital budgeted for investment among the three plants (refer to fig. 12.17). Thus, the solution procedure is relatively simple.

Stage 3 (Plant A)

Input States S_3	Decisions D_3	Returns R_3	Output States S_2	Optimal Returns, Prior Stages $f_2^*(S_2)$	Total Returns $R_3 + f_2^*(S_2)$	
5	0	0	5	15	15	
	2	6	3	10	16	$f_3^*(S_3=5)$
	3	8	2	7	15	
	4	9	1	4	13	

Transition Function: $S_2 = S_3 - D_3$

Recursion Function: $f_3(S_3) = R_3 + f_2^*(S_2)$

The column heading descriptions for stage 3 are similar to the descriptions given for stage 2. Again, investment of $1 million at plant A is not a feasible alternative. Total returns are calculated in a manner similar to stage 2, yielding an optimal return of $16 million.

$$f_3^*(S_3) = \underset{D_3}{\text{Max}}\{R_3 + f_2^*(S_2)\}$$

$$= \underset{D_3}{\text{Max}}\{R_3 + f_2^*(S_3 - D_3)\}$$

$$= \underset{D_3}{\text{Max}}\left\{\begin{matrix} 0 + 15 \\ 6 + 10 \\ 8 + 7 \\ 9 + 4 \end{matrix}\right\}$$

$$= \underset{D_3}{\text{Max}}\left\{\begin{matrix} 15 \\ 16 \\ 15 \\ 13 \end{matrix}\right\}$$

$$= 16 \text{ (for } D_3 = 2)$$

The overall allocation problem has now been solved yielding a maximum overall return of \$16 million. Note that the optimal value for D_3, from the stage 3 analysis, is an investment of \$2 million at plant *A* (under the column heading D_3 in the previous table for stage 3). The stage 3 analysis also shows that the value of S_2 associated with this optimal solution is \$3 million. Recall that at stage 2 we determined the optimal solution for each value of S_2. Therefore, returning to stage 2, for an input state value of 3, we find the optimal value of D_2 to be 0, associated with $f_2^*(S_2=3)$. Thus, the optimal solution is to invest nothing at plant *B*.

The value of S_1 associated with $f_2^*(S_2=3)$ is 3. We therefore return to the stage 1 decision table and identify the set of shaded values associated with $f_1^*(S_1=3)$. The optimal decision at stage 1 is to invest \$3 million with an associated return of \$10 million.

The overall solution can now be summarized as follows:

Stage	Plant	Optimal Decision D_n^*	Return Associated With Optimal Decision
3	*A*	2	6
2	*B*	0	0
1	*C*	3	10
		Total Investment 5	Total Return 16

Note that if the problem involved *K* capital to be allocated among *N* plants, the same solution procedure would be followed using dynamic programming for *N* stages.

A final step in the analysis of the dynamic programming solution to the problem, which can be easily performed, is a sensitivity analysis of the solution results for lesser quantities of available capital. For example, suppose the company decided to invest only \$4 million, rather than \$5 million. It is necessary to recompute only the stage 3 analysis since stages 1 and 2 already contain the information needed for a solution to this problem. The following table shows the new stage 3 analysis for an input state value of \$4 million available capital.

Stage 3 (\$4 Million Total Capital)

Input States S_3	Decisions D_3	Returns R_3	Output States S_2	Optimal Returns, Prior Stages $f_2^*(S_2)$	Total Returns $R_3 + f_2^*(S_2)$	
4	0	0	4	12	12	
	2	6	2	7	13	$f_3^*(S_3=4)$
	3	8	1	4	12	
	4	9	0	0	9	

The maximum return is shown as \$13 million for a D_3^* value of 2. The associated S_2 value is 2. Backtracking to stage 2, we find that for $S_2 = 2$ the optimal solution is $D_2 = 0$. The associated S_1 is 2. From stage 1 we find the optimal solution for $S_1 = 2$ is $D_1 = 2$. Thus, in summary, the optimal solution for total investment capital of \$4 million is

Stage	Plant	D_n^*	R_n^*
3	A	2	6
2	B	0	0
1	C	2	7
		4	13

A similar approach is used to determine the optimal allocation of capital among plants for the case in which only \$3 million total capital is available. The following table gives the new stage 3 analysis.

Stage 3 (\$3 Million Total Capital)						
Input States S_3	Decisions D_3	Returns R_3	Output States S_2	Optimal Returns, Prior Stages $f_2^*(S_2)$	Total Returns $R_3 + f_2^*(S_2)$	
3	0	0	3	10	10	$f_3^*(S_3=4)$
	2	6	1	4	10	$f_3^*(S_3=4)$
	3	8	0	0	8	

The stage 3 analysis results in alternate optimal solutions ($D_3^* = 0$ or 2). In order to determine the associated alternate optimal solution values for D_1 and D_2, we simply backtrack for both $S_2 = 3$ and $S_2 = 1$. If $D_3 = 0$, then $S_2 = 3$, the associated optimal value for D_2 is 0. If $D_3 = 2$, then $S_2 = 1$, the associated optimal value for D_2 is 0. Using the same approach to backtrack to stage 1, we find the alternate optimal solution to be as follows:

		Alternate 1		Alternate 2	
Stage	Plant	D_n^*	R_n^*	D_n^*	R_n^*
3	A	0	0	2	6
2	B	0	0	0	0
1	C	3	10	1	4
Totals		3	10	3	10

A similar approach can be used to perform sensitivity analysis on the solution results for all available capital amounts, from K down to the smallest amount considered possible. The optimal solutions for $K = 5$ through $K = 1$, in increments of 1, are summarized as follows:

Available Capital K	Optimal Decisions Plant A D_3^*	Plant B D_2^*	Plant C D_1^*	Total Return
5	2	0	3	16
4	2	0	2	13
3	{0	0	3}	10
	{2	0	1}	
2	0	0	2	7
1	0	0	1	4

In summary, note that if the problem had involved N plants, the dynamic programming solution would require evaluation of N stages. Stage 2 in the example problem is a prototype for stages 2, 3, . . . , $N - 1$ of an N stage problem, and stages 1 and N would be similar to the example problem.

The prototype dynamic programming example presented could be applied to a wide variety of resource allocation problems as long as the decision variable (and state variable) could be restricted to integer values. The problem might be described, for example, as allocation of workers to projects, machines to jobs, salesmen to territories, floor space to departments, advertising campaign budget to products, and, in general, resources to activities.

Multiplicative Return Function Problem

The following example is actually another version of an allocation problem in which the stage returns are multiplied rather than added; otherwise, it is quite similar to the previous example. The general model is given as follows:

$$\text{Minimize} \prod_{n=1}^{N} R_n = R_1 \cdot R_2 \cdot R_3 \cdot \ldots \cdot R_N$$

subject to

$$\sum_{n=1}^{N} D_n = K$$

where

D_n are nonnegative integers

The definitions for K, N, n, and D_n are generally the same as given in the previous example. The description for R_n will be given in the following example.

Example 12.2 Research Failure Problem

The federal Department of Energy has four research teams working on four energy research projects. The DOE is concerned with minimizing the probability of failure of the energy research. The estimated probability of failure for each research team is given as follows:

Research Team			
1	2	3	4
.60	.80	.45	.75

Thus, the overall probability of total failure is the product of the individual failure probabilities, or .162.

The DOE has decided that the probability of research failure is too high and has allocated therefore an additional three scientists to the research. The estimated probabilities of failure for each research team for zero, one, two, or three additional scientists, are given as follows:

Number of Additional Scientists	Probability of Failure Research Team			
	1	2	3	4
0	.60	.80	.45	.75
1	.40	.50	.20	.45
2	.20	.30	.15	.30
3	.10	.20	.10	.15

The problem is to determine how many scientists to allocate to which teams. Intuition would seem to indicate allocating additional scientists to the teams that currently have the highest probability of failure, teams 2 and 4. However, the DOE has decided to analyze the problem by dynamic programming. The problem is therefore decomposed into four stages, one for each research team. The four subproblems are to determine how many additional scientists to allocate to team 1, team 2, team 3, and team 4. The stage returns are defined as the probability of team failure for a particular allocation. Three additional scientists are available, and the objective is to minimize the joint probability of research failure.

The stage 1 decision analysis is given in the following table, which corresponds to team 1. Since stage 1 is the last stage of the dynamic programming problem (see fig. 12.17 for an example), it is obvious that the optimal decision at this stage will be to allocate any remaining scientists to team 1. Thus, D_1^* will always equal S_1. Therefore, only the optimal solutions for each input state value are given in the table.

Stage 1 (Team 1)			
S_1	D_1^*	R_1	
0	0	.6	$f_1^*(S_1=0)$
1	1	.4	$f_1^*(S_1=1)$
2	2	.2	$f_1^*(S_1=2)$
3	3	.1	$f_1^*(S_1=3)$

The stage 2 decision analysis is shown in the following table. The S_2 values are the possible remaining scientists to allocate. The D_2 values are the decision alternatives. R_2 values are the probabilities of failure associated with different allocation decisions for team 2. The value of S_1 is determined as $S_2 - D_2 = S_1$ (the transition function describing the number of remaining scientists after the stage 2 decision). The $f_1^*(S_1)$ values are the optimal decision returns (probability of failure) at stage 1, given the value of S_1. The total return for stage 2 is therefore given as the product of $R_2 \cdot f_1^*(S_1)$, which the DOE wishes to minimize. The optimal solution for each value of S_2 is identified in the table by $f_2^*(S_2 = \cdot)$.

Stage 2 (Team 2)						
S_2	D_2	R_2	S_1	$f_1^*(S_1)$	$R_2 \cdot f_1^*(S_1)$	
0	0	.8	0	.6	.48	$f_2^*(S_2=0)$
1	0	.8	1	.4	.32	
	1	.5	0	.6	.30	$f_2^*(S_2=1)$
2	0	.8	2	.2	.16	$f_2^*(S_2=2)$
	1	.5	1	.4	.20	
	2	.3	0	.6	.18	
3	0	.8	3	.1	.08	$f_2^*(S_2=3)$
	1	.5	2	.2	.10	
	2	.3	1	.4	.12	
	3	.2	0	.6	.12	

Stage 3 is given in the next table. The tabulation and computational procedure followed is quite similar to the stage 2 decision analysis. In this case we must compute, for each value of S_3,

$$f_3^*(S_3) = \underset{D_3}{\text{Min}} \{R_3 \cdot f_2^*(S_2)\}$$

where

$$S_2 = S_3 - D_3.$$

Stage 3 (Team 3)						
S_3	D_3	R_3	S_2	$f_2^*(S_2)$	$R_3 \cdot f_2^*(S_2)$	
0	0	.45	0	.48	.216	$f_3^*(S_3=0)$
1	0	.45	1	.30	.135	
	1	.20	0	.48	.096	$f_3^*(S_3=1)$
2	0	.45	2	.16	.072	
	1	.20	1	.30	.060	$f_3^*(S_3=2)$
	2	.15	0	.48	.072	
3	0	.45	3	.08	.036	
	1	.20	2	.16	.032	$f_3^*(S_3=3)$
	2	.15	1	.30	.045	
	3	.10	0	.48	.048	

Stage 4 is given in the following table, which shows that the optimal decision at stage 4 is to allocate zero scientists to team 4 ($D_4^* = 0$). The minimum overall joint probability is shown to be .0240 for the optimal allocation of the three additional scientists.

Stage 4 (Team 4)						
S_4	D_4	R_4	S_3	$f_3^*(S_3)$	$R_4 \cdot f_3^*(S_3)$	
3	0	.75	3	.032	.0240	$f_4^*(S_4=3)$
	1	.45	2	.060	.0270	
	2	.30	1	.096	.0288	
	3	.15	0	.216	.0324	

By backtracking the overall solution is determined as follows. The value of S_3, which is associated with the optimal decision at stage 4, is 3. Returning to stage 3, for an input state value of 3, the optimal solution is found to be $D_3^* = 1$ (for $S_3 = 3$). The S_2 value associated with $f_3^*(S_3=3)$ is 2. Returning to the stage 2 table, we find the optimal solution to be $D_2^* = 0$. The S_1 value associated with $f_2^*(S_2=2)$ is 2. Returning to stage 1, we see that $D_1^* = 2$ (for $S_1 = 2$).

The optimal solution is summarized as follows:

Team (Stage)	Number of Additional Scientists Allocated	Return (Probability of Failure) Associated with Optimal Decisions
1	2	.20
2	0	.80
3	1	.20
4	0	.75
	Sum = 3	Product = .024

An interesting aspect of the solution is that it is contrary to the intuitive solution initially reached prior to solving the problem by dynamic programming, which, you will recall, was to allocate scientists to teams 2 and 4 since they have the highest initial probability of failure.

Sensitivity analysis can also be performed to determine the optimal solutions related to allocation of only two scientists or one scientist by reformulating stage 4 for each case.

The stage 4 decision analysis for allocation of only two scientists is given in the following table. The optimal decision, read from stage 4, and backtracking through stages 3, 2, and 1, which were previously optimized for every possible state input, yields the overall optimal allocation of two scientists. The optimal decision at stage 4 is $D_4^* = 1$. The value of S_3 associated with the optimal decision at stage 4 is 1. Returning to stage 3, we see that the optimal solution (when $S_3 = 1$) is $D_3^* = 1$. We need not backtrack further since we have exhausted our supply of scientists ($D_4^* = 1$ and $D_3^* = 1$). Note in stage 3 that the value of S_2 (the output of remaining scientists for remaining stages 2 and 1) is zero for $f_3^*(S_3 = 1)$.

Stage 4 (Allocation of Two Additional Scientists)

S_4	D_4	R_4	S_3	$f_3^*(S_3)$	$R_4 \cdot f_3^*(S_3)$	
2	0	.75	2	.060	.0450	
	1	.45	1	.096	.0432	$f_4^*(S_4 = 2)$
	2	.30	0	.216	.0648	

The optimal solution for allocation of only two scientists is as follows:

Team	Allocation	Return
1	0	.60
2	0	.80
3	1	.20
4	1	.45
	Sum = 2	Product = .0432

An interesting feature of the sensitivity analysis to note is that by reducing the number of additional scientists from three to two, the mix of teams receiving allocations changes from teams 1 and 3 to teams 3 and 4.

Recomputation of stage 4 for an allocation of only one additional scientist reveals that the scientist should be allocated to team 3, with a resulting optimal total return of .0720. The sensitivity of total return (overall joint probability of research failure) to different levels of additional scientists is shown as follows:

Number of Additional Scientists	Total Return (Probability of Research Failure)	Decisions
0	.1620	No additional scientists
1	.0720	One additional scientist to team 3
2	.0432	One additional scientist to team 3 and one to team 4
3	.0240	Two additional scientists to team 1 and one to team 3

Network Problem

The following example is commonly referred to as the *stagecoach* problem and is frequently used as a primary illustration of the basic concepts of dynamic programming.

Example 12.3 Routing Problem

This type of problem can be illustrated as a network, as shown in figure 12.18. A traveler during the 1800s wished to determine the optimal stagecoach route to take from San Francisco to New York. The options were limited in those days. The traveler would have to travel by four different stagecoaches during the overall journey. Initially at San Francisco, the traveler could choose to travel to three different cities. Upon completion of the first leg of the journey the traveler could again select from among three different destinations. After completing the second leg of the trip, the traveler must limit the next destination to two cities. When the third stagecoach ride was completed, the traveler would then travel from that city to the final destination, New York.

The network diagram in figure 12.18 illustrates the overall routing problem. San Francisco is denoted by node 1, and New York is denoted by node 10. Nodes 2 through 9 represent intermediate cities. The arrows of the network represent travel options, given that the traveler is at a particular city. The stagecoach fare for each travel option is given by the numbers along the arrows. The problem is to determine which stagecoach to take on each of the four legs of the journey in order to minimize total travel cost.

The dynamic programming representation of the problem is also given at the top of figure 12.18. The traveler must make four decisions as to which route to follow prior to each leg of the journey. Thus, the problem is decomposed into four

Figure 12.18 The network and dynamic programming model of the stagecoach routing problem.

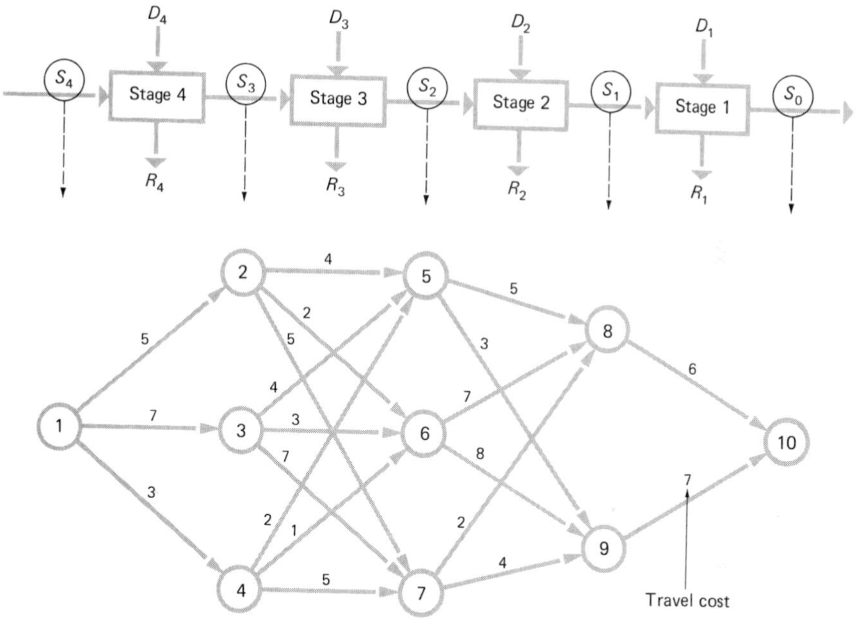

stages where decisions must be made (i.e., which stagecoach to take). Note that in this example the *state* is the *location* of the traveler. Therefore, the stage 4 input state (S_4) is defined as the initial location of the traveler, $S_4 = 1$. Likewise, after selecting a stagecoach route for the first leg of the journey, the traveler will travel to state 3, which refers to city 2, 3, or 4. Depending upon the decision, S_3 will equal 2, 3, or 4. The same explanation follows for the remainder of the journey (and the states of the dynamic programming representation). The traveler will terminate the journey at the destination $S_0 = 10$, city 10.

The problem is solved by dynamic programming by starting with stage 1 (the last leg of the journey) and working backward to the overall optimal solution at stage 4 (the first leg of the journey). The stage 1 decision analysis is indeed trivial since there is only one option, given that the traveler is at city 8 or city 9. In either case, the traveler selects the stagecoach from that city to New York. The stage 1 decisions and returns are given in the following table. Note that the decisions are denoted by $i \rightarrow j$ where i is the starting city and j is the destination city.

Stage 1

S_1	D_1^*	R_1	
8	$8 \rightarrow 10$	6	$f_1^*(S_1 = 8)$
9	$9 \rightarrow 10$	7	$f_1^*(S_1 = 9)$

We therefore move to the stage 2 decision analysis given in the next table, where the traveler is assumed to be at city 5, 6, or 7. The traveler must now decide whether to take the stagecoach to city 8 or city 9. Thus, the state 2 values may be S_2 = 5, 6, or 7, and the decision alternatives range over $D_2 = S_2 \rightarrow 8$ and $S_2 \rightarrow 9$. (In this case, the route $i \rightarrow j$ is equally defined by the route $S_2 \rightarrow j$.)

Stage 2

S_2	D_2	R_2	S_1	$f_1^*(S_1)$	$R_2 + f_1^*(S_1)$	
5	5→8	5	8	6	11	
	5→9	3	9	7	10	$f_2^*(S_2=5)$
6	6→8	7	8	6	13	$f_2^*(S_2=6)$
	6→9	8	9	7	15	
7	7→8	2	8	6	8	$f_2^*(S_2=7)$
	7→9	4	9	7	11	

Note that in stage 2 the identification of the decision alternatives, $i \rightarrow j$, are equivalent to $S_2 \rightarrow S_1$. In general, the decision alternatives at stage n are represented by $S_n \rightarrow S_{n-1}$. S_n is the current city location, and S_{n-1} is the destination for the possible route for one leg of the journey. The stage 2 analysis shows that the optimal route to New York from city 5 is 5→9→10; from city 6, it is 6→8→10; and from city 7, it is 7→8→10. The stage 3 decision analysis is given in the following table:

Stage 3

S_3	D_3	R_3	S_2	$f_2^*(S_2)$	$R_3 + f_1^*(S_2)$	
2	2→5	4	5	10	14	
	2→6	2	6	13	15	
	2→7	5	7	8	13	$f_3^*(S_3=2)$
3	3→5	4	5	10	14	$f_3^*(S_3=3)$
	3→6	3	6	13	16	
	3→7	7	7	8	15	
4	4→5	2	5	10	12	$f_3^*(S_3=4)$
	4→6	1	6	13	14	
	4→7	5	7	8	13	

The stage 3 decision analysis determines the minimum cost route to New York for travel from city 2, 3, or 4 by first computing the sum of the cost of the upcoming leg of the journey to its termination city (city 5, 6, or 7) plus the cost of travel from that termination city to the final destination by the *optimal route*. That is, the sum of the cost from city S_3 to S_2 plus the least-cost route from city S_2 to New York. This cost is given by $R_3 + f_2^*(S_2)$, where R_3 is known for each $S_3 \rightarrow S_2$ route and S_2 is the end point for this leg of the journey. The optimal route for each S_3 location is determined by

$$f_3^*(S_3) = \underset{D_3}{\text{Min}} \{R_3 + f_2^*(S_2)\}.$$

Given that the traveler is located at city 2, the optimal route is 2→7→8→10. If the traveler is at city 3, the least-cost route to take is 3→5→9→10, and from city 4, the best combination is 4→5→9→10. Thus, even if the traveler arbitrarily decides which city to travel to from San Francisco (from city 1 to city 2, 3, or 4), the traveler could then be assured of an optimal route to follow from any one of those cities. The traveler might, for example, decide that the risk of a stagecoach holdup is too great for the routes 1→2 or 1→4. The stage 3 analysis then provides the least-cost route from city 3 to New York. This point again illustrates Bellman's principle of optimality that states that regardless of the initial state and the initial decision, the optimal solution is one that provides the optimal route from that state to the destination. The stage 4 decision analysis is given in the following table.

Stage 4

S_4	D_4	R_4	S_3	$f_3^*(S_3)$	$R_4 + f_3^*(S_3)$	
1	1→2	5	2	13	18	
	1→3	7	3	14	21	
	1→4	3	4	12	15	$f_4^*(S_4 = 1)$

Stage 4 shows that the minimum cost for the optimal route from San Francisco to New York is \$15. (Travel was cheap in those days.) By backtracking from stage 4 through stage 1, we find the optimal route to be 1→4→5→9→10. Note that there is no sensitivity analysis possible for this problem since the initial input state value (S_4) denotes a location rather than a resource quantity.

As a final point, regarding the reduction in computational effort required by dynamic programming versus exhaustive enumeration, the number of combinations of different routes that would have to be evaluated in this problem by exhaustive enumeration is eighteen ($3 \times 3 \times 2 \times 1$). Let us suppose that a particular routing problem involves three alternatives from each starting point and the number of starting points is eight rather than four as in the stagecoach example. The evaluation of this problem by exhaustive enumeration requires $3^7 = 2{,}187$ combinations. (This assumes that the final destination is one location, thus the terminal stage offers only one alternative, as is also the case in the stagecoach example.) Solution by dynamic programming offers a significant computational advantage.

Knapsack Problem

The following prototype is generally referred to as the knapsack problem. The problem is to determine how many of each of several different types of items to put into a knapsack in order to maximize the total value of items packed without exceeding the capacity of the knapsack. Capacity is frequently defined in terms of total weight, and each type of item has a specified weight and value.

The general model formulation for this prototype problem is given as follows:

$$\text{Maximize } \sum_{n=1}^{N} v_n D_n$$

$$\text{subject to } \sum_{n=1}^{N} w_n D_n \leq K$$

and D_n are nonnegative integers

where

K = total capacity (i.e., total weight limit)

N = number of different types of items

n = index denoting item type n

D_n = solution value for number of type n items to pack

v_n = unit value of item type n

w_n = unit weight of item type n

Example 12.4 Cargo Loading Problem

A cargo plane is leaving for Alaska with a remaining capacity of 5 tons for additional cargo. The XZN Corporation wishes to rush several pieces of equipment along on the plane. The weights and values (in $100s) of each of three types of equipment are given as follows:

Item (n)	Unit Weight w_n	Unit Value v_n
1	2 tons	$65
2	3	80
3	1	30

The problem is to determine how many of each of the three types of equipment to ship on the cargo plane in order to maximize the value of the shipment without exceeding the weight limit of 5 tons. The problem will be solved by dynamic programming, where each stage corresponds to a decision as to the number of units of item n to ship.

The stage 1 decision analysis is presented in the following table. The state input value is the remaining capacity (in terms of weight) for item 1, which may range from a maximum of 5 to 0. The decision variable, D_1, represents the number of type 1 items to load.

Stage 1 (Item 1)				
S_1	D_1^*	W_1	R_1	
5	2	4	130	$f_1^*(S_1=5)$
4	2	4	130	$f_1^*(S_1=4)$
3	1	2	65	$f_1^*(S_1=3)$
2	1	2	65	$f_1^*(S_1=2)$
1	0	0	0	$f_1^*(S_1=1)$
0	0	0	0	$f_1^*(S_1=0)$
$W_1 = 2\,D_1$			$R_1 = 65\,D_1$	

Note that the value of D_1 is constrained by the input weight capacity available, and, in general, the upper limit for the value of D_1 is given as

$$D_1 \leq \left[\frac{S_1}{w_1}\right], \text{ where } w_1 = 2.$$

$[S_1/w_1]$ is defined as the largest *integer* value possible without exceeding the capacity constraint. The values given under the column heading W_1 are $[S_1/w_1]$—the maximum number of type 1 items times the unit weight that does not exceed the weight capacity S_1.

Also, note that only the optimal values for D_1 are given in the stage 1 table since the firm would completely use any remaining capacity at this stage. The functions defining the values for W_1 and R_1 are given at the bottom of the table ($W_1 = 2D_1$ and $R_1 = 65D_1$).

The stage 2 decision analysis is given in the following table. In each case, the value of D_2 is limited to a maximum integer value of $[S_2/w_2]$ or $[S_2/3]$. The values of R_2 are described by $80D_2$. In general, each value for total return given in the far right-hand column of the table is computed as

$$f_2(S_2, D_2) = R_2 + f_1^*(S_1),$$

where

$$R_2 = v_2\,D_2 = 80D_2,$$

and

$$S_1 = S_2 - w_2\,D_2 = S_2 - 3D_2.$$

The column of values under W_2 summarizes the computations for $w_2 \cdot D_2$.

Stage 2 (Item 2)

S_2	D_2	W_2	R_2	S_1	$f_1^*(S_1)$	$R_2+f_1^*(S_1)$	
5	1	3	80	2	65	145	$f_2^*(S_2=5)$
	0	0	0	5	130	130	
4	1	3	80	1	0	80	
	0	0	0	4	130	130	$f_2^*(S_2=4)$
3	1	3	80	0	0	80	$f_2^*(S_2=3)$
	0	0	0	3	65	65	
2	0	0	0	2	65	65	$f_2^*(S_2=2)$
1	0	0	0	1	0	0	$f_2^*(S_2=1)$
0	0	0	0	0	0	0	$f_2^*(S_2=0)$

$W_2 = 3D_2$ $\quad R_2 = 80D_2$ $\quad S_1 = S_2 - W_2$

Thus, the return function can be written as

$$f_2(S_2, D_2) = v_2D_2 + f_1^*(S_2 - w_2D_2)$$
$$= 80D_2 + f_1^*(S_2 - 3D_2).$$

And, finally, the optimal decisions for each possible state input value are computed as

$$f_2^*(S_2) = \underset{D_2 \leq [S_2/w_2]}{\text{Max}} \{R_2 + f_1^*(S_1)\}$$
$$= \underset{D_2 \leq [S_2/w_2]}{\text{Max}} \{v_2D_2 + f_1^*(S_2 - w_2D_2)\}$$
$$= \underset{D_2 \leq [S_2/3].}{\text{Max}} \{80D_2 + f_1^*(S_2 - 3D_2)\}$$

Thus, the recursive return function for the knapsack problem is basically the same as the allocation problem presented earlier. However, in this case, the computational procedure for determining the stage n return is

$$R_n = v_nD_n$$

and the transition function is defined as

$$S_{n-1} = S_n - w_nD_n.$$

The stage 3 decision analysis is given in the following table. The optimal solution yields a maximum value of 160. The corresponding decision for $f_3^*(S_3=5) = 160$ is $D_3^* = 1$. Also, the value of S_2 associated with the optimal solution is 4. Returning to stage 2, for $S_2 = 4$, we find an optimal decision for D_2 of 0. This optimal solution, $f_2^*(S_2=4)$, has a value for S_1 of 4. The optimal value for D_1, associated with $f_1^*(S_1=4)$, is $D_1^* = 2$.

Stage 3 (Item 3)

S_3	D_3	W_3	R_3	S_2	$f_2^*(S_2)$	$R_3+f_2^*(S_2)$	
5	5	5	150	0	0	150	
	4	4	120	1	0	120	
	3	3	90	2	65	155	
	2	2	60	3	80	140	
	1	1	30	4	130	160	$f_3^*(S_3=5)$
	0	0	0	5	145	145	

$W_3 = 1D_3$ $\qquad$ $R_3 = 30D_3$ $\qquad$ $S_2 = S_3 - W_3$

The optimal solution is summarized as follows:

Equipment Type	Number of Items	Value (in \$100s)	Weight (in tons)
1	2	130	4
2	0	0	0
3	1	30	1
	3	160	5

Sensitivity analysis can be performed to determine how many of which items would be loaded if the capacity is less than 5 tons. By successively repeating the stage 3 analysis for total input (capacity) of 4, 3, 2, and 1, we arrive at the following optimal cargo loading solutions:

Available Capacity (S_4)	Number of Items D_1^*	D_2^*	D_3^*	Total Return
5	2	0	1	160
4	2	0	0	130
3	1	0	1	95
2	1	0	0	65
1	0	0	1	30

Scheduling Problem

The following example illustrates a production and inventory scheduling problem. It is not a prototype for scheduling problems per se; however, it does demonstrate several of the features common to scheduling problems.

The basic model formulation for a production and inventory problem will be presented first, followed by an example problem solved by dynamic programming.

The following variable definitions for the production and inventory scheduling problem are given as

S_n = beginning inventory, period n—input variable

D_n = production quantity, period n—decision variable

q_n = quantity demanded, period n—specified parameter

K_n = production capacity, period n—specified parameter

W_n = warehouse or storage capacity, period n—specified parameter

R_n = total production and inventory holding cost, period n. For example, assuming that total production cost includes a fixed setup cost (FC) plus a variable production cost per unit (VC), and inventory holding cost is a constant cost per unit per period held (HC), then the total production and inventory holding cost can be described by the following return function:

$$R_n = \begin{cases} FC + VC \cdot D_n + HC \cdot (S_n + D_n - q_n), \text{ if } D_n > 0 \\ 0 + HC \cdot (S_n + D_n - q_n), \text{ if } D_n = 0. \end{cases}$$

Note, that quantity demanded, q_n, is to be filled from beginning inventory S_n plus production D_n in period n, and the inventory holding cost for period n is charged against the period n "ending" inventory, which is defined as

$$S_n + D_n - q_n.$$

The basic model formulation for this problem is then given by the following:

$$\text{Minimize} \sum_{n=1}^{N} R_n \qquad (\text{where } R_n = \text{production and inventory cost function})$$

subject to

$$D_n \leqslant K_n, \text{ for } n = 1, \ldots, N \qquad \text{(production capacity)}$$

$$S_n + D_n - q_n \leqslant W_n, \text{ for } n = 1, \ldots, N \qquad \text{(storage capacity)}$$

$$S_n + D_n \geqslant q_n, \text{ for } n = 1, \ldots, N \qquad \text{(demand requirement)}$$

where

D_n, S_n are nonnegative integers.

The following inventory transition function must hold,

$$S_{n-1} = S_n + D_n - q_n,$$

where S_{n-1} is the *ending* inventory for period n, and, likewise, the *beginning* inventory for the following period (where, $n-1$ is defined as the period *following* period n). Finally, the beginning inventory for the initial period of the planning horizon must be specified (which may be zero), and the ending inventory for the last period of the planning horizon may be specified to equal zero or some other desired quantity.

Example 12.5 Production and Inventory Planning Problem

The Apco manufacturing firm produces small quantities of a specialized piece of equipment. They currently have orders for fourteen pieces of the equipment, with no expectation of receiving any further orders within the next several months. The firm's customers have requested delivery according to the following schedule:

Delivery Month	Number of Items
January	2
February	5
March	3
April	4

Apco can manufacture a maximum of five pieces of equipment per month at a cost of \$50 setup cost plus \$20 per unit production cost. They also have available storage capacity for a maximum of four pieces of equipment, which they estimate involves a carrying cost of \$4 per unit held from one month to the next.

The firm wishes to determine the optimal production and inventory holding schedule for the planning period of January through April. They have decided to use dynamic programming to solve the problem. They currently have zero units in inventory, and they wish to plan for zero ending inventory in April.

The problem will be solved by beginning with the last month, April, as stage 1 and working backward to the first month, January, as stage 4. Since the firm wishes to have zero ending inventory in April, the optimal stage 1 decision is to produce the quantity differential between beginning inventory (S_1) and the amount required to meet demand in that month (4 units).

The stage 1 decision analysis is given in the following table. If the beginning inventory is four units (the maximum storage capacity), the firm will produce nothing and fill demands for that month from inventory. If the beginning inventory is zero, the firm will produce four units at a cost of \$50 + \$20 × 4, or \$130. The optimal decisions for each possible input (beginning inventory level) are given by $f_1^*(S_1 = \cdot)$.

Stage 1 (April: Demand = 4)

Beginning Inventory S_1	Quantity Produced D_1	Ending Inventory S_0	Production Cost R_1	
4	0	0	0	$f_1^*(S_1 = 4)$
3	1	0	70	$f_1^*(S_1 = 3)$
2	2	0	90	$f_1^*(S_1 = 2)$
1	3	0	110	$f_1^*(S_1 = 1)$
0	4	0	130	$f_1^*(S_1 = 0)$

Beginning Inventory = Ending Inventory from March (Stage 2)
Ending Inventory = Beginning Inventory + Quantity Produced − Demand
or $S_0 = S_1 + D_1 - 4$
Production Cost = Setup Cost + (Production Cost) (Quantity Produced)
or $R_1 = 50 + 20D_1$, for $D_1 > 0$
$= 0$, for $D_1 = 0$

The stage 2 decision analysis is given in the following table. The range of possible values for the input variable, S_2, is from 0 to 4 (where 4 is the maximum inventory storage capacity). The values of D_2 (production quantity in stage 2 for March) are limited by the following constraints:

1. $D_2 \leq 5$ (production capacity)
2. $S_2 + D_2 - 3 \leq 4$ (storage capacity for ending inventory)
3. $S_2 + D_2 \geq 3$ (demand requirements for March)

Thus, if beginning inventory S_2 is 4, the maximum production quantity D_2 is 3 due to constraint 2. Likewise, when S_2 is 0, the minimum value for D_2 is 3 in order to satisfy requirement 3. In any event, the maximum value for D_2 is 5, according to constraint 1.

Stage 2 (March: Demand = 3)

Beginning Inventory S_2	Quantity Produced D_2	Ending Inventory S_1	Production Cost $50 + 20D_2$	Inventory Holding Cost $4S_1$	Stage 2 Production and Inventory Cost R_2	Previous Stage Optimal Decision, Given S_1 $f_1^*(S_1)$	Total Return $R_2 + f_1^*(S_1)$	
4	3	4	110	16	126	0	126	
	2	3	90	12	102	70	172	
	1	2	70	8	78	90	168	
	0	1	0	4	4	110	114	$f_2^*(S_2 = 4)$
3	4	4	130	16	146	0	146	
	3	3	110	12	122	70	192	
	2	2	90	8	98	90	188	
	1	1	70	4	74	110	184	
	0	0	0	0	0	130	130	$f_2^*(S_2 = 3)$
2	5	4	150	16	166	0	166	$f_2^*(S_2 = 2)$
	4	3	130	12	142	70	212	
	3	2	110	8	118	90	208	
	2	1	90	4	94	110	204	
	1	0	70	0	70	130	200	
1	5	3	150	12	162	70	232	
	4	2	130	8	138	90	228	
	3	1	110	4	114	110	224	
	2	0	90	0	90	130	220	$f_2^*(S_2 = 1)$
0	5	2	150	8	158	90	248	
	4	1	130	4	134	110	244	
	3	0	110	0	110	130	240	$f_2^*(S_2 = 0)$

Transition Function: $S_1 = S_2 + D_2 - 3$

Return Function: $f_2(S_2, D_2) = R_2 + f_1^*(S_1)$, where $R_2 = 50 + 20D_2 + 4S_1$, for $D_2 > 0$

$= 0 + 4S_1$, for $D_2 = 0$

The transition function links stage 2 to the previously evaluated stage 1 by $S_1 = S_2 + D_2 - 3$ (i.e., March's ending inventory = March's beginning inventory + production − demand.) The total return for stage 2 is given by

$$f_2(S_2, D_2) = R_2 + f_1^*(S_1)$$

where

$$R_2 = \begin{cases} 50 + 20D_2 + 4S_1, \text{ for } D_2 > 0 \\ 0 + 4S_1, \text{ for } D_2 = 0 \end{cases}$$

and

$$S_1 = S_2 + D_2 - 3.$$

Thus, the total recursive return function can be written, for each combination of S_2 and D_2, as

$$f_2(S_2, D_2) = \begin{cases} 50 + 20D_2 + 4(S_2 + D_2 - 3) + f_1^*(S_2 + D_2 - 3), \text{ for } D_2 > 0, \\ 0 + 4(S_2 + D_2 - 3) + f_1^*(S_2 + D_2 - 3), \text{ for } D_2 = 0. \end{cases}$$

For each value of the input variable S_2, we determine the optimal (minimum) cost as

$$f_2^*(S_2) = \underset{D_2}{\text{Min}} \{R_2 + f_1^*(S_1)\}.$$

The optimal solutions for each S_2 are denoted by $f_2^*(S_2 = \cdot)$ in the stage 2 table.

The stage 3 (February) decision analysis is given in the following table. The range of possible values for D_3 are determined in a manner similar to stage 2.

1. $D_3 \leq 5$ (production capacity)
2. $S_3 + D_3 - 5 \leq 4$ (storage capacity for ending inventory)
3. $S_3 + D_3 \geq 5$ (demand requirements for February)

Note that constraints 2 and 3 can be combined into the following constraint:

$$5 \leq S_3 + D_3 \leq 9$$

And in general, for each stage

$$q_n \leq (S_n + D_n) \leq (W_n + q_n)$$

demand ≤ (beginning inventory + production) ≤ (storage capacity + demand).

Stage 3 (February: Demand = 5)

Beginning Inventory S_3	Quantity Produced D_3	Ending Inventory S_2	Production Cost $50+20D_3$	Inventory Holding Cost $4S_2$	Stage 3 Production and Inventory Cost R_3	Previous Stage Optimal Decision, Given S_2 $f_2^*(S_2)$	Total Return $R_3+f_2^*(S_2)$	
4	5	4	150	16	166	114	280	
	4	3	130	12	142	130	272	$f_3^*(S_3=4)$
	3	2	110	8	118	166	284	
	2	1	90	4	94	220	314	
	1	0	70	0	70	240	310	
3	5	3	150	12	162	130	292	$f_3^*(S_3=3)$
	4	2	130	8	138	166	304	
	3	1	110	4	114	220	334	
	2	0	90	0	90	240	330	
2	5	2	150	8	158	166	324	$f_3^*(S_3=2)$
	4	1	130	4	134	220	354	
	3	0	110	0	110	240	350	
1	5	1	150	4	154	220	374	
	4	0	130	0	130	240	370	$f_3^*(S_3=1)$
0	5	0	150	0	150	240	390	$f_3^*(S_3=0)$

Transition Function: $S_2 = S_3 + D_3 - 5$

Return Function: $f_3(S_3, D_3) = R_3 + f_2^*(S_2)$, where $R_3 = 50 + 20D_3 + 4S_2$, for $D_3 > 0$

$= 0 + 4S_2$, for $D_3 = 0$

The stage 4 (January) decision analysis is given in the table on page 551. The only value for S_4 is zero because the firm has no beginning inventory at the beginning of the planning horizon. Thus, the optimal solution is identified in the stage 4 table by $f_1^*(S_4=0) = \$454$ for a production quantity of $D_4^* = 5$. The associated output state value for S_3 is 3 (the ending inventory in January and beginning inventory for February). Backtracking to stage 3, for $S_3 = 3$, the optimal decision is $D_3^* = 5$ with $S_2 = 3$.

For $f_2^*(S_2=3)$, the optimal decision is $D_2^* = 0$, with an associated $S_1 = 0$. The optimal production quantity at stage 1, given a beginning inventory of 0, is $D_1^* = 4$.

The overall solution is summarized as follows:

(n) Stage	Month	(q_n) Demand	(D_n^*) Production	$(S_n + D_n^* - q_n)$ Ending Inventory	Production Cost	Inventory Cost	Total Cost
4	January	2	5	3	150	12	162
3	February	5	5	3	150	12	162
2	March	3	0	0	0	0	0
1	April	4	4	0	130	—	130
	Totals	14	14		430	24	454

A form of sensitivity analysis can be performed on the previous problem by assuming that some beginning inventory was available at the beginning of the planning horizon. Thus, stage 4 could be solved for input values of $S_4 = 1, 2, 3$, or 4, and the optimal strategies identified for each case. Likewise, the problem solution approach need not assume that production and/or warehouse capacities are constant over the planning horizon. A different production and warehouse capacity can be used for each month. Finally, the form of the production cost function can take on a wide variety of forms. For example, production costs might be most appropriately defined by a quadratic or U-shaped cost curve. The basic approach to solution is similar to the example presented.

Forward Versus Backward Recursion

All of the examples presented have employed the backward recursion approach to problem solution—beginning with the last stage (identified as stage 1) and working backward to the final solution at stage N. Alternatively, it is also possible to start at the first stage (stage N) and work *forward* for the solution (i.e., from left to right). This would seem to make sense, especially for problems where the stages represent time periods. For such cases, forward recursion would start with period 1 and work forward to the last period of the planning horizon.

Contrary to intuition, however, the forward computational approach is usually less efficient than the backward recursion approach that has been presented. This occurs because the state transformation for forward recursion is generally more complex. In the end, both approaches yield equivalent results. The decision as to forward or backward recursion can be determined by the individual's preference and the structure of the problem encountered.

Stage 4 (January: Demand = 2)

Beginning Inventory S_4	Quantity Produced D_4	Ending Inventory S_3	Production Cost $50+20D_4$	Inventory Holding Cost $4S_3$	Stage 4 Production and Inventory Cost R_4	Previous Stage Optimal Decision, Given S_3 $f_3^*(S_3)$	Total Return $R_4+f_3^*(S_3)$	
0	5	3	150	12	162	292	454	$f_4^*(S_4=0)$
	4	2	130	8	138	324	462	
	3	1	110	4	114	370	484	
	2	0	90	0	90	390	480	

Transition Function: $S_3 = S_4 + D_4 - 2$

Return Function: $f_4(S_4, D_4) = R_4 + f_3^*(S_3)$, where $R_4 = 50 + 20D_4 + 4S_3$, for $D_4 > 0$

$= 0 + 4S_3$, for $D_4 = 0$

Multiple State Variables

The examples presented have included a single state variable, or, more specifically, a one-dimensional state variable. For example, problems have been considered in which the input state to each stage represented the remaining quantity of resource available, the amount of cargo capacity available, the location of a traveler, the workforce level, and so forth.

Suppose, however, that a decision maker is faced with the problem of allocation of two resources, given mathematically as follows:

$$\text{Maximize} \sum_{n=1}^{N} R_n$$

subject to

$$\sum_{n=1}^{N} D_n^1 \leq K$$

and

$$\sum_{n=1}^{N} D_n^2 \leq M$$

This is quite similar to the capital budgeting example presented in example 12.1. However, in addition to K capital, there is also a second resource of total quantity M that also constrains the solution.

Thus, there are two state variables that must be accounted for at each stage of the solution procedure. Let us define S_n^1 as the first state variable for the first resource of K quantity, and S_n^2 as the second state variable for the second resource of M quantity. Assuming that we can describe the transition functions by $S_{n-1}^1 = S_n^1 - D_n^1$ and $S_{n-1}^2 = S_n^2 - D_n^2$, the general recursion relation for this problem is given by

$$\begin{aligned} f_n(S_n^1, S_n^2) &= R_n + f_{n-1}^*(S_{n-1}^1, S_{n-1}^2) \\ &= R_n + f_{n-1}^*(S_n^1 - D_n^1, S_n^2 - D_n^2). \end{aligned}$$

Conceptually, the inclusion of multiple states does not present a problem in dynamic programming; however, from a practical point of view it does present significant difficulties. For problems requiring multiple states (or a multidimensional state variable), the solution procedure in dynamic programming becomes considerably more difficult. That is, the number of computations required and the information retention requirements increase dramatically as the number of states is increased. The information storage requirements increase geometrically as the dimension of the state variable increases linearly. For example, if each state variable takes on twenty values, then for two state variables it would be necessary to evaluate

$20^2 = 400$ combinations, three state variables would require $20^3 = 8,000$ combinations, four state variables would require $20^4 = 160,000$ combinations, and so on. This problem is aptly referred to by Bellman as "the curse of dimensionality." For these reasons, problem analysis by dynamic programming is usually limited to one or, at most, two states.

Finite Versus Infinite Horizons

All of the examples presented have assumed a finite planning horizon, (i.e., a specified number of stages). However, the intended planning horizon may be infinite. There are several possible approaches to this problem.

First, many problems exhibit cyclical behavior, such as sales demands over the period of a year. Thus, it might be possible to obtain a solution to the dynamic programming problem where the planning horizon included one full set of fluctuating demands (i.e., one year) and apply this problem indefinitely into the future.

A second approach that has been suggested is to make use of discounting (i.e., in the case of cash flows, discounting extends the solution beyond some lengthy point into the future so that the infinite planning horizon becomes insignificant).

Finally, an approach frequently suggested for problems in which the stages represent time periods is to simply update the dynamic programming model and solution at the beginning of each *new* period (or stage). Thus, after each period of "experience," the decision maker would be able to respecify with certainty the input state to the newly defined first stage.

Summary

This chapter has presented the fundamental concepts of dynamic programming. Since dynamic programming is an *approach* to problem solving rather than a technique or algorithm, this chapter has included a number of concepts that must be grasped prior to the study of specific applications. The first section of the chapter should serve not only as an introduction to dynamic programming but also as a source of reference as you proceed through the section on application examples.

The second section of the chapter presents several of the best-known examples of dynamic programming applications. These include allocation problems, multiplicative return problems, network routing problems, the knapsack problem, and scheduling problems.

The presentation of these various examples indicates the wide variety of complex problem forms to which dynamic programming can be applied. In fact, many of the more complex problems encountered in topic areas covered by other chapters in this text can also be solved using dynamic programming. However, it should always be remembered that because dynamic programming is a solution approach and not a technique it often requires a great deal more modeling insight and expertise than some of the other methods presented in this text.

References

Bellman, R. *Dynamic Programming.* Princeton, N.J.: Princeton University Press, 1957.

Bellman, R., and Dreyfus, S. E. *Applied Dynamic Programming.* Princeton, N.J.: Princeton University Press, 1962.

Dallenbach, H. G., and George, J. A. *Introduction to Operations Research Techniques.* Boston: Allyn and Bacon, 1978.

Hillier, F. S., and Lieberman, G. J. *Operations Research.* 2d ed. San Francisco: Holden-Day, 1974.

Howard, R. A. *Dynamic Programming and Markov Processes.* New York: John Wiley & Sons, 1960.

Loomba, N. P., and Turban, E. *Applied Programming for Management.* New York: Holt, Rinehart and Winston, 1974.

Nemhauser, G. L. *Introduction to Dynamic Programming.* New York: John Wiley & Sons, 1966.

Wagner, H. M. *Principles of Operations Research.* Englewood Cliffs, N.J.: Prentice-Hall, 1969.

Problems

1. Refer to example 12.1, the capital budgeting problem, in which the ABC Company has budgeted \$5 million for capital improvements to be allocated among three plants. The \$5 million is to be allocated in \$1 million block amounts, with a maximum of \$4 million to any one plant. Assume that the capital allocation problem is modified as follows: Each plant can make use of any amount of capital between 0 and \$4 million, in block amounts of \$1 million, with the following expected returns:

Proposed Levels of Capital Investment (in \$ millions)	Discounted Present Value of Increase in Cash Flow (in \$ millions)		
	Plant *A*	Plant *B*	Plant *C*
0	0	0	0
1	2	3.5	4
2	6	5	7
3	8	7	10
4	9	9	11

a. Using dynamic programming, determine the optimal allocation of \$5 million capital among the three plants.

b. Determine the optimal allocation of capital among the three plants if only \$4 million capital is available for investment.

c. Illustrate the problem graphically as a dynamic programming model, showing stages, decisions, returns, and the transition function.

2. The Easy Rider Bus Line has purchased six additional buses that it plans to use on three routes. However, the bus line has not decided how many of the new buses to assign to each of the three routes. They have developed estimates of additional profit per week for various alternatives shown as follows:

	Additional Profit Per Week ($)		
Number of Buses Assigned	Route *A*	Route *B*	Route *C*
0	0	0	0
1	350	100	225
2	450	250	300
3	500	450	475
4	525	650	600
5	450	700	650
6	400	750	600

a. Use dynamic programming to determine the optimal assignment of buses to each route.
b. Determine the optimal assignment if only five buses are available.
c. Illustrate the problem graphically as a dynamic programming model, showing stages, decisions, returns, and the transition function.

3. The city police department must determine the optimal allocation of twelve new police officers to four precincts. At least one officer must be allocated to each of the four precincts, and no more than four officers can be allocated to any one precinct. The police department has developed estimates of the number of crimes that can be expected to occur per eight-hour period, given various numbers of allocated officers, shown as follows:

Number of Allocated Patrolmen	Number of Crimes Per Eight-Hour Period			
	Precinct *A*	Precinct *B*	Precinct *C*	Precinct *D*
1	40	11	30	20
2	39	8	26	18
3	36	7	23	16
4	32	6	22	14

a. Use dynamic programming to determine the optimal allocation of officers to precincts in order to minimize total number of crimes per eight-hour period.
b. Assume that only eleven new officers are available to allocate; determine the optimal allocation of police officers.
Hint for (*a*) and (*b*): Be sure to carefully define the constraints for the range of values that D_n and S_n can take on at each stage.

4. The Millco Company has four machines on which it can produce three products (X, Y, and Z). All four machines can be set up to produce all three products. However, when a machine is set up to produce one of the three products, a production run of one week is always scheduled. Each week the company must determine how many machines to schedule for each of the three products, based on sales forecasts for the week. The following table provides a forecast for the three products that has been reduced to a forecast of the coming week's profit, given the number of machines scheduled to produce each of the various products.

	Week's Forecasted Profit ($)		
Number of Machines Scheduled	Product X	Product Y	Product Z
0	0	0	0
1	1,000	1,500	500
2	1,900	2,500	1,600
3	2,700	3,200	2,800
4	3,400	3,500	4,000

Use dynamic programming to determine the optimal number of machines to schedule for production of each of the three products for the coming week.

5. Refer to example 12.2, the research failure problem, in which three additional scientists are to be allocated to a research project involving four research teams. The objective is to allocate the three additional scientists in such a way as to minimize the overall probability of research failure. Assume that the probabilities of failure for various numbers of allocated scientists to each research team have been modified as follows:

	Probability of Failure			
Number of Additional Scientists	Team 1	Team 2	Team 3	Team 4
0	.6	.7	.45	.75
1	.4	.5	.25	.45
2	.2	.3	.15	.30
3	.1	.2	.10	.15

a. Use dynamic programming to determine the optimal allocation of three additional scientists to the four research teams, in order to minimize overall probability of project failure.
b. Assume that only two additional scientists are available for allocation. Determine the alternate optimal solutions for number of scientists to allocate to each team.

6. A piece of electronic equipment consists of four components (A, B, C, and D) connected in series. If any one of the four components fail, the entire piece of equipment will not function. The reliability of each component is described in terms of the probability that the component will *not* fail, and the reliability of the entire piece of equipment is described in terms of the *product* of the component probabilities. The reliability of each component can be improved by installing more than one unit of a component (i.e., one or more spare backup components). If the original component fails, one of the spare units is automatically switched into the circuit to replace the failed unit. The firm owning the piece of electronic equipment plans to spend up to $600 to add spare backup units to some of the components of the system. However, the cost of the spare units differs for each component and the effect of adding spare units differs for each component, as follows:

Number of Spare Units Installed (x)	Component Reliability (Based on the Installation of x Spare Units)			
	A	*B*	*C*	*D*
0	.80	.60	.90	.70
1	.85	.81	.93	.90
2	.90	.99	.95	.98
Cost Per Spare Unit for Various Components	$100	300	100	200

Given this information, use dynamic programming to determine how many spare units of each component should be installed in order to maximize the probability the piece of equipment will not fail, given a budget allocation of $600. Hint: The decision variable is the number of spare units to install; whereas the state variable is dollars available for purchase of spare units. Therefore, if D_n is used to represent the decision variable, and c_n is used to represent the cost per spare unit at stage n, then, in general, the state variable transition function can be represented by $S_{n-1} = S_n - c_nD_n$.

7. Assume that the network illustrated in the following figure represents an oil pipeline network, where distances (in hundreds of miles) from node i to node j are shown along the network branches. Use dynamic programming to determine the shortest route over which to pump the oil, from source node 1 to destination node 18.

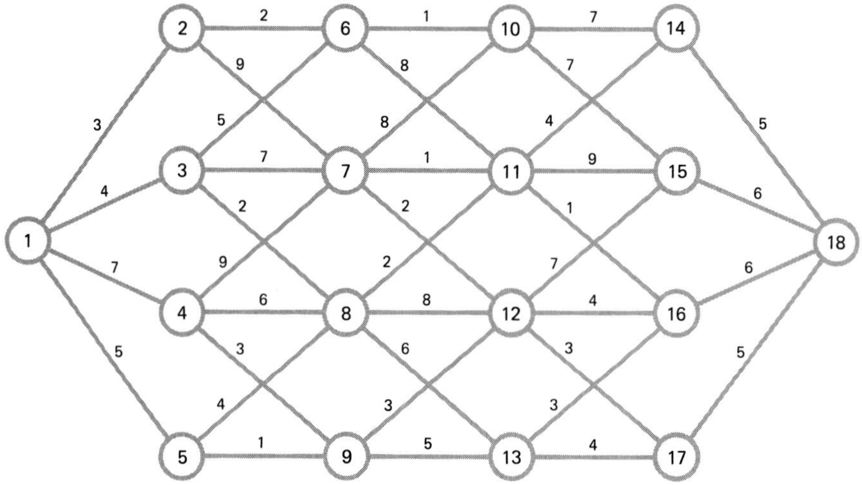

8. Assume that the network illustrated in problem 7 does not represent an existing oil pipeline network but rather the alternative sites for pumping stations (nodes) and associated feasible routes (branches) for pipelines. You may ignore the distance figures shown on the branches of the figure. Given the costs of constructing pumping stations and the costs of laying pipelines shown in the following tables, use dynamic programming to determine the minimum cost for pumping station sites and associated pipeline routes. Note that the source pumping station at node 1 already exists, and node 18 is the oil tank farm (destination) to which the pipeline must be connected. All costs are given in thousands of dollars.

Construction Costs of Pumping Stations

Station Site (Node)	Construction Cost	Station Site (Node)	Construction Cost	Station Site (Node)	Construction Cost	Station Site (Node)	Construction Cost
2	40	6	56	10	45	14	60
3	67	7	55	11	80	15	69
4	53	8	75	12	50	16	58
5	70	9	47	13	65	17	72

Costs of Laying Pipeline

Pipeline Route $(i-j)$	Cost	Pipeline Route $(i-j)$	Cost	Pipeline Route $(i-j)$	Cost	Pipeline Route $(i-j)$	Cost	Pipeline Route $(i-j)$	Cost
1–2	20	2–6	10	6–10	47	10–14	30	14–18	10
1–3	47	2–7	29	6–11	15	10–15	49	15–18	35
1–4	39	3–6	23	7–10	31	11–14	37	16–18	26
1–5	36	3–7	48	7–11	20	11–15	41	17–18	50
		3–8	40	7–12	33	11–16	25		
		4–7	34	8–11	21	12–15	43		
		4–8	31	8–12	44	12–16	39		
		4–9	27	8–13	30	12–17	45		
		5–8	46	9–12	21	13–16	47		
		5–9	38	9–13	40	13–17	36		

9. Reconsider example 12.4, the cargo loading problem, and assume that the plane has a remaining capacity of 11 tons rather than 5 tons. The unit weights and values remain unchanged from the chapter example.

   Use dynamic programming to complete the following:

   a. Determine how many of each of the three types of equipment to ship on the cargo plane in order to maximize the value of the cargo carried.
   b. Assume that one unit of item 2 *must* be included on the plane. Show how to obtain the optimal solution, given this constraint, without reworking all three stages of the problem.
   c. Assume that the capacity is 11 tons and constraint (*b*) is not applied, but the value of item 3 is revalued to \$33 per unit. Determine the optimal number of each unit to ship.

10. Refer to example 12.5, the production and inventory planning problem, in which the Apco manufacturing firm wishes to determine the optimal production and inventory plan for the coming four months. Given the information provided in the chapter, complete the following. Assume that the firm can manufacture a maximum of four pieces of equipment per month. Determine the optimal production and inventory schedule for the four months, assuming that all demand must be met.

11. Assume that the Apco firm in example 12.5 has three units in inventory at the end of December. Determine the optimal production and inventory plan for the four-month planning period.

12. Refer again to example 12.5. Assume that the maximum inventory capacity is two units rather than four units. Determine the optimal production and inventory plan.

13. A construction firm must use several pieces of specialized earth-moving equipment over the next five weeks. Since the construction firm does not expect to use the equipment on most construction projects, it has decided to rent the equipment from a large equipment rental firm rather than purchase the equipment. The number of units of equipment needed for the next five weeks are forecasted as follows:

Week	1	2	3	4	5
Number of Units Required	4	6	7	3	5

The actual rent paid for equipment is not considered since the decision has been made to rent the equipment. However, the costs of obtaining different numbers of units each week and the cost of holding excess units must be considered. A piece of equipment must be rented for a minimum of one week. The equipment rental firm charges a fixed fee of $400 for preparation of equipment (regardless of the number of units rented) each time one or more units are rented, plus a delivery charge of $300 per unit of equipment. The construction firm has estimated the cost of holding excess units of the equipment (over requirements) to be $350 per unit per week. Use dynamic programming to determine the least-cost solution for number of units of equipment to be delivered and held each week over the five-week period.

Hint: Assume that the decision variable, D_n, is defined as the number of units to hold in week n, and r_n is the number of units required in week n. Then, the range of values to be considered for D_n in any n is

$$r_n \leqslant D_n \leqslant 7.$$

Likewise, the state input value for any given week will be the value of the decision variable for the previous week.

14. Reconsider problem 13 for the case where the cost of holding excess units of the equipment is $450 per unit per week rather than the previously stipulated $350.

15. Reconsider problem 13 for the case where the cost of holding excess units of the equipment is $550 per unit per week rather than $350.

16. Reconsider problem 13 for the case where the cost of holding excess units of the equipment is $550 per unit per week and also the cost of returning equipment to the rental firm is $100 per unit returned.

17. The construction firm in problem 13 has concluded that it could get along with one unit less than the forecasted needs in either or both of the weeks 2 and 3 but only by incurring the additional shortage cost (for overtime work) of $300 per unit of shortage. Use dynamic programming to determine the least-cost schedule of rental equipment. Hint: Note that the lower limit of the range of possible solution values for the decision variable, for weeks 2 and 3, must be revised to include one unit less than the requirements for those weeks.

13
Goal Programming

In chapter 2, linear programming models were developed within a general framework that encompassed a single objective function. In most cases, the objective was to maximize profit or minimize cost. However, organizations have varied objectives according to their character, type, function, philosophy of management, and size. Although profit maximization, which is regarded in classical economic theory as the sole purpose of the business firm, is one of the most widely accepted management objectives, it is not always the only objective. In fact, business firms frequently place higher priorities on noneconomic objectives than on profit maximization. Firms often seek a ''satisfactory'' level of profit while pursuing such noneconomic objectives as social responsibility, social contributions, public relations, labor relations, and environmental protection. Many public organizations, such as government agencies, have no profit objective at all but rather a myriad of social objectives. In other words, organizations often have multiple objectives.

Nobel laureate Herbert A. Simon states that today's manager does not attempt to optimize; instead, the manager/decision maker tries to satisfice. An optimizer typically seeks the best possible outcome for a single objective, such as profit maximization. A satisficer alternatively attempts to attain a satisfactory level of achievement for several objectives. There have been a variety of methods developed for multiple objective decision making, such as multiattribute utility analysis, multiple criteria linear programming, heuristic search methods, simulation models, goal programming, and learning models. **Goal programming** is one of the most promising and appropriate techniques for modeling modern decision-making problems, which reflects Simon's theory of ''satisficing.'' It is a powerful tool that draws upon the highly developed and tested technique of linear programming but at the same time provides a simultaneous solution to a complex system of competing objectives. A major advantage of goal programming over other techniques in dealing with real-world decision problems is that it reflects the way managers actually make decisions. In other words, goal programming allows the decision maker to incorporate the environmental, organizational, and managerial considerations into the model through goal levels and priorities.

Goal programming, a concept originally introduced by Charnes and Cooper and further developed by Ijiri, Lee, and others, is very similar to the traditional linear programming model. It is implicit within this system that the objectives may be incommensurable (i.e., they may not be based on the same units of measure). A company's goals of maximizing profit and minimizing pollution can be considered incommensurable objectives because the first goal, profit, is defined in terms of dollars, while the pollution goal is defined in terms of tons of chemical wastes. Goal programming can be employed for decision problems with a single goal (objective) and multiple subgoals, as well as cases having multiple goals and subgoals. Within the goal programming model, goals may be achieved only at the expense of other goals. Although, it may not be possible to optimize every goal, goal programming attempts to obtain satisfactory levels of goal attainment that represent the best possible combination of goal achievements. This necessitates the establishment of a weighting system for the goals such that lower-ranked (or weighted) goals are considered only after higher-ranked goals have been satisfied or have reached the point beyond which no further improvement is desirable. These weights can be either ordinal or cardinal.

Since goal programming is a form of linear programming, goal programming models must be formulated under the same limitations, assumptions, and conditions as linear programming (linearity, divisibility, certainty, etc.). Further, like linear programming, goal programming problems can be solved using the simplex method only in a modified form.

Goal programming has been widely applied to decision problems in business organizations, government agencies, and nonprofit institutions. Example applications include advertising media planning, workforce planning, production scheduling, academic resource allocation, financial decision making, economic policy analysis, transportation logistics, marketing strategy planning, environmental protection, health care planning, and many others.

Example 13.1 Product Mix Problem

The following production problem was first given as a linear programming example in chapter 2 (example 2.1) to illustrate linear programming modeling. In this case, the same general production situation is employed; however, multiple objectives are defined instead of a single objective.

A manufacturing company produces three products, 1, 2, and 3. The three products have resource requirements as follows:

	Resource Requirements		
	Labor (hr./unit)	Materials (lb./unit)	Profit ($/unit)
Product 1	5	4	3
Product 2	2	6	5
Product 3	4	3	2

At present the firm has a normal production capacity of 240 hours of labor available daily and a daily supply of 400 pounds of material.

This problem was originally formulated in example 2.1 as

Maximize $Z = 3x_1 + 5x_2 + 2x_3$

subject to

$$5x_1 + 2x_2 + 4x_3 \leqslant 240$$
$$4x_1 + 6x_2 + 3x_3 \leqslant 400$$
$$x_1, x_2, x_3 \geqslant 0.$$

Notice that this model has a single objective function of profit maximization. However, now consider the situation where management has developed the following set of multiple goals, arranged in order of their importance to the firm.

1. Due to labor relations difficulties, management desires to avoid underutilization of normal production capacity (i.e., no layoffs of workers).
2. Management has established a satisfactory profit level of \$500 per day.
3. Overtime is to be minimized as much as possible.
4. Management wants to minimize the purchase of additional materials due to handling and storage problems.

The firm's management desires to achieve these goals as closely as possible. In order to reflect these multiple goals, the previous linear programming model must be reformulated into a goal programming model. First, the goal constraints must be developed.

Labor Utilization

The first goal relates to the labor hours utilized in the production of the three products. Management has decided to avoid underutilization of labor. In order to reflect the possibility of underutilization of labor (as well as overtime), the original linear programming constraint is reformulated as

$$5x_1 + 2x_2 + 4x_3 + d_1^- - d_1^+ = 240.$$

The two new variables, d_1^- and d_1^+, are referred to as **deviational variables,** which represent the number of hours less than 240 (d_1^-, underutilization) and the number of hours exceeding 240 (d_1^+, overtime) for the amount of production determined by the values of x_1, x_2, and x_3. For example, if the final solution is $x_1 = 10$, $x_2 = 40$, and $x_3 = 20$, the total labor utilization would be 210 hours. This, in turn, would mean $d_1^+ = 0$ and $d_1^- = 30$ hours. With this level of production, labor capacity would be underutilized by 30 hours. Alternatively, if $x_1 = 20$, $x_2 = 40$, and $x_3 = 50$, the total labor utilization would be 380 hours. This results in $d_1^+ = 140$ hours and $d_1^- = 0$, or 140 hours of overtime.

Implicit in this analysis is the fact that one of the deviational variables, d_1^- or d_1^+, must always be zero in the solution. In other words, it is not physically possible to have both underutilization and overutilization at the same time. However, consider the case where labor utilization is exactly 240 hours. In this case, d_1^- and d_1^+ both equal zero—there is neither overutilization or underutilization of labor. One of the fundamental relationships in goal programming is that in a given goal constraint one or both of the deviational variables must always be zero.

Now that the labor constraint for production, which reflects the possibility of underutilization or overtime, has been formulated, the goal of avoiding underutilization must be specified. This is accomplished in the objective function as follows:

$$\text{Minimize } Z = P_1 d_1^-$$

P_1 is the preemptive priority designation for this goal. The term $P_1 d_1^-$ reflects the fact that the first priority goal of the firm is to minimize d_1^-, the underutilization of labor. Thus, when solving this problem, the first goal is to minimize d_1^- or drive it to zero if possible.

There is also another goal associated with this constraint, the minimization of overtime (d_1^+). The fact that management has ranked this goal third, is reflected in the objective function as follows:

$$\text{Minimize } Z = P_1 d_1^- + \boldsymbol{P_3 d_1^+}$$

P_3 designates minimization of d_1^+, overtime, as the third priority goal. Now the objective function reflects management's desire to achieve both of these goals; however, one is more important than the other. It should be noted here that the objective function Z is not represented by a unidimensional value such as profit or cost. Instead, Z represents a multidimensional function composed of various priority factors and associated incommensurable objective criteria.

Profit Level

Management's second goal is to achieve the satisfactory profit level of $500. This goal constraint is thus formulated as

$$3x_1 + 5x_2 + 2x_3 + d_2^- - d_2^+ = 500,$$

where d_2^- is underachievement of the profit goal and d_2^+ is overachievement of the profit goal. The goal is reflected in the objective function by minimizing d_2^-, underachievement of profit, at the second priority level.

$$\text{Minimize } Z = P_1 d_1^- + \boldsymbol{P_2 d_2^-} + P_3 d_1^+$$

In other words, management is perfectly content to allow d_2^+, overachievement, to assume any value possible (the more profit the better), as long as the goal of at least $500 is achieved by minimizing d_2^-.

Purchase of Materials

Management's final goal is that daily material purchases in excess of 400 pounds be minimized. Formulating the material requirement as a goal constraint results in

$$4x_1 + 6x_2 + 3x_3 + d_3^- - d_3^+ = 400,$$

where d_3^- is the underutilization of normal material requirements and d_3^+ is the purchase of extra materials. The goal is reflected in the objective function by minimizing d_3^+ at the fourth priority level.

$$\text{Minimize } Z = P_1d_1^- + P_2d_2^- + P_3d_1^+ + P_4d_3^+$$

The term $P_4d_3^+$ reflects management's desire to minimize the purchase of extra materials at a level of achievement below the other three goals.

The goal programming model for this problem can be summarized as

$$\text{Minimize } Z = P_1d_1^- + P_2d_2^- + P_3d_1^+ + P_4d_3^+$$

subject to

$$\begin{aligned} 5x_1 + 2x_2 + 4x_3 + d_1^- - d_1^+ &= 240 \\ 3x_1 + 5x_2 + 2x_3 + d_2^- - d_2^+ &= 500 \\ 4x_1 + 6x_2 + 3x_3 + d_3^- - d_3^+ &= 400 \\ x_1, x_2, x_3, d_1^-, d_1^+, d_2^-, d_2^+, d_3^-, d_3^+ &\geq 0. \end{aligned}$$

Solution of this problem requires that the deviations from the goals specified in the objective function be minimized. The value of the deviational variable associated with the highest preemptive priority, d_1^-, must first be minimized to the fullest possible extent. When no further improvement is possible or desired for this goal, the value of the deviational variable associated with the next highest priority factor, d_2^-, is minimized, and so on. The solution procedure is a modified simplex approach. It should be pointed out once again that the objective function Z is not a unidimensional but a multidimensional function. In other words, Z represents the sum of unattained portions of each of the goals at different priority levels.

Example 13.2 Weighted Goals

In this example, an additional capability of goal programming, the ability to weight goals within the same priority level, is demonstrated.

A small manufacturing firm produces washers and dryers. Production of either product requires one hour of production time. The plant has a normal production capacity of forty hours per week. A *maximum* of twenty-four washers and thirty dryers can be stored per week. The profit margin for a washer is \$80 and \$40 for a dryer. The manager has established the following goals arranged in order of their priority.

P_1: Avoid underutilization of normal production capacity.

P_2: Produce as many washers and dryers as possible. However, since the profit margin for a washer is twice that of a dryer, the manager has twice as much desire to achieve the production of washers as dryers.

P_3: Minimize overtime as much as possible.

Production Capacity

The first goal constraint reflects the production requirements for both products.

$$x_1 + x_2 + d_1^- - d_1^+ = 40,$$

where x_1 and x_2 are the respective number of washers and dryers produced. The deviational variable, d_1^-, reflects underutilization of the normal production capacity of forty hours per week, while d_1^+ represents overtime. Priority goals 1 and 3 can be reflected as

$$\text{Minimize } Z = P_1 d_1^- + P_3 d_1^+.$$

Storage Constraints

The production goal constraints for this problem are

$$x_1 + d_2^- = 24$$

$$x_2 + d_3^- = 30.$$

In the first of these goal constraints, d_2^- reflects the underachievement in the production goal for washers, while d_3^- in the second goal constraint is the underachievement of the production goal for dryers. However, notice that d_2^+ and d_3^+ for the production goals have been eliminated. This reflects the fact that these goal levels represent *maximum* values (i.e., storage capacities) not to be exceeded. As such, this demonstrates the capability in goal programming to compensate for those cases in which underachievement or overachievement of goal levels is not possible. This type of constraint is referred to as a system constraint in that deviation in both the positive and negative direction is prohibited. In effect, system constraints accomplish the same thing as $\leq$, $=$, or $\geq$ linear programming constraints.

The second priority goal is reflected in the objective function as follows:

$$\text{Minimize } Z = P_1 d_1^- + P_3 d_1^+ + 2P_2 d_2^- + P_2 d_3^-$$

These two new terms in the objective function, $2P_2 d_2^-$ and $P_2 d_3^-$, reflect the second priority goals for minimizing the underachievement of the production goals. However, these goals are *weighted* within the second priority level by the relative profit of the two products. This means that the minimization of d_2^- is twice as important as the minimization of d_3^-. (However, both priority 2 level goals are not as important as priority 1, the minimization of d_1^-.)

The goal programming model for this problem is formulated as

$$\text{Minimize } Z = P_1 d_1^- + 2P_2 d_2^- + P_2 d_3^- + P_3 d_1^+$$

subject to

$$\begin{aligned} x_1 + x_2 + d_1^- - d_1^+ &= 40 \\ x_1 \qquad\qquad + d_2^- &= 24 \\ x_2 \qquad + d_3^- &= 30 \\ x_1, x_2, d_1^-, d_1^+, d_2^-, d_3^- &\geq 0. \end{aligned}$$

Example 13.3 *Deviational Variable Goal Constraint*

Consider example 13.2 with the added goal that overtime not exceed ten hours per week, if possible, at a priority 4 level. Recall the production requirements goal constraint

$$x_1 + x_2 + d_1^- - d_1^+ = 40.$$

In this equation, d_1^+ reflects overtime. Our new goal is that overtime be restricted to ten hours, which is formulated as

$$d_1^+ + d_4^- - d_4^+ = 10.$$

This new equation is a perfectly acceptable form in goal programming. The deviational variables d_4^- and d_4^+ denote the underachievement and overachievement of the overtime goal level.

Another way to formulate the same goal constraint in terms of decision variables is by adding the allowed overtime of ten hours to the original production requirement goal as follows:

$$x_1 + x_2 + d_4^- - d_4^+ = 50$$

The new objective function becomes

$$\text{Minimize } Z = P_1 d_1^- + 2P_2 d_2^- + P_2 d_3^- + P_3 d_1^+ + P_4 d_4^+.$$

This fourth priority goal specifies that the amount of overtime in excess of ten hours is to be minimized. This goal is not incongruous with the third priority goal of minimizing overtime. It is quite feasible for management to want to first avoid overtime if it can but, if it cannot, then to limit overtime to ten hours.

The new goal programming model is

Minimize $Z = P_1d_1^- + 2P_2d_2^- + P_2d_3^- + P_3d_1^+ + P_4d_4^+$

subject to

$$\begin{aligned} x_1 + x_2 + d_1^- - d_1^+ &= 40 \\ x_1 \qquad\qquad + d_2^- &= 24 \\ x_2 \qquad + d_3^- &= 30 \\ d_1^+ + d_4^- - d_4^+ &= 10 \\ x_j, d_i^-, d_i^+ &\geq 0. \end{aligned}$$

Example 13.4 Recreational Facility Funding

A city parks and recreation authority has been given a federal grant of \$600,000 to expand its public recreation facilities. Four different types of facilities have been demanded by city council members speaking for their constituents: gymnasiums, athletic fields, tennis courts, and swimming pools. In fact the demand by various communities has been for seven gyms, ten athletic fields, eight tennis courts, and twelve swimming pools. However, each facility costs a certain amount, requires a certain number of acres, and has an expected usage. These parameters are summarized in the following table:

Facility	Cost (\$)	Required Acres	Expected Usage (people/week)
Gymnasium	\$80,000	4	1,500
Athletic Field	24,000	8	3,000
Tennis Court	15,000	3	500
Swimming Pool	40,000	5	1,000

The park authority has presently located fifty acres of land for construction (although more land could be located if necessary).

The authority has established the following list of prioritized goals:

P_1: The authority must spend the total grant or the amount not spent will be returned to the federal government.

P_2: The park authority desires the facilities be used by 20,000 people or more weekly.

P_3: The park authority wants to avoid securing extra land other than the fifty acres presently available.

P_4: They would like to meet the demands of the city council members for the new facilities. However, this priority should be weighted according to number of people estimated to use each facility.

P_5: If the authority must secure more land, they desire to limit it to ten acres.

Funding Constraint

The cost requirements for each facility are shown in the following goal constraint:

$$80{,}000x_1 + 24{,}000x_2 + 15{,}000x_3 + 40{,}000x_4 + d_1^- = 600{,}000,$$

where x_1, x_2, x_3, and x_4 are the number of facilities of each type to be constructed. The deviational variable d_1^- is the portion of the grant not spent. The deviational variable d_1^+ has been eliminated since the grant has a specified limit of \$600,000, and it is assumed additional funding is not available. The first priority goal is reflected in the objective function as follows:

$$\text{Minimize } Z = P_1d_1^-$$

Facilities Use

The expected usage for each facility is formulated as

$$1{,}500x_1 + 3{,}000x_2 + 500x_3 + 1{,}000x_4 + d_2^- - d_2^+ = 20{,}000.$$

The deviational variables, d_2^- and d_2^+, are the respective amounts of weekly underutilization or overutilization of the facilities. The priority 2 goal of minimizing underutilization is shown in the objective function as

$$\text{Minimize } Z = P_1d_1^- + P_2d_2^-.$$

Land Requirements

The land requirements for each facility type are reflected in the following equation:

$$4x_1 + 8x_2 + 3x_3 + 5x_4 + d_3^- - d_3^+ = 50$$

The deviational variables represent the amount of land used less than fifty acres, d_3^-, and the excess above fifty acres, d_3^+. Recall also that the park authority desires that the amount of land in excess of fifty acres be limited, if possible, to ten acres.

$$d_3^+ + d_4^- - d_4^+ = 10$$

This latter goal is reflected in the objective function by the minimization of d_4^+ at the priority 5 level. This goal as well as the priority 3 goal is shown in the objective function as

$$\text{Minimize } Z = P_1d_1^- + P_2d_2^- + P_3d_3^+ + P_5d_4^+.$$

Facility Demand

The demand for facilities is shown by the following four goal constraints:

$$x_1 + d_5^- - d_5^+ = 7$$
$$x_2 + d_6^- - d_6^+ = 10$$
$$x_3 + d_7^- - d_7^+ = 8$$
$$x_4 + d_8^- - d_8^+ = 12$$

The deviational variables represent the construction of less or more facilities than the number of each type demanded. The priority 4 goal of minimizing the negative deviation from the goal levels (i.e., facility demand) is weighted in the objective function by the relative amount of expected usage for each facility.

$$\text{Minimize } Z = P_1d_1^- + P_2d_2^- + P_3d_3^+ + 3P_4d_5^- + 6P_4d_6^- + P_4d_7^- + 2P_4d_8^- + P_5d_4^+$$

The complete goal programming model for this problem is formulated as follows:

$$\text{Minimize } Z = P_1d_1^- + P_2d_2^- + P_3d_3^+ + 3P_4d_5^- + 6P_4d_6^- + P_4d_7^- + 2P_4d_8^- + P_5d_4^+$$

subject to

$$\begin{aligned}
80{,}000x_1 + 24{,}000x_2 + 15{,}000x_3 + 40{,}000x_4 + d_1^- &= 600{,}000 \\
1{,}500x_1 + 3{,}000x_2 + 500x_3 + 1{,}000x_4 + d_2^- - d_2^+ &= 20{,}000 \\
4x_1 + 8x_2 + 3x_3 + 5x_4 + d_3^- - d_3^+ &= 50 \\
d_3^+ + d_4^- - d_4^+ &= 10 \\
x_1 + d_5^- - d_5^+ &= 7 \\
x_2 + d_6^- - d_6^+ &= 10 \\
x_3 + d_7^- - d_7^+ &= 8 \\
x_4 + d_8^- - d_8^+ &= 12 \\
x_j, d_i^-, d_i^+ &\geq 0
\end{aligned}$$

General Goal Programming Model

The previous four examples have demonstrated the general goal programming model formulation, which can be summarized as

$$\text{Minimize } Z = \sum_{k=0}^{K} \sum_{i=1}^{m} P_k \, (w_{ik}^- d_i^- + w_{ik}^+ d_i^+)$$

subject to

$$\sum_{j=1}^{n} a_{ij} x_j + d_i^- - d_i^+ = b_i \; (i = 1, 2, \ldots, m)$$

$$x_j, d_i^-, d_i^+ \geq 0,$$

where P_k is the preemptive priority weight ($P_k >>> P_{k+1}$) assigned to goal k ($k=0$ is reserved for system constraints); w_{ik}^- and w_{ik}^+ are numerical (differential) weights assigned to the deviational variables of goal i at a given priority level k; d_i^- and d_i^+ represent the negative and positive deviations; a_{ij} is the technological coefficient of x_j in goal i; and b_i is the ith goal level.

Modified Simplex Method of Goal Programming

In this chapter, a modified simplex procedure is introduced to solve goal programming problems. The simplex method is an algorithmic method that employs an iterative process of obtaining the optimal solution through progressive operations. The simplex solution procedure for goal programming problems is very similar to the simplex method of linear programming. However, several distinct differences between the types of models require modification of the simplex process. For this reason, the simplex-based method of goal programming is often referred to as the *modified simplex method*. An example serves as the best way to explain the modified simplex method of goal programming.

Example 13.5 Product Mix Problem

An electronics firm produces color television sets. The company has two production lines. The production rate for line one is 2 sets per hour and for line two it is 1.5 sets per hour. The regular production capacity is forty hours a week for each line. The profit from a television set is $100. The manager of the firm wants to determine the number of hours to run each line during a week and has set the following goals for the next week. They are ranked according to their priority.

1. Meet a production goal of 180 sets for the week.
2. Limit the overtime operation of line one to five hours.
3. Avoid the underutilization of regular working hours for both lines. Differential weights should be assigned according to the production rate of each line.

4. Limit the sum of overtime operation for both lines. Again, differential weights should be assigned to each line according to the relative cost of an overtime hour. It is assumed that the cost of operation is identical for the two production lines.

Before the complete model is formulated, there are a few points to consider. First, the third goal implies that the company has a policy of no involuntary layoffs. Since the productivity of line one is 2 sets per hour as compared to only 1.5 sets for line two, the manager wishes to avoid the underutilization of regular working hours on line one more than line two. The productivity goals are weighted accordingly—2 is assigned to d_2^- and 1.5 to d_3^-. Since it is easier to deal with integers, these values can be doubled so that the ratio becomes 4 to 3. Second, the criterion for determining the differential weights in the fourth goal is the relative cost of overtime. The production rates ratio for the lines is 2 to 1.5. Therefore, the relative cost resulting from an hour of overtime for line two is greater than that for line one. The relative cost of overtime ratio for the two lines will be 3 to 4.

With the experience gained in the model formulation section, we can formulate the following model of the problem:

$$\text{Minimize } Z = P_1d_1^- + P_2d_4^+ + 4P_3d_2^- + 3P_3d_3^- + 4P_4d_3^+ + 3P_4d_2^+$$

subject to

$$\begin{aligned} 2x_1 + 1.5\,x_2 + d_1^- - d_1^+ &= 180 \\ x_1 \qquad\quad + d_2^- - d_2^+ &= 40 \\ x_2 + d_3^- - d_3^+ &= 40 \\ d_2^+ + d_4^- - d_4^+ &= 5 \\ x_j,\ d_i^-,\ d_i^+ &\geq 0 \end{aligned}$$

The Initial Tableau

Table 13.1 presents the initial tableau of the goal programming problem. The basic assumption in formulating the initial tableau of goal programming is identical to that of linear programming. We assume that the initial solution is at the origin, where values of all decision variables are zero. In the first constraint, therefore, the total production from the two lines is zero, since $x_1 = x_2 = 0$. Naturally, there cannot be any overachievement of the production goal ($d_1^+ = 0$); therefore, underachievement of the production goal (d_1^-) is 180 units. The variable d_1^- thus is entered in the solution basis and b_1^* becomes 180. By the same token, d_2^- and d_3^- are also in the solution basis. According to the last constraint ($d_2^+ + d_4^- - d_4^+ = 5$) and since line one is not in operation, d_2^+ has to be zero. The overtime operation of the line in excess of five hours (d_4^+) must also be zero. Consequently, d_4^- has the b_4^* value of 5, as shown in table 13.1. In the initial tableau of goal programming, negative deviational variables (d_i^-) always appear in the solution basis.

Table 13.1 Initial tableau

c_b \ c_j					P_1	$4P_3$	$3P_3$			$3P_4$	$4P_4$	P_2
	basis	b_i^*	x_1	x_2	d_1^-	d_2^-	d_3^-	d_4^-	d_1^+	d_2^+	d_3^+	d_4^+
P_1	d_1^-	180	2	3/2	1				−1			
$4P_3$	d_2^-	40	(1)			1				−1		
$3P_3$	d_3^-	40		1			1				−1	
0	d_4^-	5						1		1		−1
$z_j - c_j$	P_4	0								−3	−4	
	P_3	280	4	3						−4	−3	
	P_2	0										−1
	P_1	180	2	3/2					−1			

First, in goal programming, the purpose of the objective function is to minimize the unattained portions of each of the goals. This is achieved by minimizing the deviational variables through the use of certain preemptive priority factors and differential weights. There is no profit maximization or cost minimization per se in the objective function. Therefore, the preemptive factors and differential weights are the c_j used in linear programming.

Second, the objective function is expressed by assigning priority factors to certain variables. These preemptive priority factors are multidimensional because they are ordinal rather than cardinal values. In other words, priority factors at different levels are not commensurable. This implies that the simplex criterion (z_j or $z_j - c_j$) cannot be expressed by a single row as is done in the case of linear programming. Rather, the simplex criterion becomes a matrix of $k \times n$ size, where k represents the number of preemptive priority levels and n is the number of variables, including both decision and deviational variables.

Third, since the simplex criterion is expressed as a matrix rather than a row, we must design a new procedure for identifying the pivot column. The relationship between the preemptive priority factors is $P_k >>> P_{k+1}$, which means that P_k always takes priority over P_{k+1}. It is therefore clear that the selection procedure of the pivot column must consider the level of priorities.

Now let us examine c_j. In goal programming, c_j is represented by the preemptive priority factors and the differential weights as shown by the goal programming objective function. Most goal programming problems involve a large number of variables. For that reason, in order to make the tableau easier to read, empty spaces are left in the table where zero should appear.

The simplex criterion ($z_j - c_j$) is a 4×10 matrix because we have four priority levels and ten variables (2 decision, 8 deviational) in the model. The goal programming procedure first achieves the most important goal to the fullest possible extent, then considers the next order goal, and so on. The selection of the pivot column should be based on the per unit contribution rate of each variable in achieving the most important goal. When the first goal is completely attained, the pivot column selection criterion will be based on the achievement rate for the second goal, and so on. The preemptive priority factors are listed from the lowest to the highest so that the pivot column can be easily identified at the bottom of the tableau. In order to decrease the cumbersome size of the modified simplex tableau, we have omitted the matrix of z_j altogether.

The goal programming problem is a minimization problem. In the minimization problem of linear programming, the z_j value in the right-hand-side (b_i^*) column of the simplex criterion represents the total cost of the solution. By utilizing the same calculation procedure used in linear programming $[z_j(b_i^*) = \sum_{i=1}^{k} c_b b_i^*]$, we can obtain the z_j value as

$$z_j(b_i^*) = (P_1 \times 180) + (4P_3 \times 40) + (3P_3 \times 40) + (0 \times 5)$$

$$= 180P_1 + 280P_3.$$

The $z_j - c_j$ values ($P_4 = 0$, $P_3 = 280$, $P_2 = 0$, and $P_1 = 80$) in the b_i^* column represent the unattained portion of each goal. For example, in the initial tableau, where the two production lines are not in operation, the second and the fourth goals are already completely attained. How can this be possible? Examining the objective function, we can find that the second goal is to minimize the overtime operation of line one in excess of five hours, and the fourth goal is to minimize the total overtime operation of the two lines. Since we are not operating the lines at this point (at the origin), there can be no overtime operation. Consequently, we have already attained the second and fourth goals. The underachievement of the first goal is 180 because the unfulfilled production goal for television sets is 180 units. For the third goal, the underachievement of the goal is 280. Recall that the differential weights of 4 and 3 have been assigned to the underutilization of the normal production capacity of forty hours for each line. Since these two subgoals are commensurable and are at the same preemptive priority level, this procedure is considered appropriate. However, it is not as easy to interpret the underachievement of 280 for the third goal as for other attained goals where no differential weights are assigned.

Now let us examine the calculation of $z_j - c_j$ in table 13.1. We have already said that c_j (c_b) values represent the priority factors assigned to deviational variables and that z_j values are products of the sum of c_b times the b_i^* column coefficients. Thus, z_j value in the x_1 column is $P_1 \times 2 + 4P_3 \times 1$, or $2P_1 + 4P_3$. The c_j value in the x_1 column is zero, as shown by the blank in the c_j row. Therefore, $z_j - c_j$ for the x_1 column is $2P_1 + 4P_3$. Since P_1 and P_3 are not commensurable, we must list them separately in the P_1 and P_3 rows in the simplex criterion ($z_j - c_j$). Consequently, the $z_j - c_j$ value will be 2 in the P_1 row and 4 in the P_3 row in the x_1 column. By employing the same procedure, $z_j - c_j$ of the x_2 column can be derived: $(P_1 \times 3/2 + 3P_3 \times 1) - 0$, or $3/2\ P_1 + 3P_3$. For the following three columns in table 13.1 (d_1^-, d_2^-, and d_3^-), $z_j - c_j$ is zero since z_j values are identical to the respective c_j values.

For the d_4^- column, $z_j - c_j$ is zero because z_j and c_j are both zero. For the d_1^+ column, we can calculate the z_j value of $-P_1$ from the tableau. Since the c_j value of the column is 0, $z_j - c_j$ will be $-P_1$. The d_2^+ column has $z_j = -4P_3$ and

$c_j = 3P_4$. Thus, $z_j - c_j$ is $-4P_3 - 3P_4$. Now we can calculate $z_j - c_j$ for the d_3^+ and d_4^+ columns as $-3P_3 - 4P_4$ and $-P_2$, respectively (as shown in table 13.1).

As mentioned earlier, we have combined the calculation procedure for identifying z_j and $z_j - c_j$ values in the modified simplex tableau. The procedure requires more mental calculations, but it makes the tableau somewhat smaller and less cumbersome. This is especially true if the problem under consideration is a very complex one. For example, if a problem containing five preemptive priorities and twenty-five variables is being analyzed, the $z_j - c_j$ value of the 5×25 matrix can be calculated in one operation.

The First Iteration

The criterion used to determine the pivot column is the rate of contribution of each variable in achieving the most important goal (P_1). In other words, the column with the largest positive $z_j - c_j$ value at the P_1 level will be selected as the pivot column. In table 13.1, there are two positive values in the x_1 and x_2 columns. Since there is a larger value in the x_1 column (2 versus 3/2), x_1 is selected as the pivot column. The pivot row is the row with the minimum nonnegative value, which is arrived at by dividing the b_i* values by the positive coefficients in the pivot column. The coefficient 1 is circled in table 13.1 to indicate that it is the pivot element at the intersection of the pivot column and the pivot row. By entering x_1 into the solution base, the underutilization of the regular production capacity of line one and the underachievement of the production goal are affected. That is, d_2^- leaves the basis (becomes zero) and d_1^- is reduced from 180 to 100, as described below.

By utilizing the regular simplex procedure, the first tableau is revised to obtain the second tableau shown in table 13.2. Production line one is in operation for forty hours and produces 80 television sets. Therefore, the underachievement of the production goal is now 100 sets, as shown by the b_i* value in the d_1^- row. We have also completely minimized the underutilization of normal production capacity of line one, and, therefore, d_2^- has been removed from the solution base. The calculation of new coefficients in goal programming is usually easier than in linear programming because in goal programming there are many coefficients with the unit value 1.

Table 13.2 Second tableau

c_b \ c_j	basis	b_i^*	x_1	x_2	P_1 d_1^-	$4P_3$ d_2^-	$3P_3$ d_3^-	d_4^-	d_1^+	$3P_4$ d_2^+	$4P_4$ d_3^+	P_2 d_4^+
P_1	d_1^-	100		3/2	1	−2			−1	2		
0	x_1	40	1			1				−1		
$3P_3$	d_3^-	40		1			1				−1	
0	d_4^-	5						1		(1)		−1
$z_j - c_j$	P_4	0								−3	−4	
	P_3	120		3		−4					−3	
	P_2	0										−1
	P_1	100		3/2		−2			−1	2		

Let us examine table 13.2 more closely. The $z_j - c_j$ values in the b_i^* column ($P_4 = 0$, $P_3 = 120$, $P_2 = 0$, $P_1 = 100$) indicate that the unattained portion of the first goal has decreased considerably—80 to be exact. This is encouraging because the goal programming model is a minimization problem and the value of $z_j - c_j$ should decrease at each step toward the optimal point. As our immediate concern is the achievement of the most important goal, we should examine whether $z_j - c_j$ has decreased at the P_1 level at the end of each step. When $z_j - c_j$ at the P_1 level is completely minimized to zero, our attention should then be focused on the $z_j - c_j$ value at the P_2 level, and so on. In table 13.2, $z_j - c_j$ at the P_3 level has also decreased by the amount 160, as line one is put into operation at its normal capacity of forty hours.

The Second Iteration

The pivot column is identified as d_2^+ in table 13.2. The pivot row of d_4^- is determined by the usual procedure. The best way to further achieve the most important goal is by providing overtime operation to line one. Thus, line one will be in operation for a total of forty-five hours, as shown in table 13.3 (the third tableau).

Table 13.3 Third tableau

c_b \ c_j	basis	b_i^*	x_1	x_2	P_1 d_1^-	$4P_3$ d_2^-	$3P_3$ d_3^-	d_4^-	d_1^+	$3P_4$ d_2^+	$4P_4$ d_3^+	P_2 d_4^+
P_1	d_1^-	90		3/2	1	−2		−2	−1			(2)
0	x_1	45	1			1		1				−1
$3P_3$	d_3^-	40		1			1				−1	
$3P_4$	d_2^+	5						1		1		−1
$z_j - c_j$	P_4	15						3			−4	−3
	P_3	120		3		−4					−3	
	P_2	0										−1
	P_1	90		3/2		−2		−2	−1			2

The Third Iteration

The above solution indicates that operation of line one for forty-five hours (i.e., production of 90 television sets) has further reduced the underachievement of the production goal from the previous solution by 10 sets. However, in the process, the fourth goal is no longer completely attained as line one has five hours of overtime. The pivot column is d_4^+ and the pivot row is d_1^-, as shown in table 13.3.

The Fourth Iteration

Table 13.4 presents the fourth simplex tableau. This solution indicates the production goal is now completely attained. However, production line one is in operation for a total of ninety hours (fifty hours of overtime), while line two is not even in operation as yet. Now we can easily identify x_2 as the pivot column and d_3^- as the pivot row. The results of the fourth iteration are given in table 13.5.

Table 13.4 Fourth tableau

c_j / c_b	basis	b_i^*	x_1	x_2	P_1 d_1^-	$4P_3$ d_2^-	$3P_3$ d_3^-	d_4^-	d_1^+	$3P_4$ d_2^+	$4P_4$ d_3^+	P_2 d_4^+
P_2	d_4^+	45		3/4	1/2	−1		−1	−1/2			1
0	x_1	90	1	3/4	1/2				−1/2			
$3P_3$	d_3^-	40		1 (circled)			1				−1	
$3P_4$	d_2^+	50		3/4	1/2	−1			−1/2	1		
$z_j - c_j$	P_4	150		9/4	3/2	−3			−3/2		−4	
	P_3	120		3		−4					−3	
	P_2	45		3/4	1/2	−1		−1	−1/2			
	P_1	0			−1							

The Fifth Iteration

Table 13.5 presents the fifth simplex tableau. Production line two is in operation for forty hours. Thus, the operation hours of production line one have been reduced from ninety to sixty. This solution greatly reduces the goal attainment of P_2, P_3, and P_4. As a matter of fact, the third goal (minimization of underutilization of normal operation hours of the two production lines) is now completely attained as $x_1 = 60$ and $x_2 = 40$.

Table 13.5 Fifth tableau

c_j / c_b	basis	b_i^*	x_1	x_2	P_1 d_1^-	$4P_3$ d_2^-	$3P_3$ d_3^-	d_4^-	d_1^+	$3P_4$ d_2^+	$4P_4$ d_3^+	P_2 d_4^+
P_2	d_4^+	15			1/2	−1	−3/4	−1	−1/2		3/4 (circled)	1
0	x_1	60	1		1/2		−3/4		−1/2		3/4	
0	x_2	40		1			1				−1	
$3P_4$	d_2^+	20			1/2	−1	−3/4		−1/2	1	3/4	
$z_j - c_j$	P_4	60			3/2	−3	−9/4		−3/2		−7/4	
	P_3	0				−4	−3					
	P_2	15			1/2	−1	−3/4	−1	−1/2		3/4	
	P_1	0			−1							

Since P_2 is still not completely attained, the pivot column selection should be made at this level. The largest $z_j - c_j$ is found in the d_3^+ column, which is selected as the pivot column. The pivot row is d_4^+. The results of the fifth iteration are given in the sixth (and final) tableau.

The sixth simplex tableau is presented in table 13.6. The solution indicates that line one is in operation for forty-five hours ($x_1 = 45$) and line two for sixty hours ($x_2 = 60$). Production line one has a total overtime operation of five hours ($d_2^+ = 5$) and line two has twenty hours of overtime ($d_3^+ = 20$). The degree of goal attainment for this solution indicates that the first three goals are completely achieved but the fourth goal could not be achieved, $z_j - c_j\,(P_4) = 95$. This result is due to the fact that overtime operations are required in order to achieve the production goal. In other words, the fourth goal is sacrificed in order to achieve the most important goal.

Table 13.6 Sixth tableau (optimal solution)

c_b \ c_j	basis	b_i^*	x_1	x_2	P_1 d_1^-	$4P_3$ d_2^-	$3P_3$ d_3^-	d_4^-	d_1^+	$3P_4$ d_2^+	$4P_4$ d_3^+	P_2 d_4^+
$4P_4$	d_3^+	20			2/3	−4/3	−1	−4/3	−1/3		1	4/3
0	x_1	45	1			1		1	−1/4			−1
0	x_2	60		1	2/3	−4/3		−4/3	−1/3			4/3
$3P_4$	d_2^+	5						1	−1/4	1		−1
$z_j - c_j$	P_4	95			8/3	−16/3	−4	−7/3	−25/12			7/3
	P_3	0				−3	−3					
	P_2	0										−1
	P_1	0			−1							

Table 13.6 presents the most satisfactory solution to the problem. It is optimal in the sense that it enables the decision maker to attain the goals as closely as possible within the given decision constraints and priority structure. The fourth goal is not completely attained, as shown in table 13.6, because there is at least one positive $z_j - c_j$ value at the P_4 level, while there are no positive $z_j - c_j$ values at the P_1, P_2, and P_3 levels. Two positive values still remain in the $z_j - c_j$ matrix, 8/3 in the d_1^- column and 7/3 in the d_4^+ column. Obviously, we can attain the fourth goal to a greater extent if we introduce d_1^- or d_4^+ into the solution basis. We find, however, a negative value (−1) at the P_1 level in the d_1^- column and also a negative value (−1) at the P_2 level in the d_4^+ column. This implies that if we introduce d_1^- into the solution we can improve achievement of the fourth goal at the expense of the first goal. By the same token, if we introduce d_4^+, it would also improve the fourth goal at the expense of the second goal. Thus, we cannot introduce either d_1^- or d_4^+ into the solution. A positive $z_j - c_j$ at a given priority level may be used in selecting a pivot column *only* when there is no negative element at a higher priority level.

From an analysis of $z_j - c_j$ values, we can determine where conflict exists among goals. Conflict exists between the first and fourth goals in column d_1^-, and between the second and fourth goals in column d_4^+. Now the decision maker can precisely determine how he or she must rearrange the priority structure if the underachieved goals at the lower levels are to be completely attained. This process provides an opportunity to evaluate the soundness of the decision maker's priority structure for the goals. Furthermore, from an analysis of the coefficients in the main body of the tableau, the decision maker can identify the exact tradeoffs between goals. For example, in table 13.6, we can see that if we introduce 30 units of d_1^- into the solution, the fourth goal will be improved by 80. However, this procedure will "undo" the first goal by 30 television sets. The marginal substitution ratio in this case is 1:1. The same type of analysis can also be made in the d_4^+ column. An analysis of the final solution tableau provides a great deal of information and insight about the decision environment and the decision maker's priority structure of goals.

Graphical Analysis of the Goal Programming Solution

Figure 13.1 provides a graphical analysis of example 13.5, the product mix problem. In order to graph the goal programming model, the goal constraint, $d_2^+ + d_4^- - d_4^+ = 5$, must be transformed to an appropriate form containing the decision variables x_1 and x_2. This is done by letting $d_2^+ = 5 - d_4^- + d_4^+$ and substituting the equation into the goal constraint for production hours on line one.

$$x_1 + d_2^- - d_2^+ = 40$$

$$x_1 + d_2^- - (5 - d_4^- + d_4^+) = 40$$

and

$$x_1 + d_2^- + d_4^- - d_4^+ = 45$$

However, the term d_2^- is zero (since the b_i* already exceeds 40); therefore, it can be eliminated, which leaves

$$x_1 + d_4^- - d_4^+ = 45.$$

Figure 13.1 contains a graph of the goal constraints and the direction of positive and negative deviation for each. The feasible solution space of the first priority goal of minimizing d_1^- is indicated by the area above the production goal constraint *CG*. The second goal is to minimize d_4^+, which eliminates the area to the right of the line *BE*. This leaves the area above *EG* as the feasibility area. As long as production takes place within this area, the first two priority goals will be completely achieved.

The third goal is to minimize the underutilization of regular working hours for both lines. However, it is more important to meet the goal for line one than for line two, since line one has a higher rate of productivity (i.e., 2:1.5). As such, the feasible solution space is reduced to the area above *EF*. To achieve the third goal for the two production lines, either point *E* or *F* is satisfactory.

Figure 13.1 Graphical analysis of the goal programming solution procedure. Initial solution, 0; second solution, A; third solution, B; fourth solution, C, fifth solution, D; optimal solution, E.

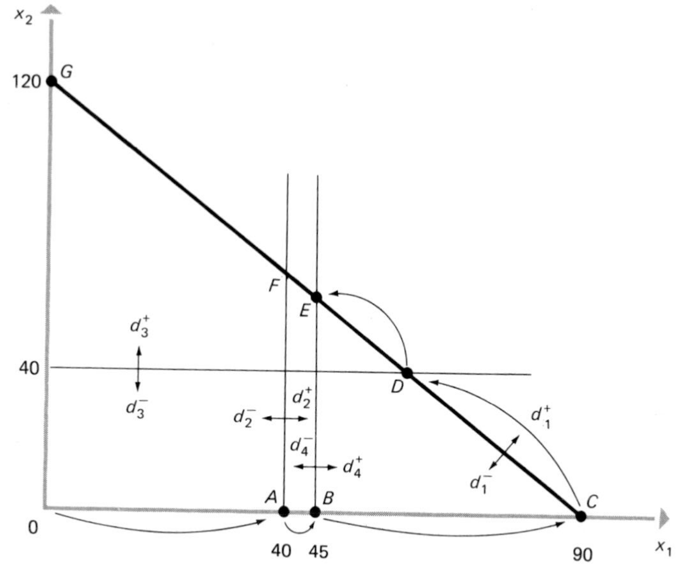

Now the final selection is between points E and F. The fourth goal is to minimize overtime operation of the two production lines as much as possible. Since the productivity rate of an overtime hour for line two is lower than that of line one (1.5:2), minimization of overtime for line two should be given a greater weight. At point E, production line two has fewer overtime hours than at point F. Thus, point E is our optimal point. At point E, the solution is $x_1 = 45$, $x_2 = 60$, $d_2^+ = 5$, $d_3^+ = 20$, and all other variables are zero. At this solution point, the degree of goal attainment is as follows: P_1, P_2, and P_3 are completely attained, but P_4 is not completely attained because production line one has five hours of overtime ($d_2^+ = 5$) and production line two has twenty hours of overtime ($d_3^+ = 20$). This is the same solution as that obtained in table 13.6. In general, our analysis of figure 13.1 replicated the solution steps of the modified simplex method for the example problem.

Steps of the Simplex Method of Goal Programming

Now that we have illustrated the modified simplex method, we can summarize the solution steps as follows:

1. Set up the initial tableau for the goal programming model. Assume that the initial solution is at the origin. Therefore, all the negative deviational variables in the model constraints should initially enter the solution basis. List the b_i*

values and the coefficients of all variables in the main body of the table. Also list the preemptive priority factors and differential weights to the appropriate variables by examining the objective function. In the simplex criterion ($z_j - c_j$), list priority levels in the basis column, from the lowest at the top to the highest at the bottom. The z_j values must be calculated and recorded in the b_i* column. The last step is to calculate $z_j - c_j$ values for each column, starting with the first decision variable to the last positive deviational variable.

2. Determine the new entering variable (pivot column). First, find the highest priority level that has not been completely attained by examining the z_j values in the b_i* column. When the priority level is determined, identify the variable column that has the largest positive $z_j - c_j$ value without a negative value at a higher priority. The variable in that column will enter the solution basis in the next iteration. If there is a tie between the largest positive values in $z_j - c_j$ at the highest priority level, check the next lower priority levels and select the column that has a greater value at the lower priority level. If the tie cannot be broken, arbitrarily choose a column.
3. Determine the exiting variable from the solution basis. This process is identical to finding the pivot row in the normal simplex procedure. If a tie exists when b_i* values are divided by the coefficients, find the row that has the variable with the higher priority factor. This procedure enables the attainment of higher order goals first, and thereby reduces the number of iterations.
4. Determine the new solution. First find the new b_i* values and coefficients of the pivot row by dividing the previous values by the pivot element (i.e., the element at the intersection of the pivot row and the pivot column). Then find the new values for all other rows by using the calculation procedure, old value − (intersectional element of that row × new value in the pivot row in the same column). Now complete the table by finding z_j and $z_j - c_j$ values for the priority rows.
5. Determine whether the solution is optimal. First analyze the goal attainment level of each goal by checking the z_j value for each priority row. If the z_j values are all zero, it is the optimal solution. If there exists a positive value of z_j, examine the $z_j - c_j$ coefficients for that row. If there are positive $z_j - c_j$ values in the row, determine whether there are negative $z_j - c_j$ values at a higher priority level in the same column. If there are negative $z_j - c_j$ values at a higher priority level for the positive $z_j - c_j$ values in the row of interest, the most satisfactory solution has been obtained. If there exists a positive $z_j - c_j$ value at a certain priority level and there is no negative $z_j - c_j$ value at a higher priority level in the same column, the most satisfactory solution has not been obtained. Therefore, return to step 2 and continue.

Figure 13.2 illustrates the solution process for goal programming problems.

Figure 13.2 Flowchart of the solution process of goal programming.

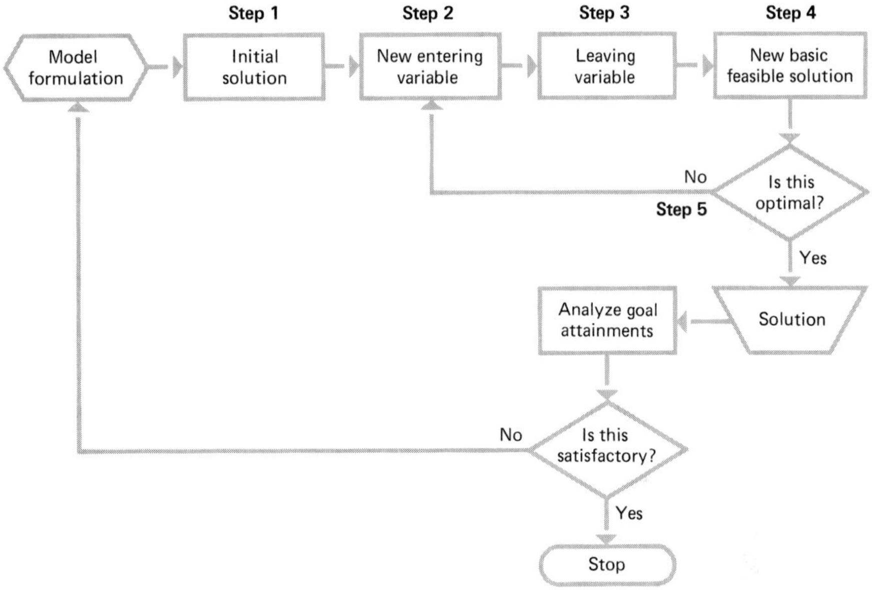

Some Complications and Their Resolutions

Nonpositive Values

To understand the problem of nonpositive b_i values, consider the following goal constraint:

$$-5x_1 - x_2 + d_1^- - d_1^+ = -25$$

In the initial tableau of simplex goal programming, it is assumed that the solution is at the origin. Therefore, the deviational variable d_1^- takes on the value of -25. However, as in the regular simplex method, the modified simplex method requires the nonnegativity condition for variables (x_j, d_i^-, $d_i^+ \geqslant 0$); thus, $d_1^- = -25$ is not permissible. In order to facilitate the initial solution, multiply both sides by -1. The goal constraint becomes

$$5x_1 + x_2 + d_1^+ - d_1^- = 25.$$

If the goal is to achieve exactly -25 from the original constraint, it can easily be achieved by minimizing both d_1^- and d_1^+ at the same priority level. However, if the goal is to make the constraints produce -25 or greater, d_1^- must be minimized in the original equation, but in the revised goal constraint d_1^+ should be minimized to achieve the same effect. Similarly, to assume the value of -25 or less from the constraint, d_1^+ must be minimized in the revised equation.

Tie for Entering Variable

During the iterations of any goal programming problem, it is quite possible that two or more columns can have exactly the same positive $z_j - c_j$ value at the highest unattained goal level. As explained previously in this chapter, when such a case occurs, the determination of the pivot column, and consequently the entering basic variable, is based on the $z_j - c_j$ values at the lower priority levels. If the tie cannot be broken, selection between the contending variables can be made arbitrarily. The other variable will generally be introduced into the solution basis in a subsequent iteration.

Tie for Exiting Variable

To determine the variable that will leave the solution basis, b_i^* values must be divided by the coefficients in the pivot column and the row with the minimum nonnegative quotient must be determined. If there are two or more rows with identical minimum nonnegative values, the problem of degeneracy arises. The resolution of degeneracy should be decided by determining which row has the variable with the higher priority factor. By selecting the variable with the higher priority factor as the exiting variable, the solution process can be shortened, as the higher priority goals will be attained faster.

Unbounded Solution

It is possible that lack of restraints produces an unrealistic priority structure and, thus, may allow one or more variables to increase without limit. In most real-world problems, however, this situation rarely occurs, since goals tend to be set at higher levels than those easily attained within the existing decision environment. If an unbounded solution occurs, it also provides insight in analyzing the decision maker's goal structure. It is often the case when an unbounded solution is obtained that important constraints have been omitted from the problem.

Multiple Optimal Solutions

It is possible that two or more points provide solutions that attain exactly the same level of goals. Such an occasion never occurs as long as (1) there is only a single deviational variable (single goal) at each preemptive priority level, (2) differential weights are assigned among subgoals at the same priority level, and (3) there exists a conflict among the goals.

Infeasible Solution

A model yields an infeasible solution when *all* system constraints are not satisfied. This result indicates that conflict exists among system constraints. In order to resolve the problem of infeasibility, the system constraints must be carefully analyzed to determine whether or not the conflict can be resolved.

Advanced Topics in Goal Programming

Thus far we have discussed the basic concepts, model formulation examples, and solution methods of goal programming. In this section, we will briefly discuss several advanced topics in goal programming.

Sensitivity Analysis

As we have seen in linear programming (chap. 4), an analysis of the effects of parameter changes after determining the optimal solution is also an important part of any solution process. Sensitivity analysis can also be very valuable in goal programming. Since there usually exists some degree of uncertainty concerning the model parameters in real-world problems—for example, priority factors (P_k), goal levels (b_i), and technological coefficients (a_{ij})—sensitivity analysis can provide valuable information in a goal programming solution process.

There have been several studies published concerning the duality of goal programming. However, the value of duality is not as apparent in goal programming as in linear programming. One important reason is the fact that management goals are not subject to random or irrational changes as opposed to changes of c_j in linear programming models. In other words, if a decision maker regards a particular goal as the most important goal, he or she most likely would not be interested in a systematic analysis of changes in the optimal solution as the priority 1 goal descends all the way to the least important level. Another reason is the fact that other information obtained from a dual model can be easily derived from the final simplex tableau of the primal solution. For example, the analysis of trade-offs between two conflicting goals can be easily accommodated by the sensitivity analysis without the dual model. In real-world situations, many parameters change simultaneously and, thus, a simple analysis based on certain information derived from a dual model has very little value.

Integer Goal Programming Methods

In many practical decision problems with multiple conflicting objectives, the decision variables make sense only if they assume discrete values. The decision variables in this situation can be people, construction crews, equipment components, assembly lines, indivisible investment alternatives, public works projects, etc. Discrete variables can be easily obtained by simply rounding off the values of the decision variables in the solution obtained by the regular goal programming algorithm. However, the procedure of rounding off to the nearest integer frequently yields either an infeasible or a nonoptimal solution, and if the variable values are small numbers, such as those in 0–1 programs, it can produce gross errors. Thus, there is a need to develop efficient integer goal programming techniques.

Interactive Goal Programming

The ordinal solution approach based on the preemptive priorities makes goal programming a powerful decision aid. Yet, this very feature also makes it difficult to analyze the trade-offs among the goals. An equally important analysis for managerial decisions studies the effects of changes in goal levels (b_i) and technological coefficients (a_{ij}), addition or deletion of constraints, and addition or deletion of decision variables.

Perhaps the best way to analyze simultaneous changes in the model parameters is an interactive mode where the decision maker and the goal programming model interact via a computer terminal. The interactive approach can perform an on-line analysis of the effect of changes in model parameters, as well as a complete sensitivity analysis of the optimal solution. The interactive goal programming approach provides a systematic process in which the decision maker seeks the most satisfactory solution. This process allows the decision maker to reformulate the model and systematically compare the solutions in terms of their achievement of multiple objectives.

Decomposition Goal Programming

Decomposition analysis was originally discussed as a computational device for solving large-scale linear programs. Recently, however, decomposition analysis has received increasing attention because of two important characteristics: (1) the decomposition technique can be utilized for resource allocation in a decentralized organization, and (2) it provides management in decentralized organizations with insights for developing organizational structure and information systems.

One of the major deficiencies of previous decomposition methods has been their inability to consider multicriteria decomposition problems due to the decomposition methods' reliance on linear programming formulation. Lee and Rho have developed decomposition goal programming algorithms to facilitate multicriteria decomposition problems. The algorithms are also effective in providing managerial implications involved in the decomposition process that can be useful in analyzing organizational development and information systems.

Separable Goal Programming

The modified simplex method is effective in solving linear goal programming problems. For nonlinear problems, however, it is not possible to apply the simplex algorithm. The optimal solution for nonlinear programs can either be any point along a curved boundary hypersurface of the feasible solution space or any point within the feasible solution space.

Presently, there is no general or universal approach for efficiently solving all general classes of nonlinear programming problems. It appears that the most promising approach to solving nonlinear programming problems is the transformation of the original problem into an acceptable linear approximation form that permits the application of the simplex algorithm. The separable programming approach can be adapted to handle multiple objective optimization problems through goal programming.

Chance-Constrained Goal Programming

Chance-constrained goal programming is an effective technique for determining solutions that *satisfice* multiple criteria decision problems that involve elements of risk and uncertainty associated with technological coefficients (a_{ij}) and levels of resources or goals (b_i). Three basic chance-constrained goal programming approaches have been developed. The first and second approaches present separate derivations that assume that only the technological coefficients (a_{ij}) or resource and/or goal levels (b_i) are random variables. The third approach presents a model that considers the combined effect of random a_{ij} and b_i. Using the general chance-constrained goal programming model, an equivalent nonlinear deterministic model can be derived for each of the approaches in a format that is amenable to the separable goal programming model.

Summary

Models developed for managerial decision analysis have often neglected or ignored the unique organizational environment, bureaucratic decision process, and multiple conflicting natures of organizational objectives. However, in reality these are important factors that greatly influence the decision process. In this chapter, the goal programming approach is presented as a tool for the satisfactory consideration and resolution of multiple objectives, while permitting an explicit consideration of the existing decision environment.

Developing and solving the goal programming model points out where some managerial goals cannot be achieved and where trade-offs must be made because of limited resources. Furthermore, this type of model allows the decision maker to critically review the priority structure in view of the solution derived by the model.

References

Arthur, J. L., and Ravindran, A. "An Efficient Goal Programming Algorithm Using Constraint Partitioning and Variable Elimination." *Management Science* 24 (1978) 867–68.

Charnes, A., and Cooper, W. W. *Management Models and Industrial Applications of Linear Programming.* New York: John Wiley & Sons, 1961.

Dyer, J. S. "Interactive Goal Programming." *Management Science* 19 (1972) 62–70.

Ignizio, J. P. *Goal Programming and Extensions.* Lexington, Massachusetts: Lexington Books, 1976.

Ijiri, Y. *Management Goals and Accounting for Control.* Chicago: Rand-McNally, 1965.

Jaaskelainen, V. "A Goal Programming Model of Aggregate Production Planning." *Swedish Journal of Economics,* no. 2 (1969), pp. 14–29.

Kornbluth, J. S. H. "A Survey of Goal Programming." *Omega* 1 (1973).

Lee, S. M. "Decision Analysis Through Goal Programming." *Decision Sciences* 2 (1971) 172–80.

Lee, S. M. *Goal Programming for Decision Analysis.* Philadelphia: Auerbach Publishers, 1972.

Lee, S. M. *Goal Programming Methods for Multiple Objective Integer Programs.* Atlanta: American Institute of Industrial Engineers, 1979.

Lee, S. M., and Clayton, E. R. "A Goal Programming Model for Academic Resource Allocation." *Management Science* 18 (1972) 395–408.

Lee, S. M., and Morris, R. "Integer Goal Programming Methods." In *Multiple Criteria Decision Making,* edited by M. Starr and M. Zeleny, pp. 273–89. TIMS Studies in the Management Sciences, 6. Amsterdam: North-Holland, 1977.

Simon, H. A. "A Behavioral Model of Rational Choice." *Quarterly Journal of Economics* 69 (1955) 99–118.

Problems

1. Consider the following goal programming graph problem:

$$\text{Minimize } Z = P_1d_1^+ + P_2d_2^- + P_2d_3^- + P_3d_2^+ + P_3d_3^+ + P_4d_4^+$$

subject to

$$\begin{aligned} 3x_1 + 3x_2 + d_1^- - d_1^+ &= 120 \\ x_1 + \quad d_2^- - d_2^+ &= 10 \\ x_2 + d_3^- - d_3^+ &= 15 \\ x_1 + \quad d_4^- - d_4^+ &= 5 \end{aligned}$$

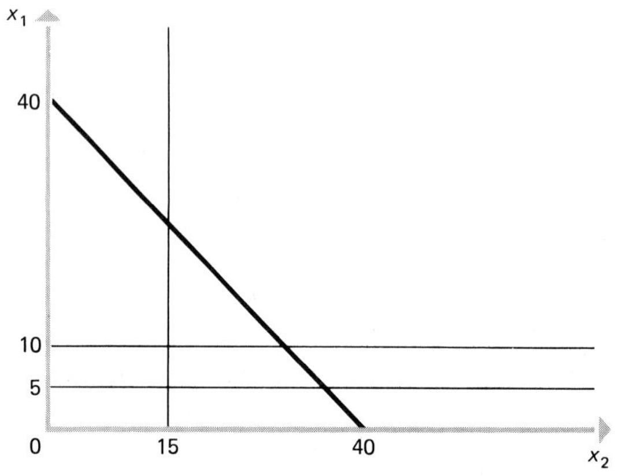

a. Are all the goals satisfied?
b. If not, which goals are not satisfied and by how much?
c. Describe the final solution listing all the variables in the problem.

2. Set up the initial tableau for problem 1 and complete one iteration (two tableaus) of the simplex method.

3. An electronics firm produces two types of radios, AM and FM. According to past experience, production of either type of radio requires an average of one hour in the plant. The plant has a normal production capacity of forty hours a week. The marketing department reports that, because of the limited sales force, a maximum of twenty-four AM and twenty-eight FM radios can be sold per week. The unit profits are $15 per AM radio and $10 per FM radio. The president of the company has set the following multiple goals, listed in the order of their importance:

   1. Avoid any underutilization of normal production capacity.
   2. Achieve the sales goals of twenty-four AM and twenty-eight FM radios. Assign differential weights according to the unit profits.
   3. Minimize the overtime operation of the plant as much as possible.

a. In this problem, if the manager of the firm had only a single goal of profit maximization within the normal production capacity and sales constraints, how would you set up a goal programming model?
b. Formulate a goal programming model for the problem and solve it by the simplex method.

4. A furniture company produces three products: desks, tables, and chairs. All furniture is produced in the central plant. To produce a desk requires three hours in the plant, a table takes two hours, and a chair requires only one hour. The regular plant capacity is forty hours a week. According to the marketing department, the maximum number of desks, tables, and chairs that can be sold per week are ten, ten, and twelve, respectively. The president of the firm has established the following goals according to their importance:

   1. Avoid any underutilization of production capacity.
   2. Meet the order of a retail store for seven desks and five chairs.
   3. Avoid overtime operation of the plant beyond ten hours.
   4. Achieve the sales goals of ten desks, ten tables, and twelve chairs.
   5. Minimize the overtime operation as much as possible.

   Solve the problem through two iterations (three tableaus) of the simplex method.

5. An electronics company produces two types of television sets, color and black and white. The production of a color set requires 10 hours of skilled labor and one hundred hours of unskilled labor. The production of a black-and-white set requires five hours of skilled labor and 150 hours of unskilled labor. The company has 100 hours of skilled labor and 1,500 hours of unskilled labor normally available per month for the production of television sets. It is confirmed from the market study that the maximum number of color and black-and-white sets that can be sold are seventy units and forty-five units per month, respectively. The profit margin from the sale of a color set is $20, whereas it is $15 from a black-and-white set. The company has set the following goals in the order of their importance:

   1. Avoid the overutilization of skilled labor since skilled labor is hard to obtain in the labor market.
   2. Minimize the underutilization of unskilled labor.
   3. Meet the demand as much as possible. Assign weights according to the unit profit of each product.
   4. Limit overutilization of unskilled labor to 100 hours.

   a. Formulate a goal programming model.
   b. Solve the problem through two iterations (three tableaus) of the simplex method.
   c. Is the solution in the third tableau optimal? Why or why not?

6. A sportswear firm produces two types of bathing suits, regular and bikini. The production of all bathing suits is done in a modern sewing center. A regular bathing suit requires an average of five minutes and a bikini requires an average of eight minutes in the sewing center. The two shifts of the sewing center combine for a normal operation period of eighty hours per week. The unit profits for the bathing suits are $2.00 for regular and $2.50 for bikini. The president of the company wishes to achieve the following goals, which are listed in order of importance:

   1. Achieve the profit goal of $2,000 for the week.
   2. Limit the overtime operation of the sewing center to eight hours.
   3. Meet the sales goal for each type of bathing suit: regular, 500; bikini, 400.
   4. Avoid any underutilization of regular operation hours of the sewing center.

      a. Formulate a goal programming model for this problem.
      b. What will be the change in the objective function if the president decides to achieve the sales goal exactly as stated?
      c. Ignore part (*b*) and solve the original problem through one iteration of the simplex method.

7. A department store plans to schedule its annual advertising. The total budget is set at $200,000. The store can purchase local radio spots at $100 per spot, local television spots at $500 per spot, and local newspaper advertising at $200 per ad. The payoff from each advertising medium is a function of its audience size and audience characteristics. The generally accepted objective criterion for advertising is audience points. The audience points for the three advertising vehicles are

Radio:	30 points per spot
TV:	150 points per spot
Newspaper:	150 points per ad.

   The president of the firm has established the following goals for the advertising campaign in order of their importance:

   1. The total budget should not exceed $200,000.
   2. The contract with the local television station requires that the firm spend at least $30,000 in television ads. Meet this contract.
   3. The corporate advertising policy prohibits annual newspaper ad expenditures in excess of $50,000.
   4. Maximize the audience points for the advertising campaign.

   Formulate a goal programming model for this problem.

8. A midwestern granary specializes in the sale of wheat. The firm has definite information concerning the cost at which it can buy and the price at which it can sell the wheat during the next four months. The sale of wheat is restricted by the storage capacity of the firm. The normal capacity of the firm's storage facility is three thousand bushels (overloading of two thousand bushels is allowed in emergencies). The estimated cost c_i and the price p_i during the next four months are given as follows:

	Months			
	1	2	3	4
Cost (c_i)	$4	4	4	7
Price (p_i)	6	7	5	6

The quantity of the purchase is assumed to be based entirely upon the revenue generated from sales. It is also assumed that sales are made at the beginning of the month, followed by purchases. At the beginning of the first month there are two thousand bushels of wheat in the warehouse. The president of the firm has the following multiple goals, listed in ordinal importance with respect to what he desires to achieve in the next four months:

1. In the first month, only the normal capacity of the warehouse should be used.
2. The firm should have at least $20,000 for purchases at the beginning of the fourth month.
3. The firm should reserve at least $2,000 in each month for emergency purposes.
4. The firm should maximize total profit during the entire four-month period.

Formulate a goal programming model for this problem.

9. A clothing store, which is a branch of a larger store in a nearby city, specializes in sales of men's quality clothing. The store is presently operating with the full-time manager, who works on salary, and eight part-time salespeople, who earn an hourly wage of $1.40 plus a 20% discount on any clothes they purchase in the store. Among the part-time salespeople, four are experienced in selling men's clothing and the others are new to the job.

Each month the store receives a sales quota. The manager breaks it down into her quota and the quota for the part-time salespeople as a group. For the next month, the store has received a sales quota of $25,000. The manager has allotted $13,000 to herself and $12,000 to the part-time staff. From records of past experience, the manager sells an average of $54.40 worth of clothing per hour. The four experienced part-time salespeople sell an average of $32.25 per hour, and the inexperienced salespeople sell an average of $26.25 per hour. The manager's regular working schedule per month has been 188 hours and for each part-time sales person it has been 50 hours. The manager realizes, however, that she has to put in many extra hours to meet the monthly quotas. She would like to limit her overtime hours to 44 so that the part-time salespeople get enough hours to meet their quota and to earn sufficient wages.

As an incentive to the manager and other employees, the main store offers bonus and commission plans. The manager receives 3% bonus on the total sales volume that the store achieves above its sales quota for each month. The manager's objective is to earn an average $50 per month from this bonus plan. The part-time salespeople receive a 5% commission on all sales that they make over their quota. The bonus is then split equally among the salespeople. The manager feels that if part-time salespeople put forth a determined effort, they should be able to earn about $10 each in additional commission per month. The manager's goals are listed in ordinal ranking of importance:

1. The store must meet its sales quota of $25,000 for the month.
2. The manager desires to meet her sales quota of $13,000 for the month.
3. The manager would like to limit her overtime to 44 hours for the month.
4. The part-time salespeople must meet their group sales quota of $12,000 for the month.
5. The manager wants the part-time salespeople to work a total of at least 400 hours for the month.
6. The manager would like to earn $50 in bonus and would also like to see the part-time salespeople earn a commission of $10 each.
7. If possible, the manager would like to work no more than 188 hours for the month.
8. The manager wants to minimize the total extra hours that part-time salespeople work in the month.

Formulate a goal programming model for this problem.

10. Your grandmother has just won $200,000 in a lottery. Because of her advanced age you plan to "have fun" investing in the following five alternatives: stock options, real estate, bonds, savings accounts, and diamonds. Real estate and bonds yield an estimated 15% and 10% per year, respectively, while the savings account yields 6%. Since options and diamonds are risky, you cannot assume they will have any yield. You have established the following goals, in order of importance.

    1. Minimize the risk by diversifying the investment. No more than 40% of the total investment should be in any one plan.
    2. Since diamonds are rumored to be profitable, try to invest at least $50,000 in this plan.
    3. The amount invested in speculative ventures (options and diamonds) should not exceed the amount invested in safer plans.
    4. Guarantee that your grandmother will earn an annual yield of at least $25,000 on the investments.

    Formulate a goal programming model that will determine the amount of money to be invested in the various plans.

11. An electronics firm produces two products, record players and tape recorders. The production of both products is done in two separate machine centers. Each record player requires 2 hours in machine center *A* and 1 hour in machine center *B*. Each tape recorder requires 1 hour in machine center *A* and 3 hours in machine center *B*. In addition, each product requires some in-process inventory. The per-unit, in-process inventory requirements are $50 per record player and $30 per tape recorder.

The firm has the normal monthly operation hours of 120 for machine center *A* and 150 for machine center *B*. The average monthly in-process inventory is $3,800. According to the marketing department, the forecasted sales for the record player and tape recorder are fifty and seventy units, respectively, for the coming month.

The president of the firm has the following multiple goals:

1. Achieve the sales goal of fifty record players for the month.
2. Not more than $4,200 may be tied up in in-process inventory.
3. Avoid any underutilization of regular operation hours of both machine centers (no differential weights are required).
4. Limit the overtime operation of machine center *A* to 20 hours.
5. Achieve the sales goal of seventy tape recorders.
6. Limit the sum of overtime for both machine centers (no differential weights are required).

1. If the president's only concern is to maximize profit, how would you set up a linear programming model within the limits of normal monthly production capacity, average inventory level, and forecasted sales?
2. Formulate a goal programming model and solve through three tableaus of the simplex method.

12. The local school district was handed a special order from the state supreme court that racial balance must be achieved among the three schools in the district through extensive busing of pupils. The problem is summarized as follows:

Area \ School	A	B	C	Pupils
1	$ 4	8	8	400 white 200 black
2	16	24	16	300 white 300 black
3	8	16	24	100 white 500 black
Capacity	500	600	400	

The dollar amounts represent the busing cost per pupil from each area to each school. The capacity figures are in terms of normal capacity to provide "quality education." The number of children in each area is divided into two groups, white and black.

The local school district has established the following goals in ordinal ranking of importance:

1. Busing more than thirty minutes (at a cost of $20 or more) should be avoided.
2. Provide educational opportunity for every child.
3. Achieve the racial balance among schools.
4. Overcrowding among the schools should be equally (proportionally) shared among schools.
5. Total transportation cost should be minimized.

Formulate a goal programming model that will determine the optimal busing schedule for the children in the district.

13. Solve the following goal programming problem using the modified simplex method.

$$\text{Minimize } Z = P_1d_1^- + P_2d_4^+ + 5P_3d_2^- + 3P_3d_3^- + P_4d_1^+$$

subject to

$$x_1 + x_2 + d_1^- - d_1^+ = 80$$
$$x_1 + d_2^- = 70$$
$$x_2 + d_3^- = 45$$
$$x_1 + x_2 + d_4^- - d_4^+ = 90$$
$$x_j,\ d_i^-,\ d_i^+ \geq 0$$

14. Solve the following goal programming problem using the modified simplex method.

$$\text{Minimize } Z = P_1d_1^- + P_2d_4^+ + 2P_3d_2^- + P_3d_3^- + P_4d_2^+ + 3P_4d_3^+$$

subject to

$$5x_1 + 2x_2 + d_1^- - d_1^+ = 5{,}500$$
$$x_1 + d_2^- - d_2^+ = 800$$
$$x_2 + d_3^- - d_3^+ = 320$$
$$d_2^+ + d_4^- - d_4^+ = 100$$
$$x_j,\ d_i^-,\ d_i^+ \geq 0$$

15. Solve the following goal programming problem using the modified simplex method.

$$\text{Minimize } Z = P_1d_1^- + P_2d_2^+ + 6P_3d_3^+ + 5P_3d_4^+ + 6P_4d_4^- + 5P_4d_3^-$$

subject to

$$\begin{aligned} 5x_1 + 6x_2 + d_1^- - d_1^+ &= 120 \\ x_2 + d_2^- - d_2^+ &= 11 \\ x_1 + d_3^- - d_3^+ &= 8 \\ x_2 + d_4^- - d_4^+ &= 8 \\ x_j, d_i^-, d_i^+ &\geq 0 \end{aligned}$$

14

Integer and Zero-One Programming

One of the requirements of linear and goal programming techniques is **divisibility**. In other words, each model variable can take on any nonnegative, continuous value in the solution. The divisibility requirement does not present any serious problem in most practical problems. For example, it is quite acceptable to use 1.59 hours in machine center *A*, to put 0.29 ounces of syrup in a bottle of soft drink, and to produce 1.27 tons of steel.

In certain decision problems, however, the divisibility assumption is totally unrealistic and unacceptable. For example, a solution requiring 2.29 dams on a river system has no practical meaning. In this case, either 2 or 3 dams must be assigned (but not 2.29). In a typical production assignment problem, the assignment of people to machines must be made in terms of whole numbers. It is impossible to consider assigning 1.39 people to .75 machines. These types of problems require integer values for the model variables.

In certain problems, costs and/or returns may function in a stepwise manner. Such variables do not move continuously with quantity but rather move discretely up or down when a certain quantity level is reached. This is not a continuous function but an either-or case where integer solutions are required.

There are special cases of integer problems that restrict integer variables to values of either zero or one. For example, capital budgeting, construction scheduling, and assignment problems are good examples of zero-one programming problems. A problem may be set up so that a decision maker must either accept or reject a proposed investment opportunity. Partial acceptance or rejection cannot be considered. In such a case, if the project is accepted, the decision variable equals one, and if it is rejected, the decision variable equals zero. In like manner, if a construction project is completed by the end of period t, the decision variable is indicated as the value one. If it is not completed at time t, the decision variable is zero.

One method of achieving an integer solution is by rounding off the fractional values of the optimal solution. This is possible, however, only when the b_i* value of the constraints can be readily changed. It is not a simple task to round off the fractional values of the basic variables while satisfying the given set of constraints.

A special solution technique, referred to as integer programming, has been developed for solving this type of problem.

The integer programming model requires the following characteristics: (1) a linear objective function, (2) a set of linear constraints, (3) nonnegativity constraints for model variables, and (4) integer value constraints for certain variables. When the model requires all integer values for the basic solution variables, it is generally referred to as an all-integer or *pure-integer* problem. If the model requires only certain variables to be integers, it is called a *mixed-integer* problem. When a problem requires only values of zero or one for the decision variables, it is called a *zero-one integer* problem.

There have been various solution approaches to integer programming problems suggested during the past twenty-five years. We shall discuss several of these approaches in this chapter.

Rounding Approach

A simple and sometimes practical approach to solving an integer programming problem is to round off the values of the decision variables derived by the regular linear programming procedure. This approach is certainly easy and practical in terms of economy of effort, time, and cost required to derive a solution through the integer programming method. As a matter of fact, the rounding approach may be a very effective technique for large integer programming problems where computational costs are extremely high or for problems where the solution values of decision variables are large. For example, rounding off the solution value for the number of paper clips to be produced from 12,450.2 to 12,450.0 would probably be acceptable. However, the major pitfall of this approach is that the solution derived by this method may not be the true optimal integer solution. In other words, the rounded-off solution may be inferior to the true integer optimal solution, or it may be an infeasible solution. This could be of great consequence if the number of submarines to be constructed was rounded off to the nearest whole number.

The following three problems are given to illustrate the rounding procedure:

Problem 1

Maximize $Z = \$100x_1 + \$90x_2$

subject to

$$10x_1 + 7x_2 \leq 70$$

$$5x_1 + 10x_2 \leq 50$$

$$x_1, x_2 \geq 0$$

Problem 2

Minimize $Z = \$200x_1 + \$400x_2$

subject to

$$10x_1 + 25x_2 \geq 100$$

$$3x_1 + 2x_2 \geq 12$$

$$x_1, x_2 \geq 0$$

Problem 3

$$\text{Maximize } Z = \$80x_1 + \$100x_2$$

subject to

$$4x_1 + 2x_2 \leqslant 12$$
$$x_1 + 5x_2 \leqslant 15$$
$$x_1, x_2 \geqslant 0$$

A comparison of the standard simplex solution with no integer restrictions, rounded integer, and optimal integer solutions for these three problems is shown in table 14.1. The first problem is a maximization problem, in which the rounded solution yields a total profit of \$680, only \$20 less than the \$700 yielded by the optimal integer solution.

Table 14.1 Comparison of problem solutions

Problem	Standard Linear Programming Relaxed Solution	Rounded Integer Solution	Optimal Integer Solution
1	$x_1 = 5.38$ $x_2 = 2.31$ $Z = 746.15$	$x_1 = 5$ $x_2 = 2$ $Z = 680$	$x_1 = 7$ $x_2 = 0$ $Z = 700$
2	$x_1 = 1.82$ $x_2 = 3.27$ $Z = 1{,}672.73$	$x_1 = 2$ $x_2 = 3$ Infeasible	$x_1 = 3, x_2 = 3$ or $x_1 = 5, x_2 = 2$ $Z = 1{,}800$
3	$x_1 = 2.14$ $x_2 = 1.71$ $Z = 343$	$x_1 = 2$ $x_2 = 2$ Infeasible	$x_1 = 0$ $x_2 = 3$ $Z = 300$

Problem 2 is a minimization problem in which the rounded solution is infeasible. This points out that although the rounding approach is simple, it can sometimes lead to an infeasible solution. To avoid infeasibility, the simplex solution values with no integer restrictions (referred to as the *relaxed solution*) in a minimization problem must be rounded *up* to the nearest integer value. For example, in problem 2, if a rounded-up solution of $x_1 = 2$ and $x_2 = 4$ had been used, the solution would have been feasible. Alternatively, in a maximization problem, the relaxed simplex solution values would be rounded *down*. Problem 3 demonstrates this case.

In the third problem, the rounded-off solution is also infeasible. However, as indicated in problem 2, if the optimal relaxed solution value of $x_1 = 2.14$ and $x_2 = 1.71$ had been rounded down to $x_1 = 2$ and $x_2 = 1$, this solution would be feasible. This can be verified by examining each of the model constraints with the rounded-down values of the decision variables.

The Z value for this infeasible solution is 360, which is greater than the optimal noninteger solution (343). This can never be the case. The relaxed noninteger simplex solution will always yield the maximum Z value since the solution is on the boundary of the feasible solution space at the extreme corner point. Thus, it is the maximum integer or noninteger solution that can be possibly obtained. This is also the reason we can only round down for a maximization problem (and up for a minimization problem). By rounding down, we are assured that the integer solution will remain in the feasible solution area, although we will always get a lower Z value.

A method similar to the rounding approach is the trial-and-error procedure. Using this method, the decision maker examines each of the integer solutions in comparison with the linear programming solution and selects the solution that optimizes the objective function. This method is not very effective when the problem involves a large number of variables and constraints. Furthermore, checking the feasibility of each rounded solution can be very time consuming.

Integer Programming Solution Methods

Graphical Approach

An integer programming problem that involves only two decision variables can be solved by the graphical approach. This approach is identical to the graphical method of linear programming in all aspects except that the optimal solution must meet the integer requirements. Perhaps the easiest approach to solving a two-dimensional integer programming problem is to use graph paper and plot a collection of lattice integer points within the area of feasible solutions. The following problem serves as an example of the graphical solution approach.

Example 14.1 Furniture Production Problem

A furniture company manufactures dining tables and desks. Production of tables and desks takes place in two departments, cutting and finishing. The company plans its operations on a weekly basis. A dining table requires ten hours in the cutting department and five hours in the finishing department. A desk requires seven hours in the cutting department and ten hours in the finishing department. The firm has a weekly production capacity of seventy hours in the cutting department and fifty hours in the finishing department. A dining table contributes a \$100 profit, and a desk contributes a \$90 profit. The firm wants to determine the optimal number of tables and desks to produce in order to maximize total profit. A noninteger solution is not acceptable for this problem.

We can formulate the problem as an integer programming model.

Maximize $Z = \$100x_1 + \$90x_2$

subject to

$$10x_1 + 7x_2 \leq 70$$
$$5x_1 + 10x_2 \leq 50$$
$$x_1, x_2 = 0 \text{ or nonnegative integers}$$

where

x_1 = number of dining tables

x_2 = number of desks

This model is similar to a standard linear programming model. The only difference is that the last constraint requires the decision variables to take on nonnegative integer values or zero.

The graphical solution to the furniture production problem is presented in figure 14.1. The area of feasible solutions for the linear programming problem is *OABC*. The optimal linear programming solution can be identified as point *B*, where $x_1 = 5.38$, $x_2 = 2.31$, and $Z = \$746.15$. In order to identify the integer optimal solution to the problem, we must retreat from the noninteger optimal point (point *B*) toward the origin with the slope of the iso-profit function (–9/10). This slope is parallel to the slope of the line that passes through the noninteger optimal point. The optimal integer solution is the first integer point to intersect with the iso-profit function. This point is *A*, where $x_1 = 7$, $x_2 = 0$, $Z = \$700$, as shown in figure 14.1.

Figure 14.1 Graphical solution of the furniture production problem.

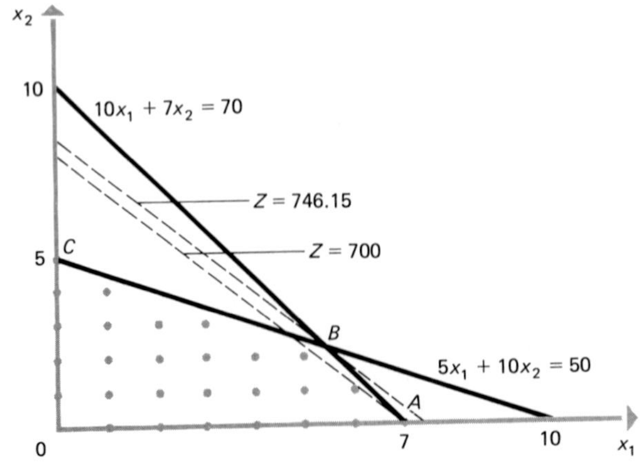

Gomory Approach

Integer programming is a special variant of the standard linear programming approach. Consequently, an optimal integer solution can be derived through the simplex method with some modifications. The modification required for integer programming is the construction of the area of feasible solutions covering all lattice points. This can be accomplished by adding new constraints to the problem and constructing *cutting planes*. This approach was originally proposed by R. E. Gomory. As an initial step in integer programming, a supplementary Gomory constraint must be determined for the simplex solution.

The steps of the Gomory approach are summarized as follows:

1. Solve the problem by the standard linear programming approach using the simplex method. If a problem is so simple that it can be easily solved by the graphical approach, the Gomory approach is not necessary.
2. Examine the optimal solution. If all basic variables have integer values (b_i*), the integer optimal solution is derived and solution process is complete. If one or more basic variables have fractional values, proceed to step 3.
3. Construct a Gomory constraint (a cutting plane) and find a new optimal solution through the dual simplex procedure. Return to step 2.

The branch-and-bound method has become the industry standard for computer codes for integer programming, and real-world applications seem to suggest that the branch-and-bound method is more efficient than the Gomory approach. Thus, the detailed solution procedure of the Gomory approach will not be presented here.

Branch-and-Bound Method

Integer programming problems quite frequently have upper and/or lower bounds for the decision variables. Since the bounded integer programming problem has a finite number of feasible integer solutions, an enumeration procedure serves as a sensible method for determining an optimal solution for this type of problem.

The branch-and-bound method was initially developed by Land and Doig, and it was further studied by Little et al. and other researchers. This technique is quite useful in solving integer, mixed-integer, and zero-one integer problems.

The basic steps of the branch-and-bound method (for a maximization problem) can be summarized as follows:

1. Solve the integer programming problem by the standard simplex method with the integer restrictions relaxed.
2. Examine the optimal solution. If the basis variables that have integer requirements are integers, the optimal integer solution is obtained. If one or more basis variables do not satisfy integer requirements, proceed to step 3.
3. The set of feasible noninteger solution values is branched into subsets (subproblems). The purpose of branching is to eliminate continuous solutions that do not satisfy the integer requirements of the problem. The branching is achieved by introducing mutually exclusive constraints that are necessary to satisfy integer requirements while making sure that no feasible integer solution is excluded.

4. For each subset, the optimal relaxed solution value of the objective function is determined as the upper bound. The best *integer* solution becomes the lower bound. (Initially, this is the rounded-down relaxed solution.) Those subsets having upper bounds that are less than the current lower bound are excluded from further analysis. A feasible integer solution that is as good or better than the upper bound for any subset is sought. If such a solution exists, it is optimal. If such a solution does not exist, a subset with the best upper bound is selected to branch on. Return to step 3.

To illustrate the branch-and-bound method, consider the following problem:

Maximize $Z = 3x_1 + 5x_2$

subject to

$$\begin{aligned} 2x_1 + 4x_2 &\leq 25 \\ x_1 &\leq 8 \\ 2x_2 &\leq 10 \\ x_1, x_2 &= 0 \text{ or nonnegative integers} \end{aligned}$$

The optimal relaxed simplex solution to this problem is $x_1 = 8$, $x_2 = 2.25$, and $Z = 35.25$. This solution represents the initial upper bound. The lower bound is the rounded-down solution of $x_1 = 8$, $x_2 = 2$, and $Z = 34$. In the branch-and-bound method, we divide the problem into two parts in order to search for the possible integer solution values for x_1 and x_2. To accomplish this, the variable with the noninteger solution value that has the greatest fractional part is selected. Since in this solution only x_2 has a fractional part it is selected. In order to eliminate the fractional part of 2.25 (the value of x_2), two new constraints are created. These constraints represent the two new parts to the problem. In this case, the two integer values closest to 2.25 are 2 and 3. Thus, we obtain two new problems by introducing two mutually exclusive constraints, $x_2 \leq 2$ and $x_2 \geq 3$, which are described in the following as parts *A* and *B*. These constraints effectively eliminate all possible fractional values for x_2 between 2 and 3. In effect, they serve to reduce the feasible solution space such that a fewer number of finite integer solutions are evaluated in the problem.

Part *A*

Maximize $Z = 3x_1 + 5x_2$

subject to

$$\begin{aligned} 2x_1 + 4x_2 &\leq 25 \\ x_1 &\leq 8 \\ 2x_2 &\leq 10 \quad \text{(redundant)} \\ x_2 &\leq 2 \\ x_1, x_2 &\geq 0 \end{aligned}$$

Part B

$$\text{Maximize } Z = 3x_1 + 5x_2$$

subject to

$$2x_1 + 4x_2 \leq 25$$
$$x_1 \leq 8$$
$$2x_2 \leq 10$$
$$x_2 \geq 3$$
$$x_1, x_2 \geq 0$$

Parts *A* and *B* are solved with integer restrictions relaxed by the simplex method. (The graphical solutions for the two parts are shown in figure 14.2.) The simplex solutions are

Part *A*: $x_1 = 8, x_2 = 2, Z = 34$

Part *B*: $x_1 = 6.5, x_2 = 3, Z = 34.5$

Figure 14.2 Graphical solutions of part A and part B of the sample problem.

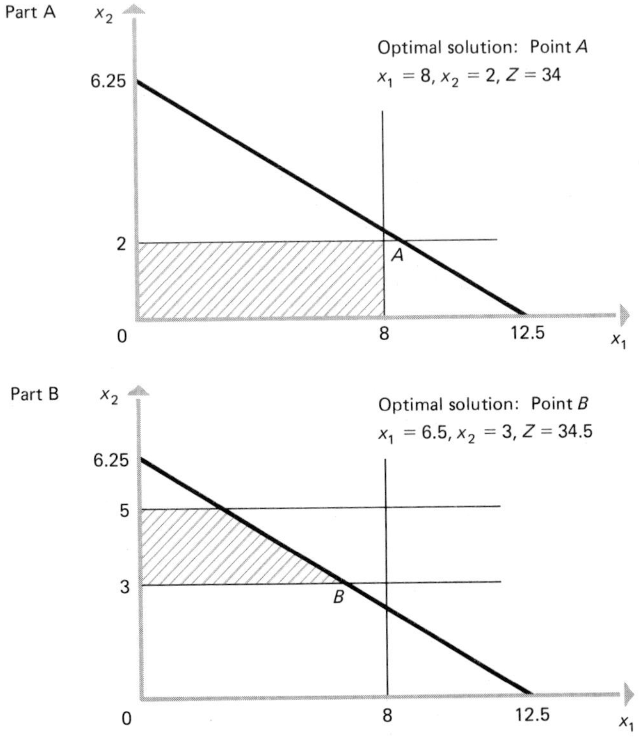

Part A yields an all-integer solution. For part A the upper *and* lower bounds are now $Z = 34$. The part B noninteger solution warrants a further search because its solution has a total profit that is greater than the part A upper bound. It is quite possible that a further search may yield an all-integer solution with total profit exceeding the part A upper bound of 34.

We branch part B into two subparts, $B1$ and $B2$, the first with the constraint $x_1 \leq 6$ and the other with $x_1 \geq 7$. The two subproblems are stated as follows:

Part *B*1

Maximize $Z = 3x_1 + 5x_2$

subject to

$$\begin{aligned} 2x_1 + 4x_2 &\leq 25 \\ x_1 &\leq 8 \quad \text{(redundant)} \\ 2x_2 &\leq 10 \\ x_2 &\geq 3 \\ x_1 &\leq 6 \\ x_1, x_2 &\geq 0 \end{aligned}$$

Part *B*2

Maximize $Z = 3x_1 + 5x_2$

subject to

$$\begin{aligned} 2x_1 + 4x_2 &\leq 25 \\ x_1 &\leq 8 \\ 2x_2 &\leq 10 \\ x_2 &\geq 3 \\ x_1 &\geq 7 \\ x_1, x_2 &\geq 0 \end{aligned}$$

The graphical solutions for the two subproblems are shown in figure 14.3. The simplex solutions are

Part *B*1: $x_1 = 6$, $x_2 = 3.25$, $Z = 34.25$

Part *B*2: infeasible.

Figure 14.3 Graphical solutions of part B1 and part B2.

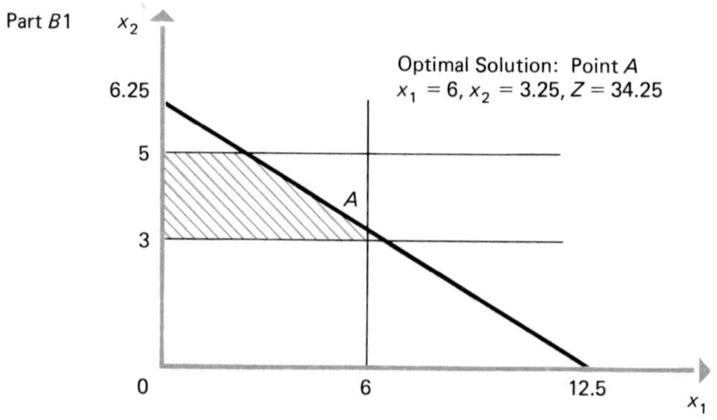

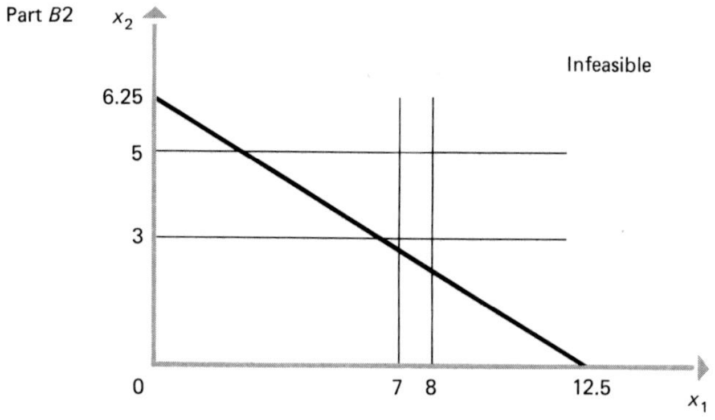

Since part $B1$ yields a total profit greater than 34 (the previously computed upper bound for part A), it must be further branched into two sub-subproblems, with the constraints $x_2 \leq 3$ and $x_2 \geq 4$. The two sub-subproblems are indicated as parts $B1a$ and $B1b$.

Part *B*1*a*

Maximize $Z = 3x_1 + 5x_2$

subject to

$$
\begin{aligned}
2x_1 + 4x_2 &\leq 25 \\
2x_2 &\leq 10 \quad \text{(redundant)} \\
x_2 &\geq 3 \\
x_1 &\leq 6 \\
x_2 &\leq 3 \\
x_1, x_2 &\geq 0
\end{aligned}
$$

Part *B1b*

Maximize $Z = 3x_1 + 5x_2$

subject to

$$2x_1 + 4x_2 \leqslant 25$$

$$2x_2 \leqslant 10$$

$$x_2 \geqslant 3 \quad \text{(redundant)}$$

$$x_1 \leqslant 6$$

$$x_2 \geqslant 4$$

$$x_1, x_2 \geqslant 0$$

The optimal simplex solutions are

Part *B1a*: $x_1 = 6$, $x_2 = 3$, $Z = 33$

Part *B1b*: $x_1 = 4.25$, $x_2 = 4$, $Z = 33.5$

The two preceding solutions have upper bounds ($Z = 33$ and $Z = 33.5$) that are inferior to the solution yielded by part *A*. Therefore, the optimal integer solution is $x_1 = 8$, $x_2 = 2$, $Z = 34$, which was yielded by part *A*.

In the branching and searching procedure, further analysis is stopped when (1) a subproblem results in an inferior solution as compared with the upper bounds already identified and (2) further branching yields infeasible solutions.

When the search is completed, the integer solution with the highest value of the objective function (in a maximization problem) is selected as the optimal solution. The entire branch-and-bound procedure for this problem is shown in figure 14.4.

Figure 14.4 Complete branch-and-bound solution of the sample problem.

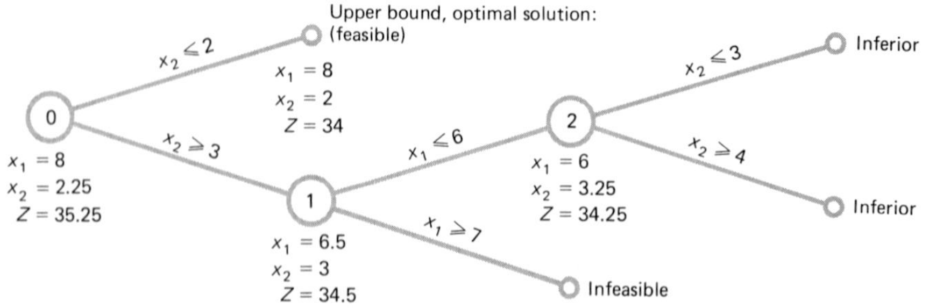

Example 14.2 Assignment Problem

The assignment problem defined in the following table illustrates an application of the branch-and-bound method to a minimization problem. (However, recall that in chapter 5, a method for solving the assignment problem that yields integer solutions was also presented.) The objective of the problem is to assign each of the four employees to each of the four machines in such a manner that the total cost of the work is minimized. This problem consists of a 4 × 4 matrix. Therefore, there are 4! = 24 feasible solutions.

	Machines			
Employee	*A*	*B*	*C*	*D*
1	$10	$15	$16	$ 9
2	14	14	8	10
3	11	9	11	18
4	13	13	15	12

To apply the branch-and-bound method, a tight lower bound on the total cost should be established for all twenty-four feasible solutions. One way to determine this tight lower bound is by summing the minimum costs of each column, without considering whether or not this amount corresponds to a feasible solution. In this example, the sum of the minimum costs in respective columns is 10 + 9 + 8 + 9 = 36.

Since any of the four employees can be assigned to machine *A*, all feasible solutions can be initially branched into four subsets. Then, the lower bound is computed for each of the four subsets. If employee 1 is assigned to machine *A*, there will be 3! = 6 feasible solutions. The lower bound for these six feasible solutions is determined by summing the cost of assigning employee 1 to machine *A* and the minimum costs of the three remaining columns (columns *B*, *C*, and *D* without row 1). For example, the lower bound for the subset of assigning employee 1 to machine *A* will be 10 + (9 + 8 + 10) = 37. This calculation is shown in the following table:

	Machine			
Employee	*A*	*B*	*C*	*D*
1	(10)			
2		14	(8)	(10)
3		(9)	11	18
4		13	15	12

Similarly, the lower bound for the subset of assigning employee 2 to machine A is $14 + (9 + 11 + 9) = 43$, which is shown in the next table:

Employee	Machine A	B	C	D
1		15	16	(9)
2	(14)			
3		(9)	(11)	18
4		13	15	12

The lower bounds for the remaining two subsets can be calculated in a similar manner. The lower bounds for the four subsets are listed in the following table:

Subsets	Lower Bounds
1*A*	$10 + (9 + 8 + 10) = 37$ ←lower bound
2*A*	$14 + (9 + 11 + 9) = 43$
3*A*	$11 + (13 + 8 + 9) = 41$
4*A*	$13 + (9 + 8 + 9) = 39$ ←upper bound

The minimum cost of assignment among the lower bounds of the four subsets is 37, as shown by subset 1*A*. This amount is selected as the *lower* bound in the first step. The minimum value among the lower bounds of the feasible solutions (if there are any at this step) is selected as the *upper* bound. Subsets 3*A* and 4*A* are both feasible solutions. Therefore, the lower bound of subset 4*A* (39) is chosen as the upper bound. Subsets 2*A* and 3*A* have lower bounds greater than the identified upper bound of 39. Consequently, these two subsets are eliminated from further branching.

The analysis of the problem thus far is shown in figure 14.5. Subset 1*A*, which has the current lower bound, is selected for further branching. Thus, subset 1*A* is identified by the circled node 1. Employee 1 has been assigned to machine *A*. The next step is the assignment of one of the remaining employees (2, 3, and 4) to machine *B*. If employee 2 is assigned to machine *B*, the lower bound for this subset is the sum of assignment costs of 1*A*, 2*B* and the minimum costs of the remaining two columns, after deleting rows 1 and 2. For example, the lower bound for the subset 1*A* and 2*B* is $10 + 14 + (11 + 12) = 47$, as shown in the following table:

Employee	Machine A	B	C	D
1	(10)			
2		(14)	8	10
3		9	(11)	18
4		13	15	(12)

Figure 14.5 First step of the branch-and-bound solution.

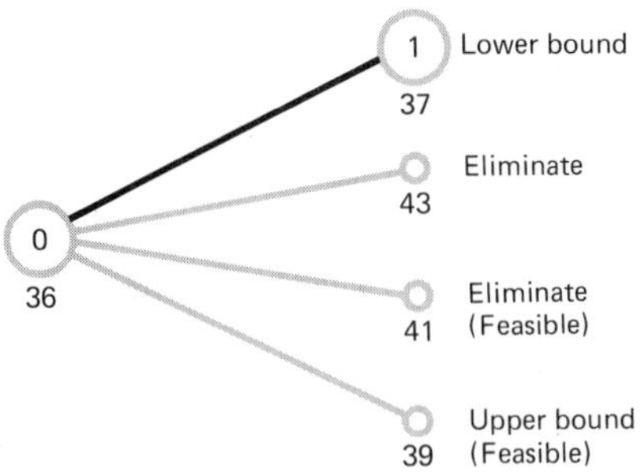

The lower bounds for the remaining two subsets can be calculated in the same manner, so that the bounds of the three subsets are as follows:

Subsets	Lower Bound
1*A*-2*B*	10 + 14 + (11 + 12) = 47
1*A*-3*B*	10 + 9 + (8 + 10) = 37 ← lower bound
1*A*-4*B*	10 + 13 + (8 + 10) = 41

Among the three lower bounds calculated, the minimum is found at subset 1*A*-3*B*. Thirty-seven becomes the new lower bound. The lower bounds for the remaining two subsets, 1*A*-2*B* and 1*A*-4*B*, are greater than the upper bound identified in the first step (39 for subset 4*A*). Therefore, we can eliminate subsets 1*A*-2*B* and 1*A*-4*B* from further analysis. The results of the second step of the analysis are shown in figure 14.6.

Figure 14.6 Second step of the branch-and-bound solution.

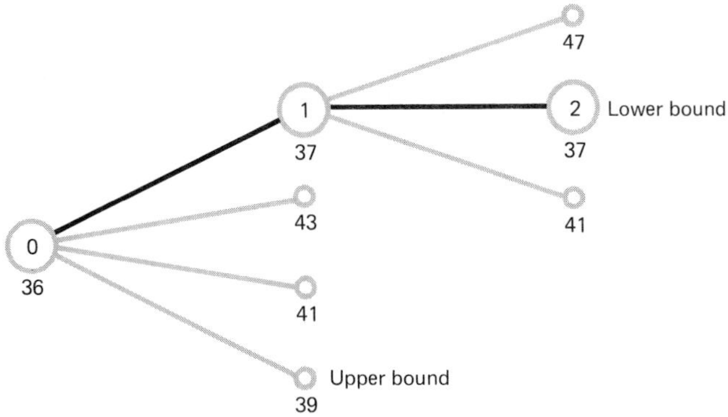

Two more employees are still waiting for assignment to machines *C* and *D*. The third-step branching must begin from the new lower bound identified by the circled node 2. There are only two possible ways to branch 2! = 2. The two possible assignments are 1*A*-3*B*-2*C*-4*D* and 1*A*-3*B*-2*D*-4*C*. If employee 2 is assigned to machine *C*, the lower bound will be 10 + 9 + 8 + (12) = 39. On the other hand, if employee 4 is assigned to machine *C*, the lower bound will be 10 + 9 + 15 + (10) = 44. The preceding two subsets are both feasible solutions to the problem. Since the first subset (1*A*-3*B*-2*C*-4*D*) indicates a lower total assignment cost than the second subset (1*A*-3*B*-2*D*-4*C*), it is selected for comparison with the upper bound (39). The lower bound (39) of subset 1*A*-3*B*-2*C*-4*D* is not greater than the upper bound (39). Therefore, this subset is an optimal solution. However, since the lower bound is equal to the upper bound, the subset that yielded the upper bound is also an optimal solution. When we inspect the two solutions, we can identify the two optimal solutions shown in the following table:

Assignment 1		Assignment 2	
1 to *A*	$10	1 to *D*	$ 9
2 to *C*	8	2 to *C*	8
3 to *B*	9	3 to *B*	9
4 to *D*	12	4 to *A*	13
Total Cost	$39	Total Cost	$39

The complete branch-and-bound analysis for the problem is shown in figure 14.7. If the total costs of the final two subsets (1*A*-3*B*-2*C*-4*D* and 1*A*-3*B*-2*D*-4*C*) exceed the upper bound (39), these solutions must be eliminated from further consideration. Then a new node with the minimum lower bound, which is less than the upper bound, should be selected for further branching. If no node meets this requirement, then the subset that yields the upper bound is the optimal solution.

Figure 14.7 Complete branch-and-bound solution of the assignment problem.

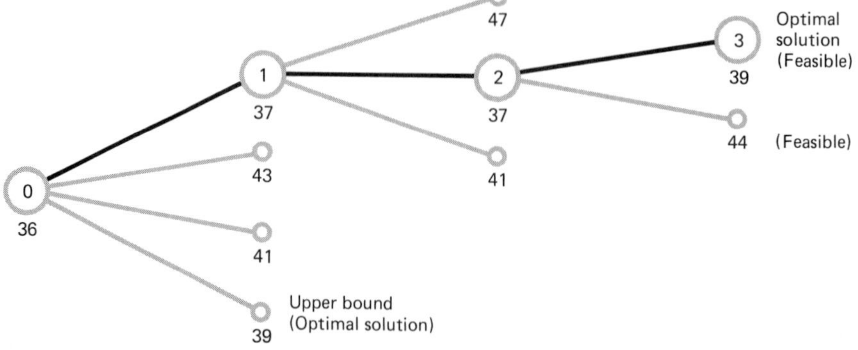

The branch-and-bound method can also be applied to a maximization case of the assignment problem. The procedure is exactly the same as the one just presented. The only difference is that the calculation process for the upper and lower bounds is the reverse of the process for the minimization case.

Zero-One Programming

Many real-world problems require integer solutions with decision variables of zero or one. Assignment, capital budgeting, project scheduling, fixed-cost, location-allocation, and traveling salesmen problems are good examples of this type. Rather than applying the branch-and-bound algorithm, we can use a different algorithm that takes advantage of the 0–1 system constraint characteristics.

The zero-one problem can be stated as

$$\text{Minimize } Z = \sum_{j=1}^{n} c_j x_j$$

subject to

$$\sum_{j=1}^{n} a_{ij} x_j \leq b_i \quad (i = 1, 2, \ldots, m)$$

$$x_j = 0 \text{ or } 1.$$

Example 14.3 Capital Budgeting Problem

A corporation is considering six possible investment opportunities. The following table presents pertinent information about the investment projects:

Projects	Initial Outlay ($000)	New Managerial Staff Need	Average Annual Cash Flow ($000)	Annual Accounting Profit ($000)	Net Present Value ($000)
1	$210	3	$45	$40	$100
2	340	5	75	70	190
3	150	2	35	33	80
4	60	1	10	18	30
5	540	8	150	120	220
6	350	3	100	80	150
Requirement or Maximum Available	Maximum 1,000	Maximum 12	Minimum 100	Minimum 100	Maximize

In addition, projects 3 and 4 are mutually exclusive pollution control activities. Furthermore, project 6 is contingent upon the prior acceptance of project 1. The model can be formulated as follows:

$$\text{Maximize } Z = 100x_1 + 190x_2 + 80x_3 + 30x_4 + 220x_5 + 150x_6$$

subject to

$$\begin{aligned}
210x_1 + 340x_2 + 150x_3 + 60x_4 + 540x_5 + 350x_6 &\leqslant 1{,}000 \\
3x_1 + 5x_2 + 2x_3 + x_4 + 8x_5 + 3x_6 &\leqslant 12 \\
45x_1 + 75x_2 + 35x_3 + 10x_4 + 150x_5 + 100x_6 &\geqslant 100 \\
40x_1 + 70x_2 + 33x_3 + 18x_4 + 120x_5 + 80x_6 &\geqslant 100 \\
x_3 + x_4 &\leqslant 1 \\
x_6 - x_1 &\leqslant 0 \\
x_j &= 0 \text{ or } 1
\end{aligned}$$

Although the model is not exactly in the desired form (all constraints should be $\leqslant$), as we shall see later, the general idea of formulating a capital budgeting problem can be clearly seen in this example.

Example 14.4 Either-Or Constraints

A farmer is considering one of two possible new markets for the farm's operation: dog food or cattle feed. The production processes for the two new products under consideration differ significantly. The farmer has established the following production constraints:

$$2x_1 + 4x_2 + x_3 \leqslant 30 \quad \text{dog food process} \tag{14.1}$$

$$10x_1 + 8x_2 \leqslant 180 \quad \text{cattle feed} \tag{14.2}$$

where

x_1 = bushels of corn

x_2 = bushels of wheat

x_3 = horse meat (100 pounds)

Either constraint (14.1) or (14.2) is applicable only if the firm decides to produce dog food or cattle feed, respectively. In order to accommodate the two either-or constraints in the model, we can transform them into the following two constraints:

$$2x_1 + 4x_2 + x_3 \leqslant 30 + yM \tag{14.3}$$

$$10x_1 + 8x_2 \leqslant 180 + (1 - y)M \tag{14.4}$$

where

y = 0–1 variable

M = an arbitrarily large value

If the contribution rate (c_j) assigned to y is zero, the either-or constraints are as follows:

1. If $y = 0$, then constraint (14.3) becomes a binding constraint, while constraint (14.4) becomes redundant as its right-hand-side value increases.
2. If $y = 1$, then constraint (14.4) becomes the binding constraint, while constraint (14.3) becomes a redundant constraint.

This procedure can be utilized for many different types of either-or type situations. Consider the following cases:

The first case involves inconsistent directions for constraints. It is possible that two mutually exclusive constraints can have different inequality directions as shown:

$$\sum_{j=1}^{n} a_{1j}x_j \leqslant b_1 \tag{14.5}$$

$$\sum_{j=1}^{n} a_{2j}x_j \geqslant b_2 \tag{14.6}$$

Constraint (14.6) can be changed to a $\leqslant$ constraint by multiplying both sides by -1.

$$\sum_{j=1}^{n} -a_{2j}x_j \leqslant -b_2 \tag{14.7}$$

Now constraints (14.5) and (14.7) can be transformed into

$$\sum_{j=1}^{n} a_{1j}x_j \leqslant b_1 + yM$$

$$\sum_{j=1}^{n} -a_{2j}x_j \leqslant -b_2 + (1-y)M$$

or

$$\sum_{j=1}^{n} a_{1j}x_j \leqslant b_1 + yM$$

$$\sum_{j=1}^{n} a_{2j}x_j \geqslant b_2 - (1 - y)M.$$

The second either-or case involves a minimum quantity for a certain variable. In many situations, a certain decision variable makes sense only when its quantity reaches a certain minimum level L. For example, production of petroleum makes sense only when a well produces at least so many barrels a day; shipment of a certain product to a foreign country is considered only when the order meets a certain minimum quantity. If the decision variable under consideration is x_k, the situation can be described as

$$x_k = 0 \quad \text{or} \quad x_k \geq L.$$

Although the nonnegativity constraint ($x_k \geq 0$) is assumed, for the sake of convenience, we can rewrite the constraints as

$$x_k \leq 0 \quad \text{or} \quad x_k \geq L.$$

Then following the previous procedure,

$$x_k \leq 0 + yM$$
$$x_k \geq L - (1 - y)M$$
$$y = 0, 1.$$

Example 14.5 At Least *k* of *r* Constraints Must Hold

The either-or type of mutually exclusive constraints presents a special situation in the case where at least k of r constraints must hold. Suppose these constraints are as follows:

$$\sum_{j=1}^{n} a_{ij}x_j \leq b_i \qquad i = 1, 2, \ldots, r$$

As with the either-or constraints, the 0–1 variable y_i and an arbitrarily large value M can be used to transform the constraint into the following:

$$\sum_{j=1}^{n} a_{ij}x_j \leq b_i + y_iM \qquad i = 1, 2, \ldots, r$$

If $y_i = 0$, then the ith constraint becomes binding as it approaches b_i. If $y_i = 1$, then the ith constraint becomes redundant as its b_i becomes very large ($b_i + M$).

In order to guarantee that at least k of r constraints must hold, we can introduce the following additional constraint:

$$\sum_{i=1}^{r} y_i \leq r - k$$

Suppose a model has the following constraints:

$$x_1 + x_2 + x_3 \leq 10$$
$$4x_1 + x_2 - x_3 \leq 12$$
$$x_2 + 2x_3 \leq 8$$
$$3x_1 - x_2 + x_3 \leq 9$$

These constraints can be converted to

$$x_1 + x_2 + x_3 \leq 10 + y_1M$$
$$4x_1 + x_2 - x_3 \leq 12 + y_2M$$
$$x_2 + 2x_3 \leq 8 + y_3M$$
$$3x_1 - x_2 + x_3 \leq 9 + y_4M$$
$$y_i = 0, 1.$$

If only one constraint must hold (all constraints are mutually exclusive), then the following additional constraint is needed:

$$y_1 + y_2 + y_3 + y_4 = 4 - 1 = 3$$

If at least three constraints must hold, then the additional constraint required is

$$y_1 + y_2 + y_3 + y_4 \leq 4 - 3$$

or

$$y_1 + y_2 + y_3 + y_4 \leq 1.$$

Example 14.6 Fixed-Cost Problem

In undertaking various management activities, it is common to incur fixed costs (fixed-charge or setup cost). In such cases, the objective function is the minimization of the total cost, which is the sum of variable cost and fixed cost, related to a management activity.

Indicate x_j as the level of activity j, k_j as the fixed cost of $x_j>0$, and c_j as the variable cost of activity j. The total cost is determined as follows:

$$Z = f_1(x_1) + f_2(x_2) + \cdots + f_n(x_n)$$

where

$$f_i(x_j) = \begin{cases} k_j + c_jx_j, \text{ if } x_j > 0 \\ 0, \text{ if } x_j = 0 \end{cases}$$
$$x_j \geq 0.$$

As with the mutually exclusive constraints, the 0–1 variable y_j and a large value M can be utilized in the following fashion for the fixed charge problem:

$$\text{Minimize } Z = \sum_{j=1}^{n}(c_jx_j + k_jy_j)$$

subject to original constraints and

$$x_j \leq My_j \quad (j=1, 2, \ldots, n)$$
$$y_j \leq 1$$
$$y_j \geq 0, \text{ and } y_j \text{ is an integer}$$

In this model, the system constraint $x_j \leq My_j$ can be converted to $x_j - My_j \leq 0$ for the actual solution process. Some solution methods require the identification of y_j simply as 0–1 variables, while others require an explicit formulation as $y_j \leq 1$, $y_j \geq 0$, and y_j is an integer for $j=1, 2, \ldots, n$.

Consider the following production case. A company is considering three different products with the following characteristics:

Product	Fixed Cost	Unit Profit
1	\$100 if $x_1>0$, \$ 0 if $x_1=0$	\$5
2	\$150 if $x_2>0$, \$ 0 if $x_2=0$	\$7
3	\$ 75 if $x_3>0$, \$ 0 if $x_3=0$	\$4

The production constraints are

$$4x_1 + 6x_2 + x_3 \leq 2{,}000$$
$$2x_1 + 2x_2 + 3x_3 \leq 1{,}500.$$

The problem can now be formulated as

$$\text{Maximize } Z = 5x_1 - 100y_1 + 7x_2 - 150y_2 + 4x_3 - 75y_3$$

subject to

$$4x_1 + 6x_2 + x_3 \leq 2{,}000$$
$$2x_1 + 2x_2 + 3x_3 \leq 1{,}500$$
$$x_1 - 10{,}000y_1 \leq 0$$
$$x_2 - 10{,}000y_2 \leq 0$$
$$x_3 - 10{,}000y_3 \leq 0$$
$$y_j \leq 1 \quad \text{for all } j$$
$$x_j, y_j \geq 0 \quad \text{for all } j$$
$$y_j = \text{an integer.}$$

Now let us consider a slight modification of the fixed-cost problem. Suppose that a firm is considering three different products for the upcoming planning horizon. The pertinent information is given in the following table:

Product	Unit Contribution	Direct Labor Requirement
1	\$15	5 hr.
2	12	4
3	20	7

The fixed cost of the production facility is based on the amount of labor (number of people working in the production plant and their equipment needs). The industrial engineering department estimates the following steps of fixed costs as a function of the direct labor requirements in the production process:

Fixed Costs	Direct Labor Requirement
\$200,000	up to 30,000 hr.
300,000	30,000–50,000 hr.
400,000	50,000–100,000 hr.

The production scheduling model can be formulated as follows:

$$\text{Maximize } Z = 15x_1 + 12x_2 + 20x_3 - 200{,}000y_1 - 300{,}000y_2 - 400{,}000y_3$$

subject to normal production constraints and

$$5x_1 + 4x_2 + 7x_3 \leq 30{,}000y_1 + 50{,}000y_2 + 100{,}000y_3$$

$$y_1 + y_2 + y_3 = 1$$

$$y_j \leq 1$$

$$y_j \leq 0, \text{ and } y_j \text{ is an integer}$$

In this model, constraint $y_1 + y_2 + y_3 = 1$ guarantees that only one fixed cost schedule will be selected, based on the appropriate direct labor requirement.

Example 14.7 Location-Allocation Problem

Another interesting application of zero-one programming is the location-allocation problem. The problem usually involves multiple market areas (states, warehouses, distribution centers, or other geographical areas), multiple facility locations, known demand at various markets, and known transportation costs from potential facilities to destinations.

For the sake of simplicity, let us assume that each potential facility location site will permit only one type of plant to be built to produce one product. The variables for the problem are defined as follows:

x_{ij} = quantity of the product transported from facility i to area j
c_{ij} = transportation per unit of product from facility i to area j
K_i = production capacity at facility i
F_i = total fixed cost (amortized construction and operating costs) at facility i
D_j = demand for the product at market area j
y_i = 1, if facility location i is selected, 0 otherwise

The model can be developed as follows:

$$\text{Minimize } Z = \sum_{i=1}^{m}\sum_{j=1}^{n} c_{ij}x_j + \sum_{i=1}^{m} F_i y_i$$

subject to

$$\sum_{j=1}^{n} x_{ij} \leq K_i y_i, \quad i = 1, 2, \ldots, m$$

$$\sum_{i=1}^{m} x_{ij} \geq D_j, \quad j = 1, 2, \ldots, n$$

$$y_i \leq 1$$

$$y_i \geq 0, \text{ and } y_i \text{ is an integer}$$

There are many applications of the location-allocation model. Problems for determining the location of health care facilities (clinics or hospitals), schools, police precincts, fire stations, and computer facilities are good examples. Other variations include the so-called set-covering case where the addition of new facility sites or closing of some existing facilities can be evaluated.

Example 14.8 Traveling Salesman Problem

The traveling salesman problem is concerned with the minimization of total travel cost (distance, time, expenses, or a combination of these). The decision variable x_{ijk} equals 1 if the journey includes a travel from location i to location j in leg k, otherwise x_{ijk} equals 0.

Consider a simple case where there are four locations (e.g., cities, states, sales districts, campuses, military installations, factories). Suppose the home location is defined as node 1 and the locations to be visited are numbered 2, 3, and 4 as shown in figure 14.8.

Figure 14.8 Locations and routes of the traveling salesman problem.

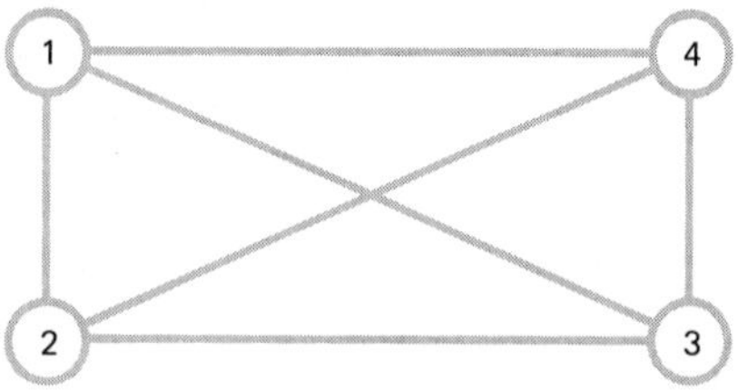

There are six possible routes for the salesperson to visit locations 2, 3, and 4 from node 1.

Travel plan 1:	(1→2)	(2→3)	(3→4)	(4→1)
Leg:	1	2	3	4
Travel plan 2:	(1→2)	(2→4)	(4→3)	(3→1)
Leg:	1	2	3	4
Travel plan 3:	(1→3)	(3→2)	(2→4)	(4→1)
Leg:	1	2	3	4
Travel plan 4:	(1→3)	(3→4)	(4→2)	(2→1)
Leg:	1	2	3	4
Travel plan 5:	(1→4)	(4→2)	(2→3)	(3→1)
Leg:	1	2	3	4
Travel plan 6:	(1→4)	(4→3)	(3→2)	(2→1)
Leg:	1	2	3	4

The travel plan from one location to another is often termed an **arc.**

The problem involves four basic types of constraints. The first set of constraints guarantees that each of the n locations is visited only once, starting from and ending at location (node) 1.

$$\sum_{j=2}^{n} x_{1j1} = 1 \tag{14.8}$$

$$\sum_{i=2}^{n} \sum_{j=2}^{n} x_{ijk} = 1 \quad k = 2, 3, \ldots, n-1;\ i \neq j \tag{14.9}$$

$$\sum_{i=2}^{n} x_{i1n} = 1 \tag{14.10}$$

A second set of constraints assures that there is exactly one departure from each of the n locations.

$$\sum_{j=1}^{n}\sum_{k=2}^{n} x_{ijk} = 1 \qquad i = 2, 3, \ldots, n;\ i \neq j \tag{14.11}$$

If $j=1,\ k=n$ or if $k=n,\ j=1$

The condition imposed in constraint (14.11) assures that the person would return home on the last leg. In developing a real-world traveling salesman model, equations of type (14.11) should be written out first and variables eliminated that do not satisfy the conditions. For example, suppose $n = 4$ and $i = 2$; the equation is

$$x_{212} + x_{222} + x_{232} + x_{242} + x_{213} + x_{223} + x_{233}$$
$$+ x_{243} + x_{214} + x_{224} + x_{234} + x_{244} = 1.$$

Since $i \neq j$, it eliminates x_{222}, x_{223}, and x_{224}. The condition if $j=1,\ k=n$ or if $k=n,\ j=1$ further eliminates x_{212}, x_{213}, x_{234}, and x_{244}. Thus, the equation becomes

$$x_{232} + x_{242} + x_{233} + x_{243} + x_{214} = 1.$$

A third set of constraints assures that only one leg ends at each of the n locations.

$$\sum_{i=1}^{n}\sum_{k=1}^{n-1} x_{ijk} = 1 \qquad j = 2, 3, \ldots, n;\ i \neq j \tag{14.12}$$

If $i=1,\ k=1$ or if $k=1,\ i=1$

The final set of constraints guarantees that if leg k ends at location j, leg $k+1$ must start from the same location j.

$$x_{1j1} = \sum_{p=2}^{n} x_{jp2} \qquad j = 2, 3, \ldots, n;\ i \neq j \tag{14.13}$$

$$\sum_{i=2}^{n} x_{ijk} = \sum_{p=2}^{n} x_{jpk+1} \qquad \begin{cases} j = 2, 3, \ldots, n;\ i \neq j \\ k = 2, 3, \ldots, n-2 \end{cases} \tag{14.14}$$

$$\sum_{k=2}^{n} x_{ijn-1} = x_{j1n} \qquad j = 2, 3, \ldots, n;\ i \neq j \tag{14.15}$$

Constraint (14.13) assures that leg 2 can start from location j only if leg 1 ended at location j. Constraint (14.14) is basically the same as the first leg shown in (14.13) and last leg shown in (14.15), except that it is a more general formulation.

The objective function of the model is the minimization of total travel cost, c_{ij}, associated with traveling from location i to location j.

$$\text{Minimize } Z = \sum_{i=1}^{n}\sum_{j=1}^{n}\sum_{k=1}^{n} c_{ij}x_{ijk} \quad i \neq j$$

The traveling salesman model can be adapted to represent such problems as political campaigns, truck routing, inspection tours, and production scheduling. Although the logic of model formulation can be easily seen, the actual solution of the real-world traveling salesman problem is not as simple. Usually, such problems are complex with large numbers of decision variables and constraints. There has, however, been some progress in developing efficient algorithms and computer programs to solve the traveling salesman problem during the past several years.

Example 14.9 Knapsack Problem

The knapsack problem is a classic application problem of integer programming. This problem involves filling a knapsack with a given capacity (volume or weight) by selecting certain items from a given number of available articles. Usually, the available quantity of each item is limited to one unit and each item has certain characteristics in terms of weight, volume, and relative benefits (utilities). The objective of the problem is to determine the optimal combination of items that should be packed in the knapsack to maximize the total benefit within the given knapsack capacity constraints.

Suppose a boy scout is packing his knapsack for a camping trip. He is considering ten different items for the trip. Their values for the trip and weights are shown in the following table:

Item	Value	Weight
Compass/watch	300 points	.15 lb.
Jar of peanut butter	200	.5
Portable burner	75	4
Canteen	225	2.5
Sleeping bag	250	5
Dried meat	125	2
Fishing gear	75	4
Movie camera	25	1.2
Portable television	10	2
Radio	50	.8

The maximum limit of weight allowed each scout is fifteen pounds. Furthermore, there should be at least one food item packed in the knapsack and not more than one item among cameras, television, and radio. The model can be formulated in the following manner:

$$\text{Maximize } Z = 300x_1 + 200x_2 + 75x_3 + 225x_4 + 250x_5 + 125x_6 + 75x_7 + 25x_8 + 10x_9 + 50x_{10}$$

subject to

$$.15x_1 + .5x_2 + 4x_3 + 2.5x_4 + 5x_5 + 2x_6 + 4x_7 + 1.2x_8 + 2x_9 + .8x_{10} \leq 15$$

$$x_2 + x_6 \geq 1$$

$$x_8 + x_9 + x_{10} \leq 1$$

$$x_j = 0 \text{ or } 1 \text{ for all } j$$

There have been many variations of the knapsack problem for real-world applications. The cargo loading problem is a very good example of a variation of the knapsack problem. The knapsack problem can be expanded by allowing additional constraints and possible inclusion of more units of item j.

The knapsack problem is computationally challenging as the total number of possible combinations of n items is 2^n. For example, a problem with 5 items has thirty-two different combinations, a problem with 10 items has one thousand twenty-four, and a problem with 30 items would have over one billion possible solution combinations.

Implicit Enumeration Method

You should now be quite familiar with some of the many real-world problems that require all decision variables to be either values of zero or one. This section contains a discussion of the implicit enumeration method for solving the zero-one problem. Egon Balas has developed an algorithm that analyzes all solutions (feasible and infeasible), although the vast majority of solutions are enumerated only implicitly. The implicit enumeration method is based on Balas' additive algorithm and Glover's backtracking method, which was implemented to the Balas algorithm by Geoffrion.

The technique approach is to start the solution process with an optimal (actually even better-than-optimal) but infeasible solution. The procedure then forces the solution toward feasibility while maintaining an optimal solution. The implicit enumeration method is not based on the usual simplex method but a binary branch-and-bound procedure. The bounding is accomplished by keeping the best feasible solution as the optimality test criterion for new solutions. The branching is performed through the feasibility test and the assignment of the binary value to solution variables.

The contribution rates (c_j) in the objective function should be nonnegative, $c_j \geq 0$. Actually, this condition is not restrictive because if $c_j < 0$, x_j can be replaced by $1 - x_j$, where $x_j = 0$ or 1. This way x_j has a positive contribution rate in the objective function. This substitution must be made in the constraints as well.

In order to examine the solution procedure in a systematic manner, the following variables are defined:

A = the set of all decision variables

V_j = the set of all decision variables that have been assigned a value of either 0 or 1 at jth iteration

$A - V_j$ = the set of free variables (i.e., those that have not entered the solution, as yet, after the jth iteration)

I_j = the set of free decision variables that could possibly improve the solution at the jth iteration

$\overline{Z}$ = current upper bound value of the objective function

The general solution procedure for the implicit enumeration method is summarized as follows:

1. Set all variables as free variables ($V_0 = \emptyset$). They are implicitly equal to zero. If this solution is feasible, the optimal solution is found. Otherwise, determine the initial upper bound of $\overline{Z}$ when $x_j = 1$ for all j.
2. Find the set of constraints violated when partial solution V_j is implemented. If no constraint is violated, set all free variables to zero. This is a feasible solution ($I_j = \emptyset$). If the solution's value of the objective function is less than the previous $\overline{Z}$, it becomes the new upper bound $\overline{Z}$. Proceed to step 3. If some constraints are still violated, find the value of the objective function for the solution F and set $\overline{Z} - F$ as the objective coefficient limit. Proceed to step 4.
3. The solution is "fathomed." When a solution cannot be improved any further, it is said to be fathomed. The backtracking procedure is to be initiated. The last variable added to the solution with a value of 1 (the rightmost positive element in V_j) is made 0 but left in the solution set (not a free variable). Drop any elements to the right. Return to step 2.
4. Find I_j, the set of improving variables, by evaluating each of the free variables for two criteria: (1) feasibility test 1—it should have a positive coefficient in some violated constraints; and (2) optimality test—the objective function coefficient should be less than the limit $\overline{Z} - F$.

   If $I_j = \emptyset$, check all elements in V_j. If they are all negative, terminate the solution. The current upper bound feasible solution, if there is one, is the optimal solution. If all elements in V_j are not negative, return to step 3.

   If $I_j \neq \emptyset$, proceed to step 5.
5. Check the feasibility test 2. This test determines whether or not all violated constraints can be made feasible if some or all variables in I_j are made 1 in each of those violated constraints, where these variables have positive coefficients.

   If yes, select the variable in I_j with the greatest coefficient sum and enter it into V_j. Return to step 2.

   If no, check all elements in V_j. If they are all negative, terminate the solution. The current upper bound feasible solution, if there is one, is the optimal solution. If all elements in V_j are not negative, return to step 3.

Consider the following example problem:

$$\text{Minimize } Z = 2x_1 + x_2 + 3x_3 + 2x_4 + 4x_5$$

subject to

$$\begin{aligned}
x_1 + 2x_2 + x_3 + x_4 + 2x_5 &\geq 4 \\
7x_1 + x_2 - 3x_4 + 3x_5 &\geq 2 \\
-3x_1 + 3x_2 + 2x_3 - x_5 &\geq -1 \\
x_j &= 0 \text{ or } 1 \text{ for all } j
\end{aligned}$$

The number of possible solution combinations for this problem is $2^5 = 32$. The implicit enumeration method for the problem is applied as follows:

Iteration 0

$$\begin{aligned}
A &= (1,2,3,4,5) \\
V_0 &= \emptyset \\
A - V_0 &= (1,2,3,4,5) \\
I_0 &= (1,2,3,4,5) \\
Z &= 12 \text{ (initial upper bound) infeasible}
\end{aligned}$$

Since the goal is to minimize the objective function and since all contribution coefficients (c_j) are positive, a good place to start the solution is where all $x_j = 0$. Thus, $A = (1,2,3,4,5)$ and the V_0 set is empty. $A - V_0$, or the set of free variables, is (1,2,3,4,5). The initial upper bound $\overline{Z}$ is found by making all $x_j = 1$ in the objective function. This solution ($V_0 = \emptyset$) is, of course, infeasible.

To determine the set of improving variables, I_0, rearrange the constraints in the following manner:

$$\underbrace{x_1 + 2x_2 + x_3 + x_4 + 2x_5 \geq 4}_{f_1} \tag{14.16}$$

$$\underbrace{7x_1 + x_2 - 3x_4 + 3x_5 \geq 2}_{f_2} \tag{14.17}$$

$$\underbrace{-3x_1 + 3x_2 + 2x_3 - x_5 \geq -1}_{f_3} \tag{14.18}$$

Then

$$\begin{aligned}
f_1 &= -4 + x_1 + 2x_2 + x_3 + x_4 + 2x_5 \geq 0 \\
f_2 &= -2 + 7x_1 + x_2 - 3x_4 + 3x_5 \geq 0 \\
f_3 &= 1 - 3x_1 + 3x_2 + 2x_3 - x_5 \geq 0
\end{aligned}$$

Since $x_j = 0$ at iteration 0,

$f_1 = -4 \ngeq 0$ violated constraint

$f_2 = -2 \ngeq 0$ violated constraint

$f_3 = 1 \geqslant 0$ unviolated constraint.

The improving variable candidates are those with positive coefficients (feasibility test 1) in the first two constraints.

		x_1		x_2		x_3		x_4		x_5	
$f_1 =$	-4	$+$	$1(0)$	$+$	$2(0)$	$+$	$1(0)$	$+$	$1(0)$	$+ \; 2(0)$	$\ngeq 0$
$f_2 =$	-2	$+$	$7(0)$	$+$	$1(0)$			$-$	$3(0)$	$+ \; 3(0)$	$\ngeq 0$
Sums of coefficients			8		3		1		-2	5	

Thus, $I_0 = (1,2,3,4,5)$. Perform feasibility test 2 by checking whether or not the two violated constraints can be made feasible by making variables in I_0 that have positive coefficients in the first and second constraints equal 1. The calculations are as follows:

Constraint 1: $f_1 = -4 + 1(1) + 2(1) + 1(1) + 1(1) + 2(1) = 3 \geqslant 0$

Constraint 2: $f_2 = -2 + 7(1) + 1(1) \qquad -3(0) + 3(1) = 9 \geqslant 0$

Thus, the partial solution passes the feasibility test. Note that variables with negative coefficients (x_4 in constraint 2) are not assigned the value of 1.

Since the procedure is to add one variable at a time to V_j in search of a feasible solution, the entering variable should be the one that moves a solution closest to feasibility. Since a variable may have positive coefficients in some constraints and negative coefficients in others, its addition to the solution may be "helpful" in some constraints and "harmful" in others. To find an overall measure, determine the sum of the constraint coefficients for each of the free variables in the violated constraints. In the example, x_1 is easily determined as the most attractive candidate since the sum of its coefficients is the greatest. The optimality test, or the objective function coefficient test, is not needed here as a feasible solution is not yet found.

Iteration 1

$V_1 = (+1)$ infeasible solution

$A - V_1 = (2,3,4,5)$

$I_1 = (2,3,4,5)$

With $x_1 = (+1)$, the solution becomes $x_1 = 1$, $x_2 = x_3 = x_4 = x_5 = 0$. The + sign in front of 1 indicates that a value of 1 has been assigned to x_1. When a variable has been assigned a value of 0, its subscript will be preceded by a − sign. Once again check feasibility test 1 as follows:

		x_1	x_2	x_3	x_4	x_5	
$f_1 =$	-4	$+ 1(1)$	$+ 2(0)$	$+ 1(0)$	$+ 1(0)$	$+ 2(0)$	$= -3 \ngeq 0$
$f_2 =$	-2	$+ 7(1)$	$+ 1(0)$		$- 3(0)$	$+ 3(0)$	$= 5 \geq 0$
$f_3 =$	1	$- 3(1)$	$+ 3(0)$	$+ 2(0)$		$- 1(0)$	$= -2 \ngeq 0$
Sum of coefficients in constraints 1 and 3			5	3	1	1	

The first and third constraints are still not satisfied. Thus, the solution is infeasible. The feasibility test 2 for the two violated constraints is

$$\text{Constraint 1: } f_1 = -4 + 1(1) + 2(1) + 1(1) + 1(1) + 2(1) = 3 \geq 0$$

$$\text{Constraint 3: } f_3 = 1 - 3(1) + 3(1) + 2(1) = 3 \geq 0.$$

$I_1 = (2,3,4,5)$, and x_2 is the entering variable as the sum of its coefficients is the greatest. It should again be noted that since the upper bound $\overline{Z}$ is not that of a feasible solution, it is not necessary to perform the optimality test.

Iteration 2

$$V_2 = (+1, +2) \quad \text{infeasible solution}$$
$$A - V_2 = (3,4,5)$$
$$I_2 = (3,4,5)$$

By entering the improving variable x_2 into the solution, the result can be determined as follows:

		x_1	x_2	x_3	x_4	x_5	
$f_1 =$	-4	$+ 1(1)$	$+ 2(1)$	$+ 1(0)$	$+ 1(0)$	$+ 2(0)$	$= -1 \ngeq 0$
$f_2 =$	-2	$+ 7(1)$	$+ 1(1)$		$- 3(0)$	$+ 3(0)$	$= 6 \geq 0$
$f_3 =$	1	$- 3(1)$	$+ 3(1)$	$+ 2(0)$		$- 1(0)$	$= 1 \geq 0$
Coefficients in constraint 1				1	1	2	

This solution is still not feasible. I_2 (3,4,5) and the entering variable at the next iteration should be x_5.

Iteration 3

$$V_3 = (+1, +2, +5) \quad \text{feasible solution}$$
$$A - V_3 = (3{,}4)$$
$$I_3 = \emptyset \text{ fathomed}$$
$$\overline{Z} = 7$$

The feasibility of the solution can be examined again as follows:

$$\begin{array}{lllllll} & & x_1 & x_2 & x_3 & x_4 & x_5 \\ f_1 = & -4 & + 1(1) & + 2(1) & + 1(0) & + 1(0) + & 2(1) = 1 \geq 0 \\ f_2 = & -2 & + 7(1) & + 1(1) & & - 3(0) & + 3(1) = 9 \geq 0 \\ f_3 = & 1 & - 3(1) & + 3(1) & + 2(0) & & - 1(1) = 0 \geq 0 \end{array}$$

This solution is feasible as all constraints are satisfied. The solution is $x_1 = 1, x_2 = 1, x_5 = 1, x_3 = 0, x_4 = 0$, and $Z = 7$. As this solution is feasible, adding any new variable (making either $x_3 = 1$ or $x_4 = 1$) only increases the total cost. Thus, $I_3 = \emptyset$ and the solution is fathomed. It should be noted that we have implicitly completed the enumeration of all solutions in which $x_1 = x_2 = x_5 = 1$.

Iteration 4

$$V_4 = (+1, \ +2, \ -5) \quad \text{infeasible solution}$$
$$A - V_4 = (3{,}4)$$
$$I_4 = (3{,}4)$$

As the solution at iteration 3 was fathomed, the backtracking procedure should be initiated. The rightmost positive element in V_3 (X_5) should be made 0 but left in the solution set as described in step 3 of the solution procedure. Going back to step 2 of the solution procedure, analyze the feasibility and optimality of the solution. Of course, this solution is basically the same one evaluated at iteration 2. At that iteration, the improving variable set was identified as $I_2 = (3,4,5)$. Since x_5 is no longer a free variable, I_4 equals (3,4). The upper bound has now been derived from a feasible solution, and the improving variables must also pass the optimality test. The objective function coefficients of the improving variables should be less than $\overline{Z} - F$. The value of the objective function for the partial solution $V_2 = (+1, \ +2)$ is 3. Thus $\overline{Z} - F = 7 - 3 = 4$. Either variable qualifies as an entering variable.

	x_3	x_4
Objective function coefficients	3	2

The feasibility test 2 (step 5) must be performed whether or not the violated constraint ($f_1 = -1 \not\geq 0$) can be made feasible, if variables in I_4 are made 1. The test shows that with the solution $(+1, +2, -5, +3, +4)$, $f_1 = 1 \geq 0$. The coefficients of x_3 and x_4 are same value (1). Thus, enter x_4, which has a smaller objective function coefficient.

Iteration 5

$$V_5 = (+1, +2, -5, +4) \quad \text{feasible solution}$$
$$A - V_5 = (3)$$
$$I_5 = \emptyset \quad \text{fathomed}$$
$$\bar{Z} = 5$$

The feasibility of the solution can be checked as follows:

		x_1	x_2	x_3	x_4	x_5	
$f_1 =$	-4	$+\ 1(1)$	$+\ 2(1)$	$+\ 1(0)$	$+\ 1(1)$	$+\ 2(0)$	$= 0 \geq 0$
$f_2 =$	-2	$+\ 7(1)$	$+\ 1(1)$		$-\ 3(1)$	$+\ 3(0)$	$= 3 \geq 0$
$f_3 =$	1	$-\ 3(1)$	$+\ 3(1)$	$+\ 2(0)$		$-\ 1(0)$	$= 1 \geq 0$

This solution is also feasible, but the value of the objective function is 2 less than the previous upper bound. Thus, the new upper bound $\bar{Z} = 5$. We have completed implicit enumeration of all solutions with $x_1 = x_2 = x_4 = 1$.

Iteration 6

$$V_6 = (+1, +2, -5, -4) \quad \text{infeasible solution}$$
$$A - V_6 = (3)$$
$$I_6 = \emptyset \quad \text{fathomed}$$

The variables in the $A - V_6$ set (only x_3 in this case) should be tested for feasibility and optimality. Constraint 1 is the only constraint violated $f_1 = -1 \not\geq 0$ (see the solution at iteration 2). The x_3 variable easily passes the feasibility test 1 as it has a positive coefficient in f_1. The optimality test shows that the objective function coefficient of x_3, ($c_3 = 3$) is greater than $Z - F = 2$. Thus, x_3 does not pass the optimality test.

Iteration 7

$$V_7 = (+1, -2) \quad \text{infeasible solution}$$
$$A - V_7 = (3,4,5)$$
$$I_7 = (4)$$

The feasibility of this solution was tested at iteration 1. The optimality test should be performed for the three free variables against $\overline{Z}-F = 3$. Only x_4 passes the test.

Iteration 8

$$V_8 = (+1,-2,+4) \quad \text{infeasible solution}$$
$$A-V_8 = (3,5)$$
$$I_8 = \emptyset \quad \text{fathomed}$$

The feasibility test 1 of the solution is shown in the following:

		x_1	x_2	x_3	x_4	x_5	
$f_1 =$	-4	$+\ 1(1)$	$+\ 2(0)$	$+\ 1(0)$	$+\ 1(1)$	$+\ 2(0)$	$= -2 \ngeq 0$
$f_2 =$	-2	$+\ 7(1)$	$+\ 1(0)$		$-3\ (1)$	$+\ 3(0)$	$= 2 \geq 0$
$f_3 =$	1	$-\ 3(1)$	$+\ 3(0)$	$+\ 2(0)$		$-\ 1(0)$	$= -2 \ngeq 0$
Sum of coefficients in constraints 1 and 3				3		1	

Constraints 1 and 3 are violated. The optimality test is performed for the two free variables, x_3 and x_5, that have positive coefficients in the violated constraints. Since $\overline{Z}-F = 5-4=1$, neither variable passes the test. Thus, $I_8 = \emptyset$.

Iteration 9

$$V_9 = (+1,-2,-4) \quad \text{infeasible solution}$$
$$A-V_9 = (3,5)$$
$$I_9 = \emptyset$$

It is already known from iteration 7 that the variables x_3 and x_5 do not pass the optimality test.

Iteration 10

$$V_{10} = (-1) \quad \text{infeasible solution}$$
$$A-V_{10} = (2,3,4,5)$$
$$I_{10} = (2,3,4,5)$$

This solution is basically the same as the one analyzed at iteration 0. The feasibility test 1 is as follows:

		x_1	x_2	x_3	x_4	x_5		
$f_1 =$	-4	$+ 1(0)$	$+ 2(0)$	$+ 1(0)$	$+ 1(0)$	$+ 2(0)$	$=$	$-4 \ngeq 0$
$f_2 =$	-2	$+ 7(0)$	$+ 1(0)$		$- 3(0)$	$+ 3(0)$	$=$	$-2 \ngeq 0$
$f_3 =$	1	$- 3(0)$	$+ 3(0)$	$+ 2(0)$		$- 1(0)$	$=$	$1 \geqslant 0$
Sum of coefficients in constraints 1 and 2		3	1	-2	5			

All the free variables pass the optimality test, $c_j < (\bar{Z} - F) = 5$. The feasibility test 2 shows that $f_1 = -4 + 1(0) + 2(1) + 1(1) + 1(1) + 2(1) = 1 \geqslant 0$; $f_2 = -2 + 7(0) + 1(1) - 3(0) + 3(1) = 2 \geqslant 0$.

Iteration 11

$$V_{11} = (-1, +5) \quad \text{infeasible solution}$$
$$A - V_{11} = (2,3,4)$$
$$I_{11} = \emptyset \quad \text{fathomed}$$

This solution violates only constraint 1, $f_1 = -2 \ngeq 0$. All of the free variables satisfy the feasibility test. However, none passes the optimality test, $c_j < (\bar{Z} - F) = 5 - 4 = 1$. Thus, the solution is fathomed.

Iteration 12

$$V_{12} = (-1, -5) \quad \text{infeasible solution}$$
$$A - V_{12} = (2,3,4)$$
$$I_{12} = \emptyset \quad \text{fathomed}$$

All free variables face the feasibility test 1 and optimality tests. The feasibility test 2 of the violated constraints indicates the following:

$$f_1 = -4 + 1(0) + 2(1) + 1(1) + 1(1) + 2(0) = 0 \quad \geqslant 0$$
$$f_2 = -2 + 7(0) + 1(1) \qquad - 3(0) + 3(0) = -1 \geqslant 0$$

This solution is therefore fathomed. Since all elements in V_{12} are negative, the solution procedure should be terminated.

The optimal solution is the incumbent solution that has the current upper bound. The optimal solution is therefore $x_1 = x_2 = x_4 = 1$, $x_3 = x_5 = 0$, $Z = 5$, as identified at iteration 5.

As the final step, check the entire solution combinations as shown in the following table:

Solutions	x_1	x_2	x_3	x_4	x_5	Feasibility	$\bar{Z}$
1	0	0	0	0	0	No	
2	0	0	0	0	1	No	
3	0	0	0	1	0	No	
4	0	0	0	1	1	No	
5	0	0	1	0	0	No	
6	0	0	1	0	1	No	
7	0	0	1	1	0	No	
8	0	0	1	1	1	No	
9	0	1	0	0	0	No	
10	0	1	0	0	1	Yes	5
11	0	1	0	1	0	No	
12	0	1	0	1	1	No	
13	0	1	1	0	0	No	
14	0	1	1	0	1	Yes	8
15	0	1	1	1	0	No	
16	0	1	1	1	1	No	
17	1	0	0	0	0	No	
18	1	0	0	0	1	No	
19	1	0	0	1	0	No	
20	1	0	0	1	1	No	
21	1	0	1	0	0	No	
22	1	0	1	0	1	No	
23	1	0	1	1	0	No	
24	1	0	1	1	1	No	
25	1	1	0	0	0	No	
26	1	1	0	0	1	Yes	7
27	1	1	0	1	0	Yes	5
28	1	1	0	1	1	Yes	9
29	1	1	1	0	0	Yes	6
30	1	1	1	0	1	Yes	10
31	1	1	1	1	0	Yes	8
32	1	1	1	1	1	Yes	12

The optimal solution is identified as solution 27. There is also an alternate optimal solution identified as solution 10. If you are interested in alternate optimal solutions, the criterion of the optimality test can be modified from $c_j < \bar{Z} - F$ to $c_j \leq \bar{Z} - F$ for the free variables. The complete solution network for the problem is shown in figure 14.9. The solutions explicitly enumerated are shown by bold lines. Figure 14.10 presents a flow diagram of the implicit enumeration procedure followed in solving the sample problem.

Figure 14.9 Solution network of the sample problem.

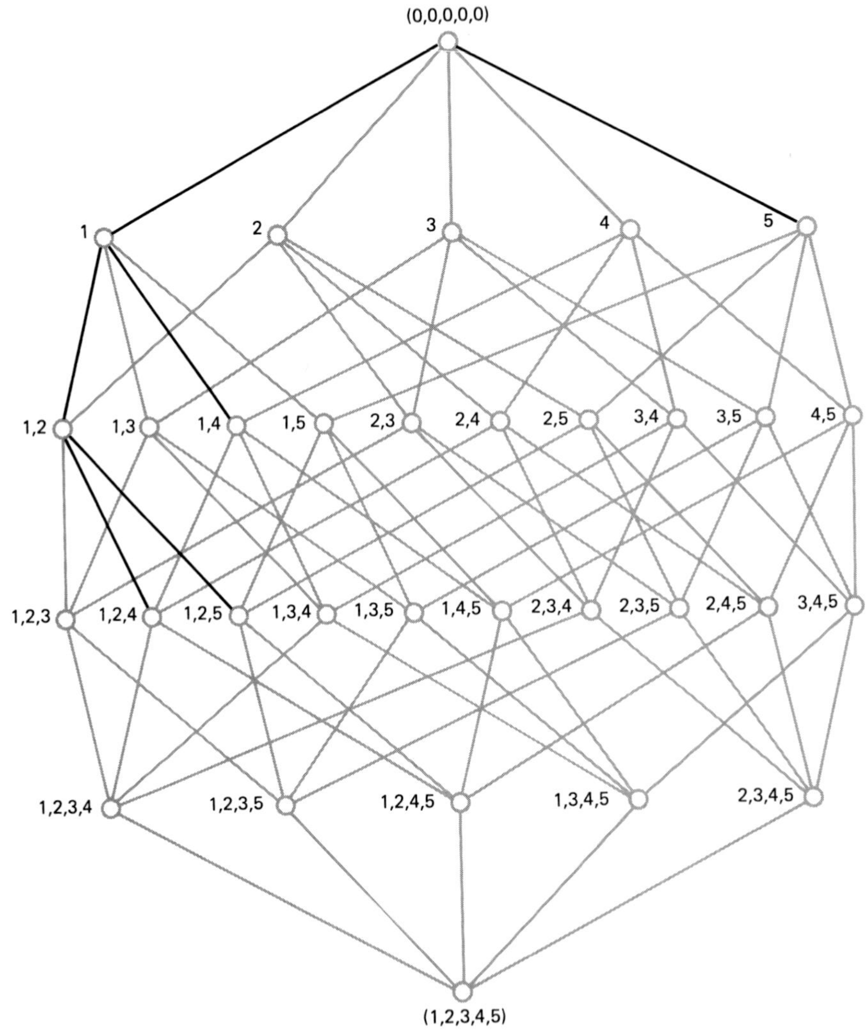

Figure 14.10 Flow diagram of the implicit enumeration procedure.

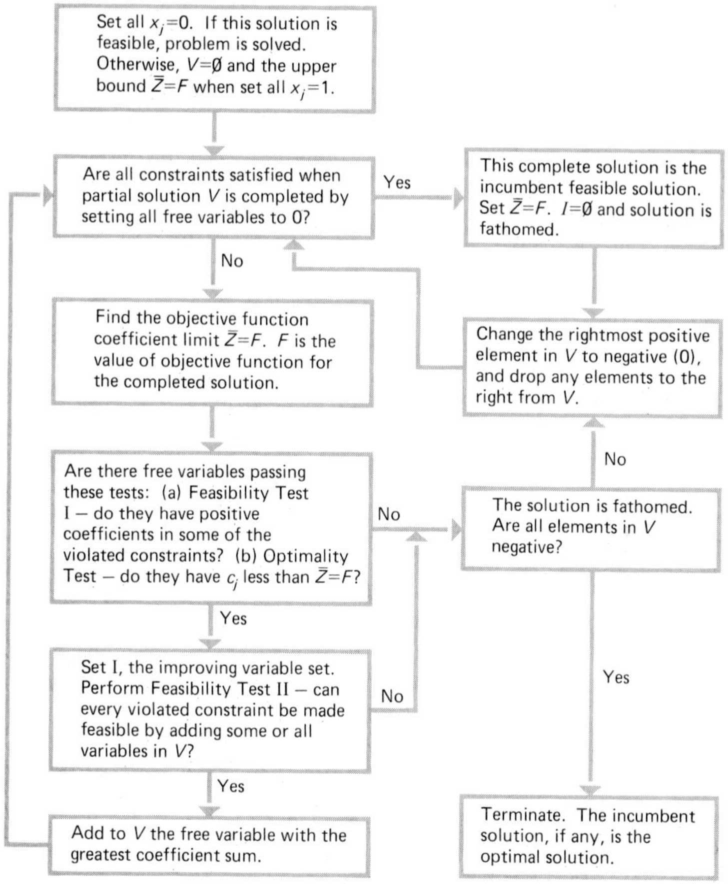

Some Complications of the Zero-One Problem

Because the standard zero-one programming problem requires $c_j \geqslant 0$ and the constraints to be all $\geqslant$ constraints, the following complications can arise.

A Maximization Problem

If the problem under consideration is a maximization problem, the objective function can be transformed into a minimization function by simply multiplying it by -1. The solution procedure can proceed in the usual manner.

Negative Contribution Rates

As discussed earlier, if x_j has a negative objective function coefficient $(-c_j)$, then x_j can be easily replaced by $1-x_j$. Thus, $-c_jx_j = -c_j(1-x_j) = -c_j + x_j$, and the objective function coefficient becomes positive.

Equality or ≤ Constraints

A ≤ constraint can be easily converted to a ≥ constraint by multiplying both sides by −1. Any equality constraint can be converted in the following manner:

If

$$f_i = b_i,$$

then

$$f_i \leq b_i \quad \text{and} \quad f_i \geq b_i$$

or

$$f_i \geq b_i \quad \text{and} \quad -f_i \leq -b_i$$

It should be clear that each equality constraint will be replaced by two inequality constraints. If the problem under consideration has a small number of equality constraints, this procedure is quite satisfactory. If, however, the problem has a large number of equality constraints, this procedure will make the problem very complex.

The following is an alternate approach:

Given

$$\begin{aligned} f_1 &= b_1 \\ f_2 &= b_2 \\ &\cdot \\ &\cdot \\ &\cdot \\ f_m &= b_m, \end{aligned}$$

then

$$\begin{aligned} f_1 &\geq b_1 \\ f_2 &\geq b_2 \\ &\cdot \\ &\cdot \\ &\cdot \\ f_m &\geq b_m \end{aligned}$$

and

$$f_1 + f_2 + \ldots + f_m \leq b_1 + b_2 + \ldots + b_m$$

This procedure converts m equality constraints to only $m+1$ inequality constraints.

Variable Elimination

Variable elimination is not a complication of the zero-one problem but rather a procedure to make the problem simpler (and reduce solution combinations) by reducing one decision variable in the model (in the objective function and constraints) when there is an equality constraint. Consider the following example:

Given constraint

$$x_1 + 2x_2 + 5x_3 = 10$$
$$x_j = 0,1$$

then,

$$x_1 = 10 - 2x_2 - 5x_3$$

since,

$$x_1 \geqslant 0, \quad 10 - 2x_2 - 5x_3 \geqslant 0 \quad \text{or} \quad -2x_2 - 5x_3 \geqslant -10$$

since

$$x_1 \leqslant 1, \quad 10 - 2x_2 - 5x_3 \leqslant 1 \quad \text{or} \quad 2x_2 + 5x_3 \geqslant 9$$

Summary

In this chapter we examined various integer programming problem examples, their model formulations and solution methods. There are many real-world problems that can be formulated as integer programming models. Integer programming problems are intellectually stimulating and interesting to analyze. However, such problems cannot always be easily solved by the solution methods discussed in this chapter. The difficulty involved in integer programming problems is not the formulation of the model but the efficient solution of these problems. The techniques discussed in this chapter work well for problems involving few variables. However, even with the powerful computers available today, many larger integer problems are difficult to solve by integer programming algorithms. When these techniques are applied to larger real-world problems, the solution process can be very complex, time consuming, and costly. These solution methods are meant to converge in a finite number of steps. Yet this finite number of steps has often been found to be prohibitive in terms of computation time or shortage requirements. The hope is that, in the future, continued research will produce improved solution methods for integer programming problems.

References

Balas, E. "An Additive Algorithm for Solving Linear Programs with Zero-One Variables." *Operations Research* 13 (1965): 517–46.

Baumol, W. J. *Economic Theory and Operations Analysis*. Englewood Cliffs, N.J.: Prentice-Hall, 1965.

Budnick, F. S.; Mozena, R.; and Vollman, T. E. *Principles of Operations Research*. Homewood, Illinois: Richard D. Irwin, 1977.

Dantzig, G. B. "On the Significance of Solving Linear Programming Problems with Some Integer Variables." *Econometrica* 28 (1960): 30–44.

Geoffrion, A. M. "Integer Programming by Implicit Enumeration and Balas' Method." *SIAM Review* 9 (1967): 178–90.

Glover, F. "A Multiphase Dual Algorithm for the Zero-One Integer Programming Problem." *Operations Research* 13 (1965): 879–919.

Gomory, R. E. "An Algorithm for Integer Solutions to Linear Programs." In *Recent Advances in Mathematical Programming*. Edited by R. L. Graves and P. Wolfe. New York: McGraw-Hill, 1963.

Hartley, R. V. *Operations Research: A Managerial Emphasis*. Pacific Palisades, Calif.: Goodyear Publishing Co., 1976.

Hillier, F. S., and Lieberman, G. J. *Introduction to Operations Research*. 2d ed. San Francisco: Holden-Day, 1975.

Kwak, N. K. *Mathematical Programming with Business Applications*. New York: McGraw-Hill, 1973.

Land, A. H., and Doig, A. G. "An Automatic Method of Solving Discrete Programming Problems." *Econometrica* 28 (1960): 497–520.

Lawler, E. L., and Wood, D. W. "Branch-and-Bound Methods—A Survey." *Operations Research* 14 (1966): 699–719.

Little, J. D. C., et al. "An Algorithm for the Traveling Salesman Problem." *Operations Research* 11 (1963): 972–89.

Loomba, N. P., and Turban, E. *Applied Programming for Management*. New York: Holt, Rinehart and Winston, 1974.

McMillan, C., Jr. *Mathematical Programming*. New York: John Wiley & Sons, 1970.

Mitten, L. G. "Branch-and-Bound Methods: General Formulation and Properties." *Operations Research* 18 (1970): 24–34.

Plane, D. R., and McMillan, C., Jr. *Discrete Optimization*. Englewood Cliffs, N.J.: Prentice-Hall, 1971.

Wagner, H. *Principles of Operations Research*. 2d ed. Englewood Cliffs, N.J.: Prentice-Hall, 1975.

Problems

1. A production manager faces the problem of job allocation of two production crews. The production rate of crew 1 is five units per hour and six units for crew 2. The normal working hours for each crew is eight hours per day. If the firm requires overtime operations, each crew can work up to eleven hours according to union contract. The firm has a special contract with a customer to provide a minimum of 120 units of the product the next day.

   The union contract calls for working arrangements where each crew should work at least eight hours per day and any overtime not exceeding three hours should be in terms of increments of an hour. The operating costs are \$200 for crew 1 and \$220 for crew 2.

a. Formulate a linear programming model for this problem.
b. Solve the problem by the simplex method.
c. The problem requires an integer solution. Solve the problem by the rounding approach and compare it with the graphical solution.

2. The following problem requires an integer solution. Solve it by the branch-and-bound method.

Maximize $Z = \$4x_1 + \$3x_2$
subject to

$$x_1 + x_2 \leq 30$$
$$3x_1 + x_2 \leq 75$$
$$x_1 + 2x_2 \leq 50$$
$$x_1, x_2 = 0 \text{ or nonnegative integers}$$

3. The dietician at the local hospital is planning the breakfast menu for the maternity ward patients. The dietician is planning a special nonfattening diet and has chosen cottage cheese and scrambled eggs for breakfast. The primary concern in planning the breakfast is the vitamin E and iron requirements of the new mothers.

According to the American Medical Association (AMA), new mothers should get at least 12 milligrams of vitamin E and 24 milligrams of iron from breakfast (fictitious figures). The AMA handbook reports that a scoop of cottage cheese contains 3 milligrams of vitamin E and 3 milligrams of iron. An average scoop of scrambled egg contains 2 milligrams of vitamin E and 8 milligrams of iron. In accordance with the AMA handbook, the dietician also recommends that new mothers should eat at least two scoops of cottage cheese for their breakfast. The dietician considers this as one of the model constraints.

The hospital accounting department estimates that a scoop of cottage cheese and a scoop of scrambled egg each costs five cents. The dietician is attempting to determine the optimal breakfast menu that will satisfy all the nutritional requirements and minimize total cost. The cook insists that only full scoops of food be served, which necessitates an integer solution. Determine the optimal integer solution to the problem.

4. Solve the diet problem presented in problem 3, using the branch-and-bound technique.

5. Consider the following problem:

$$\text{Maximize } Z = \$4x_1 + \$20x_2$$

subject to

$$x_1 + 10x_2 \leq 20$$
$$x_1 \leq 2$$
$$x_1, x_2 = 0 \text{ or nonnegative integers}$$

Solve the problem by the branch-and-bound technique.

6. Solve the following mixed-integer programming problem:

$$\text{Maximize } Z = 2x_1 + 3x_2$$

subject to

$$2x_1 + 4x_2 \leq 25$$
$$x_1 \leq 8$$
$$2x_2 \leq 10$$

x_1, s_1, s_3 without integer requirements

x_2 and s_2 with integer requirements

7. A central dispatcher for the local police department has just received five calls for police investigation. Examining the location map, the dispatcher notes that there are five patrol cars available for investigation. The following table indicates the distances between each patrol car and the trouble spots. The objective of the problem is to minimize total travel time for the patrol cars to respond to the five calls. Solve the problem by the branch-and-bound technique.

	Trouble Spot				
Patrol Car	1	2	3	4	5
A	18	14	10	14	17
B	22	18	8	9	14
C	15	25	12	15	25
D	20	16	16	22	12
E	16	28	10	14	15

8. Solve the following problem by the branch-and-bound technique (or you may solve it graphically).

$$\text{Maximize } Z = 3x_1 + 4x_2$$

subject to

$$x_1 + x_2 \leqslant 500$$
$$x_1 + x_2 \geqslant 400$$
$$x_1 - 2x_2 = 0$$
$$6x_1 - 4x_2 \geqslant 0$$
$$x_1, x_2 = 0 \text{ or nonnegative integers}$$

9. A marine transport company has four of its oceangoing freighters scheduled to arrive in port. The ships carry different cargoes from several foreign countries. There are four possible berths at which the vessels can be docked to unload their cargo. Each of the four berths is equipped with different cargo loading and unloading facilities. Given the characteristics of the cargoes and the facilities available at each berth, the manager has estimated the number of hours required to unload each of the ships at each of the four berths. This information is given in the following table:

	Ships			
Berths	1	2	3	4
A	8	14	20	8
B	12	16	16	12
C	16	8	28	12
D	9	12	19	15

a. Formulate a zero-one programming model for the problem.
b. Determine the optimal assignments that will minimize the number of hours.

10. Use the branch-and-bound technique to find the optimal solution to the following employee-machine assignment problem. Cost data are given as follows:

	Machines			
Employee	A	B	C	D
1	$180	$ 10	$ 96	$146
2	138	28	166	172
3	114	186	4	158
4	14	154	150	46

11. A chemical company is considering six possible investment opportunities. The following table presents pertinent information about the investment projects:

Projects	Initial Outlay ($000)	New Managerial Staff Need	Average Annual Cash Flow ($000)	Annual Accounting Profit ($000)	Net Present Value ($000)
1	$ 700	6	$200	$160	$300
2	1,080	16	300	240	440
3	120	2	20	36	60
4	300	4	70	66	160
5	680	10	150	140	380
6	420	6	90	80	200
Requirement or Maximum Available	Maximum 2,000	Maximum 24	Minimum 200	Minimum 200	Maximize

In addition, projects 3 and 4 are mutually exclusive pollution control activities. Furthermore, project 1 is contingent upon the prior acceptance of project 6. Formulate a zero-one programming model for this problem.

12. A boy scout is trying to pack his knapsack for a forthcoming camping trip. He is considering ten different items for the trip. Their values for the trip and weights are shown below.

Item	Value for Camping	Weight
1. Compass/watch	600 points	.15 lb.
2. Jar of peanut butter	400	1
3. Portable burner	150	4
4. Canteen	450	5
5. Sleeping bag	500	10
6. Dried meat	250	5
7. Fishing gear	150	7
8. Movie camera	50	4
9. Portable television	20	8
10. Radio	100	2

The maximum limit of weight allowed for each scout is 20 pounds. Furthermore, there should be at least one food item packed in the knapsack and not more than one item among cameras, television, and radio. Formulate this problem as a zero-one programming model.

13. Given the following information, formulate a zero-one programming model and solve the problem using the branch-and-bound technique.

	Machine				
Men	*A*	*B*	*C*	*D*	
1	$20	$30	$32	$36	1
2	28	26	32	20	1
3	22	18	16	36	1
4	26	26	22	18	1
	1	1	1	1	

14. Solve the following zero-one problem:

$$\text{Minimize } Z = 6x_1 + 3x_2 + 9x_3 + 6x_4 + 12x_5$$

subject to

$$3x_1 + 6x_2 + 3x_3 + 3x_4 + 6x_5 \geq 12$$
$$21x_1 + 3x_2 - 9x_4 + 9x_5 \geq 6$$
$$-9x_1 + 9x_2 + 6x_3 - 3x_5 \geq -3$$
$$x_j = 0 \text{ or } 1$$

15

Advanced Topics in Linear Programming

Linear models play a prominent role in management science. Perhaps the single most important factor for the widespread real-world application of linear models is their efficient solution algorithm. It is not unusual to see large problems (i.e., problems with five hundred constraints and two thousand decision variables) routinely formulated and solved by available computer codes.

In this chapter we will examine several advanced topics of linear programming that have further enhanced the value of linear programming as a decision-making tool. More specifically, this chapter focuses on the following topics: parametric linear programming, the revised simplex method, decomposition methods, and stochastic programming.

Parametric Linear Programming

Sensitivity analysis and parametric programming refer to the same basic postoptimal analysis that evaluates the relationship between the optimal solution and changes in the model parameters. As discussed in chapter 4, sensitivity analysis is concerned with the analysis of discrete changes in the parameters, and it is fairly well developed. Parametric linear programming is also a form of postoptimality analysis. However, it is concerned with the continuous change of one or more model parameters (c_j and/or b_i) and is not as well developed as sensitivity analysis.

The major motivation for the development of postoptimality analysis is that simple changes in the parameters can be checked without re-solving the model. Furthermore, information obtained from postoptimality analysis can be valuable for managerial planning and decision making. For example, if the optimal solution is not very sensitive to change in the unit contribution rate of a product, there is no justification for spending a great deal of effort to more accurately estimate its future contribution rate. With the availability of various interactive linear programming approaches, a simple sensitivity check of the optimal solution is no longer the primary role of postoptimal analysis.

Parametric Analysis of the Contribution Rates (c_j)

Changes in the contribution rates (c_j) may be entirely based on exogenous factors, such as economic conditions, changing supply levels of materials, or a strike by the labor force. It is also possible that changes may be due to internal decisions, such as transferring workers from one department to another or shifting equipment from one activity to another.

When changes in c_j occur, the objective function of the original problem ($Z = \sum_{j=1}^{n} c_j x_j$) is changed to

$$Z = \sum_{j=1}^{n} (c_j + \alpha_j \theta) x_j,$$

where α_j = relative rates at which the coefficient θ is being changed and θ = increase or decrease of the coefficient of contribution rates.

The purpose of parametric programming for the contribution rate is to find the optimal solution (and the value of the objective function) as θ increases or decreases gradually from zero (the original solution).

The parametric programming procedure can be outlined as follows:

1. Solve the problem by the regular simplex method with $\theta = 0$.
2. By utilizing the sensitivity analysis procedure (chap. 4), analyze the change in c_j by $\Delta c_j = \alpha_j \theta$.
3. Increase or decrease θ until one of the nonbasic variable columns has nonnegative $c_j - z_j$ ($z_j - c_j$ in a minimization problem). If no such column exists, stop.
4. Use this nonbasic column as the pivot column (entering variable) and find a new optimal solution. Return to step 3.

Consider the following simple linear programming problem:

$$\text{Maximize } Z = 5x_1 + 12x_2$$
$$x_1 + 2x_2 \leq 20$$
$$x_1 \leq 12$$
$$x_2 \leq 6$$
$$x_1, x_2 \geq 0$$

The graphic solution of the problem is presented in figure 15.1, and the simplex solution is shown in table 15.1. The optimal solution is $x_1 = 8$, $x_2 = 6$, $s_2 = 4$, and $Z = 112$. Suppose now that $\alpha_1 = 2$ and $\alpha_2 = -1$ for this problem. The objective function becomes $Z = (5 + 2\theta)x_1 + (12 - \theta)x_2$. By replacing these contributions rates in the final simplex tableau, we obtain table 15.2.

Figure 15.1 Graphic solution of the linear programming problem.

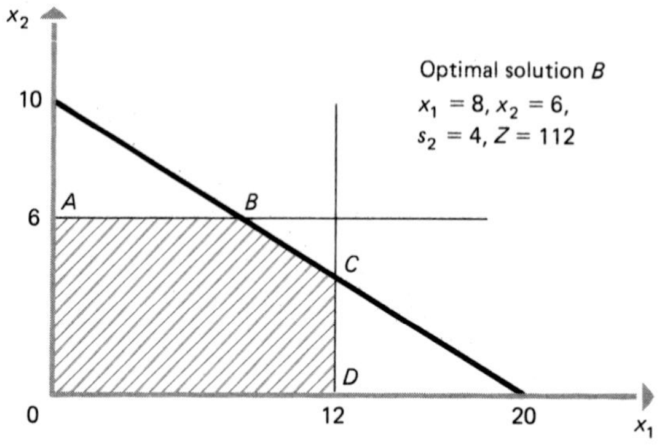

Table 15.1 Simplex solution

c_b \ c_j	basis	b_i^*	5 x_1	12 x_2	0 s_1	0 s_2	0 s_3
0	s_1	20	1	2	1	0	0
0	s_2	12	1	0	0	1	0
0	s_3	6	0	(1)	0	0	1
	z_j	0	0	0	0	0	0
	$c_j - z_j$		5	12	0	0	0
0	s_1	8	(1)	0	1	0	−2
0	s_2	12	1	0	0	1	0
12	x_2	6	0	1	0	0	1
	z_j	72	0	12	0	0	12
	$c_j - z_j$		5	0	0	0	−12
5	x_1	8	1	0	1	0	−2
0	s_2	4	0	0	−1	1	2
12	x_2	6	0	1	0	0	1
	z_j	112	5	12	5	0	2
	$c_j - z_j$		0	0	−5	0	−2

Table 15.2 Simplex solution with revised objective function

c_b \ c_j	basis	b_i^*	$5+2\theta$ x_1	$12-\theta$ x_2	0 s_1	0 s_2	0 s_3
$5+2\theta$	x_1	8	1	0	1	0	-2
0	s_2	4	0	0	-1	1	2
$12-\theta$	x_2	6	0	1	0	0	1
	z_j	$112+10\theta$	$5+2\theta$	$12-\theta$	$5+2\theta$	0	$2-5\theta$
	c_j-z_j		0	0	$-5-2\theta$	0	$-2+5\theta$

Remember, of course, that if $\theta=0$, the previous optimal solution remains optimal ($x_1=8$, $x_2=6$, $s_2=4$, and $Z=112$). However, if θ is allowed to increase or decrease, the previous optimal solution may no longer be optimal. The optimality test performed in the simplex method determines whether c_j-z_j values in all nonbasic variable columns are nonpositive. In other words, in table 15.2 the c_j-z_j values in the two nonbasic variable columns, s_1 and s_3, should be nonpositive.

s_1 column: $-5-2\theta \leqslant 0$

s_3 column: $-2+5\theta \leqslant 0$

As long as these conditions are met, the current optimal solution will remain optimal. Also, the range of θ within which the current solution remains as optimal can be determined as follows:

s_1 column: $-5-2\theta \leqslant 0,\ \theta \geqslant -\dfrac{5}{2}$ lower bound

s_3 column: $-2+5\theta \leqslant 0,\ \theta \leqslant \dfrac{2}{5}$ upper bound

The previous optimal solution is valid if $-\frac{5}{2} \leqslant \theta \leqslant \frac{2}{5}$. If $\theta = -\frac{5}{2}$ or $\theta = \frac{2}{5}$, the problem would have an alternate optimal solution. Also, if $\theta < -\frac{5}{2}$, then s_1 becomes the entering variable as its $c_j - z_j > 0$, and if $\theta > \frac{2}{5}$, then s_3 would be the pivot column as its $c_j-z_j > 0$.

To perform the parametric analysis, the sensitivity analysis procedure is used. The only difference between the two methods is that the changes in the c_j parameters are expressed in terms of θ instead of a specific discrete number. If θ is allowed to increase past $\theta = \frac{2}{5}$, s_3 enters the solution base. The new solution can be found by the primal simplex method as shown in the *second tableau* of table 15.3. The new solution is $x_1 = 12$, $x_2 = 4$, $s_3 = 2$, and $Z = 108 + 20\theta$.

Table 15.3 Simplex tableaus when θ is increased

c_b \ c_j	basis	b_i^*	$5+2\theta$ x_1	$12-\theta$ x_2	0 s_1	0 s_2	0 s_3
$5+2\theta$	x_1	8	1	0	1	0	-2
0	s_2	4	0	0	-1	1	(2)
$12-\theta$	x_2	6	0	1	0	0	1
	z_j	$112+10\theta$	$5+2\theta$	$12-\theta$	$5+2\theta$	0	$2-5\theta$
	c_j-z_j		0	0	$-5-2\theta$	0	$-2+5\theta$
$5+2\theta$	x_1	12	1	0	0	1	0
0	s_3	2	0	0	$-1/2$	$1/2$	1
$12-\theta$	x_2	4	0	1	(1/2)	$-1/2$	0
	z_j	$108+20\theta$	$5+2\theta$	$12-\theta$	$6-\theta/2$	$-1+5\theta/2$	0
	c_j-z_j		0	0	$-6+\theta/2$	$1-5\theta/2$	0
$5+2\theta$	x_1	12	1	0	0	1	0
0	s_3	6	0	1	0	0	1
0	s_1	8	0	2	1	-1	0
	z_j	$60+24\theta$	$5+2\theta$	0	0	$5+2\theta$	0
	c_j-z_j		0	$12-\theta$	0	$-5-2\theta$	0

This solution shown in the second tableau in table 15.3 is valid when $\frac{2}{5} \leqslant \theta \leqslant 12$:

$$s_1 \text{ column:} \quad -6 + \frac{1}{2}\theta \leqslant 0, \; \theta \leqslant 12 \quad \text{upper bound}$$

$$s_2 \text{ column:} \quad 1 - \frac{5}{2}\theta \leqslant 0, \; \theta \geqslant \frac{2}{5} \quad \text{lower bound}$$

If θ is further increased beyond $\theta = 12$, s_1 becomes the entering variable and an additional iteration results in a new solution as shown in the third tableau of table 15.3. The new solution is $x_1 = 12$, $s_1 = 8$, $s_3 = 6$, and $Z = 60 + 24\theta$. The limits for θ within which this solution is valid are determined by computing the following:

$$x_2 \text{ column:} \quad 12 - \theta \leqslant 0, \quad \theta \geqslant 12$$

$$s_2 \text{ column:} \quad -5 - 2\theta \leqslant 0, \; \theta \geqslant -\frac{5}{2}$$

Thus, since $\theta \geq -5/2$ and $\theta \geq 12$, the solution has no upper limit for θ, and the solution is therefore valid when $12 \leq \theta \leq \infty$. This completes the analysis of optimal solutions when θ is increased.

Refer back to table 15.2, and check the solution when θ is allowed to decrease. As already indicated, if $\theta < -\frac{5}{2}$, s_1 becomes the entering variable as its $c_j - z_j$ becomes positive. Table 15.4 presents the new solution, $x_2 = 6$, $s_1 = 8$, $s_2 = 12$, and $Z = 72 - 6\theta$. The limits for θ within which this solution is valid are determined by computing the following:

$$x_1 \text{ column:} \quad 5 + 2\theta \leq 0,\ \theta \leq -\frac{5}{2}$$

$$s_3 \text{ column:} \quad -12 + \theta \leq 0,\quad \theta \leq 12$$

Table 15.4 Simplex tableaus when θ is decreased

c_b \ c_j	basis	b_i^*	$5+2\theta$ x_1	$12-\theta$ x_2	0 s_1	0 s_2	0 s_3
$5+2\theta$	x_1	8	1	0	(1)	0	-2
0	s_2	4	0	0	-1	1	2
$12-\theta$	x_2	6	0	1	0	0	1
	z_j	$112+10\theta$	$5+2\theta$	$12-\theta$	$5+2\theta$	0	$2-5\theta$
	$c_j - z_j$		0	0	$-5-2\theta$ ↑	0	$-2+5\theta$
0	s_1	8	1	0	1	0	-2
0	s_2	12	1	0	0	1	0
$12-\theta$	x_2	6	0	1	0	0	1
	z_j	$72-6\theta$	0	$12-\theta$	0	0	$12-\theta$
	$c_j - z_j$		$5+2\theta$	0	0	0	$-12+\theta$

Thus, since $\theta \leq -5/2$ and $\theta \leq 12$, the solution has no lower limit for θ, and the solution is therefore valid when $-\infty \leq \theta \leq -5/2$. This completes the analysis of optimal solutions when θ is decreased.

In figure 15.2, the value of the optimal solution is presented as a function of θ. The function is linear and its form is convex. The four line segments in figure 15.2 correspond to the four corner points (A, B, C, D) in figure 15.1. The numbers on the line segments represent the rates of increase in the value of the objective function in relation to the per unit increase of θ. A closer analysis can be made from the following information:

Value of θ	Value of Objective Function	Basic Variables
$\theta < -\frac{5}{2}$	$72-6\theta$	X_2, S_1, S_2
$\theta = -\frac{5}{2}$	$\$87 = 72 - 6\theta$ $87 = 112 + 10\theta$	X_2, S_1, S_2 X_1, X_2, S_2
$-\frac{5}{2} \leqslant \theta \leqslant \frac{2}{5}$	$112+10\theta$	X_1, X_2, S_2
$\theta = \frac{2}{5}$	$\$116 = 112 + 10\theta$ $116 = 108 + 20\theta$	X_1, X_2, S_2 X_1, X_2, S_3
$\frac{2}{5} \leqslant \theta \leqslant 12$	$108+20\theta$	X_1, X_2, S_3
$\theta = 12$	$\$348 = 108 + 20\theta$ $348 = 60 + 24\theta$	X_1, X_2, S_3 X_1, S_1, S_3
$\theta > 12$	$60+24\theta$	X_1, S_1, S_3

Figure 15.2 Parametric analysis of contribution rates.

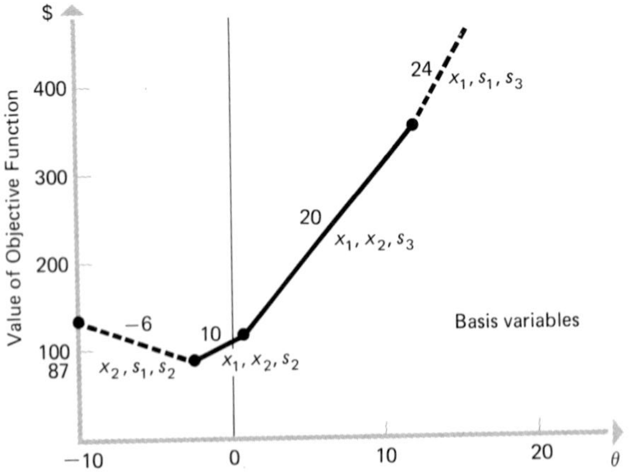

Parametric programming for the contribution rate is based on a relatively simple procedure that determines a sequence of optimal bases by the primal simplex method. At each solution, computation is performed to determine the range of θ parameter within which the current basic solution remains optimal. Through the simplex iterative procedure, new solutions and their corresponding ranges of θ are determined. The result of the contribution rate parametrics provides valuable information for managerial decision making.

Parametric Analysis of Resources

If the b_i parameters change continuously, the b_i parametric analysis can be employed. The only modification to be made in the linear programming model is to replace b_i by $(b_i + d_i\theta)$ as shown in the following:

$$\text{Maximize } Z = \sum_{j=1}^{n} c_j x_j$$

subject to

$$\sum_{j=1}^{n} a_{ij} x_j \leqslant b_i + d_i\theta, \; i = 1, 2, \ldots, m$$

The goal of the b_i parametrics is to identify optimal solutions as a function of θ. The solution procedure is quite similar to that utilized for the contribution rate parametrics, because of the fact that changes in b_i are equivalent to changes in c_j of the dual model.

The steps of the procedure can be summarized as follows:

1. Solve the problem by the regular simplex method with $\theta = 0$.
2. By utilizing the sensitivity analysis procedure, analyze the change in b_i by $\Delta b_i = d_i\theta$.
3. Increase or decrease θ until the b_i value of one of the basic variables becomes negative. If no such variable exists, stop.
4. Use this basic variable row as the pivot row (leaving variable), and find a new optimal solution by the dual simplex method. Return to step 3.

To illustrate the general procedure, let us consider the same problem analyzed in figure 15.1 and table 15.1.

$$\text{Maximize } Z = 5x_1 + 12x_2$$

subject to

$$\begin{aligned} x_1 + 2x_2 &\leqslant 20 \\ x_1 &\leqslant 12 \\ x_2 &\leqslant 6 \\ x_1, x_2 &\geqslant 0 \end{aligned}$$

Suppose that the second and third constraints represent the sales capacities in terms of availability of products, market size, and sales force of the company. If it can be assumed that the sales capacity can be transferred from the second product to the first product, after such an exchange, the b_i values would be changed to $(12+\theta)$ for the second constraint and $(6-\theta)$ for the third constraint. The decision maker is attempting to determine the optimal contribution the company can obtain for each θ.

Since the final simplex tableau for the problem has already been presented (table 15.2), it can easily be modified by introducing $b_2^* = b_2 + \theta$ and $b_3^* = b_3 - \theta$. Increasing the b_i value by θ in the second constraint is the same as setting its slack variable $s_2 = -\theta$. Conversely, decreasing the b_i value of the third constraint by θ is equivalent to setting $s_3 = \theta$. By making these changes, the new b_i^* values in the final simplex tableau can be obtained. For example, from table 15.2 the following can be obtained:

$$x_1 \text{ row:} \quad x_1 + s_1 - 2s_3 = 8,\ x_1 + s_1 - 2(\theta) = 8,\ x_1 + s_1 = 8 + 2\theta$$

$$s_2 \text{ row:} \quad -s_1 + s_2 + 2s_3 = 4,\ -s_1 - \theta + 2\theta = 4,\ -s_1 = 4 - \theta$$

$$x_2 \text{ row:} \quad x_2 + s_3 = 6,\ x_2 + \theta = 6,\ x_2 = 6 - \theta$$

Table 15.5 presents the final simplex tableau with the new b_i^* values.

Table 15.5 Final simplex tableau with new b_i^*

C_b \ C_j	basis	b_i^*	5 x_1	12 x_2	0 s_1	0 s_2	0 s_3
5	x_1	$8+2\theta$	1	0	1	0	−2
0	s_2	$4-\theta$	0	0	−1	1	2
12	x_2	$6-\theta$	0	1	0	0	1
	Z_j	$112-2\theta$	5	12	5	0	2
	$C_j - Z_j$		0	0	−5	0	−2

Since changes in b_i affect only the intercepts of constraints (iso-profit function and constraint slopes remain the same), it is only necessary to check the feasibility of the solution. Thus, the solution is optimal as long as it is feasible. The feasibility conditions are:

x_1: $8 + 2\theta \geq 0,\ \theta \geq -4$ lower limit

s_2: $4 - \theta \geq 0,\ \theta \leq 4$ upper limit

x_2: $6 - \theta \geq 0,\ \theta \leq 6$.

Since the goal is to determine the range of θ within which the current solution remains optimal, the lower limit is the maximum value of θ when θ is greater than or equal to a given value and the upper limit is the minimum value of θ when θ is less than or equal to a given value. Thus, the range is $-4 \leq \theta \leq 4$, within which the current solution is feasible and optimal. The value of the objective function within the range is $112 - 2\theta$.

When $\theta = -4$, x_1 becomes zero, and when $\theta = 4$, s_2 becomes zero. If this range is extended, the problem becomes infeasible and the dual simplex method must be utilized to identify a new feasible solution. For example, if θ is allowed to increase so that $\theta > 4$, then s_2 becomes negative. By following the dual simplex method procedure, the s_2 row becomes the pivot row. The pivot column can be identified by determining the following:

$$\text{Min } \frac{c_j - z_i}{a_{ki}} \text{ for } a_{ki} < 0,$$

where a_{ki} is the coefficient in the kth row where the basic variable is negative and in the ith nonbasic variable column.

If θ is allowed to increase beyond $\theta = 4$, the basic variable s_2 will have a negative b_i^* value. s_2 then becomes the pivot row. The pivot column is the s_1 column since it has the only negative coefficient in the s_2 row. Table 15.6 presents a new solution derived by the dual simplex method. The new solution is $x_1 = 12 + \theta$, $x_2 = 6 - \theta$, $s_1 = -4 + \theta$, and $Z = 132 - 7\theta$.

Table 15.6 Dual simplex solution with increased b_i^*

c_b \ c_j	basis	b_i^*	5 x_1	12 x_2	0 s_1	0 s_2	0 s_3
5	x_1	$8 + 2\theta$	1	0	1	0	−2
0	s_2	$4 - \theta$	0	0	(−1)	1	2
12	x_2	$6 - \theta$	0	1	0	0	1
	z_j	$112 - 2\theta$	5	12	5	0	2
	$c_j - z_j$		0	0	−5	0	−2
5	x_1	$12 + \theta$	1	0	0	1	0
0	s_1	$-4 + \theta$	0	0	1	−1	−2
12	x_2	$6 - \theta$	0	1	0	0	1
	z_j	$132 - 7\theta$	5	12	0	5	12
	$c_j - z_j$		0	0	0	−5	−12

The new solution is feasible within the range of $-12 \leq \theta \leq 6$.

x_1 row: $12 + \theta \geq 0,\ \theta \geq -12$

x_2 row: $6 - \theta \geq 0,\ \theta \leq 6$

It is not necessary to evaluate the s_1 row since it has just been entered into the solution base. If θ is allowed to increase beyond $\theta = 6$, the x_2 row will have a negative b_i^* value. Thus, x_2 becomes the leaving variable. However, the entering variable cannot be determined as there is no negative coefficient in the x_2 row. Therefore, the problem becomes infeasible when $\theta > 6$.

Check also the solution when θ is allowed to decrease. As identified earlier, the solution derived by the regular simplex method (when $\theta = 0$) is feasible and optimal within the range $-4 \leq \theta \leq 4$. The lower limit is found in the x_1 row. Using the dual simplex method, a new solution can be found when $\theta < -4$. The leaving variable is x_1, and the entering variable is s_3, as shown in table 15.7. The new solution is $x_2 = 10$, $s_2 = 12 + \theta$, $s_3 = -4 - \theta$, and $Z = 120$.

The new solution identified in table 15.7 is feasible within the range of $-12 \leq \theta \leq -4$. If $\theta < -12$, the solution becomes infeasible as the b_i^* value of the s_2 row becomes negative. However, since there is no negative coefficient in the s_2 row, the solution becomes infeasible when $\theta < -12$.

Table 15.7 Dual simplex solution with decreased b_i^*

c_b \ c_j	basis	b_i^*	5 x_1	12 x_2	0 s_1	0 s_2	0 s_3
5	x_1	$8+2\theta$	1	0	1	0	(−2)
0	s_2	$4-\theta$	0	0	−1	1	2
12	x_2	$6-\theta$	0	1	0	0	1
	z_j	$112-2\theta$	5	12	5	0	2
	$c_j - z_j$		0	0	−5	0	−2
0	s_3	$-4-\theta$	−1/2	0	−1/2	0	1
0	s_2	$12+\theta$	1	0	0	1	0
12	x_2	10	−1/2	1	−1/2	0	0
	z_j	120	6	12	6	0	0
	$c_j - z_j$		−1	0	−6	0	0

Figure 15.3 presents the value of the optimal solution as a function of θ. This function is linear and its form is concave. A closer analysis can be made from the following information:

Value of θ	Value of Objective Function	Basic Variables
$\theta < -12$	Infeasible	—
$\theta = -12$	\$120	x_2, s_2, s_3
$-12 < \theta \leq -4$	120	x_2, s_2, s_3
$-4 \leq \theta \leq 4$	$112-2\theta$	x_1, x_2, s_2
$4 \leq \theta \leq 6$	$132-7\theta$	x_1, x_2, s_1
$\theta > 6$	Infeasible	—

Figure 15.3 Parametric analysis of b_i values.

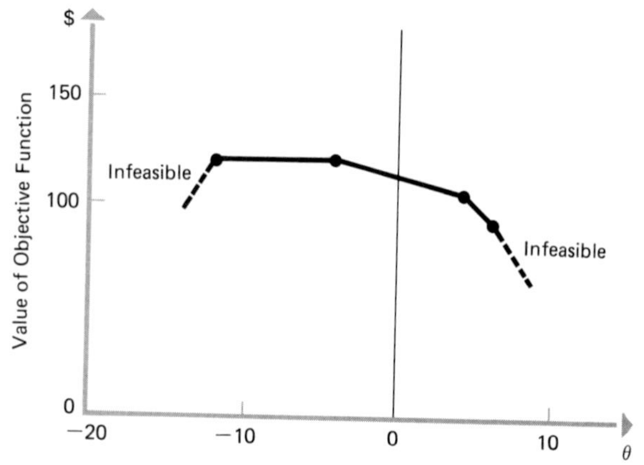

In this section, we have examined the effects of continuous or systematic changes in the c_j or b_i parameters of a linear programming model, which can provide additional information that is useful for managerial decision analysis.

Revised Simplex Method

In the standard simplex method, the iterative process moves from one corner point solution to another corner point solution that is as good as or better than the previous solution. In the process, the simplex algorithm recalculates the entire tableau at each iteration. Since all numbers and elements are not needed at each step of the iterative process, this computational procedure is not very efficient, especially for the computer-based solution procedure. The only elements that are relevant at each iterative step are the contribution rates, the coefficients of the pivot column, and the b_i^* values. A process of obtaining only needed information without recalculating and storing all numbers in the tableau is necessary to make the solution process more efficient. The revised simplex method has been developed to meet this goal.

The revised simplex method is basically a shortcut algorithm that is capable of obtaining the optimal solution with fewer calculations than the standard simplex method. It is especially efficient for solving large problems on a computer.

The revised simplex method relies on matrix manipulation. The basic procedure proceeds directly from the inverse of one basis to the inverse of the new basis. The general model of linear programming in the matrix form is

Maximize $Z = CX$

subject to

$$AX \leq b$$

$$X \geq 0.$$

C is the row vector of contribution rates associated with X, $C=[c_1, c_2, \ldots, c_n]$. X and b are the column vectors of decision variables and resources (b_i).

$$X = \begin{bmatrix} x_1 \\ x_2 \\ \cdot \\ \cdot \\ \cdot \\ x_n \end{bmatrix}, \qquad b = \begin{bmatrix} b_1 \\ b_2 \\ \cdot \\ \cdot \\ \cdot \\ b_m \end{bmatrix},$$

A is the matrix of technological coefficients.

$$A = \begin{bmatrix} a_{11} & a_{12} & \cdots & a_{1n} \\ a_{21} & a_{22} & \cdots & a_{2n} \\ \cdot & \cdot & & \cdot \\ \cdot & \cdot & & \cdot \\ \cdot & \cdot & & \cdot \\ a_{m1} & a_{m2} & \cdots & a_{mn} \end{bmatrix}$$

If an initial basic feasible solution can be derived with the use of slack and/or artificial variables, then the basic matrix is an identity matrix. The basic feasible solutions at other iterations will consist of decision, slack, or artificial variables. Assume the following basic matrix:

$$B = \begin{bmatrix} b_{11} & b_{12} & \cdots & b_{1m} \\ b_{21} & b_{22} & \cdots & b_{2m} \\ \cdot & \cdot & & \cdot \\ \cdot & \cdot & & \cdot \\ \cdot & \cdot & & \cdot \\ b_{m1} & b_{m2} & \cdots & b_{mn} \end{bmatrix}$$

Only the basic variable coefficients are included, and all nonbasic coefficients are eliminated as the nonbasic variables are set equal to zero. The set of equations for the basic variables is

$$BX_B = b.$$

In order to solve $BX_B = b$, proceed as follows:

$$\begin{aligned} B^{-1}BX_B &= B^{-1}b \quad \text{(multiplying both sides by } B^{-1}\text{)} \\ X_B &= B^{-1}b \end{aligned}$$

If C_B is denoted as the vector representing contribution rates of the basic variables, the value of the objective function for the basic solution becomes

$$Z = C_BX_B = C_BB^{-1}b.$$

Now, denote the content of the simplex tableau by S in such a manner that

$$S = \begin{bmatrix} a_{11} & a_{12} & \cdots & a_{1n} & x_1 \\ a_{21} & a_{22} & \cdots & a_{2n} & x_2 \\ \cdot & \cdot & & \cdot & \cdot \\ \cdot & \cdot & & \cdot & \cdot \\ \cdot & \cdot & & \cdot & \cdot \\ a_{m1} & a_{m2} & \cdots & a_{mn} & x_n \\ c_1 - z_1 & c_2 - z_2 & \cdots & c_n - z_n & z \end{bmatrix}$$

The right-hand column of the partitioned matrix S presents the basic variables (X_B), and the bottom row presents the simplex criterion and the value of the objective function.

It can now be shown that

$$S_i = \hat{B}_i^{-1} \hat{A},$$

where S_i is the simplex tableau at the ith iteration.

$$\hat{B} = \begin{bmatrix} B_i & 0 \\ C_B & 1 \end{bmatrix} \quad \text{and} \quad \hat{A} = \begin{bmatrix} A & b \\ C & 0 \end{bmatrix}$$

where

B_i = basic matrix at ith iteration.
C_B = contribution rates vector of the basic variables
0 = a zero vector
1 = a unit vector
A = technological coefficient matrix of the original model
C = contribution rates vector of the original objective function
b = vector of the original rhs values

Thus, the simplex tableau at any iteration can be easily constructed from the data of the initial model (A, b, and C) and the inverse of the current basic matrix ($\hat{B}_i^{-1}$).

A Revised Simplex Solution

In order to provide a simple illustration as to how the revised simplex method works, consider the following problem:

Maximize $Z = 100x_1 + 80x_2$

subject to

$$2x_1 + 4x_2 \leq 80$$
$$3x_1 + x_2 \leq 60$$
$$x_1, x_2 \geq 0$$

Step 1 Determine the initial solution. By introducing the slack variables, the two constraints can be transformed as follows:

$$2x_1 + 4x_2 + s_1 = 80$$
$$3x_1 + x_2 + s_2 = 60$$

Since the initial solution is at the origin ($x_1 = x_2 = 0$), the basic variables are s_1 and s_2. Thus,

$$B_1 = \begin{bmatrix} 1 & 0 \\ 0 & 1 \end{bmatrix} .$$

Step 2 Determine B_1^{-1}. Since the initial solution basis B_1 is an identity matrix, its inverse is $B_1^{-1} = B_1$.

Step 3 Determine $\hat{B}_1^{-1}$. As defined,

$$\hat{B}_1 = \begin{bmatrix} B_1 & 0 \\ C_{B_1} & 1 \end{bmatrix}$$

Its inverse is

$$\hat{B}_1^{-1} = \begin{bmatrix} B_1^{-1} & 0 \\ -C_{B_1} B^{-1} & 1 \end{bmatrix} .$$

It is known that $C_{B_1} = [0\ 0]$ since the contribution rates of the two slack variables (basic variables at the initial solution) are zero. Thus, $-C_{B_1}B_1^{-1} = [0\ 0]$.

$\hat{B}_1^{-1}$ can be expressed as follows:

B_1^{-1}

$$\hat{B}_1^{-1} = \left[\begin{array}{cc|c} 1 & 0 & 0 \\ 0 & 1 & 0 \\ \hline 0 & 0 & 1 \end{array}\right]$$

$-C_{B_1}B^{-1}$

Step 4 Determine $\hat{A}$. As defined earlier,

$$\hat{A} = \left[\begin{array}{c|c} A & b \\ \hline C & 0 \end{array}\right] .$$

For the example problem,

$$\hat{A} = \left[\begin{array}{cc|c} 2 & 4 & 80 \\ 3 & 1 & 60 \\ \hline 100 & 80 & 0 \end{array}\right] .$$

Step 5 Construct the simplex tableau and test optimality. The initial revised simplex tableau takes the form shown in table 15.8.

Table 15.8 Revised simplex tableau

basis	$\hat{B}_i^{-1}$	Decision Variables	b_i^*
$c_j - z_j$			Z

Determine the simplex criterion ($c_j - z_j$) for a maximization problem and $z_j - c_j$ for a minimization problem) for each column. There are two alternative approaches that can be used in selecting the entering variable (pivot column). The first approach is to select the first positive $c_j - z_j$ column as the pivot column, and the second approach is to use the normal simplex procedure where the largest $c_j - z_j$ value column is selected. The first approach saves some computational work as $c_j - z_j$ values for all columns need not be calculated. The second approach, on the other hand, usually requires fewer iterations. We shall use the second approach, which is the same as the one used in the standard simplex algorithm. If no positive $c_j - z_j$ is found, the solution is optimal. The value of $c_j - z_j$ is calculated by finding the product of the bottom row of $\hat{B}_1^{-1}$ and the columns of $\hat{A}$, as follows:

$$c_1 - z_1 = [0 \; 0 \; 1] \begin{bmatrix} 2 \\ 3 \\ 100 \end{bmatrix} = 100$$

$$c_2 - z_2 = [0 \; 0 \; 1] \begin{bmatrix} 4 \\ 1 \\ 80 \end{bmatrix} = 80$$

The value of the objective function for a given solution is found by multiplying the same bottom row of $\hat{B}_1^{-1}$ by the b column of $\hat{A}$ ($Z = C_B X_B = C_B B^{-1} b$).

$$Z = [0 \; 0 \; 1] \begin{bmatrix} 80 \\ 60 \\ 0 \end{bmatrix} = 0$$

All $c_j - z_j$ and Z values computed should be entered in the appropriate locations as shown in table 15.9.

Table 15.9 B_1^{-1} and $c_j - z_j$ in the revised simplex tableau

basis	$\hat{B}_1^{-1}$ s_1 s_2		x_1 x_2	b_i^*
s_1	1 0	0		
s_2	0 1	0		
$c_j - z_j$	0 0	1	100 80	0

↑ Pivot Column

Test the optimality of the solution. The optimality test is the same as the one employed in the standard simplex procedure. If $c_j - z_j$ values of the nonbasic variables are zero or negative, an optimal solution has been obtained. Otherwise, proceed to step 6. Since the nonbasic variables indicate positive $c_j - z_j$ values, the solution is not optimal. The x_1 column is identified as the pivot column as it has the largest $c_j - z_j$ value.

Step 6 Determine the leaving variable. To complete the first solution, the following procedures should be followed.

The first step is to determine the new coefficients of the pivot column ($\hat{A}$) by multiplying the $\hat{B}_1^{-1}$ rows by the pivot column (x_1 in this case) in $\hat{A}$.

$$[1 \;\; 0 \;\; 0] \begin{bmatrix} 2 \\ 3 \\ 100 \end{bmatrix} = 2$$

$$[0 \;\; 1 \;\; 0] \begin{bmatrix} 2 \\ 3 \\ 100 \end{bmatrix} = 3$$

$$[0 \;\; 0 \;\; 1] \begin{bmatrix} 2 \\ 3 \\ 100 \end{bmatrix} = 100$$

The resulting elements in the x_1 column are

$$\begin{bmatrix} 2 \\ 3 \\ 100 \end{bmatrix}$$

These elements are entered in the tableau as shown in table 15.10.

Table 15.10 The complete initial revised simplex tableau

basis	$\hat{B}_1^{-1}$	x_1 x_2	b_i^*
s_1 s_2	1 0 0 0 1 0	2 (3)	80 60
$c_j - z_j$	0 0 1	100	0

Since the elements of the pivot column are known, b_i^* values must also be determined before the pivot row can be identified. The values of b_i^* can be determined by multiplying the $\hat{B}_1^{-1}$ row by the b column of $\hat{A}$.

$$[1\ \ 0\ \ 0]\begin{bmatrix}80\\60\\0\end{bmatrix} = 80$$

$$[0\ \ 1\ \ 0]\begin{bmatrix}80\\60\\0\end{bmatrix} = 60$$

$$[0\ \ 0\ \ 1]\begin{bmatrix}80\\60\\0\end{bmatrix} = 0$$

The resulting b_i^* values are

$$\begin{bmatrix}80\\60\\0\end{bmatrix}$$

These values are also entered in Table 15.10.

The pivot row (leaving variable) is determined in the same manner as the standard simplex method. Since the minimum nonnegative value is obtained in the s_2 row when b_i^* values are divided by the coefficient elements in the pivot column (the x_1 column), s_2 is the leaving variable.

The pivot element is the circled value 3, which is at the intersection of the pivot column and the pivot row.

Step 7 Determine the next basis inverse, $\hat{B}_2^{-1}$. The procedure for calculating $\hat{B}_2^{-1}$ directly from $\hat{B}_1^{-1}$ is similar to the transformation method used in the standard simplex method. The pivot row (s_2) elements are divided by the pivot element (3) to obtain the new values in the $\hat{B}_2^{-1}$ column. The second row of $\hat{B}_2^{-1}$ becomes [0 1/3 0] as shown in table 15.11. The new b_i^* value for the row is obtained in the same manner.

Old values in the pivot row		Pivot element
$\hat{B}_1^{-1}$	b_i^*	
[0 1 0]	60	3

Table 15.11 The second solution tableau

basis	$\hat{B}_2^{-1}$			x_1	x_2	b_i^*
s_1	1	−2/3	0	0	(10/3)	40
x_1	0	1/3	0	1	1/3	20
$c_j - z_j$	0	−100/3	1	0	140/3	2,000

New values in the corresponding row of $\hat{B}_2^{-1}$ are determined by dividing the old value by the pivot element.

B_2^{-1}	b_i^*
[0 1/3 0]	20

All other nonpivot rows in $\hat{B}_1^{-1}$ can be transformed by the same rule used in the standard simplex method as shown in the following:

Old values in the s_1 row

$\hat{B}_1^{-1}$	b_i^*	Intersectional element
[1 0 0]	80	2

New values in the corresponding row of B_2^{-1}

$\hat{B}_2^{-1}$	b_i^*
[1 −2/3 0]	40

These values are also entered in table 15.10.

The same procedure is used for the $c_j - z_j$ row.

Old values in the $c_j - z_j$ row	Intersectional element
[0 0 1]	100

New values in the $c_j - z_j$ row

[0 −100/3 1]

These values are also entered in table 15.11.

Step 8 The following represents a new test of optimality. The optimality of the new solution, $B_2 = (s_1, x_1)$, should also be tested by checking the $c_j - z_j$ values. The $c_j - z_j$ values are obtained by multiplying the bottom row of $\hat{B}_2^{-1}$ ($c_j - z_j$ row) by the columns of $\hat{A}$, as follows:

$$[0 \quad -100/3 \quad 1] \begin{bmatrix} 2 \\ 3 \\ 100 \end{bmatrix} = 0 \quad (x_1 \text{ column})$$

$$[0 \quad -100/3 \quad 1] \begin{bmatrix} 4 \\ 1 \\ 80 \end{bmatrix} = 140/3 \quad (x_2 \text{ column})$$

Since $c_j - z_j$ for the x_2 column is positive, an optimal solution has not yet been found.

Step 9 Find the next solution. In order to identify the elements in the x_2 column, multiply the $\hat{B}_2^{-1}$ rows by the x_2 column elements in $\hat{A}$.

$$[1 \quad -2/3 \quad 0] \begin{bmatrix} 4 \\ 1 \\ 80 \end{bmatrix} = 10/3$$

$$[0 \quad 1/3 \quad 0] \begin{bmatrix} 4 \\ 1 \\ 80 \end{bmatrix} = 1/3$$

$$[0 \quad -100/3 \quad 1] \begin{bmatrix} 4 \\ 1 \\ 80 \end{bmatrix} = 140/3$$

It can also be determined that $Z = C_B X_B = C_B \hat{B}_2^{-1} b = 2{,}000$. These elements are also entered in table 15.11.

The s_1 row is identified as the pivot row (entering variable) in table 15.11. A new solution can be derived by following the same procedures.

<u>Pivot row $\hat{B}_3^{-1}$</u>

Old values $\hat{B}_2^{-1}$, $[1 \quad -2/3 \quad 0]$ Pivot element (10/3)

New values $\hat{B}_3^{-1} = [3/10 \quad -1/5 \quad 0]$

<u>x_1 row $\hat{B}_3^{-1}$</u>

Old values $\hat{B}_2^{-1}$, $[0 \quad 1/3 \quad 0] - (1/3 \times \text{new value in the pivot row})$

New values $\hat{B}_3^{-1} = [-1/10 \quad 2/5 \quad 0]$

<u>$c_j - z_j$ row</u>

Old values: $[0 \quad -100/3 \quad 1] - (140/3 \times \text{new value in the pivot row})$

New values: $[-14 \quad -24 \quad 1]$

x_1 column $\hat{B}_3^{-1}\hat{A}x_1$

$$[3/10 \quad -1/5 \quad 0]\begin{bmatrix}2\\3\\100\end{bmatrix} = 0$$

$$[-1/10 \quad 2/5 \quad 0]\begin{bmatrix}2\\3\\100\end{bmatrix} = 1$$

$$[-14 \quad -24 \quad 1]\begin{bmatrix}2\\3\\100\end{bmatrix} = 0$$

x_2 column $\hat{B}_3^{-1}\hat{A}x_2$

$$[3/10 \quad -1/5 \quad 0]\begin{bmatrix}4\\1\\80\end{bmatrix} = 1$$

$$[-1/10 \quad 2/5 \quad 0]\begin{bmatrix}4\\1\\80\end{bmatrix} = 0$$

$$[-14 \quad -24 \quad 0]\begin{bmatrix}4\\1\\80\end{bmatrix} = 0$$

b_i^* column

$$[3/10 \quad -1/5 \quad 0]\begin{bmatrix}80\\60\\0\end{bmatrix} = 12 \qquad (x_2 \text{ row})$$

$$[-1/10 \quad 2/5 \quad 0]\begin{bmatrix}80\\60\\0\end{bmatrix} = 16 \qquad (x_1 \text{ row})$$

$$Z = C_B X_B = 2{,}560$$

Thus, the complete tableau can be constructed as shown in table 15.12. This solution is the optimal solution as there is no positive $c_j - z_j$ value in the nonbasic variable columns (in this case only s_1 and s_2). It should be noted that the unit vector 1 in the third column should not be confused with nonbasic variable column values.

Table 15.12 Final optimal solution tableau

basis	$\hat{B}_3^{-1}$			x_1	x_2	b_i^*
x_2	3/10	−1/5	0	0	1	12
x_1	−1/10	2/5	0	1	0	16
$c_j - z_j$	−14	−24	1	0	0	2,560

The revised simplex method is an efficient algorithm for solving linear programming problems when a computer is utilized. It is especially superior in its computational capability as compared to the standard simplex method when the number of decision variables is several times larger than the number of constraints.

The Russian Algorithm of Linear Programming

In the January, 1979, issue of the Russian journal *Doklady*, a young Russian mathematician, L. G. Khachian, published the abstract of an article "Polynomial Algorithm for Solving Linear Programming." Since then, there has been much praise, criticism, and discussion of the Russian algorithm, also known as Khachian's algorithm or polynomial-time algorithm of linear programming. As a matter of fact, many newspapers and science magazines carried sensational front-page headlines, such as "A Soviet Discovery Rocks World of Mathematics" (*New York Times*, November 7, 1979).

Briefly, what Khachian has accomplished is to prove that linear programming problems can be solved in polynomial-time rather than exponential-time of the simplex technique. The Russian algorithm is also an iterative technique as is the simplex method. However, it is based on the concept of ellipsoidal manipulation in an Euclidian n-dimensional space. The iterative process takes the form of finding half-ellipsoids within an ellipsoid that contains the smallest residual for the iteration. A new ellipsoid is then circumscribed around the half-ellipsoid, and a new half-ellipsoid is found that contains the next smallest residual for this iteration. At this point, the residual is examined for its magnitude. This process continues until the residual is equal to zero or the number of iterations is equal to a preset number.

The Russian algorithm is basically a set of successive approximations to the optimal solution. The result it provides will not necessarily be exact. Thus, the magnitude of the inexactness and the tolerance of the system for this inexactness will determine whether or not the solution is accurate enough for the problem under consideration.

It appears that there is a general agreement among management scientists that the Russian algorithm is mathematically neat and interesting. However, the practicality of the algorithm appears to be limited. Many scientists, who evaluated the computational efficiency of the Russian algorithm against the simplex algorithm, reported at the 1979 Joint Conference of Operations Research Society of America and the Institute of Management Science in Washington, D.C., that the simplex method was far superior to the Russian algorithm. One important reason appears to be the fact that currently available simplex-based methods do not necessarily solve a problem in exponential-time due to many computational improvements that have been made over the years. An experiment by George Dantzig indicated that a particular linear programming problem could be solved in about 30 minutes by the simplex method but it would require about 50 million years on the computer by the Russian algorithm.

Today, most management scientists believe that the Russian algorithm will not become an effective solution technique for linear programming. However, some scientists still believe that the algorithm may prove to be effective for solving dynamic programming and nonlinear programming problems. The true value of the Russian algorithm can be determined only through further research of this technique.

Decomposition Approaches

Large-Scale Systems

As management science techniques are further refined and computer capabilities increase, many large-scale models can be developed for complex managerial problems. Technological advances have been remarkable in the area of linear programming application. Today, commercial computer codes of linear programming are available that are capable of solving problems with up to six thousand constraints and a virtually unlimited number of variables. These programs can solve most linear programming models developed for real-world problems. However, there have been cases where real-world problems have exceeded the computational capabilities of even these programs. Decomposition methods have been developed as computational devices for solving certain structured, large-scale linear programs. In this section, we will discuss decomposition methods, with special emphasis on the modified **Kornai-Liptak method.**

Many large-scale linear programs have certain structural patterns in terms of their zero and nonzero technological coefficients in the constraints. Thus, large-scale systems theory attempts to devise solution algorithms that exploit the unique structure of these problems. In this section, several of the most common structures of large-scale systems, which are shown in figure 15.4, will be discussed.

Figure 15.4 Large-scale system coefficient structures.

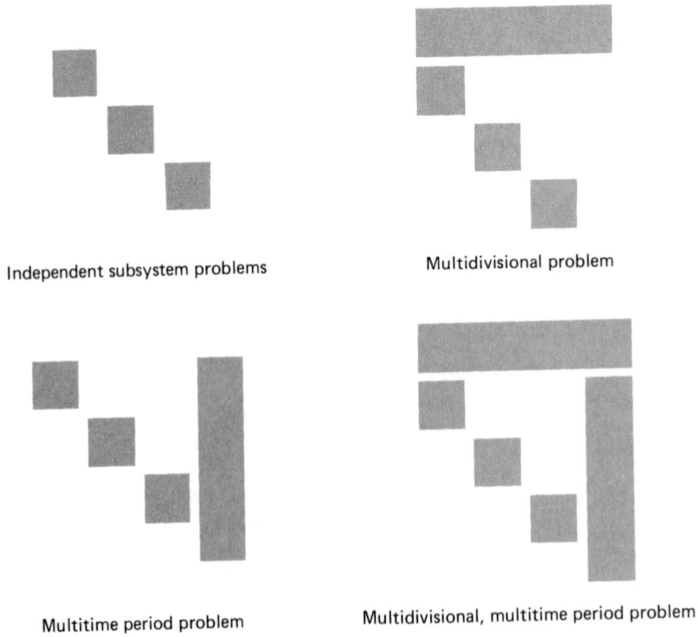

Independent Subsystems

The model of a holding company that has several completely independent organizations under its umbrella without any centralized control is based on independent subsystems. Thus, the model appears as follows:

$$\text{Maximize } Z = \sum_{j=1}^{r} c_j x_j + \sum_{j=r+1}^{s} c_j x_j + \sum_{j=s+1}^{q} c_j x_j$$

subject to

$$\sum_{j=1}^{r} a_{ij}\, x_j \leqslant b_i \; (i = 1, 2, \ldots, m),$$

$$\sum_{j=r+1}^{s} a_{ij} x_j \leqslant b_i \; (i = m+1, m+2, \ldots, t),$$

$$\sum_{j=s+1}^{q} a_{ij} x_j \leqslant b_i \; (i = t+1, t+2, \ldots, u),$$

$$x_j \geqslant 0$$

In this model there is no common constraint in which most of the decision variables appear. As a matter of fact, neither the decision variables $x_i, x_2, \ldots, x_r$, the variables $x_{r+1}, x_{r+2}, \ldots, x_s$, nor the variables $x_{s+1}, x_{s+2}, \ldots, x_q$ appear in the same constraint. Therefore, the variables are independent. The problem can thus be solved as three smaller, separate problems.

Multidivisional Problems

The multidivisional problems are perhaps the most prevalent large-scale systems. The special feature of these problems is the decentralized organizational structure. Each division has certain operational autonomy in optimizing its operations. However, certain overall policies, control, and coordination are needed to allocate organizational resources among the divisions. The model of such a problem appears as a primal block angular form as shown in figure 15.4.

The multidivisional problem can be easily envisioned when we consider the Department of Defense with its semiautonomous departments of the Army, Air Force, Navy, and Marine Corps. A similar example of a large business firm is General Motors with its various divisions, Buick, Chevrolet, Oldsmobile, and Cadillac.

A multidivisional model can be expressed as

$$\text{Maximize } Z = \sum_{j=1}^{n} c_j x_j$$

subject to

$$\sum_{j=1}^{n} a_{ij} x_j \leq b_i \ (i = 1, 2, \ldots, m),$$

$$\sum_{j=1}^{n} c_{qj} x_j \leq d_q \ (q = m+1, m+2, \ldots, u), \text{ divisional constraints}$$

$$x_j \geq 0.$$

Suppose a firm has two production divisions with the following operational requirements:

Division 1

Products and Resource Requirements

Resources	1	2	3	Resources Available
A	6	2	3	20
B	2	3	0	12
C	1	4	2	16
Unit Contribution	$10	12	8	

Division 2

Products and Resource Requirements

Resources	4	5	6	Resources Available
D	8	4	7	30
E	10	15	8	60
F	3	8	4	24
Unit Contribution	$14	16	12	

If the two divisions are completely independent, their individual linear programming models are as follows:

Division 1

$$\text{Maximize } Z = 10x_1 + 12x_2 + 8x_3$$

subject to

$$\begin{aligned} 6x_1 + 2x_2 + 3x_3 &\leq 20 \\ 2x_1 + 3x_2 &\leq 12 \\ x_1 + 4x_2 + 2x_3 &\leq 16 \\ x_1, x_2, x_3 &\geq 0 \end{aligned}$$

Division 2

$$\text{Maximize } Z = 14x_4 + 16x_5 + 12x_6$$

subject to

$$\begin{aligned} 8x_4 + 4x_5 + 7x_6 &\leq 30 \\ 10x_4 + 15x_5 + 8x_6 &\leq 60 \\ 3x_4 + 8x_5 + 4x_6 &\leq 24 \\ x_4, x_5, x_6 &\geq 0 \end{aligned}$$

However, there are common organizational resources (e.g., advertising, training and development) that must be shared by the two divisions as shown in the following table:

	Products and Resource Requirements						
Resources	1	2	3	4	5	6	Resources Available
G	4	2	1	0	6	3	40
H	2	0	4	2	1	2	36

Thus, the resulting model is

$$\text{Maximize } Z = 10x_1 + 12x_2 + 8x_3 + 14x_4 + 16x_5 + 12x_6$$

subject to

$$\begin{aligned} 4x_1 + 2x_2 + x_3 + 6x_5 + 3x_6 &\leq 40 \\ 2x_1 + 4x_3 + 2x_4 + x_5 + 2x_6 &\leq 36 \\ 6x_1 + 2x_2 + 3x_3 &\leq 20 \\ 2x_1 + 3x_2 &\leq 12 \\ x_1 + 4x_2 + 2x_3 &\leq 16 \\ 8x_4 + 4x_5 + 7x_6 &\leq 30 \\ 10x_4 + 15x_5 + 8x_6 &\leq 60 \\ 3x_4 + 8x_5 + 4x_6 &\leq 24. \\ x_j &\geq 0 \end{aligned}$$

Multitime-Period Problems

Like multidivisional problems, multitime-period problems are almost decomposable into separable subproblems. Each subproblem in this case seeks to optimize the organizational operation in a given time period within the planning horizon. Yet, there is a need for common constraints to coordinate the activities in various time periods in order to optimize the operation for the entire planning horizon.

As an illustration, consider a case where an agribusiness firm purchases and sells corn in large quantities as shown in the following table:

Planning Period	Purchase Price (per 1,000 bushels)	Selling Price (per 1,000 bushels)	Maximum Expected Sales (per 1,000 bushels)
1	\$2,000	2,050	2,000
2	2,100	2,200	2,800
3	2,200	2,400	1,700

The corn is assumed to be available for purchase at the beginning of each time period but can be sold throughout the time period. If the corn is to be stored in elevators for sale during a later time period, a total cost of \$100 per one thousand bushels is incurred for storage, handling, and shrinkage. The firm has a contract with a local elevator company for storage space for 2.5 million bushels at any given time. The firm wishes to sell all the corn by the end of period 3.

The problem variables are defined as follows:

x_i = amount of corn (1,000 bushels) purchased in period i

y_i = amount of corn (1,000 bushels) sold in period i

s_{ij} = amount of corn (1,000 bushels) stored in period i for sale in period j

Now, the model can be formulated as follows:

$$\text{Maximize } Z = -2{,}000x_1 + 2{,}050y_1 - 100s_{12} - 200s_{13} - 2{,}100x_2 + 2{,}200y_2 - 100s_{23} - 2{,}200x_3 + 2{,}400y_3$$

subject to

$$\begin{aligned}
x_1 &\leqslant 2{,}500 \\
x_1 - y_1 - s_{12} - s_{13} &= 0 \\
y_1 &\leqslant 2{,}000 \\
s_{12} + x_2 - y_2 - s_{23} &= 0 \\
-s_{12} + y_2 &\leqslant 0 \\
s_{12} + s_{13} + x_2 &\leqslant 2{,}500 \\
y_2 &\leqslant 2{,}800 \\
s_{13} + s_{23} + x_3 - y_3 &= 0 \\
s_{13} + s_{23} + x_3 &\leqslant 2{,}500 \\
y_3 &\leqslant 1{,}700 \\
x_i, y_i, s_{ij} &\geqslant 0
\end{aligned}$$

This model contains three subproblems, where the subproblem for period i is developed by deleting s_{ij} variables and keeping only x_i and y_i variables from the entire model. Thus, the storage variables, s_{ij}, become the linking variables for the three time periods of the planning horizon. The structure of the model can be visualized in table 15.13.

Table 15.13 Multitime-period problem structure

x_1	y_1	x_2	y_2	x_3	y_3	s_{12}	s_{13}	s_{23}
+1								
+1	−1					−1	−1	
	+1							
		+1	−1			+1		−1
			+1			−1		
		+1				+1	+1	
			+1					
				+1	−1		+1	+1
				+1			+1	+1
					+1			

Multidivisional, Multitime-Period Problems

In real-world situations, many problems may occur that possess both multidivisional and multitime-period characteristics simultaneously. For example, a large agricultural grain dealer with multiple divisions may want to design a multiyear planning model that would take advantage of fluctuating grain prices. The multidivisional, multitime-period problem contains many subproblems, each of which is concerned with achieving an optimal level of operations for a given division at a given time period. These subproblems are also linked to common constraints and common variables as shown in figure 15.4. The linking constraints, as shown in the multidivisional problem, coordinate the divisional operations by allocating organizational resources. The linking variables coordinate the operation of each division during the time periods in the planning horizon.

Decomposition Methods

The decomposition algorithm, originally developed by Dantzig and Wolfe as a computational device for solving large-scale linear programs, has received increasing attention in recent years. This is mainly attributed to two important characteristics of the decomposition technique: (1) it effectively handles resource allocation problems in decentralized organizations, and (2) it provides managerial implications in decentralized organizations in terms of the developments of organizational structure and information systems.

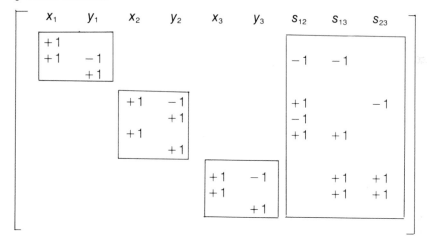

There are basically two different approaches to the decomposition technique. First is the **price directive method** developed by Dantzig and Wolfe (DW). The second is the **resource directive method** developed by Kornai and Liptak (KL). These methods are sometimes referred to by different names. The price directive method is also called the *column generation technique,* and another name for the resource directive method is the *direct distribution technique*. A variety of models based on the decomposition principle have been developed. Some of them have followed the philosophy of Dantzig and Wolfe, and others have followed that of Kornai and Liptak. The category of DW algorithms includes models developed by Balas, Hass, Whinston, and Jennergen. Models of Zschan, Weitzman, and Freeland are classified under the category of the KL algorithm.

The decomposition technique is generally applied to the following type of structured linear programming problems:

$$\text{Maximize } Z = c_1x_1 + c_2x_2 + \ldots + c_nx_n$$

subject to

$$\begin{aligned}
a_1x_1 + a_2x_2 + \ldots a_nx_n &\leq b_0 \\
B_1x_1 \qquad\qquad\qquad &\leq b_1 \\
B_2x_2 \qquad\qquad &\leq b_2 \\
&\vdots \\
B_nx_n &\leq b_n,
\end{aligned}$$

where x_j is a $(m_j \times 1)$ vector of jth activity, c_j is a $(1 \times m_j)$ vector of the objective function coefficient for the jth activity, a_j is a $(r_o \times m_j)$ matrix, B_j is a $(r_j \times m_j)$ matrix, and b_j is a $(r_o \times 1)$ vector of resources.

This model represents the decision problem facing a two-level, multidivisional organization with n divisions. There are two types of resources, b_0 and b_j. The variable b_0 represents the corporate resources that are managed by the central unit and shared by all divisions. The variable b_j represents the jth divisional resources that cannot be shared with other divisions. The variables a_j and B_j are the technology matrices for the jth division.

Dantzig-Wolfe Method

The DW algorithm is an iterative process where the central unit generates shadow prices, and divisional units use these shadow prices to generate their proposals. These proposals are sent to the central unit for the generation of new shadow prices. The process continues until the system reaches an equilibrium. The optimal solution is the convex combination of proposals generated by each division.

The central unit generates shadow prices by solving the following master problem:

$$\text{Maximize } Z = \sum_i \sum_j c_i x_i^j \beta_i^j$$

subject to

$$\sum_i \sum_j a_i x_i^j \beta_i^j = b_0$$

$$\sum_j \beta_i^j = 1, \text{ for } i = 1, \ldots, n$$

$$x_j, \beta_i^j > 0,$$

where β_i^j is a coefficient of the convex combination for x_i^j, the ith extreme point of the convex set $B_i x_i = b_i$, i.e., $x_i = \sum_j x_i^j \beta_i^j$.

Each division generates proposals by solving the following subproblem:

$$\text{Maximize } (c_i - a_i v_o)\, x_i$$

subject to

$$B_i x_i \leqslant b_i$$

$$x_i \geqslant 0,$$

where v_o is the dual variable associated with corporate resources b_0.

The Dantzig-Wolfe algorithm starts with the central unit's pricing of corporate resources. Each division uses these prices to solve its divisional problem and submits its proposal to the central unit. The central unit evaluates all the divisional proposals and forms new prices for corporate resources. The process continues until it reaches an equilibrium. The final decision is made by the central unit, which combines divisional proposals in a certain proportion. Thus, it may be noted that the central unit acts both as a price control board setting prices and as a planning board making the final decision. Divisions are not allowed to choose the final decisions. They are only used as a tool for decision making by the central unit. It has been said, therefore, that the DW algorithm should not really be construed as a decentralized planning system. Rather, it should be accepted as a centralized planning system within a framework of a decentralized structure. According to Dantzig, it is ''central planning without complete information at the center.''

There has been extensive treatment of the Dantzig-Wolfe method in management science texts (see especially Bradley, Hax, and Magnanti; Hillier and Lieberman; Kim; and Wagner). Therefore, a detailed discussion of the decomposition method will not be presented in this text.[1]

1. Interested readers should study illustrative examples in Loomba and Turban, *Applied Programming for Management,* pp. 149–57 and Kim, *Introduction to Linear Programming,* pp. 387–96.

The DW and KL algorithms differ in their underlying philosophies, as well as the manner in which the model is decomposed. It is generally recognized that the KL algorithm has advantages over the DW algorithm in terms of managerial implications that can be obtained from the solution. However, KL is inferior to DW in terms of its computational efficiency.

As pointed out by Kornai, the KL algorithm has *one* computational advantage over DW. Computations carried out at the central unit are considerably simpler in KL because the allocation of corporate resources to divisions in certain proportions for each resource is handled separately. However, in DW, the master problem, which integrates all the divisions and corporate resources, must be solved. Nevertheless, the DW algorithm has the following three decisive advantages over KL: (1) the DW algorithm is finite while KL is not; (2) the DW algorithm offers more rapid convergence to the optimal solution than KL; and (3) the value of the objective function converges monotonically in DW, but it fluctuates in KL.

There are three basic weaknesses inherent in the KL algorithm. These weaknesses involve the (1) computation of bidding prices, (2) allocation of resources, and (3) stopping rule. The KL algorithm employs an averaging technique in the computation of bidding prices for resources and in the allocation of resources. However, this averaging technique can result in unsound allocation of resources and can cause a wild fluctuation of current solutions. This is because the averaging technique is based on an erroneous and arbitrary conceptual base, as will be shown in the following.

First, in computing bidding prices, the KL algorithm uses the averaging technique, which gives equal weights to all past shadow prices generated by a division. The rationale for giving equal weights to all past shadow prices has no logical basis. For the present allocation decision, the shadow prices bidding for the previous system of allocation are irrelevant, and only the bidding for the present system of allocation is relevant.

Secondly, in allocating resources, the KL algorithm also uses an averaging technique that takes the average of all the past allocations as the amount of present allocation. This scheme is devised by KL to avoid a back-and-forth movement of resources from one division to the other. However, this averaging technique is very arbitrary. Another drawback to the method for allocating resources also exists. The KL algorithm reallocates more than one resource per division at a time. This method distorts the picture of the shadow price system. It may be noted that the system of shadow prices is dependent on that of resource allocation. In other words, a change in the amount of allocation for any one resource brings about the change in the shadow prices of other resources. Thus, it is not a good idea to change the amount of allocation in more than one resource at a time, as the effect of change in one resource allocation on the shadow price of other resources is not considered.

Finally, the stopping rule in the KL algorithm is based upon a comparison with a predetermined critical value, δ. It is not possible, however, to determine the reasonable size of δ.

The modified KL algorithm devised by Lee and Rho rectifies the inherent weaknesses of the original KL algorithm. The technique utilizes the present price system in computing bidding prices for resource allocation. Thus, only present prices are considered for the resource allocation. In the actual allocation of resources, it is extremely difficult to determine exactly how much each allocation should be. However, since at least the range of optimal resource allocation quantities is known, it is possible to take the mean value of the range as an approximate allocation. Thus, the modified KL algorithm uses the binary search technique, which determines the middle of upper and lower bounds of the optimal allocation as the resource allocation quantity. The stopping rule of the modified KL algorithm terminates iterations when the percentage difference of two successive current solutions is smaller than a predetermined critical ratio.

The KL algorithm decomposes the central unit and divisions vertically. Thus, each decomposed divisional model becomes

$$\text{Maximize } Z_i = c_i x_i$$

subject to

$$\begin{aligned} a_i x_i &\leq b_o^i \\ B_i x_i &\leq b_i \\ x_i &\geq 0, \end{aligned}$$

where b_o^i is the allocation of corporate resources to division i (i.e., $\sum_{i=1}^{n} b_o^i = b_o$).

Define a vector $V_o^i(N)$ and sets R_i, S_j and T as follows:

$$V_o^i(N) = \begin{bmatrix} v_{o1}^i(N) \\ v_{o2}^i(N) \\ \vdots \\ v_{om_o}^i(N), \end{bmatrix} \quad i = 1, 2, \ldots, n$$

$$R_i = \{v_{oi}^1(N), v_{oi}^2(N), \ldots, v_{oi}^n(N)\} \qquad i = 1, \ldots, m$$

$$S_j = \{v_{o1}^j(N), v_{o2}^j(N), \ldots, v_{o_{mo}}^j(N)\} \quad j = 1, \ldots, n$$

$$T = \bigcup_{i=1}^{m_o} R_i = \bigcup_{j=1}^{n} S_j,$$

where $v_{oi}^j(N)$ is the shadow price of $b_{oi}^j(N)$, ith corporate resource allocated to division i at the Nth iteration.

The steps of the modified KL algorithm are as follows: Initially, determine the resource allocation $b^j_{oi}(0)$, the upper bound $b^j_{ui}(0)$, and the lower bound $b^j_{1i}(0)$ of the optimal resource allocation for all divisions and resources.

$$b^j_{oi}(0) = b_{oi}/n$$

$$b^j_{ui}(0) = b_{oi}, \qquad i = 1, 2, \ldots, m_o$$

$$b^j_{1i}(0) = 0, \qquad j = 1, 2, \ldots, n$$

where b_{oi} is the ith corporate resource.

Step 1 Each division solves its subproblem based on the previous allocation $b^i_o(N-1)$ and obtains the values of shadow prices $V^i_o(N)$ and current solutions $Z_i(N)$.

If $ZD < \pi$, proceed to step 3. Otherwise, proceed to step 2.

$$ZD = \frac{|Z(N) - Z(N-1)|}{Z(N-1)},$$

where

π is a predetermined critical ratio.

Step 2 If $T = \emptyset$, return to step 1. Otherwise, let t and c be integers such that $|v^c_{ot}(N)| = \max\limits_{i,j} \{|v^j_{oi}(N)|\}$.

And if $v^c_{ot}(N) = 0$, return to step 1.

If $v^c_{ot}(N) > 0$, let $v^r_{ot} = v^c_{ot}(N)$, $v^s_{ot} = \min\limits_k \{v^k_{ot}(N)\}$.

If $v^c_{ot}(N) < 0$, let $v_{ot} = v^c_{ot}(N)$, $v^r_{ot} = \max\limits_k \{v^k_{ot}(N)\}$.

Determine upper bounds $b^r_{ut}(N)$ and $b^s_{ut}(N)$ and lower bounds $b^r_{lt}(N)$ and $b_{lt}(N)$ on the optimal allocation and actual allocations $b^r_{ot}(N)$ and $b^s_{ot}(N)$ of the tth resource for the rth and s^{th} divisions:

$$b^r_{ut}(N) = b^r_{ut}(N-1) \qquad b^s_{ut}(N) = b^s_{ot}(N-1)$$

$$b^r_{lt}(N) = b^r_{ot}(N-1) \qquad b^s_{lt}(N) = b^s_{lt}(N-1)$$

$$b_t = \min\left[\frac{\{b^r_{ut}(N) - b^r_{lt}(N)\}}{2} \quad \frac{\{b^s_{ut}(N) - b^s_{lt}(N)\}}{2}\right]$$

$$b^r_{ot}(N) = b^r_{ot}(N-1) + b_t \qquad b^s_{ot}(N) = b^s_{ot}(N-1) - b_t$$

Remove S_r and S_s from T, and repeat step 2.

Step 3 The optimal solution is found: $Z \text{ opt} = \min \{(z(1), z(2), \ldots z(N)\}$.

Stochastic Linear Programming

The general linear programming problem is deterministic. The model is formulated and solved with a given set (usually the mean values) of parameters (contribution rates c_j, technological coefficients a_{ij}, and the quantity of available resources b_i). This general assumption makes linear programming an extremely easy technique to use. However, this assumption is also the primary problem in the practical application of linear programming. The true values of model parameters are usually not known until after the decision based on the linear programming solution is actually implemented. Although preliminary analysis of the problem may provide fairly good estimates, it is impossible to predict accurate values of the model parameters. The primary reason for this is that often all or some of the parameters may be random variables, which are influenced by random events in the decision environment.

We have already discussed sensitivity analysis and parametric programming, which can be used for examining the effect of changes in the model parameters. One shortcoming of these methods is that each change made is assumed to be independent of any other change. Hence, an analysis of the effect of simultaneous changes is not possible. Another disadvantage of these methods is their inability to take into account the complete randomness of the parameters as suggested by specific probability distributions.

There have been many different approaches suggested for formulating the linear programming problem under uncertainty. However, their common characteristic is the difficulty of solution. There has been no general solution method for linear programming problems under uncertainty, such as the simplex algorithm for the deterministic linear programming problem. There have been basically two distinct approaches to formulating linear programming problems under uncertainty. The first approach, which is generally referred to as stochastic programming, attempts to solve the problem through making one or more decisions by selecting model parameters at different points in time. Although this approach sounds very logical, its practical application is enormously complex, especially when the model is large and involves a number of time periods. The second approach, called chance-constrained programming, involves the formulation of a deterministic equivalent model to the problem under uncertainty and solution by the simplex method. This method is especially attractive as it can be solved by the powerful simplex technique.

Characteristically, stochastic programming problems evolve as nonlinear when several of the parameters become random. This attribute directly affects the difficulty of solving the problem. We will discuss only three basic approaches: (1) **sequential stochastic programming,** (2) **nonsequential stochastic programming,** and (3) **chance-constrained programming.**

Sequential Stochastic Programming

Sequential stochastic programming (SSP) solves problems under uncertainty that involve making two or more decisions at different points in time with the condition that at least one of the later decisions depends not only on an earlier decision but also on the value of random parameters "observed" in the time intervening between the two decisions. This technique has also been called the two-stage approach since the model parameters are fixed in the first stage. After the random event occurs over time, the parameters can be revised according to decision rules to account for the resolved uncertainties. The general version of the two-stage (sequential) stochastic model may be written in the general form.

$$\text{Maximize or Minimize } Z = \sum_{j=1}^{K} E(c_j)x_j + \sum_{q=1}^{Q} P_q(c_{qj}x_{qj})$$

subject to

$$\sum_{j=1}^{K} a_{ij}x_j = b_i, \qquad i = 1, \ldots, g \text{ (first stage)}$$

$$\sum_{j=1}^{K} a_{qij}x_j + \sum_{j=K+1}^{M} a_{qij}x_{qj} = b_{qj} \text{ (second stage decision rules)}$$

$$x_j \geq 0 \qquad i = g+1, \ldots, m$$

$$q = 1, \ldots, Q$$

$$x_{qj} \geq 0 \qquad j = 1, \ldots, K$$

In this model, x_j $(j=1, \ldots, k \leq n)$ represents fixed levels of x in the first stage; the constraints i contain only first stage variables for deterministic a_{ij} and b_i; x_j $(j=K+1, \ldots, n)$ represents levels of x after all random values are known; Q is a finite number of possible sets of values for c_j $(j=1+1, \ldots, n)$ and a_{ij}, b_i $(i=g+1, \ldots, m)$. The probability of occurrence is denoted by P_q $(q=1, 2 \ldots, Q)$.

The primary difficulty in using the sequential approach is related to the vast proportions the resulting model can achieve, where additional variables and constraints are necessary to formulate the model. These additions make the problem more complex, resulting in a large incremental amount of computation. This drawback reduces the pragmatic application of the sequential stochastic programming model to real-world applications.

Nonsequential Stochastic Programming

The nonsequential approach to stochastic programming is a one-stage technique that does not allow for intermediate revisions in the model formulation. One method used in this approach is the expected value approach, which transforms the original nonlinear, probabilistic problem into a deterministic linear programming model. Essentially the expected value is used in place of a random variable (parameter) and is slightly more realistic than the deterministic mean value approach.

This technique is primarily used in replacing the cost coefficients (c_j) of the objective function where the problem reduces to one of minimizing (or maximizing) the expected cost (profit). The solution obtained is generally greater than the actual optimal solution in the minimization case and less than the actual optimal solution for the maximization case.

Chance-Constrained Programming

A special approach to sequential stochastic programming, referred to as chance-constrained programming, was pioneered and later extended by Charnes and Cooper. Chance-constrained programming is concerned with selecting certain random variables as functions of random variables with known distributions. The approach attempts to maximize a functional of both classes of random variables subject to constraints on these variables which must be maintained at prescribed levels of probability.

The primary purpose of the chance-constrained method is to reduce the problem of planning in light of an uncertain future. In developing the chance-constrained stochastic model, Charnes and Cooper derived a deterministic equivalence to the original stochastic problem and employed the simplex algorithm as the vehicle for computation. The logic behind the chance-constrained model is similar to the conventional statistical significance tests where a prescribed level of confidence (based on a normal distribution) is used to establish a penalty for violating the test.

The general formulation of the chance-constrained model is as follows:

$$\text{Maximize or Minimize } Z = \sum_{j=1}^{K} E(c_j)x_j$$

subject to

$$\sum_{j=1}^{K} a_{ij}x_j = b_i, \qquad i = 1, \ldots, g$$

$$P\left[\sum_{j=1}^{K} a_{ij}x_j \leq b_i\right] \geq 1 - \alpha_i, \; i = 1, \ldots, m$$

$$x_j \geq 0$$

where α_i = risk level for constraint i and $0 \leq \alpha_i \leq 1$ for each level of b_i ($i = g + 1, \ldots, m$); c_j and b_i are all random variables; all parameters are normally distributed with known means and variances. The general model can be extended to show deterministic models for each case that shows c_j, a_{ij}, and b_i as random variables.

There are several desirable attributes that make chance-constrained programming a powerful stochastic programming technique. First, the original stochastic problem can be transformed into an equivalent deterministic model. Second, the resulting deterministic model is the same size and structure as the original problem formulation. Third, the equivalent model, while nonlinear, can be approximated with a simplex-based nonlinear programming model, such as the separable programming technique. Computational speed and efficiency is a direct spin-off of advantages two and three.

Another property that makes this technique appealing is that the only information necessary for each random variable b_i is the $(1-\alpha_i)$ fractile for the unconditional distribution of the b_i value. The ability to handle larger-scale problems also provides the chance-constrained programming method an advantage over other existing stochastic programming techniques. Important contributions have been made in extending the original model formulation and employing the model in practical applications. Charnes and Cooper have developed a chance-constrained programming model to analyze the risk and uncertainty in a time-phased transport problem based on the decision rules involving independent normal variates.

Linear Programming and Input-Output Analysis

The input-output model was developed by Leontief in the early 1930s. The model is intended to analyze economic interdependence among industries at the regional or national level. The input-output model is especially valuable for analyzing, forecasting, and planning business and/or economic activities. Linear programming has been applied in solving both static and dynamic formulations of large-scale input-output models. For example, suppose an input-output model has been developed for economic development planning of underdeveloped countries. In such a model, the objective function is to maximize national production subject to the available workforce, balance of payment, capital, and income distribution.[2]

Summary

In this chapter, we have discussed several important advanced topics of linear programming. Parametric programming is concerned with analysis of the effects of continuous and systematic change in the model parameters on the optimal solution. The revised simplex method is a shortcut solution method that requires fewer computations in solving the linear programming problem. This algorithm is especially valuable when a large problem is solved by electronic computer. The decomposition method is primarily concerned with breaking up a large-scale linear program into several less complex subproblems and formulating a master problem that ties the subproblems together. Although the primary motivation of the decomposition method is to simplify the large problem, it can make important contributions in terms of managerial implication, organizational structure, and information systems in a large decentralized organization.

2. Interested readers should consult works of Dorfman et al., Leontief, Loomba and Turban, and Wagner.

References

Arrow, K. J., and Hurwicz, L. "Decentralization and Computation in Resource Allocation." In *Essays in Economics and Econometrics*. Edited by R. P. Font. Chapel Hill, N.C.: University of North Carolina Press, 1960.

Bradley, S. P.; Hax, A. C.; and Magnanti, T. L. *Applied Mathematical Programming*. Reading, Mass.: Addison-Wesley Publishing Co., 1977.

Burton, R. M.; Damon, W. W.; and Loughridge, D. W. "The Economics of Decomposition: Resource Allocation Versus Transfer Pricing." *Decision Sciences* 5 (1974): 297–310.

Charnes, A.; Clower, R. W.; and Kortanek, K. O. "Effective Control Through Coherent Decentralization with Preemptive Goals." *Econometrica* 35 (1967).

Charnes, A., and Cooper, W. W. "Chance-Constrained Programming." *Management Science* 6 (1959): 73–79.

———. *Management Models and Industrial Applications of Linear Programming*. New York: John Wiley & Sons, 1961.

Charnes, A., and Lemke, C. E. "Minimization of Nonlinear Separable Convex Functions." *Naval Research Logistics Quarterly* 1 (1954): 301–12.

Dantzig, G. B., and Wolfe, P. "Decomposition Principle for Linear Programs." *Operations Research* 8 (1960): 101–11.

———. *Linear Programming and Extensions*. Princeton, N.J.: Princeton University Press, 1963.

Dorfman, R.; Samuelson, P. A.; and Solow, R. M. *Linear Programming and Economic Analysis*. New York: McGraw-Hill, 1958.

Geoffrion, A. M. "Primal Resource-Directive Approaches for Optimizing Nonlinear Decomposable Systems." *Operations Research* 18 (1970): 377–403.

Grinold, R. C. "Steepest Ascent for Large-Scale Linear Programs. *SIAM* Review 14 (1972): 447–64.

Hillier, F. S., and Lieberman, G. J. *Introduction to Operations Research*. 3rd ed. San Francisco: Holden-Day, 1980.

Ijiri, Y. *Management Goals and Accounting for Control*. Chicago: Rand-McNally & Co., 1965.

Khachian, L. G. "Polynomial Algorithm for Solving Linear Programming." *Doklady* 1 (1979): 191–94.

Kim, C. *Introduction to Linear Programming*. New York: Holt, Rhinehart and Winston, 1971.

Kornai, J. *Mathematical Planning of Structural Decisions*. Amsterdam: North-Holland, 1969.

Kornai, J., and Liptak, T. "Two-Level Planning." *Econometrica* 33 (1965).

Lee, S. M., and Rho, B. H. "The Modified Kornai-Liptak Decomposition Algorithm." *Computers and Operations Research* 6 (1979): 39–45.

Leontief, W. W. *Input-Output Economics*. New York: Oxford Book Co., 1970.

Loomba, N. P., and Turban, E. *Applied Programming for Management*. New York: Holt, Rinehart and Winston, 1974.

McMillan, C. *Mathematical Programming*. New York: John Wiley & Sons, 1970.

Malinvaud, E. "Decentralized Procedures for Planning." In *Activity Analysis in the Theory of Growth and Planning*. Edited by E. Malinvaud and M. Bacharach. New York: Macmillan, 1967.

Miller, C. E. "The Simplex Method for Local Separable Programming." In *Recent Advances in Mathematical Programming*. Edited by R. L. Graves and P. Wolfe. New York: McGraw-Hill, 1963.

von Neumann, J., and Morgenstern, O. *Theory of Games and Economic Behavior*. 3rd ed. Princeton, N.J.: Princeton University Press, 1953.

Wagner, H. M. *Principles of Operations Research*. 2d ed. Englewood Cliffs, N.J.: Prentice-Hall, 1975.

Problems

1. Consider the following problem:

$$\text{Maximize } Z = 5x_1 + 12x_2$$

subject to

$$\begin{aligned} x_1 + 2x_2 &\leq 20 \\ x_1 &\leq 12 \\ x_2 &\leq 6 \\ x_1, x_2 &\geq 0 \end{aligned}$$

Solve the parametric linear programming problem assuming that the objective function is given by

$$Z(\theta) = (5 + 3\theta)\, x_1 + (12 - 6\theta)\, x_2.$$

2. Graphically plot the parametric analysis derived in problem 1 with the value of the objective function on the vertical axis and θ on the horizontal.

3. Consider the following problem:

$$\text{Maximize } Z(\theta) = 20x_1 + 16x_2$$

subject to

$$\begin{aligned} 4x_1 + 6x_2 &\leq 48 \\ 2x_1 + x_2 &\leq 20 \\ x_1, x_2 &\geq 0 \end{aligned}$$

Assume that it is possible to modify the objective function by the shifting of resources between the activities. Thus the unit profit of x_2 can be increased above 16 but only at the expense of reducing the unit profit of x_1 below 20 by twice the amount of the increase for x_2. Formulate the new objective function.

4. Consider the same problem given in problem 1.

$$\text{Maximize } Z = 5x_1 + 12x_2$$

subject to

$$\begin{aligned} x_1 + 2x_2 &\leq 20 \\ x_1 &\leq 12 \\ x_2 &\leq 6 \\ x_1, x_2 &\geq 0 \end{aligned}$$

Solve the parametric linear programming problem assuming that the right-hand-side values are changed to $(20 + \theta)$ for the first constraint, $(12 - \theta)$ for the second constraint, and $(6 - \theta)$ for the third constraint.

5. Provide a graphical interpretation of the solution to problem 4.

6. Solve the following problem using parametric linear programming to examine systematic changes in the right-hand-side values of θ for $0 \leqslant \theta \leqslant 25$.

   Maximize $Z(\theta) = 10x_1 + 5x_2$

   subject to

$$2x_1 \leqslant 20 + 4\theta$$
$$x_1 + x_2 \leqslant 25 - \theta$$
$$x_2 \leqslant 10 + 2\theta$$
$$x_1, x_2 \geqslant 0$$

7. Solve the following problem by the revised simplex method:

   Maximize $Z = 10x_1 + 8x_2$

   subject to

$$4x_1 + 6x_2 \leqslant 48$$
$$2x_1 + x_2 \leqslant 20$$
$$x_1, x_2 \geqslant 0$$

8. Solve the following problem by the revised simplex method:

   Maximize $Z = 70x_1 + 80x_2$

   subject to

$$2x_1 - x_2 \leqslant 20$$
$$x_1 + x_2 \leqslant 14$$
$$x_1 + 2x_2 \leqslant 20$$
$$x_1, x_2 \geqslant 0$$

9. Solve the following problem by the revised simplex method:

   Maximize $Z = 2x_1 + 3x_2$

   subject to

$$2x_1 + 5x_2 \geqslant 30$$
$$4x_1 + 2x_2 \geqslant 28$$
$$x_1, x_2 \geqslant 0$$

10. The Beatrice Corporation has three production divisions with the following operational requirements:

Division 1

Products and Resources Requirements

Resources	1	2	3	Resources Available
A	9	6	18	60
B	0	9	6	36
C	6	12	3	48
Unit Contribution	$24	36	30	

Division 2

Products and Resources Requirements

Resources	4	5	6	Resources Available
D	21	12	24	90
E	24	45	30	180
F	12	24	9	72
Unit Contribution	$42	48	36	

Division 3

Products and Resources Requirements

Resources	7	8	9	Resources Available
G	40	28	52	160
H	34	64	46	226
I	28	46	22	130
Unit Contribution	$78	94	76	

Suppose there are common organizational resources that must be shared by the three divisions as shown in the following table:

Products and Resource Requirements

Resources	1	2	3	4	5	6	7	8	9	Resources Available
J	12	6	3	0	18	9	15	3	12	150
K	6	0	12	6	3	6	10	4	8	130
L	20	8	16	8	24	20	30	10	25	300

Formulate a decomposition linear programming model for the multidivisional problem.

11. The National Cranberry Company purchases and sells cranberries in large quantities. The cranberries are assumed to be available for purchase at the beginning of each time period but can be sold throughout the time period. If the cranberries are to be stored for sale during a later time period, a total cost of $200 per one thousand barrels is incurred. The company has a contract with a local firm for storage space for five million barrels at any given time. The company wishes to sell all the cranberries by the end of period 3. Formulate a linear programming model for the multitime-period problem from the following data.

Planning Period	Purchase Price (per 1,000 barrels)	Selling Price (per 1,000 barrels)	Maximum Expected Sales (per 1,000 barrels)
1	$4,000	4,100	4,000
2	4,200	4,400	5,600
3	4,400	4,800	3,400

12. Give an example of a corporate situation in which the decomposition method would be useful.

16

Nonlinear Programming

A large portion of this book, in particular chapters 2 through 5, has been devoted to the methods of linear optimization. This is due, in large part, to the development of powerful methods for solution of linear models, including the simplex method and the specialized solution algorithms for transportation and assignment models. Highly efficient computer programs have been developed using specially developed versions of these algorithms, for solution of large-scale, real-world applications.

Extensions and modifications of the linear programming models were treated in chapters 13, 14, and 15. Chapter 13 considered the fact that a single criterion, or goal, may be inadequate to reflect the real-world requirements of the problem environment. Chapter 14 introduced the case where treatment of solution variables as continuous values is unacceptable. And finally, chapter 15 presented advanced topics in linear programming. However, all of these topics relate to *linear models*, in that the assumption of linear relationships first specified in chapter 2 is still in effect.

The assumption of linear relationships is often appropriate or at least a ''good enough'' approximation for the range of values considered for the variables of a given problem. For some problems, however, nonlinear relationships (or functions) must be constructed in order to accurately reflect the structure of the problem.

The presentation of inventory models in chapter 7 included nonlinear relationships. Classical calculus was the basis for solution of these models. Chapter 12 also presented the techniques of dynamic programming for solution of nonlinear optimization problems.

The purpose of this chapter is to provide an introduction to the general topic of nonlinear programming. The topic is much too broad and advanced for more than a cursory introduction within the span of one chapter. Much of the theory of nonlinear optimization is directed toward obtaining the necessary and sufficient conditions for an optimal solution. This theory does not, however, exploit the efficiencies provided by computer solution.

Most of the modern day algorithms for solution of nonlinear programming problems have been recently developed. These algorithms are typically specialized iterative search procedures that do utilize the computer. To adequately cover each type of algorithm would require a book in itself.[1]

This chapter presents a brief overview of the classical theory of nonlinear programming, including most importantly the Kuhn-Tucker theorem, with the purpose of providing some insight into the philosophy of constrained nonlinear optimization. This presentation follows directly the concept of Lagrange multipliers, which is presented in Appendix B.

Kuhn-Tucker Conditions

The general form of the nonlinear maximization problem to be considered is as follows:

Maximize $y = f(x_1, x_2, \ldots, x_n)$

subject to

$$g_i(x_1, x_2, \ldots, x_n) \leq b_i, \quad \text{for } i = 1, 2, \ldots, m$$

and

$$x_j \geq 0, \qquad \text{for } j = 1, 2, \ldots, n$$

The problem is to maximize a linear or nonlinear objective function, f, consisting of n decision variables, subject to m linear or nonlinear constraints, $g_i \leq b_i$, and all decision variables, x_j, subject to the nonnegativity restriction.

There is no general algorithm available that will solve all problems with this basic structure. However, as previously pointed out, numerous special purpose algorithms and search procedures have been developed for special cases of the nonlinear programming problem.

The Kuhn-Tucker conditions provide the basis for recognizing candidates for an optimal solution to a nonlinear programming problem.[2] These conditions are based upon the classical calculus methods of solution, which are introduced in Appendix B.

Recall that when y is a function of one variable, x, (i.e., $y = f(x)$), in order to maximize y, $dy/dx = 0$ must be determined. As long as $f(x)$ is differentiable, this yields a candidate for the maximum. If $f(x)$ is a concave function, this yields the maximum. By the same token, when $y = f(x_1, x_2, \ldots, x_n)$, the candidates for the maximum can be determined by computing $\partial y/\partial x_j = 0$, for $j = 1, 2, \ldots, n$, and solving these equations simultaneously for the values of x_j. Again, if $f(x_1, x_2, \ldots, x_n)$ is a concave function, this yields a maximum.[3]

1. For an excellent in-depth presentation of nonlinear optimization techniques, refer to Luenberger, *Introduction to Linear and Nonlinear Programming*.
2. Kuhn and Tucker, "Nonlinear Programming," pp. 481–92.
3. To be more precise, the function must be "strictly" concave excluding the case where $f(x_1, x_2, \ldots, x_n)$ is a linear function.

When the nonnegativity restrictions, $x_j \geqslant 0$ ($j = 1, 2, \ldots, n$), are introduced, they may force the value of one or more $x_j = 0$. For such cases, the value of $\partial y/\partial x_j$ may be forced to take on a negative value. Thus, in summary, the maximum of $y = f(x_1, x_2, \ldots, x_n)$ is obtained where $\partial y/\partial x_j = 0$, if $x_j^* > 0$; or $\partial y/\partial x_j \leqslant 0$, if $x_j^* = 0$; when $f(x_1, x_2, \ldots, x_n)$ is a concave function.

It will become apparent that the conditions set forth by Kuhn and Tucker are variations of these classical conditions. Prior to presenting the Kuhn-Tucker conditions, the Lagrange multiplier will be reviewed (see also Appendix B).

The Lagrange multiplier function is formed as follows:

Given

$$y = f(x_1, x_2, \ldots, x_n)$$

subject to

$$g_i(x_1, x_2, \ldots, x_n) \leqslant b_i, \; i = 1, 2, \ldots, m$$

and

$$x_j \geqslant 0, \quad j = 1, 2, \ldots, n$$

The Lagrangian expression, denoted by L, is given as

$$L = f(x_1, x_2, \ldots, x_n) - \sum_{i=1}^{m} \lambda_i [g_i(x_1, x_2, \ldots, x_n) - b_i].$$

Stated more succinctly, given that f and g_i are functions of n decision variables, x_j ($j = 1, 2, \ldots, n$), the Lagrange multiplier function is given as

$$L = f - \sum_{i=1}^{m} \lambda_i (g_i - b_i)$$

where

m = the number of constraints ($i = 1, 2, \ldots, m$)

λ_i = the Lagrange *multiplier*.

The Kuhn-Tucker conditions assume that the nonlinear problem has been formulated as a Lagrange multiplier expression, and differentiated with respect to x_j ($j = 1, 2, \ldots, n$) and λ_i ($i = 1, 2, \ldots, m$). For example, if the general problem includes two decision variables and two constraints, as follows,

$$y = f(x_1, x_2)$$

subject to

$$g_1(x_1, x_2) \leq b_1$$

$$g_2(x_1, x_2) \leq b_2$$

and

$$x_1, x_2 \geq 0$$

the Lagrangian expression is

$$L = f(x_1, x_2) - \lambda_1[g_1(x_1, x_2) - b_1] - \lambda_2[g_2(x_1, x_2) - b_2].$$

The classical approach to solution of the Lagrange multiplier expression requires solving the following equations simultaneously,

$$\frac{\partial L}{\partial x_1} = 0, \frac{\partial L}{\partial x_2} = 0, \frac{\partial L}{\partial \lambda_1} = 0, \frac{\partial L}{\partial \lambda_2} = 0.$$

Given the preceding discussion, the Kuhn-Tucker conditions, which must be satisfied to yield candidates for an optimal solution, are given as follows:

where

$$\frac{\partial L}{\partial x_j} = \frac{\partial f}{\partial x_j} - \sum_{i=1}^{m} \lambda_i \frac{\partial g_i}{\partial x_j}, \quad j = 1, 2, \ldots, n$$

$$x_j^* \left(\frac{\partial L}{\partial x_j}\right) = 0, \quad j = 1, 2, \ldots, n \qquad (1a)$$

$$\frac{\partial L}{\partial x_j} \leq 0, \quad j = 1, 2, \ldots, n \qquad (1b)$$

$$\lambda_i[g_i(x_1^*, x_2^*, \ldots, x_n^*) - b_i] = 0, \quad i = 1, 2, \ldots, m \qquad (2a)$$

$$g_i(x_1^*, x_2^*, \ldots, x_n^*) - b_i \leq 0, \quad i = 1, 2, \ldots, m \qquad (2b)$$

and all $x_j^* \geq 0$, $\lambda_i \geq 0$. (3)

Note that (2*b*) is the $\partial L/\partial \lambda_i$.

These conditions are interpreted by the following restatements:

$$\text{If } x_j^* > 0, \text{ then } \frac{\partial L}{\partial x_j} = 0, \quad j = 1, 2, \ldots, n \tag{1a}$$

$$\text{If } x_j^* = 0, \text{ then } \frac{\partial L}{\partial x_j} \leq 0, \quad j = 1, 2, \ldots, n \tag{1b}$$

$$\text{If } \lambda_i > 0, \text{ then } g_i(x_1^*, x_2^*, \ldots, x_n^*) - b_i = 0, \quad i = 1, 2, \ldots, m \tag{2a}$$

$$\text{If } \lambda_i = 0, \text{ then } g_i(x_1^*, x_2^*, \ldots, x_n^*) - b_i \leq 0, \quad i = 1, 2, \ldots, m \tag{2b}$$

$$\text{and all } x_j^* \geq 0, \lambda_i \geq 0 \tag{3}$$

Note that the requirements for $\partial L/\partial x_j$ are essentially the same as those for $\partial y/\partial x_j$ given previously. Further note that when the Lagrange multiplier function is formulated from $g_i \leq b_i$ to $\lambda_i(g_i - b_i)$, it is *assumed* that the inequality may be temporarily stated as an equality. If the solution value of λ_i is positive, ($\lambda_i > 0$), this indicates that the solution is bound by constraint i, and, therefore, the equality assumption is acceptable (see again the discussion of the Lagrange multiplier in Appendix *B*). However, if the value of $\lambda_i = 0$, the term $(g_i - b_i)$ must be allowed to be equal to or less than zero, since the solution is not bound by constraint i (i.e., $g_i < b_i$). Thus, the Kuhn-Tucker conditions (2*a*) and (2*b*) are defined for each constraint, i, by

(2*a*) Binding constraint (boundary point optimization)
If $\lambda_i > 0$, then $g_i - b_i = 0$, i.e., $g_i = b_i$, for $(x_1^*, x_2^*, \ldots, x_n^*)$.
(2*b*) Nonbinding constraint (interior point optimization)
If $\lambda_i = 0$, then $g_i - b_i \leq 0$, i.e., $g_i \leq b_i$, for $(x_1^*, x_2^*, \ldots, x_n^*)$.

The economic interpretation of the λ_i is analogous to the dual variables of linear programming, and it is the λ_i that are referred to as the Lagrangian *multipliers*. It can be shown that $\partial f^*/\partial b_i = \lambda_i$ (i.e., the "value" associated with relaxing constraint i is given by λ_i).

However, satisfaction of the Kuhn-Tucker conditions only yields the acceptable candidates for an optimal solution. The candidates must then be evaluated further to determine the global optimal solution, which is analogous to the single decision variable case where solution of $dy/dx = 0$ yields one candidate. The limits of the domain must then be evaluated to determine the global optimal solution, unless $y = f(x)$ is known to be concave in which case $dy/dx = 0$ yields x^*. This leads to the following extensions of the Kuhn-Tucker theorem.

If $f(x_1, x_2, \ldots, x_n)$ is a concave function, and if $g_i(x_1, x_2, \ldots, x_n)$ for $i = 1, 2, \ldots, m$, are convex functions, then the results obtained by employing the Lagrangian function, which satisfy the Kuhn-Tucker conditions, will result in an optimal solution. For example, if the objective function is known to be a quadratic cone function, subject to all linear constraints (yielding a convex feasible solution space), then satisfaction of the Kuhn-Tucker conditions will yield an optimal solution. This corollary was also presented and proven by Kuhn and Tucker. (See Appendix B for a discussion of concavity and convexity.)

In summary, the Kuhn-Tucker conditions are necessary, but, in general, are not sufficient. Furthermore, these conditions provide only a *test* for optimality and are not a procedure for finding a solution.

Example 16.1 Nonlinear Maximization Problem

Consider the following nonlinear maximization problem:

$$\text{Maximize } y = 8x_1^2 + 2x_2^2$$

subject to

$$x_1^2 + x_2^2 \leqslant 9$$

and

$$x_1, x_2 \geqslant 0$$

Forming the Lagrangian expression yields

$$L = 8x_1^2 + 2x_2^2 - \lambda(x_1^2 + x_2^2 - 9).$$

Next form the Kuhn-Tucker conditions, given in the following order: (*a*) for $x_1^* > 0$; (*b*) for $x_2^* > 0$; (*c*) for $\lambda > 0$; followed by (*d*) for $x_1^* = 0$; (*e*) for $x_2^* = 0$; and (*f*) for $\lambda = 0$.

$$x_1\left(\frac{\partial L}{\partial x_1}\right) = x_1(16x_1 - 2\lambda x_1) = 0, \quad \text{for } x_1^* > 0 \qquad (a)$$

$$x_2\left(\frac{\partial L}{\partial x_2}\right) = x_2(4x_2 - 2\lambda x_2) = 0, \quad \text{for } x_2^* > 0 \qquad (b)$$

$$\lambda(x_1^2 + x_2^2 - 9) = 0, \quad \text{for } \lambda > 0 \qquad (c)$$

$$\frac{\partial L}{\partial x_1} = 16x_1 - 2\lambda x_1 \leqslant 0, \quad \text{for } x_1^* = 0 \qquad (d)$$

$$\frac{\partial L}{\partial x_2} = 4x_2 - 2\lambda x_2 \leqslant 0, \quad \text{for } x_2^* = 0 \qquad (e)$$

$$x_1^2 + x_2^2 - 9 \leqslant 0, \quad \text{for } \lambda = 0 \qquad (f)$$

The previous discussion of the Kuhn-Tucker conditions has distinguished between solution values for x_j and λ_i in terms of $x_j = 0$ or $x_j > 0$ and $\lambda_i = 0$ or $\lambda_i > 0$. Thus, in general, any Lagrangian formulation of a nonlinear programming problem with n decision variables and m constraints can yield 2^{m+n} possible combinations of solutions (i.e., the n decision variables, x_j, may be either zero or nonzero, and the m Lagrangian multiplier variables, λ_i, may be either zero or nonzero). Thus, for the problem at hand, there are $2^3 = 8$ combinations of solution values for x_1, x_2, and λ that must be considered. The cases are summarized as follows:

Case	x_1	x_2	λ	Must Satisfy Kuhn-Tucker Conditions
1	$= 0$	$= 0$	$= 0$	(*d*, *e*, *f*)
2	$= 0$	$= 0$	> 0	(*d*, *e*, *c*)
3	$= 0$	> 0	$= 0$	(*d*, *b*, *f*)
4	> 0	$= 0$	$= 0$	(*a*, *e*, *f*)
5	$= 0$	> 0	> 0	(*d*, *b*, *c*)
6	> 0	$= 0$	> 0	(*a*, *e*, *c*)
7	> 0	> 0	$= 0$	(*a*, *b*, *f*)
8	> 0	> 0	> 0	(*a*, *b*, *c*)

In order for a solution case to qualify as a candidate for the optimal solution, it must satisfy the Kuhn-Tucker conditions noted in the right-hand column of the table. The conditions are tested by substituting the case solution values into the relevant condition expressions.

Case 1: $x_1 = 0, x_2 = 0, \lambda = 0$

Conditions	Test	Result
(*d*)	$0 \leq 0$	OK
(*e*)	$0 \leq 0$	OK
(*f*)	$-9 \leq 0$	OK

None of the required Kuhn-Tucker conditions are violated for this case, therefore it is theoretically a candidate for the optimal solution. However, it is clearly not a logical choice for a maximization problem. This case is presented for purposes of illustrating the testing of all possible combinations for a solution.

Case 2: $x_1 = 0, x_2 = 0, \lambda > 0$

Conditions	Test	Result
(*d*)	$0 \leq 0$	OK
(*e*)	$0 \leq 0$	OK
(*c*)	$-9 = 0$	Not true, therefore a violation

Condition c is violated, $x_1^2 + x_2^2 - 9$ or $(0)^2 + (0)^2 - 9$ clearly does not equal zero. Recall from the previous presentation of Lagrange multipliers that λ only takes on a positive value when the solution is bound by the constraint. Since x_1 and x_2 are zero for this case, the constraint is not binding. Again, this case is given for illustration of the testing of all possible cases. Normally this combination would be discarded by observation without formal testing.

Case 3: $x_1 = 0, x_2 > 0, \lambda = 0$

Note that since $\lambda = 0$, this implies an interior solution for $x_2 > 0$, with $x_1 = 0$. An interior solution for x_2 indicates that the solution is not bound by the constraint. Conditions d, b, and f must be tested. Starting with condition d, $16x_1 - 2\lambda x_1 = 0$ (for $x_1 = 0$), which satisfies the requirement that $16x_1 - 2\lambda x_1 \leq 0$. For condition b,

$$x_2(4x_2 - 2\lambda x_2) = 0 \Rightarrow x_2^2(4 - 2\lambda) = 0.$$

Since $x_2 > 0$, $4 - 2\lambda = 0$. This implies that $\lambda = 2$, which violates the case assumption that λ is equal to zero.

For condition f, $x_1^2 + x_2^2 - 9 \leq 0$, or $x_2^2 - 9 \leq 0$, or $x_2^2 \leq 9$. Since $\lambda > 0$, we have a boundary solution; thus, the solution value of x_2 is 3.

The following is a summary of case 3:

Conditions	Test	Result
(*d*)	$0 \leq 0$	OK
(*b*)	$\lambda = 2$	Violation of $x_2(4x_2 - 2\lambda x_2) = 0$, for $x_2 > 0$
(*f*)	$(3)^2 - 9 \leq 0$	OK

Case 4: $x_1 > 0, x_2 = 0, \lambda = 0$

Similar to case 3, $\lambda = 0$ implies an interior solution for $x_1 > 0$, with $x_2 = 0$. We obtain similar results also for condition a.

$$x_1(16x_1 - 2\lambda x_1) = 0 \Rightarrow x_1^2(16 - 2\lambda) = 0,$$

Since $x_1 > 0$, $16 - 2\lambda = 0$. This implies that $\lambda = 8$, which violates the case assumption that $\lambda = 0$.

Conditions	Test	Result
(*a*)	$\lambda = 8$	Violation of $x_1(16x_1 - 2\lambda x_1) = 0$
(*e*)	$0 \leq 0$	OK
(*f*)	$(3)^2 - 9 \leq 0$	OK

Case 5: $x_1 = 0, x_2 > 0, \lambda > 0$

This case assumes a boundary solution ($\lambda > 0$) for $x_2 > 0$, with $x_1 = 0$. After having tested case 3, for $x_1 = 0$ and $x_2 > 0$, we can easily determine the outcome for this case.

Conditions	Test	Result
(*d*)	$0 \leq 0$	OK
(*b*)	$\lambda = 2$	OK for $x_2(4x_2 - 2\lambda x_2) = 0$ and $x_2 > 0$
(*c*)	$x_2 = 3$	OK for $\lambda(x_1^2 + x_2^2 - 9) = 0$. Since $\lambda = 2$ and $x_1 = 0$, $x_2^2 = 9 \Rightarrow x_2 = 3$.

Thus, case 5 yields a candidate for the optimal solution.

Case 6: $x_1 > 0, x_2 = 0, \lambda > 0$

Again, you may refer back to the test of case 4, where $x_1 > 0$ and $x_2 = 0$. For condition *a*, $x_1(16x_1 - 2\lambda x_1) = 0$, $x_1 > 0$ and $\lambda = 8$. For condition *e*, $4x_2 - 2\lambda x_2 \Rightarrow 0 \leq 0$ (ok). For condition *c*, $\lambda(x_1^2 + x_2^2 - 9) = 0 \Rightarrow 8(x_1^2 - 9) = 0$. Thus, $x_1^2 - 9 = 0 \Rightarrow x_1 = 3$.

Conditions	Test	Result
(*a*)	$\lambda = 8$	OK
(*e*)	$0 \leq 0$	OK
(*c*)	$x_1 = 3$	OK

Case 6 yields a possible candidate for the optimal solution.

Case 7: $x_1 > 0, x_2 > 0, \lambda = 0$

Conditions *a*, *b*, and *f* apply for case 7. Testing case *a* yields $x_1(16x_1 - 2\lambda x_1) = 0 \Rightarrow \lambda = 8$, which is a violation of the assumption that $\lambda = 0$. Condition *b* yields $x_2(4x_2 - 2\lambda x_2) = 0 \Rightarrow \lambda = 2$, which violates the condition that $\lambda = 0$. Condition *f*, $x_1^2 + x_2^2 - 9 = 0$, does not violate the assumption that $x_1 > 0$ and $x_2 > 0$.

Conditions	Test	Result
(*a*)	$\lambda = 8$	Violation of $x_1(16x_1 - 2\lambda x_1) = 0$
(*b*)	$\lambda = 2$	Violation of $x_2(4x_2 - 2\lambda x_2) = 0$ (and λ cannot = 8 *and* 2)
(*f*)	$x_1^2 + x_2^2 = 9$	OK

Case 8: $x_1 > 0$, $x_2 > 0$, $\lambda > 0$

This case assumes that both x_1 and x_2 are nonzero, with the optimal solution on the boundary created by the constraint, since $\lambda > 0$. Testing yields the following:

Conditions	Test	Result
(a)	$\lambda = 8$	Violation
(b)	$\lambda = 2$	Violation
(c)	$x_1^2 + x_2^2 = 9$	OK

After testing the eight combinations of possible solution values for x_1, x_2 and λ, the resulting candidates are summarized and evaluated as follows:

Case	(x_1, x_2, λ)	Results of Testing Kuhn-Tucker Conditions	Value of Solution (y)
1	(0, 0, 0)	OK for $x_1 = 0$, $x_2 = 0$, $\lambda = 0$	$y = 0$
2	(0, 0, > 0)	Violation	NA
3	(0, > 0, 0)	Violation	NA
4	(> 0, 0, 0)	Violation	NA
5	(0, > 0, > 0)	OK for $x_2 = 3$, $\lambda = 2$, $x_1 = 0$	$y = 2(3)^2 = 18$
6	(> 0, 0, > 0)	OK for $x_1 = 3$, $\lambda = 8$, $x_2 = 0$	$y = 8(3)^2 = 72$*
7	(> 0, > 0, 0)	Violation	NA
8	(> 0, > 0, > 0)	Violation	NA

NA = Not Allowed

Therefore, the problem yields three candidates that satisfy the Kuhn-Tucker conditions (cases 1, 5, and 6), and the optimal solution is given at $x_1^* = 3$, $x_2^* = 0$, $y^* = 72$, with the associated solution value for $\lambda = 8$.

The interpretation of λ is $\partial y/\partial b_i$ equals the rate of improvement in y for incremental relaxation of b_i (the right-hand side of the constraint). For example, given the current constraint of $x_1^2 + x_2^2 \leq 9$, if it were changed to $x_1^2 + x_2^2 \leq 10$, since $x_2^* = 0$, the solution value for x_1^* would be $\sqrt{10}$. Substituting into $y = 8x_1^2 + 2x_2^2 = 8x_1^2 = 8\left(\sqrt{10}\right)^2 = 80$. Note that this value for y is exactly 8 greater than the previous value. The economic interpretation is analogous to the dual variables in linear programming.

For more complex problems (more decision variables or more constraints), it may be extremely difficult to obtain the optimal solution directly from the Kuhn-Tucker conditions as illustrated by the previous example. These conditions, nevertheless, provide the necessary information for testing possible solutions for candidacy as an optimal solution. With the aid of modern high-speed computers, more complex problems can be evaluated through partial enumeration procedures. Equally important, the Kuhn-Tucker conditions provide much of the necessary theoretical insights for development of specialized algorithms for particular nonlinear problems.

Quadratic Programming

A special class of nonlinear programming problems includes the case where (1) the objective function is a concave quadratic function and (2) the constraints are all linear. Formulation of the Kuhn-Tucker conditions, therefore, results in a set of linear expressions for solution. This set of linear expressions makes solution by the simplex method possible.

Preparation of the quadratic programming problem for solution by the simplex method is presented, as well as several required modifications in problem formulation for this special case.

Recall that Kuhn-Tucker conditions (1*a*) and (1*b*) were given as follows:

$$x_j^* \left(\frac{\partial L}{\partial x_j}\right) = 0, \text{ for } x_j^* > 0 \tag{1a}$$

$$\frac{\partial L}{\partial x_j} \leq 0, \text{ for } x_j^* = 0 \tag{1b}$$

These conditions are now restated simply as

$$\frac{\partial L}{\partial x_j} = 0, \text{ for all } x_j^*.$$

However, additional terms are added to the Lagrange multiplier expression to include the nonnegativity requirements ($x_j \geq 0$) and to allow the preceding modification in (1*a*) and (1*b*).

Formulation of the Lagrangian expression and the subsequent Kuhn-Tucker conditions, including the preceding modifications, is illustrated for the general problem including two decision variables (x_1, x_2).

Given the quadratic programming problem:

Maximize $y = f(x_1, x_2)$

subject to

$$g_1(x_1, x_2) \leq b_1$$

and

$$x_1 \geq 0, x_2 \geq 0 \Rightarrow -x_1 \leq 0, -x_2 \leq 0$$

The problem is restated as

Maximize $y = f(x_1, x_2)$

subject to

$$g_1(x_1, x_2) - b_1 \leq 0$$

and

$h_1(x_1) \leq 0$ where $h_1(x_1)$ is $-x_1$

$h_2(x_2) \leq 0$ where $h_2(x_2)$ is $-x_2$.

The Lagrangian expression is given as follows:

$$L = f(x_1, x_2) - \lambda_1[g_1(x_1, x_2) - b_1] - \mu_1[h_1(x_1)] - \mu_2[h_2(x_2)]$$

Letting $f = f(x_1, x_2)$, $g_1 = g_1(x_1, x_2)$, and since $h_1(x_1) = -x_1$ and $h_2(x_2) = -x_2$, the Lagrangian expression can be written as

$$L = f - \lambda_1(g_1 - b_1) + \mu_1 x_1 + \mu_2 x_2$$

where

λ_1 = the Lagrange multiplier for g_1 (the original problem constraint)

μ_1 = the Lagrange multiplier for h_1 (the nonnegativity requirement for x_1)

μ_2 = the Lagrange multiplier for h_2 (the nonnegativity requirement for x_2).

The Kuhn-Tucker conditions are, therefore, as follows:

$$\frac{\partial L}{\partial x_1} = \frac{\partial f}{\partial x_1} - \lambda_1 \frac{\partial g_1}{\partial x_1} + \mu_1 = 0 \qquad (1)$$

$$\frac{\partial L}{\partial x_2} = \frac{\partial f}{\partial x_2} - \lambda_1 \frac{\partial g_1}{\partial x_2} + \mu_2 = 0 \qquad (2)$$

$$g_1 - b_1 \leqslant 0 \qquad (3)$$

$$\lambda_1(g_1 - b_1) = 0 \qquad (4)$$

$$\mu_1 x_1 = 0 \qquad (5)$$

$$\mu_2 x_2 = 0 \qquad (6)$$

$$x_1, x_2, \lambda_1, \mu_1, \mu_2 \geqslant 0 \qquad (7)$$

Condition (3) is next converted to an equality by introducing a slack variable, s_1, to yield

$$g_1 - b_1 + s_1 = 0. \qquad (3)$$

Therefore, since $g_1 - b_1 = -s_1$, condition (4) can also be rewritten, by substitution, as $\lambda_1(g_1 - b_1) = \lambda_1(-s_1) = \lambda_1 s_1$:

$$\lambda_1 s_1 = 0 \qquad (4)$$

Thus, in general, the Kuhn-Tucker conditions for the quadratic programming problem including n decision variables and m constraints are given as follows:

$$\frac{\partial L}{\partial x_j} = \frac{\partial f}{\partial x_j} - \sum_{i=1}^{m} \lambda_i \frac{\partial g_i}{\partial x_j} + \mu_j = 0, \; j = 1, 2, \ldots, n$$

from (1) and (2) (a)

$g_i - b_i + s_i = 0, \; i = 1, 2, \ldots, m$ from (3) (b)

$\lambda_i s_i = 0, \; i = 1, 2, \ldots, m$ from (4) (c)

$\mu_j x_j = 0, \; j = 1, 2, \ldots, n$ from (5) and (6) (d)

all $x_j, \lambda_i, \mu_j, s_i \geq 0$ from (7) (e)

Conditions (a) and (b) are linear, whereas conditions (c) and (d) are nonlinear. This general problem, however, can be solved using the simplex procedure by including the linear equations generated by (a) and (b) in the simplex tableau and further stipulating that both λ_i and s_i (for any i) will never be basic variables at the same time and that both μ_j and x_j (for any j) will follow the same restriction.

The final requirement to form an initial basic solution is to add artificial variables to all linear expressions generated by (a). These equations are then solved in terms of the artificial variables to form the objective function, which is to be minimized (i.e., the objective is to drive the artificial variables out of the basis).

Example 16.2 Quadratic Maximization Problem

The preceding presentation is illustrated for the following quadratic programming example:

Maximize $y = 4x_1 + 6x_2 - 2x_1^2 - 2x_1x_2 - 2x_2^2$

subject to

$$x_1 + 2x_2 \leq 2$$

and

$$x_1, x_2 \geq 0$$

The Lagrangian multiplier expression is given as

$$L = 4x_1 + 6\,x_2 - 2x_1^2 - 2x_1x_2$$
$$- 2x_1^2 - \lambda_1(x_1 + 2x_2 - 2) + \mu_1 x_1 + \mu_2 x_2.$$

Note: The term $+\mu_1 x_1$ is obtained by the conversion of the nonnegativity restriction, $x_1 \geq 0$, to the form $-x_1 \leq 0$. Thus, the term, $-\mu_1(-x_1)$, becomes $+\mu_1 x_1$, and similarly for $+\mu_2 x_2$.

Thus, the Kuhn-Tucker conditions for the problem are

$$\frac{\partial L}{\partial x_1} = 4 - 4x_1 - 2x_2 - \lambda_1 + \mu_1 = 0 \qquad (a_1)$$

$$\frac{\partial L}{\partial x_2} = 6 - 2x_1 - 4x_2 - 2\lambda_1 + \mu_2 = 0 \qquad (a_2)$$

$$x_1 + 2x_2 - 2 + s_1 = 0 \qquad (b)$$

$$\lambda_1 s_1 = 0 \qquad (c)$$

$$\mu_1 x_1 = 0 \qquad (d_1)$$

$$\mu_2 x_2 = 0. \qquad (d_2)$$

Equations (a_1), (a_2), and (b) are rewritten with the artificial variables added in (a_1) and (a_2) to yield

$$4x_1 + 2x_2 + \lambda_1 - \mu_1 + A_1 = 4 \qquad (a_1)$$

$$2x_1 + 4x_2 + 2\lambda_1 - \mu_2 + A_2 = 6 \qquad (a_2)$$

$$x_1 + 2x_2 + s_1 = 2. \qquad (b)$$

The preceding problem will now be solved via the simplex method with (a_1), (a_2), and (b) as the tableau constraints. The objective function is developed as follows:

Minimize $A_1 + A_2 \equiv$ Maximize $-A_1 - A_2$

where

$$-A_1 = -4 + 4x_1 + 2x_2 + \lambda_1 - \mu_1$$
$$-A_2 = -6 + 2x_1 + 4x_2 + 2\lambda_1 - \mu_2$$

and therefore, the objective function in terms of the decision variables, x_j, and the Lagrange multiplier variables, λ_i, is as follows:

Maximize $Z = -10 + 6x_1 + 6x_2 + 3\lambda_1 - \mu_1 - \mu_2$

The linear programming problem to be solved via the simplex method is as follows:

$$\text{Maximize } Z = 6x_1 + 6x_2 + 3\lambda_1 - \mu_1 - \mu_2 + 0A_1 + 0A_2 + 0s_1$$

subject to

$$4x_1 + 2x_2 + \lambda_1 - \mu_1 + A_1 = 4$$
$$2x_1 + 4x_2 + 2\lambda_1 - \mu_2 + A_2 = 6$$
$$x_1 + 2x_2 + s_1 = 2$$

and

$\lambda_1 s_1 = 0$ (i.e., either λ_1 or s_1 must be nonbasic in solution)

$\mu_1 x_1 = 0$ (i.e., either μ_1 or x_1 must be nonbasic in solution)

$\mu_2 x_2 = 0$ (i.e., either μ_2 or x_2 must be nonbasic in solution)

and

$$x_1, x_2, \lambda_1, \mu_1, \mu_2 \geq 0$$

The simplex solution to the formulated problem requires three iterations. The initial simplex tableau is shown in table 16.1.

Table 16.1 Initial simplex tableau

c_b \ c_j	basis	b_i^*	6 x_1	6 x_2	3 λ_1	−1 μ_1	−1 μ_2	0 A_1	0 A_2	0 s_1
0	A_1	4	4	2	1	−1	0	1	0	0
0	A_2	6	2	4	2	0	−1	0	1	0
0	s_1	2	1	2	0	0	0	0	0	1
	z_j	0	0	0	0	0	0	0	0	0
	$c_j - z_j$		6	6	3	−1	−1	0	0	0

The three iterations of the solution are summarized as follows:

	Basis	
Iteration	Entering Variable	Leaving Variable
1	x_1	A_1
2	x_2	s_1
3	λ_1	A_2

The final simplex tableau is shown in table 16.2.

Table 16.2 Final simplex tableau

c_b \ c_j	basis	b_i^*	6 x_1	6 x_2	3 λ_1	−1 μ_1	−1 μ_2	0 A_1	0 A_2	0 s_1
6	x_1	1/3	1	0	0	−1/3	1/6	1/3	−1/6	0
3	λ_1	1	0	0	1	0	−1/2	0	1/2	−1
6	x_2	5/6	0	1	0	1/6	−1/12	−1/6	1/12	1/2
	z_j	10	6	6	3	−1	−1	1	1	0
	$c_j - z_j$		0	0	0	0	0	−1	−1	0

The final simplex tableau indicates that the nonbasic variables μ_1, μ_2, and s_1 can be entered into the basis without changing the value of z_j. However, μ_1 cannot be entered without removing x_1, due to condition (d_1). The same is true for μ_2 versus x_2, and for s_1 versus λ_1. Note that in each case, the a_{ij} value at the intersection of the subject pair of variables is a negative value (see the shaded values in table 16.2). Thus, this solution can proceed no further. Also, note that the solution value for z_j in the final tableau is 10. Recall that the value of Z, initially calculated as $Z = -A_1 - A_2$, was equal to $-10 + 6x_1 + 6x_2 + 3\lambda_1 - \mu_1 - \mu_2$. Therefore, the solution value for Z is $-10 + z_j$, or $-10 + 10 = 0$. This will always result since the only objective is to drive the artificials out of the basic solution.

Thus, the solution yielded is

$$x_1^* = 1/3,\ x_2^* = 5/6,\ \lambda_1 = 1.$$

The value of y^* is calculated as

$$y^* = 4x_1 + 6x_2 - 2x_1^2 - 2x_1x_2 - 2x_2^2 = 75/18 = 4.1667.$$

The preceding approach always yields an optimal solution to a quadratic programming problem if the quadratic objective function is concave. If the objective function is convex for a minimization problem, the optimal solution will also be obtained. The preceding example included a concave objective function, therefore the solution obtained was optimal. Numerous solution approaches for the quadratic programming problem have been proposed. This approach is only one variation among several.

Standard Quadratic Form

Frequently, the quadratic programming problem is reformulated into the *standard quadratic form,* and the Kuhn-Tucker conditions are derived from this form. The standard quadratic form is given as follows:

$$\text{Maximize } y = \sum_{j=1}^{n} c_j x_j - \frac{1}{2} \sum_{j=1}^{n} \sum_{k=1}^{n} q_{jk} x_j x_k$$

subject to

$$\sum_{j=1}^{n} a_{ij} x_j \leqslant b_i, \quad i = 1, 2, \ldots, m$$

and

$$x_j \geqslant 0, \quad j = 1, 2, \ldots, n$$

where

q_{jk} are given constants such that $q_{jk} = q_{kj}$

Convex Programming

Another special class of nonlinear programming problems includes the case where the objective function is a concave function and all the constraints are convex functions. Thus, the convexity of the (nonlinear) constraint functions implies that the set of feasible solutions forms a convex set. These conditions greatly simplify the requirements for obtaining the optimal solution to such problems.

One rather well-known technique developed for solution of convex programming problems is the Sequential Unconstrained Minimization Technique (SUMT). This procedure first reformulates the problem into a minimization form, subject to all $\geqslant$ constraints. It then deals with the objective function and the constraints simultaneously by combining them into a single function (the approach for this formulation procedure is beyond the desired scope of this text). The solution is then obtained using a gradient search procedure or some similar method.

Gradient Search Methods

As initially pointed out in this chapter, many of the modern day solution methods being employed for nonlinear programming problems exploit the efficiencies available from use of the high-speed computer. Basically, these methods make use of the vector of the partial derivatives of the objective function, known as the **gradient.**

These methods can be compared to mountain climbing where the climber successively searches for the peak of the mountain by adopting a policy of going from point *A* to point *B*, when *B* appears to be the highest point in the neighborhood of *A*. The search is continued until the summit is reached (no more improvement in the objective function can be made).

Of course, problems are encountered when more than one peak exists over the domain of the possible solution. Problems are encountered in connection with convergence, stopping rules, parameter selection, and computerization. Numerous such techniques, however, have been proposed and used. You are referred to Luenberger for extensive discussion of these topics.

Summary

This chapter has presented an introduction to the topic of nonlinear programming. The basic classical theory underlying nonlinear programming has been reviewed, including reformulation of the problem into the Lagrangian expression and testing for candidates using the Kuhn-Tucker conditions. Although the Kuhn-Tucker conditions do not provide a solution approach for nonlinear programming problems, they do provide considerable insight into the general nature of such problems.

An approach for reformulation of a quadratic programming problem and solution using the simplex method was presented. This problem with a concave quadratic objective function, subject to all linear constraints, is the simplest of nonlinear programming problems.

Convex-programming gradient search methods were discussed briefly. Considerable progress has been made in these areas, and a variety of algorithms and search techniques are available for these cases. In summary, there is no efficient all-purpose solution method available for nonlinear programming problems; however, research in this area is actively continuing.

References

Hillier, F. S., and Lieberman, G. J. *Operations Research*. 2d ed. San Francisco: Holden-Day, 1974.

Kuhn, H. W., and Tucker, A. W. "Nonlinear Programming." In *Proceedings of the Second Berkeley Symposium on Mathematical Statistics and Probability*. Edited by Jerzy Neyman. Berkeley: University of California Press, 1951.

Loomba, N. P., and Turban, E. *Applied Programming for Management*. New York: Holt, Rinehart and Winston, 1974.

Luenberger, D. G. *Introduction to Linear and Nonlinear Programming*. Reading, Mass.: Addison-Wesley, 1973.

McMillan, C., Jr. *Mathematical Programming*. 2d ed. New York: John Wiley & Sons, 1975.

Taha, H. A. *Operations Research, An Introduction*. 2d ed. New York: MacMillan, 1976.

Problems

1. Given the following nonlinear programming problem, use the Kuhn-Tucker conditions to derive the optimal solution:

$$\text{Maximize } y = x_1^2 + 2x_2^2 + 11x_1 + 15x_2 + 45$$

subject to

$$5x_1 + 7x_2 \leqslant 400$$
$$x_1 + 3x_2 \leqslant 120$$
$$x_1, x_2 \geqslant 0$$

2. Consider the following nonlinear programming problem:

$$\text{Maximize } y = -x_1^2 - x_2^2 + 4x_1 + 8x_2$$

subject to

$$x_1 + x_2 \leqslant 2$$
$$x_1, x_2 \geqslant 0$$

Determine the optimal solution making use of the Kuhn-Tucker conditions.

3. Make use of the Kuhn-Tucker conditions to determine the optimal solution to the following nonlinear programming problem:

$$\text{Minimize } y = x_1^2 + 4x_1x_2 + 4x_2^2$$

subject to

$$x_1 - x_2 \geqslant 3$$
$$x_1, x_2 \geqslant 0$$

4. Given the following nonlinear programming problem, determine the optimal solution using the Kuhn-Tucker conditions:

$$\text{Minimize } y = -12x_1 - 15x_2 + 3x_1^2 + .5x_2^2 + 1{,}000$$

subject to

$$x_1 + x_2 \geqslant 35$$
$$x_1, x_2 \geqslant 0$$

5. Use the Kuhn-Tucker conditions to derive the optimal solution to the following nonlinear programming problem:

$$\text{Minimize } y = 4(x_1 - 2)^2 + 2(x_2 - 3)^2$$

subject to

$$\begin{aligned} 2x_1 + x_2 &\leq 6 \\ x_1 + 3x_2 &\leq 15 \\ x_1 + x_2 &\geq 1 \\ x_1, x_2 &\geq 0 \end{aligned}$$

6. Given the following quadratic programming problem, formulate and solve the problem using the simplex method:

$$\text{Minimize } y = x_1^2 + 3x_2^2 - x_1x_2 - 4x_2 + 4$$

subject to

$$\begin{aligned} x_1 + x_2 &\leq 1 \\ x_1, x_2 &\geq 0 \end{aligned}$$

7. Formulate and solve the following quadratic programming problem using the simplex method:

$$\text{Maximize } y = -3x_1^2 - 4x_2^2 - 4x_1x_2 + 3x_1 + 4x_2$$

subject to

$$\begin{aligned} 8x_1 + 6x_2 &\leq 3 \\ x_1, x_2 &\geq 0 \end{aligned}$$

8. Use the simplex method to determine the solution to the following quadratic programming problem:

$$\text{Minimize } y = 2x_1^2 + 2x_2^2 - 2x_1x_2 - 6x_1$$

subject to

$$\begin{aligned} x_1 + x_2 &\leq 2 \\ x_1, x_2 &\geq 0 \end{aligned}$$

9. Solve the following quadratic programming problem using the simplex method:

$$\text{Maximize } y = -2x_1^2 + 3x_1 + 4x_2$$

subject to

$$\begin{aligned} x_1 + 2x_2 &\leq 4 \\ x_1 + x_2 &\leq 2 \\ x_1, x_2 &\geq 0 \end{aligned}$$

10. Given the following quadratic programming problem, show the steps for formulation of the initial simplex tableau.

Minimize $y = 1.5x_1 + 3x_2^2 + x_3^2$

subject to

$$x_1 + x_2 + 2x_3 \geq 20$$

$$x_1 + x_3 \geq 10$$

$$x_1, x_2, x_3 \geq 0$$

11. Consider the following quadratic programming problem:

Maximize $y = 3x_1^2 + 2x_2^2 + 2x_3^2 + 2x_1x_2 + 2x_2x_3 - 5x_1 - 3x_2 + x_3$

subject to

$$x_1 + 2x_2 + 3x_3 \leq 6$$

$$x_1 + x_2 + x_3 \geq 1$$

$$x_1, x_2, x_3 \geq 0$$

Formulate the initial simplex tableau for solution using the simplex method.

Part

6

Implementation

17

Implementation of Management Science

Since the end of World War II a significant number of quantitative techniques have been developed for the practical solution of management problems. In the previous chapters of this text, a broad spectrum of these techniques has been reviewed and some of the more prominent and traditional ones have been analyzed in-depth. For the most part, the successes of these management science techniques have been numerous.[1] In a survey by Gaither, it was found that approximately one-half of the 275 firms responding to a questionnaire used management science/operations research techniques.[2] Of the firms that applied these techniques, 80% rated the results very good, while 11% rated the results excellent.

In this text, the presentation of the various techniques has emphasized the description and development of the mathematical structures of the techniques. Yet model construction represents only one part of the management science process. In this process, the system first is analyzed and the problem formulated, then the model is constructed and results are achieved and tested, and finally, *the model is implemented*. As such, it would be negligent to conclude this text without providing some insight into this final step of the modeling process, *implementation*.

Implementation is an essential part of the management science process for the simple reason that if the model is not applied to some practical end, the desired results will not be forthcoming. The development of a model is pursued, after all, for the purpose of increasing a system's efficiency as measured by cost reduction, resource utilization, profit, etc. If the model does not come to fruition in the form of its successful use, then the effort expended in its development is wasted.

Implementation often is not a simple task but rather a complex and difficult achievement. In fact, implementation is frequently referred to as the "problem of implementation." The difficulty of implementation has only recently been perceived as a potential problem. Although the new techniques developed during and immediately following World War II showed promise of future success, the evolution

1. Jan H. Huysman, "Operations Research Implementation and the Practice of Management," in *Implementing Operations Research/Management Science*, eds. R. L. Schultz and D. P. Slevin, p. 273.

2. Gaither, "The Adoption of Operations Research Techniques by Manufacturing Organizations," pp. 797–813.

of management science was initially slow. It was not until the decade of the sixties that the rapid development of new techniques and applications of these techniques began to appear. The advancement of computer technology enabled the practical application of many sophisticated management science techniques to various operational problems. During this period, many computer firms developed "canned" programs and sophisticated information systems that facilitated the easy, rapid and economical application of management science techniques.

During the 1960s, a corresponding growth of management science was experienced in academic institutions. Only a few universities entered the decade with formal degree programs encompassing management science-related topics for the business/management student. However, by the end of the decade, numerous schools had developed such programs, and, in fact, were emphasizing their development. Thus, college graduates armed with management science training and capabilities moved into the business environment. This resulted in an increased appreciation and understanding of the potential of management science among all management personnel. This, in turn, created a conducive atmosphere for further growth of management science within the business community. An understanding of the role, value, and limitations of management science began to emerge. As a result, many firms established their own management science staffs.

However, rapid growth is often accompanied by problems, and this has been true of the evolution of management science. Both management scientists and managers have begun to question the extent to which these techniques are being applied. A feeling is emerging that the full potential of management science and accompanying computer facilities is not being realized. There is an increased tendency to believe that many models either fail upon implementation or are never implemented at all. Thus, a great deal of attention has been focused on the problem of implementation. (As evidence of this increased attention, Wysocki, in a recently developed "bibliography of implementation," identified approximately two-hundred journal articles devoted to the subject of implementation written in the past six years.[3] This represents almost 75% of the total research output on this topic.)

The purposes of this chapter are to first define implementation in order to provide a framework for the analysis of the variables and factors that have an effect on successful implementation, and then to discuss some of the strategies developed by researchers in the field to insure successful implementation.

Implementation Defined

Implementation is a complex subject and, as a result, a number of varied definitions exist. We will review several of the more popular and traditional definitions. One definition provided by Churchman and Shainblatt holds that implementation is "the manner in which the manager may come to use the results of scientific effort" and that the problem of implementation is "determining what activities of the scientist and manager are most appropriate to bring about an effective relation-

3. Wysocki, "OR/MS Implementation Research: A Bibliography," pp. 37–41.

ship."[4] A similar definition by Schultz and Slevin states that implementation "refers to the actual use of operations research/management science output by managers that *influences* their decision processes."[5]

The common thread between these two definitions is that implementation exists when the model or its results are in use *and* that implementation presupposes some interface or link between the management scientist and the manager. However, it can be assumed with some degree of certainty that the manager does not perceive implementation to occur unless some degree of success in attaining the manager's objectives is achieved (i.e., unless the model does what it was intended to do.) Conversely, the management scientist may perceive that implementation is achieved (i.e., it is successful), if the model is used at all. In other words, some form of perceived success must be present for implementation to have occurred.

A somewhat different and expanded view of implementation suggests that implementation is a *continuous process* encompassing not only the final use of the model, but also problem formulation, model development and construction, and model testing. In this framework, the "experiences" gained from implementation provide feedback to different stages in the management science modeling process. Thus, the model evolves through the implementation process. The basic premise of this approach is that successful implementation is dependent upon success at each of the various stages of the modeling process. If the problem is not formulated properly, if the model is not constructed correctly, if the results are not valid, then the implementation step will not be successfully achieved. Within this framework, initial management involvement in the management science process enhances the possibility of successful implementation.

The notion of implementation being a continuous, ongoing process is supported by the research of Rubenstein et al.[6] and Markland and Newett.[7] Markland and Newett have proposed that management science projects include six "life phases": prebirth, introduction, transition, maturity, death, and resurrection. These phases represent a life cycle for the project from its inception to its eventual disuse and rediscovery. These authors then demonstrate that various implementation criteria are important at various phases in the life cycle. The important point to be gained from this research is that eventual successful implementation is dependent on occurrences during each phase of the project.

As can be seen from these various views of implementation, it is difficult to develop a single, specific definition. However, we can surmise that implementation encompasses certain characteristics: (1) it is achieved by successful use of the model, although success is a matter of degree and must be evaluated by the party involved, (2) it is based on an interface between the management scientist and the manager, (3) it must be considered at each phase of the management science process (i.e., life of the project), and (4) it is an ongoing, dynamic process.

4. Churchman and Shainblatt, "The Researcher and the Manager: A Dialectic of Implementation," pp. 869–87.

5. Schultz and Slevin, "Implementation and Management Innovations," in *Implementing Operations Research/Management Science,* p. 6.

6. Rubenstein et al., "Some Organizational Factors Related to Effectiveness of Management Science Groups in Industry," pp. B508–18.

7. Markland and Newett, "A Subjective Taxonomy for Evaluating the Stages of Management Science Research," pp. 31–39.

The Implementation Problem

Now that we have developed a working definition of what constitutes implementation, we must turn our thoughts to why, on occasion, it becomes a problem. In other words, it is important to identify those variables and the relationships among those variables that inhibit successful implementation. This, in turn, will facilitate the development of strategies to overcome the problems.

When the problem of implementation was first encountered by managers and management scientists, the proposed causes were somewhat opinionated and superficial. Some of these proposed causes included personality and training differences between managers and management scientists, ill-defined problems and improper model formulation, models too sophisticated for the problems to be solved, lack of understanding of management and decision-making processes by the management scientist, and a lack of understanding of management science techniques by managers.

Grayson perceived five basic reasons for not utilizing management science techniques:

1. Shortage of time—techniques are time consuming and decision making often must be made spontaneously.
2. Inaccessibility of data—data is not always available to the manager when and where it is needed.
3. Resistance to change—the organization must often be changed to create an atmosphere for the use of management science techniques.
4. Long response time—management scientists are not geared to working in a manager's time frame. It takes too long to develop models.
5. Invalidating simplifications—management scientists strip away much of the real-world problem with simplifying assumptions.[8]

Several observations can be made regarding the proposed causes of unsuccessful implementation of management science techniques. First, the proposed causes were often opinions based, in many cases, on practical experiences, and, as such, they tended to be narrow in scope. Although such problems do occur in individual cases, they tend to be generalizations that are inappropriate when applied to the problem of implementation as a whole. Second, these problems are not criticisms of the techniques themselves but rather criticisms of the manner in which the techniques are developed into specific models and applied. This is an underlying characteristic of the analysis of implementation that has been consistently present since the initial recognition that a problem of implementation existed.

As is the case with many forms of problem analysis, attempts to explain the problem of implementation passed quickly from generalization to directed research. One of the earliest examples of a concerted study of the factors related to the success or failure of implementation was conducted by Rubenstein et al. This study resulted in a compilation of ten factors effecting implementation:

1. How much management supports and understands the management science activity.
2. How receptive the recipients of the management science activity are.

8. Grayson, "Management Science and Business Practice," pp. 41–48.

3. The technical and organizational capabilities of the management science group.
4. At what level the management science group is located in the organization.
5. The amount of influence the management science group has in the organization.
6. The reputation of the management science staff.
7. The amount of resources allocated to management science.
8. How relevant management science is to what the organization needs.
9. The amount of opposition to management science and its level in the organization.
10. How the organization as a whole perceives the success of the management science group.[9]

These factors tend to reflect the relationship of the management science group to the surrounding organization. As such, they describe general conditions that should exist in a positive context, at least in part, for implementation to be successful. Alternatively, Little identified several characteristics that can enhance implementation if they exist *in the model:* simplicity, robustness, ease of control, adaptiveness, completeness, and ease of communication.[10]

Viewing the implementation problem from a practitioner's point of view, Harvey, in a survey of thirty-one companies, has identified a set of twenty-three factors that affect the success or failure of implementation.[11] These factors are further subdivided into three categories of characteristics regarding management, the problem, and the management science team and the solution. With regard to management, these factors include such items as management's experience with sophisticated quantitative models, the management climate for innovation, change and conflict, management's use of quantitative criteria for evaluation, and the time frame for decision making. In terms of the problem, factors that relate to the nature of objectives and the manner in which they are stated are considered, while characteristics of the management science team include the sensitivity of the management science group to the organization and the responsibility for implementation which includes the recognition of the problems implementation can cause.

Harvey also noted, however, that the problem of implementation does not consist of any one specific group of characteristics. That is, the problem characteristics vary from organization to organization and from model to model.

Also during the late 1960s, a period devoted to examining the problem of implementation, a somewhat different but insightful view was presented by Churchman and Shainblatt that had as its emphasis the manager/management scientist interface. In their study, four positions related to the problem of implementation are identified:

1. separate function position
2. communication position
3. persuasion position
4. mutual understanding position[12]

9. Rubenstein, et al., ''Some Organizational Factors Related to Effectiveness of Management Science Groups in Industry,'' pp. B508–18.
10. Little, J. D. C., ''Models and Managers: The Concept of a Decision Calculus,'' *Management Science,* 16, 8 (April, 1970), pp. B466–85.
11. Harvey, ''Factors Making for Implementation Success and Failure,'' pp. B312–21.
12. Churchman and Schainblatt, ''The Researcher and the Manager: A Dialectic of Implementation,'' pp. B69–87.

The essential aspect of the four positions is the concept of understanding between the manager and management scientist. In the first position, the separate function reflects no understanding between manager and management scientist as a precondition for implementation. The second and third positions represent one party's understanding of the other. The fourth position asserts that a necessary condition for implementation is mutual understanding between manager and management scientist. This last position is the most popular and most generally agreed upon as a requirement of implementation.

The most recent developments in the research of the implementation problem have taken a behavioral approach. An excellent summary of these behaviorally oriented research models is presented by Schultz and Slevin in the first text devoted exclusively to implementation.[13] All the behavioral models are similar in that ''some measure of implementation, a dependent variable, is explained by a set of so-called independent variables.''[14] Twelve different models are presented that encompass, overall, approximately sixty dependent variables related to implementation.

These models highlight the numerous variables and relationships that have been identified as being related to the problem of implementation. They further emphasize the extensive depth and degree of the research now being performed in this area. For the purpose of determining the causes of the problem of implementation, these models, as well as the other studies identified in this section, demonstrate rather conclusively that there is no set group of factors or reasons for the failure of implementation. Rather, the problem and its causes are, in many cases, unique to a particular firm or business environment. As a result, it is difficult to propose one specific strategy for assuring successful implementation. In effect, a strategy must be tailored to fit the particular situations—an effective strategy should encompass those particular characteristics unique to the organization, the particular problem, and the model.

Strategies for Successful Implementation

Numerous strategies have been proposed for attaining successful implementation as might be expected in light of the many variables related to the problem. These strategies are based upon a team approach, where a number of individuals with different backgrounds and training are drawn into the implementation process to compensate for the different behavioral factors.[15] In addition to the manager and management scientist, the ''team'' might include computer scientists, people from the operating area, and nontechnical people (i.e., personnel staff).

13. Schultz and Slevin, eds., *Implementing Operations Research/Management Science*.
14. Ibid., ''Implementation and Management Innovation,'' pp. 3–20.
15. Shycon, ''All Around the Model,'' pp. 33–35.

Lucas suggests a three-step strategy as follows:

1. The system is designed in conjunction with the proposed uses. In fact, the user takes the lead in development.
2. Consideration of system's or model's impact on the user, organization, and work area (group) during design.
3. Design a simple and easily understandable model.[16]

Huysmans divides implementation strategies into "three categories focusing on the achievement of":

1. Management action—management is not closely involved in development. Models are typically well structured, routine, low level.
2. Management change—the manager must have a basic understanding of the model. This is the most frequent case. The models are higher level and strategic. They stimulate alternative solutions on the part of the managers.
3. Recurring use of the approach—the ultimate test of the model is its continued use. Requires a strong manager—management scientist relationship and the management science staff is an effective part of the organizational design.[17]

These are several examples of potential strategies that attempt to reflect the different causes of the problem of implementation. An example of the development and use of an implementation strategy is presented in Davis and Taylor.[18] (However, it should be kept in mind that this is only one example of a particular strategy that was effective for a single firm.)

Organizational Change

The strategies developed for implementation encompass the concept of simulation gaming and the general model of implementation developed by Zand and Sorensen.[19] One of the basic premises underlying many of the models of implementation presented earlier is that implementation often necessitates behavioral *change* on the part of the manager. A lack of change promotes stability and continuity within the organization, leading to feelings of comfortableness and safeness. Within this framework, however, management and labor functions often become routinized and habitual. When change becomes imminent, it is resisted since it is perceived as a threat to the security of the organization.

The hypothesis that organizational change is a major factor in implementation is supported by the research of Zand and Sorensen. These researchers have found

16. H. C. Lucas, Jr., "Behavioral Factors in System Implementation," in *Implementing Operations Research/Management Science,* pp. 203–16.
17. Huysmans, "Operations Research Implementation and the Practice of Management," in *Implementing Operations Research/Management Science,* pp. 273–89.
18. A complete presentation of this case is presented in Davis and Taylor, "Addressing the Implementation Problem: A Gaming Approach," pp. 677–87.
19. Zand and Sorensen, "Theory of Change and the Effective Use of Management Science," pp. 532–45.

that a high level of implementation success results only when organizational members adapt to the required change. Their research further shows that the organizational change process required for implementation follows a predefined change theory developed by Lewin.[20] Viewed in an implementation framework, the Lewin theory defines the change process as a three-step procedure (see fig. 17.1).

1. "unfreezing" of the present system
2. "changing"
3. "refreezing" of the new system.

Figure 17.1 The Lewin change process.

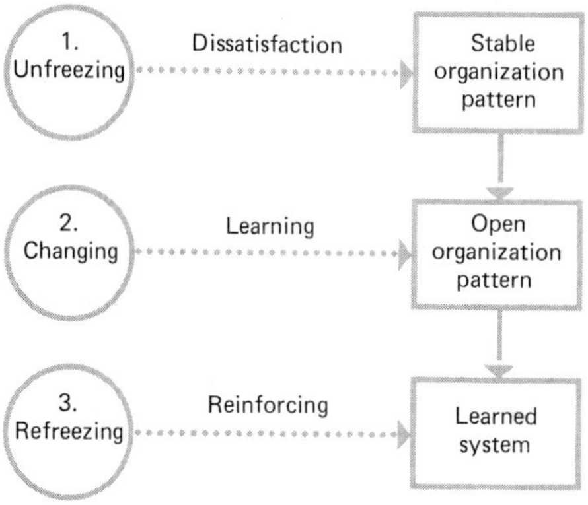

The initial step, unfreezing, attempts to overcome the resistance to change by encouraging dissatisfaction with current behavior. Generally, the manager exhibits a preference for a familiar technique or methodology and rejects one that is unfamiliar. If the manager feels threatened by the new technique being implemented, he or she will go to great lengths to avoid it. However, if the manager becomes dissatisfied with the current way of doing things, he or she will be more receptive to new methods. Thus, a "desire to learn new behavior" is generated that leads to effective change.

Change is often resisted because the manager is asked to relinquish something familiar and valuable. Thus, the old behavior must be "dissolved" (i.e., the stable organization pattern is "unfrozen") before a new behavior pattern can be learned. Unfreezing of old behavior must be achieved so that the process of change can continue.

The second step, changing, is the actual learning of new behavioral patterns. The initial step of unfreezing creates an environment for change wherein the manager is open to new behavior patterns. Change is normally achieved via learning of the new process or technique, which can be used in place of old methods discredited in the unfreezing process.

20. Lewin, "Group Decision and Social Change," pp. 197–211.

The final step, refreezing, is the reestablishment of a stable atmosphere, which has been previously upset in the unfreezing phase. This necessitates reinforcing the manager in the new behavior pattern so that he or she feels both successful and comfortable. If this step is not accomplished, it is likely that the manager will slip back into the original behavior pattern.

Through empirical testing, Zand and Sorensen found that the degree of application of the Lewin theory explains the degree of success of application in implementation. Specifically, these authors found that a high level of unfreezing, changing, and refreezing results in a high level of success, while low levels of the change process result in low levels of success.

The Lewin theory of change successfully identifies the process by which implementation of management science techniques can be achieved. However, the theory of change does not specifically identify how to achieve the change cycle. In other words, no procedure is suggested for achieving unfreezing, change, and refreezing.

As a tool for achieving organizational change, the concept of a *change agent* has been suggested by several researchers. The change agent is usually a neutral individual who mediates between the management scientist and the manager to facilitate change. Often, however, a change agent is a staff or liaison group since successful implementation is often a result of group effectiveness in producing organizational change. In some cases, the management scientist is identified as the change agent. Whatever the case, there is a great deal of uncertainty as to the true identity of a change agent.

Certainly a change agent of some type must exist. An individual, a group, or some action-based event must be incorporated in the Lewin process to facilitate unfreezing, changing, and refreezing within the organization.

Regardless of its identity, the change agent must act as a catalyst in the implementation process by instructing the manager in the new technique and carrying him or her through the implementation process. To demonstrate the concept of a change agent within the Lewin change process, a *simulation game* will be presented as the change agent. The simulation game demonstrates how each step of the change process is initiated and successfully achieved.

Simulation Games

Gaming is the use of a computerized simulation model to permit participants to make decisions and observe the behavior of the system as a result of those decisions. As such, a *simulation game* should not be confused with game theory, which was discussed in chapter 8. A gaming model consists of a simulated environment that mirrors the characteristics of the actual system under analysis. Historically, games have served as a means of studying human behavior, a training device for management personnel, and an instructional aid in university business schools. Simulation games that simulate business environments are often employed at the undergraduate level in finance, management policy, and production and operations management courses.

The simulation game is an on-line computer system that complements the steps of the Lewin theory:

1. unfreezing via game/system introduction
2. changing via game playing
3. refreezing via on-line deployment of the system

The initial step of introducing the game occurs in the form of a management training session. The game is employed to demonstrate improved conditions that could result through use of the new technique (i.e., the achievement of newly defined higher objectives or easier achievement of present ones). After demonstrating to a manager what can be accomplished, the manager usually becomes dissatisfied with the present level of output.

The second step, game playing, involves employing the game model as a teaching device. The game offers an alternative to a manager's previous behavior pattern. By actually playing the game, a manager begins to learn the new technique and hopefully becomes more receptive to it. In this step, the unfreezing process continues and may actually mesh with the change step. Old behavior patterns gradually change as new patterns are learned and as the manager becomes more and more dissatisfied with the previous system.

As part of the change process, a manager may be required to develop new objectives. However, if goals and objectives are successfully displayed as a manager becomes familiar with the game, the new goals can be easily learned.

The third step in the gaming procedure is the development of the new technique as an on-line computer system similar to the game used to demonstrate the system. This step enables a manager to continue to use the familiar mode of implementation that was introduced in the learning process. In effect, a manager continues to play the game. The value of the on-line system becomes apparent as it allows a manager to progress through the Lewin steps via one vehicle of learning and implementation. A feeling of continuity is generated that contributes to the success of the implementation process.

A representative framework of the gaming methodology and its relationship to the three-step Lewin change process is depicted in figure 17.2.

The component parts of this gaming system approach are defined as follows:

1. *Establish system objectives.* System objectives are the goals or desired results sought from the system to be implemented. By establishing objectives that require a high level of output from a manager's area of responsibility, the unfreezing step in the change process begins. A manager becomes dissatisfied and uncomfortable in his or her current situation.
2. *Abstract game development.* Development of an abstract game is part of a three-step phase that also requires identification of the present system and a comparative analysis between that system and the abstract game. The game is abstract in that it does not necessarily mirror the present system. Developing the game in this manner enables a management scientist to conceptualize a system without management input and bias.

Figure 17.2 The game/system simulator.

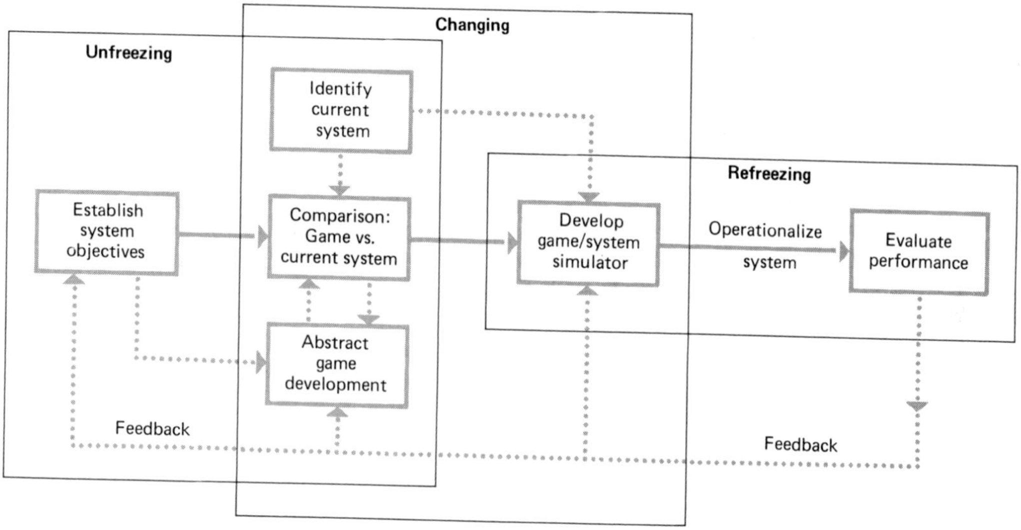

3. *Identification of the system.* This activity provides a basis for comparative analysis (i.e., comparison of the abstract game and the current system). It further provides both the management scientist and the manager with a common point of departure (i.e., basis for discussion).
4. *Comparison of the game and the current system.* By comparing the abstract game with the present system, a manager is able to gain a new perspective. A manager is forced into feeling dissatisfaction with the present system, while being offered an alternative approach. This further enhances the unfreezing step. By taking full advantage of the game environment, the unfreezing step can be finalized and the change step can be initiated. The structure of the gaming activity involves game play followed by critique sessions in which a manager participates via group discussion and/or private questionnaire. The critique sessions have a two-fold effect. First, they enable a manager/participant to voice opinions and ask questions, actions that should promote the learning process. Secondly, the critique sessions offer feedback to the management scientist. This provides input that a management scientist can use to alter the abstract game to reflect a compromised system. By repeating the game playing/critique session cycle several times, a participant begins to learn the fundamentals of the system, while the management scientist refines and develops the system. This process initiates the change step.
5. *Game/system simulator.* In this activity of the gaming framework, a simulation model of the actual system is developed. By employing the model as a game, a manager is in reality learning the actual system that will be operationalized. This activity completes the change step by exposing the new system to the recipient and initiates the refreezing steps by demonstrating the system's effectiveness in achieving results.

6. *Evaluation of performance*. At this stage, the system has reached operationality, and the recipient is involved in its use. However, a management scientist must be careful to remain involved with the implementation process until the manager has completed the refreezing process. This involves evaluating the system to determine if it meets specifications and achieves desired results. Discrepancies must be corrected through the feedback process before the manager relapses to the previous system. When all problems are sufficiently resolved, the refreezing step is completed.

This simulation gaming approach has been found to be highly successful in facilitating the implementation of systems. The game/system cycle tends to force the manager through the Lewin steps, thus minimizing the amount of regression from step to step. In effect, the game meshes the unfreezing-changing-refreezing cycle, creating a smooth continuous change process. This points out the fact that the Lewin steps need not be performed distinctly; that is, it is not necessary to complete each step before the next one is started.

The use of a computerized instructional tool like the simulation game model also has other benefits. It involves the manager in the development of the model via the on-line characteristic of the system. The on-line operation encourages the exploration of "what if" questions and the use of computer-generated information. Managers become aware of previously unknown computer capabilities, which can develop an inclination to further experimentation. This is the ultimate accolade of any implementation process—the ability to not only successfully implement the present model but to create an interest in other management science techniques.

Another important benefit that should be promoted in the implementation process is positive and negative feedback between the manager and the management science group. Managers are often able to discover problems and inconsistencies that the management scientist might not notice. Thus, the implementation process becomes continuous.

Cost of Implementation

An often overlooked, but important aspect of implementation is the cost in time and required resources. The financial cost, workforce requirements, and computer cost required to develop and use a simulation game can be very high. In fact, the costs involved usually make this particular implementation strategy prohibitive for all but the largest firms. Thus, any form of implementation strategy, as well as the management science model, must be carefully analyzed to determine if the benefits to be gained from implementation will exceed the costs.

The cost of the management science model itself can be a factor in determining whether it should be implemented or not. The easiest costs to determine are the direct workforce requirements necessary to develop the model (and this is not always easy to forecast). However, the implementation of management science models often disrupts normal operational activities and can result in temporary decreased output and productivity, lost sales, and disrupted production schedules. These costs are more difficult to forecast and to assign an economic value. The implementation of a model can also disrupt the manager's schedule and consume valuable time that might be spent more profitably elsewhere.

In terms of benefits from the model, it must be determined with some degree of certainty if the benefits accruing from implementation will exceed the costs. The benefits resulting from the model are obviously measured in terms of increased productivity, profits, efficiency, and reduced cost. In addition, it must always be considered that failure to implement results in little or no benefit and the wasted cost of model development and implementation. Previously, we have considered the problem of implementation only in regard to the model not being used without considering the potential financial losses. Considered in light of these losses, the problem of implementation can take on new magnitude.

Management Science Within the Organization

One of the variables identified in several of the models on implementation relates to the location of management science within the organization. Such factors as the existence of a management science staff, the location of the management science service within the organizational structure, the size of the management science staff, and the status of the management science group, are important factors in attaining successful implementation. Many larger- and medium-size firms have management science departments or staffs concerned exclusively with problem solving and model development. However, although these staffs can be quite large, containing as many as thirty members, quality is primarily the determining factor in achieving implementation.

The management science staff can exist at numerous locations within the organizational structure. For example, it can be contained at the top management level, the corporate level, or the operational level. Some firms have management science groups at each of these levels of the organization. The organizational officer to whom the management science staff reports to is basically determined by the location of the staff in the organization. There does not appear, however, to be a typical organizational location for management science. The position of the staff in the firm and the political strength of the organizational member in charge of the management science function can be major factors in achieving implementation.

This discussion of the management science staff should not indicate that management science does not exist in those firms where there is no staff or department. In some instances, a member or several members of the management staff perform the management science function. This will become more and more prevalent in the future as a result of increased training in management science techniques at the college level. Both undergraduate business majors and M.B.A. students will be more prepared in the future to develop and implement management science models. Although, in the cases where a staff does not exist and the manager/management scientist is constrained by lack of time and resources, the manager has the advantage of being totally involved in the management science process; thus, enhancing implementation.

Summary

The purpose of this chapter has been to make you aware of and familiar with the problems that can arise when attempting to implement management science models based on the quantitative techniques presented in this text. As such, implementation has been defined, and the various reasons that often render it a problem have been analyzed.

Although the successes of management science are many and more successes will be forthcoming in the future, there is a need for continued emphasis and awareness of the problem of implementation. It would be negligent to ignore the full potential of management science because obstacles to implementation could not be overcome. However, this chapter as well as numerous other sources indicate that the problem has been recognized, that solutions are being sought, and that research will be continued in the future.

References

Churchman, C., and Shainblatt, A. A. "The Researcher and the Manager: A Dialectic of Implementation." *Management Science* 11 (1965): B69–87.

Davis, K. R., and Taylor, B. W. "Addressing the Implementation Problem: A Gaming Approach." *Decision Sciences* 7 (1976): 677–87.

Gaither, N. "The Adoption of Operations Research Techniques by Manufacturing Organizations." *Decision Sciences* 6 (1975): 797–813.

Grayson, C. J., Jr. "Management Science and Business Practice." *Harvard Business Review* 51 (1973): 41–48.

Harvey, A. "Factors Making for Implementation Success and Failure." *Management Science* 16 (1970): B312–21.

Lewin, K. "Group Decision and Social Change." In *Readings in Social Psychology*. Edited by E. Maccoby, T. M. Newcomb, and E. L. Hartley. New York: Holt, Rinehart and Winston, 1947, pp. 197–211.

Little, J. D. C. "Models and Managers: The Concept of a Decision Calculus." *Management Science* 16 (1970): B466–85.

Markland, R. E., and Newett, R. J. "A Subjective Taxonomy for Evaluating the Stages of Management Science Research." *Interfaces* 2 (1972): 31–39.

Rubenstein, A. H.; Radnor, M.; Baker, N. R.; Heiman, D. K.; and McColly, J. B. "Some Organizational Factors Related to Effectiveness of Management Science Groups in Industry." *Management Science* 13 (1967): B508–18.

Schultz, R. L., and Slevin, D. P., eds. *Implementing Operations Research/Management Science*. New York: Elsevier, 1975.

Shycon, H. N. "All Around the Model." *Interfaces* 2 (1972): 33–35.

Wysocki, R. K. "OR/MS Implementation Research: A Bibliography." *Interfaces* 9 (1979): 37–41.

Zand, D. E., and Sorensen, R. E. "Theory of Change and the Effective Use of Management Science." *Administrative Science Quarterly* 20 (1975): 532–45.

Study Questions

1. Develop your own definition of *implementation*.

2. Discuss implementation as a continuous process that occurs throughout the life of a management science project.

3. Discuss the reasons why implementation often becomes a problem.

4. List and discuss the various strategies that can be employed to enhance successful implementation.

5. Discuss *change theory* as a framework for achieving successful implementation.

6. Identify some of the specific costs that might accompany management science implementation.

7. Indicate the different levels within the organization at which the management science staff could exist, and discuss the advantages and disadvantages of each.

8. Give your opinion as to the optimal makeup of a management science staff (i.e., what specialties should be encompassed by a management science staff?).

9. Define the four positions related to the problem of implementation that occur between the manager and management scientist.

10. Consider the example models developed in previous chapters.

    a. Examples 2.2 and 2.3 in chapter 2
    b. The check processing network in chapter 6
    c. Example 12.2 in chapter 12
    d. Example 13.4 in chapter 13

    Discuss the problems that might develop with the implementation of each of these models.

11. In Lucas's three-step strategy for achieving successful implementation, the third step is to design a simple and easily understandable model. Is this always a feasible task? Based on your experiences in model development gained from this text, discuss the ways in which this third step can be achieved.

12. Identify the various forms that a change agent can take.

13. Based on the information provided in this chapter, develop your own strategy for attaining successful implementation and devise an example to demonstrate your strategy.

14. Discuss the degree to which you perceive differences in personality and training between managers and management scientists to be a cause of implementation problems. Identify some of these differences.

15. Why is the manager often viewed as more resistant to change than the management scientist?

Appendix A

Introduction to Matrix Methods

A matrix is a rectangular array of numbers arranged into rows and columns. A matrix is usually denoted by enclosing the array of numbers in brackets or parentheses, as follows:

$$\begin{bmatrix} 1 & 3 & 5 \\ 2 & 7 & 6 \end{bmatrix} \text{ or } \begin{pmatrix} 1 & 3 & 5 \\ 2 & 7 & 6 \end{pmatrix}$$

The general form of a matrix can be designated by an array of symbols as entries. These symbols are usually lowercase roman or italic letters with two subscripts, shown as follows:

$$\begin{bmatrix} a_{11} & a_{12} & a_{13} & \cdots & a_{1n} \\ a_{21} & a_{22} & a_{23} & \cdots & a_{2n} \\ \cdot & \cdot & \cdot & & \cdot \\ \cdot & \cdot & \cdot & & \cdot \\ \cdot & \cdot & \cdot & & \cdot \\ a_{m1} & a_{m2} & a_{m3} & \cdots & a_{mn} \end{bmatrix}$$

This array is called an m by n matrix because it contains m rows and n columns. In general, each element is denoted by a_{ij}, where i = row location and j = column location.

A matrix is often denoted by a single capital roman or italic letter. For example, the preceding matrix of a_{ij} elements can also be denoted by the capital letter A.

A matrix as a whole does not have a numerical value. However, the values in the matrix can be useful in representing a particular numerical problem. For example, the matrix elements can represent the following transition probabilities for a Markov process:

$$P = \begin{bmatrix} p_{11} & p_{12} & p_{13} \\ p_{21} & p_{22} & p_{23} \\ p_{31} & p_{32} & p_{33} \end{bmatrix} = \begin{bmatrix} .6 & .3 & .1 \\ .2 & .5 & .3 \\ .4 & .4 & .2 \end{bmatrix}$$

A matrix with the same number of rows and columns is called a *square matrix*. Such a matrix is referred to as an m by m or n by n matrix. The Markov transition probability matrix in chapter 9 is such a matrix.

A matrix with only one row is referred to as a *row vector*, and a matrix with only one column is referred to as a *column vector*. The state values of a Markov process are generally given as a row vector, such as

$$S = [s_1, s_2, s_3].$$

Matrix Addition and Subtraction

Two or more matrices can be added (or subtracted) only if they are of the same dimensions (same number of rows and columns). Matrices of equal dimensions are added by adding the corresponding elements of each matrix array. Likewise, subtraction is accomplished by subtracting the elements of one array from the corresponding elements of another.

Consider, for example, the following 2 by 3 matrices:

$$A = \begin{bmatrix} 2 & 3 & 1 \\ 4 & 7 & 5 \end{bmatrix} \qquad B = \begin{bmatrix} 1 & 2 & 6 \\ 5 & 2 & 3 \end{bmatrix}$$

Determine C, where

$$\begin{aligned} C &= A + B \\ &= \begin{bmatrix} 2 & 3 & 1 \\ 4 & 7 & 5 \end{bmatrix} + \begin{bmatrix} 1 & 2 & 6 \\ 5 & 2 & 3 \end{bmatrix}. \end{aligned}$$

By adding the corresponding elements of each matrix, we obtain

$$C = \begin{bmatrix} 2+1 & 3+2 & 1+6 \\ 4+5 & 7+2 & 5+3 \end{bmatrix} = \begin{bmatrix} 3 & 5 & 7 \\ 9 & 9 & 8 \end{bmatrix}.$$

As an illustration of matrix subtraction, determine D, where

$$\begin{aligned} D &= A - B \\ &= \begin{bmatrix} 2 & 3 & 1 \\ 4 & 7 & 5 \end{bmatrix} - \begin{bmatrix} 1 & 2 & 6 \\ 5 & 2 & 3 \end{bmatrix}. \end{aligned}$$

By subtracting the elements of matrix B from the corresponding elements of A, we obtain

$$D = \begin{bmatrix} 2-1 & 3-2 & 1-6 \\ 4-5 & 7-2 & 5-3 \end{bmatrix} = \begin{bmatrix} 1 & 1 & -5 \\ -1 & 5 & 2 \end{bmatrix}.$$

Matrix Multiplication

Two matrices can be multiplied only if the number of *columns* of the *first* matrix is equal to the number of *rows* of the *second* matrix. For example, if we wish to determine the product of A and B, the number of columns of matrix A must equal the number of rows of matrix B. In general, the new matrix obtained by $A \times B$ is not the same as $B \times A$. Thus,

$$A \times B \neq B \times A$$

The number of elements in the matrix obtained as the product of the two original matrices is determined by the number of rows in the first matrix and the number of columns in the second matrix.

The requirements for multiplying one matrix by another and the resulting dimensions of the product matrix are summarized as follows:

Multiply matrix A times matrix B to yield matrix C

$$C = A \times B$$

1. The number of columns of matrix A must equal the number of rows of matrix B.

$$\text{Number of columns}_A = \text{Number of rows}_B$$

2. The dimensions of matrix C are dependent on the number of rows of matrix A and the number of columns of matrix B.

$$\text{Dimensions: Number of rows}_A \times \text{Number of columns}_B$$

3. The elements of the new matrix C, formed by multiplying A times B, are given by

$$c_{ij} = \sum_{k=1}^{r} a_{ik} \cdot b_{kj}, \; i = 1, \ldots, m; \; j = 1, \ldots, n,$$

where

it is assumed that A is an m by r matrix, and B is an r by n matrix.

Note that the required condition that the number of columns of A be equal to the number of rows of B is met (the number of columns of A equals r and the number of rows of B equals r). Further note that the resulting dimensions of the product matrix C are m rows by n columns, which is equal to the number of rows of A and the number of columns of B.

The computational procedure for determining the c_{ij} elements of the product matrix is illustrated by the following:

Determine

$$C = A \times B,$$

where

$$A = \begin{bmatrix} 2 & 3 & 4 \\ 4 & 2 & 5 \end{bmatrix}$$

$$B = \begin{bmatrix} 1 & 3 \\ 6 & 3 \\ 5 & 1 \end{bmatrix}.$$

Note that the number of columns of A is equal to the number of rows of B. The resulting product matrix will be a 2 by 2 matrix (two rows in A and two columns in B) of the general form

$$C = \begin{bmatrix} c_{11} & c_{12} \\ c_{21} & c_{22} \end{bmatrix}.$$

The elements of the product matrix are computed such that the ijth element of C is equal to the sum of the ith row elements of A times the jth column elements of B. This is given symbolically by

$$c_{11} = a_{11} \cdot b_{11} + a_{12} \cdot b_{21} + a_{13} \cdot b_{31}$$
$$c_{12} = a_{11} \cdot b_{12} + a_{12} \cdot b_{22} + a_{13} \cdot b_{32}$$
$$c_{21} = a_{21} \cdot b_{11} + a_{22} \cdot b_{21} + a_{23} \cdot b_{31}$$
$$c_{22} = a_{21} \cdot b_{12} + a_{22} \cdot b_{22} + a_{23} \cdot b_{32}.$$

The multiplication procedure is summarized by

$$C = \begin{bmatrix} (\text{1st row of } A \times \text{ 1st column of } B) & (\text{1st row of } A \times \text{ 2nd column of } B) \\ (\text{2nd row of } A \times \text{ 1st column of } B) & (\text{2nd row of } A \times \text{ 2nd column of } B) \end{bmatrix}$$

Performing the multiplication,

$$C = A \times B = \begin{bmatrix} 2 & 3 & 4 \\ 4 & 2 & 5 \end{bmatrix} \cdot \begin{bmatrix} 1 & 3 \\ 6 & 3 \\ 5 & 1 \end{bmatrix}$$

$$= \begin{bmatrix} 2 \cdot 1 + 3 \cdot 6 + 4 \cdot 5 & 2 \cdot 3 + 3 \cdot 3 + 4 \cdot 1 \\ 4 \cdot 1 + 2 \cdot 6 + 5 \cdot 5 & 4 \cdot 3 + 2 \cdot 3 + 5 \cdot 1 \end{bmatrix}$$

$$= \begin{bmatrix} 2 + 18 + 20 & 6 + 9 + 4 \\ 4 + 12 + 25 & 12 + 6 + 5 \end{bmatrix}$$

$$C = \begin{bmatrix} 40 & 19 \\ 41 & 23 \end{bmatrix}.$$

Consider the following example in which two 2 by 2 matrices are multiplied, first as $A \times B$ and then as $B \times A$:

$$A = \begin{bmatrix} 2 & 3 \\ 1 & 4 \end{bmatrix} \qquad B = \begin{bmatrix} 5 & 8 \\ 7 & 6 \end{bmatrix}$$

$$A \times B = \begin{bmatrix} 2 & 3 \\ 1 & 4 \end{bmatrix} \cdot \begin{bmatrix} 5 & 8 \\ 7 & 6 \end{bmatrix} = \begin{bmatrix} 10 + 21 & 16 + 18 \\ 5 + 28 & 8 + 24 \end{bmatrix} = \begin{bmatrix} 31 & 34 \\ 33 & 32 \end{bmatrix}$$

$$B \times A = \begin{bmatrix} 5 & 8 \\ 7 & 6 \end{bmatrix} \cdot \begin{bmatrix} 2 & 3 \\ 1 & 4 \end{bmatrix} = \begin{bmatrix} 10 + 8 & 15 + 32 \\ 14 + 6 & 21 + 24 \end{bmatrix} = \begin{bmatrix} 18 & 47 \\ 20 & 45 \end{bmatrix}$$

Although the requirement that the number of columns of the first matrix equals the number of rows of the second matrix is satisfied in each case, the resulting product matrix from $A \times B$ is not the same as $B \times A$.

Consider the following case in which the first matrix is a row vector, while the second matrix is a 3 by 3 matrix:

$$A = [100 \;\; 200 \;\; 300] \qquad B = \begin{bmatrix} .1 & .7 & .2 \\ .3 & .5 & .2 \\ .8 & .1 & .1 \end{bmatrix}$$

The product of $A \times B$ is computed by the same procedure. The number of rows of the new product matrix is one (number of rows of A), and the number of columns of the product matrix is three (number of columns of B). Thus, the resulting product matrix is a 1 by 3 row vector.

The product of $A \times B$ is given by

$$A \times B = [100 \;\; 200 \;\; 300] \cdot \begin{bmatrix} .1 & .7 & .2 \\ .3 & .5 & .2 \\ .8 & .1 & .1 \end{bmatrix}$$

$$= [10 + 60 + 240 \quad 70 + 100 + 30 \quad 20 + 40 + 30]$$

$$= [310 \;\; 200 \;\; 90].$$

This example illustrates a Markov process in which A is the state vector and B is the matrix of transition probabilities. The resulting product matrix (row vector) is the system state vector after one transition period.

Simultaneous Solution of a System of Linear Equations

A system of n linear equations with n unknowns can often be more easily solved by using matrix methods. For example, assume we wish to solve the following system of linear equations simultaneously for the values of x_1, x_2, and x_3.

$$\begin{aligned} x_1 + 3x_2 + 2x_3 &= 13 \\ 4x_1 - 2x_2 + 2x_3 &= 14 \\ 2x_1 + x_2 + x_3 &= 9 \end{aligned}$$

This set of linear equations can be expressed in matrix form as

$$\begin{bmatrix} 1 & 3 & 2 \\ 4 & -2 & 2 \\ 2 & 1 & 1 \end{bmatrix} \cdot \begin{bmatrix} x_1 \\ x_2 \\ x_3 \end{bmatrix} = \begin{bmatrix} 13 \\ 14 \\ 9 \end{bmatrix}.$$

If we define the first matrix of coefficients as A, the second matrix of variables as X, and the third matrix of right-hand-side values as B, we have

$$A \times X = B.$$

This can be verified by multiplying matrix A times matrix X (column vector). The initial set of linear equations are obtained.

An intuitive illustration of the matrix solution to the set of simultaneous linear equations is given first. Consider the following ordinary algebraic equation:

$$2y = 10$$

The solution for y is obtained by multiplying both sides of the equation by the reciprocal of 2, as follows:

$$(1/2)2y = (1/2)10,$$

which yields

$$y = 5.$$

In general, if we have

$$ay = b,$$

then the solution for y is obtained by

$$(1/a)ay = (1/a)b.$$

Note that on the left-hand-side of the equation, $(1/a)a$ reduces to 1. This is important for purposes of understanding the following discussion.

For the case of a matrix representation of this type of problem, such as solving for X where

$$A \times X = B,$$

both sides of the equation must be multiplied by a matrix term that reduces A to a matrix form similar to that obtained from $(1/a)a$.

Identity Matrix

The identity matrix acts in matrix multiplication in the same way as the number 1 acts in the multiplication of ordinary algebra. That is, multiplication of a matrix by an identity matrix leaves the original matrix unchanged, just as $1 \times a = a$ in ordinary algebra. Thus, where the identity matrix is denoted by I,

$$I \times A = A.$$

The identity matrix is always square (number of rows equals number of columns) and consists of ones in the diagonal from upper left to lower right (the *main diagonal*) and zeros elsewhere. An example of a 3 by 3 identity matrix is given as follows:

$$I = \begin{bmatrix} 1 & 0 & 0 \\ 0 & 1 & 0 \\ 0 & 0 & 1 \end{bmatrix}$$

The statement that $I \times A = A$ is illustrated by the following:

If

$$A = \begin{bmatrix} 3 & 2 \\ 5 & 1 \\ 6 & 4 \end{bmatrix},$$

then

$$I \cdot A = \begin{bmatrix} 1 & 0 & 0 \\ 0 & 1 & 0 \\ 0 & 0 & 1 \end{bmatrix} \cdot \begin{bmatrix} 3 & 2 \\ 5 & 1 \\ 6 & 4 \end{bmatrix}$$

$$= \begin{bmatrix} 3+0+0 & 2+0+0 \\ 0+5+0 & 0+1+0 \\ 0+0+6 & 0+0+4 \end{bmatrix} = \begin{bmatrix} 3 & 2 \\ 5 & 1 \\ 6 & 4 \end{bmatrix} = A.$$

Therefore, in order to solve for X in the matrix equation, $A \times X = B$, we must multiply both sides of the equation by a term that reduces A to an identity matrix. When A is reduced to an identity, we have $I \times X$ or simply X remaining on the left side of the equation. This is analogous to multiplying both sides of the equation, $ay = b$, by the reciprocal of a in algebra.

Inverse of a Matrix

The inverse of the matrix A is analogous to the reciprocal of a in algebra. The inverse (or reciprocal) of the matrix A is denoted by A^{-1}. Thus, it can be seen that

$$A^{-1} \times A = I,$$

which is analogous to $(1/a)a = 1$ in algebra.

Thus, we can see that the solution to $A \times X = B$ is given by

$$A^{-1} \times A \times X = A^{-1} \times B,$$

which yields

$$I \times X = A^{-1} \times B$$

or

$$X = A^{-1} \times B.$$

The inverse of matrix A is obtained by

$$A^{-1} = \frac{A_{adj}}{|A|},$$

where

A_{adj} = the adjoint of matrix A

$|A|$ = the determinant of matrix A.

Determinant of a Matrix

A determinant is a square array of elements that has a numerical value. The determinant of A is denoted by $|A|$.

A second order determinant is a square array of numbers in two rows and two columns. In general, a second order determinant can be denoted by

$$|A| = \begin{vmatrix} a_{11} & a_{12} \\ a_{21} & a_{22} \end{vmatrix}.$$

The value of $|A|$ is determined as

$$a_{11} \cdot a_{22} - a_{21} \cdot a_{12}.$$

The product of the elements in the diagonal from upper left to lower right is first computed. From this is subtracted the product of the elements in the diagonal from lower left to upper right. For example, the value of the following determinant is given by

$$|A| = \begin{vmatrix} 3 & 1 \\ 4 & 2 \end{vmatrix} = 3 \cdot 2 - 4 \cdot 1 = 6 - 4 = 2.$$

A third order determinant is a square array of numbers in three rows and three columns. In general, it is denoted by

$$|A| = \begin{vmatrix} a_{11} & a_{12} & a_{13} \\ a_{21} & a_{22} & a_{23} \\ a_{31} & a_{32} & a_{33} \end{vmatrix}.$$

The value of the third order determinant is determined by

$$(a_{11} \cdot a_{22} \cdot a_{33} + a_{12} \cdot a_{23} \cdot a_{31} + a_{13} \cdot a_{21} \cdot a_{32})$$
$$- (a_{31} \cdot a_{22} \cdot a_{13} + a_{32} \cdot a_{23} \cdot a_{11} + a_{33} \cdot a_{21} \cdot a_{12}).$$

The preceding computation can be easily grasped by rewriting the determinant as follows:

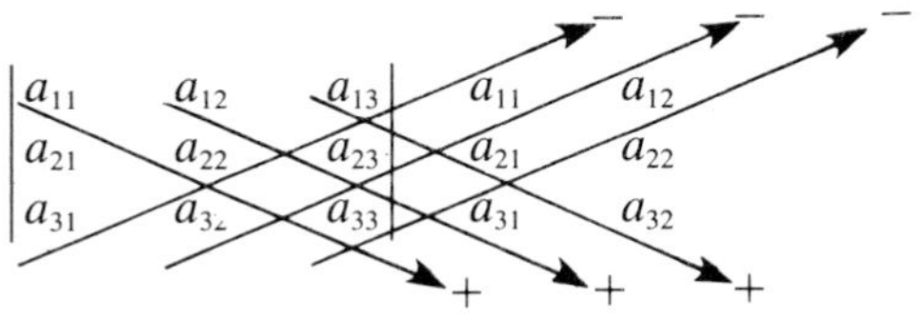

The first two columns of the determinant have been rewritten to the right of the determinant. The product of the elements in each of the three underscored diagonals from upper left to lower right are first computed and summed. Then, the product of the elements in each of the three underscored diagonals from lower left to upper right are computed and summed. Finally, the second sum is subtracted from the first sum.

For example, the value of the following third order determinant is given by

$$|A| = \begin{vmatrix} 3 & 2 & 4 \\ 5 & 1 & 3 \\ 2 & 6 & 2 \end{vmatrix}$$
$$= (3 \cdot 1 \cdot 2 + 2 \cdot 3 \cdot 2 + 4 \cdot 5 \cdot 6) - (2 \cdot 1 \cdot 4 + 6 \cdot 3 \cdot 3 + 2 \cdot 5 \cdot 2)$$
$$= (6 + 12 + 120) - (8 + 54 + 20)$$
$$= 138 - 82$$
$$= 56.$$

The same general approach can be used to evaluate determinants of higher order. For example, a fourth order determinant involves four diagonals in each direction.

Adjoint of a Matrix

The adjoint of the matrix A is denoted by A_{adj} and is determined by

$$A_{adj} = A^T_{cof},$$

where

A^T_{cof} = the transpose of the matrix of cofactors.

Transpose of a Matrix

The transpose of a matrix is a matrix that is formed by interchanging the rows and columns of the matrix. The transpose of the matrix A is denoted by A^{T}. For example,

if

$$A = \begin{bmatrix} 3 & 4 & 8 \\ 5 & 1 & 2 \end{bmatrix},$$

then

$$A^{T} = \begin{bmatrix} 3 & 5 \\ 4 & 1 \\ 8 & 2 \end{bmatrix}.$$

Cofactor Matrix

A cofactor matrix is a square matrix whose elements are cofactors of the corresponding elements of the matrix A. The cofactor elements of the cofactor matrix will be denoted by a'_{ij}. For any element a_{ij} of the matrix A, there is a corresponding cofactor element a'_{ij} (for corresponding values of i and j). The general form for the matrix A and the corresponding cofactor matrix are given as

$$A = \begin{bmatrix} a_{11} & a_{12} & a_{13} \\ a_{21} & a_{22} & a_{23} \\ a_{31} & a_{32} & a_{33} \end{bmatrix}, \; A_{cof} = \begin{bmatrix} a'_{11} & a'_{12} & a'_{13} \\ a'_{21} & a'_{22} & a'_{23} \\ a'_{31} & a'_{32} & a'_{33} \end{bmatrix}.$$

The elements of the cofactor maxtrix A are determined by the following:

$$a'_{ij} = (-1)^{i+j} \cdot |D_{ij}|,$$

where

$|D_{ij}|$ = the determinant of the submatrix obtained by deleting row i and column j from matrix A.

Suppose we wish to determine the cofactor element corresponding to the element a_{11} of the matrix A. First delete the elements of row 1 and column 1 from matrix A, which yields the determinant of the remaining elements, as follows:

$$|D_{ij}| = \begin{bmatrix} a_{11} & a_{12} & a_{13} \\ a_{21} & a_{22} & a_{23} \\ a_{31} & a_{32} & a_{33} \end{bmatrix} = \begin{vmatrix} a_{22} & a_{23} \\ a_{32} & a_{33} \end{vmatrix}.$$

Then compute the cofactor for a_{11} as

$$a'_{11} = (-1)^{1+1} \cdot \begin{vmatrix} a_{22} & a_{23} \\ a_{32} & a_{33} \end{vmatrix}.$$

Note that the term $(-1)^{i+j}$ for the 3 by 3 matrix can be summarized as

$$\begin{pmatrix} +1 & -1 & +1 \\ -1 & +1 & -1 \\ +1 & -1 & +1 \end{pmatrix},$$

which is obtained by $(-1)^{1+1} = +1$, $(-1)^{1+2} = -1$, $(-1)^{1+3} = +1$, $(-1)^{2+1} = -1$, etc.

Assume that the matrix of interest is given by

$$A = \begin{bmatrix} 4 & 1 & 5 \\ 2 & 8 & 6 \\ 3 & 5 & 7 \end{bmatrix}.$$

The determinants of the submatrices obtained by deleting row i and column j are given as follows:

$$|D_{11}| = \begin{vmatrix} 8 & 6 \\ 5 & 7 \end{vmatrix} = 26, \quad |D_{12}| = \begin{vmatrix} 2 & 6 \\ 3 & 7 \end{vmatrix} = -4, \quad |D_{13}| = \begin{vmatrix} 2 & 8 \\ 3 & 5 \end{vmatrix} = -14$$

$$|D_{21}| = \begin{vmatrix} 1 & 5 \\ 5 & 7 \end{vmatrix} = -18, \quad |D_{22}| = \begin{vmatrix} 4 & 5 \\ 3 & 7 \end{vmatrix} = 13, \quad |D_{23}| = \begin{vmatrix} 4 & 1 \\ 3 & 5 \end{vmatrix} = 17$$

$$|D_{31}| = \begin{vmatrix} 1 & 5 \\ 8 & 6 \end{vmatrix} = -34, \quad |D_{32}| = \begin{vmatrix} 4 & 5 \\ 2 & 6 \end{vmatrix} = 14, \quad |D_{33}| = \begin{vmatrix} 4 & 1 \\ 2 & 8 \end{vmatrix} = 30$$

Thus, the matrix of cofactor elements is given by the product of $(-1)^{i+j}$ and $|D_{ij}|$.

$$A_{cof} = \begin{bmatrix} (+1)\cdot(26) & (-1)\cdot(-4) & (+1)\cdot(-14) \\ (-1)\cdot(-18) & (+1)\cdot(13) & (-1)\cdot(17) \\ (+1)\cdot(-34) & (-1)\cdot(14) & (+1)\cdot(30) \end{bmatrix}$$

$$= \begin{bmatrix} 26 & 4 & -14 \\ 18 & 13 & -17 \\ -34 & -14 & 30 \end{bmatrix}$$

Now return to our original statement of the matrix inverse, given as

$$A^{-1} = \frac{A_{adj}}{|A|} = \frac{(\text{adjoint of matrix } A)}{(\text{determinant of matrix } A)}$$

$$= \frac{A^T_{cof}}{|A|} = \frac{(\text{cofactor matrix for } A \text{ transposed})}{(\text{determinant of matrix } A)}.$$

By way of illustration, the inverse will be determined for the set of simultaneous linear equations given at the beginning of this section.

$$A = \begin{bmatrix} 1 & 3 & 2 \\ 4 & -2 & 2 \\ 2 & 1 & 1 \end{bmatrix}$$

The cofactor matrix is determined to be

$$A_{cof} = \begin{bmatrix} -4 & 0 & 8 \\ -1 & -3 & 5 \\ 10 & 6 & -14 \end{bmatrix}.$$

Transposing the cofactor matrix yields

$$A^T_{cof} = \begin{bmatrix} -4 & -1 & 10 \\ 0 & -3 & 6 \\ 8 & 5 & -14 \end{bmatrix} = A_{adj}.$$

Thus, we have the numerator for our determination of the inverse of A.

The determinant of A is given by

$$A = \begin{vmatrix} 1 & 3 & 2 \\ 4 & -2 & 2 \\ 2 & 1 & 1 \end{vmatrix} = (-2 + 12 + 8) - (-8 + 2 + 12)$$

$$= 18 - 6 = 12.$$

We have as the inverse of the matrix A,

$$A^{-1} = \frac{1}{12} \cdot \begin{bmatrix} -4 & -1 & 10 \\ 0 & -3 & 6 \\ 8 & 5 & -14 \end{bmatrix}$$

$$= \begin{bmatrix} -1/3 & -1/12 & 5/6 \\ 0 & -1/4 & 1/2 \\ 2/3 & 5/12 & -7/6 \end{bmatrix}.$$

It was previously shown that, given $A \times X = B$, the solution for X is

$$A^{-1} \times A \times X = A^{-1} \times B$$
$$I \times X = A^{-1} \times B$$
$$X = A^{-1} \times B.$$

Recall that the right-hand-side values of the simultaneous linear equations were given as the column vector.

$$B = \begin{bmatrix} 13 \\ 14 \\ 9 \end{bmatrix}$$

Therefore, we can solve for X as

$$A^{-1} \times B = \begin{bmatrix} -1/3 & -1/12 & 5/6 \\ 0 & -1/4 & 1/2 \\ 2/3 & 5/12 & -7/6 \end{bmatrix} \cdot \begin{bmatrix} 13 \\ 14 \\ 9 \end{bmatrix}$$

$$= \begin{bmatrix} (-1/3)(13) + (-1/12)(14) + (5/6)(9) \\ (0)(13) + (-1/4)(14) + (1/2)(9) \\ (2/3)(13) + (5/12)(14) + (-7/6)(9) \end{bmatrix}$$

$$= \begin{bmatrix} -13/3 - 7/6 + 45/6 \\ 0 - 7/2 + 9/2 \\ 26/3 + 35/6 - 63/6 \end{bmatrix}$$

$$= \begin{bmatrix} 12/6 \\ 2/2 \\ 24/6 \end{bmatrix}.$$

Thus,

$$X = \begin{bmatrix} 2 \\ 1 \\ 4 \end{bmatrix}$$

or

$$x_1 = 2, x_2 = 1, \text{ and } x_3 = 4.$$

As a final note, it should be pointed out that the computations can be simplified by multiplying through by 1/12 as the last step, as follows:

$$A^{-1} \times B = \frac{1}{|A|} \cdot A_{adj} \cdot B = \frac{1}{12} \cdot \begin{bmatrix} -4 & -1 & 10 \\ 0 & -3 & 6 \\ 8 & 5 & -14 \end{bmatrix} \cdot \begin{bmatrix} 13 \\ 14 \\ 9 \end{bmatrix}$$

$$= \frac{1}{12} \cdot \begin{bmatrix} 24 \\ 12 \\ 48 \end{bmatrix} = \begin{bmatrix} 2 \\ 1 \\ 4 \end{bmatrix}$$

The Gauss-Jordan Elimination Procedure

An alternative method for determining the inverse of a matrix is the Gauss-Jordan elimination method. This method can also be used to solve systems of linear equations and, in fact, is often used as an alternative to the simplex tableau method for solving linear programming problems.

The Gauss-Jordan method consists of the following general steps. Given a set of linear equations, an equivalent set of equations with the same solution set can be generated by replacing one of the original equations with another equation.

The replacement equation is computed as the sum of a replaced equation plus some multiple of any of the other equations in the original set.

As an example of the Gauss-Jordan method, consider the following set of equations:

$$4x_1 + 8x_2 = 160 \quad (1)$$
$$6x_1 + 4x_2 = 120 \quad (2)$$

It is desired to have this set of equations in the following general form:

$$1x_1 + 0x_2 = A$$
$$0x_1 + 1x_2 = B,$$

which is, in effect, the solution of the original set of equations.

In order to achieve this transformation, we must first change the coefficient of x_1 in the first equation to 1 rather than 4. This can be accomplished by dividing equation (1) through by 4, which yields

$$x_1 + 2x_2 = 40 \quad (1a)$$
$$6x_1 + 4x_2 = 120. \quad (2)$$

The next step is to make the coefficient of x_1 in equation (2) zero instead of 6. To achieve this, equation (1*a*) is multiplied by -6 and added to equation (2) as follows:

$$-6x_1 - 12x_2 = -240 \quad (1a) \times -6$$
$$6x_1 + 4x_2 = 120 \quad (2)$$
$$0x_1 - 8x_2 = -120 \quad (2a)$$

Replacing equation (2) in the original system with this sum (2*a*) yields

$$x_1 + 2x_2 = 40 \quad (1a)$$
$$0x_1 - 8x_2 = -120. \quad (2a)$$

Now, it is desired to transform the x_2 coefficients to 1 and 0 just as we did with the x_1 coefficients. First, divide equation (2*a*) by -8, which yields the following set of equations:

$$x_1 + 2x_2 = 40 \quad (1a)$$
$$0x_1 + x_2 = 15 \quad (2b)$$

This leaves only the x_2 coefficient in equation (1a) to be changed from 2 to 0. This can be accomplished by multiplying equation (2b) by -2 and adding it to equation (1a) as follows:

$$
\begin{array}{rcll}
x_1 + 2x_2 &=& 40 & (1a) \\
0x_1 - 2x_2 &=& -30 & (2b) \times -2 \\
\hline
x_1 + 0x_2 &=& 10 & (1b)
\end{array}
$$

Replacing equation (1a) with this sum (1b) results in the following set of equations:

$$x_1 + 0x_2 = 10 \qquad (1b)$$

$$0x_1 + x_2 = 15 \qquad (2b)$$

or $x_1 = 10$, $x_2 = 15$

This is the new form we desired to transform the original set of equations to, and thus it is the solution set to the original equations.

This same process can be employed to find the inverse of a matrix. First, set up the problem in the following form:

$$\underset{A}{\begin{bmatrix} 4 & 8 \\ 6 & 4 \end{bmatrix}} \quad \underset{I}{\begin{bmatrix} 1 & 0 \\ 0 & 1 \end{bmatrix}}$$

Now perform the Gauss-Jordan steps on both of these matrices simultaneously. First divide the first line by 4.

$$\underset{A}{\begin{bmatrix} 1 & 2 \\ 6 & 4 \end{bmatrix}} \quad \underset{I}{\begin{bmatrix} 1/4 & 0 \\ 0 & 1 \end{bmatrix}}$$

Now, multiply the first line by -6 and add this to the second line.

$$\underset{A}{\begin{bmatrix} 1 & 2 \\ 0 & -8 \end{bmatrix}} \quad \underset{I}{\begin{bmatrix} 1/4 & 0 \\ -3/2 & 1 \end{bmatrix}}$$

Next, divide the second line by -8.

$$\underset{A}{\begin{bmatrix} 1 & 2 \\ 0 & 1 \end{bmatrix}} \quad \underset{I}{\begin{bmatrix} 1/4 & 0 \\ 3/16 & -1/8 \end{bmatrix}}$$

Finally, multiply the second line by -2 and add to the first line.

$$\underset{I}{\begin{bmatrix} 1 & 0 \\ 0 & 1 \end{bmatrix}} \quad \underset{A^{-1}}{\begin{bmatrix} -1/8 & 1/4 \\ 3/16 & -1/8 \end{bmatrix}}$$

The preceding computations result in A^{-1}, the inverse of the original matrix. To check this result using the original set of equations, $Ax = B$, where

$$B = \begin{bmatrix} 160 \\ 120 \end{bmatrix}.$$

Compute the following:

$$x = A^{-1}B$$

and thus,

$$\begin{bmatrix} x_1 \\ x_2 \end{bmatrix} = \begin{bmatrix} -1/8 & 1/4 \\ 3/16 & -1/8 \end{bmatrix} \begin{bmatrix} 160 \\ 120 \end{bmatrix}$$

$$\begin{bmatrix} x_1 \\ x_2 \end{bmatrix} = \begin{bmatrix} 10 \\ 15 \end{bmatrix},$$

which is the original solution previously computed.

Now, let us apply the Gauss-Jordan process to determine the inverse of the 3×3 matrix found by using the method of cofactors in the previous section.

$$\overset{A}{\begin{bmatrix} 1 & 3 & 2 \\ 4 & -2 & 2 \\ 2 & 1 & 1 \end{bmatrix}} \quad \overset{I}{\begin{bmatrix} 1 & 0 & 0 \\ 0 & 1 & 0 \\ 0 & 0 & 1 \end{bmatrix}}$$

Since a_{11} is already 1, the first step is to make $a_{21} = 0$. This is achieved by multiplying the first line by -4 and adding it to the second line.

$$\overset{A}{\begin{bmatrix} 1 & 3 & 2 \\ 0 & -14 & -6 \\ 2 & 1 & 1 \end{bmatrix}} \quad \overset{I}{\begin{bmatrix} 1 & 0 & 0 \\ -4 & 1 & 0 \\ 0 & 0 & 1 \end{bmatrix}}$$

Now in order to make a_{31} equal to zero, multiply the first line by -2 and add to the third line.

$$\overset{A}{\begin{bmatrix} 1 & 3 & 2 \\ 0 & -14 & -6 \\ 0 & -5 & -3 \end{bmatrix}} \quad \overset{I}{\begin{bmatrix} 1 & 0 & 0 \\ -4 & 1 & 0 \\ -2 & 0 & 1 \end{bmatrix}}$$

Next, the a_{i2} values must be transformed to 0, 1, 0. Divide the second line by -14.

$$\overset{A}{\begin{bmatrix} 1 & 3 & 2 \\ 0 & 1 & 3/7 \\ 0 & -5 & -3 \end{bmatrix}} \quad \overset{I}{\begin{bmatrix} 1 & 0 & 0 \\ 2/7 & -1/14 & 0 \\ -2 & 0 & 1 \end{bmatrix}}$$

Next, multiply the second line by -3 and add to the first line, and then multiply the second line by 5 and add to the third line.

$$\overset{A}{\begin{bmatrix} 1 & 0 & 5/7 \\ 0 & 1 & 3/7 \\ 0 & 0 & -6/7 \end{bmatrix}} \quad \overset{I}{\begin{bmatrix} 1/7 & 3/14 & 0 \\ 2/7 & -1/14 & 0 \\ -4/7 & -5/14 & 1 \end{bmatrix}}$$

Finally, the a_{i3} values must be changed 0, 0, 1. First divide the third line by $-6/7$.

$$\overset{A}{\begin{bmatrix} 1 & 0 & 5/7 \\ 0 & 1 & 3/7 \\ 0 & 0 & 1 \end{bmatrix}} \quad \overset{I}{\begin{bmatrix} 1/7 & 3/14 & 0 \\ 2/7 & -1/14 & 0 \\ 2/3 & 5/12 & -7/6 \end{bmatrix}}$$

Next, multiply the third line by $-3/7$ and add to the second line, and multiply the third line by $-5/7$ and add to the first line.

$$\overset{I}{\begin{bmatrix} 1 & 0 & 0 \\ 0 & 1 & 0 \\ 0 & 0 & 1 \end{bmatrix}} \quad \overset{A^{-1}}{\begin{bmatrix} -1/3 & -1/12 & 5/6 \\ 0 & -1/4 & 1/2 \\ 2/3 & 5/12 & -7/6 \end{bmatrix}}$$

Thus, the inverse, A^{-1}, is obtained by the Gauss-Jordan steps as opposed to the method shown in the previous section.

Solving Linear Programming Problems by the Gauss-Jordan Method

As noted in chapter 3, the simplex method is based on the principles of matrix algebra. In fact, the simplex procedure basically follows the steps of the Gauss-Jordan method just presented. In this section the solution of a linear programming problem by the Gauss-Jordan steps will be demonstrated. As an example, the linear programming model presented in chapter 3 and solved via the simplex method in tables 3.2–3.13 will be used. The formulation for this example is

$$\text{Maximize } Z = 100x_1 + 80x_2$$

subject to

$$\begin{aligned} 2x_1 + 4x_2 &\leqslant 80 \\ 3x_1 + x_2 &\leqslant 60 \\ x_1, x_2 &\geqslant 0. \end{aligned}$$

As in the simplex method, the first step is to transform the inequalities into equalities. Also, the objective function must be put into proper form for the Gauss-Jordon solution method by having all variables on the left side of the equality sign.

$$Z - 100x_1 - 80x_2 = 0 \quad (0)$$

$$2x_1 + 4x_2 + s_1 = 80 \quad (1)$$

$$3x_1 + x_2 + s_2 = 60 \quad (2)$$

The Gauss-Jordan steps will be applied to the problem in equation form instead of transforming the equations into matrix form. This will allow us to more readily observe the similarities between the algebraic approach and the simplex method. However, it is important to note that the identity matrix is formed by the slack variables s_1 and s_2.

As in the simplex method, the variable that enters the solution must first be identified. By observing the objective function in its original form, it is apparent that x_1 will contribute the greatest amount, 100, to the achievement of the objective. Therefore, it is selected as the entering variable.

Now that x_1 is selected as the entering variable, the leaving variable must be selected. This is achieved by solving for x_1 in both constraint equations, while the other variables are assumed to be zero.

$$2x_1 + 4(0) + 0 = 80 \quad (1)$$

$$3x_1 + 1(0) + 0 = 60 \quad (2)$$

Therefore,

$x_1 = 40$ in equation (1)

$x_1 = 20$ in equation (2).

This indicates that s_2 should be eliminated. As we move along the x_1 axis in figure 3.1, s_1 in equation (1) and s_2 in equation (2) are approaching zero (i.e., we are using up those previously unused resources). Since x_1 is equal to 20 in equation (2), which is less than $x_1 = 40$ in equation (1), it means that s_2 in equation (2) will reach zero first. As in the simplex process, we have determined which constraint is most constraining. Thus, s_2 is the leaving variable.

Now the steps of the Gauss-Jordan process are applied in order to reestablish the identity matrix with x_1 in the basis. This is achieved when the coefficient for x_1 is zero in equations (0) and (1) and one in equation (2). Recall that equation (2) is selected because s_2 is the leaving variable.

Step 1 Since x_1 must have a coefficient of 1 in equation (2), divide this equation by 3. This results in a new equation, (2*a*).

$$x_1 + \frac{1}{3}x_2 + \frac{1}{3}s_2 = 20 \quad (2a)$$

Step 2 The variable x_1 must have a coefficient of zero (i.e., x_1 is eliminated) in equation (1). To achieve this multiply equation (2*a*) by 2 and subtract from (1).

$$2x_1 + 4x_2 + s_1 = 80 \qquad (1)$$

$$-2x_1 - \frac{2}{3}x_2 - \frac{2}{3}s_2 = -40 \qquad (2a)\times 2$$

$$\frac{10}{3}x_2 + s_1 - \frac{2}{3}s_2 = 40 \qquad (1a)$$

Step 3 The variable x_1 must also be eliminated from equation (0). This can be accomplished by multiplying equation (2*a*) by 100 and adding it to equation (0).

$$Z - 100x_1 - 80x_2 = 0 \qquad (0)$$

$$100x_1 + \frac{100}{3}x_2 + \frac{100}{3}s_2 = 2{,}000 \qquad (2a)\times 100$$

$$Z - \frac{140}{3}x_2 + \frac{100}{3}s_2 = 2{,}000 \qquad (0a)$$

The new set of equations is now

$$Z - \frac{140}{3}x_2 + \frac{100}{3}s_2 = 2{,}000 \qquad (0)$$

$$\frac{10}{3}x_2 + s_1 - \frac{2}{3}s_2 = 40 \qquad (1)$$

$$x_1 + \frac{1}{3}x_2 + \frac{1}{3}s_2 = 20. \qquad (2)$$

Comparing this set of equations with the corresponding simplex tableau (table *A*.1) shows that the same relationships exist.

Table *A*.1 Completed second simplex tableau

c_b \ c_j	basis	b_i*	100 x_1	80 x_2	0 s_1	0 s_2
0	s_1	40	0	10/3	1	−2/3
100	x_1	20	1	1/3	0	1/3
	z_j	2,000	100	100/3	0	100/3
	$c_j - z_j$		0	140/3	0	−100/3

Observing the objective function in general form for our new set of equations,

$$Z = \frac{140}{3} x_2 - \frac{100}{3} s_2 + 2{,}000$$

It can be seen that x_2 is the only remaining variable that has a positive coefficient and, thus, will increase profit.

The leaving variable is selected by solving for x_2 in both equations (1) and (2), and setting all other variables equal to zero.

$$+ \frac{10}{3} x_2 + 0 - \frac{2}{3}(0) = 40 \qquad (1)$$

$$0 + \frac{1}{3} x_2 \qquad + \frac{1}{3}(0) = 20 \qquad (2)$$

Therefore,

$x_2 = 12$ in equation (1)

$x_2 = 60$ in equation (2).

Thus, equation (1) is most constrained and s_1 is the leaving variable. As such, the Gauss-Jordan steps are used to reestablish the identity matrix with x_2 in the solution basis. This is accomplished when x_2 has a coefficient of one in equation (1) and a coefficient of zero in equations (0) and (2).

Step 1 Since x_2 must have a coefficient of 1 in equation (1), multiply this equation by $\frac{3}{10}$.

$$x_2 + \frac{3}{10} s_1 - \frac{1}{5} s_2 = 12 \qquad (1a)$$

Step 2 Eliminate x_2 in equation (2) by multiplying equation (1*a*) by $\frac{1}{3}$ and subtracting from equation (2).

$$x_1 + \frac{1}{3} x_2 \qquad + \frac{1}{3} s_2 = 20 \qquad (2)$$

$$- \frac{1}{3} x_2 - \frac{1}{10} s_1 + \frac{1}{15} s_2 = -4 \qquad (1a) \times 1/3$$

$$x_1 \qquad - \frac{1}{10} s_1 + \frac{2}{5} s_2 = 16 \qquad (2a)$$

Step 3 Eliminate x_2 in equation (0) by multiplying equation (1a) by 140/3 and adding it to equation (0).

$$Z - \frac{140}{3}x_2 \qquad + \frac{100}{3}s_2 = 2{,}000 \qquad (0)$$

$$\frac{140}{3}x_2 + 14s_1 - \frac{28}{3}s_2 = 560 \qquad (1a) \times 140/3$$

$$Z \qquad + 14s_1 + 24\ s_2 = 2{,}560 \qquad (0a)$$

The new set of equations is

$$Z \qquad + 14\ s_1 + 24\ s_2 = 2{,}560 \qquad (0)$$

$$x_2 + \frac{3}{10}s_1 - \frac{1}{5}s_2 = 12 \qquad (1)$$

$$x_1 \qquad - \frac{1}{10}s_1 + \frac{2}{5}s_2 = 16. \qquad (2)$$

The corresponding simplex tableau is shown in table *A*.2.

Table *A*.2 Completed third simplex tableau

c_b \ c_j	basis	b_i^*	100 x_1	80 x_2	0 s_1	0 s_2
80	x_2	12	0	1	3/10	−1/5
100	x_1	16	1	0	−1/10	2/5
	z_j	2,560	100	80	14	24
	$c_j - z_j$		0	0	−14	−24

Again notice the similarity between the simplex tableau and the Gauss-Jordan equations.

Analyzing the objective function, in regular form,

$$Z = -14s_1 - 24s_2 + 2{,}560,$$

it can be seen that there is no variable that will increase the value of the objective function. Thus, the optimal solution has been reached.

$$x_1 = 16$$

$$x_2 = 12$$

$$Z = 2{,}560$$

The advantage in employing the simplex procedure is that it is more systematic because it provides distinct steps for each iteration. This, in turn, reduces the chances for error and the necessity of ascertaining the appropriate multiples required to achieve the Gauss-Jordan steps.

Appendix B
Calculus-Based (Classical) Optimization

The essential concept of classical optimization is the slope, or rate of change of a functional relationship. In the analysis of mathematical models of real-world systems decision makers are most often interested in determining the optimal values of one or more decision variables. The mathematical model generally consists of the decision variables and their functional relationship to some other dependent variable, such as total output, total profit, or total cost.

In determining the optimal solution, it is necessary to obtain a general equation of the slope of the mathematical function relating the dependent variable to the decision variables. An intuitive understanding of this requirement can be gained by examining the following problem.

Assume that a production process involving one product and one resource input is to be analyzed. The objective is to maximize the dependent variable, output. The problem is to determine the value of the decision variable, resource input, which will maximize output. The functional relationship of productive output to resource input is illustrated in figure *B*.1.

Figure *B*.1 Optimal resource input and output.

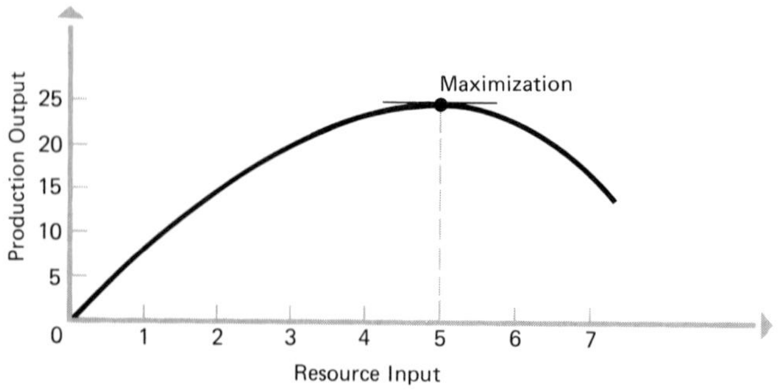

Figure $B.1$ illustrates the standard production function model of economic theory in which productive output increases as resource input increases up to a point, after which diminishing returns are experienced.

Production output is maximized at the point where the curve (the functional relationship of output to input) stops rising and begins to fall. The *slope* of the curve at the point of maximum output is therefore zero. Thus, a general equation of the slope, for all possible values of resource input, would allow us to set the slope equation equal to zero and solve for the input value that maximizes output. This concept is the essence of classical optimization.

Slope of a Function

The slope of a curve or its equivalent, the rate of change of a mathematical function, is the central concept of differential calculus. The slope of a straight line, $y = f(x)$, can be easily determined by selecting any two points along the x axis, such as x_1 and x_2, and calculating the corresponding change in y (called Δy) relative to the change in x (called Δx). If the slope is defined as b and y_1 and y_2 are defined as the two functional values corresponding to x_1 and x_2, respectively, the slope is

$$b = \frac{\Delta y}{\Delta x} = \frac{y_2 - y_1}{x_2 - x_1}.$$

The slope of a straight line is illustrated in figure $B.2$.

Figure B.2 Slope of a straight line.

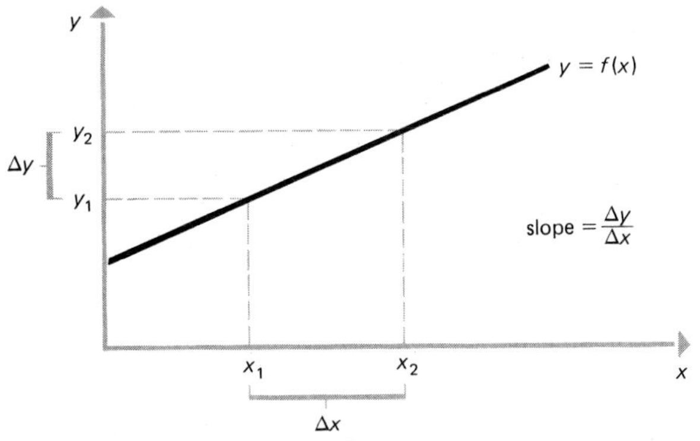

Note the equation at the end of the straight line describing the relationship of y to x in figure $B.2$, $y = f(x)$, which is read as y equals a function of x. In figure $B.2$, $y_1 = f(x_1)$ and $y_2 = f(x_2)$. Also $\Delta y = y_2 - y_1$ and $\Delta x = x_2 - x_1$. Now, if $\Delta x = x_2 - x_1$, then solving for x_2 we have $x_2 = x_1 + \Delta x$. Therefore, since $y_2 = f(x_2)$, it is also $y_2 = f(x_1 + \Delta x)$. The formula for the slope can be written as

$$b = \frac{\Delta y}{\Delta x} = \frac{f(x_1 + \Delta x) - f(x_1)}{\Delta x}.$$

The slope of the straight line, $y = f(x)$, is the same regardless of how small a change occurs in x and Δx. The preceding equation is a general equation for the *average* rate of change in y relative to x. However, if we let Δx approach zero ($\Delta x \to 0$) but never quite equal zero, we obtain the *instantaneous* rate of change in y for a given value of x. This is written as

$$\lim_{\Delta x \to 0} \frac{f(x_1 + \Delta x) - f(x_1)}{\Delta x} = \text{instantaneous rate of change in } f(x) \text{ at } x = x_1.$$

This is very important since the average rate of change for a curved line is not the same as the instantaneous rate of change. And it is the slope of a curve at a given point that is of interest in classical optimization. To determine the slope of a curve at a point, first determine the slope of a straight line tangent to the curve at the point of interest.

Using figure $B.3$ as an example, note that as Δx becomes smaller and smaller ($\Delta x \to 0$), the straight line passing through point P pivots downward until it is tangent to the curve $f(x)$ at point P, which corresponds to x_1. Therefore, the slope of the curved line at x_1 is given by the preceding slope equation for a straight line when Δx is infinitesimally small. It is, for all practical purposes, at the point $x = x_1$.

Figure *B*.3 Slope at a given point.

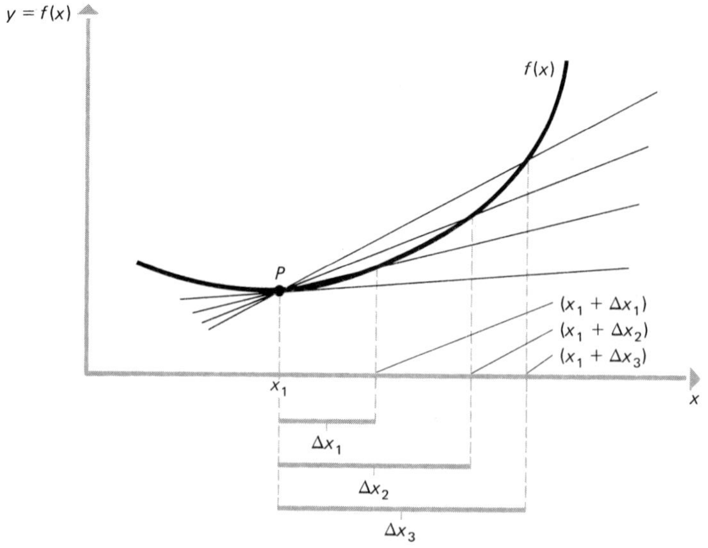

Differentiation

The special kind of formula for slope given in the preceding section is called a **derivative,** and the process of calculating it is called **differentiation.** In general, the derivative of a function, $y = f(x)$, is given as

$$\lim_{\Delta x \to 0} \frac{f(x + \Delta x) - f(x)}{\Delta x} = \text{instantaneous rate of change in } f(x) \text{ for any } x.$$

Again, this process obtains a general equation of the slope of a curve for all points along the curve. The slope at a specific point on the curve is obtained by substituting into the slope equation the specific value of x corresponding to the point of interest on the curve.

Derivatives are denoted by several different symbols. For example, the following symbols all indicate the derivatives of the function $y = f(x)$:

$$y', f'(x), f', \frac{dy}{dx}, \frac{d}{dx}f(x), D_x y, D_x f(x)$$

The symbols most often used in this text to denote derivative are y', $f'(x)$, and dy/dx.

As an example, suppose that the functional relationship of output to input is,

$$y = f(x) = 10x - x^2.$$

The general model for the slope of this equation for any value of x is given by determining the derivative of this function. First note that if $f(x) = 10x - x^2$, then $f(x_1) = 10x_1 - x_1^2$, and, likewise, $f(b) = 10b - b^2$ and $f(x + \Delta x) = 10(x + \Delta x) - (x + \Delta x)^2$. The derivative of the function can be written as

$$\lim_{\Delta x \to 0} \frac{f(x + \Delta x) - f(x)}{\Delta x}$$

$$= \lim_{\Delta x \to 0} \frac{[10(x + \Delta x) - (x + \Delta x)^2] - [10x - x^2]}{\Delta x}$$

$$= \lim_{\Delta x \to 0} \frac{10\Delta x - 2x\Delta x - (\Delta x)^2}{\Delta x}$$

$$= \lim_{\Delta x \to 0} 10 - 2x - \Delta x.$$

Therefore, as $\Delta x \to 0$, you obtain $f'(x) = 10 - 2x$.

Thus, by differentiation the general model for the slope of the function $f(x) = 10x - x^2$ has been obtained. By substituting any value for x, the slope of $f(x)$ at that point can be obtained. For example, for $x = 5$, the point of maximum output is obtained, since the slope equals $10 - 2(5) = 0$.

Rules of Differentiation

Fortunately, rules have been developed for determining the derivative of a function that are considerably easier to use than the approach illustrated in the previous section. The rules do, however, differ depending upon the nature of the function to be differentiated. In the following rules, the derivative is denoted by $f'(x)$.

1. *The derivative of a constant.* If $f(x) = k$, where k is a constant, then $f'(x)$ is

   $$f'(k) = 0.$$

   The derivative of a constant is zero.
2. *The derivative of a variable.* If $f(x) = x$, where x is a variable, then $f'(x)$ is

   $$f'(x) = 1.$$

   The derivative of a variable with respect to itself is 1.
3. *The derivative of a variable raised to a power.* If $f(x) = x^n$, where x is a variable and n is a positive integer, then $f'(x)$ is

   $$f'(x^n) = nx^{n-1} .$$

   The derivative of a variable raised to a positive integer power is the product of the original power times the variable raised to the original power minus one.
4. *The derivative of a constant times a function.* If $f(x) = k \cdot g(x)$, where k is a constant, then $f'(x)$ is

   $$f'[k \cdot g(x)] = k \cdot g'(x) .$$

   The derivative of a constant times a function is equal to the constant times the derivative of the function.
5. *The derivative of the sum (or difference) of two functions.* If $f(x) = g(x) + h(x)$, then $f'(x)$ is

   $$f'[g(x) + h(x)] = g'(x) + h'(x)$$

   and

   $$f'[g(x) - h(x)] = g'(x) - h'(x) .$$

   The derivative of the sum (or difference) of two equations is the sum (or difference) of the derivatives of the two equations.
6. *The derivative of the product of two functions.* If $f(x) = g(x) \cdot h(x)$, then $f'(x)$ is

   $$f'[g(x) \cdot h(x)] = g(x) \cdot h'(x) + h(x) \cdot g'(x) .$$

   The derivative of the product of two functions is the product of the first function times the derivative of the second function plus the second function times the derivative of the first function.

7. *The derivative of the quotient of two functions.* If $f(x) = \dfrac{g(x)}{h(x)}$, then $f'(x)$ is

$$f'\left[\frac{g(x)}{h(x)}\right] = \frac{h(x) \cdot g'(x) - g(x) \cdot h'(x)}{[h(x)]^2}.$$

The derivative of the quotient of two functions is the denominator times the derivative of the numerator minus the numerator times the derivative of the denominator all divided by the denominator squared.

8. *The derivative of a function of a function (a composite function).* In order to demonstrate this method we will also use the notation for a derivative $f'(x) = dy/dx$, where $y = f(x)$.

This rule of differentiation is determined by the **chain rule**, which states that if $y = f[g(x)]$, otherwise stated as $f[u]$ where $u = g(x)$, then $f'[g(x)] = f'[u] \cdot g'(x)$, more commonly given as

$$\frac{dy}{dx} = \frac{dy}{du} \cdot \frac{du}{dx}.$$

The derivative of the composite function $f[g(x)]$ is given by setting $g(x) = u$ and differentiating $f(u)$ with respect to u, and multiplying times the derivative with respect to x of $g(x)$. In other words,

$$\frac{df[g(x)]}{dx} = \frac{d\,f(u)}{du} \cdot \frac{d\,g(x)}{dx}.$$

9. *The derivative of the exponential function.* If $f(x) = e^x$, where e is the base of the natural logarithms $= 2.71828$, then $f'(x)$ is

$$f'(e^x) = e^x$$

The derivative of e^x is itself.

More generally, making use of rule 8, if $f[g(x)] = e^u$, where $u = g(x)$, then

$$f'(e^u) = e^u \cdot \frac{du}{dx}, \text{ or } f'[e^{g(x)}] = e^{g(x)} \cdot g'(x).$$

10. *The derivative of the natural logarithm.* If $f(x) = 1n\, x$, where $1n = \log_e$, then $f'(x)$ is

$$f'(1n\, x) = \frac{1}{x}.$$

The derivative of the natural log of x is $\dfrac{1}{x}$.

More generally, making use of rule 8, if $f[g(x)] = 1n\, u$, where $u = g(x)$, then

$$f'[1n\, u] = \frac{1}{u} \cdot \frac{du}{dx}, \text{ or } f'[1n\, g(x)] = \frac{1}{g(x)} \cdot g'(x).$$

Integration

Thus far, the derivative of $f(x)$, $f'(x)$, has been discussed. However, another useful calculus tool is the **integral** of $f(x)$, which equals the area under a curve defined by $f(x)$. The integral of a function within the range a, b is written as

$$\int_a^b f(x)\,dx.$$

This function reflects the area under the curve in figure B.4.

Figure *B*.4 Integral of $f(x)$.

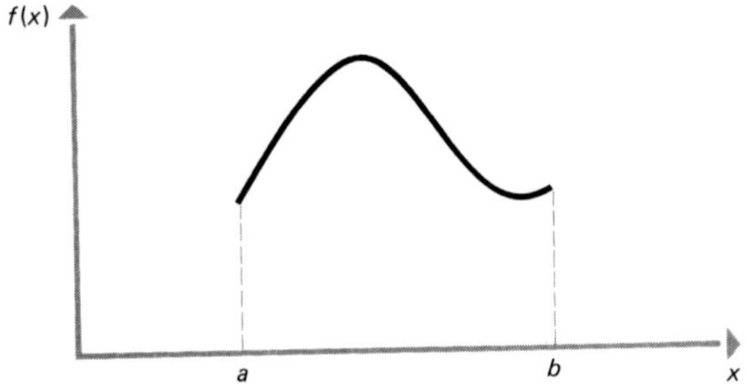

Some of the more commonly used integration formulas (for different functions, $f(x)$) are summarized as follows:

$$\int_a^b dx = x\Big|_a^b = b - a$$

$$\int_a^b k\,dx = kx\Big|_a^b = k(b - a)$$

$$\int_a^b [f(x) + g(x)]\,dx = \int_a^b f(x)\,dx + \int_a^b g(x)\,dx$$

$$\int_a^b kf(x)\,dx = k\int_a^b f(x)\,dx$$

Given that $f(x) = x^n$, the following generalization can be made:

$$\int_a^b x^n dx = \frac{x^{n+1}}{n+1}\Bigg|_a^b = \frac{b^{n+1}}{n+1} - \frac{a^{n+1}}{n+1}$$

Consider the following example distribution contained in figure B.5.

Figure *B*.5 Example of an integral curve.

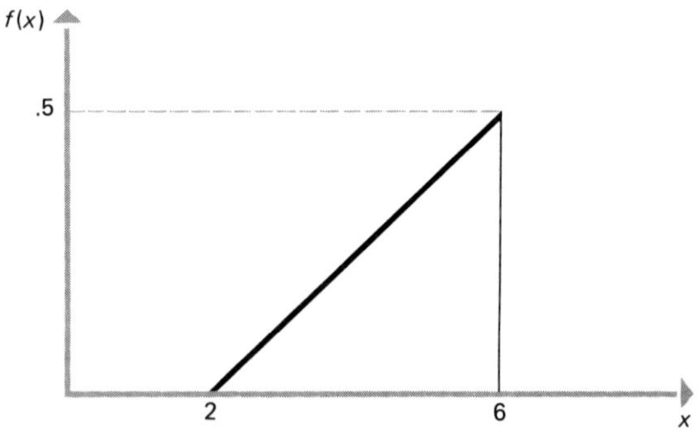

The curve in this figure is defined as

$$f(x) = -\frac{1}{4} + \frac{x}{8}, \quad 2 \leq x \leq 6.$$

Therefore, the integral of $f(x)$ is

$$\begin{aligned} \frac{-1}{4}\int_2^6 dx + \frac{1}{8}\int_2^6 xdx &= \left.\frac{-1x}{4}\right|_2^6 + \left.\frac{x^2}{16}\right|_2^6 \\ &= \left[\left(\frac{-6}{4}\right) - \left(\frac{-2}{4}\right)\right] + \left[\left(\frac{36}{16}\right) - \left(\frac{4}{16}\right)\right] \\ &= 1, \end{aligned}$$

which is the area under the curve, $f(x) = -\frac{1}{4} + \frac{x}{8}$.

Higher Order Derivatives

It has been shown that when a function is differentiated another function is obtained. It is reasonable, therefore, to assume that the equation that is the derivative of the initial function can also be differentiated. For example, when $f(x) = 10x - x^2$ is differentiated we obtain $f'(x) = 10 - 2x$, which is the general model for the slope, or rate of change of $f(x)$. If we differentiate $f'(x)$, we obtain $f''(x) = -2$, which is the rate of change in $f'(x)$ and also the rate of acceleration in $f(x)$. In fact, the process of successive differentiation can be carried out as far as desired as long as there remains some function to differentiate. The successive derivatives of $f(x)$ are denoted by $f'(x)$, $f''(x)$, $f'''(x)$, and so on.

By way of example, consider a high-powered dragster, which contains enough fuel to operate 11 seconds and must travel one quarter mile (1,320 ft.). Assume that the distance traveled, d, from the starting point after t seconds is given by the equation $d = t^3$. Determine the vehicle's speed (velocity) at any point in time after leaving the start line by differentiating $d = t^3$ to obtain the general model for rate of change, which is $d' = 3t^2$. Likewise, the acceleration of the dragster at any point in time after starting is the second derivative of $d = t^3$, which is obtained by differentiating $d' = 3t^2$ to yield $d'' = 6t$.

The distance traveled, the instantaneous speed, and the acceleration after t seconds from the starting point are given in the following table:

Seconds from Start t	Distance Traveled (ft.) $d = t^3$	Speed (ft./sec.) $d' = 3t^2$	Acceleration (ft./sec.^{2}) $d'' = 6t$
1	1	3	6
4	64	48	24
7	343	147	42
10	1,000	300	60
10.97	1,320	361	65.8
11	1,331	363	66

Therefore, just as the vehicle passes the quarter-mile point (very close to 11 seconds after starting), it would be traveling at a speed of about 361 feet per second (or 246 miles per hour) and it would be accelerating at a rate of about 65.8 feet per second (or 44.87 miles per hour).

You will see in the following section that the second derivative is also valuable for determining whether a maximum or a minimum value has been calculated when the slope equation is set equal to zero in solving for the optimal value of the decision variable. For more complex functions, higher derivatives may be used to determine whether a maximum or a minimum value has been found.

Maxima and Minima

At this point in our discussion, we return to some practical aspects of the use of calculus. The purpose of using differential calculus is to determine maximum and minimum values of functions (models). Consider the function illustrated in figure *B*.6.

Figure *B*.6 Maxima and minima.

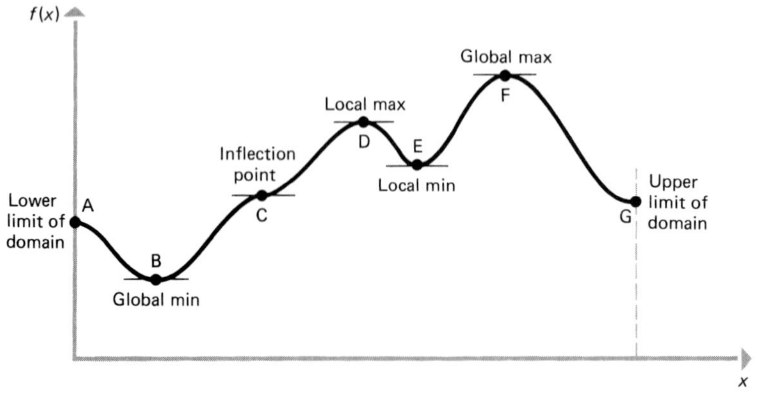

Figure $B.6$ illustrates a function of the variable x. Also illustrated are several new terms. The **domain** is the range of values of x. The value of the function for the lower limit of the domain of x is given as A; whereas the value of the function for the upper limit of the domain of x is given as G. These are sometimes referred to as **endpoints.** The domain limits (or endpoints) fall in a general category called **stationary** or **critical points.**

Some points other than endpoints are also stationary (critical) points. A point (other than an endpoint) on $f(x)$ is considered stationary only if the first derivative of the function is equal to zero at that point. That is, $f'(x) = 0$. All of the points B through F satisfy this condition. Two subsets of the stationary point category are **inflection points** and **extreme points.** Extreme points, or extrema, are further identified as either **local** or **global** extrema. In our analysis it is global extrema (or **absolute** extrema) that are of primary interest. Finally, extrema are either maximum or minimum.

In profit maximization, we would generally attempt to determine the global maximum, whereas in cost minimization the global minimum is of interest. It is important to point out that the global maximum or minimum of a function can be located at the lower or upper limits of the domain of the decision variable. In the illustration, however, this is not the case.

A *necessary condition* for identifying a stationary point, other than an endpoint, is to calculate the first derivative of the function, set the first derivative equation equal to zero, and solve for the unknown (in this case, x). As previously pointed out, this is also a necessary condition for determining the extrema of a function. That is,

$$f'(x) = 0 \quad \text{for } x = x^*,$$

where x^* is defined as a value of x for which we have an extrema. To determine whether we have a relative maximum, a relative minimum, or a point of inflection requires further differentiation. Note that relative maximum (minimum) simply indicates that it may be either a local or a global maximum (minimum).

The following represents a *sufficient condition* for x^* to be a relative *minimum*.

$$f''(x) > 0 \quad \text{at } x = x^*$$

That is, the second derivative evaluated for the value x^* must be greater than zero. Likewise, a sufficient condition for x^* to be a relative maximum is

$$f''(x) < 0 \quad \text{at } x = x^*.$$

That is, the second derivative evaluated for the value x^* must be less than zero.

For the case in which the second derivative is equal to zero, $f''(x) = 0$, it *generally* indicates a point of inflection. However it may be necessary to examine higher derivatives. The general procedure for this case is as follows. Find the value of the lowest order derivative that is *not zero* evaluated at x^*. If the *order* of the lowest order derivative is even, the second order derivative rules apply. If the order of the lowest order derivative is odd, the critical point is an inflection point.

The preceding discussion is summarized in its simplest form in figure $B.7$. (Differentiation will *not* identify these points as extrema; only by comparison with other extrema can they be identified as local or global maximum or minimum.)

Figure *B*.7 Determination of critical points.

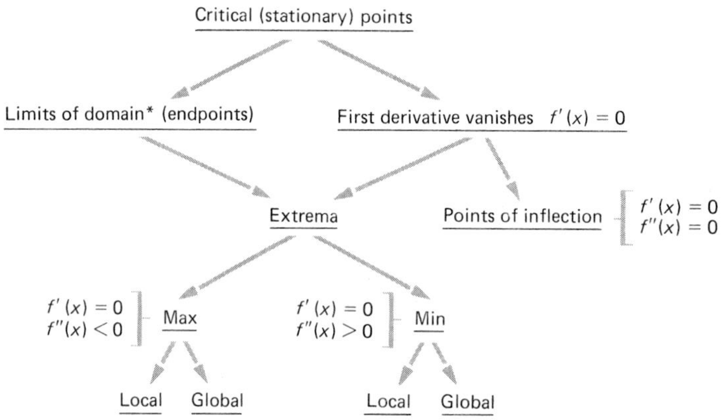

For a function with multiple critical points, it is necessary to compare the value of the function for the various extrema (including the limits of the domain) in order to determine the global (or absolute) maximum and minimum.

In summary, the goal is to determine the absolute (global) maximum and minimum for the function $y = f(x)$ in which the domain of x is given as $a \leq x \leq b$. The hypothetical function is illustrated in figure $B.8$.

Figure *B*.8 Identification of extrema.

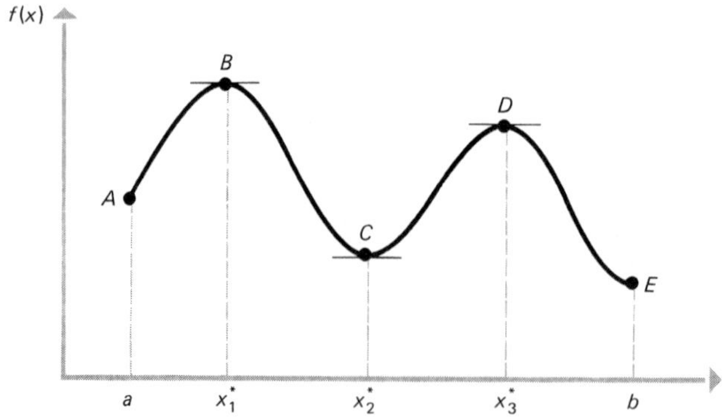

The following is a step-by-step summary of the previous discussion:

1. Necessary Conditions
   a. Calculate the equation for the first derivative. Compute $f'(x)$.
   b. Set the first derivative equation equal to zero. Set $f'(x) = 0$.
   c. Solve the equation of step $1b$ for the value of x^*. Solve $f'(x) = 0$.
2. Sufficient Conditions
   a. Calculate the equation for the second derivative. Compute $f''(x)$.
   b. Solve the equation of step $2a$ for the value of x^* obtained in step $1c$. Solve $f''(x^*)$.
   c. If $f''(x^*)$ is negative, we have a relative maximum at x^*.
      If $f''(x^*)$ is positive, we have a relative minimum at x^*.
      If $f''(x^*)$ is equal to zero, we generally have a point of inflection.
3. Determine Global Maximum and Minimum
   a. Substitute the values of x^* into the original equation. Determine $f(x^*)$. That is, solve for the value of y at $x = x^*$.
   b. Substitute the value of a and b into the original equation. Determine $f(a)$, $f(b)$.
   c. Compare all maxima to determine global maximum.
      Compare all minima to determine global minimum.

For the function illustrated in figure B.8, we obtain three values for x^* in step $1c$ (points B, C, and D on the function). There then are two cases in which step $2c$ yields a negative value and one case in which it yields a positive value—$f''(x_1^*) < 0$, $f''(x_3^*) < 0$, $f''(x_2^*) > 0$. Thus, we have two relative maximums (points B and D) and one relative minimum (point C). By substituting a, x_1^*, x_2^*, x_3^*, and b into $f(x)$ to obtain the values A, B, C, D, and E, we can determine the global maximum and minimum by inspection.

Some further discussion regarding the nature of functions commonly found in business problems is warranted at this point. It is much easier to deal with the problem of determining maximum or minimum values when the functions are either convex or concave. Both types of functions are illustrated in figure B.9.

Figure *B*.9 Convex and concave functions.

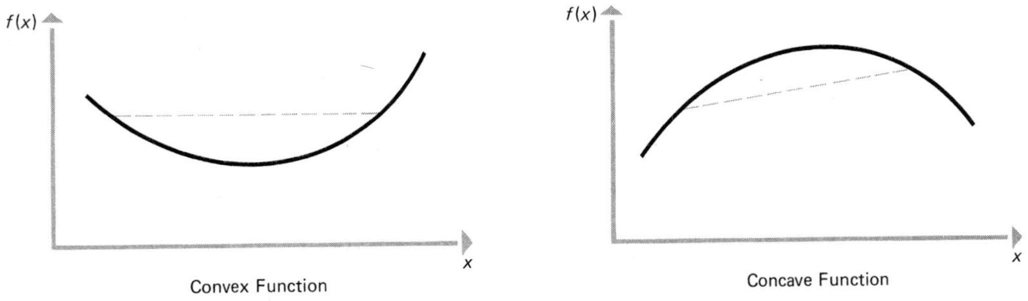

A function is said to be convex if a straight line connecting any two points on that function falls entirely above the function. A function is said to be concave if a straight line connecting any two points on that function falls entirely below the function.

If a convex function exists, the first derivative set equal to zero must yield at least a local minimum. The limit of the domain may still be the absolute minimum. Likewise, if a concave function exists, the first derivative set equal to zero must yield a local maximum.

For many cases in business analysis, the function is assumed to be either concave or convex. Therefore, the most frequently encountered problem involves computing the first derivative, equating it to zero, and solving for the extrema and then computing the second derivative and evaluating for the value of x^* to determine whether the value is a maximum or a minimum. Although the optimal value generally does not occur at a limit of the domain for unconstrained optimization problems, the optimal value for constrained optimization problems is very likely to occur at the intersection of the objective function and a constraint, which is actually the redefined limit of the domain for the function being optimized.

Consider the following example of a profit maximization problem:

$$Z = f(TR, TC)$$
$$= TR - TC$$

where

Z = total profit

TR = total revenue

TC = total cost

Total revenue is a function of price and quantity sold.

$$TR = f(P, Q)$$
$$= P \cdot Q$$

where

P = price

Q = quantity sold

Total cost is assumed to be a function of fixed cost, variable cost, and quantity.

$$TC = f(FC, VC, Q)$$
$$= FC + VC \cdot Q$$

where

FC = fixed cost

VC = variable cost per unit

Q = quantity sold

In addition, quantity sold is assumed to be a function of price (demand function).

$$Q = f(P)$$
$$= a - b \cdot P$$

where

$$P = \text{price}$$
$$a \text{ and } b = \text{parameters of the demand function}$$

Figure B.10 illustrates the demand function.

Figure B.10 Demand function.

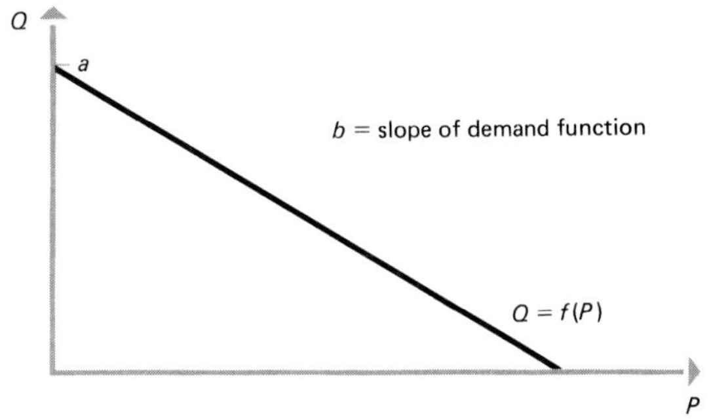

Thus, $a - b \cdot P$ can be substituted back into the total revenue and total cost functions where Q appears, as follows:

$$TR = P \cdot Q$$
$$= P(a - b \cdot P)$$
$$= aP - b \cdot P^2$$
$$TC = FC + VC \cdot Q$$
$$= FC + VC(a - b \cdot P)$$
$$= FC + a \cdot VC - b \cdot P \cdot VC$$

Substituting back into the original profit equation,

$$Z = TR - TC$$
$$= (a \cdot P - b \cdot P^2) - (FC + a \cdot VC - b \cdot P \cdot VC)$$
$$= a \cdot P - b \cdot P^2 - FC - a \cdot VC + b \cdot P \cdot VC.$$

The profit equation is now defined in terms of one decision variable, price. This functional relationship is illustrated in figure $B.11$.

Figure *B*.11 Profit function.

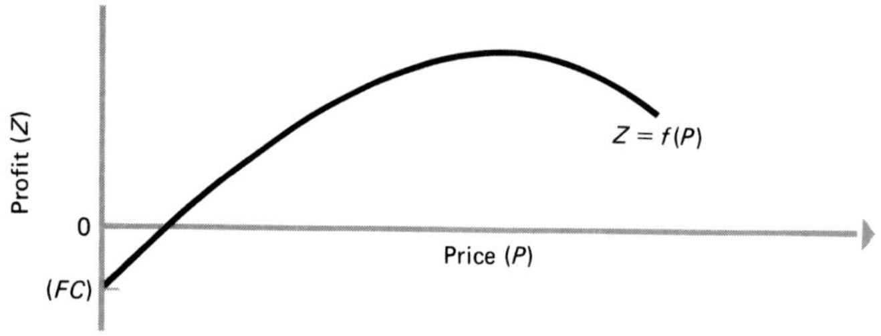

The optimal price to charge can now be determined using calculus, as follows:

First derivative: $\dfrac{dZ}{dP} = a - 2b \cdot P + b \cdot VC$

Set equal to zero: $a - 2b \cdot P + b \cdot VC = 0$

Solve for P: $2b \cdot P = a + b \cdot VC$

$$P = \frac{a + b \cdot VC}{2b}$$

Second derivative: $\dfrac{d^2Z}{dP^2} = -2b$

Therefore, we have a maximum.

The optimal price to charge is $(a + b \cdot VC)/2b$, which maximizes total profit (Z).

Assume the following:

Demand function: $Q = a - bP = 10 - 2P$

Fixed costs: $FC = \$1$

Variable costs: $VC = \$3$ per unit

The model is determined as follows:

$$P = \frac{10 + 2(3)}{2(2)}$$

$P^* = \$4.00$ (where the * denotes the optimum value for P)

Note, the example values could have been used from the beginning, as follows:

$$
\begin{aligned}
Z &= TR - TC \\
&= P \cdot Q - FC - VC \cdot Q \\
&= P(10 - 2 \cdot P) - 1 - 3(10 - 2 \cdot P) \\
&= 10 \cdot P - 2 \cdot P^2 - 1 - 30 + 6 \cdot P \\
&= -2P^2 + 16P - 31 \\
\frac{dZ}{dP} &= -4P + 16
\end{aligned}
$$

$$-4P + 16 = 0$$

$$P^* = 4$$

Note that fixed costs do not affect the answer. It is the *change* in profits relative to *change* in price that is important.

The optimal value for quantity to be sold and the maximum profit can also be determined as

$$
\begin{aligned}
Q &= 10 - 2 \cdot P \\
&= 10 - 2(4) \\
Q^* &= 2 \text{ units} \\
Z &= P \cdot Q - FC - VC \cdot Q \\
&= (4)(2) - 1 - (3)(2) \\
Z^* &= \$1.
\end{aligned}
$$

This process has converted the profit equation from a function of two variables into a function of one variable in order to determine the optimal solution. This, however, is not always possible. The following discussion of partial differentiation addresses itself to this problem.

Partial Differentiation

Thus far, we have considered functions of one variable. That is, the dependent variable is a function of only one independent (or decision) variable, $y = f(x)$. We will now consider functions of more than one independent variable, $y = f(x_1, x_2, \ldots, x_n)$.

For example, presume that total sales of a product is a function of not only price but also of advertising.

$$S = f(P, A)$$

where

S = total sales

P = price

A = advertising

First observe what happens to sales when price varies but advertising is kept at a constant level. Figure *B*.12 illustrates the relationship of sales to price, with advertising held constant.

Figure *B*.12 Relationship of sales to price.

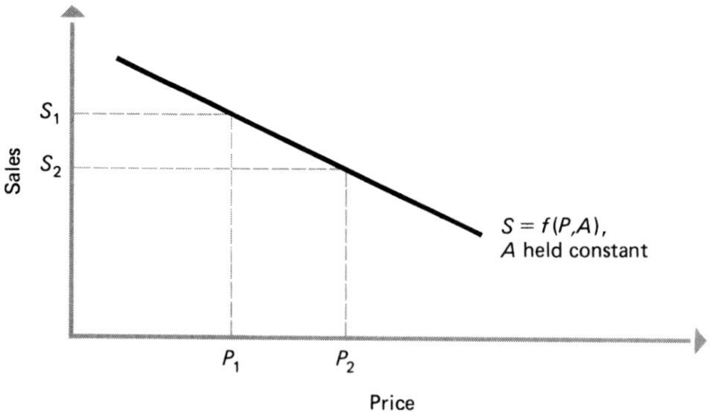

The next step is to hold price constant and observe the behavior of sales as the level of advertising varies. This is illustrated in figure *B*.13.

Figure *B*.13 Relationship of sales to advertising.

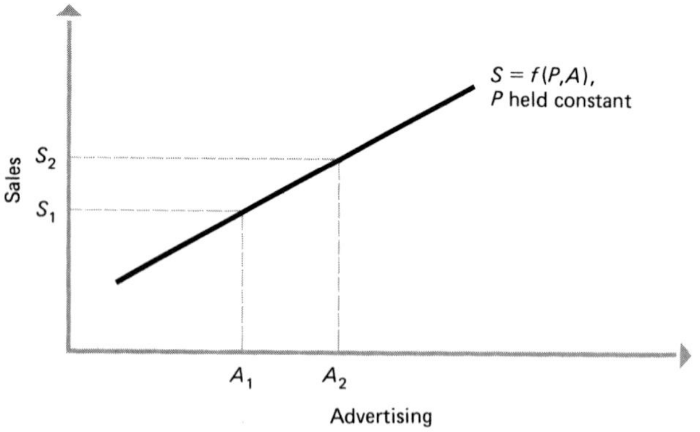

The preceding analysis is illustrated on a three-dimensional graph (fig. *B*.14) to show the simultaneous relationship of sales to price and advertising. Figure *B*.14 illustrates sales as a function of two variables, price and advertising.

Figure B.14 Relationship of sales to price and advertising.

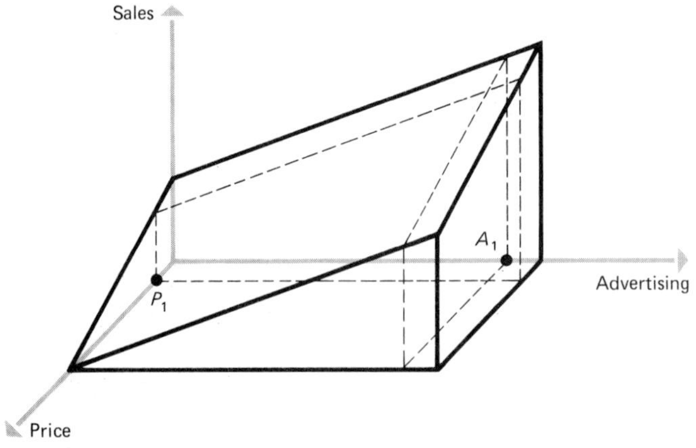

The dotted line connected to P_1 is a two-dimensional plane illustrating the increase in sales as advertising increases for a constant price (P_1). Likewise, the dotted line connected to A_1 is a two-dimensional plane illustrating the decrease in sales as price increases for a constant level of advertising (A_1). It is apparent from figure *B*.14 that maximum sales are obtained at end points of the domain for price and advertising, where price equals zero and advertising equals the maximum amount available. It is also obvious that this is not a profit maximizing model since where price equals zero, revenue is also zero. This does, however, illustrate the analysis of a function of more than one variable.

Recall that if the optimal value for a function is not at an endpoint, the function must be differentiated, set equal to zero, and solved for the optimal value of the independent variable. If there is more than one independent variable, however, **partial differentiation** must be employed. Partial differentiation treats all but one of the independent variables as a constant and then proceeds as in ordinary differentiation. This is analogous to the preceding discussion where advertising was first held constant to observe sales as a function of price and then price was held constant to observe sales as a function of advertising.

Partial derivatives provide a general model of the slope of a function relative to one independent variable at a time. The partial derivative of y with respect to x_1 is given as $\partial y/\partial x_1$. Note that we have simply exchanged the lowercase Greek letter delta (∂) for d in the derivative notation. For a graphical illustration of a similar case, see figure *B*.15.

Figure B.15 Three-dimensional view of $y = f(x_1, x_2)$.

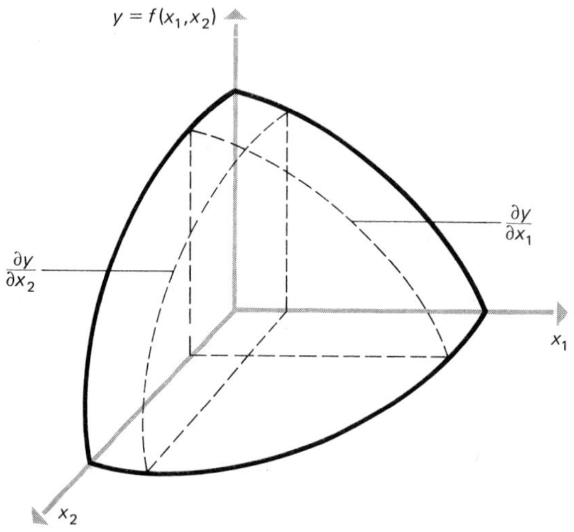

Assume the following equation:

$$y = 2x_1^2 + 3x_2^2 - 8x_1 - 12x_2 + 25$$

The partial derivatives of this equation are

$$\frac{\partial y}{\partial x_1} = 4x_1 - 8$$

$$\frac{\partial y}{\partial x_2} = 6x_2 - 12.$$

In the first case, x_2 is assumed to be a constant. Since the derivative of a constant is 0, the x_2 terms both go to zero. Likewise, in the second case, x_1 is a constant, and it goes to zero when differentiated.

Using the same approach for determining the optimal values of the independent variables as was used previously, set the first derivatives to zero and solve, as follows:

$$4x_1 - 8 = 0$$

$$6x_2 - 12 = 0$$

thus,

$$4x_1 = 8$$

$$x_1^* = 2$$

$$6x_2 = 12$$

$$x_2^* = 2$$

Therefore the optimal value of both x_1 and x_2 is 2. Substituting into the original equation,

$$\begin{aligned} y &= 2x_1^2 + 3x_2^2 - 8x_1 - 12x_2 + 25 \\ &= 2(2)^2 + 3(2)^2 - 8(2) - 12(2) + 25 \\ &= 8 + 12 - 16 - 24 + 25 \\ y^* &= 5. \end{aligned}$$

Now determine whether this value is a relative maximum or a relative minimum. Determine the second partial derivative of each equation with respect to each independent variable, as follows:

$$\frac{\partial^2 y}{\partial x_1^2} = \frac{\partial(4x_1 - 8)}{\partial x_1} = 4$$

$$\frac{\partial^2 y}{\partial x_2^2} = \frac{\partial(6x_2 - 12)}{\partial x_2} = 6$$

Since each of the second partial derivatives is greater than zero, it is probable that the value is a relative minimum (this is consistent with the rules for the single variable case discussed previously). However, one additional test must be performed to insure that it is indeed a relative minimum. The following equation must also be satisfied:

$$\frac{\partial^2 y}{\partial x_1^2} \cdot \frac{\partial^2 y}{\partial x_2^2} - \left[\frac{\partial^2 y}{\partial x_1\, \partial x_2}\right]^2 > 0$$

The term $\partial^2 y/\partial x_1\, \partial x_2$ is called the **cross partial derivative** and is simply the first partial derivative with respect to x_1 and the partial derivative of that answer with respect to x_2.

$$\frac{\partial^2 y}{\partial x_1\, \partial x_2} = \frac{\partial\left[\dfrac{\partial y}{\partial x_1}\right]}{\partial x_2}$$

thus,

$$\frac{\partial y}{\partial x_1} = 4x_1 - 8$$

$$\frac{\partial^2 y}{\partial x_1\, \partial x_2} = \frac{\partial(4x_1 - 8)}{\partial x_2} = 0$$

Remember, you are differentiating $4x_1 - 8$ with respect to x_2. Therefore treat x_1 as a constant and obtain a second partial derivative, with respect to x_2, of zero. Substituting back into the previous equation,

$$\frac{\partial^2 y}{\partial x_1^{\,2}} \cdot \frac{\partial^2 y}{\partial x_2^{\,2}} - \left[\frac{\partial^2 y}{\partial x_1\, \partial x_2}\right]^2$$

$$= 4 \cdot 6 - (0)$$

$$= 24, \text{ which satisfies } > 0.$$

Since the computation satisfies the equation's requirements, we accept the conclusion that the value is a relative minimum.

In summary, for cases involving more than one independent variable, determine the first partial derivative for each of the independent variables, set each equal to zero, and solve simultaneously for the optimal values. In order to determine whether the value obtained is a relative maximum or a relative minimum, the following rules must be satisfied:

Relative Maximum

$$\frac{\partial^2 y}{\partial x_1^{\,2}} < 0, \; \frac{\partial^2 y}{\partial x_2^{\,2}} < 0 \text{ and } \frac{\partial^2 y}{\partial x_1^{\,2}} \cdot \frac{\partial^2 y}{\partial x_2^{\,2}} - \left[\frac{\partial^2 y}{\partial x_1\, \partial x_2}\right]^2 > 0$$

Relative Minimum

$$\frac{\partial^2 y}{\partial x_1^{\,2}} > 0, \; \frac{\partial^2 y}{\partial x_2^{\,2}} > 0 \text{ and } \frac{\partial^2 y}{\partial x_1^{\,2}} \cdot \frac{\partial^2 y}{\partial x_2^{\,2}} - \left[\frac{\partial^2 y}{\partial x_1\, \partial x_2}\right]^2 > 0$$

If $\frac{\partial^2 y}{\partial x_1^{\,2}} \cdot \frac{\partial^2 y}{\partial x_2^{\,2}} - \left[\frac{\partial^2 y}{\partial x_1\, \partial x_2}\right]^2 < 0$, you have what is known as a **saddle point** (neither a max nor a min). It is, for the two independent variable case, analogous to a point of inflection for the one independent variable case. The exploration of this and other possible results are beyond the scope of this appendix.

Consider the following example. Suppose a manufacturer of cars and trucks wishes to determine the optimal quantity of each to produce. The following relationship has been determined.

$$Z = f(TR, TC)$$
$$= TR - TC$$

where

Z = total profit

TR = total revenue

TC = total cost

The revenue function is given as follows:

$$TR = f(P_1, P_2, x_1, x_2)$$
$$= P_1 \cdot x_1 + P_2 \cdot x_2$$

where

P_1 = price for cars

P_2 = price for trucks

x_1 = quantity of cars

x_2 = quantity of trucks

The cost function is given as follows:

$$TC = f(FC, VC_1, VC_2, VC_3, x_1, x_2)$$
$$= FC + VC_1 \cdot x_1 + VC_2 \cdot x_2 + VC_3 \cdot x_1 \cdot x_2$$
$$= 0 + 12 \cdot x_1 + 8 \cdot x_2 + 4x_1 \cdot x_2$$

where

FC = fixed cost

VC_1 = variable cost for cars

VC_2 = variable cost for trucks

VC_3 = variable cost for simultaneous production of cars and trucks

It is assumed that fixed cost equals zero and that there is variable cost associated with simultaneous production of both cars and trucks. The demand functions are given as

$$x_1 = 80/3 - P_1/3$$
$$x_2 = 30 \quad - P_2/2$$

which can be solved for in terms of P_1 and P_2 as

$$P_1 = 80 - 3x_1$$
$$P_2 = 60 - 2x_2.$$

Restating the profit function,

$$Z = TR - TC$$
$$= P_1 \cdot x_1 + P_2 \cdot x_2 - (FC + VC_1 \cdot x_1 + VC_2 \cdot x_2 + VC_3 \cdot x_1 x_2)$$
$$= (80 - 3x_1)x_1 + (60 - x_2)x_2 - (12x_1 + 8x_2 + 4x_1 x_2)$$
$$= 80x_1 - 3x_1^2 + 60x_2 - 2x_2^2 - 12x_1 - 8x_2 - 4x_1 x_2$$
$$Z = 68x_1 - 3x_1^2 + 52x_2 - 2x_2^2 - 4x_1 x_2.$$

Now compute the partial derivatives, set them equal to zero, and solve simultaneously for x_1^* and x_2^*.

$$\frac{\partial Z}{\partial x_1} = 68 - 6x_1 - 4x_2$$

$$\frac{\partial Z}{\partial x_2} = 52 - 4x_2 - 4x_1$$

Remember, in the last term, to first treat x_2 as a constant and differentiate with respect to x_1, as follows:

$$\frac{\partial(-4x_2 \cdot x_1)}{\partial x_1} = -4x_2,$$

where $4x_2$ is treated as a constant. Likewise, in the last term, for the second of the partial derivatives, treat x_1 as a constant and differentiate with respect to x_2, as follows:

$$\frac{\partial(-4x_1 \cdot x_2)}{\partial x_2} = -4x_1$$

In order to set each partial derivative equal to zero and solve for x_1^* and x_2^*, we must solve the two equations (each containing x_1 and x_2) simultaneously, as follows:

$$68 - 6x_1 - 4x_2 = 0$$
$$52 - 4x_2 - 4x_1 = 0,$$

which yields

$$6x_1 + 4x_2 = 68$$
$$4x_1 + 4x_2 = 52.$$

Subtracting the equations,

$$2x_1 = 16$$
$$x_1^* = 8.$$

Substituting back,

$$4(8) + 4x_2 = 52$$
$$4x_2 = 20$$
$$x_2^* = 5.$$

Next, test to insure that you have obtained a maximum for x_1 and x_2, as follows:

$$\frac{\partial^2 Z}{\partial x_1^2} = -6$$

$$\frac{\partial^2 Z}{\partial x_2^2} = -4$$

Since both are negative, it appears that a maximum exists.. Finally, we must satisfy

$$\frac{\partial^2 Z}{\partial x_1^2} \cdot \frac{\partial^2 Z}{\partial x_2^2} - \left(\frac{\partial^2 Z}{\partial x_1 \partial x_2}\right)^2 > 0$$

$$\frac{\partial^2 Z}{\partial x_1 \partial x_2} = \frac{\partial(68 - 6x_1 - 4x_2)}{\partial x_2} = -4$$

therefore,

$$(-6)(-4) - (-4)^2$$
$$= 24 - 16$$
$$= 8, \text{ which satisfies } > 0.$$

Thus, we have determined the optimal quantity of cars and trucks to produce to maximize profits.

$$Z = 68(8) - 3(8)^2 + 52(5) - 2(5)^2 - 4(8)(5)$$
$$= 544 - 192 + 260 - 50 - 160$$
$$Z^* = \$402$$

We did not bother to investigate the end points (limits of the domain for x_1 and x_2). Why? Because if x_1 or x_2 is allowed to go to zero, this obviously reduces profits. And, if x_1 or x_2 is increased to its maximum possible value ($x_1 = 80/3$, $x_2 = 30$, as given by the demand functions), the price must go to zero, which also obviously reduces profits.

Constrained Optimization

Thus far, we have considered only optimization of unconstrained functions. That is, we have given no specific attention to restrictions or limitations on the possible values a decision variable can take on.[1] We now consider the more likely case in which one or more *constraints* (restrictions) must also be satisfied while optimizing

1. This is not completely true since it has been stated that there must be some domain of possible values that x can take on (i.e., $a \leq x \leq b$), which is, in effect, a restriction.

the stated function. The function to be optimized is referred to as the *objective function*. In other words, the objective is to optimize that function subject to other functional constraints. Often the objective function is also referred to as the *criterion function* — the criterion by which the model to be optimized is evaluated. Such a constraint did exist in the profit maximization example in which we assumed quantity demanded was a linear function of price ($Q = a - b \cdot P$).

Objective Function
Profit function:

$$\text{Maximize } Z = TR - TC$$
$$= P \cdot Q - FC - VC \cdot Q$$

Constraining Function
Demand Function:

subject to

$$Q = a - b \cdot P$$

Substituting the demand (constraining) function into the profit (objective) function yields

$$\text{Maximize } Z = P(a - b \cdot P) - FC - VC(a - b \cdot P)$$
$$= a \cdot P - b \cdot P^2 - FC - a \cdot VC + b \cdot P \cdot VC.$$

This process converts a constrained objective function of two independent variables (P,Q) into an unconstrained objective function of one variable. The next step is to apply the techniques of calculus to determine the optimal solution. In those cases where an equality constraint exists, it is often possible to approach the problem in this manner.

However, such models often contain inequality constraints rather than equality constraints. A simple example of an inequality constraint is the nonnegativity restriction. For example,

$$\text{Maximize } y = f(x)$$

subject to

$$x \geqslant 0.$$

The nonnegativity constraint is illustrated in figure B.16. This sort of situation can occur when the first derivative is set equal to zero and solved for x, yielding two solutions for x ($-x^*$, $+x^*$). At this point, simply discard the $-x^*$ as a possible solution since it violates the initially specified constraint ($x \geqslant 0$).

Figure B.16 Nonnegativity constraint.

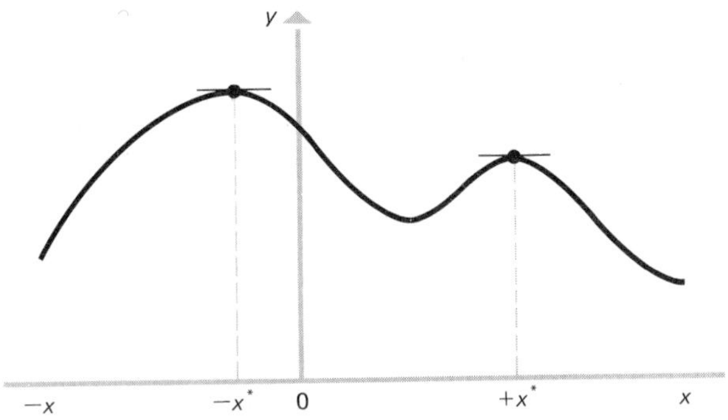

Now return to the initial output maximization example in which you solved for the optimal input in order to maximize output, as follows:

Maximize $y = 10x - x^2$

where

y = output

x = input

First derivative: $y' = 10 - 2x$

Set equal to zero: $10 - 2x = 0$

Solve for x: $x^* = 5$

Now, suppose there is a maximum of six units of input available. The problem becomes

Maximize $y = 10x - x^2$

subject to

$x \leq 6.$

The goal is to maximize the objective function while satisfying the restriction that input is equal to or less than six units. It can be seen from the preceding computations for x^* that the constraint is not violated; therefore, the solution is still $x^* = 5$.

However, consider the following problem:

Maximize $y = 10x - x^2$

subject to

$x \leq 4$

This maximization problem is illustrated graphically in figure B.17.

Figure B.17 Optimal point bound by a constraint.

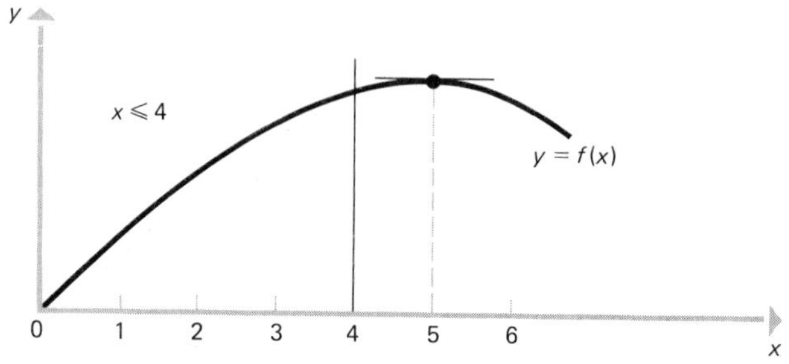

It is now apparent that the optimal solution obtained by the calculus method, which yields $x^* = 5$, is infeasible; that is, it violates the constraint. It is also apparent from the graphical portrayal of the problem that the optimal solution is at the point $x^* = 4$.

Normally you would proceed to solve for the calculus solution as in the unconstrained case and then check to see if it violates the constraint. If the calculus solution ($x^* = 5$) does violate the constraint, check to see if the solution occurs at the boundary created by the constraint. This is analogous to checking the limits of the domain discussed previously. Thus $x^* = 4$ is found to be the optimal solution, yielding $y^* = 24$.

The *region of feasible solution* is defined by the following:

Maximize $y = 10x - x^2$

subject to

$$x \leqslant 4$$

$$x \geqslant 0$$

The shaded region in figure B.18 represents the area of feasible solution.

Figure B.18 Area of feasible solution.

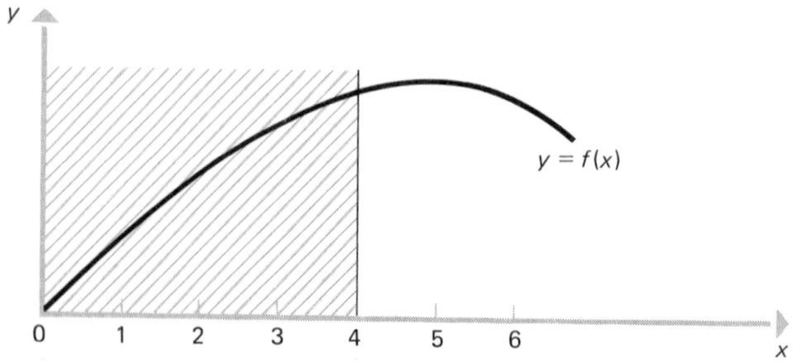

The region of feasible solution points out that when maximizing the function $y = 10x - x^2$, the conditions $0 \leqslant x \leqslant 4$ must also be satisfied. It does not make sense to assume negative input quantities, and the maximum input quantity available is four units. In fact, it is probably illogical to assume zero input; thus, the constrained domain of x is determined to be $0 < x \leqslant 4$ (the value of x does not include zero).

If it is further determined that a minimum of two units of input can be used, up to a maximum of four units, the problem becomes

Maximize $y = 10x - x^2$
subject to

$$x \geqslant 2$$
$$x \leqslant 4.$$

Recall that the solution $x^* = 5$, which was determined by the calculus approach, was discarded because it violated the constraint $x \leqslant 4$. If the feasible solution had not been determined by a graph of the function, the following steps could be performed to arrive at the same feasible solution:

1. Determine the value of y for $x = 2$.

$$y = 10(2) - (2)^2$$
$$y = 16$$

2. Determine the value of y for $x = 4$.

$$y = 10(4) - (4)^2$$
$$y = 24$$

Again the optimal solution is $x^* = 4$, which yields $y^* = 24$.

Now return to the profit optimization example in which we had a function of two independent variables.

$$Z = 68x_1 - 3x_1^2 + 52x_2 - 2x_2^2 - 4x_1x_2$$

The partial derivatives with respect to x_1 and x_2 were determined to be

$$\frac{\partial Z}{\partial x_1} = 68 - 6x_1 - 4x_2$$

$$\frac{\partial Z}{\partial x_2} = 52 - 4x_2 - 4x_1.$$

The partial derivatives were set equal to zero and the two equations were solved simultaneously.

$$68 - 6x_1 - 4x_2 = 0$$
$$52 - 4x_2 - 4x_1 = 0$$
$$x_1^* = 8$$
$$x_2^* = 5$$

Computation of the second order conditions (second derivative tests) yields

$$\frac{\partial^2 Z}{\partial x_1} = -6 < 0$$

$$\frac{\partial^2 Z}{\partial x_2} = -4 < 0$$

$$\frac{\partial^2 Z}{\partial x_2} \cdot \frac{\partial^2 Z}{\partial x_2} - \left(\frac{\partial^2 Z}{\partial x_1 \partial x_2}\right)^2 = 8 > 0.$$

This process insures that a maximum exists for Z at the points $x_1^* = 8$ and $x_2^* = 5$, which yields $Z^* = 402$.

There is generally an implicit assumption that the decision variables are nonnegative ($x_1 \geq 0$, $x_2 \geq 0$). Now assume that x_1 cannot exceed a value of 6. This is specified as follows:

Maximize $Z = 68x_1 - 3x_1^2 + 52x_2 - 2x_2^2 - 4x_1x_2$
subject to
$x_1 \leq 6$

The solution for x_1 can be determined by examining a two-dimensional graph of Z with respect to x_1, as illustrated in figure B.19.

Figure B.19 Profit with respect to x_1.

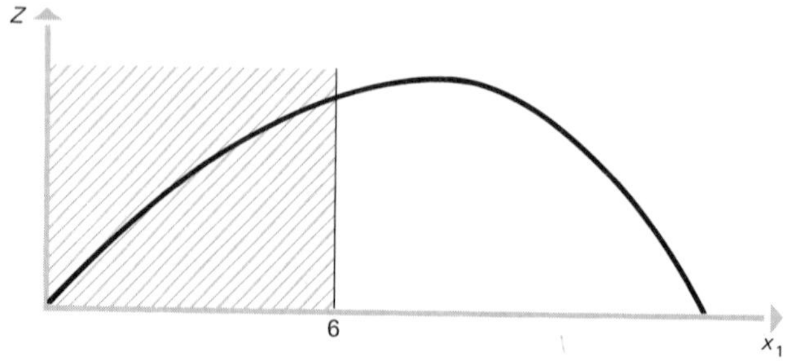

It is apparent that the optimal value of x_1 is 6. But what about x_2? Also examine a two-dimensional graph of Z with respect to x_2, as illustrated in figure B.20.

Figure *B*.20 Profit with respect to x_2.

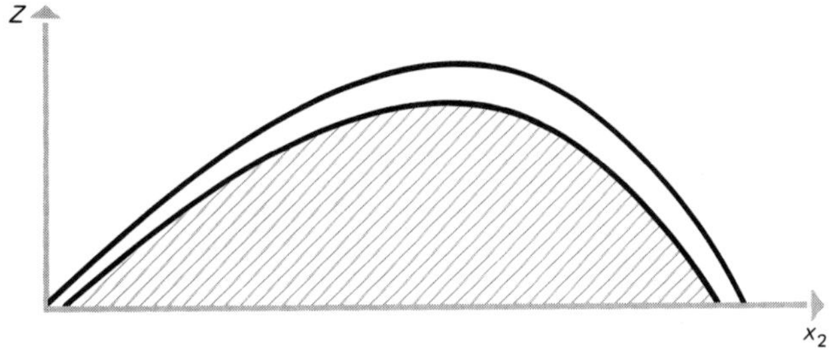

It can be seen that part of the three-dimensional function has been sliced off by the constraint $x_1 \leq 6$. The shaded portion of the two-dimensional curve illustrated in figure B.20 shows the remaining curve that can be optimized with respect to x_2.

If $x_1^* = 6$ is substituted into the original equation,

$$Z = 68(6) - 3(6)^2 - 52x_2 - 2x_2^2 - 4(6)x_2$$
$$= 300 + 28x_2 - 2x_2^2$$

This equation results in an unconstrained function of one variable that can be solved in the usual manner.

$$\frac{\partial Z}{\partial x_2} = 28 - 4x_2 = 0$$
$$28 - 4x_2 = 0$$
$$x_2^* = 7$$

We have arrived at an optimal solution for the constrained problem of $x_1^* = 6$ and $x_2^* = 7$ (as opposed to $x_1^* = 8$ and $x_2^* = 5$ for the unconstrained case). Substituting into the original profit equation, $Z^* = 68(6) - 3(6)^2 + 52(7) - 2(7)^2 - 4(6)(7) = 398$ (as opposed to $Z^* = 402$ previously obtained).

With the aid of graphs, the optimal solution has been determined with relative ease. However, if the objective function and associated constraint are not graphed, it is not apparent whether or not the optimal solution is, in fact, bound by the constraint. For example, consider the following problem:

$$\text{Maximize } Z = 68x_1 - 3x_1^2 + 52x_2 - 2x_2^2 - 4x_1x_2$$

subject to

$$x_1 \leq 9$$

The problem is illustrated graphically in figure B.21.

Figure B.21 Optimal solution bound by a constraint.

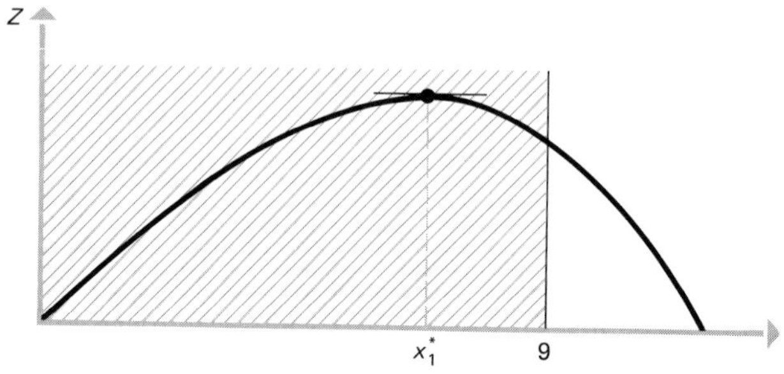

It is apparent from the graph that the constraint $x_1 \leq 9$ does not restrict the peak of the profit function. Thus, mere substitution of the value $x_1^* = 9$ into the equation and solving for x_2^*, as done previously, yields a less-than-optimal solution.

First the unconstrained problem must be solved to determine $x_1^* = 8$ and $x_2^* = 5$, and then observe whether the alternate solution for $x_1^* = 9$ (and x_2^* equals the solution obtained by differentiation) provides a better solution. If it can be assumed that the profit function is concave (which is often the case), it can be seen that if $x_1^* = 8$, then $x_1^* = 9$ is beyond the optimal point. Therefore, $x^* = 9$ is discarded. The only other alternative approach is the graphical approach, which can be tedious or even impossible for more than two independent variables.

Thus, it is seen that investigating the intersection of the objective function and the constraint does not always yield the optimal constrained solution. There is a need for an analytic procedure for determining the optimal value of a function subject to constraints that distinguishes between the cases where the constraint is binding and where it is not binding. The method of Lagrange multipliers is presented as such a technique.

Lagrange Multipliers

The method of Lagrange multipliers enables us to convert an objective function, along with its associated constraints, into a single unconstrained function. The advantage of using this approach is twofold. In the first place, it is often easier to solve a constrained optimization problem using Lagrange multipliers versus the method of substitution previously illustrated. Secondly, the method of Lagrange multipliers yields an additional solution value that determines whether or not the constraint is binding on the solution. That is, the Lagrange multiplier indicates whether the optimal solution is on the boundary formed by the constraint or at some interior point. In any event, the Lagrange multiplier approach yields only a *candidate* for the optimal solution, similar to the calculus solution approach. It must still be insured that the global optimal value is not at some critical point not identified by differentiation (i.e., investigate limits of the domain, such as the case where $x_1 = 0$, $x_2 = 0$, etc.). Figure B.22 illustrates these characteristics.

Figure B.22 Candidates for the global optimal solution.

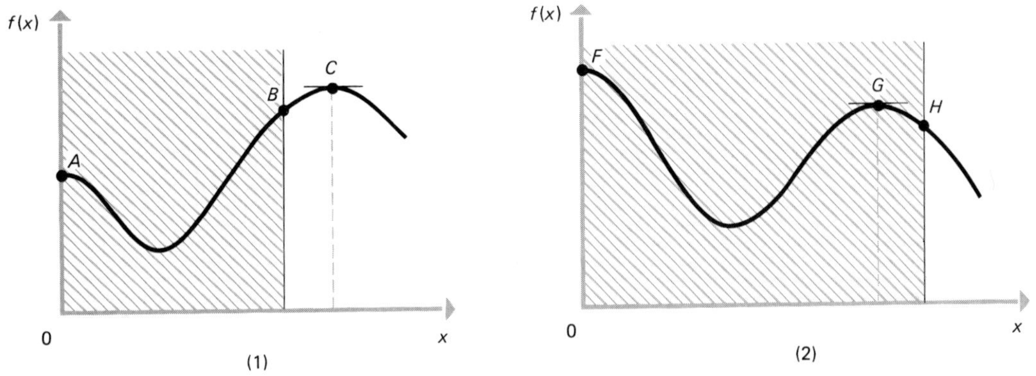

In the first graph, the global optimal solution is obviously bound by the constraint. The Lagrange multiplier approach yields point B as the candidate for the optimal solution, and it also indicates that a better solution could be obtained (point C) if the constraint did not exist. It does *not*, however, insure that point B is better than point A. In the second graph, the Lagrange multiplier approach yields H as the candidate for the (local) optimal solution, but it also indicates that the constraint has no effect on the solution (the solution is not bound by the constraint). We can, therefore, go back and determine the unconstrained optimal value by regular methods of calculus to yield point G. Note, however, that the global optimal value is at point F. Only direct evaluation of the function at its end points (for $x = 0$ in this case) is sufficient to identify the global optimal value here.

The Lagrange multiplier approach for converting the objective function and associated constraints into a single unconstrained function is as follows:

a. Given the problem

$$\text{Maximize } y = f(x_1, x_2)$$

subject to

$$g(x_1) = b.$$

b. Convert $g(x_1) = b$ to $g(x_1) - b = 0$.

c. Convert to Lagrangian form as follows:

$$\text{Maximize } L = f(x_1, x_2) - \lambda \cdot [g(x_1) - b]$$

In this conversion process, the constraint is first equated to zero and then multiplied by a variable, λ, and that product is subtracted from the original objective function. The variable λ is known as the Lagrange multiplier, and it is the solution value of λ that indicates whether or not the solution obtained is bound by the constraint.

Note that $g(x_1) - b = 0$, thus $\lambda \cdot [g(x_1) - b] = 0$, and, therefore, $L = f(x_1, x_2) - 0$, which is the same as the original objective function. If, however, the function $L = f(x_1,x_2) - \lambda \cdot [g(x_1) - b]$ is solved in terms of each of the independent variables, you will have determined a candidate for the optimal solution while satisfying the constraint $g(x_1) = b$.

First consider a problem subject to an equality constraint, as follows:

$$\text{Maximize } y = 5x_1 + 4x_2 + x_1x_2 - x_1^2 - x_2^2 + 10$$

subject to

$$x_1 + x_2 = 5$$

First convert $x_1 + x_2 = 5$ to $x_1 + x_2 - 5 = 0$. The Lagrangian multiplier can then be formulated as

$$\text{Maximize } L = 5x_1 + 4x_2 + x_1x_2 - x_1^2 - x_2^2 + 10 - \lambda(x_1 + x_2 - 5).$$

Next, proceed to calculate the partial derivatives with respect to x_1, x_2, and λ, set them equal to zero, and solve the equations simultaneously.

$$\frac{\partial L}{\partial x_1} = 5 + x_2 - 2x_1 - \lambda = 0 \tag{1}$$

$$\frac{\partial L}{\partial x_2} = 4 + x_1 - 2x_2 - \lambda = 0 \tag{2}$$

$$\frac{\partial L}{\partial \lambda} = -(x_1 + x_2 - 5) = 0 \tag{3}$$

Subtracting equation (2) from equation (1), we get

$$1 - 3x_1 + 3x_2 = 0. \tag{4}$$

Multiplying equation (3) by 3 and subtracting from equation (4),

$$6x_2 = 14.$$

Thus,

$$x_2^* = 2.333.$$

Substituting x_2^* into equation (3), we get

$$x_1^* = 2.667.$$

Substituting x_1^* and x_2^* into equation (1) [or equation (2)] yields

$$\lambda^* = 2.$$

Finally, substitute x_1^* and x_2^* into the original objective function to get

$$y^* = 26.33.$$

The solution is a global optimal value since the equality constraint requires that the sum of x_1 and x_2 *must* equal 5; thus, there is no need to investigate end points.

The interpretation of λ is as follows. If a small amount is added to the right-hand-side of the constraint, $x_1 + x_2 = 5$, to yield $x_1 + x_2 = 5 + \Delta$, the value of the objective function is increased in the optimal solution by the amount $\lambda \cdot \Delta$. For example, if the constraint is changed to $x_1 + x_2 = 6$ (add one unit to the right-hand side), we can expect to increase y^* by 2 to yield $y^* = 26.33 + 2.00 = 28.33$.

Lambda (λ) may be interpreted as the marginal opportunity cost associated with constraining the solution. Note in this case that λ is a *positive* value. This indicates that the optimal solution is constrained from achieving its unconstrained optimal value. If λ were *negative*, this would indicate that the constraint was *beyond* the optimal unconstrained solution. For the case of the equality constraint, however, the optimal solution by definition would still be on the constraint boundary. But, a negative λ would indicate that the solution is beyond the unconstrained optimal point; therefore, there is no point in increasing the right-hand-side value.

The preceding problem is illustrated in figure *B*.23 on a two-dimensional graph in which x_1 and x_2 are the axes. To yield a third dimension, you must visualize another axis (the y axis) coming straight out of the page toward you.

Figure *B*.23 Optimal solution bound by a constraint.

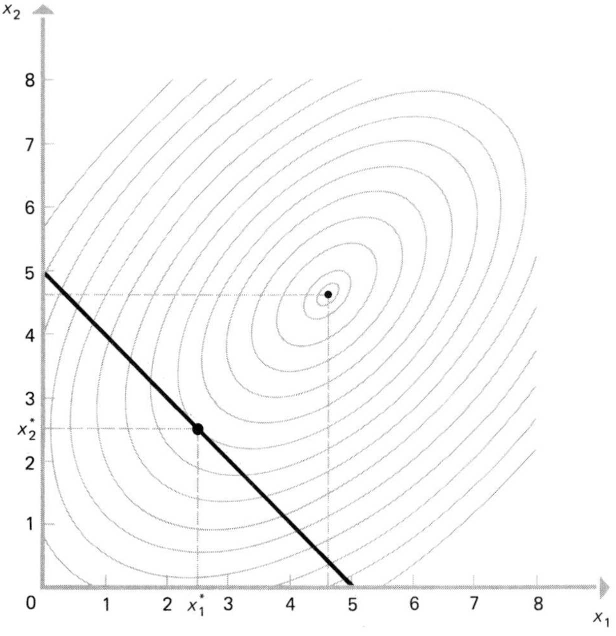

In figure $B.23$, each circular line, known as *contour line* (or trace line), is successively higher (nearer to you) as it approaches the center point. The center point is the peak of the "hill" and represents the unconstrained optimal solution. The constraint $x_1 + x_2 = 5$ is illustrated by the line connecting $x_1 = 5$ and $x_2 = 5$. The point at which the constraint line touches the contour line (of the objective function) is the constrained optimal solution. Note the values of the axes variables, $x_1^* = 2.66$ and $x_2^* = 2.333$. At their point of intersection, the height of the objective function is equal to $y^* = 26.33$.

If the constraint is changed to $x_1 + x_2 = 12$, the constraint line lies beyond the peak. The solution is still on the constraint line since it is an equality constraint, but the value of λ is negative, indicating that the solution cannot be improved by increasing the value on the right-hand-side of the constraint.

Although the Lagrange multiplier method is generally assumed to be used for equality constraints only (for theoretical reasons that are beyond the scope of this chapter); we will illustrate how it can also be used for inequality constraints.

Assume the following problem:

$$\text{Maximize } y = 5x_1 + 4x_2 + x_1x_2 - x_1^2 - x_2^2 + 10$$

subject to

$$x_1 + x_2 \leqslant 5$$

Reviewing figure $B.23$ and the previous calculations, it is apparent that the optimal solution is again the same as before. However, the area of feasible solution, rather than lying on the constraint line, is now the entire triangle enclosed by the constraint and the two axes. The positive value for λ indicates that the solution could be improved if it were not bound by the constraint; thus, the solution is on the boundary line.

Consider the following problem:

$$\text{Maximize } y = 5x_1 + 4x_2 + x_1x_2 - x_1^2 - x_2^2 + 10$$

subject to

$$x_1 + x_2 \leqslant 12$$

This problem defines an area of feasible solution that includes the unconstrained optimal solution, as illustrated in figure $B.24$.

Figure B.24 Optimal solution not bound by a constraint.

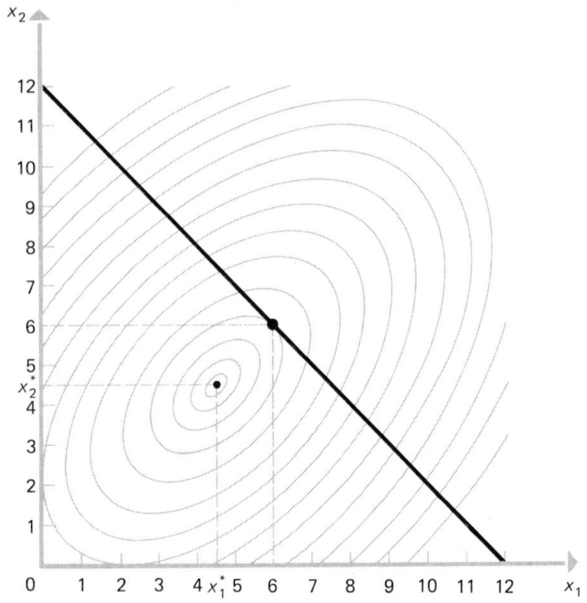

The problem is solved via the Lagrange multiplier approach by simply setting $x_1 + x_2$ equal to 12 and proceeding as before.

$$\text{Maximize } L = 5x_1 + 4x_2 + x_1x_2 - x_1^2 - x_2^2 + 10 - \lambda\,(x_1 + x_2 - 12)$$

$$\frac{\partial L}{\partial x_1} = 5 + x_2 - 2x_1 - \lambda = 0$$

$$\frac{\partial L}{\partial x_2} = 4 + x_1 - 2x_2 - \lambda = 0$$

$$\frac{\partial L}{\partial \lambda} = -(x_1 + x_2 - 12) = 0$$

Solving the equations simultaneously yields

$$x_1^* = 6.167$$
$$x_2^* = 5.833$$
$$y^* = 28.08$$
$$\lambda^* = -1.50.$$

It can be seen from the graph that the global optimal value in the area of the feasible solution is not on the boundary of the constraint. However, by changing the constraint from $x_1 + x_2 \leq 12$ to $x_1 + x_2 = 12$ in the formulation of the Lagrangian function, the solution is restricted to the boundary. However, the *negative* solution value of λ indicates that the solution value is beyond the unconstrained optimal solution. Therefore, return to the original objective function and determine the optimal solution, ignoring the constraint, as follows:

$$\text{Maximize } y = 5x_1 + 4x_2 + x_1x_2 - x_1^2 - x_2^2 + 10$$

$$\frac{\partial y}{\partial x_1} = 5 + x_2 - 2x_1 = 0$$

$$\frac{\partial y}{\partial x_2} = 4 + x_1 - 2x_2 = 0$$

Solving the equations simultaneously yields

$$x_1^* = 4.667$$

$$x_2^* = 4.333$$

$$y^* = 30.33.$$

The value of λ is calculated as zero, indicating that the optimal solution is not bound by the constraint.

In summary, for inequality constraints, proceed as follows:

1. Assume the inequality holds as an equality, and use the Lagrange multiplier approach to determine an initial optimal solution candidate.
2. If λ is positive ($\lambda > 0$), the optimal solution is bound by the constraint and we have a global optimal solution (assuming it is not at an end point).
3. If λ is negative ($\lambda < 0$), the global optimal solution is not bound by the constraint. Return to optimize the objective function, ignoring the constraint.

Take special note of the following. For a maximization problem, if $\lambda > 0$, the constraint binds the solution, and if $\lambda \leq 0$, the optimal solution is an *interior* solution. This refers only to $\leq$ constraints. For $\geq$ constraints, the reverse is true. That is, if $\lambda < 0$, the constraint binds the solution, and if $\lambda \geq 0$, the constraint does not bind the solution. In dealing with a minimization problem, the procedure again reverses itself. If the constraint is $\leq b$ and if $\lambda < 0$, the constraint is binding, and if $\lambda \geq 0$, the constraint is not binding. Finally, for minimization, if the constraint is $\geq b$ and if $\lambda > 0$, constraint is binding, and if $\lambda \leq 0$, constraint is not binding.

This appendix has considered problems involving only one linear constraint of the equality and inequality types. It is also possible to consider objective functions that are subject to more than one linear constraint and/or nonlinear constraints. Refer to chapter 16 for a discussion of such problems.

Appendix C
Probability Theory

This appendix presents a general review of probability theory. It is likely that you have had prior exposure to at least some of this material in previous statistics courses. However, many of the topics covered in the text, such as decision theory and games, queueing, inventory, Markov theory, simulation, and PERT analysis, are based extensively on probability. As such, a review of the basic fundamentals of probability theory will enhance the presentation of the remaining textual material. For those who have had limited exposure to probability and are interested in a more in-depth presentation of some topics, the references at the end of this appendix should be consulted.

Concepts and Definitions

Before proceeding to a general discussion of probability theory, several basic concepts must be defined including experiments, outcomes, sample space, and events.

Sample data is obtained from an **experiment,** which is defined as a predetermined process, the results of which are not known with certainty (i.e., subject to chance). The result of an experiment is referred to as an **outcome.** The number of outcomes of an experiment can vary and be either finite or infinite, depending on the experiment. The set of all possible outcomes of an experiment is known as the **sample space.** Given this definition, an outcome is often referred to as a sample point. An **event** is a subset of outcomes from the sample space.

In order to demonstrate these definitions, consider the experiment of tossing a die. The sample space for this experiment consists of six possible outcomes represented by the six faces of the die—1,2,3,4,5,6. The outcomes of this experiment are both finite and discrete. (*Discrete* refers to the fact that the outcomes are "countable" integers rather than continuous.) One possible event for this experiment is the occurrence of a "5" on a single toss of the die. Another possible event is the occurrence of two outcomes summing to six in two tosses of the die, which would be realized with outcomes of (1,5), (2,4), (3,3), (4,2), or (5,1).

Two or more events are said to be *mutually exclusive* if there is no outcome jointly contained between them. For example, the sample space, S, for tossing a die is

$$S = \{1,2,3,4,5,6\}.$$

If event $A = \{2,3,4\}$ and event $B = \{5,6\}$, then A and B are mutually exclusive events—there is no intersection between them. The notation for this occurrence is

$$A \cap B = \phi.$$

The notation, $\cap$, means that the intersection between A and B is realized; however, in this case it is null (ϕ).

Mutually exclusive events can also be shown pictorially via a **Venn diagram.** Figure C.1 shows Venn diagrams for A and B in mutually exclusive and nonmutually exclusive conditions.

Figure C.1 (*A*) Venn diagram for mutually exclusive events. (*B*) Venn diagram for nonmutually exclusive events.

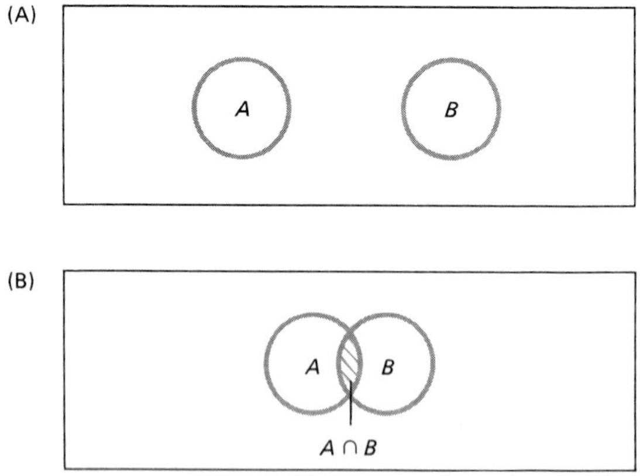

Alternatively, the notation $A \cup B$ signifies that event A or B or both occur. This is referred to as a **union** of two events, which, in turn, produces the event $E = A \cup B$. If event A or B occurs, then event E also occurs. Figure C.2 is a Venn diagram of the union of two events.

Figure C.2 Venn diagram for the union of two events.

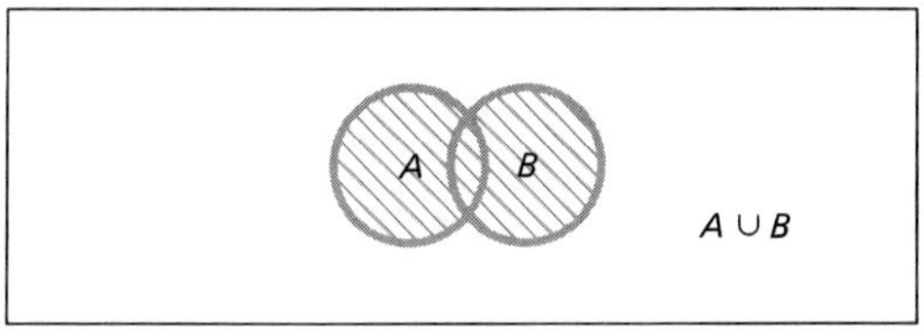

Two events are said to be mutually exclusive and *exhaustive* if they do not intersect but do take up the entire sample space. For example, in the die tossing experiment if event $A = \{1,2,3\}$ and $B = \{4,5,6\}$ then A and B are mutually exclusive and exhaustive (i.e., the two events have no common sample point and they take up the entire sample space). The notation for this condition is

$$A \cap B = \phi$$

$$A \cup B = S.$$

The intersection of A and B is nonexistent and the union of A and B is the sample space, S. Figure C.3 is a Venn diagram showing mutually exclusive and exhaustive events.

Figure C.3 Venn diagram for mutually exclusive and exhaustive events.

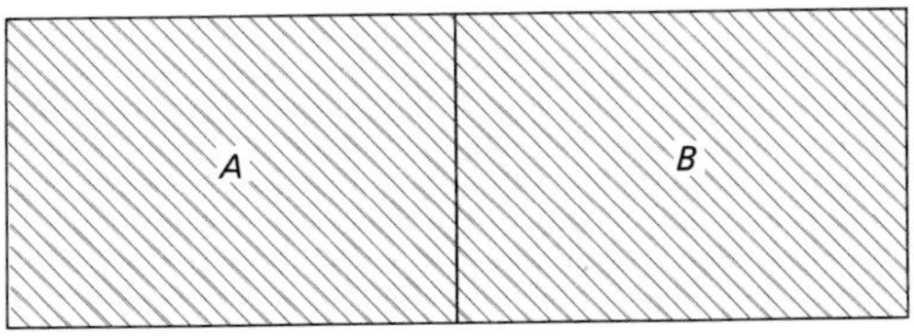

The Elements of Probability

Probability is a term that is part of the normal vocabulary of nearly everyone, and, it is employed so frequently that everyone has at least a general notion of what it means. A theoretical definition of probability is more difficult to develop.

The most commonly recognized definition of probability is that it is the frequency with which an event occurs out of a number of trials of an experiment.

More specifically, this is known as an *objective probability*. In probabilistic notation, the probability of an event A is $P(A)$, where $P(A)$ is equal to the number of outcomes, n, of the event A divided by the total number of trials of an experiment, N.

$$P(A) = \lim_{N \to \infty} n/N$$

However, probabilities are often assigned to events that are not conducive to experimentation. For example, when a meteorologist states that there is an 80% chance of rain, a sportscaster quotes odds on a football game, or a businessperson states that there is a 60% chance of closing a deal, a number of trials of an experiment have not been conducted to develop these probabilities. Rather, *subjective probabilities* have been employed. A subjective probability is not related to the measured frequency with which an event has occurred, but the assumed likelihood of an event occurring. The subjective probability estimate can be based on past experience or knowledge about circumstances surrounding the event or the event itself.

Regardless of the strict definition of probability (or the lack of one), certain principles can be stated about probabilities. These principles or "laws" of probability are described as follows:

1. The probability of each event in the sample space occurring is positive or zero.

   $$P(A) \geq 0$$

2. The sum of the probabilities of all possible outcomes in the sample space is 1. For sample space S,

   $$P(S) = 1.0.$$

   For example, in the die experiment, the sample space consists of six outcomes, $S = \{1,2,3,4,5,6\}$. The probability of each outcome is 1/6; thus,

   $$P(S) = 1/6 + 1/6 + 1/6 + 1/6 + 1/6 + 1/6 = 1.0.$$

3. The probability of a null set is zero.

   $$P(\phi) = 0$$

4. The probability of an event, A, is equal to the sum of the probabilities of the outcomes belonging to event A. If $O_{i \to n}$ are the outcomes in event A, then

   $$P(A) = P(O_1) + P(O_2) + \ldots + P(O_n).$$

   For example, in the die tossing experiment, if event $A = \{1,5\}$ and $P(1) = 1/6$ and $P(5) = 1/6$, then $P(A) = 1/6 + 1/6 = 2/3$.

5. The probability of a union between events $(A \cup B)$ is equal to

$$P(A \cup B) = P(A) + P(B) - P(A \cap B).$$

This is known as the *addition law* of probability. In the die tossing experiment, if $A = \{1,2,3\}$ and $B = \{3,4\}$, then $P(A) = 1/2$ and $P(B) = 1/3$. The probability of the intersection of A and B is the probability of 3 as an outcome, $P(A \cap B) = P(3)$. However, by simply summing events A and B the probability of a 3 is added twice; thus, it must be subtracted out.

$$\begin{aligned} P(A \cup B) &= 1/2 + 1/3 - 1/6 \\ &= 2/3 \end{aligned}$$

6. If A and B are mutually exclusive events, then $P(A \cap B) = 0$. The addition law becomes

$$P(A \cup B) = P(A) + P(B).$$

For example, in the die experiment if $A = \{1,5\}$ and $B = \{2\}$, then $P(A \cup B) = 1/3 + 1/6 = 1/2$.

7. The *conditional probability* law denotes the probability of event A given the occurrence of event B. The conditional probability has the notation $P(A|B)$ and is defined as

$$P(A|B) = \frac{P(A \cap B)}{P(B)}.$$

The concept of conditional probabilities is based on the notion that if information is obtained about one event following its occurrence, it will alter the likelihood of a second event in the experiment. In other words, $P(A|B)$ is the altered (or new) probability of A given information gained from the occurrence of B.

For example, consider three production plants, A, B, and C. It is known that plant A produces 2% defective items; plant B, 1% defective items; and plant C, 3% defective items. Thus, the conditional probability, $P(D|A) = .02$, is the probability of a defective item given the item came from plant A.

8. Given the formula for the conditional probability, $P(A|B)$, the following manipulation can be made regarding $P(A \cap B)$:

$$P(A \cap B) = P(A|B)P(B)$$

This is known as the *multiplicative law of probability*.

9. If the probability of A is not affected by the occurrence of B (i.e., they are not related), then A and B are said to be *independent*. If two events, A and B, are independent, the conditional probability is

$$P(A|B) = P(A)$$

and the multiplicative law becomes

$$P(A \cap B) = P(A)P(B).$$

As an example of independence, consider an experiment where one card is selected from a deck of fifty-two cards and replaced. If event A is defined as drawing a club and event B is defined as drawing an ace, then

$$P(A) = 13/52 = 1/4$$

$$P(B) = 4/52 = 1/13.$$

The probability of drawing both an ace and a club is the probability of drawing just one card—the ace of clubs,

$$P(A \cap B) = 1/52.$$

From the conditional probability law,

$$P(A|B) = \frac{P(A \cap B)}{P(B)}$$

$$P(A|B) = \frac{1/52}{1/13} = 1/4$$

Now, since

$$P(A) = 1/4 = P(A|B),$$

the events are independent. In other words, the event B, selecting an ace, does not affect event A, selecting a club.

Bayes' Theorem

In the die tossing experiment, the probability of each outcome in the sample space, $S = \{1,2,3,4,5,6\}$, is 1/6. This probability is referred to as a *prior probability* since it is known prior to conducting the experiment and, thus, before any information is obtained from the experiment. *Posterior probabilities,* on the other hand, are conditional probabilities, based on new information obtained from performing trials of an experiment. As such, posterior probabilities are a means of revising prior probabilities to reflect new information. The formula for determining the posterior probability (i.e., revising prior probabilities) is known as Bayes' theorem (or law) and is given by

$$P(A_i|O) = \frac{P(A_i)P(O|A_i)}{\sum_{i=1}^{n} P(A_i)P(O|A_i)}$$

where

A_i = a set of n mutually exclusive and exhaustive events

O = an outcome of an experiment

$P(A_i)$ = the prior probability for event i

$P(O|A_i)$ = the conditional probability of outcome, O, given the occurrence of A_i.

Note that $P(O|A_i)$ conforms to a conditional probability as previously defined. While $P(A_i|O)$ is also conditional, it reverses the sequence of events.

The following example demonstrates the application of Bayes' theorem. A company produces a product in three production plants. Plant A produces 20% of the product, plant B produces 50%, and plant C produces 30%. At each plant a different percentage of the output is defective. Plant A produces 2% defective products; plant B, 1%; and plant C, 3%. Given that one unit of product selected from a day's production is defective, it is desired to know the probability that it came from plant B.

The prior and conditional probabilities for this situation are

$$P(A) = .20 \qquad P(D|A) = .02$$
$$P(B) = .50 \qquad P(D|B) = .01$$
$$P(C) = .30 \qquad P(D|C) = .03.$$

Given these probabilities, the problem is to determine the posterior probability that a defective unit came from plant B, $P(B|D)$. Applying Bayes' theorem,

$$P(B|D) = \frac{P(B)P(D|B)}{P(A)P(D|A) + P(B)P(D|B) + P(C)P(D|C)}$$
$$= \frac{(.50)(.01)}{(.20)(.02) + (.50)(.01) + (.30)(.03)}$$
$$= \frac{.005}{.018}$$
$$P(B|D) = .278.$$

Bayes' theorem introduces an important concept in probability theory—the fact that additional information can alter prior probabilities. In fact, Bayes' theorem is the basis for a rather complex field of study known as Bayesian decision analysis. As such, the complex topic of Bayesian analysis is treated lightly in this appendix.

Random Variables

A function that associates outcomes of an experiment to real numbers is a *random variable*. For example, in the die tossing experiment, the set of outcomes is {1,2,3,4,5,6}. If the experiment is defined as observing the number of 2s that come up in four tosses, the results of the experiment take on the numerical values, 0, 1, 2, 3, or 4. While these values are not events, they do correspond to events. If X is defined as a random variable representing the number of 2s that will occur in four tosses of a die, then X will equal 0, 1, 2, 3, or 4. Now suppose the four tosses are made and one 2 occurs, then $X = 1$.

The term *random variable* is derived from the fact that a variable, X, can take on different values selected by a random process (i.e., the particular value that X assumes is a random occurrence). In probabilistic notation, $P(x)$ is the probability that the random variable, X, will equal some value (denoted by the lower case x).

Two types of random variables exist, continuous and discrete. A discrete random variable takes on only specific, integer number values in its range, while a continuous random variable can take on *all* real values in its range (i.e., an infinite number of possible values). For example, in the die tossing experiment, the random variables are discrete since the outcomes (the die faces) are countable integers. However, measures such as time or weight are continuous random variables.

Probability Distributions

Discrete Distribution

If X is a discrete random variable, the assignment of probabilities to each value of x that can occur is referred to as a discrete probability distribution. The probability that X (the random variable) will take on a particular value, x, is known as a *probability distribution* and is defined by

$$p(x) = P(X=x).$$

For the die tossing experiment, the probability that the face value will be 2 is 1/6, or

$$p(2) = P(X=2) = 1/6.$$

The entire probability distribution for this experiment is given in the following table:

	X					
	1	2	3	4	5	6
p(x)	1/6	1/6	1/6	1/6	1/6	1/6

The graphical representation of this distribution is shown in figure C.4.

Figure C.4 Discrete distribution.

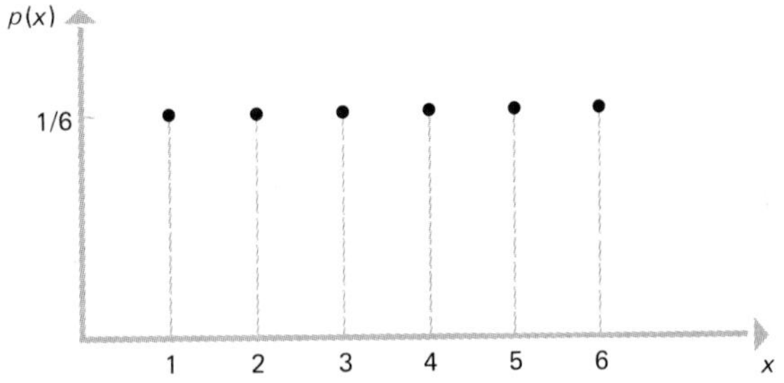

The probability distribution for a discrete random variable must also satisfy the following conditions. First, all probabilities of the random variable are positive or zero.

$$0 \leq p(x) \leq 1.0, \qquad -\infty < x < \infty$$

Second, the sum of all probabilities for the random variable must sum to 1.0.

$$\Sigma p(x) = 1.0$$

Both of these conditions are reflected in the die tossing experiment and can be easily verified.

An alternative measure of probability is the *cumulative distribution,* which is the probability that the random variable X has a value less than or equal to x. The cumulative distribution has the notation, $F(x)$, and is defined as

$$F(x) = P(X \leq x).$$

For example, in the die experiment, suppose it is desired to determine the probability that the face value will be 3 or less. The cumulative probability is

$$F(3) = P(X \leq 3) = P(X = 1) + P(X = 2) + P(X = 3)$$
$$P(X \leq 3) = 1/6 + 1/6 + 1/6$$
$$P(X \leq 3) = 1/2.$$

Graphically, the cumulative distribution for $P(X \leq 3)$ is a step function, which is shown in figure C.5.

Figure C.5 Cumulative distribution.

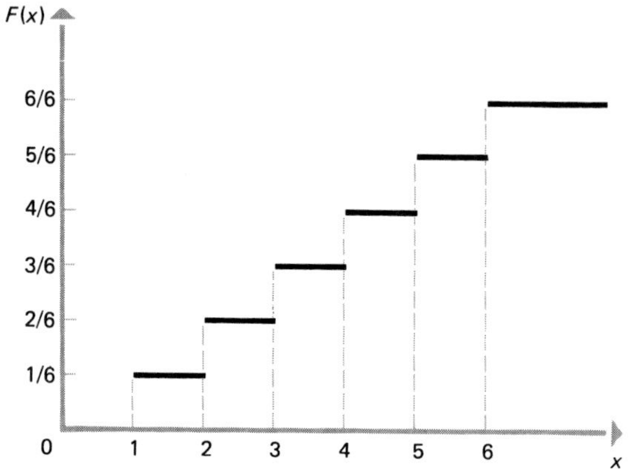

A third probability measure is the *complementary distribution function, G(x)*, which is defined as

$$G(x) = 1 - F(x)$$

or

$$G(x) = 1 - P(X \leq x)$$
$$G(x) = P(X > x).$$

The complementary distribution defines the probability that the random variable X is greater than some value x. For the die experiment, the probability that the face value will be greater than 4 is

$$G(4) = P(X > 4) = P(X = 5) + P(X = 6)$$
$$P(X > 4) = 1/6 + 1/6$$
$$P(X > 4) = 1/3.$$

Also, since

$$G(x) = 1 - F(x),$$
$$1/3 = 1 - F(x)$$
$$F(x) = 2/3.$$

To illustrate these alternative measures of the discrete probability distribution, consider the following example. A store owner has determined the demand for a product as 0, 1, 2, 3, or 4 units per day. Based on prior sales the probability of each value, 0, 1, 2, 3, 4, for the random variable, demand, is 0.10, 0.20, 0.10,

0.30, and 0.30, respectively. The probability distribution for demand, the cumulative distribution, and the complementary distribution are computed in the following table:

Demand x	Probability Distribution $p(x)$	Cumulative Distribution $F(x)=P(X\leq x)$	Complementary Distribution $G(x)=P(X>x)$
0	0.10	0.10	0.90
1	0.20	0.30	0.70
2	0.10	0.40	0.60
3	0.30	0.70	0.30
4	0.30	1.00	0.00
	1.00		

Continuous Distribution

The probability distribution for a continuous random variable is somewhat different than for a discrete random variable since a continuous random variable is not finite within its range (i.e., an infinite number of real values exist in the defined range of a continuous random variable). As such, a prior probability cannot be assigned to any one distinct value of the random variable since there are an infinite number of values likely to occur. Alternatively, continuous probabilities must be mapped across the range of the random variable according to a function.

For a continuous random variable, X, probabilities are defined according to a function, $f(x)$, referred to as the *probability density function.* It must meet the following conditions:

$$0 \leq f(x) \leq 1.0, \quad -\infty < x < \infty$$

$$\int_{-\infty}^{\infty} f(x)\, dx = 1.0$$

The first condition indicates that the probability of any value of the random variable must be nonnegative. The second condition shows that the sum of the probability of the sample space defined by $f(x)$ equals 1.0. Notice that this second condition is accomplished by integrating $f(x)$, which computes the area under the curve mapped by $f(x)$. As such, for a probability density function, the area under the curve must be 1.0.

For example, suppose a production manager has determined that a machine breakdown will occur sometime between 0 and 4 years. The probability density function of the time of a breakdown has been defined as

$$f(x) = \frac{x}{8}, \quad 0 \leq x \leq 4.$$

Figure C.6 is a graphical representation of this function. Notice that $f(x)$ is defined such that $\int_0^4 f(x)\, dx = 1.0$.

Figure C.6 Probability density function.

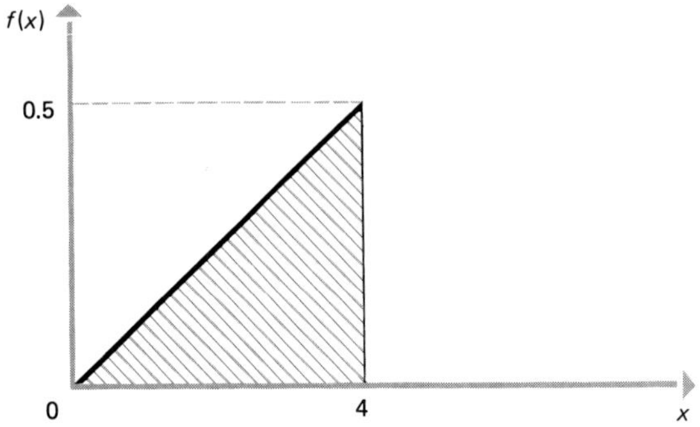

The *cumulative density function* for a continuous random variable is also extremely useful. Recall that for a discrete probability distribution the cumulative distribution is defined as

$$F(x) = P(X \leqslant x) = \sum_{x} P(x).$$

For the continuous density function, $f(x)$, this relationship translates to

$$F(x) = \int_{-\infty}^{x} f(x)\,dx.$$

This is a logical extension since integrating $f(x)$ within a defined range determines the sum of the area under the curve mapped by $f(x)$. This is demonstrated in figure $C.7$.

Figure C.7 Cumulative density function for a continuous random variable.

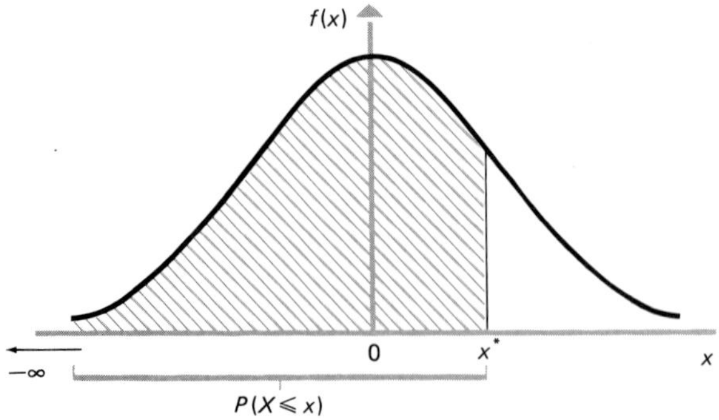

Integrating the function $f(x)$ in the defined range determines the area under the curve up to x, which corresponds to the probability that the random variable X is less than or equal to x.

$$F(x) = P(X \leq x) = \int_{-\infty}^{x} f(x)\, dx.$$

Recalling the machine breakdown example, the probability that the time of a machine breakdown is less than or equal to x years is

$$F(x) = \int_{o}^{x} \frac{x}{8}\, dx.$$

Integrating $f(x)$,

$$F(x) = \frac{x^2}{16},\ 0 \leq x \leq 4.$$

The graph of this cumulative density function is shown in figure $C.8$.

Figure C.8 Cumulative density function.

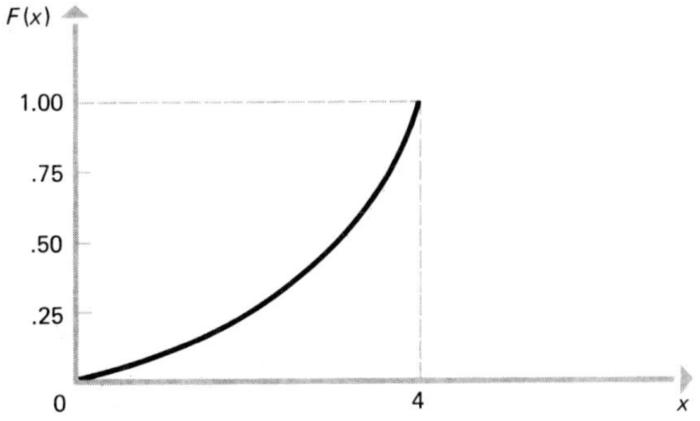

In the machine breakdown example, if the manager desires to know the probability that a breakdown will occur in three years or less the following computation is performed:

$$F(x) = P(X \leq 3) = \int_{o}^{3} \frac{x}{8}\, dx$$

$$= \frac{x^2}{16}\Bigg|_0^3$$

$$= .56$$

If the probability that X is greater than x is desired (i.e., the complementary density function), then

$$G(x) = 1 - F(x).$$

For this example, the probability that the time of a breakdown is greater than three years is

$$G(x) = 1 - F(x) = 1 - \frac{x^2}{16}$$

or

$$G(x) = 1 - .56 = .44.$$

The cumulative density function also enables the computation of another important probability measure, the probability that x is in the interval (a,b).

$$P(a \leqslant x \leqslant b) = \int_a^b f(x)\, dx$$

This probability is shown on the graph of the breakdown example in figure C.9.

Figure C.9 Probability of x occurring in the interval (a,b).

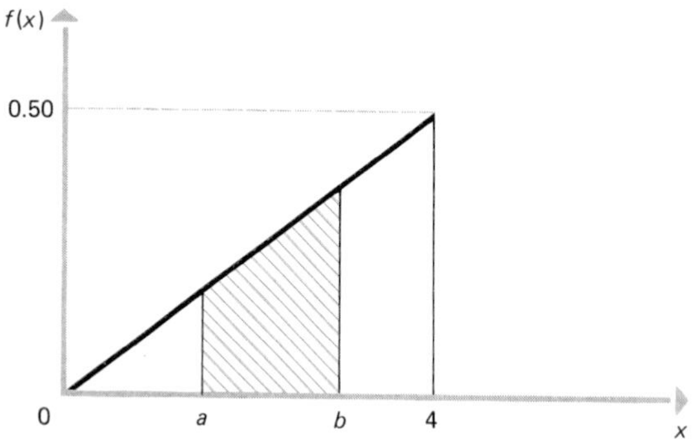

From figure C.9 it can be observed that the determination of $P(a \leqslant x \leqslant b)$ is the same as computing $F(b) - F(a)$, where

$$F(a) = \int_0^a f(x)\, dx$$

$$F(b) = \int_0^b f(x)\, dx.$$

By subtracting the area in the interval $(0,a)$ from the area $(0,b)$, the remaining area is in the interval (a,b), which yields

$$P(a \leqslant x \leqslant b) = F(b) - F(a).$$

Expected Value of a Random Variable

One of the most useful measures for describing a probability distribution is the *expected value* (alternatively referred to as the weighted average of the distribution, the *mean*, and the *first moment* of the distribution). The expected value, $E(X)$, of a discrete random variable, X, is defined by

$$E(X) = \sum_x xp(x).$$

The expected value of a continuous random variable is defined as

$$E(X) = \int_x xf(x)\,dx.$$

Expected value is demonstrated in the following product demand example, which was also employed in the section on discrete distributions. Demand alternatives and probabilities are shown in the following table:

Demand x	$p(x)$
0	0.10
1	0.20
2	0.10
3	0.30
4	0.30

The expected value of demand, x, is computed as

$$\begin{aligned} E(X) &= (0)(0.10) + (1)(0.20) + (2)(0.10) + (3)(0.30) + (4)(0.30) \\ &= 0 + 0.2 + 0.2 + 0.9 + 1.2 \\ E(X) &= 2.5. \end{aligned}$$

This value is the weighted average of the x values shown in the table.

As an example of the expected value for a continuous random variable, consider the following density function:

$$f(x) = \frac{x}{3},\ 0 \leq x \leq 3$$

The expected value is computed as

$$\int_0^3 \frac{x}{3}\,dx = \frac{x^2}{6}\bigg|_0^3 = 9/6 - 0 = 1.5.$$

Expectation has a number of useful properties, which are summarized as follows:

1. $E(a) = a$, where a is a constant. For example, if $a = 4$, $E(4) = 4$.
2. $E(aX) = aE(X)$. If $a = 3$, then $E(3X) = 3E(X)$.
3. $E(X + a) = E(X) + a$. For example, $E(X + 2) = E(X) + 2$.
4. $E(X + Y) = E(X) + E(Y)$, where X and Y are two random variables (i.e., the expected value of a sum is the sum of the expected values).
5. $E(XY) = E(X)E(Y)$, if X and Y are independent random variables.

Variance and Standard Deviation

The variance of a random number, X, is a measure of the dispersion or spread of X. The variance for a discrete random variable is defined as

$$V(X) = E(X^2) - [E(X)]^2.$$

In other words, the variance is the weighted average of the deviations from the expected values, squared. The square root of the variance is the standard deviation.

For a continuous random variable the variance is defined as

$$V(X) = \int_x [X - E(X)]^2 f(x)\, dx.$$

However, the variance can also be defined as

$$V(X) = \int_x x^2 f(x)\, dx - [E(X)]^2$$

and

$$V(X) = E(X^2) - [E(X)]^2,$$

which is the same function defined for a discrete random variable.

Again consider the product demand example. The following table summarizes the computation of the variance and standard deviation.

x	x^2	$f(x)$	$xf(x)$	$x^2f(x)$
0	0	0.10	0.0	0.0
1	1	0.20	0.2	0.2
2	4	0.10	0.2	2.4
3	9	0.30	0.9	2.7
4	16	0.30	1.2	4.8
			$E(X) = 2.5$	$E(X)^2 = 8.1$

$$V(X) = 8.10 - (2.5)^2$$
$$V(X) = 8.10 - 6.85$$
$$V(X) = 1.25$$
$$\text{Standard deviation} = \sqrt{1.25}$$
$$= 1.8$$

The variance of an expected value has the following properties:

1. $V(aX) = a^2V(X)$, where a is a constant.
2. $V(X + b) = V(X)$.
3. $V(X + Y) = V(X) + V(Y)$, where X and Y are independent random variables.
4. $V(X + Y) = V(X) + V(Y) + 2\text{Cov}(X,Y)$, where X and Y are dependent random variables.

Some additional properties can be defined for dependent random variables. For two random variables, X and Y, the *covariance* is a measure of the degree of dependence between X and Y. Covariance is defined as

$$\text{Cov}(X,Y) = E([X - E(X)][Y - E(Y)])$$
$$= E(XY) - E(X)E(Y).$$

Recall from the discussion of the properties of expectation that for independent random variables, X and Y,

$$E(XY) = E(X)E(Y).$$

Thus, the covariance is zero for independent random variables. However, if the covariance is computed to be zero, it does not always hold that X and Y are independent.

An additional measure of the dependence between two random variables, X and Y, that can be computed from the variance is the correlation coefficient, ρ, defined as

$$\rho = \frac{\text{Cov}(X,Y)}{\sqrt{V(X)V(Y)}}.$$

Discrete Probability Distributions

A number of well-known distributions are available and are used extensively in stochastic management science techniques, such as queueing, inventory control, and simulation. In this section, some of the more prominent discrete distributions will be briefly reviewed. These will be followed by a review of some of the more well-known continuous distributions.

Discrete Uniform Distribution

Recall that in the die tossing experiment there were six possible outcomes, $s = \{1,2,3,4,5,6\}$, each with an equal likelihood of occurrence. Thus, the probability of each outcome was 1/6. This is an example of a *discrete uniform distribution*, which has the following general form:

$$p(x) = \frac{1}{n}, \quad x = 1, 2 \ldots n,$$

where n is the number of outcomes in the sample space. In other words, for any possible value of the discrete random variable X between 1 and n, the probability of the outcome, x, is the same, $1/n$.

The expected value and variance are defined as

$$E(X) = \frac{n}{2}$$

$$V(X) = \frac{n^2 - 1}{12}.$$

Binomial Distribution

In the examples employed thus far, only experiments in which each trial has more than two possible outcomes have been considered. However, in a *binomial* experiment, each trial can have only two outcomes. For example, if in the die tossing experiment, the six outcomes are divided into two events, A and B, where $A = \{1,2,3\}$ and $B = \{4,5,6\}$, it would be a binomial experiment. Likewise, tossing a coin has two outcomes, heads or tails, which qualifies it as a binomial experiment. A binomial experiment has the following properties:

1. The experiment consists of n trials.
2. Each trial results in one of two possible outcomes, success or failure.
3. The probability of a successful outcome, p, is the same for each trial. The probability of failure is $1 - p = q$.
4. The trials are independent.

The trials in an experiment that satisfy these properties are referred to as *Bernoulli trials*. As an example of Bernoulli trials (and the binomial properties), consider an experiment where a coin is tossed ten times. The experiment consists of ten Bernoulli trials, in which each trial has two outcomes, heads (i.e., success) and tails (i.e., failure). The probability of success is 1/2 for each of the ten trials (i.e., $p = 1/2$) and the probability of a failure is $1 - p = q = 1/2$. The trials are obviously independent.

For an experiment with n independent Bernoulli trials, each with a probability of success, p, and, probability of failure, q, the probability that the experiment will result in exactly x successes and $n - x$ failures is

$$p(x) = \binom{n}{x} p^x q^{n-x}, \text{ where } q = 1-p.$$

The term $\binom{n}{x}$ is a permutation that computes the number of successes, x, in n trials and $\binom{n}{x} = \frac{n!}{x!(n-x)!}$. The terms n and p are constant parameters, while x is a random variable. The probability of an outcome having x successes and $n - x$ failures is given by $p^x(1 - p)^{n-x}$ (or, $p^x q^{n-x}$).

The expected value or mean number of successes for a binomial experiment consisting of n trials is defined as

$$E(X) = np.$$

The variance of x is

$$V(X) = npq.$$

The following example demonstrates the binomial distribution. A quality control process calls for sampling large lots of a product as they come off the production line. If the lots are known to contain 10% defective items, what is the probability of getting two defective items out of ten items drawn from a lot?

In this experiment, drawing a defective item is a success, and the probability of a success is 10% (i.e., $p = 0.10$). Thus, for ten trials,

$$p(2) = \binom{10}{2}(0.10)^2(0.90)^8$$

$$p(2) = .387.$$

If the experiment is altered to reject the lot if two or more defects are found, the probability of acceptance is

$$\begin{aligned} p(x \leqslant 1) &= p(0) + p(1) \\ &= \binom{10}{0}(0.10)^0(0.90)^{10} + \binom{10}{1}(0.10)^1(0.90)^9 \\ &= .736. \end{aligned}$$

Thus, the probability of rejection is

$$\begin{aligned} p(x \geqslant 2) &= 1 - p(x \leqslant 1) \\ &= 1 - .736 \\ &= .264. \end{aligned}$$

Tables exist that give probabilities for specific parameter values, as is the case with almost all probability distributions (discrete and continuous).

Poisson Distribution

If, in the binomial experiment, p is extremely small and n very large, the binomial distribution can be approximated by the *poisson distribution*. The properties of the poisson distribution are the same as those of the binomial distribution. The poisson distribution is given by

$$p(x) = \frac{\lambda^x e^{-\lambda}}{x!}$$

where

x = a discrete random variable

$\lambda = np$ = the expected value or mean

$e = 2.718.$

Since p is very small, it is close to 0; thus, as p approaches 0, q approaches 1. The variance is defined as

$$\begin{aligned} V(X) &= npq \\ &= np(1) \\ V(X) &= np. \end{aligned}$$

The poisson distribution is useful because of the fact that binomial tables are not generally available for $n > 100$; however, many business applications exist for experiments with $n > 100$.

The poisson distribution is also useful in problems where the number of events occurring in a time period are being counted. As such, it is used in queueing models to represent the arrivals of customers to a service facility, λ_t, where λ is the rate at which arrivals occur and t is the length of the period.

Consider the following example. Automobiles arrive at a bank teller's window at random times but at an average rate of fifteen customers per hour. It is desired to know the probability that twenty-five cars will arrive at the facility in an hour. Since an hour is a continuous parameter, it contains an infinite number of time increments, n. Since there are an infinite number of arrival times, n, the probability that any one time will occur is extremely small. Thus, λ represents the average arrival rate, $\lambda = np = 15$. As such,

$$P(x = 25) = \frac{(15)^{25} e^{-15}}{25!} = .005.$$

Continuous Probability Distributions

Continuous Uniform Distribution

The continuous uniform distribution is analagous to the discrete case in that the outcomes of an experiment are equally likely to occur. However, since the distribution defines a continuous random variable, there are an infinite number of values in the range of the distribution; thus, the probability of any one value is zero. As such, the distribution is defined as

$$f(x) = \frac{1}{b-a}, \quad a \leqslant x \leqslant b.$$

The expected value of the distribution (the mean) is

$$E(x) = \frac{a + b}{2}.$$

The variance is

$$V(x) = \frac{(b-a)^2}{12}.$$

For example, consider a uniform distribution over the range (0,10). The probability density function is

$$f(x) = \frac{1}{10}, \quad 0 \leqslant x \leqslant 10.$$

It is worthwhile to point out that the cumulative density function is the integral of $f(x)$.

$$F(x) = \int_0^x \frac{1}{10}\,dx = \frac{x}{10}, \quad 0 \leqslant x \leqslant 10$$

The probability density function and the cumulative density function for this example are shown in figure $C.10$.

Figure C.10 Cumulative density function.

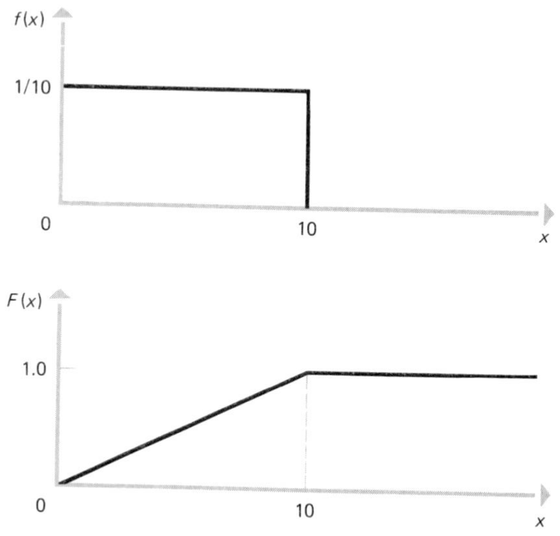

Normal Distribution

As the number of trials, n, of a binomial experiment increases, the binomial distribution becomes a continuous and symmetric bell-shaped curve known as the *normal distribution*. The probability density function of the normal distribution is

$$f(x) = \frac{e^{-(x-\mu)^2/2\sigma^2}}{\sigma\sqrt{2\pi}},$$

where, μ and σ^2, the mean and variance of the random variable x, determine the shape of the distribution.

The normal distribution has the following properties:

1. $f(x)$ is a continuous curve.
2. It is symmetrical about the dependent axis as shown in figure $C.11$.

Figure C.11 Normal distribution curve.

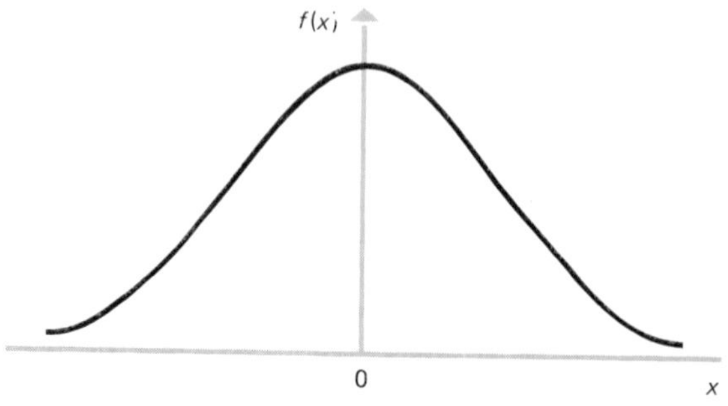

3. The total probability area under the curve is 1.0.
4. The probability of a single point occurring is zero. Therefore, only the probability of a single point falling within a range can be determined.

The normal distribution is the most important continuous distribution primarily because it approximates the probability distributions of a number of physical phenomena in the real world. For example, diameters of machine parts are approximately normally distributed. Also, regardless of the shape of the original population, the sampling distribution of means of a fixed sample size approaches a normal shape as the size of the sample increases. This extremely important property is known as the *central limit theorem,* which states that if random samples of size n are drawn from a population with mean, μ, and standard deviation, σ, then when n is large, the sample mean $\bar{x}$ will be approximately normally distributed with mean, μ, and standard deviation, $\sigma/\sqrt{n}$. As n increases, the approximation becomes more accurate.

This enables us to convert a normally distributed random variable, X, to a standard normal variable, Z, for specific values of x, as

$$Z = \frac{x - \mu}{\sigma}.$$

Thus, for any values, μ and σ, the value of Z will determine the area under the normal curve (i.e., the distance in standard normal units for $\mu = 0$ to Z). Z values are listed in standard normal tables in conjunction with their associated probabilities.

Consider the following example. The life expectancy of a machine part is normally distributed with a mean of 200 days and a standard deviation of 30 days. The purchaser of these parts wants to know the probability that a part will last longer than 250 days. Figure C.12 presents a schematic of the problem. The shaded area represents the desired probability.

Figure C.12 Example of a normal distribution.

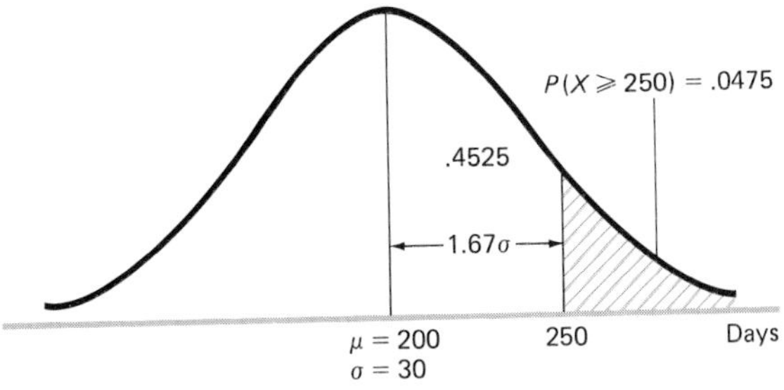

To find the solution, the value of Z is computed.

$$Z = \frac{x - \mu}{\sigma}$$
$$= \frac{250 - 200}{30}$$
$$= 1.67$$

By looking at a standard normal table (see table $D.3$), the Z value of 1.67 is seen to correspond to a probability of .95254. However, this is not the desired probability but rather the probability that the life expectancy is equal to or less than 250 days. Since the area under the normal curve is 1.0 (which is also the probability) and since the normal curve is symmetrical, the area desired is

$$P(x > 250) = 1.0 - P(x \leq 250)$$
$$= 1.0 - .95254$$
$$= .04746.$$

Now suppose the purchaser wants to know the probability of a part having a life expectancy between 175 and 240 days. This probability corresponds to the sum of the two areas shown as A_1 and A_2 in figure $C.13$.

Figure C.13 Sum of two areas in a normal distribution.

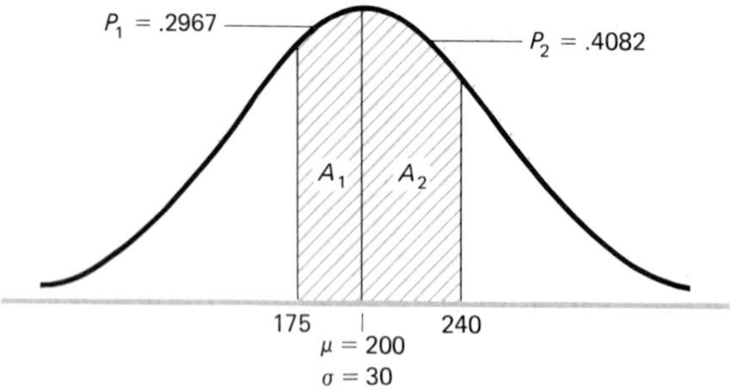

For area A_2, the Z value is

$$Z = \frac{240 - 200}{30} = 1.33,$$

and the corresponding probability for $Z = 1.33$, in table D.3, is .9082. Thus, the A_2 area is given by $P(x \leq 240) - P(x \leq 200) = P(Z \leq 1.33) - P(Z \leq 0.0) = .9082 - .5000 = .4082$ (shown as P_2 in fig. C.13).

For area A_1, the Z value is $(175-200)/30 = .83$ (disregarding the negative sign since the normal curve is symmetric), and the A_1 area is similarly computed to be .2967 (shown as P_1 in fig. C.13).

Thus, the solution is

$$P(175 \leq x \leq 240) = P_1 + P_2$$
$$= .2967 + .4082$$
$$= .7049.$$

Exponential Distribution

The *exponential distribution* (also known as the negative exponential distribution) is employed extensively in queueing theory to describe random variables that reflect durations or waiting times. The probability density function for the exponential distribution is

$$f(x) = \lambda e^{-\lambda x},$$

where x is values of a continuous random variable and λ is a predetermined parameter.

The probability density function for the exponential distribution has the form shown in figure $C.14$.

Figure C.14 Exponential distribution.

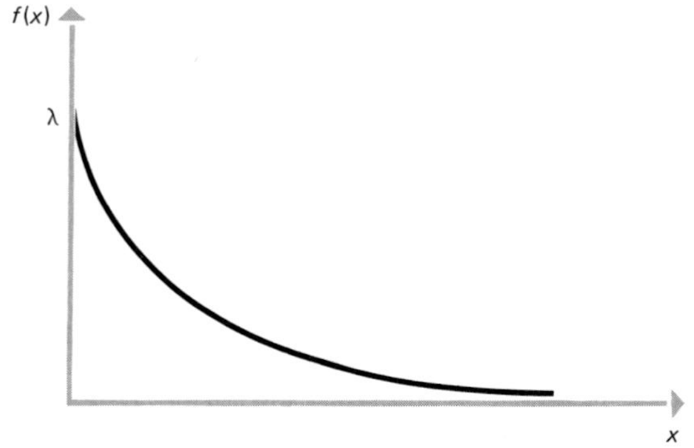

The cumulative density function is also widely used and has the following form:

$$F(x) = 1 - e^{-\lambda x}$$

The expected value and variance of the exponential distribution is

$$E(X) = \frac{1}{\lambda}$$

$$V(X) = \frac{1}{\lambda^2}.$$

As an example of the exponential distribution and its similarity to the poisson distribution, consider the bank teller situation described for the poisson distribution. In that example, an average of fifteen customers per hour arrive at the teller's window. After one customer arrives, the next customer will arrive, on the average, in 1/15th of an hour. The probability that after one customer arrives it will take longer than x minutes for the next one to arrive is expressed by the exponential distribution.

For the poisson distribution, the number of customers arriving at the teller's window is a random variable and the time frame is a fixed parameter. Alternatively, in the exponential distribution, the number of successes is equal to one and the time frame is a continuous random variable.

Other Continuous Distributions

The *Erlang distribution,* a generalization of the exponential distribution, is employed extensively in queueing theory to measure service times. The probability density function of the Erlang distribution is

$$f(x) = \frac{\lambda^r x^{r-1} e^{-\lambda x}}{(r-1)!}.$$

Notice that when $r = 1$ this function becomes the exponential density function.

The *gamma distribution* is a generalization of the Erlang distribution (for cases where r is not an integer). The *chi-square* (χ^2) *distribution* is a special case of the gamma distribution that is used for testing statistical hypotheses relating to frequencies and validity.

Another important distribution used extensively in management science is the *beta distribution*. The beta distribution describes random variables whose values lie in a range (a,b). As such, it is employed in PERT (project scheduling) to describe activity time durations when only a range (or interval) of times can be subjectively determined. This distribution is illustrated in chapter 6.

References

Chou, Y. *Statistical Analysis*. 2d ed. New York: Holt, Rinehart and Winston, 1975.

Cramer, H. *The Elements of Probability Theory and Some of Its Applications*. New York: John Wiley & Sons, 1955.

Dixon, W. J., and Massey, F. J. *Introduction to Statistical Analysis*. 3d ed. New York: McGraw-Hill, 1969.

Hays, W. L., and Winkler, R. L. *Statistics: Probability, Inference, and Decision*. New York: Holt, Rinehart and Winston, 1970.

Mendenhall, W., and Reinmuth, J. E. *Statistics for Management and Economics*. 2d ed. North Scituate, Massachusetts: Duxbury Press, 1974.

Neter, J.; Wasserman, W.; and Whitmore, G. A. *Fundamental Statistics for Business and Economics*. 4th ed. Boston: Allyn & Bacon, 1973.

Sasaki, K. *Statistics for Modern Business Decision Making*. Belmont, Calif.: Wadsworth Publishing Co., 1969.

Spurr, W. A., and Bonini, C. P. *Statistical Analysis for Business Decisions*. Homewood, Ill.: Richard D. Irwin, 1973.

Appendix D
Tables

Table *D*.1 Poisson probability values

	λ									
r	0.10	0.20	0.30	0.40	0.50	0.60	0.70	0.80	0.90	1.00
0	.9048	.8187	.7408	.6703	.6066	.5488	.4966	.4493	.4066	.3679
1	.0905	.1637	.2222	.2681	.3033	.3293	.3476	.3595	.3659	.3679
2	.0045	.0164	.0333	.0536	.0758	.0988	.1217	.1438	.1647	.1839
3	.0002	.0011	.0033	.0072	.0126	.0198	.0284	.0383	.0494	.0613
4	.0000	.0001	.0003	.0007	.0016	.0030	.0050	.0077	.0111	.0153
5	.0000	.0000	.0000	.0001	.0002	.0004	.0007	.0012	.0020	.0031
6	.0000	.0000	.0000	.0000	.0000	.0000	.0001	.0002	.0003	.0005
7	.0000	.0000	.0000	.0000	.0000	.0000	.0000	.0000	.0000	.0001

	λ									
r	1.10	1.20	1.30	1.40	1.50	1.60	1.70	1.80	1.90	2.00
0	.3329	.3012	.2725	.2466	.2231	.2019	.1827	.1653	.1496	.1353
1	.3662	.3614	.3543	.3452	.3347	.3230	.3106	.2975	.2842	.2707
2	.2014	.2169	.2303	.2417	.2510	.2584	.2640	.2678	.2700	.2707
3	.0738	.0867	.0998	.1128	.1255	.1378	.1496	.1607	.1710	.1804
4	.0203	.0260	.0324	.0395	.0471	.0551	.0636	.0723	.0812	.0902
5	.0045	.0062	.0084	.0111	.0141	.0176	.0216	.0260	.0309	.0361
6	.0008	.0012	.0018	.0026	.0035	.0047	.0061	.0078	.0098	.0120
7	.0001	.0002	.0003	.0005	.0008	.0011	.0015	.0020	.0027	.0034
8	.0000	.0000	.0001	.0001	.0001	.0002	.0003	.0005	.0006	.0009
9	.0000	.0000	.0000	.0000	.0000	.0000	.0001	.0001	.0001	.0002

r	λ 2.10	2.20	2.30	2.40	2.50	2.60	2.70	2.80	2.90	3.00
0	.1225	.1108	.1003	.0907	.0821	.0743	.0672	.0608	.0550	.0498
1	.2572	.2438	.2306	.2177	.2052	.1931	.1815	.1703	.1596	.1494
2	.2700	.2681	.2652	.2613	.2565	.2510	.2450	.2384	.2314	.2240
3	.1890	.1966	.2033	.2090	.2138	.2176	.2205	.2225	.2237	.2240
4	.0992	.1082	.1169	.1254	.1336	.1414	.1488	.1557	.1622	.1680
5	.0417	.0476	.0538	.0602	.0668	.0735	.0804	.0872	.0940	.1008
6	.0146	.0174	.0206	.0241	.0278	.0319	.0362	.0407	.0455	.0504
7	.0044	.0055	.0068	.0083	.0099	.0118	.0139	.0163	.0188	.0216
8	.0011	.0015	.0019	.0025	.0031	.0038	.0047	.0057	.0068	.0081
9	.0003	.0004	.0005	.0007	.0009	.0011	.0014	.0018	.0022	.0027
10	.0001	.0001	.0001	.0002	.0002	.0003	.0004	.0005	.0006	.0008
11	.0000	.0000	.0000	.0000	.0000	.0001	.0001	.0001	.0002	.0002
12	.0000	.0000	.0000	.0000	.0000	.0000	.0000	.0000	.0000	.0001

r	λ 3.10	3.20	3.30	3.40	3.50	3.60	3.70	3.80	3.90	4.00
0	.0450	.0408	.0369	.0334	.0302	.0273	.0247	.0224	.0202	.0183
1	.1397	.1304	.1217	.1135	.1057	.0984	.0915	.0850	.0789	.0733
2	.2165	.2087	.2008	.1929	.1850	.1771	.1692	.1615	.1539	.1465
3	.2237	.2226	.2209	.2186	.2158	.2125	.2087	.2046	.2001	.1954
4	.1733	.1781	.1823	.1858	.1888	.1912	.1931	.1944	.1951	.1954
5	.1075	.1140	.1203	.1264	.1322	.1377	.1429	.1477	.1522	.1563
6	.0555	.0608	.0662	.0716	.0771	.0826	.0881	.0936	.0989	.1042
7	.0246	.0278	.0312	.0348	.0385	.0425	.0466	.0508	.0551	.0595
8	.0095	.0111	.0129	.0148	.0169	.0191	.0215	.0241	.0269	.0298
9	.0033	.0040	.0047	.0056	.0066	.0076	.0089	.0102	.0116	.0132
10	.0010	.0013	.0016	.0019	.0023	.0028	.0033	.0039	.0045	.0053
11	.0003	.0004	.0005	.0006	.0007	.0009	.0011	.0013	.0016	.0019
12	.0001	.0001	.0001	.0002	.0002	.0003	.0003	.0004	.0005	.0006
13	.0000	.0000	.0000	.0000	.0001	.0001	.0001	.0001	.0002	.0002
14	.0000	.0000	.0000	.0000	.0000	.0000	.0000	.0000	.0000	.0001

r	λ 4.10	4.20	4.30	4.40	4.50	4.60	4.70	4.80	4.90	5.00
0	.0166	.0150	.0136	.0123	.0111	.0101	.0091	.0082	.0074	.0067
1	.0679	.0630	.0583	.0540	.0500	.0462	.0427	.0395	.0365	.0337
2	.1393	.1323	.1254	.1188	.1125	.1063	.1005	.0948	.0894	.0842
3	.1904	.1852	.1798	.1743	.1687	.1631	.1574	.1517	.1460	.1404
4	.1951	.1944	.1933	.1917	.1898	.1875	.1849	.1820	.1789	.1755
5	.1600	.1633	.1662	.1687	.1708	.1725	.1738	.1747	.1753	.1755
6	.1093	.1143	.1191	.1237	.1281	.1323	.1362	.1398	.1432	.1462
7	.0640	.0686	.0732	.0778	.0824	.0869	.0914	.0959	.1002	.1044
8	.0328	.0360	.0393	.0428	.0463	.0500	.0537	.0575	.0614	.0653
9	.0150	.0168	.0188	.0209	.0232	.0255	.0281	.0307	.0334	.0363
10	.0061	.0071	.0081	.0092	.0104	.0118	.0132	.0147	.0164	.0181
11	.0023	.0027	.0032	.0037	.0043	.0049	.0056	.0064	.0073	.0082
12	.0008	.0009	.0011	.0013	.0016	.0019	.0022	.0026	.0030	.0034
13	.0002	.0003	.0004	.0005	.0006	.0007	.0008	.0009	.0011	.0013
14	.0001	.0001	.0001	.0001	.0002	.0002	.0003	.0003	.0004	.0005
15	.0000	.0000	.0000	.0000	.0001	.0001	.0001	.0001	.0001	.0002

r	λ 5.10	5.20	5.30	5.40	5.50	5.60	5.70	5.80	5.90	6.00
0	.0061	.0055	.0050	.0045	.0041	.0037	.0033	.0030	.0027	.0025
1	.0311	.0287	.0265	.0244	.0225	.0207	.0191	.0176	.0162	.0149
2	.0793	.0746	.0701	.0659	.0618	.0580	.0544	.0509	.0477	.0446
3	.1348	.1293	.1239	.1185	.1133	.1082	.1033	.0985	.0938	.0892
4	.1719	.1681	.1641	.1600	.1558	.1515	.1472	.1428	.1383	.1339
5	.1753	.1748	.1740	.1728	.1714	.1697	.1678	.1656	.1632	.1606
6	.1490	.1515	.1537	.1555	.1571	.1584	.1594	.1601	.1605	.1606
7	.1086	.1125	.1163	.1200	.1234	.1267	.1298	.1326	.1353	.1377
8	.0692	.0731	.0771	.0810	.0849	.0887	.0925	.0962	.0998	.1033
9	.0392	.0423	.0454	.0486	.0519	.0552	.0586	.0620	.0654	.0688
10	.0200	.0220	.0241	.0262	.0285	.0309	.0334	.0359	.0386	.0413
11	.0093	.0104	.0116	.0129	.0143	.0157	.0173	.0190	.0207	.0225
12	.0039	.0045	.0051	.0058	.0065	.0073	.0082	.0092	.0102	.0113
13	.0015	.0018	.0021	.0024	.0028	.0032	.0036	.0041	.0046	.0052
14	.0006	.0007	.0008	.0009	.0011	.0013	.0015	.0017	.0019	.0022
15	.0002	.0002	.0003	.0003	.0004	.0005	.0006	.0007	.0008	.0009
16	.0001	.0001	.0001	.0001	.0001	.0002	.0002	.0002	.0003	.0003
17	.0000	.0000	.0000	.0000	.0000	.0001	.0001	.0001	.0001	.0001

r	λ 6.10	6.20	6.30	6.40	6.50	6.60	6.70	6.80	6.90	7.00
0	.0022	.0020	.0018	.0017	.0015	.0014	.0012	.0011	.0010	.0009
1	.0137	.0126	.0116	.0106	.0098	.0090	.0082	.0076	.0070	.0064
2	.0417	.0390	.0364	.0340	.0318	.0296	.0276	.0258	.0240	.0223
3	.0848	.0806	.0765	.0726	.0688	.0652	.0617	.0584	.0552	.0521
4	.1294	.1249	.1205	.1161	.1118	.1076	.1034	.0992	.0952	.0912
5	.1579	.1549	.1519	.1487	.1454	.1420	.1385	.1349	.1314	.1277
6	.1605	.1601	.1595	.1586	.1575	.1562	.1546	.1529	.1511	.1490
7	.1399	.1418	.1435	.1450	.1462	.1472	.1480	.1486	.1489	.1490
8	.1066	.1099	.1130	.1160	.1188	.1215	.1240	.1263	.1284	.1304
9	.0723	.0757	.0791	.0825	.0858	.0891	.0923	.0954	.0985	.1014
10	.0441	.0469	.0498	.0528	.0558	.0588	.0618	.0649	.0679	.0710
11	.0244	.0265	.0285	.0307	.0330	.0353	.0377	.0401	.0426	.0452
12	.0124	.0137	.0150	.0164	.0179	.0194	.0210	.0227	.0245	.0263
13	.0058	.0065	.0073	.0081	.0089	.0099	.0108	.0119	.0130	.0142
14	.0025	.0029	.0033	.0037	.0041	.0046	.0052	.0058	.0064	.0071
15	.0010	.0012	.0014	.0016	.0018	.0020	.0023	.0026	.0029	.0033
16	.0004	.0005	.0005	.0006	.0007	.0008	.0010	.0011	.0013	.0014
17	.0001	.0002	.0002	.0002	.0003	.0003	.0004	.0004	.0005	.0006
18	.0000	.0001	.0001	.0001	.0001	.0001	.0001	.0002	.0002	.0002
19	.0000	.0000	.0000	.0000	.0000	.0000	.0001	.0001	.0001	.0001

r	λ 7.10	7.20	7.30	7.40	7.50	7.60	7.70	7.80	7.90	8.00
0	.0008	.0007	.0007	.0006	.0006	.0005	.0005	.0004	.0004	.0003
1	.0059	.0054	.0049	.0045	.0041	.0038	.0035	.0032	.0029	.0027
2	.0208	.0194	.0180	.0167	.0156	.0145	.0134	.0125	.0116	.0107
3	.0492	.0464	.0438	.0413	.0389	.0366	.0345	.0324	.0305	.0286
4	.0874	.0836	.0799	.0764	.0729	.0696	.0663	.0632	.0602	.0573
5	.1241	.1204	.1167	.1130	.1094	.1057	.1021	.0986	.0951	.0916
6	.1468	.1445	.1420	.1394	.1367	.1339	.1311	.1282	.1252	.1221
7	.1489	.1486	.1481	.1474	.1465	.1454	.1442	.1428	.1413	.1396
8	.1321	.1337	.1351	.1363	.1373	.1381	.1388	.1392	.1395	.1396
9	.1042	.1070	.1096	.1121	.1144	.1167	.1187	.1207	.1224	.1241
10	.0740	.0770	.0800	.0829	.0858	.0887	.0914	.0941	.0967	.0993
11	.0478	.0504	.0531	.0558	.0585	.0613	.0640	.0667	.0695	.0722
12	.0283	.0303	.0323	.0344	.0366	.0388	.0411	.0434	.0457	.0481
13	.0154	.0168	.0181	.0196	.0211	.0227	.0243	.0260	.0278	.0296
14	.0078	.0086	.0095	.0104	.0113	.0123	.0134	.0145	.0157	.0169

r	7.10	7.20	7.30	7.40	7.50	7.60	7.70	7.80	7.90	8.00
15	.0037	.0041	.0046	.0051	.0057	.0062	.0069	.0075	.0083	.0090
16	.0016	.0019	.0021	.0024	.0026	.0030	.0033	.0037	.0041	.0045
17	.0007	.0008	.0009	.0010	.0012	.0013	.0015	.0017	.0019	.0021
18	.0003	.0003	.0004	.0004	.0005	.0006	.0006	.0007	.0008	.0009
19	.0001	.0001	.0001	.0002	.0002	.0002	.0003	.0003	.0003	.0004
20	.0000	.0000	.0001	.0001	.0001	.0001	.0001	.0001	.0001	.0002
21	.0000	.0000	.0000	.0000	.0000	.0000	.0000	.0000	.0001	.0001

λ

r	8.10	8.20	8.30	8.40	8.50	8.60	8.70	8.80	8.90	9.00
0	.0003	.0003	.0002	.0002	.0002	.0002	.0002	.0002	.0001	.0001
1	.0025	.0023	.0021	.0019	.0017	.0016	.0014	.0013	.0012	.0011
2	.0100	.0092	.0086	.0079	.0074	.0068	.0063	.0058	.0054	.0050
3	.0269	.0252	.0237	.0222	.0208	.0195	.0183	.0171	.0160	.0150
4	.0544	.0517	.0491	.0466	.0443	.0420	.0398	.0377	.0357	.0337
5	.0882	.0849	.0816	.0784	.0752	.0722	.0692	.0663	.0635	.0607
6	.1191	.1160	.1128	.1097	.1066	.1034	.1003	.0972	.0941	.0911
7	.1378	.1358	.1338	.1317	.1294	.1271	.1247	.1222	.1197	.1171
8	.1395	.1392	.1388	.1382	.1375	.1366	.1356	.1344	.1332	.1318
9	.1256	.1269	.1280	.1290	.1299	.1306	.1311	.1315	.1317	.1318
10	.1017	.1040	.1063	.1084	.1104	.1123	.1140	.1157	.1172	.1186
11	.0749	.0776	.0802	.0828	.0853	.0878	.0902	.0925	.0948	.0970
12	.0505	.0530	.0555	.0579	.0604	.0629	.0654	.0679	.0703	.0728
13	.0315	.0334	.0354	.0374	.0395	.0416	.0438	.0459	.0481	.0504
14	.0182	.0196	.0210	.0225	.0240	.0256	.0272	.0289	.0306	.0324
15	.0098	.0107	.0116	.0126	.0136	.0147	.0158	.0169	.0182	.0194
16	.0050	.0055	.0060	.0066	.0072	.0079	.0086	.0093	.0101	.0109
17	.0024	.0026	.0029	.0033	.0036	.0040	.0044	.0048	.0053	.0058
18	.0011	.0012	.0014	.0015	.0017	.0019	.0021	.0024	.0026	.0029
19	.0005	.0005	.0006	.0007	.0008	.0009	.0010	.0011	.0012	.0014
20	.0002	.0002	.0002	.0003	.0003	.0004	.0004	.0005	.0005	.0006
21	.0001	.0001	.0001	.0001	.0001	.0002	.0002	.0002	.0002	.0003
22	.0000	.0000	.0000	.0000	.0001	.0001	.0001	.0001	.0001	.0001

r	λ 9.10	9.20	9.30	9.40	9.50	9.60	9.70	9.80	9.90	10.00
0	.0001	.0001	.0001	.0001	.0001	.0001	.0001	.0001	.0001	.0000
1	.0010	.0009	.0009	.0008	.0007	.0007	.0006	.0005	.0005	.0005
2	.0046	.0043	.0040	.0037	.0034	.0031	.0029	.0027	.0025	.0023
3	.0140	.0131	.0123	.0115	.0107	.0100	.0093	.0087	.0081	.0076
4	.0319	.0302	.0285	.0269	.0254	.0240	.0226	.0213	.0201	.0189
5	.0581	.0555	.0530	.0506	.0483	.0460	.0439	.0418	.0398	.0378
6	.0881	.0851	.0822	.0793	.0764	.0736	.0709	.0682	.0656	.0031
7	.1145	.1118	.1091	.1064	.1037	.1010	.0982	.0955	.0928	.0901
8	.1302	.1286	.1269	.1251	.1232	.1212	.1191	.1170	.1148	.1126
9	.1317	.1315	.1311	.1306	.1300	.1293	.1284	.1274	.1263	.1251
10	.1198	.1210	.1219	.1228	.1235	.1241	.1245	.1249	.1250	.1251
11	.0991	.1012	.1031	.1049	.1067	.1083	.1098	.1112	.1125	.1137
12	.0752	.0776	.0799	.0822	.0844	.0866	.0888	.0908	.0928	.0948
13	.0526	.0549	.0572	.0594	.0617	.0640	.0662	.0685	.0707	.0729
14	.0342	.0361	.0380	.0399	.0419	.0439	.0459	.0479	.0500	.0521
15	.0208	.0221	.0235	.0250	.0265	.0281	.0297	.0313	.0330	.0347
16	.0118	.0127	.0137	.0147	.0157	.0168	.0180	.0192	.0204	.0217
17	.0063	.0069	.0075	.0081	.0088	.0095	.0103	.0111	.0119	.0128
18	.0032	.0035	.0039	.0042	.0046	.0051	.0055	.0060	.0065	.0071
19	.0015	.0017	.0019	.0021	.0023	.0026	.0028	.0031	.0034	.0037
20	.0007	.0008	.0009	.0010	.0011	.0012	.0014	.0015	.0017	.0019
21	.0003	.0003	.0004	.0004	.0005	.0006	.0006	.0007	.0008	.0009
22	.0001	.0001	.0002	.0002	.0002	.0002	.0003	.0003	.0004	.0004
23	.0000	.0001	.0001	.0001	.0001	.0001	.0001	.0001	.0002	.0002
24	.0000	.0000	.0000	.0000	.0000	.0000	.0000	.0001	.0001	.0001

r	λ 11.0	12.0	13.0	14.0	15.0	16.0	17.0	18.0	19.0	20.0
0	.0000	.0000	.0000	.0000	.0000	.0000	.0000	.0000	.0000	.0000
1	.0002	.0001	.0000	.0000	.0000	.0000	.0000	.0000	.0000	.0000
2	.0010	.0004	.0002	.0001	.0000	.0000	.0000	.0000	.0000	.0000
3	.0037	.0018	.0008	.0004	.0002	.0001	.0000	.0000	.0000	.0000
4	.0102	.0053	.0027	.0013	.0006	.0003	.0001	.0001	.0000	.0000
5	.0224	.0127	.0070	.0037	.0019	.0010	.0005	.0002	.0001	.0001
6	.0411	.0255	.0152	.0087	.0048	.0026	.0014	.0007	.0004	.0002
7	.0646	.0437	.0281	.0174	.0104	.0060	.0034	.0019	.0010	.0005
8	.0888	.0655	.0457	.0304	.0194	.0120	.0072	.0042	.0024	.0013
9	.1085	.0874	.0661	.0473	.0324	.0213	.0135	.0083	.0050	.0029

r	λ 11.0	12.0	13.0	14.0	15.0	16.0	17.0	18.0	19.0	20.0
10	.1194	.1048	.0859	.0663	.0486	.0341	.0230	.0150	.0095	.0058
11	.1194	.1144	.1015	.0844	.0663	.0496	.0355	.0245	.0164	.0106
12	.1094	.1144	.1099	.0984	.0829	.0661	.0504	.0368	.0259	.0176
13	.0926	.1056	.1099	.1060	.0956	.0814	.0658	.0509	.0378	.0271
14	.0728	.0905	.1021	.1060	.1024	.0930	.0800	.0655	.0514	.0387
15	.0534	.0724	.0885	.0989	.1024	.0992	.0906	.0786	.0650	.0516
16	.0367	.0543	.0719	.0866	.0960	.0992	.0963	.0884	.0772	.0646
17	.0237	.0383	.0550	.0713	.0847	.0934	.0963	.0936	.0863	.0760
18	.0145	.0256	.0397	.0554	.0706	.0830	.0909	.0936	.0911	.0844
19	.0084	.0161	.0272	.0409	.0557	.0699	.0814	.0887	.0911	.0888
20	.0046	.0097	.0177	.0286	.0418	.0559	.0692	.0798	.0866	.0888
21	.0024	.0055	.0109	.0191	.0299	.0426	.0560	.0684	.0783	.0846
22	.0012	.0030	.0065	.0121	.0204	.0310	.0433	.0560	.0676	.0769
23	.0006	.0016	.0037	.0074	.0133	.0216	.0320	.0438	.0559	.0669
24	.0003	.0008	.0020	.0043	.0083	.0144	.0226	.0329	.0442	.0557
25	.0001	.0004	.0010	.0024	.0050	.0092	.0154	.0237	.0336	.0446
26	.0000	.0002	.0005	.0013	.0029	.0057	.0101	.0164	.0246	.0343
27	.0000	.0001	.0002	.0007	.0016	.0034	.0063	.0109	.0173	.0254
28	.0000	.0000	.0001	.0003	.0009	.0019	.0038	.0070	.0117	.0181
29	.0000	.0000	.0001	.0002	.0004	.0011	.0023	.0044	.0077	.0125
30	.0000	.0000	.0000	.0001	.0002	.0006	.0013	.0026	.0049	.0083
31	.0000	.0000	.0000	.0000	.0001	.0003	.0007	.0015	.0030	.0054
32	.0000	.0000	.0000	.0000	.0001	.0001	.0004	.0009	.0018	.0034
33	.0000	.0000	.0000	.0000	.0000	.0001	.0002	.0005	.0010	.0020
34	.0000	.0000	.0000	.0000	.0000	.0000	.0001	.0002	.0006	.0012
35	.0000	.0000	.0000	.0000	.0000	.0000	.0000	.0001	.0003	.0007
36	.0000	.0000	.0000	.0000	.0000	.0000	.0000	.0001	.0002	.0004
37	.0000	.0000	.0000	.0000	.0000	.0000	.0000	.0000	.0001	.0002
38	.0000	.0000	.0000	.0000	.0000	.0000	.0000	.0000	.0000	.0001
39	.0000	.0000	.0000	.0000	.0000	.0000	.0000	.0000	.0000	.0001

r	λ 25.0	30.0	40.0	50.0	75.0	100.0
0	.0000	.0000	0	0	0	0
1	.0000	.0000	0	0	0	0
2	.0000	.0000	0	0	0	0
3	.0000	.0000	0	0	0	0
4	.0000	.0000	0	0	0	0
5	.0000	.0000	0	0	0	0
6	.0000	.0000	.0000	0	0	0
7	.0000	.0000	.0000	0	0	0
8	.0001	.0000	.0000	0	0	0
9	.0001	.0000	.0000	0	0	0
10	.0004	.0000	.0000	0	0	0
11	.0008	.0000	.0000	.0000	0	0
12	.0017	.0001	.0000	.0000	0	0
13	.0033	.0002	.0000	.0000	0	0
14	.0059	.0005	.0000	.0000	0	0
15	.0099	.0010	.0000	.0000	0	0
16	.0155	.0019	.0000	.0000	0	0
17	.0227	.0034	.0000	.0000	0	0
18	.0316	.0057	.0000	.0000	0	0
19	.0415	.0089	.0001	.0000	0	0
20	.0519	.0134	.0002	.0000	0	0
21	.0618	.0192	.0004	.0000	0	0
22	.0702	.0261	.0007	.0000	0	0
23	.0763	.0341	.0012	.0000	0	0
24	.0795	.0426	.0019	.0000	0	0
25	.0795	.0511	.0031	.0000	0	0
26	.0765	.0590	.0047	.0001	.0000	0
27	.0708	.0655	.0070	.0001	.0000	0
28	.0632	.0702	.0100	.0002	.0000	0
29	.0545	.0726	.0138	.0004	.0000	0
30	.0454	.0726	.0185	.0007	.0000	0
31	.0365	.0703	.0238	.0011	.0000	0
32	.0286	.0659	.0298	.0017	.0000	0
33	.0217	.0599	.0361	.0026	.0000	0
34	.0159	.0529	.0425	.0038	.0000	0
35	.0114	.0453	.0485	.0054	.0000	0
36	.0079	.0378	.0539	.0075	.0000	0
37	.0053	.0306	.0583	.0102	.0000	0
38	.0035	.0242	.0614	.0134	.0000	0
39	.0023	.0186	.0629	.0172	.0000	0

r	25.0	30.0	λ 40.0	50.0	75.0	100.0
40	.0014	.0139	.0629	.0215	.0000	0
41	.0009	.0102	.0614	.0262	.0000	0
42	.0005	.0073	.0585	.0312	.0000	.0000
43	.0003	.0051	.0544	.0363	.0000	.0000
44	.0002	.0035	.0495	.0412	.0000	.0000
45	.0001	.0023	.0440	.0458	.0001	.0000
46	.0001	.0015	.0382	.0498	.0001	.0000
47	.0000	.0010	.0325	.0530	.0001	.0000
48	.0000	.0006	.0271	.0552	.0002	.0000
49	.0000	.0004	.0221	.0563	.0003	.0000
50	.0000	.0002	.0177	.0563	.0005	.0000
51	.0000	.0001	.0139	.0552	.0007	.0000
52	.0000	.0001	.0107	.0531	.0011	.0000
53	.0000	.0000	.0081	.0501	.0015	.0000
54	.0000	.0000	.0060	.0464	.0021	.0000
55	.0000	.0000	.0043	.0422	.0028	.0000
56	.0000	.0000	.0031	.0376	.0038	.0000
57	.0000	.0000	.0022	.0330	.0050	.0000
58	.0000	.0000	.0015	.0285	.0065	.0000
59	.0000	.0000	.0010	.0241	.0082	.0000
60	.0000	.0000	.0007	.0201	.0103	.0000
61	.0000	.0000	.0004	.0165	.0126	.0000
62	.0000	.0000	.0003	.0133	.0153	.0000
63	.0000	.0000	.0002	.0105	.0182	.0000
64	.0000	.0000	.0001	.0082	.0213	.0000
65	0	.0000	.0001	.0063	.0246	.0000
66	0	.0000	.0000	.0048	.0279	.0001
67	0	.0000	.0000	.0036	.0313	.0001
68	0	.0000	.0000	.0026	.0345	.0002
69	0	.0000	.0000	.0019	.0375	.0002
71	000	.0000	.0000	.0014	.0402	.0003
72	0	.0000	.0000	.0010	.0424	.0004
73	0	.0000	.0000	.0007	.0442	.0006
74	0	0	.0000	.0005	.0454	.0008
	0	0	.0000	.0003	.0460	.0011
75	0	0	.0000	.0002	.0460	.0015
76	0	0	.0000	.0001	.0454	.0020
77	0	0	.0000	.0001	.0442	.0026
78	0	0	.0000	.0001	.0425	.0033
79	0	0	.0000	.0000	.0404	.0042

r	λ 25.0	30.0	40.0	50.0	75.0	100.0
80	0	0	.0000	.0000	.0379	.0052
81	0	0	.0000	.0000	.0350	.0064
82	0	0	.0000	.0000	.0321	.0078
83	0	0	.0000	.0000	.0290	.0094
84	0	0	.0000	.0000	.0259	.0112
85	0	0	.0000	.0000	.0228	.0132
86	0	0	.0000	.0000	.0199	.0154
87	0	0	.0000	.0000	.0172	.0176
88	0	0	.0000	.0000	.0146	.0201
89	0	0	0	.0000	.0123	.0225
90	0	0	0	.0000	.0103	.0250
91	0	0	0	.0000	.0085	.0275
92	0	0	0	.0000	.0069	.0299
93	0	0	0	.0000	.0056	.0322
94	0	0	0	.0000	.0044	.0342
95	0	0	0	.0000	.0035	.0360
96	0	0	0	.0000	.0027	.0375
97	0	0	0	.0000	.0021	.0387
98	0	0	0	.0000	.0016	.0395
99	0	0	0	.0000	.0012	.0399
100	0	0	0	.0000	.0009	.0399
101	0	0	0	.0000	.0007	.0395
102	0	0	0	.0000	.0005	.0387
103	0	0	0	.0000	.0004	.0376
104	0	0	0	0	.0003	.0361
105	0	0	0	0	.0002	.0344
106	0	0	0	0	.0001	.0325
107	0	0	0	0	.0001	.0303
108	0	0	0	0	.0001	.0281
109	0	0	0	0	.0000	.0258
110	0	0	0	0	.0000	.0234
111	0	0	0	0	.0000	.0211
112	0	0	0	0	.0000	.0188
113	0	0	0	0	.0000	.0167
114	0	0	0	0	.0000	.0146
115	0	0	0	0	.0000	.0127
116	0	0	0	0	.0000	.0110
117	0	0	0	0	.0000	.0094
118	0	0	0	0	.0000	.0079
119	0	0	0	0	.0000	.0067

			λ			
r	25.0	30.0	40.0	50.0	75.0	100.0
120	0	0	0	0	.0000	.0056
121	0	0	0	0	.0000	.0046
122	0	0	0	0	.0000	.0038
123	0	0	0	0	.0000	.0031
124	0	0	0	0	.0000	.0025
125	0	0	0	0	.0000	.0020
126	0	0	0	0	.0000	.0016
127	0	0	0	0	.0000	.0012
128	0	0	0	0	.0000	.0010
129	0	0	0	0	.0000	.0007
130	0	0	0	0	.0000	.0006
131	0	0	0	0	.0000	.0004
132	0	0	0	0	.0000	.0003
133	0	0	0	0	.0000	.0003
134	0	0	0	0	.0000	.0002
135	0	0	0	0	.0000	.0001
136	0	0	0	0	.0000	.0001
137	0	0	0	0	.0000	.0001
138	0	0	0	0	.0000	.0001

Table D.2 Values of e^x and e^{-x}

x	e^x	e^{-x}	x	e^x	e^{-x}
0.00	1.000	1.000	3.00	20.086	0.050
0.10	1.105	0.905	3.10	22.198	0.045
0.20	1.221	0.819	3.20	24.533	0.041
0.30	1.350	0.741	3.30	27.113	0.037
0.40	1.492	0.670	3.40	29.964	0.033
0.50	1.649	0.607	3.50	33.115	0.030
0.60	1.822	0.549	3.60	36.598	0.027
0.70	2.014	0.497	3.70	40.447	0.025
0.80	2.226	0.449	3.80	44.701	0.022
0.90	2.460	0.407	3.90	49.402	0.020
1.00	2.718	0.368	4.00	54.598	0.018
1.10	3.004	0.333	4.10	60.340	0.017
1.20	3.320	0.301	4.20	66.686	0.015
1.30	3.669	0.273	4.30	73.700	0.014
1.40	4.055	0.247	4.40	81.451	0.012
1.50	4.482	0.223	4.50	90.017	0.011
1.60	4.953	0.202	4.60	99.484	0.010
1.70	5.474	0.183	4.70	109.95	0.009
1.80	6.050	0.165	4.80	121.51	0.008
1.90	6.686	0.150	4.90	134.29	0.007
2.00	7.389	0.135	5.00	148.41	0.007
2.10	8.166	0.122	5.10	164.02	0.006
2.20	9.025	0.111	5.20	181.27	0.006
2.30	9.974	0.100	5.30	200.34	0.005
2.40	11.023	0.091	5.40	221.41	0.005
2.50	12.182	0.082	5.50	244.69	0.004
2.60	13.464	0.074	5.60	270.43	0.004
2.70	14.880	0.067	5.70	298.87	0.003
2.80	16.445	0.061	5.80	330.30	0.003
2.90	18.174	0.055	5.90	365.04	0.003
3.00	20.086	0.050	6.00	403.43	0.002

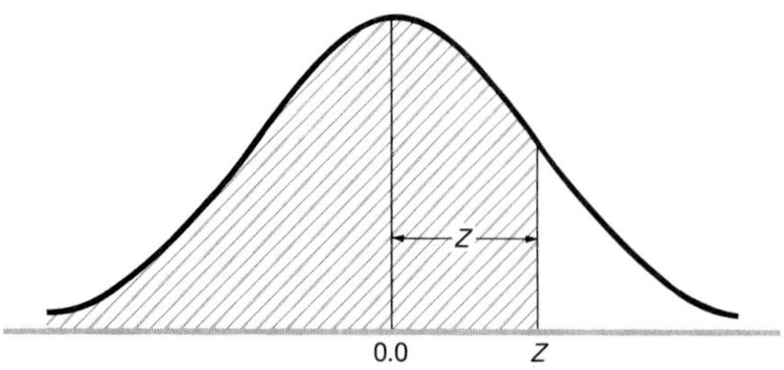

Table *D*.3 Normal probability values for values of *Z*

Z	.00	.01	.02	.03	.04	.05	.06	.07	.08	.09
0.0	.50000	.50399	.50798	.51197	.51595	.51994	.52392	.52790	.53188	.53586
0.1	.53983	.54380	.54776	.55172	.55567	.55962	.56356	.56749	.57142	.57535
0.2	.57926	.58317	.58706	.59095	.59483	.59871	.60257	.60642	.61026	.61409
0.3	.61791	.62172	.62552	.62930	.63307	.63683	.64058	.64431	.64803	.65173
0.4	.65542	.65910	.66276	.66640	.67003	.67364	.67724	.68082	.68439	.68793
0.5	.69146	.69497	.69847	.70194	.70540	.70884	.71226	.71566	.71904	.72240
0.6	.72575	.72907	.73237	.73536	.73891	.74215	.74537	.74857	.75175	.75490
0.7	.75804	.76115	.76424	.76730	.77035	.77337	.77637	.77935	.78230	.78524
0.8	.78814	.79103	.79389	.79673	.79955	.80234	.80511	.80785	.81057	.81327
0.9	.81594	.81859	.82121	.82381	.82639	.82894	.83147	.83398	.83646	.83891
1.0	.84134	.84375	.84614	.84849	.85083	.85314	.85543	.85769	.85993	.86214
1.1	.86433	.86650	.86864	.87076	.87286	.87493	.87698	.87900	.88100	.88298
1.2	.88493	.88686	.88877	.89065	.89251	.89435	.89617	.89796	.89973	.90147
1.3	.90320	.90490	.90658	.90824	.90988	.91149	.91309	.91466	.91621	.91774
1.4	.91924	.92073	.92220	.92364	.92507	.92647	.92785	.92922	.93056	.93189
1.5	.93319	.93448	.93574	.93699	.93822	.93943	.94062	.94179	.94295	.94408
1.6	.94520	.94630	.94738	.94845	.94950	.95053	.95154	.95254	.95352	.95449
1.7	.95543	.95637	.95728	.95818	.95907	.95994	.96080	.96164	.96246	.96327
1.8	.96407	.96485	.96562	.96638	.96712	.96784	.96856	.96926	.96995	.97062
1.9	.97128	.97193	.97257	.97320	.97381	.97441	.97500	.97558	.97615	.97670
2.0	.97725	.97784	.97831	.97882	.97932	.97982	.98030	.98077	.98124	.98169
2.1	.98214	.98257	.98300	.98341	.98382	.98422	.98461	.98500	.98537	.98574
2.2	.98610	.98645	.98679	.98713	.98745	.98778	.98809	.98840	.98870	.98899
2.3	.98928	.98956	.98983	.99010	.99036	.99061	.99086	.99111	.99134	.99158
2.4	.99180	.99202	.99224	.99245	.99266	.99286	.99305	.99324	.99343	.99361
2.5	.99379	.99396	.99413	.99430	.99446	.99461	.99477	.99492	.99506	.99520
2.6	.99534	.99547	.99560	.99573	.99585	.99598	.99609	.99621	.99632	.99643
2.7	.99653	.99664	.99674	.99683	.99693	.99702	.99711	.99720	.99728	.99736
2.8	.99744	.99752	.99760	.99767	.99774	.99781	.99788	.99795	.99801	.99807
2.9	.99813	.99819	.99825	.99831	.99836	.99841	.99846	.99851	.99856	.99861

z	.00	.01	.02	.03	.04	.05	.06	.07	.08	.09
3.0	.99865	.99869	.99874	.99878	.99882	.99886	.99899	.90893	.99896	.99900
3.1	.99903	.99906	.99910	.99913	.99916	.99918	.99921	.99924	.99926	.99929
3.2	.99931	.99934	.99936	.99938	.99940	.99942	.99944	.99946	.99948	.99950
3.3	.99952	.99953	.99955	.99957	.99958	.99960	.99961	.99962	.99964	.99965
3.4	.99966	.99968	.99969	.99970	.99971	.99972	.99973	.99974	.99975	.99976
3.5	.99977	.99978	.99978	.99979	.99980	.99981	.99981	.99982	.99983	.99983
3.6	.99984	.99985	.99985	.99986	.99986	.99987	.99987	.99988	.99988	.99989
3.7	.99989	.99990	.99990	.99990	.99991	.99991	.99992	.99992	.99992	.99992
3.8	.99993	.99993	.99993	.99994	.99994	.99994	.99994	.99995	.99995	.99995
3.9	.99995	.99995	.99996	.99996	.99996	.99996	.99996	.99996	.99997	.99997

Table *D*.4 *P*(0) for multichannel poisson/exponential queueing process: probability of zero in system

$R=\lambda/(S\times\mu)$	Number of Channels: *S*								
R	2	3	4	5	6	7	8	9	10	15
0.02	0.96079	0.94177	0.92312	0.90484	0.88692	0.86936	0.85215	0.83527	0.81873	0.74082
0.04	0.92308	0.88692	0.85215	0.81873	0.78663	0.75578	0.72615	0.69768	0.67032	0.54881
0.06	0.88679	0.83526	0.78663	0.74082	0.69768	0.65705	0.61878	0.58275	0.54881	0.40657
0.08	0.85185	0.78659	0.72615	0.67032	0.61878	0.57121	0.52729	0.48675	0.44983	0.30119
0.10	0.81818	0.74074	0.67031	0.60653	0.54881	0.49659	0.44933	0.40657	0.36788	0.22313
0.12	0.78571	0.69753	0.61876	0.54881	0.48675	0.43171	0.38289	0.33960	0.30119	0.16530
0.14	0.75439	0.65679	0.57116	0.49657	0.43171	0.37531	0.72628	0.28365	0.24660	0.12246
0.16	0.72414	0.61838	0.52720	0.44931	0.38289	0.32628	0.27804	0.23693	0.20190	0.09072
0.18	0.69492	0.58214	0.48660	0.40653	0.33959	0.28365	0.23693	0.19790	0.16530	0.06721
0.20	0.66667	0.54795	0.44910	0.36782	0.30118	0.24659	0.20189	0.16530	0.13534	0.04979
0.22	0.63934	0.51567	0.41445	0.33277	0.26711	0.21437	0.17204	0.13807	0.11080	0.03688
0.24	0.61290	0.48519	0.38244	0.30105	0.23688	0.18636	0.14660	0.11532	0.09072	0.02732
0.26	0.58730	0.45640	0.35284	0.27233	0.21007	0.16200	0.12492	0.09632	0.07427	0.02024
0.28	0.56250	0.42918	0.32548	0.24633	0.18628	0.14082	0.10645	0.08045	0.06081	0.01500
0.30	0.53846	0.40346	0.30017	0.22277	0.16517	0.12241	0.09070	0.06720	0.04978	0.01111
0.32	0.51515	0.37913	0.27676	0.20144	0.14644	0.10639	0.07728	0.05612	0.04076	0.00823
0.34	0.49254	0.35610	0.25510	0.18211	0.12981	0.09247	0.06584	0.04687	0.03337	0.00610
0.36	0.47059	0.33431	0.23505	0.16460	0.11505	0.08035	0.05609	0.03915	0.02732	0.00452
0.38	0.44928	0.31367	0.21649	0.14872	0.10195	0.06981	0.04778	0.03269	0.02236	0.00335
0.40	0.42857	0.29412	0.19929	0.13433	0.09032	0.06065	0.04069	0.02729	0.01830	0.00248
0.42	0.40845	0.27559	0.18336	0.12128	0.07998	0.05267	0.03465	0.02279	0.01498	0.00184
0.44	0.38889	0.25802	0.16860	0.10944	0.07080	0.04573	0.02950	0.01902	0.01225	0.00136
0.46	0.36986	0.24135	0.15491	0.09870	0.06265	0.03968	0.02511	0.01587	0.01003	0.00101
0.48	0.35135	0.22554	0.14221	0.08895	0.05540	0.03442	0.02136	0.01324	0.00826	0.00075
0.50	0.33333	0.21053	0.13043	0.08010	0.04896	0.02984	0.01816	0.01104	0.00671	0.00055
0.52	0.31579	0.19627	0.11951	0.07207	0.04323	0.02586	0.01544	0.00920	0.00548	0.00041
0.54	0.29870	0.18273	0.10936	0.06477	0.03814	0.02239	0.01311	0.00767	0.00448	0.00030
0.56	0.28205	0.16986	0.09994	0.05814	0.03362	0.01936	0.01113	0.00638	0.00366	0.00022
0.58	0.26582	0.15762	0.09119	0.05212	0.02959	0.01673	0.00943	0.00531	0.00298	0.00017
0.60	0.25000	0.14599	0.08306	0.04665	0.02601	0.01443	0.00799	0.00441	0.00243	0.00012

$R = \lambda/(Sx\mu)$	Number of Channels: S								
R	2	3	4	5	6	7	8	9	10	15
0.62	0.23457	0.13491	0.07550	0.04167	0.02282	0.01243	0.00675	0.00366	0.00198	0.00009
0.64	0.21951	0.12438	0.06847	0.03715	0.01999	0.01069	0.00570	0.00303	0.00161	0.00007
0.66	0.20482	0.11435	0.06194	0.03304	0.01746	0.00918	0.00480	0.00251	0.00131	0.00005
0.68	0.19048	0.10479	0.05587	0.02930	0.01522	0.00786	0.00404	0.00207	0.00106	0.00004
0.70	0.17647	0.09569	0.05021	0.02590	0.01322	0.00670	0.00338	0.00170	0.00085	0.00003
0.72	0.16279	0.08702	0.04495	0.02280	0.01144	0.00570	0.00283	0.00140	0.00069	0.00002
0.74	0.14943	0.07875	0.04006	0.01999	0.00986	0.00483	0.00235	0.00114	0.00055	0.00001
0.76	0.13636	0.07087	0.03550	0.01743	0.00846	0.00407	0.00195	0.00093	0.00044	0.00001
0.78	0.12360	0.06335	0.03125	0.01510	0.00721	0.00341	0.00160	0.00075	0.00035	0.00001
0.80	0.11111	0.05618	0.02730	0.01299	0.00610	0.00284	0.00131	0.00060	0.00028	0.00001
0.82	0.09890	0.04933	0.02362	0.01106	0.00511	0.00234	0.00106	0.00048	0.00022	0.00000
0.84	0.08696	0.04280	0.02019	0.00931	0.00423	0.00190	0.00085	0.00038	0.00017	0.00000
0.86	0.07527	0.03656	0.01700	0.00772	0.00345	0.00153	0.00067	0.00029	0.00013	0.00000
0.88	0.06383	0.03060	0.01403	0.00627	0.00276	0.00120	0.00052	0.00022	0.00010	0.00000
0.90	0.05263	0.02491	0.01126	0.00496	0.00215	0.00092	0.00039	0.00017	0.00007	0.00000
0.92	0.04167	0.01947	0.00867	0.00377	0.00161	0.00068	0.00028	0.00012	0.00005	0.00000
0.94	0.03093	0.01427	0.00627	0.00268	0.00113	0.00047	0.00019	0.00008	0.00003	0.00000
0.96	0.02041	0.00930	0.00403	0.00170	0.00070	0.00029	0.00012	0.00005	0.00002	0.00000
0.98	0.01010	0.00454	0.00194	0.00081	0.00033	0.00013	0.00005	0.00002	0.00001	0.00000

Table *D*.5 Random numbers

39 65 76 45 45	19 90 69 64 61	20 26 36 31 62	58 24 97 14 97	95 06 70 99 00
73 71 23 70 90	65 97 60 12 11	31 56 34 19 19	47 83 75 51 33	30 62 38 20 46
72 20 47 33 84	51 67 47 97 19	98 40 07 17 66	23 05 09 51 80	59 78 11 52 49
75 17 25 69 17	17 95 21 78 58	24 33 45 77 48	69 81 84 09 29	93 22 70 45 80
37 48 79 88 74	63 52 06 34 30	01 31 60 10 27	35 07 79 71 53	28 99 52 01 41
02 89 08 16 94	85 53 83 29 95	56 27 09 24 43	21 78 55 09 82	72 61 88 73 61
87 18 15 70 07	37 79 49 12 38	48 13 93 55 96	41 92 45 71 51	09 18 25 58 94
98 83 71 70 15	89 09 39 59 24	00 06 41 41 20	14 36 59 25 47	54 45 17 24 89
10 08 58 07 04	76 62 16 48 68	58 76 17 14 86	59 53 11 52 21	66 04 18 72 87
47 90 56 37 31	71 82 13 50 41	27 55 10 24 92	28 04 67 53 44	95 23 00 84 47
93 05 31 03 07	34 18 04 52 35	74 13 39 35 22	68 95 23 92 35	36 63 70 35 33
21 89 11 47 99	11 20 99 45 18	76 51 94 84 86	13 79 93 37 55	98 16 04 41 67
95 18 94 06 97	27 37 83 28 71	79 57 95 13 91	09 61 87 25 21	56 20 11 32 44
97 08 31 55 73	10 65 81 92 59	77 31 61 95 46	20 44 90 32 64	26 99 76 75 63
69 26 88 86 13	59 71 74 17 32	48 38 75 93 29	73 37 32 04 05	60 82 29 20 25
41 47 10 25 03	87 63 93 95 17	81 83 83 04 49	77 45 85 50 51	79 88 01 97 30
91 94 14 63 62	08 61 74 51 69	92 79 43 89 79	29 18 94 51 23	14 85 11 47 23
80 06 54 18 47	08 52 85 08 40	48 40 35 94 22	72 65 71 08 86	50 03 42 99 36
67 72 77 63 99	89 85 84 46 06	64 71 06 21 66	89 37 20 70 01	61 65 70 22 12
59 40 24 13 75	42 29 72 23 19	06 94 76 10 08	81 30 15 39 14	81 83 17 16 33
63 62 06 34 41	79 53 36 02 95	94 61 09 43 62	20 21 14 68 86	84 95 48 46 45
78 47 23 53 90	79 93 96 38 63	34 85 52 05 09	85 43 01 72 73	14 93 87 81 40
87 68 62 15 43	97 48 72 66 48	53 16 71 13 81	59 97 50 99 52	24 62 20 42 31
47 60 92 10 77	26 97 05 73 51	88 46 38 03 58	72 68 49 29 31	75 70 16 08 24
56 88 87 59 41	06 87 37 78 48	65 88 69 58 39	88 02 84 27 83	85 81 56 39 38
22 17 68 65 84	87 02 22 57 51	68 69 80 95 44	11 29 01 95 80	49 34 35 86 47
19 36 27 59 46	39 77 32 77 09	79 57 92 36 59	89 74 19 82 15	08 58 94 34 74
16 77 23 02 77	28 06 24 25 93	22 45 44 84 11	87 80 61 65 31	09 71 91 74 25
78 43 76 71 61	97 67 63 99 61	80 45 67 93 82	59 73 19 85 23	53 33 65 97 21
03 28 28 26 08	69 30 16 09 05	53 58 47 70 93	66 56 45 65 79	45 56 20 19 47
04 31 17 21 56	33 73 99 19 87	26 72 39 27 67	53 77 57 68 93	60 61 97 22 61
61 06 98 03 91	87 14 77 43 96	43 00 65 98 50	45 60 33 01 07	98 99 46 50 47
23 68 35 26 00	99 53 93 61 28	52 70 05 48 34	56 65 05 61 86	90 92 10 70 80
15 39 25 70 99	93 86 52 77 65	15 33 59 05 28	22 87 26 07 47	86 96 98 29 06
58 71 96 30 24	18 46 23 34 27	85 13 99 24 44	49 18 09 79 49	74 16 32 23 02
93 22 53 64 39	07 10 63 76 35	87 03 04 79 88	08 13 13 85 51	55 34 57 72 69
78 76 58 54 74	92 38 70 96 92	52 06 79 79 45	82 63 18 27 44	69 66 92 19 09
61 81 31 96 82	00 57 25 60 59	46 72 60 18 77	55 66 12 62 11	08 99 55 64 57
42 88 07 10 05	24 98 65 63 21	47 21 61 88 32	27 80 30 21 60	10 92 35 36 12
77 94 30 05 39	28 10 99 00 27	12 73 73 99 12	49 99 57 94 82	96 88 57 17 91

Table *D*.6 The chi-square distribution values

df	.995	.990	.975	.950	.050	.025	.010	.005
	Probability that the χ^2 value will be exceeded							
1	—	—	—	.004	3.84	5.02	6.63	7.88
2	.01	.02	.05	.10	5.99	7.38	9.21	10.60
3	.07	.11	.22	.35	7.81	9.35	11.34	12.84
4	.21	.30	.48	.71	9.49	11.14	13.28	14.86
5	.41	.55	.83	1.15	11.07	12.83	15.09	16.75
6	.68	.87	1.24	1.64	12.59	14.45	16.81	18.55
7	.99	1.24	1.69	2.17	14.07	16.01	18.48	20.28
8	1.34	1.65	2.18	2.73	15.51	17.53	20.09	21.96
9	1.73	2.09	2.70	3.33	16.92	19.02	21.67	23.59
10	2.16	2.56	3.25	3.94	18.31	20.48	23.21	25.19
11	2.60	3.05	3.82	4.57	19.68	21.92	24.72	26.76
12	3.07	3.57	4.40	5.23	21.03	23.34	26.22	28.30
13	3.57	4.11	5.01	5.89	22.36	24.74	27.69	29.82
14	4.07	4.66	5.63	6.57	23.68	26.12	29.14	31.32
15	4.60	5.23	6.26	7.26	25.00	27.49	30.58	32.80
16	5.14	5.81	6.91	7.96	26.30	28,85	32.00	34.27
17	5.70	6.41	7.56	8.67	27.59	30.19	33.41	35.72
18	6.26	7.01	8.23	9.39	28.87	31.53	34.81	37.16
19	6.84	7.63	8.91	10.12	30.14	32.85	36.19	38.58
20	7.43	8.26	9.59	10.85	31.41	34.17	37.57	40.00
21	8.03	8.90	10.28	11.59	32.67	35.48	38.93	41.40
22	8.64	9.54	10.98	12.34	33.92	36.78	40.29	42.80
23	9.26	10.20	11.69	13.09	35.17	38.08	41.64	44.18
24	9.89	10.86	12.40	13.85	36.42	39.36	42.98	45.56
25	10.52	11.52	13.12	14.61	37.65	40.65	44.31	46.93
26	11.16	12.20	13.84	15.38	38.89	41.92	45.64	48.29
27	11.81	12.88	14.57	16.15	40.11	43.19	46.96	49.64
28	12.46	13.56	15.31	16.93	41.34	44.46	48.28	50.99
29	13.12	14.26	16.05	17.71	42.56	45.72	49.59	52.34
30	13.79	14.95	16.79	18,49	43.77	46.98	50.89	53.67
40	20.71	22.16	24.43	26.51	55.76	59.34	63.69	66.77
50	27.99	29.71	32.36	34.76	67.50	71.42	76.15	79.49
60	35.53	37.48	40.48	43.19	79.08	83.30	88.38	91.95
70	43.28	45.44	43.76	51.74	90.53	95.02	100.43	104.22
80	51.17	53.54	57.15	60.39	101.88	106.63	112.33	116.32
90	59.20	61.75	65.65	69.13	113.14	118.14	124.12	128.30
100	67.33	70.06	74.22	77.93	124.34	129.56	135.81	140.17

Index

d

e